POLITICS, POWER AND THE COMMON GOOD

AN INTRODUCTION TO POLITICAL SCIENCE

SECOND EDITION

ERIC MINTZ
SIR WILFRED GRENFELL COLLEGE,
MEMORIAL UNIVERSITY OF NEWFOUNDLAND

DAVID CLOSE
MEMORIAL UNIVERSITY OF NEWFOUNDLAND

OSVALDO CROCI
MEMORIAL UNIVERSITY OF NEWFOUNDLAND

D1415799

Toronto

Library and Archives Canada Cataloguing in Publication

Mintz, Eric
  Politics, power and the common good : an introduction to
political science/Eric Mintz, David Close, Osvaldo Croci. —2nd ed.

Includes bibliographical references and index.
ISBN 978-0-13-239362-1

  1. Political science—Textbooks.   I. Close, David, 1945–
II. Croci, Osvaldo   III. Title.

JA66.M55 2008   320   C2007-905598-2

ISBN-13: 978-0-13-239362-1
ISBN-10: 0-13-239362-X

Vice-President, Editorial Director: Gary Bennett
Senior Acquisitions Editor: Laura Forbes
Executive Marketing Manager: Judith Allen
Senior Developmental Editor: Jennifer Murray
Production Editors: Susan Broadhurst, Söğüt Y. Güleç
Copy Editor: Susan Broadhurst
Proofreader: John Firth
Production Coordinator: Avinash Chandra
Composition: Integra
Permissions and Photo Research: Julie Pratt
Art Director: Julia Hall
Cover Design: Miguel Acevedo
Cover Image: Getty Images/Photographer's Choice RR/Sergei Kozak

Statistics Canada information is used with the permission of the Minister of Industry, as Minister responsible for Statistics Canada. Information on the availability of the wide range of data from Statistics Canada can be obtained from Statistics Canada's Regional Offices, its World Wide Web site at http://www.statcan.ca, and its toll-free access number 1-800-263-1136.

  4 5   12 11 10

Printed and bound in USA.

To the memory of my parents, Sidney and Sally Mintz

E.M.

To Rosa

D.C.

To my teachers and the sternest teacher of all, life,
whose lessons are usually learned too late.

O.C.

BRIEF CONTENTS

CONTENTS

PREFACE

Politics is a fascinating subject and one that affects all of our lives. We decided to write this textbook in order to provide students with an interesting, easy-to-read, and straightforward introduction to politics. Our goal has been to offer a clear explanation of the basics of politics, while at the same time raising challenging questions that will encourage students to think deeply about the contemporary political world. Although it is important to understand the politics and governing of our own country, globalization is making it equally important to understand what is happening in the world at large and how this affects our lives in Canada.

Some students are turned off by politics because they see it as an activity involving people who seek personal benefits or glory. The overblown rhetoric, distortions, and lies of government leaders, the exaggerations and unfulfilled promises of the politicians who seek our votes, and the violence and wars that have been justified with dubious political ideals are certainly sufficient to lead us to a skeptical view of politics.

However, there is another side to the story. Politics can and should also be about how we might best achieve what is good for our communities and the world as a whole. Humanity faces many important challenges—for example, how to establish and expand human rights, protect the environment, reduce poverty, and create a more peaceful world. Political actions and decisions are very important in dealing with such challenges. In order to act effectively in political life, it is essential to understand how the political world works. We need to examine different views about how political communities should be organized and the values they should pursue.

In this book, we provide the basic knowledge that every citizen should have—from understanding the political parties that seek our votes to the way that Canada's parliamentary system works. But politics is about more than the institutions of governing. As you read this text, you will learn about the contending perspectives that are used to understand the world, the problems of the five-sixths of the world that lives in poverty, the global political system of the twenty-first century, and much more.

The authors of this book do not claim to have all of the answers to political problems. Nor do we want to promote a particular political perspective. Instead, our goal is to introduce our readers to the analysis of politics and government and raise important political questions to ponder and discuss.

The pedagogy of this text has been carefully developed. For example:

- A unique feature of this book is the *vignettes* that open each chapter with an interesting and often provocative story that relates to the content of the chapter. Among the vignettes are the controversy about whether Catalonia and Quebec are nations, terrorism and the "clash of civilizations," the 2007 election of the Scottish Nationalist Party, and the near defeat of a minority government in Canada.
- *Boxes* in each chapter offer special focus on key theoretical issues and provide global and Canadian examples. These boxes deal with such topics as the bungled effort to bring democracy to Iraq, whether Canada is a nation-state, why the majority of young people don't vote, and the extent to which the position of women has improved.
- To help students effectively structure their reading, we have provided *Chapter Objectives* at the start and a *Summary and Conclusion* at the end of each chapter.
- *Key terms* are printed in bold in the text, defined in the margin for instant reference, listed at the end of each chapter, and compiled in the end-of-book Glossary.
- The *Discussion Questions* at the end of each chapter are designed to spark critical thought and discussion.
- The *Further Reading* section, also at the end of each chapter, steers students toward references that will expand their understanding of the chapter's topics. *Weblinks* in the margins provide additional research resources.
- The text's *graphics*—photos, figures, tables, and cartoons—are sure to illuminate concepts discussed in the text and capture students' interest.

New to this Edition

We have been very pleased with the response to the first edition of *Politics, Power and the Common Good*. The preparation of a second edition has provided us with an opportunity not only to update the textbook, but also to make improvements throughout the book. This second edition features several new topics, including:

- Citizenship and identity politics (Chapter 2)
- Religious fundamentalism (Chapter 6)
- Terrorism, guerrilla insurgency, and revolution (Chapter 12)

- General perspectives on the policy process and policy outcomes (Chapter 17)
- Foreign policy (Chapter 20)

The treatment of a number of important topics has been expanded, including:

- Globalization (Chapter 2)
- Social democracy (Chapter 5)
- Decline of parties (Chapter 9)
- European Union (Chapter 14)
- Local governments (Chapter 14)
- Semi-presidential systems (Chapter 16)

The organization of some topics has been modified to increase clarity:

- Discussion of the New Right has been integrated into the section on conservatism in Chapter 5.
- Discussion of social movements has shifted to Chapter 11 (collective action), with Chapter 12 now focusing on various forms of unconventional political activity.
- Parliamentary and presidential systems are now discussed in separate chapters (Chapters 15 and 16).
- Discussion of public administration has moved to Chapter 17.

Finally, the definitions of some basic concepts such as politics, power, the common good, and nationalism have been modified or clarified.

Supplements

The supplements package for this book has been carefully created to enhance the topics discussed in the text.

Instructor's Resource CD-ROM (IRCD). This instructor resource CD includes the *Instructor's Manual, Test Item File,* and *PowerPoint Presentations.*

Instructor's Manual. For each chapter of the text, this manual provides sample lecture outlines, clarification of potentially confusing terms and ideas, and a description of the major themes. In addition, it includes sample course outlines and lecture schedules.

Powerpoint Presentations. This instructor resource contains key points and lecture notes to accompany each chapter in the text.

Test Item File. This test bank contains more than 900 multiple choice, true/false, short answer, and essay questions.

Mytest. The test bank is also available as a MyTest, a powerful assessment generation program that helps instructors easily create and print quizzes, tests, exams, as well as homework or practice handouts. Questions and tests can be authored online, allowing instructors ultimate flexibility and the ability to manage assessments efficiently anywhere, at any time. The MyTest can be accessed by visiting **www.pearsonmytest.com/**.

Companion Website. This student resource features chapter objectives and study questions, as well as links to interesting material and information from other sites on the Web that reinforce and enhance the content of each chapter. The companion website can be accessed at **www.pearsoned.ca/mintz**.

ACKNOWLEDGEMENTS

Writing a textbook is somewhat of a parasitic activity. We have ransacked the books and articles of our esteemed colleagues for ideas that we hope we have explained in an interesting and accessible way to readers unfamiliar with the theories and jargon of the discipline. We have attempted to cite what we have borrowed from the extensive literature of political science and related disciplines. If we have overlooked someone's contributions, we extend our apologies and ask that we be informed so that proper acknowledgement can be made in the next edition.

We would like to thank the many political science professors who provided detailed and helpful suggestions by reviewing the first edition of this book and the draft chapters of the second edition. Among these reviewers were the following individuals (in alphabetical order): Duane Bratt, Mount Royal College; Paul Gecelovsky, University of Lethbridge; Harold Jansen, University of Lethbridge; Dimitrios Karmis, University of Ottawa; Ayla Kilic, Okanagan College; Jocelyne Praud, University of Regina; Meir Serfaty, Brandon University; Elizabeth Smythe, Concordia University College of Alberta; and Lori Turnbull, Dalhousie University.

We would also like to thank the many people at Pearson Education Canada whose professional expertise and enthusiasm have been essential in developing this text. In particular, we would like to thank Jennifer Murray, Senior Developmental Editor; Christine Cozens, Executive Acquisitions Editor; Susan Broadhurst, Production Editor and Copy Editor; and John Firth, Proofreader. Finally, we would like to thank Tami Thirlwell, whose original cartoons were specially designed for this book.

Eric Mintz would like to thank Leigh Kelloway for her assistance in updating the references and for comments on a couple of chapters. As with the first edition, Diane Mintz helped in a variety of ways to ensure that this book is clearly written and easy to understand. She also provided a greatly appreciated and comfortable home environment during the lengthy process of revising this text. Eric would also like to thank Kaila and Aaron for their encouragement and support.

David Close would like to thank Sherrill Pike for reading and commenting on the chapters he drafted. He also appreciates the support of the Political Science Department at Memorial University of Newfoundland for his work.

Osvaldo Croci would like to thank Livianna Tossutti for many interesting political discussions and his colleagues at Memorial University for making the atmosphere in the Political Science Department professional but also enjoyable, and thus ideal for research.

We look forward to receiving comments and suggestions from students, teaching assistants, professors, and other readers to help us in writing the next edition. Please send comments to emintz@swgc.ca with the subject line "politics text."

A Great Way to Learn and Instruct Online

The Pearson Education Canada Companion Website is easy to navigate and is organized to correspond to the chapters in this textbook. Whether you are a student in the classroom or a distance learner you will discover helpful resources for in-depth study and research that empower you in your quest for greater knowledge and maximize your potential for success in the course.

Companion Website

[www.pearsoned.ca/mintz]

Enter

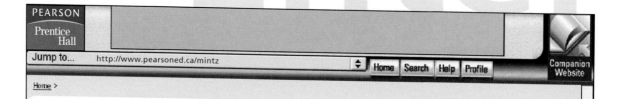

PEARSON
Prentice
Hall

Jump to... | http://www.pearsoned.ca/mintz | Home | Search | Help | Profile

Companion
Website

Home >

Companion Website

Politics, Power and the Common Good, Second Edition, by Mintz, Close, and Croci

POLITICS,
POWER
AND THE
COMMON
GOOD

Student Resources

The modules in this section provide students with tools for learning course material. These modules include
- Chapter Objectives
- Chapter Quizzes
- Internet Activities
- Web Destinations

In the quiz modules students can send answers to the grader and receive instant feedback on their progress through the Results Reporter. Coaching comments and references to the textbook may be available to ensure that students take advantage of all available resources to enhance their learning experience.

PART I

INTRODUCTION

Chapter 1

UNDERSTANDING POLITICS

PHOTO ABOVE: Tens of thousands of protesters demonstrated at the Third Summit of the Americas in Quebec City, 2001. Protesters argued that the free trade pact would give private corporations the right to provide key public services.

CHAPTER OBJECTIVES

After reading this chapter you should be able to:

1. discuss the importance of politics
2. explain why conflict is a major feature of politics
3. define the concepts of power, authority, and legitimacy
4. discuss whether seeking the common good is a meaningful goal of political life
5. explain the difference between the empirical and normative analysis of politics

Tens of thousands of protesters demonstrated in Quebec City in April 2001 as government leaders and officials from thirty-four countries met to discuss the establishment of a free-trade area that would include almost all of North and South America. Generally, the protesters were peaceful. However, some of the youthful protesters hurled teddy bears, rocks, and other objects across the 3.8-kilometre-long chain-link fence that had been erected to keep protesters out of the centre of Quebec City, where the Summit of the Americas was being held. Police responded with tear gas, pepper spray, rubber bullets, and stun guns. About four hundred protesters were arrested. Fifty-seven protesters and forty-five police officers were hurt.

The protest was part of the anti-globalization movement that had shut down meetings of the World Trade Organization in Seattle in 1999 and continues to demonstrate at the meetings of various international organizations committed to developing a global free-market capitalist economy. The Quebec City protesters—including students, environmentalists, trade unionists, social activists, and nationalists from many countries, but especially from across Canada—argued that the proposed Free Trade Area of the Americas (FTAA) agreement would give private, profit-oriented corporations the right to provide such public services as education and health care and reduce governments' power to protect the environment and workers.

The events at Quebec City illustrate some important features of the nature of politics. For example, exaggeration is commonplace as interested parties struggle to affect public opinion. Members of the general public who tried to make sense of the Quebec City events received very different interpretations from government, protesters, and the media. The Canadian government claimed that the summit was a major step toward ensuring democracy throughout the Americas. Protesters asserted that the terms of a free-trade agreement would subvert democracy in the interests of big corporations. The mass media highlighted the clashes between protesters and police, but generally devoted little attention to the arguments for and against the proposed free-trade agreement.

Politics involves not only governments, legislatures, and politicians, but also a wide range of groups and individuals. Different interests, values, opinions, and perspectives are responsible for many of the conflicts that occur in politics and make achieving the common good of the political community a difficult challenge, as we discuss in this chapter.

POLITICS AND CONFLICT

Conflict and disagreement are important basic features of politics for four major reasons:

- people have different interests
- people embrace different values
- people have different identities
- people struggle for power in the political arena

Different Interests

The policies that are adopted for a political community often benefit (or harm) some members of the political community more than others. For example, the business community generally supports free trade because it expects to benefit by having better access to larger markets for its goods and services. Business executives like the fact that free-trade agreements can limit governments' ability to pass laws and regulations that restrict trade and investment. In general, the business community sees free-trade agreements as desirable because they reduce the ability of government to "interfere" in business decision making.

Unions, on the other hand, worry that free-trade agreements will make it easier for business to relocate to low-wage countries. The workers that unions represent may face the loss of their jobs or pressure to accept lower wages and poorer working conditions. And student organizations are concerned when they see proposals for free trade in services because they fear that this will lead to the erosion of publicly funded education by making it easier for profit-seeking corporations to provide educational services.

Different Values

The values that people seek to achieve through political action are undoubtedly affected by their interests. We are not surprised when we hear business people praise the free-enterprise economic system and seek to reduce government regulation of business. Nor are we surprised when students demand lower tuition fees and criticize policies that might undermine publicly funded education. Of course, people will refer to general values that have widespread support to try to justify political actions designed to advance their own personal interests. For example, business people asking for a government subsidy argue that it will be good for job creation, regional development, or Canada's technological advancement—not that it will make them richer.

Nevertheless, the values that people seek to obtain through politics are not only a product of their own interests and circumstances. Consider students who are active in the non-governmental organization Oxfam because of a concern about poverty in Africa, or who participate in the letter-writing campaigns of Amnesty International because they want to promote human rights around the world. They are not seeking benefits for themselves, but rather are acting to pursue their values. These values reflect their view of what is good for humanity.

The pursuit of values, like the pursuit of one's own interests, can be a source of political conflict. For example, the disputes between pro-life and pro-choice activists over the issue of abortion reflect differences in deeply held values. Although differences concerning interests can often be settled by compromise, it can sometimes be difficult or impossible to find an acceptable compromise when opposing values are at stake. Neither pro-life nor pro-choice groups would likely be satisfied with a compromise in which abortion was legal in certain but limited circumstances.

Fortunately, there are often a variety of general values that are widely shared within a political community. For example, most Canadians would agree that freedom, equality, justice, order, prosperity, and peace are desirable values. This does not mean that we all think about these values in the same way. For example, some people think of equality as existing when all persons have the same rights and are treated in the same way by the law. Others argue that equality exists only if each individual has the same opportunity to get ahead in life. Still others define equality in terms of an equal sharing of the wealth of the country. Thus, we may agree that equality is desirable, but disagree about its meaning and consequently what policies are desirable to achieve greater equality.

Furthermore, different people often place a different priority on the values that they share with others. For example, even though many people value both freedom and order, these values sometimes conflict. For those who place a higher value on freedom, police attempts to limit protest activity in the name of maintaining order may be viewed as unjustified. Those who place a higher value on order may expect the police to curtail protest demonstrations because of the risk of unruly behaviour.

The existence of shared values, therefore, does not eliminate disagreement over the policies that a political community should adopt. However, it can be the basis for discussion about how best to achieve the shared values and for co-operation in achieving goals based on those values.

Different Identities

People within a political community will often identify with one or more particular groups. One may, for example, think of oneself primarily as Canadian, Québécois, or Albertan; Italian-Canadian, Aboriginal, or black; gay, working class, or Muslim; female, student, or Catholic; or various combinations of such identities. Those identifying with particular groups will often evaluate the actions of government or the platforms of political parties in light of those identities. This may involve seeking redress for perceived injustices, equitable representation for their group in Parliament, assistance in preserving or developing their identity, some ability for the group to govern itself, or simply some form of recognition of the worthiness of the group.

Different identities can lead to conflict and disagreement because of the different interests or values of groups. However, the desire for recognition can also lead to disagreement. For example, the idea that the distinctive identity of Quebec society should be recognized in the Canadian constitution has resulted in serious political disagreements.

The Competitive Struggle for Power

When we think about politics, our attention is often drawn to the struggle for political power. High-profile political events such as election campaigns, the selection of the leader of a political party, and Question Period in the House of Commons can be easily understood as part of an ongoing struggle for power.

Most politicians enjoy being in positions of political power and vigorously compete to gain and maintain their positions. The desire to have power to affect or control decision making for the community and the longing for the status of high political office can be strong motivating factors for political competition. As well, some people engage in political activity because they enjoy the competition that it often involves. To work hard for a candidate or party and see them win an election can be as exciting as being on a winning hockey team.

"Don't they understand that politics is about power?"

Most political activity, however, is motivated primarily by a desire to affect the direction and policies of the political community. Power is usually a means to an end rather than a goal in itself (Easton, 1953). Even on the international level where the pursuit of power is often most evident, power is often sought to achieve particular objectives, such as protecting the security of a country, rather than for its own sake.

The extent to which the interests and values of a particular group are taken into account in decision making is strongly affected by the power that a group is able to bring to bear in affecting that decision. The demonstrators protesting in Quebec City were trying to show that they were not simply powerless individuals who could be ignored: rather, they were a group that needed to be reckoned with. By mobilizing a substantial number of determined supporters and attracting media attention, they were able to raise concerns that might otherwise have gone unnoticed. The general public was largely unaware of the Summit of the Americas and the issues involved in negotiating the FTAA until the public spectacle of the demonstrations brought it to their attention.

Raising public awareness is one way in which a group can try to affect government policies, particularly in the long run. In the short run, however, the Quebec City demonstration had little effect on the free-trade negotiations, other than encouraging government spokespersons to emphasize the democratic principles agreed to at the Summit of the Americas.[1] Other powerful forces, such as the business representatives who were directly involved in consultations about free-trade negotiations and had good access to top government officials, likely have had a greater impact on the positions taken by the Canadian government. Power is often exercised behind closed doors and is thus not visible to the casual observer.

Politics and Conflict Resolution

Although war and violent forms of conflict are a significant part of the reality of politics, most conflicts and disagreements are settled in a more peaceful fashion. Indeed, much political activity is directed at the resolution of conflicts. Governments and political parties often attempt to find compromises to try to keep different groups reasonably satisfied. In the view of British political scientist Bernard Crick (1963), politics in democratic countries involves listening to discordant interests, conciliating them, and bringing them together so that each contributes positively to the process of governing. When decisions are made after considerable discussion, consultation with groups that have differing interests and values, and efforts to find acceptable compromises, a

---

[1] In the years following the Summit, the goal of establishing the FTAA was not realized particularly because of dwindling support for the FTAA in several Latin American countries and the defeat of governments committed to that objective.

consensus about a particular course of action may develop. The use of fair and widely accepted procedures for making decisions can assist in resolving conflicts and gaining acceptance for the decisions that are made.

Because human beings are not only competitive individuals concerned with their own interests, but also social beings concerned with the well-being of the communities with which they identify, political conflicts can be resolved, particularly where shared values are present within the community. Thus although disagreement and conflict is an important feature of politics, the attention given to political conflict by the media can lead us to overlook the extent of co-operation and consensus that exists in well-functioning political communities.

BASIC CONCEPTS

Politics

Politics can be viewed as a feature of all organized human activity (Leftwich, 1983). In all groups, disagreements arise as to what should be done, and different people try to get the group to adopt the course of action they prefer. Relationships of power and authority (discussed below) are important in any group, whether a family, a business, a religious organization, or the government (Dahl, 1984). However, political science generally focuses on such characteristics as they relate to the making of governing decisions.

David Easton's definition of politics as the "authoritative allocation of values for a society" (1953, p. 129) is widely used by political scientists. The "allocation of values" refers to how the limited resources of a society (more generally, those things that are desired or valued) are allocated (distributed). By referring to the *authoritative* allocation of values, Easton suggests that what is distinctive about the allocation of values through governmental institutions is that this allocation is generally accepted as binding on all persons in the community. People feel that they should accept or obey the policies of government that affect them (Easton, 1953). Politics, in this view, "concerns all those varieties of activity that influence significantly the kind of authoritative policy adopted for a society and the way it is put into practice" (Easton, 1953, p. 128). However, while many government decisions are authoritative, governments also take actions that are not considered binding on the members of the political community. For example, governments try to persuade us to adopt healthier lifestyles and often enter into voluntary agreements with industries to reduce pollution.

POLITICS
Activity related to influencing, making, or implementing collective decisions for a political community.

For the purposes of this book, we define **politics** as activity related to influencing, making, or implementing collective decisions for a political community. Political activity includes trying to influence government decisions and policies, mobilizing support for political parties seeking to gain or maintain control of the government, and trying to change or maintain the basic characteristics of

A Broader View of Politics

We often think of political activity as involving the struggle for political power and the attempts to influence the decisions of government. But this may be too limited a focus. Consider the following example.

Various environmental groups have sought to end the clear-cutting practices of forest companies in British Columbia. Having had limited success in persuading the B.C. government to pass stricter logging regulations, they turned to other methods to achieve their objective. Europeans were encouraged to participate in a boycott of products made with B.C. lumber, and pressure was put on retail businesses such as Home Depot only to sell lumber produced in an environmentally friendly manner. These activities had considerable success, and a number of B.C. forest companies began to change their logging practices.

In many ways, these activities by environmental groups are similar to what we normally consider as political. People were mobilized to try to achieve an objective that was viewed as being in the public interest. Rather than influencing government to adopt a policy that might change the actions of logging companies, environmental groups were able to directly pressure some of the companies to change their actions to deal with a public problem. The activities of environmental groups might therefore be considered political, even though the groups decided to try to affect the decisions of private businesses rather than the decisions of government.

the political community. Raising awareness of problems affecting the political community and efforts to change political values, attitudes, and opinions can also be viewed as political. As well (as discussed in Box 1-1, A Broader View of Politics), taking action concerning problems that some believe should be the subject of collective decisions might also be considered political.

Power

Discussion and analysis of politics often focuses on power. Statements such as "the prime minister is very powerful," "big business is more powerful than ordinary citizens," and "the United States is the most powerful country in the world" are very frequently made. Determining the validity of such statements, however, can be difficult and controversial. Nevertheless, power is important in affecting what gets done in political life.

Power can be defined as the ability to achieve an objective by influencing the behaviour of others (Nye, 2004), particularly to get them to do what they would not have otherwise done.[2] Power, in this definition, is a relationship among different individuals and groups. As such, it is not easily quantifiable and changes depending on the objective being pursued and the circumstances

POWER
The ability to achieve an objective by influencing the behaviour of others, particularly to get them to do what they would not have otherwise done.

---

[2] Some political scientists prefer to use the term *influence* for the general ability to affect behaviour, leaving the term *power* to refer to the use of coercion, inducements, or manipulation to get people to act against their own desires or interests (Dahl, 1984).

involved. For example, the president of the United States may be very powerful in decisions concerning the deployment of armed forces, but less powerful when trying to change American agricultural policies.

Power does not necessarily mean that one actor controls or dominates others, although the term is generally used to refer to situations where one actor is in a stronger position than other actors. Politics typically involves considerable bargaining and negotiating among different actors. Although bargaining sometimes involves exchange among equals (as when two legislators agree to support each other's proposals), the type of bargain achieved often reflects differences in power among the parties to the bargain. For example, rich countries may be in a better position than poor countries to negotiate an international trade agreement favourable to their interests because of their greater power, even if some concessions are made to poorer countries to gain their agreement or to legitimate the agreement.

Political power can be exerted in several different ways.[3] *Coercion* involves using fear or threats of harmful consequences to achieve an outcome. For example, Nazi Germany's threat to invade Czechoslovakia in 1938 was successful in convincing the Czech government to allow Germany to annex part of its territory. If your employer threatens to fire you unless you work on behalf of a certain candidate in an election, coercive power has been used to intimidate you. *Inducements* involve achieving an outcome by offering a reward or bribe. For example, if your employer promises to give you a promotion should you decide to support a particular candidate, power has been exercised in the form of an inducement. *Persuasion* is a very important aspect of political life, as people are often involved in trying to persuade other people to think and act in particular ways. Persuasion may involve the use of truthful information to encourage people to act in accordance with their own interests or values, or the use of misleading information to manipulate people. In practice, it is often difficult to distinguish between persuasion based on truthful information and persuasion involving manipulation, as exaggeration and selective presentation of the facts are often used to make a persuasive argument. Power can also be exercised through *leadership*. For example, a country that is successful in providing wealth and harmony to its population may be better able to convince other countries to follow its example (Nye, 2004).

Power is often viewed negatively because of its association with domination. Those in governing positions have used the power they wield to establish, promote, or defend systems of economic, social, military, and ideological

---

[3] Power can be significant even when there is no intentional exercise of power. Political actors may change their behaviour because they *anticipate* that there will be negative consequences from those with greater power if they act in a particular way, even if no direct threat has been made. For example, knowing that the United States has imposed severe economic sanctions on Cuba, other Caribbean countries may be reluctant to act in ways that could result in similar consequences.

power involving domination and exploitation. As well, there are always tendencies for those with political power to use their power for their own benefit rather than for the good of the political community. In addition, those in powerful positions may become arrogant and unresponsive to the needs and desires of the population. As American Senator William Fulbright put it, "power has a way of undermining judgment, of planting delusions of grandeur in the minds of otherwise sensible people and otherwise sensible nations" (cited in Lobe, 2002, p. 3).

Power is often thought of in terms of some people, groups, or countries having *power over* others. However, we can also think about the *power to* achieve collective goals. Power is often necessary to induce people to co-operate in order to achieve objectives that benefit themselves and the political community as a whole, such as developing the economy, providing security, or protecting the environment. Such objectives may not be easily achieved by individuals, but might be achievable by using the collective power of the community organized by government. This can be illustrated by what is known as the **free rider problem**. Imagine that all persons in a community agreed they would each contribute to building a road that would benefit everyone. One miserly individual might decide not to contribute to the cost of building the road, knowing that the road would still be built with the contributions of others. However, if enough people followed this self-interested logic, the road might never be built and everyone would suffer. The use of the coercive power of government (for example, to enforce the payment of taxes) is often useful or necessary to achieve the common good. However, as Box 1-2, The Tragedy of the Commons, illustrates, there are sometimes alternatives to the use of coercive action by government to achieve the common good.

FREE RIDER PROBLEM
A problem with voluntary collective action that results because an individual can enjoy the benefits of group action without contributing.

THE DISTRIBUTION OF POWER In any society, the resources that give individuals and groups the potential to exert political power are unequally distributed. Wealth, control of important aspects of the economy, social status and prestige, official position, control of information and expertise, the ability to mobilize supporters, control of the means of force, and the ability to influence people are some of the resources that can be used for advantage in politics. Although all citizens in a democracy have some potential power through their ability to vote, other resources are less equally distributed.

Understanding the distribution of power involves more than adding up the resources available to different groups. Groups differ in how effectively they use their power resources. Some groups are more successful than others in mobilizing potential supporters, forming alliances with other groups, and appealing to the values and beliefs of the community to achieve their objectives. As Box 1-3, People Power, illustrates, mobilizing ordinary citizens around a popular cause can sometimes bring about fundamental changes.

The power of different groups is not only a product of their skill in mobilizing resources. Political institutions may be organized and operate in ways

The Tragedy of the Commons

In a famous article Garrett Hardin (1968) asks us to imagine a situation where herders allow their flocks to graze on a common pasture (that is, a pasture available freely to all members of the community). To make more money, each herder may find it profitable to purchase more cattle to graze on the common land. Eventually, the pasture will be overgrazed and all will suffer. One solution would be to privatize the commons, with the owner then charging a fee to allow each head of cattle to graze there. This would, however, not necessarily lead to the common good, as only those who could afford the fee could then graze their cattle, or the owner might convert the pasture to another, more profitable endeavour. The alternative that Hardin favours involves a coercive government ensuring that the commons is not overused.

However, Elinor Ostrom (2000), looking at a variety of real-world situations, points out that under the right circumstances co-operation among the users of a common resource, such as water or pastures, can result in the proper management of that resource. These conditions include the development of a sense of community, shared values, and mechanisms to monitor and enforce the use of the resource to ensure that no cheating occurs. In contrast to Hardin's bleak outlook, which suggests that a dictatorial, overbearing global government is needed to solve global environmental problems such as overpopulation, Ostrom's analysis points to the possibility that co-operation to achieve solutions potentially can be arrived at even when individuals are concerned with their own interests, provided that there is trust and discussion among the members of the community. To what extent this can apply to global problems remains an open question, although Ostrom suggests that co-operative institutions in combination with governments and markets can be useful in dealing with global environmental problems (Dietz, Ostrom, & Stern, 2003).

that advantage or disadvantage certain groups. For example, until recently the House of Lords, the upper chamber of the British Parliament, was designed to try to entrench the power of the aristocracy. Likewise, the method of allocating representatives to the provincial legislatures in some Canadian provinces deliberately overrepresents rural areas, thus giving the people of those areas greater potential power than if there was equal representation by population.

Analysts often disagree about how concentrated or dispersed power is in particular political communities. In part, these disagreements are a result of different perspectives about power, which can lead to different conclusions about the distribution of power and about who is powerful. Disagreements about how to analyze the distribution of power can be summarized as the **three faces of power** (see Table 1-1).

THREE FACES OF POWER
The argument that looking at who affects particular decisions is insufficient to analyze power. Power can also involve the ability to keep issues off the political agenda and the ability to affect the dominant values of society.

TABLE 1-1
THE THREE FACES OF POWER

FIRST FACE	Ability to affect decisions
SECOND FACE	Ability to ensure that issues are not raised
THIRD FACE	Ability to affect the dominant ideas of society

BOX 1-3

People Power

Those who control large corporations, occupy top government positions, or head major social organizations clearly have many resources that can be used to affect what the political community does. Occasionally, however, groups and individuals with seemingly few resources are able to bring about major changes.

The dictatorial Philippine government of Ferdinand Marcos was successfully challenged in 1986 when a very large number of people, including praying nuns, sat down in front of the army's tanks and refused to move. In Eastern Europe, peaceful demonstrations by ever-larger numbers of people helped to bring down communist regimes in 1989. Black South Africans, by engaging in a determined struggle against the white minority-controlled government and organizing international support for their cause, were eventually successful in challenging the system of apartheid that had suppressed them. Canadian Aboriginals, who in the past were ignored by the political system, have been able to make their voices heard through successful legal cases in the courts, confrontation with Canadian authorities, and building a strong moral case that they have been treated unjustly. In each case, ordinary or disadvantaged people were able to challenge the powerful through determined and skilful action, even though serious personal risks and sacrifices were involved.

Of course, "people power" is not always successful. For example, in the People's Republic of China, student-led actions to support demands for democracy were brutally suppressed by the army on orders from the Communist party leadership in 1989. Despite the outrage in many parts of the world when news coverage revealed the suppression of peaceful protest, the Chinese government did not back away from its hard-line stance.

People power. Citizens of Prague, Czechoslovakia, turned out by the hundreds of thousands in November 1989 to protest the Communist regime led by General Secretary Milos Jakes. Just one month later, the regime toppled peacefully, and the formerly Communist Assembly elected Václav Havel, leader of the pro-democracy Civic Forum, as the country's president.

THE THREE FACES OF POWER One way to assess the distribution of power is to examine which groups or individuals are most successful in affecting a variety of decisions (the "first face" of power). If, for example, one group is usually successful in getting its way, then we would conclude that political power is highly concentrated. If, on the other hand, a variety of groups representing different interests had a significant influence on decisions, or if different groups influenced different decisions, we would conclude that political power is dispersed rather than concentrated.

However, some have argued that measuring political power in terms of who influenced particular decisions does not tell us the complete story. Bachrach and Baratz (1962) point out that power can be manifested not only by winning on contentious issues, but also by ensuring that certain issues are not raised in the first place. They call this deliberate avoidance of an important problem a "non-decision." For example, the owner of a polluting factory may be said to be powerful if discussion of the pollution problem is deliberately avoided by the political leaders of the community or by the media. In other words, this "second face" of power involves exercising control over the **political agenda**, that is, the issues that are considered important and are given priority in political deliberations.

POLITICAL AGENDA
The issues that are considered important and given priority in political deliberations.

Steven Lukes (1974) argues that there is a third face of power that is ignored when we focus on who influences specific decisions and "non-decisions." Those who are able to shape the dominant ideas in a society will have a general effect on the politics of that society and the decisions that are made. If those dominant ideas work against the interests of the weaker groups in society, and result in the weaker groups acting against their own "true" interests, then power has been exercised.

Take, for example, societies where women are expected to confine themselves to domestic responsibilities such as cooking, cleaning, and raising children, while men are involved in public activities, including politics. Ideas that these "separate spheres" are "natural" or that women do not have the qualities to participate in public life might lead many women to believe that the proper role of women is different from that of men, and thus not to challenge that system. Power, in this case, has been exerted through the dominant ideas that favour the interests of men, rather than through coercion or particular governmental decisions.

A problem with Lukes' analysis is that it is often difficult and controversial to determine what a person or group's true interests are. For example, are workers who vote for a party that favours policies that give tax breaks to promote business activity acting against their true interests? Further, the assumption that the leading ideas in a society necessarily reflect and serve the interests of the dominant groups in society is contentious. For example, the traditional ideas concerning the proper role of women that reflected male dominance have been challenged in Canada and a number of other societies in recent decades Likewise, the free-market capitalist ideas that work to the advantage of big business interests, although influential, have not been wholeheartedly accepted by a substantial proportion of the population.

Nevertheless, Lukes' analysis is useful in pointing out that power not only can be thought of as the ability to directly affect the behaviour of others, but also can operate indirectly by shaping people's ideas and preferences, which, in turn, affects how they act (Hay, 1997; Nye, 2004).

THE CONCENTRATION OF POWER Studies of the distribution of power in terms of who influences the decision making in some American communities have suggested that power is not highly concentrated in a small number of hands (Dahl, 1961). In the **pluralist perspective**, a wide variety of groups has an ability to influence the decisions of government in democratic systems that allow groups the freedom to organize and take action. Some groups may have a greater ability than others to influence particular types of decisions, but no one group or set of groups has the dominant influence on most or all decisions.

Others, however, have tried to show that power in all communities is concentrated in a small number of hands, particularly in the elites that hold the top positions in the major institutions of the economy, society, and politics (Panitch, 1995). Those who take this **elitist perspective** often focus on the interconnections among elite groups, their common backgrounds, and the extent to which they have a shared outlook that would bias their key decisions (Scott, 2001). For example, C. Wright Mills (1956) argued that a power elite, consisting of the top government, business, and military leaders, was crucial in setting the direction of the United States. In Canada, John Porter (1965) found that the political elite interacted with the economic elite and shared their conservative values. Power was, in Porter's view, largely concentrated in the hands of various connected elites. There was, however, disagreement from time to time, particularly between the economic and political elites.

Generally, the pluralist view sees democratic politics as working to satisfy (though not necessarily perfectly) the wishes of a wide variety of interests in society. The elitist view is more critical, suggesting that democratic procedures hide the reality that the "true" interests of much of society are not properly served. Elites are able not only to influence government decisions and "non-decisions," but also to influence the leading ideas of the society as a whole in ways that serve their own interests. Pluralists see government as open to influence from a wide variety of groups while elitists view the ruling elites as a group that is largely "closed off" from the ruled (Evans, 2006).

Authority and Legitimacy

Authority, the right to exercise power, is of special importance in understanding politics. Those with political authority claim that they have been *authorized* (whether by God, tradition, constitutional rules, election, or some other source) to govern. Political authority that is accepted by those being governed (or at least not challenged by a significant part of the population) can be described as legitimate. Although **legitimacy** may be established by legal procedures, legitimacy (as used in political science) refers more generally to the acceptance of the right to rule of those in positions of authority whether or not it was established by law.

PLURALIST PERSPECTIVE
The freedom of individuals to establish and join groups that are not controlled by the government results in a wide variety of groups having an ability to influence the decisions of government, with no group dominant.

ELITIST PERSPECTIVE
The view that power in all communities is concentrated in a small number of hands, particularly in the elites that hold the top positions in the major institutions of the economy, society, and politics.

AUTHORITY
The right to exercise power. Those with political authority claim that they have been *authorized* to govern.

LEGITIMACY
Acceptance by the members of a political community that those in positions of authority have the right to govern.

ESTABLISHING AND MAINTAINING LEGITIMACY How is the legitimacy of a system of governing established and maintained? Why do most Canadians accept the right of a few people to make decisions for the political community, even though they may not agree with the decisions that are being made? German sociologist Max Weber (1864–1920) described three basic types of authority, each of which could try to establish its legitimacy in its own way:

- charismatic authority
- traditional authority
- legal–rational authority

CHARISMATIC AUTHORITY
Authority based on the perception that a leader has extraordinary or supernatural qualities.

Charismatic authority is based on the perception that a leader has extraordinary or supernatural qualities established through such means as performing miracles, issuing prophecies, or leading a military victory. The legitimacy of charismatic authority "rests upon the belief in magical powers, revelations and hero worship" by the followers (Weber, 1958, p. 296). Charismatic leaders, such as Mao Zedong, leader of the Chinese Communist revolution, have inspired intense devotion in their followers.

TRADITIONAL AUTHORITY
Authority based on customs that establish the right of certain persons to rule.

Traditional authority, whether exercised through the elders of a tribe or a ruling family, is based on customs that establish the right of certain persons to rule. The traditional authority of monarchs who inherited their position was often buttressed with the idea that rulers had a divinely created right to rule that

▶ Charismatic leaders, such as Mao Zedong, leader of the Chinese Communist revolution, inspire intense devotion in their followers. Charismatic authority rests upon the belief of followers in magical powers, revelations, and hero worship. The Chinese media depicted an elderly Mao supposedly performing the heroic feat of swimming across the Yangtze River to maintain his charismatic image.

was sanctified by religious authorities. Japanese emperors, for example, claimed to be descended from the sun goddess. The legitimacy of traditional authority can be based on beliefs that a certain family has always ruled and that customs are sacred practices that will bring evil consequences if violated (Weber, 1958).

Modern societies, in Weber's view, are characterized by efficient management and bureaucratic organization. The **legal–rational authority** of modern societies is based on legal rules and procedures rather than on the personal qualities or characteristics of the rulers. Authority is impersonal in the sense that it rests in official positions such as prime minister or president, rather than in the individuals holding such positions. The right of those in governing positions to rule is based on being chosen by a set of established and accepted legal procedures. Those holding official positions are expected to act in accordance with legal rules and procedures. Thus, their authority is limited. The legitimacy of the system of governing is based on a belief in the legality of the procedures for selecting those who have official duties and the legal "correctness" of the procedures that are used in governing (Weber, 1958).

LEGAL–RATIONAL AUTHORITY
The right to rule based on legal rules and procedures rather than on the personal qualities or characteristics of the rulers.

Holding free and fair elections involving all adult citizens to designate those authorized to make governing decisions is often considered to be the most effective way of establishing the legitimacy of government. Nevertheless, a "legitimacy crisis" can occur even in democratic systems (Habermas, 1975). Although an unpopular government in a democracy can be voted out, if governments are persistently ineffective in dealing with serious problems, citizens might question the legitimacy of the democratic institutions and processes in their country. For example, if the policies of successive governments led to widespread poverty and unemployment or to a collapse in the value of the currency, then the legitimacy of the system of governing might be challenged. Legitimacy can also be reduced if some groups feel that there is a long-term pattern of mistreatment by the government. In other words, legitimacy not only may require an acceptance of the procedures by which governing authorities are chosen and actions taken, but also may depend on the perceived rightfulness of how government (or more generally the system of governing) exercises its authority (Barnard, 2001). In particular, the governing authorities will have a higher level of legitimacy if their actions are perceived as being consistent with the general principles and values of the political community (Gilley, 2006).

In addition, a system of governing that is imposed on a country or on a part of the population without its consent might be viewed by as illegitimate, even if it establishes democratic procedures. For example, when a democratic system of governing was established in Germany after the First World War, some Germans doubted its legitimacy, partly because they viewed it as being imposed on the country by the victors in that war. The problem of legitimacy, combined with the failure of German governments to deal effectively with the problems the country faced, eventually contributed to the demise of the democratic system and the takeover by Adolf Hitler and the Nazi party. Likewise, conquered peoples are often unwilling to accept the authority of the governing authorities regardless of how well the authorities govern.

THE SIGNIFICANCE OF LEGITIMACY Effective governing depends not only on governing institutions having the power to force people to act in certain ways, but also on their ability to establish and maintain legitimate authority. A government that is not accepted as legitimate by a significant proportion of the population will have to devote much of its energy and resources to persuading or coercing the population to obey its laws and maintain order. All governments rely on coercion and other forms of power to some extent, but generally people feel an obligation to obey a legitimate government. Thus, a government whose rule is considered legitimate can rely more on authority than on coercion to get people to obey the laws it adopts.

Having legitimate authority gives government a powerful resource to achieve its goals. People usually obey laws, even when they find those laws against their interests or values, because they view the source of those laws as legitimate. This can potentially allow the government to act for the good of the community as a whole, even when some may object to the policies adopted. However, even though most people would agree that political authority is a necessary and desirable feature of an orderly society, questions can arise concerning whether there are circumstances in which authority should be resisted or disobeyed. What would you do if you were drafted to fight in a war that you considered unjust? Would you resist the authority of a democratically elected government that was persecuting an unpopular minority, even if that persecution were done in a legal manner?

The Common Good

Political philosophers have often viewed politics as different from other activities in that it is concerned with what is common to the community as a whole. Ensuring the good functioning of the basic activities of governing—such as maintaining order and security, providing for a just settlement of disputes, and taking actions to promote a prosperous, sustainable economy—potentially benefits all members of the political community (Wolin, 1960). Ideally politics is about seeking the **common good** of a political community.

COMMON GOOD
What is good for the entire political community.

On the surface, the concept of the common good (also referred to as the public interest) seems uncontroversial. Who would not agree that political activity should be directed toward the common good of the political community? However, in practice, determining and achieving the common good can be contentious.

The idea of the common good rests on the assumption that the members of a political community have some interests and values in common. However, contemporary political communities often feature considerable diversity such that a consensus on what is the common good may be difficult or impossible to determine. Even if there are a number of general values such as freedom, equality, order, and justice that are shared by people within the community, these values may be thought of in different ways and different people or groups may give these values different priorities. As well, the costs and benefits of actions to achieve the common good are often unequally distributed. For example, most people would agree that reducing air pollution would be for the common good of the Canadian political community. However, the costs of reducing pollution to achieve this objective may fall more heavily on some (such as factory owners and automobile users) than others. Likewise, a free school breakfast program primarily benefits those whose parents are very poor. Nevertheless, we might view such a program as being for the common good if we assume that being part of a community involves caring about others in the community and supporting policies that help others enjoy the benefits of the community.

However, in political communities where there are sharp divisions (based, for example, on economic inequality, religion, or cultural identities), the sense of being members of a shared community and a willingness to be concerned about others may be weak or non-existent. In such political communities, the notion of the common good may not be very meaningful.

Further, for those who have an **individualist perspective** on politics, the idea of the common good and how it can be achieved is rather different. This perspective assumes that human beings act primarily in accordance with their own interests—in other words, selfishly. A community is a collection of individuals each pursuing their own interests. Thus, it is naive or hopelessly idealistic to expect people (whether as voters, politicians, or government officials) to deliberately act for the common good, particularly when that involves sacrifices of their own interests. Those who hold the individualist perspective often argue that if each person is free to pursue their own interests, the result will lead to the best overall result for the members of the community. For example, as discussed in Chapter 3, many economic theorists suggest that if individuals pursue their own self-interest in a free marketplace system, the result will be the maximization of the wealth of society.

Are we concerned only with our own good? If individuals pursue their own interests, will the good of the entire community be served? Are the communities that we live in no more than a collection of independent individuals? Critics of the individualist perspective argue that humans are social beings who flourish through harmonious interaction with others. Connected to our social nature is the capability to care about others. This capability initially develops within our own family, but can extend to the social groups to which we belong, to citizens of our country, and potentially to the world as a whole. Further, the communities to which we belong—including political communities—help to shape our sense of ourselves, that is, our identity. A sense of

INDIVIDUALIST PERSPECTIVE
A perspective that views human beings as acting primarily in accordance with their own interests.

belonging to and participating in a community (or a set of communities) could be considered an important part of a fulfilling and meaningful life. People do not only have an interest in their own material well-being, but also an interest in the quality of their community and the social relations that are a part of that community (Lutz, 1999). Individuals engage in political activity not only to advance their own interests, but also to pursue the values they think should guide the actions of government (Lewin, 1991).

ACHIEVING THE COMMON GOOD?   We often look to government to achieve the common good. But how can we be assured that government will pursue the common good rather than the particular interests of those in government? In *The Republic*, the ancient Greek philosopher Plato (c. 429–c. 347 BCE) sketched out an ideal of how the common good might be achieved. This involved placing political authority in the hands of a wise philosopher–king who had been thoroughly educated in the art of governing. To ensure that such a leader would rule for the common good rather than out of personal interest, leaders would be prevented from having a family or owning property.

What might this suggest for governments and their citizens operating in the real world and not a great thinker's utopia?

In the contemporary world, democracy is often seen as the form of government most likely to actually pursue the common good. Ideally, through discussion among citizens, an informed consensus can be reached about the policies that are desirable for the common good. However, meaningful discussion is often difficult to achieve outside of small groups and small communities. Instead, there is an expectation that decisions in a democracy will tend to reflect the opinions of the majority of the population. Even if this is the case, it does not ensure that the common good of the community will be achieved. The majority is not necessarily oriented toward the common good of all members of the community, and at various times majorities have supported policies that oppress minorities.

Some suggest that a pluralist system where a large number of interest groups put forward the demands of various groups of people will result in the common good. A potential problem here is that even if government is responsive to groups representing a wide variety of interests, this does not necessarily result in the common good. Providing particular benefits to various groups that are able to exert effective pressure may not be the same as acting for the common good. If each group pursues its own interests, the good of the entire community may be ignored.

Although seeking the common good is a worthwhile objective for political life, it should be kept in mind that the claim to be acting for the common good (or other ideals) can be deceptive. Ruthless leaders have tried to justify brutal actions in the name of the long-term good of the political community. For example, the Soviet leader Joseph Stalin tried to justify his actions, which resulted in the starvation of millions of peasants, with the ideal of creating a "classless society." Fascist leaders such as Adolf Hitler and Benito Mussolini used the appeal of the good of the nation to suppress dissent and justify wars of aggression. Even in those democratic countries where individual rights are valued, appeals to the common good are sometimes made to justify repressive government actions in order to fight terrorism, subversion, and crime. In general, there is a real danger that government leaders claiming to pursue the common good of the political community as a whole will act in ways that are oppressive to some members of that community.

A QUESTION OF COMMUNITIES The common good is often thought of in terms of the country that we live in. But the common good of the country may not necessarily be the same as the common good of the other political communities to which we belong, such as provincial or local communities. Indeed, some argue that we should be concerned about the common good of humanity. The processes of globalization (discussed in Chapter 2) are creating increased interaction and interdependence among the peoples of the world. However, despite greater awareness of and concern about what happens in other parts of the world, for most of us our sense of being part of a global political community is much weaker than our sense of being Canadian. Major differences among the peoples of the world in culture and circumstances mean that there are fewer shared interests and values upon which a consensus about the common good of humanity could be based.

Some environmentalists suggest that the common good should include not only humanity (including future generations), but also the Earth as a whole, including plants, animals, and the ecosystems upon which life is based (Daly & Cobb, 1994). Protecting the environment is ultimately essential for humanity as well as for plants and animals. But, when faced with the issue of protecting the jobs of loggers or protecting the habitat of an endangered animal or plant, should the good of human beings be given greater priority than the good of other life forms? Or as parts of an interrelated whole, are all life forms, including humans, of equal inherent worth? (Devall & Sessions, 1998).

WHAT IS POLITICAL SCIENCE?

The term **political science** may sound confusing, as politics and science seem to be very different. Indeed, some universities and colleges prefer to use terms such as *political studies*, *politics*, or *government* rather than political science. However, keeping in mind that the word *science* is derived from a Latin word meaning knowledge, we could define political science simply as the systematic study of politics. As Box 1-4, The Development of Political Science, indicates, the extent to which the study of politics can and should be scientific has been a matter of dispute.

POLITICAL SCIENCE
The systematic study of politics.

BOX 1-4

The Development of Political Science

The origins of political science are often traced back about 2400 years to the works of ancient Greek philosophers Plato and Aristotle, although even before that the Chinese thinker Confucius also developed influential political ideas (Tremblay et al., 2004). Political philosophers have been concerned particularly with normative questions, but have also often been keen observers and analysts of the realities of politics and human nature. Political science as an academic discipline distinct from economics, philosophy, and law developed in the late nineteenth century and focused on the description of governmental institutions and constitutional law. In the mid twentieth century, a different approach, termed behaviouralism, was developed particularly by political scientists educated in the United States. Behaviouralism focuses on examining the actual behaviour of political actors such as voters and legislators, typically by using quantitative methods such as survey research (a sophisticated version of public opinion polls). The goal of behaviouralism is to develop a value-free scientific approach to understanding politics by developing generalizations based on empirical analysis. Criticism of

behaviouralism developed in the late 1960s on the grounds that it was not truly value-free, but rather was oriented to defending the status quo. As well, critics argued that insufficient attention was being paid to key political questions and to the importance of values, historical context, and institutions in explaining politics.

Political science today uses a variety of approaches and methods and has become more of a global endeavour than one centred on the United States. There is an increased interest in qualitative as well as quantitative methodologies. Rational choice models borrowed from economics have been widely used to try to explain political behaviour. Gender-based analyses have challenged what is perceived as the traditional male orientation of the discipline. The behavioural emphasis on rigorous scientific testing of hypotheses with empirical data has been complemented by an interest in a broader understanding and theorizing about politics and its relationship with society, the economy, and historical development. And normative and ethical concerns are important in the choice of topics that political scientists examine.

EMPIRICAL ANALYSIS
Analysis that involves explaining various aspects of politics, particularly by using careful observation and comparison to develop generalizations and testable theories.

A distinction is often made between empirical analysis and normative analysis (see Table 1-2). **Empirical analysis** involves explaining various aspects of politics, particularly by using careful observation and comparison to develop generalizations. The goal of empirical analysis is not simply to gather data to describe various features of politics and government, but also to develop testable theories that will help us to understand how politics works.

TABLE 1-2
EMPIRICAL, NORMATIVE, AND POLICY ANALYSIS: AN EXAMPLE

EMPIRICAL ANALYSIS	Why are women less likely than men to run for Parliament?
NORMATIVE ANALYSIS	Should legislatures be a microcosm of society?
POLICY ANALYSIS	What is the best way of increasing the proportion of women in Parliament?

Normative analysis involves examining ideas about how the community should be governed and what values should be pursued through politics.

In practice, the distinction between empirical and normative analysis is not as clear-cut as it seems. Political scientists are part of the world they study, and inevitably the empirical questions they choose to study and the way they go about researching those questions will be affected by their values and perspectives. Likewise, normative analyses are based on understandings of human nature and how the political world works. The combination of empirical and normative analysis is particularly evident in **policy analysis**, which involves evaluating existing policies and assessing possible alternatives to deal with particular problems. In providing practical advice, policy analysts have to consider what is feasible rather than ideal, which calls for an understanding of political realities. That is, they need to consider how best to achieve desired values under particular circumstances.

Why Study Politics?

The most basic answer to the question "Why study politics?" is simply that politics is important and that knowing about it is an essential aspect of understanding the world we live in. The politically motivated terrorist attack on the United States on September 11, 2001, illustrates how political actions can affect the world. Less dramatically, but no less importantly, decisions taken by government can affect our material well-being, the accessibility of health care, the quality of the air we breathe, and the degree of freedom we enjoy.

Understanding politics is also essential in order to take effective action to achieve our goals and ideals. Imagine that you are concerned about global climate change and would like governments to take actions to reduce the use of fossil fuels. Or perhaps you think that university tuition fees are too high and should be lowered to allow greater accessibility to higher education. Or you heard that a friend has been killed by someone who was drinking and driving and you decide that stricter laws are needed. How would you go about trying to achieve your goals? Would you write a letter to the prime minister, your member of Parliament, your member of the provincial legislature, or your local municipal council? Join a group that is taking up your cause? Organize a protest demonstration? Vote for a party that appears sympathetic to your concerns? Sit back and hope that decision-makers in government make the right decision?

Understanding politics can help you to think about the issues that arise in politics, how to achieve what is best for yourself and your community, and how to recognize some of the obstacles that hinder the achievement of your goals.

CAREER TIES Students often ask how taking political science courses or getting a degree in political science will help them in finding employment and pursuing a career. Political science would obviously be useful for anyone

NORMATIVE ANALYSIS
Analysis that involves examining ideas about how the community should be governed and what values should be pursued through politics.

POLICY ANALYSIS
Analysis that involves evaluating existing policies and assessing alternatives to deal with particular problems.

Canadian Political Science Association
www.cpsa-acsp.ca

Political Science Resources
www.psr.keele.ac.uk

contemplating a career in politics, but most of those who study politics are not budding politicians. Nevertheless, about one-fifth of Canadians work for government or its agencies. Those who work for business or non-profit organizations often interact with government and government agencies. Knowledge of government policies and regulations is useful in almost every field of endeavour. And, in an increasingly globalized world, knowledge of foreign political systems and international political organizations and agreements is very important for doing business. Taking political science courses or a degree in political science provides a good background to a wide variety of career choices.

Political science courses can also be helpful in developing general intellectual skills that are useful in one's personal development and eventual career. Such skills include developing the ability to communicate effectively, read carefully, do good research, and think critically. Political science contains a great diversity of perspectives and approaches. This diversity helps to make political science interesting, challenging, and useful in the development of general intellectual skills.

Summary and Conclusion

Politics plays a vital role in our lives and our communities. Whether or not we are interested in politics, we are affected by political decisions. Because of disagreements about what political communities should do, political activity involves mobilizing people to advance their interests and values. As well, politics involves trying to resolve conflicts in order to achieve the co-operation needed to achieve collective goals.

Politics is a complex activity. To understand what goes on in political life and the policies that result from political activity, it is necessary to examine the interests that people and groups pursue, the ideas and values that affect their activities and decisions, the identities that are important to them, and the institutions, rules, and processes that shape political activities and lead to the actions and policies of government. As well, politics in any particular political community is affected by the broader context—such as the economic and social systems—in which it operates (with government policies, in turn, affecting economic and social systems as well as individual behaviour). Of particular importance in determining the actions that governments take is the distribution of political power.

People often have a negative view of politics. When a job or a promotion goes to a person because of their contacts and family connections, or because they have flattered their employer, others often grumble that the decision was "political." Likewise, if a politician makes a decision based on trying to gain power or a personal benefit, win re-election, or reward supporters, rather than on a careful analysis of what is best for the country, the decision is often criticized for being "political." Politics, in other words, is often thought of as involving the selfish or competitive pursuit of one's own interests, without concern for others or the community as a whole.

Politics is also often viewed negatively because many people distrust governments and politicians. Governments are often criticized for being inefficient, wasteful, and prone to corruption. Some governments have supported or acquiesced in the domination and exploitation of the weak within the society that they govern. The laws and policies adopted by governments may reflect the interests and values of the dominant groups in society, resulting in the harassment, persecution, or neglect of the less powerful. As well, some governments have pursued the conquest, control, and exploitation of other countries.

There is, however, also a positive side to politics. Many people engage in political activity not only to advance their own interests or to pursue power for its own sake, but also with the hope of advancing the common good of the political community. Many governments have been able to work toward the common good by such measures as establishing peace and security within the political community, creating a fair and impartial system of justice, helping to develop their country's economy and infrastructure, and providing accessible education and health care. Governments can also promote the common good by regulating and checking the power wielded by various social and economic institutions, and thus help to protect and assist the weaker elements of society.

A key political problem is how to ensure that the power and authority of governments is used for the common good. As the famous saying of nineteenth-century British historian Lord Acton warns, "Power tends to corrupt and absolute power corrupts absolutely." Because power and authority are easily abused, it is important to ensure that those in governing positions are held accountable for their actions. Excessive concentrations of power, whether in the hands of governing authorities, police and military forces, private business, the media, or religious organizations, can be dangerous.

Political science, the systematic study of politics, has its roots in thousands of years of discussion and analysis about what is good for the communities we live in and how this good can best be achieved (Strauss, 1945). Contemporary political science is building a systematic, theoretically based understanding of politics while continuing to examine fundamental questions about the values upon which our communities should be based. Many political scientists also use their research to provide practical advice about the political processes and public policies that are for the common good.

Key Terms

Discussion Questions

1. What are the major political issues in your local, provincial, or national community? What about the global community? Do the most talked-about issues reflect the most serious problems that each of these communities faces? Are any important issues ignored?

2. Should we be concerned if political power is highly concentrated? Can we trust government to look after the common good?

3. Is it meaningful to talk about the common good in a diverse society?

4. How important is the study of politics? Is it an essential component of a good education?

5. Do all citizens have a responsibility to keep themselves informed about politics?

Further Reading

Aristotle. (E. Barker, Trans.) *Politics of Aristotle*. New York: Oxford University Press, 1973.

Dahl, R.A., & Stinebrickner, B. *Modern political analysis*, 6th ed. Upper Saddle River, NJ: Prentice Hall, 2002.

Etzioni, A. *The common good*. Oxford: Polity Press, 2004.

Goodin, R.E., & Klingemann (Eds.). *A new handbook of political science*. Oxford: Oxford University Press, 1998.

Leftwich, A. *Redefining politics: People, resources and power*. London and New York: Methuen, 1983.

Theodoulou, S.Z., & O'Brien, R. (Eds.). *Methods for political inquiry: The discipline, philosophy, and analysis of politics*. Upper Saddle River, NJ: Prentice Hall, 1999.

A number of novels provide interesting and provocative descriptions of politics in the past, present, and possible future:

Achebe, C. *A man of the people*. London: William Heinemann, 1966.

Allende, I. *Eva Luna*. New York: Bantam Press, 1987.

Anonymous. *Primary colors*. New York: Warner Books, 1996.

Atwood, M. *The handmaid's tale*. Toronto: McClelland & Stewart, 1985.

LeGuin, U.K. *The dispossessed*. New York: Avon Books, 1974.

Orwell, G. *1984*. New York: New American Library, 1948.

Warren, R.P. *All the king's men*. New York: Bantam, 1959.

Chapter 2

NATION-STATES, NATIONALISM, AND GLOBALIZATION

PHOTO ABOVE: After intense controversy, the Spanish legislature in 2006 recognized the Catalan nationality and gave expanded self-governing powers to the region of Catalonia.

1. explain the difference between a nation and a state
2. discuss the nature of the modern state
3. examine the meaning of citizenship
4. discuss the significance of identity politics
5. explain the nature and significance of nationalism
6. outline the nature and significance of globalization

On June 18, 2006, 74 percent of Catalans voting in a binding referendum supported the adoption of a revised Statute of Autonomy of Catalonia (a region of northeastern Spain with a distinct language, history, and culture), which recognized the Catalan nationality and expanded the self-governing powers of Catalonia's government. Recognizing this distinct nationality came after an intense debate within Spain and a close vote in the Spanish legislature. Indeed, in January 2006, the head of the Spanish army was fired after he threatened military intervention over the issue.

A few days later, Canadian Prime Minister Stephen Harper and his Cabinet attended the *Fête Nationale* celebrations in Quebec City. When reporters asked Harper if he would describe Quebec as a nation, he evaded the question, responding that "if the National Assembly [the Quebec legislature] wants to make such a declaration, that's its right." However, in December 2006, Harper introduced a motion that the Canadian House of Commons "recognize that the Québécois form a nation within a united Canada." Although the motion, which passed by a 266–16 margin, has no legal significance, it stirred up considerable controversy. Michael Chong resigned from the Cabinet, stating that he believed that Canada is one nation—a view widely shared by English-speaking Canadians. Other Cabinet ministers differed on the meaning of recognizing the Québécois as a nation: did it refer only to French-speaking Quebecers, most of whom share a common culture and ancestry, or did it refer to all residents of Quebec? Harper did little to clarify the meaning of the motion by stating that the Québécois are a nation "bound together by a common language, culture, and history" and that "recognition of Quebec as a nation is part of the Canadian identity" (*Globe and Mail Online*, December 19, 2006).

Disputes about whether Catalonia and Quebec are nations are not simply semantic disputes. Nor are they simply questions about the extent to which these regions are different than other parts of their countries in history, language, and culture. Rather, the term *nation* is a highly charged political term because the major form of political community in the modern world is the nation-state. Declaring a region or a group within a country to be a nation is viewed by some as undermining efforts to build a strong national identity in the country as a whole and leading eventually to the breakup of the country. Others argue that recognition of the reality that countries like Canada and Spain contain different nations that should have considerable autonomy to govern themselves, combined with a partnership in governing the country as a whole, would enhance the stability of those countries and the legitimacy of the state.

A basic political question is whether the world should be divided into self-governing political communities, each based upon a people that consider themselves a nation. Or can stable political communities be built on the recognition and political accommodation of different nations?

We begin this chapter by examining the nature of the modern state. Then we look at the concept of nation, which is often viewed as the basis of the modern state, and the idea of nationalism, which has had an important impact on how the world is organized. Finally, we discuss the processes of globalization, which many observers believe is altering human existence and eroding the significance of nation-states.

THE STATE

A **state** is an independent, self-governing political community whose governing institutions have the capability to make rules that are binding on the population residing within a particular territory. This capability to make binding rules is based ultimately on the state's coercive power. The territory of a state involves borders that are recognized by other states, or at least borders that can be defended by force if necessary. Most modern states have **jurisdiction** (exclusive governing and law-making authority) over sizable geographic areas and substantial permanent populations.

The state can be viewed as a more extensive and permanent expression of the political community than the **government**, the set of institutions that makes decisions and oversees their implementation on behalf of the state for a particular period of time[1] (Heywood, 2002). The Canadian state, for example, includes not only the Canadian government and the governments of the provinces, but also the court system, the military and police forces, the employees of the various levels of government, and state-owned corporations (termed Crown corporations in Canada). Some state institutions (such as the courts and the Bank of Canada) may be autonomous in the sense of being free of direct government control.

The term *state* is often misunderstood because regional political units equivalent to Canadian provinces are, in some countries, referred to as states. In the United States, for example, each of the thirteen British colonies that became independent states after the War of Independence (1775–1783) retained some degree of self-government after they agreed to establish the United States of America. Thus, they continued to be called states.

The term *state* can also be misleading because it may conjure up an image of a powerful, unified body. In reality, the various institutions that make up a state do not necessarily all work co-operatively in pursuit of a common interest or goal.

Sovereignty and the State

States are often described as being sovereign, meaning that they are the highest authority for their population and their territory. The idea of **sovereignty** developed in the sixteenth century as various European monarchs strove to establish themselves as the highest authority in the territory that they controlled. Conflicts between the monarchs, religious leaders, and feudal lords, each of whom had considerable governing powers, led to the idea that there should be a single highest authority in each territory in order to maintain peace and avoid civil war. In particular, the treaties comprising the Peace of Westphalia (1648), which ended the devastating Thirty Years War (based, in part, on conflicts between Protestants and Catholics), established the supreme authority of states and their monarchs.

STATE
An independent, self-governing political community whose governing institutions have the capability to make rules that are binding on the population residing within a particular territory.

JURISDICTION
The state's governing and law-making authority over a particular geographic area and population.

GOVERNMENT
The set of institutions that makes decisions and oversees their implementation of decisions on behalf of the state for a particular period of time.

SOVEREIGNTY
The principle that states have the right to govern their population and territory without outside interference.

---

[1] The term *government* refers, in the Canadian context, particularly to the prime minister and Cabinet, although the public service that works under their direction could also be considered part of the government.

In various countries, legislatures and/or the people challenged the absolute power claimed by monarchs. In Britain, the "Glorious Revolution" (1688) resulted in Parliament's removal and replacement of a monarch and established the idea that Parliament is the supreme authority. The leaders of the French Revolution (1789) proclaimed that sovereignty rested with the people. The adoption of federal systems of government in countries such as the United States, Canada, and Australia means that sovereignty in these countries is shared between the central (national) and regional (provincial or state) governments, with the constitution as the supreme source of authority. Regardless of whether sovereignty is viewed as resting in the hands of a single individual (such as a monarch), a particular organization, several sets of organizations (for example, the Canadian Parliament and provincial legislatures), the constitution, the people as a whole, or some combination of these, the modern state itself is viewed as sovereign.

SOVEREIGN STATE
A state that has the ability to govern its population and territory without outside interference.

The concept of the **sovereign state** is particularly important when we look at the relationship among states. A central principle of international law is that the states of the world are the legal equals of one another, and thus states should not interfere in the affairs of other states, unless invited to do so. In other words, states are expected to respect each other's sovereignty. States, whether large or small, powerful or weak, rich or poor, are viewed as being self-governing.

TODAY'S STATES Most of the contemporary world's people and land mass (and some of the adjoining ocean) are divided among the individual states of the world. The empires that ruled over conquered territories and peoples have been dissolved and the number of sovereign states has increased substantially (see Figure 2-1). There are, however, some anomalies.

FIGURE 2-1
THE INCREASING NUMBER OF SOVEREIGN STATES

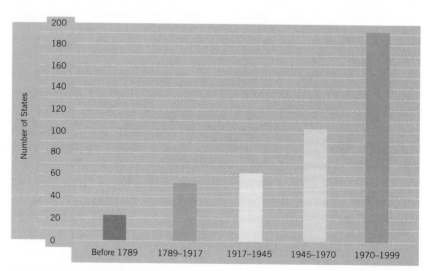

SOURCE: From *An introduction to political science: Comparative and world politics*, 4th ed. (p. 48), by R.J. Jackson and D. Jackson, 2003, Toronto: Pearson Education Canada. Adapted from data found in *World handbook of political and social indicators*, 2nd ed. (pp. 26 *ff*), 1972, New Haven: Yale University Press; *Political handbook of the world: 1890*, 1990, Binghamton, NY: CSA Publications; and the *New York Times*, 1991 to 2000.

Civil wars have occasionally shattered states, resulting in no real authority in a particular area. For example, in recent times, competing warlords in Somalia and Afghanistan have controlled much of each country, making the state ineffective or non-existent. These cases are sometimes referred to as **failed states,** in which governments cannot enforce laws, maintain order, or protect the lives of citizens. A few areas, such as some small Caribbean and Pacific islands, are still controlled by foreign countries. In other areas, control of some territory is contested or its future uncertain. For example, Israel occupies some of the territories that it captured in wars with neighbouring countries, India and Pakistan have clashed over control of Kashmir for decades, and the People's Republic of China (mainland China) claims jurisdiction over the island of Taiwan (which refers to itself as the Republic of China).

In reality, the sovereignty of states is not absolute. Because of the great disparities in power among the states of the world, it is not surprising that weaker countries have found their sovereignty limited at times. The United States, for example, has a long history of involving itself in the affairs of Caribbean and Latin American countries, including invading and overthrowing the governments of Grenada (1983) and Panama (1989). The former Soviet Union exercised tight control over the countries of Eastern Europe.

As well, various elements of the international community have taken actions to persuade states to protect human rights or to avoid potentially aggressive policies. For example, the North Atlantic Treaty Organization, including Canada, bombed Serbia (then known as Yugoslavia) in 1999, which it justified in terms of ending Serb mistreatment of ethnic Albanians in the province of Kosovo. Often such actions are controversial because of differences of opinion about whether the action was justified and whether it would have the desired effects. Serbs argued that their actions in Kosovo (which resulted in large numbers of Albanians fleeing the country, fearing for their lives) were taken to deal with terrorist activities by Albanian separatists.

FAILED STATE
A state that no longer has the capacity to maintain order.

◀ Afghanistan: a failed state. Competing warlords have exercised control over much of the country, and the state is largely ineffective. The government has a limited ability to enforce laws, maintain order, or protect the lives of citizens throughout the troubled country.

THE NATION-STATE

NATION-STATE

A sovereign state based on people living in a country who share a sense of being a member of a particular nation.

Modern states are often referred to as **nation-states**. A nation-state is a sovereign state based on people living in a country who share a sense of being a member of a particular nation. Most states claim to represent a nation, although that claim is sometimes controversial.

Nation

NATION

A group of people who share a sense of common identity and who typically believe they should be self-governing within their homeland.

The term *nation* is often confused with that of the *state*, but the two terms have different meanings. A **nation** is a group of people who have a sense of common identity and who typically believe they should be self-governing within their homeland (Suny, 2006).[2] To be self-governing does not necessarily mean that members of the nation believe they should have their own sovereign state. Self-government can involve a degree of autonomy within a country. For example, Quebecers enjoy a substantial degree of self-government within Canada through the powers of the Quebec government.

How does a sense of national identity develop among a large group of people who do not know each other? A sense of national identity can be based on people located in a particular territory who share common characteristics such as ethnicity[3] (that is, a belief in a common ancestry), language, culture, and religion. Although many countries are based on a dominant group having some of these shared characteristics, there are only a few countries (for example, Japan, Norway, and Iceland) in which the vast majority of people have the same characteristics.

A feeling of belonging to a nation can also develop from the shared experiences of living in a particular geographical area and from sharing the values, particularly the basic political values, common to the people of that area (sometimes referred to as a "civic nation"). States often try to promote this sense of national identity among their citizens through their educational systems, national holidays, and the promotion of a national culture. It can also develop through feelings of patriotism that are often associated with war or international sporting events such as the Olympics. It may be difficult, however, to

---

[2] A distinction is sometimes made between a nation in a sociological sense (that is, a people having shared characteristics and culture) and a nation in a political sense of a people in a geographical area that have or want self-government or their own sovereign state. See, for example, Trudeau (1993, pp. 72–74).

[3] The terms *ethnic group* and *ethnicity* are rather vague. Although an ethnic group is often defined as a group with common ancestry ("blood"), most ethnic groups are composed of people who have different ancestries, given the intermingling of peoples in most parts of the world. Beyond a belief in having a common ancestry, ethnic groups are often characterized as sharing such features as a common language, religion, culture, and history (Dowty, 2005). In this usage, an ethnic group is similar to a nation except that a nation, as we have defined it, includes the political objective of self-government, which an ethnic group does not necessarily seek. Canadians of Polish, Chinese, and Greek ancestry may view themselves as members of distinct ethnic groups, but do not consider themselves members of distinct nations within Canada.

create a strong, inclusive national identity in countries with deep social divisions based on such characteristics as ethnicity, language, or religion, particularly if those divisions are connected to a history of discrimination, persecution, or inequality among the different groups.

Overall, whether a result of ethnic, racial, linguistic, religious, cultural, or historic differences, there are many countries where substantial numbers of people view themselves as having a different national identity than other citizens. Even in Western Europe where the idea of the nation-state originated, there are some countries (for example, Belgium, Spain, and the United Kingdom) that could be considered **binational or multinational states**. Because there are different bases for a sense of national identity (that sometimes change over time) and because there are important implications for the governing of a country, the question of whether a country is a nation-state can be the subject of serious controversy, as discussed in Box 2-1, Is Canada a Nation-State?

BINATIONAL AND MULTINATIONAL STATES States whose population is composed of two or more nations.

The Development of National Identities

Until modern times, people tended to view themselves mainly in terms of their clan, tribe, or local community. European monarchs typically had little in common with the people they ruled, and territories changed hands as a result of dynastic marriages and conquest. In many parts of the world, clan, tribal, and local or regional identities continue to be stronger than broader national identities.

Although elements of national identity can be found before modern times, historians generally view the French Revolution of 1789 as sparking the development of a sense of nationhood among the general public. The French Revolution was based on the idea that the state is an instrument of the people (that is, the nation), with the people having the right to overthrow rulers who do not reflect the will of the people. The subsequent Napoleonic Wars helped to create a sense of unity and pride in the French nation and its citizen army, which replaced reliance on mercenaries. In reaction to the French conquest of much of continental Europe, other European peoples developed their own sense of national identity.

To some extent, the process of developing national identities has involved building upon existing ethnic identities and cultural characteristics. However, states have often made deliberate efforts to replace local and regional dialects, cultures, and identities with a national culture, language, and identity. For example, in the latter part of the nineteenth century the government of France created a French identity in the rural areas of the country by instilling patriotism through the educational system and encouraging the use of Parisian French throughout the country instead of the very distinct dialects that were spoken in various parts of France (Weber, 1976). In the United States, where persons from

BOX 2-1

Is Canada a Nation-State?

Canada was largely built on the foundations laid by three peoples: Aboriginals (who are themselves very diverse in language and culture), the French colonists of the seventeenth and eighteenth centuries, and English-speaking persons of British or Irish ancestry, many of whom came to Canada from the United States after the American War of Independence. Added to this diverse foundation are large numbers of persons from various countries in Europe, Asia, Africa, and other parts of the world, particularly since the latter part of the nineteenth century. Because of Canada's lingering ties to Britain, a sense of Canadian identity was slow to develop. Indeed, until a few decades ago, Canada lacked specifically Canadian symbols of identity such as a flag, national anthem, or even citizenship.

Most English-speaking Canadians view Canada as a nation-state, based on each resident of Canada having the same rights. With more than one-third of Canada's population tracing their ancestry to neither the British Isles nor France, Canadian governments since the early 1970s have promoted the view that Canada is a multicultural nation (that is, one nation composed of a variety of different cultural groupings) with two official languages. Since the early 1960s, many French Quebecers have developed the view that Quebec is a distinct nation with a substantial minority favouring the establishment of an independent Quebec nation-state. Aboriginal Canadians resent the privileging of those of British and French ancestry in such ideas as "two founding peoples" and "two nations." Instead, many Aboriginals view Canada as ideally being a partnership between Aboriginal First Nations and the descendants of subsequent settlers.

Thus, Canada can be considered a nation-state, a multicultural nation-state, a nation-state with one or more minority nationalities, a binational state, or a multinational state, depending upon one's perspective. The complexity of the concept of *nation* is illustrated by the fact that many Quebecers view themselves as both Québécois and Canadian without necessarily seeing one national identity as subordinate to the other.*

The question of whether Canada is a nation-state is not only a definitional argument, but also a political dispute of potentially great significance. If, for example, Quebecers are officially recognized as members of a distinct nation, this suggests that the Quebec government may need greater powers to act on behalf of the Quebec nation. Proposals in the 1980s and 1990s that the Canadian constitution recognize Quebec as a distinct society met with vigorous opposition from those who view Canada as one nation with all provincial governments having the same powers. Likewise, recognition of Aboriginal nations leads to expectations that Aboriginal governments be treated as equals to other governments in Canada, that Aboriginals be guaranteed representation in Parliament and the Supreme Court of Canada, and that Aboriginals be subject to their own laws.

---

* Likewise, many Newfoundlanders have a strong sense of a Newfoundland identity based on historic and cultural differences—an identity that is, for many, stronger than their sense of Canadian identity. Residents of other parts of Canada also have an important sense of provincial identity.

a variety of countries settled, American governments devoted considerable effort to the creation of a common sense of American identity, although blacks and Native Americans were largely excluded from the American "melting pot." Creating a national identity has often involved trying to persuade different groups to adopt the culture, language, and values of the dominant group.

Modern means of transportation, such as railways, and new forms of communication, such as mass circulation newspapers, also helped to create a sense of national identity in many countries. Smaller communities were now linked to the major cities, reducing the distinctiveness of local dialects and cultures, and ideas about the larger community could be transmitted to the population throughout the country. Likewise, the development of a national economy made local communities less insular and encouraged the flow of labour, products, and capital.

Difficulties in Creating Nation-States

In the nineteenth century, the concept of popular sovereignty (that the people should be able to govern themselves) became transformed into the idea that nations defined in cultural terms should be self-governing. After the First World War, the principle of **national self-determination** (that nations should be able to choose to be self-governing) was applied to the establishment of several new states in central and eastern Europe out of the empires that had collapsed. It was recognized, however, that it would be unrealistic to establish states strictly on the basis of the location of national cultures. Thus, attempts were made (generally unsuccessfully) to persuade new states to protect minority nationalities that resided in their territory (Harty & Murphy, 2005). The United Nations International Covenant on Economic, Social, and Cultural Rights, which came into force in 1976, establishes that "all peoples have the right to self-determination," which involves the right to "freely determine their political status and freely pursue their economic, social, and cultural development."

NATIONAL SELF-DETERMINATION
The idea that nations should have the right to determine their political status, including choosing to have their own sovereign state.

The idea of dividing the world into states based on where people with a particular national identity reside is hard to achieve. Persons sharing such an identity often do not live in well-defined geographical areas. In many parts of Eastern Europe and the Balkans, for example, different nationalities are so highly interspersed that it would be very difficult to draw boundaries that would include each nationality within its own state.

The attempt to create a single national identity within a diverse country has not been very successful in many parts of the world. The countries of Africa, for example, retained the boundaries that resulted from conquest by various European empires. These political boundaries often bear little relationship to the geographical location of peoples, languages, cultures, and religions. In other words, the boundaries are artificial, often combining very dissimilar groups into the same country. Despite efforts by the leaders of independence movements and post-independence governments to create new political identities, severe tensions often exist among peoples sharing the same country. This has helped to fuel the civil wars that have plagued a number of African countries.

Is the Nation-State the Most Desirable Form of Political Community?

In a nation-state, people have a bond with each other, and thus are more likely to feel a commitment to advancing the good of the political community. A sense of trust in government and other institutions may be easier to develop. Political compromises that are acceptable to different social groups may be easier to achieve because an appeal can be made to a common national interest (Keating, 1996). In a nation-state, rule is by members of the nation who can claim to have the good of the nation at heart and to share the basic values of the other members of the nation. The legitimacy of the state and governing authorities is less likely to be questioned when the state is based on a people that considers themselves part of a common nation. A stable democratic system may be more likely to be sustained in a nation-state. Democratic dialogue is facilitated by having a common language, culture, and basic political values. Deep divisions and the lack of a common sense of nationhood can hinder efforts to develop or maintain democracy. Nevertheless, democratic countries such as Canada, Belgium, and Spain that might be considered binational or multinational have survived and flourished despite occasional "national unity" crises.

The development of nationalist movements seeking to create a new nation-state out of a region of an existing state raises questions about whether it is desirable that nations with small populations and located in small geographical areas have their own self-governing state. Certainly, there are advantages to larger states in terms of having large internal markets, spreading the costs of government services over a large population, and having the capability to defend their country militarily. However, some small states such as the Republic of Ireland, Singapore, and Luxembourg have been successful economically and able to maintain their sovereignty. The development of economic agreements and military alliances composed of a number of countries has helped to offset some of the problems that might otherwise face small nation-states. Nevertheless, there are some nations so small and lacking in economic capabilities (such as the many Aboriginal First Nations in Canada) that establishing a sovereign state for each group that considers itself a nation is unrealistic.

NATIONALISM

NATIONALISM
The idea that that the nation-state is the best form of political community and that a nation should have its own self-governing state.

Nationalism is based on the view that the nation-state is the best form of political community and that a nation should have its own self-governing state. Nationalists seek to promote the interests, culture, and values of their particular nation, and typically argue that people's loyalty to their nation should take precedence over their other loyalties, such as to their family, tribe, clan, local community, or religion.

◄ Nationalism continues to be a powerful force in the modern world. For instance, Basque nationalists, whose homeland is divided by the international border between France and Spain, have resisted outside domination since the tenth century. Basque nationalists have sought to create an independent state through both conventional political action and terrorism.

Internet Modern History Sourcebook: Nationalism
www.fordham.edu/halsall/mod/ modsbook17.html

The Nationalism Project
www.nationalismproject.org

Nationalism has inspired a variety of movements that have arisen in opposition to existing states among those seeking to create their own independent state. For example, Basque nationalists seek to create an independent Basque state in areas of Spain and France that they consider their homeland. Nationalism has played an important role in the struggle of various peoples for liberation from exploitative foreign rule, and has led to the breakup of empires. In some cases, nationalists have sought to unite different territories that they view as being based on the same nation—as occurred in the creation of Germany and Italy in the nineteenth century. Nationalism can also take the form of trying to strengthen and unify an existing state by promoting a common culture, limiting foreign influences, and protecting domestic ownership and control of the economy. For example, Canadian nationalists have advocated limiting American economic and cultural influence on Canada through such measures as restricting foreign ownership of business and requiring that the media carry considerable Canadian content.

Types of Nationalism

A distinction is often made between ethnic nationalism and civic nationalism. **Ethnic nationalism** views common ancestry along with the cultural traditions and language associated with a particular ethnic group as the basis for a nation-state. By attempting to base a state on a particular ethnic group, ethnic nationalism can result in harassment, discrimination, and the oppression of those who do not share the characteristics of the dominant group. In some cases, as in the former Yugoslavia and Rwanda in the 1990s, it can lead to "ethnic cleansing," the forcible removal and even the massacre of people whose ethnicity differs from that of the dominant ethnic group. Ethnic nationalism can also result in war if attempts are made to seize areas in other countries where members of the

ETHNIC NATIONALISM
Nationalism based on common ancestry along with the cultural traditions and language associated with a particular ethnic group.

ethnic group live or areas that are considered the traditional homeland of the ethnic group.

Civic nationalism views shared political values and political history as the basis of a nation-state. Civic nationalism tends to be more inclusive than ethnic nationalism as it treats all permanent residents of a state as citizens regardless of their characteristics. Civic nationalists often want to create a sense of nationhood among its citizens by encouraging the adoption of a common set of political values and beliefs and promoting loyalty to the nation-state through patriotic rituals.

In practice, it is often difficult to separate the two types of nationalism. For example, contemporary Quebec nationalists often claim that their nationalism includes all residents of Quebec and is therefore civic nationalism. However, occasional comments by some prominent Quebec nationalists implying that only those descended from the original French settlers are "true" Quebecers suggests that there is also an element of ethnic nationalism.

Evaluating Nationalism

Nationalism can be viewed positively in terms of fostering the establishment and maintenance of self-governing nation-states. Throughout Africa, Asia, and Latin America, nationalist ideas encouraged people to challenge domination and exploitation by Europe's imperial powers. Contemporary nationalists suggest that nationalism can be useful in maintaining diversity in the world against the pressures for a homogeneous American or Western-dominated world. As well, nationalism may encourage the development of a sense of solidarity with others beyond one's family and local community.

On the negative side, nationalism has been an important cause of many wars and conflicts. Although some new nation-states have been created in a peaceful manner (for example, Czechoslovakia split peacefully into the Czech Republic and Slovakia in 1993), attempts to create new nation-states have often involved violent conflicts.

Extreme forms of nationalism can also encourage xenophobia—fear or hatred of other nationalities—and foster a sense of superiority that can lead to efforts to dominate weaker countries. As well, nationalism may encourage uniformity within a country and make it less cosmopolitan and vibrant. An exclusive focus on the interests of the nation can also provide a justification for the authoritarian (non-democratic) rule of those who claim to speak on behalf of the nation.

Although nationalism can encourage people to consider the common good of their own political community, it does not encourage people to think of the good of humanity as a whole. In the pursuit of national interests, the interests of others may be harmed.

CIVIC NATIONALISM
Nationalism based on the shared political values and political history of those who are citizens of a country.

CITIZENSHIP AND THE POLITICAL COMMUNITY

Connected to the development of the modern nation-state is the idea of **citizenship**—that the permanent residents are full members of the political community with certain duties and rights. A citizen is not only subject to the laws passed by the governing institutions of that state, but also shares in the power of the sovereign state (Rousseau, 1762/1968).

Those who are born in a particular country are usually considered to be citizens of that country, as are those whose parents are citizens. Those who immigrate to a new country can usually apply for citizenship after a certain period of time.[4] They may have to pass an exam testing their knowledge of their new country, including its political system, and take an oath of allegiance before becoming citizens. Although we usually think of citizenship as involving an exclusive loyalty to one country, many persons are citizens of two countries (as discussed in Box 2-2, Who Is a Citizen?).

CITIZENSHIP
The idea that the permanent residents of a country are full members of the political community, involving various duties and rights.

BOX 2-2

Who Is a Citizen?

As Israeli planes bombarded Hezbollah strongholds in Lebanon in July 2006, the Canadian government attempted to bring its citizens to safety in Canada. To the surprise of many, this involved not just a relatively small number of tourists and business travellers, but up to fifty thousand persons, many of whom had dual Lebanese and Canadian citizenship and Canadian passports. Some argued that the Canadian government should not help persons who had, in some cases, never set foot in Canada or paid Canadian taxes (although many of those evacuated at government expense were tourists). Others argued that treating those with dual citizenship differently than other Canadians was discriminatory and would create two classes of citizens.

A more fundamental question is whether individuals should be required to have citizenship status in only one country or whether dual citizenship (as allowed by Canada's Citizenship Act, 1977) is an appropriate response to increased migration and the reality of globalization. Interestingly, when Michaëlle Jean (who came to Canada from Haiti as a child) was appointed as Canada's governor general in 2005, controversy erupted when it was discovered that she was a citizen of both France and Canada. The controversy subsided when she voluntarily gave up her French citizenship. A similar controversy arose when Stéphane Dion (who has French as well as Canadian citizenship) was elected as Liberal party leader.

---

[4] Some countries, however, connect citizenship to particular characteristics. Germany and Israel, for example, allow persons from other countries the right to become citizens based on their ancestry immediately upon taking up residence. In contrast, a number of European countries have been reluctant to grant citizenship to "guest workers" from North Africa and the Middle East, even when they have resided in the country for a lengthy period of time.

Is citizenship a matter of rights for individuals (such as the right to vote and hold elected office) or does it also involve obligations to the political community? Citizens may, for example, be expected to defend their country in times of war. Governments have used this argument to justify compulsory military service and to draft men (and likely women, in the future) to fight in wars, even those that are not strictly defensive in nature. As well, since citizenship is associated with being a member of the political community, some have argued that citizens have an obligation to become informed participants in politics. Indeed, it has been suggested that citizens should put aside their personal interests and act in political life for the common good of their country (Pierson, 1996).

The concept of citizenship is often based on the view that all citizens should be equal members of the political community regardless of social status, ethnicity, gender, wealth, or other characteristics. In the past, citizenship was limited to a small segment of the population, such as males, property owners, and those born in the country. The struggles for equal political rights in the past century and a half have been successful in most countries in expanding citizenship to include most of the population of a country.

There has been increasing discussion about whether members of certain groups should have different citizenship rights because of their particular circumstances (termed "differentiated citizenship"), such as historic rights, a legacy of oppression and discrimination, or exclusion from the mainstream of society. For example, many Aboriginal tribes or nations in Canada have various rights established by treaties and other agreements between the British Crown or the Canadian government and Aboriginal chiefs. Although the nature of these rights is often in dispute and subject to lengthy negotiations, Aboriginal treaty rights are recognized in the Canadian constitution.

Some have argued that the special rights of Aboriginals eventually should be extinguished so that they can be treated the same as other Canadians (as was proposed by the Canadian government in 1969). Others have argued that Aboriginals should be self-governing nations within Canada. This could imply a form of dual citizenship in which Aboriginals are both citizens of their Aboriginal nation and citizens of Canada (Harty & Murphy, 2005). Political scientist Alan Cairns (2000) has tried to find a middle ground, termed "citizens plus," in which Aboriginal differences are recognized, but not at the expense of a strong common citizenship that would bind Canadians together.

Overall, the question of whether the conventional meaning of citizenship as equal membership in a particular political community with all persons having the same duties and rights has increasingly been raised, particularly in multinational states (Carens, 2000).

Identity Politics

A desire for recognition as members of a distinct nation within a larger country (such as Quebecers in Canada, the Scottish in the United Kingdom, and Catalans in

Spain) could be considered as part of a broader phenomenon referred to as **identity politics**. Within a variety of groups that view themselves as oppressed or marginalized from mainstream society—including women, gays and lesbians, minority ethnic groups, the disabled, and Aboriginals—movements have developed seeking recognition and respect for their group identity and the values that they associate with their group. Instead of seeking to integrate into mainstream society, those involved in identity politics often seek to express their distinctiveness and gain a degree of autonomy from the rest of the community by such measures as developing their own institutions and services, obtaining recognition of their specific rights, and having their own means of political representation. In addition, various movements connected to identity politics often seek action by government and various social institutions to combat racism, sexism, and other social problems. Likewise, they may seek to ensure that there are positive portrayals of the diversity of society in the educational system and the mass media. Overall, rather than (or in addition to) being treated as equal *individual* citizens, those involved in identity politics often seek equality for their *group*, equal consideration of their particular needs and circumstances, and the ability to nurture their group's distinctiveness (Tully, 2003).

In recent decades, Canadian governments have officially recognized the diverse cultural heritage of Canadians through a policy of multiculturalism that provides support for different groups to retain their cultures. Critics have argued that multiculturalism might conflict with individual rights (for example, by protecting cultures that discriminate against women) and might interfere with the integration of immigrants into Canadian society. Similarly, while some gays and lesbians seek to be accepted as part of the mainstream society, with the same rights as heterosexuals, others act to promote and develop their own identity and culture.

IDENTITY POLITICS
A perspective in which groups seek recognition and respect for their particular identity. Those involved in identity politics often seek to express their distinctiveness and gain a degree of autonomy from the rest of the community by developing their own institutions and services, obtaining recognition of their specific rights, and having their own means of political representation.

◀ Identity politics is not just about achieving an equitable distribution of income and opportunities for each individual in the political community, but also about gaining respect, particular rights, political power, and autonomy for specific groups.

GLOBALIZATION

The Globalization Website
www.emory.edu/SOC/globalization

GLOBALIZATION
The processes that are increasing the interconnectedness of the world.

Some analysts claim that the modern state is declining in significance. Globalization is making the boundaries of states less relevant, eroding state sovereignty, and reducing the ability of governments to determine the direction of their country. Indeed, one author predicted that by 2025 we will see the end of the nation-state, to be replaced by small units subordinate to a global economy (Ohmae, 1995).

Globalization is often described in terms of the processes that are, in effect, shrinking the world. The obstacles of space and time are being rapidly overcome by contemporary technology, such as high-speed, low-cost communications. This is increasing the interconnectedness of the world and creating a greater awareness of the world as a whole. American journalist Tom Friedman (2000, p. 9) describes globalization as

> *the inexorable integration of markets, nation-states and technologies to a degree never witnessed before—in a way that is enabling individuals, corporations and nation-states to reach around the world farther, faster, deeper and cheaper than ever before, and in a way that is enabling the world to reach into individuals, corporations and nations farther, faster, deeper, and cheaper than ever before.*

Three types of globalization are particularly important: economic globalization, cultural globalization, and political globalization.

Economic Globalization

A key aspect of globalization is the development of a global economic system. Such a development concerns manufacturing, trade, and finance. Many business corporations are becoming global in their activities; they move or contract out their production facilities to wherever goods and services can be produced at the lowest cost and sell their products and services in a variety of countries. Global trade has increased greatly in the past half-century (see Figure 2-2). The process of economic globalization has been most pronounced in the financial markets that provide a substantial proportion of the money and credit needed by business and government. Approximately $2 trillion is traded daily on the currency markets, much of it for speculative purposes (Harmes, 2004). Capital can flow instantaneously in and out of countries connected to the global financial markets. However, there is no global free market in labour, as most workers in the poorer countries cannot easily move to countries featuring high wages and full employment.

Among the advantages of economic globalization are:

- *Efficiency.* Economic wealth is maximized when countries focus on those sectors of their economy in which they are most efficient, and then trade with other countries for those products and services that they cannot produce as efficiently. As well, the pressure of global competition encourages business to be more efficient and more attentive to the desires of their customers.

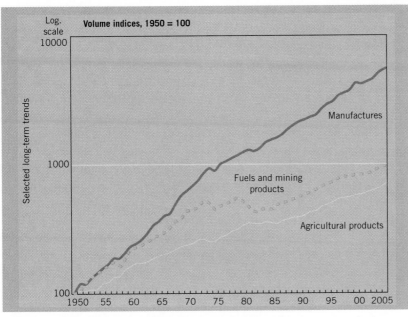

FIGURE 2-2

THE INCREASE IN GLOBAL TRADE, 1950 TO 2005 (LOG SCALE)

SOURCE: World Trade Organization, *International trade statistics, 2006,* retrieved July 15, 2007 from www.wto.org/english/res_e/statis_e/its2006_e/its06_longterm_e.pdf.

- *Access to money.* Easier access to global financial markets can help countries that are developing their economies to obtain the loans and investment capital they need.
- *Consumer prices.* Consumers benefit from the lower prices that can result from shifting the production of goods and services to areas where the costs of production are the lowest.
- *Wider variety.* Consumers enjoy access to a wider selection of goods.

Economic globalization, however, has come under considerable criticism because of several disadvantages:

- *Global inequality.* The increased wealth associated with economic globalization has gone more to the richest rather than to the poorest members of the global community. Although shifting production to some poor countries has created jobs in those countries, competition to attract those jobs has typically resulted in extremely low wages. Some countries (such as South Korea and Taiwan) have been successful in developing prosperous export-oriented economies, but many African countries have fallen behind.
- *Tax evasion.* The ease with which large amounts of money can be instantaneously transferred has resulted in wealthy individuals and corporations shifting their money to tax havens (jurisdictions that do not levy taxes) such as the Cayman Islands.

- *Concentration of power.* Globalization has substantially increased the power of the largest corporations. By threatening to shift production to other countries, they have been able to secure a variety of profitable concessions from governments, such as lower taxes and subsidies for their operations. Because of their power and mobility, it can be difficult for governments to try to ensure that large global corporations are operating for the common good. The enhanced economic power of business may result in increased pressure on governments to weaken or eliminate regulations, including those designed to protect the environment, ensure the safety of consumer products, and restrict the development of monopolies.
- *Weakening of labour.* Because many businesses can move their operations from location to location while workers are generally less able or willing to move to another country, business has generally been increasing its power at the expense of workers. The threat of a business "outsourcing" its operations to a low-wage country puts pressure on workers and unions to accept concessions such as lower wages and fewer benefits.
- *Challenges to the welfare state.* In order to increase the capability of national businesses to compete globally, governments may reduce or eliminate social benefits and programs (such as social assistance and unemployment insurance) in order to provide lower-cost labour to business, reduce taxes, or redirect government spending to programs that assist business competitiveness, particularly in education and research.
- *Economic crises snowball.* Globalization may increase the risk of serious global economic crises. Economic problems in one country can now quickly spread to other parts of the world because of the interdependence of economies, the instantaneous nature of contemporary communication, and the high level of speculation in global financial markets.

United Students against Sweatshops
www.studentsagainstsweatshops.org

Cultural Globalization

Globalization also involves the spreading of cultural products and values around the world. Advances in communications, such as the Internet, have greatly increased the interaction of people, businesses, and other organizations worldwide. Leading brands such as Coke, Pepsi, McDonald's, Taco Bell, and Nike have become familiar to people around the world. American movies, television shows, and music videos are the leading sources of entertainment in many parts of the world. CNN and BBC World are major sources of news in many countries.

Cultural globalization is often viewed as a process in which Western (and particularly American) culture is spread globally. Although the transformation of communication has given us increased access to cultures in other parts of the world, the flow of cultural communication outward from Western countries is substantially greater than the flow in the reverse direction. How many movies and television shows have you watched lately that were produced outside of North America?

Cultural globalization may have some important political effects. The spread of democracy is often attributed, in part, to the information revolution that has both spread democratic values and presented challenges to the attempts of non-democratic governments to control information and ideas. The portrayal on television of the wealth of Western societies may have contributed to the collapse of communist regimes in Eastern Europe as people compared their situation to that of their Western neighbours. On the other hand, Islamic fundamentalists may have their negative views of Western societies reinforced by what they perceive as the decadence portrayed by Western-produced movies and television.

Political Globalization

A variety of contemporary problems, including the regulation of global business and finance, global climate change, international crime and terrorism, and the spread of diseases, cannot be dealt with effectively by individual states. A variety of institutions have developed to try to coordinate the actions of states, promote free trade, and deal with global problems. In a few cases, most notably the European Union, a level of governing above that of the state has been created. In other cases, such as the North American Free Trade Agreement involving Canada, the United States, and Mexico, countries have reached agreements that affect the policies they adopt. At the global level, the United Nations and its agencies have had some success in helping states deal with global issues, although only limited success in dealing with war and other forms of violence.

There are also a large number of groups that engage in political action on a global level. Greenpeace, for example, has grown from a small Vancouver organization concerned with nuclear weapons testing in Alaska to a large international organization involved in environmental causes around the world. A concerned American, Jody Williams, made extensive use of email to mobilize a wide variety of groups and individuals around the world that successfully pressed for an international treaty banning anti-personnel land mines (although forty countries, including the United States, Russia, and China, refused to sign the treaty). Growing networks of non-governmental organizations operate on a global scale seeking to influence the policies of states (and the actions of corporations) in such areas as human rights, the environment, the status of women, and peace. International business, labour, and religious groups are also important actors on the global political stage.

Is Globalization Inevitable?

There is little doubt that we live in an era of rapid change, and that the interconnectedness of the world's population is increasing. However, as discussed in Box 2-3, Is the Significance of Globalization Exaggerated?, some critics argue that the extent and consequences of globalization have been exaggerated.

BOX 2-3

Is the Significance of Globalization Exaggerated?

Is globalization a novel feature of human existence that is rapidly transforming the world? Or is the widespread discussion of globalization since the early 1990s largely an intellectual fad? The technological changes that have brought the world much closer together in the past few decades are truly amazing. But for millions of people, particularly those in poorer countries, computers and the Internet are unaffordable; for some, even telephones and televisions are beyond their financial reach. In addition, much of the world's trade and investment involves Europe, North America, and East Asia. Globalization is an uneven phenomenon with some parts of the world more closely interconnected than others.

Globalization is not entirely a new phenomenon. Trading is a very ancient occupation. Two thousand years ago, the Romans built a large empire, as did the Han dynasty in East Asia. Spanish, Portuguese, and Dutch explorers set up a global system of trading posts in the sixteenth century. A massive slave trade bringing Africans to the Americas developed in the seventeenth century. Britain built a global empire ("where the sun never sets") in the nineteenth century. Similarly, long before modern communications and transportation, religions spread across large areas of the earth. Christianity spread throughout the Roman Empire and continued to expand its geographical reach after the empire fell. And in a relatively short time after the death of its

founder, Mohammed (632 CE), Islam spread through conquest from its home in Saudi Arabia as far as Spain and India. Likewise, large-scale migrations of people occurred well before the development of modern means of transportation.

Some features of globalization are new. In particular, the globalization of production—whereby a product (such as an automobile or a computer) is assembled from parts manufactured in many different countries—could be considered an important new feature of contemporary economic globalization (Harmes, 2004). Even so, most of the production of goods and services is still for domestic markets (Mann, 1997).

Questions have arisen as to whether a global "monoculture"—that is, a single global culture based on the cultural values of the Western world, particularly the United States—is developing. Certainly cultural diversity is diminishing and many traditional languages and cultures are endangered. American cultural products are widely distributed throughout much of the world. However, there are substantial cultural differences among various regions of the world that American movies, television shows, music, fast foods, and brand labels will not easily erase. Indeed, contemporary communications media, such as the Internet and satellite television, can help minority cultures that are spread across a variety of countries to maintain and develop their cultural values (Elkins, 1995).

Global Policy Forum
www.globalpolicy.org

Although globalization is often described as an inevitable process, various circumstances, including the policies adopted by governments, can accelerate, slow down, or even reverse the trend. For example, the economic globalization that developed in the late nineteenth and early twentieth centuries was reversed by the First World War and later by the rise of economic and political nationalism during the Great Depression of the 1930s.

On the other hand, toward the end of the Second World War, there was an agreement among the Allied powers to prevent a recurrence of nationalism by promoting freer trade, establishing several international financial institutions, and creating a mechanism for managing currency exchanges, all of which came to be known as the Bretton Woods system. The system of basically fixed currency exchange rates collapsed in the early 1970s to be replaced by a system of floating (that is, market-determined) exchange rates, which, along with the removal of restrictions on the flow of capital, encouraged the development of a large global currency market. The tendency of governments since the early 1980s to reduce the regulation of their economies, privatize publicly owned enterprises, and reduce taxes has contributed to the acceleration of the growth of a global free-market capitalist economy.

International Forum on Globalization
www.ifg.org

Globalization and the Nation-State

Is globalization seriously eroding the power of nation-states? The heightened pressures of economic competition may encourage countries to adopt policies that focus on removing barriers to the global free market, reducing the role of government in regulating the economy, and cutting the taxes that are needed to provide social benefits. The rules of trade adopted by bodies such as the World Trade Organization are aimed at trying to establish a "level playing field" in which government policies that protect domestic products and services and place barriers to trade and investment are expected to be eliminated.

Nevertheless, there is diversity among the policies adopted by different countries, reflecting continuing differences in cultures and circumstances. The relatively prosperous countries of Western Europe, for example, have generally continued to maintain a wider range of social benefits for their populations as well as higher environmental and health standards than other countries. The governments of the newly industrialized countries of East Asia are more heavily involved in directing their industries than is the case for the United States and Canada. Generally, countries have tended to adapt to globalization in different ways, and have chosen to integrate into the global economy to differing extents (Garrett, 1998).

It has been argued that globalization is eroding the power of the nation-state not only by shifting power upward to global institutions, global markets, and global corporations, but also by indirectly challenging the nation-state from below (see Box 2-4, Jihad versus McWorld). The decreasing importance of states in providing for the well-being of their people may have the effect of stimulating separatist movements. The development of organizations such as the European Union and the North American Free Trade Agreement makes it possible for some people in smaller areas, such as Scotland and Quebec, to think that belonging to such organizations will offset the disadvantages they would face by separating from a large country.

Finally, people's sense of identification with the nation-state may be reduced as an increasing proportion of people have multiple identities. This,

BOX 2-4

Jihad versus McWorld

American political scientist Benjamin Barber describes the key forces in the contemporary world as "McWorld" (globalization) and "Jihad" (a term sometimes used to refer to war against the enemies of Islam that Barber uses more generally to describe the "retribalization" of different peoples opposed to global interdependence and homogenization).

These forces "operate with equal strength in opposite directions, the one driven by parochial hatreds, the other by universalizing markets, the one recreating ancient sub-national and ethnic borders from within, the other making national borders porous from without" (Barber, 1995, p. 6). Both undermine the nation-state and the ability of democratic nation-states to pursue the common good. In Barber's view, the success of either of these trends would lead to a bleak and undemocratic political future. McWorld involves imposing an unnatural uniformity based on consumerism and the pursuit of profit, while Jihad creates intolerant communities pursuing "a bloody politics of identity" (Barber, 1995, p. 8).

As an alternative, Barber advocates working toward a loose global confederation of democratic communities, smaller than existing states, in which citizens, active in a variety of voluntary organizations, work co-operatively toward the common good.

To what extent is Barber's interpretation of contemporary politics valid? The terrorist attack on the United States in 2001 by al-Qaeda extremists seemed to show the power of Jihad. However, al-Qaeda is not based on a particular tribe, nationality, or homeland, but rather a loose network of groups located in a large number of countries generally connected by an extreme interpretation of Islam and antipathy toward the West and Western-leaning governments of Muslim states. In addition, although movements seeking independence or autonomy have developed within several countries, such movements are not necessarily inward looking. For example, many Scottish and Catalan nationalists seek to develop stronger ties with other countries. Finally, powerful nation-states (such as the United States, China, and Russia) continue to pursue their national interests. Challenges to existing nation-states (such as the jihad against existing Muslim states by extremist Islamic groups) have often proved unsuccessful.

however, is not an entirely new phenomenon, as religious, cultural, regional, local, and ethnic identities have often coexisted or competed with national identities. And although concern with human rights for all people and concern about global environmental problems may be challenging traditional notions of state sovereignty, it does not yet appear that a significant proportion of the world's population has developed a sense of global identity. Indeed, identity politics can lead to an expansion of the activities of the state. For example, although the women's movement has developed a significant global network, its demands, in various countries, have resulted in new state laws and programs such as child-care programs, laws dealing with abuse and sexual harassment, and programs to increase women's educational and employment opportunities (Mann, 1997).

Summary and Conclusion

The nation-state is often considered to be the primary basis for the way the modern world is organized. States claim to be the highest authority within a particular, well-defined territory. State sovereignty is the legal principle that states have the right to govern their population and territory without outside interference, and that they should be treated as equals on the world stage. Questions have been raised, however, whether outside intervention is justified in some instances, such as when state authorities violate the basic human rights of the people they govern.

The rationale often given for state sovereignty is that states are the political expression of a nation, and that nations should have the right to govern themselves. However, not all nations have their own state and not all states are based on a single nation. The determination of what constitutes a particular nation is often controversial. Nations are often thought of in terms of the common ancestry, language, culture, and other characteristics of a people. However, a sense of belonging to a nation can also develop among people of diverse backgrounds and characteristics living in a particular country. Governments, along with intellectuals and artists, have often created or developed myths of nationhood to try to unify the people of their country and create a common culture.

Many states are not based on a people with a single, common identity or set of characteristics. Although some binational and multinational states are stable and successful, the determination of the common good in these states can be difficult because the good of each nation needs to be taken into account to maintain the legitimacy of the state.

The political doctrine of nationalism—with its goals of trying to establish or maintain a self-governing state based on a particular nation and promoting the interests and values of that nation-state—continues to have great significance for the politics of the modern world. From a nationalist perspective, the state should look after the common good of the nation upon which it is based. In the pursuit of the good of the nation, however, the good of others or of the world as a whole may be ignored or harmed.

Associated with the development of the nation-state is the concept of citizenship. The idea that all permanent members of a political community should be equal citizens with the same rights and responsibilities has been challenged, to some extent, by the development of identity politics. Various groups, particularly those who have suffered discrimination, have sought to have their differences recognized and supported by the state. Minority nationalities, in particular, may wish to have a different relationship to the state than other citizens. This raises controversial questions as to whether efforts should be made to strengthen a sense of common citizenship or whether recognizing differences and incorporating them into the organization of the state would help to overcome the alienation that may be felt by minority nationalities (Harty & Murphy, 2005).

The contemporary state faces challenges from globalization as well as from regions and groups within the state that would like to gain greater autonomy or independence. Economic globalization reduces the ability of states to manage their economies, cultural globalization may reduce the significance of national cultural differences, and political globalization can limit state sovereignty. However, claims that the state has declined greatly in significance are exaggerated. States, although having to take globalizing tendencies into account, are still the most important political unit. The governing institutions of the state continue to play a crucial role in providing order and security; economic regulation; justice, social, health, and educational services; and other highly important aspects of our lives.

Nevertheless, politics and governing are becoming more complex as a variety of organizations beyond the state are assuming increased importance. Although a global or cosmopolitan sense of identity has been slow to develop, the development of multiple identities may be reducing the significance of the nation-state as the primary source of political identification (Castells, 2004).

Globalization presents important political challenges; in particular, how to regulate global forces so that they work for the common good of the world rather than concentrating unaccountable power in the hands of large multinational corporations or certain powerful states. Effective political institutions at the global level are needed to direct economic and technological globalization for the common good of humanity (Valaskakis, 2001). "Civilizing globalization"—in other words, trying to make globalization more equitable, environmentally sustainable, democratic, controllable, and less threatening to cultural diversity—is a key political challenge for the twenty-first century (Sandbrook, 2003). To make progress toward achieving the common good of humanity, the development of a consciousness of being part of a global community as well as citizens of a particular state may be necessary.

Key Terms

Discussion Questions

1. What should be the rights and obligations of citizens? How should citizenship be determined? Should a person be allowed to be a citizen of more than one country?

2. Should each nation be self-governing?

3. Is Canada a nation-state?

4. Will globalization make the state irrelevant?

5. Is globalization a threat to cultural values?

6. Have the economic troubles that began in 2008 affected economic globalization?

Further Reading

Bagwati, J. *In defense of globalization: With a new afterword.* Oxford: Oxford University Press, 2007.

Barber, B. *Jihad vs. McWorld: How globalization and tribalism are reshaping the world.* New York: Ballantine, 1995.

Brawley, M.R. *The politics of globalization: Gaining perspective, assessing consequences.* Peterborough, ON: Broadview, 2003.

Friedman, T. *The world is flat: A brief history of the twenty-first century.* New York: Farrar, Straus and Giroux, 2005.

Giddens, A. *Runaway world: How globalization is reshaping our lives.* New York: Routledge, 2000.

Harmes, A. *The return of the state: Protestors, power-brokers and the new global compromise.* Vancouver and Toronto: Douglas & McIntyre, 2004.

Harty, S., & Murphy, M. *In defence of multinational citizenship.* Vancouver and Toronto: UBC Press, 2005.

Held, D., & McGrew, A. (Eds.). *The global transformations reader: An introduction to the* globalization *debate,* 2nd ed. Cambridge: Polity Press, 2003.

Hirst, P., & Thompson, G. *Globalization in question: The international economy and the possibilities of governance,* 2nd ed. Cambridge: Polity Press, 1999.

Ignatieff, M. *Blood and belonging: Journeys into the new nationalism.* Toronto: Penguin, 1993.

Kymlicka, W. *Finding our way. Rethinking ethnocultural relations in Canada.* Toronto: Oxford University Press, 1998.

McBride, S. *Paradigm shift: Globalization and the Canadian state,* 2nd. ed. Halifax: Fernwood, 2005.

Smith, A.D. *Nationalism.* Cambridge, UK: Polity Press, 2001.

Stevenson, G. *Parallel paths: The development of nationalism in Ireland and Quebec.* Montreal: McGill-Queen's University Press, 2006.

Stiglitz, J.E. *Globalization and its discontents.* New York: W.W. Norton, 2002.

Weiss, L. *The myth of the powerless state.* Ithaca: Cornell University Press, 1998.

Chapter 3

GOVERNMENT, THE ECONOMY, AND POLITICAL CONFLICT

PHOTO ABOVE: Mikhail Khodorkovsky, former chief executive of Yukos, Russia's second-largest oil producer, is well known for his political opposition to President Vladimir Putin. In 2005, he was convicted of fraud and tax evasion and sentenced to nine years in jail.

1. outline the strengths and weaknesses of the free-market capitalist system

2. examine the ways in which the free-market capitalist system has been modified by modern governments

3. evaluate the controversies concerning the welfare state

4. discuss the alternatives to a free-market capitalist system

5. explain how economic issues relate to political conflicts

In October 2003, Mikhail Khodorkovsky was on his private jet at a remote airport in Siberia. With assets of more than US$16 billion, surely he had every reason to relax. Suddenly, his plane was stormed by dozens of armed security men who took him off to jail, charged with fraud, embezzlement, and tax evasion. How did Russia's richest man become a convicted criminal?

Khodorkovsky was raised in a typical two-room communal apartment and was a leader in the Communist Youth League. But as restrictions on private enterprise began to ease in the 1980s, he opened a café, established an import business, and soon emerged as an owner of Russia's first privately owned bank, Bank Menatep. When the Soviet Union disbanded in 1991 and the state-owned economy was dismantled, Bank Menatep was hired to auction off Yukos, the leading oil company. In a dubious transaction, the bank bought the company for a tiny fraction of its worth. Like a small number of so-called "oligarchs," Khodorkovsky accumulated great wealth—in part through his political connections.

Khodorkovsky, however, made the mistake of being a political opponent of Vladimir Putin, the former head of the security service elected president of Russia in 2000. Khodorkovsky's arrest occurred shortly after he purchased a newspaper and hired a journalist known to be highly critical of Putin. Putin (now prime minister) has acted to ensure that the mass media are supportive of his rule. Many Russians supported the arrest and conviction of Khodorkovsky—they suffered great hardships during the transition to capitalism and blame the oligarchs for plundering Russia's wealth. Critics, however, viewed the actions taken against Khodorkovsky as an indication that Russia was moving away from democracy. As well, by forcing Khodorkovsky to sell most of his assets to pay a massive alleged tax debt, a Russian state-owned oil company gained control of the valuable oil resources of that country.

Politics and economics are closely related. Political decisions have important effects on the distribution of wealth and people's well-being. Those with economic power often use their wealth to try to affect politics. High levels of inequality can lead to tensions between the wealthy and the rest of the population. The clash of communism and capitalism that was characteristic of much of the twentieth century has faded—most countries are now part of the global capitalist system. However, there continue to be substantial variations among countries regarding the role of the state in managing the economy and in providing for the well-being of the population.

The Russian example also indicates that, contrary to popular belief, a capitalist system is not necessarily associated with freedom and democracy. Capitalism has flourished not only in free, democratic countries, but also in strict dictatorships such as contemporary China and military-ruled Chile of the 1970s and 1980s.

This chapter examines the role of government in the economy and discusses how the well-being of the public can best be served. It also looks at the political conflicts that relate to the inequalities associated with the economic system.

THE RELATIONSHIP BETWEEN POLITICS AND THE ECONOMY

American political scientist Harold Lasswell (1936) described politics as "who gets what, when, how." Usually we think of the economic system as determining how wealth and income are distributed, but political decisions often have a substantial effect on "who gets what." In a fundamental sense, an economic system depends on the laws and regulations established by government. Without laws, no substantial economic system could exist. Those with the means of force would simply plunder the goods of those who are weaker.

The type of economic system established, maintained, and enforced by government will have a major impact on the distribution of wealth and income within a country. Although all economic systems feature an unequal distribution of goods and services (except for small communal systems where all goods are shared equally), inequalities are generally greater in free-market capitalist systems than in socialist economic systems. Government spending and taxing policies also have significant effects on the distribution of wealth and income, modifying the distribution that results from the workings of the economic system. In fact, as Table 3-1 illustrates, there is considerable variation in inequalities from country to country, in part because of governmental actions.

TABLE 3-1
THE DISTRIBUTION OF INCOME, SELECTED COUNTRIES

Notes: The Gini Index measures the extent to which the distribution differs from a perfectly equal distribution. A figure of 0.0 indicates perfect equality. A figure of 100.0 would result if all income were in the hands of one person. The data are based on different years for different countries. The figures for different countries are not strictly comparable. Some are based on distribution of income while others are based on distribution of consumption.

COUNTRY	GINI INDEX	POOREST 10%	RICHEST 10%	COUNTRY	GINI INDEX	POOREST 10%	RICHEST 10%
Japan	24.3	4.8%	21.7%	Russia	39.9	2.4%	30.6%
Sweden	25.0	3.6%	22.2%	United States	40.8	1.9%	29.9%
Czech Republic	25.4	4.3%	22.4%	Nicaragua	43.1	2.2%	33.8%
Germany	28.3	3.2%	22.1%	Turkey	43.6	2.0%	34.1%
Pakistan	30.6	4.0%	26.3%	Nigeria	43.7	1.9%	33.2%
South Korea	31.6	2.9%	22.5%	Mexico	46.1	1.6%	39.4%
Canada	32.6	2.6%	24.8%	China	46.9	1.6%	34.9%
France	32.7	2.8%	25.1%	Chile	54.9	1.4%	45.0%
Australia	35.2	2.0%	25.4%	Brazil	57.0	0.9%	44.8%
United Kingdom	36.0	2.1%	28.5%	South Africa	57.8	1.4%	44.7%
Italy	36.0	2.3%	26.8%	Sierra Leone	62.9	0.5%	43.6%
India	36.8	3.6%	31.1%				

SOURCE: Adapted from Table 2.7 Distribution of income or consumption, 2007 World development indicators, originally published by the World Bank in a volume entitled World development report 2006. To purchase a copy of World development report 2006, please visit www.worldbank.org/publications. Retrieved July 15, 2007, from http://siteresources.worldbank.org/DATASTATISTICS/RESOURCES/table2_7.pdf.

Political controversy often centres on questions related to the distribution of wealth and income, such as:

- whether government should redistribute income and wealth from the rich to the poor
- whether government should ensure that all persons have a reasonable standard of living
- whether various basic services (such as health care and education) should be available free of charge to all members of the political community and supplied by government

Politics, then, often revolves around issues related to material well-being and the regulation of economic activity. This is especially true when physical security is not seriously threatened by war or violence. Those in different economic positions (such as business owners and workers) and those in different economic circumstances (such as the rich and the poor) often have conflicting views about many government policies. Government policies affect the extent to which different groups of people are able to retain their wealth, have the basic necessities, feel secure against the hardships that may be caused by unemployment, disability, or old age, and find opportunities to develop themselves.

Not only do political decisions affect the impact of the economic system on people's lives, but the economic system affects the nature of political decisions. Those with economic power often translate that power into political power. Thus, the policies and laws of the political community may be strongly influenced by those who have dominant positions in the economic system.

THE FREE-MARKET CAPITALIST SYSTEM

The basic economic system that was developed in the nineteenth century in countries such as Britain, the United States, and Canada can be labelled as a **free-market capitalist economic system** (also often referred to as a free-enterprise system). This system involves private ownership and control of most businesses. Economic activity is coordinated mainly through market transactions, rather than by the commands of government or other authorities (Lindblom, 2001).

Key features of the free-market capitalist economic system include:

- businesses produce for the marketplace in search of profits
- consumers choose among competing products at prices determined by the marketplace
- workers supply their labour for wages determined by the marketplace

Although the use of markets to buy and sell goods is thousands of years old, markets generally played only a limited role before the modern era. Households produced food and other products primarily for their own use. In feudal societies, there was often no free labour market, and competition among businesses was severely restricted.

FREE-MARKET CAPITALIST ECONOMIC SYSTEM
An economic system involving private ownership and control of most businesses. Economic activity is coordinated primarily through market transactions, rather than by the commands of government or other authorities.

The Industrial Revolution resulted in economies that were based on the production of goods and services for sale in the marketplace. Setting up large-scale production required both a large labour force available for hire and large amounts of money (capital) to be invested in the expectation of profit. In other words, the Industrial Revolution resulted in a great increase in the markets for goods and services and the development of labour and capital markets.

Efficiency

Free-market capitalist systems can be very efficient in matching the demands of consumers with the supply of products by business (see Box 3-1, Adam Smith and the Efficiency of Free Markets). In fact, the establishment of the free-market capitalist system (replacing **mercantilist policies**) in the nineteenth century, combined with new techniques of production, was revolutionary, resulting in the mass production of consumer goods. Large-scale industrial production contributed to the growth of cities and the decline of traditional, rural ways of life.

On the surface, the free-market capitalist system does not appear very efficient. Businesses regularly go bankrupt, different companies produce the same product, and major miscalculations by business executives are common. However, if competition and entrepreneurship are strong and capital is easily available for new enterprises, the free-market capitalist system can be highly flexible. Entrepreneurs seeking new sources of profit will quickly seek financing for new endeavours, while enterprises that are not competitive, efficient, or sufficiently profitable will be shut down in favour of newer, more efficient, technologically advanced, and profitable ones. In the view of Austrian economist Joseph Schumpeter (1943), the essence of capitalism is the process of "creative destruction"—the perpetual cycle of rejecting older and less efficient products and services and replacing them with newer, more efficient ones. A drawback is that workers suffer insecurity because the company that they work for may collapse. Likewise, communities, particularly smaller communities, are harmed if a major employer becomes bankrupt or moves its operations to a different location.

Innovation

The free-market capitalist system is often praised for its innovative capabilities. It has a built-in incentive to innovate, as those who take risks with new products or processes can reap large profits. Businesses will want to adopt new technologies in order to stay ahead of their competitors. This point should be qualified, however, by noting that a variety of technological advances have also resulted from government- and military-sponsored research and development—including nuclear fission, rockets, jet engines, radar, computers, the Internet, plastics, and a variety of synthetic materials (Hedley, 2002).

MERCANTILIST POLICIES
Pursuit of the interests of the nation-state through protectionist policies, the granting of monopolies to particular merchants, and the extraction of wealth from colonies.

The Capitalism Site
www.capitalism.org

The Center for the Advancement of Capitalism
www.moraldefense.com

BOX 3-1

Adam Smith and the Efficiency of Free Markets

Scottish philosopher Adam Smith (1723–1790) provided the classic argument for a free-market system in 1776 with the publication of his book *The Wealth of Nations*.

Smith's basic argument was that a free, competitive economy is the most efficient way of producing goods. It is desirable because it maximizes the total wealth of the community. Individuals pursuing their own economic interests will be guided by the "invisible hand" of the marketplace to act in a fashion that is in the interests of the community as a whole. Smith wrote, "It is not from the benevolence of the butcher, the brewer, or the baker that we expect our dinner, but from their regard to their self-interest" (Smith, 1776/2004, p. 105). Competition among producers results in the production of goods at the lowest possible price. The signals of the marketplace lead to a balance between what goods are produced and what goods consumers desire. The marketplace, in other words, is self-regulating. Intervention by government lowers the overall level of wealth and creates special privileges for those who are able to influence government at the expense of the society as a whole. The common good is best achieved by allowing individuals to pursue their own economic self-interest.

Smith also advocated the removal of barriers to international free trade. Tariffs (taxes) on imports designed to protect domestic industries result in higher prices for consumers and special privileges for protected industries. In Smith's view, pursuing the interests of the nation-state through protectionist policies such as tariffs on imported goods to aid domestic producers, the granting of monopolies to particular merchants, and the extraction of wealth from colonies (the mercantilist policies common in the seventeenth and eighteenth centuries) hindered the creation of a prosperous and peaceful world.

For Smith, the proper role of government was to provide protection from foreign invasion and to protect property and maintain order through a system of laws. Involvement in the economy should be limited to providing certain "collective goods," such as roads, canals, education, and street lighting that are unlikely to be provided by private business (Ball & Dagger, 2004). Although Smith wanted to free the market from government regulation, he believed (unlike some of his current followers) that a community needed to be based on shared moral principles to limit greedy and selfish behaviour that could harm the common good (Lipschutz, 2004).

Critics argue that an unregulated free-market system leads to a concentration of economic power in the hands of a small number of large corporations, rather than the economy being guided by the "invisible hand" of the marketplace. As well, maximizing wealth for a community may be undesirable if it is associated with great inequalities, exploitation, poverty, and environmental degradation.

Economic Power

Problems can arise if a business or a group of businesses gains control over a sector of the economy because it can then charge exorbitant prices without the need to focus on efficiency. The highly competitive marketplace that Adam Smith envisioned has been replaced, to a considerable extent, by a system in which several hundred large and powerful corporations control a substantial proportion of the global economy. Some have expressed concerns

"The Wal-Stores are coming! The Wal-Stores are coming!"

that the rise of large business corporations will eventually result in a decline in the dynamic element of entrepreneurship (Schumpeter, 1943).

Adam Smith was aware that business could be a powerful force; for example, businesses would be tempted to collude to limit competition, or seek privileges from government. However, in his influential model of a free-market economy, individual businesses have no significant power; rather, they compete with each other to produce the goods that consumers want at the lowest possible price. In reality, large corporations have the ability to affect the economic well-being and employment opportunities of the communities and countries in which they operate. This gives them substantial potential political power. To attract or retain businesses, governments often offer special incentives such as tax exemptions, grants, and free serviced land. Because governments are concerned with maintaining a favourable investment climate, they may tailor their policies to meet the demands of the leading business interests and will try to ensure the profitability of business.

The Environment

A free-market capitalist system can create problems for the environment. The massive increase in production and consumption that has accompanied the growth of the free-market capitalist system has resulted in a greatly increased use of the world's limited resources. There has also been a major increase in the emission of wastes into the atmosphere, soil, and water as a by-product of production and consumption. The competitive pursuit of profit typically does not encourage business to spend money on pollution abatement equipment or on sustainable resource management unless required by government legislation or encouraged by the pressure of consumer boycotts. In other words, the efficiency of the free-market capitalist system in producing goods for the marketplace is not necessarily matched by efficiency in minimizing negative effects on the environment.

In the long run, protection of the natural environment and conservation of natural resources are important for business as well as the public. However, individual businesses may be reluctant to take costly measures to limit their negative impact on the environment unless they can be assured that their competitors will take similar actions. Thus, government action is often needed to protect the environment.

CorpWatch: Holding Corporations Accountable
www.corpwatch.org

Short-term Focus

Individual businesses are often focused on maintaining and enhancing their profitability in the short term. Corporations whose shares trade on the stock market are particularly concerned with ensuring that each of their quarterly reports shows a positive performance. This means in some cases that insufficient attention is given to long-term planning.

Inequality

Concern has also been expressed about the distribution of the wealth created by the free-market capitalist system. This system tends to generate considerable disparities in income and wealth. For example, top corporate officers typically earn many times as much as the workers in their company (see Box 3-2, Business Reward$: Nortel and Enron). In a pure free-market system with very limited government, individuals who are unable to find employment or lack skills for which there is a strong demand may find themselves dependent upon charity to survive.

Government Involvement in the Free-Market Economy

Even in countries with a basically free-market capitalist system, governments are major economic actors. Governments collect a sizable proportion of a country's income through taxation to fund its operations and services and to transfer to individuals for various purposes. As Table 3-2 indicates, government expenditure relative to the size of the economy tends to be higher in the richer countries than in the poorer countries.

BOX 3-2

Business Reward$: Nortel and Enron

During the 1990s, the top executives of large North American corporations not only were able to obtain very large increases in annual salaries, but also received options to buy shares in their companies at discounted prices. Stock options, the argument went, were needed to ensure that top executives had a stake in the companies they were running; executives should share in the profits their efforts generated. However, when the high-technology stock market bubble of the 1990s burst, the huge amount of wealth garnered by top executives began to be questioned.

Consider John Roth, the former head of Canadian-based Nortel Networks, North America's largest telecommunications manufacturer. Roth cashed in $135 million of stock options in 2000. Soon afterwards, shareholders, including pension funds, saw Nortel shares plummet from a peak of more than $120 to less than $1 a share. Tens of thousands of workers were laid off and Nortel lost US$27.3 billion in 2001. Despite his very poor business decisions, Roth, who was pushed out of his position in 2001, had been compensated very generously.

Interestingly, the problems at Nortel continued under his successor, Frank Dunn. Although Dunn and other senior executives received huge bonuses when Nortel returned to profitability in 2003, it was subsequently discovered that profits had been greatly overstated by the company. Dunn and other executives were fired in 2004 amid investigations of Nortel's accounting practices, lawsuits, and criminal probes.

The corruption that can exist in the business world was highlighted by the scandal at Enron, the seventh-largest company in the United States. With the assistance of senior personnel at one of the world's largest accounting firms, top executive officers were able to make their company appear to be highly profitable. These dishonest accounting practices boosted the price of the company's stock so that top executive officers could sell their stock options at highly inflated prices. Enron subsequently went bankrupt in 2001, leaving its shareholders, including its workers, with huge losses. Enron's top executives had secretly sold their shares before the collapse of the company, even as they were encouraging their employees to buy more shares.

Nortel and Enron are not isolated cases. Similar accusations have been made concerning a number of major corporations. Although the pursuit of profit can result in efficiency and innovation, it can also lead to unproductive forms of greed and exploitation.

PROTECTING CONSUMERS Why are governments, even in countries with basically free-market capitalist economies, active in the economy? One reason is that various sectors of the economy do not feature a substantial level of competition. Governments have at times taken action to try to restore competition and to protect consumers. For example, American and European governments took legal action against Microsoft Corporation, alleging that it engages in anti-competitive practices that allow it to dominate the Internet browser and software markets. Some Canadian provinces regulate the price of gasoline and some other petroleum products because of concerns that limited competition may result in price gouging.

TABLE 3-2
**TOTAL GOVERNMENT
SPENDING IN SELECTED
COUNTRIES**

COUNTRY	GOVERNMENT EXPENDITURE AS % OF GDP	COUNTRY	GOVERNMENT EXPENDITURE AS % OF GDP
Sweden	56.7	United States	36.4
Denmark	54.8	Nigeria	35.4
France	53.7	Turkey	35.4
Austria	50.1	Australia	35.3
Belgium	49.6	Russia	33.6
Hungary	49.4	Romania	31.1
Italy	47.8	South Korea	28.1
Germany	47.0	Egypt	26.7
Netherlands	46.6	South Africa	26.3
Norway	45.9	Mexico	23.5
Czech Republic	44.3	Argentina	20.9
United Kingdom	44.0	Brazil	20.9
Poland	42.9	China	20.8
Canada	39.9	Chile	20.4
New Zealand	39.2	Indonesia	19.1
Spain	38.8	India	16.3
Japan	37.3	Pakistan	16.0
Switzerland	36.6	Bangladesh	14.2

Notes: *GDP* is Gross Domestic Product. *Government expenditure* includes government spending, transfers to individuals, and spending by state-owned enterprises.

SOURCE: *Compiled from 2007* Index of economic freedom *by The Heritage Foundation, 2007; retrieved July 15, 2007, from www.heritage.org/research/features/index.*

Governments also have adopted a variety of business regulations to protect consumers and to try to ensure that they have the information they need
to make informed choices in the marketplace. For example, government
inspection and regulation of food products is important in protecting the
health of consumers. Likewise, requiring that food products be labelled with
information about ingredients and nutritional values is essential for persons
with allergies and other medical conditions, as well as for those who wish to
pursue a healthy lifestyle. Before such regulations, few businesses voluntarily
provided such information and many products were unsafe.

PROTECTING THE ENVIRONMENT Government regulation of business
activity can be very useful in protecting the environment. Limitations on dis-
charges of pollutants, elimination of the use of some highly toxic chemicals,
requirements that renewable resources be managed in a sustainable manner,
and protection of natural areas and endangered species may "interfere"
with economic decision making, but are necessary limitations on economic
freedom.

PROTECTING WORKERS Government plays an important role in the relations between business and labour. To prevent workers from being exploited
by business, most contemporary governments legislate the minimum wage

that workers must receive, set limits on the hours of work, require that vacation time be provided, and establish safety standards for workplaces. As well, to try to avoid the bitter conflicts that often occurred between business and labour, governments provide a legal basis for unions to bargain collectively on behalf of workers, and establish rules and procedures concerning the relationship between unions and management.

KEEPING THINGS MOVING Business activity in a free-market capitalist economy tends to go through cycles of expansion and contraction ("boom" and "bust"). **Keynesian economic policies** and **monetarism**, as described in Box 3-3, Avoiding the Economic Roller Coaster, provide different perspectives on how to achieve sustained growth without high levels of inflation or unemployment.

KEYNESIAN ECONOMIC POLICIES
The idea that government can smooth out the ups and downs of the free-market economy by stimulating the economy when private business investment is low, and cooling down the economy when excessive investment is creating inflation.

MONETARISM
An economic perspective based on the view that government's role in the economy should be largely restricted to controlling the supply of money.

ASSISTANCE TO BUSINESS Most governments provide support for various sectors of the economy. For example, governments often provide subsidies to fledgling industries, to industries that are vital to the country's economy or military capabilities, and to high-technology industries that are considered to be the wave of the future. As well, governments often provide various forms of assistance to sectors of the economy that are experiencing decline, such as textile, steel, and shipbuilding industries, or that have very volatile fortunes, such as agriculture. Governments also often provide loans and subsidies to encourage businesses to locate in the less economically developed areas of a country.

INVOLVEMENT OR INTERFERENCE? Government involvement in the economy is sometimes described as interference with the free market. Excessive regulation can reduce the flexibility of the free-market system. High taxes can reduce the competitiveness of business in the global marketplace and result in the emigration of persons with specialized skills (the "brain drain"). Price controls can lead to shortages and insufficient investment for future demand to be met.

Government involvement in the economy, however, is not necessarily harmful to the free market and the interests of business. Government restrictions on monopolies can help to encourage a competitive market. Government provision or funding of research and development (R&D) can be of major assistance to business in a technological age. The provision of some public services by government, such as education, hospitals, and parks, does remove some activities from the market. However, the general interests of business, as well as the population as a whole, are served by providing a healthy and educated workforce and by ensuring a higher quality of life. Indeed, the public provision of health care is less expensive than private provision, thus saving money for those businesses that provide health care benefits to their employees. Health, safety, and environmental regulations may limit some business activities, but are for the common good of all parts of society in the long run.

BOX 3-3

Avoiding the Economic Roller Coaster: Keynes and Friedman

British economist John Maynard Keynes (1883–1946) and American economist Milton Friedman (1912–2006) both put forward ideas to keep economies operating on a relatively even keel, but they had different thoughts on the role that government should play.

During the Depression of the 1930s, when business activity collapsed and unemployment rates skyrocketed, Keynes developed the idea that government could smooth out the ups and downs of the free-market economy. Keynesian economic policies involve stimulating the economy (by spending money and/or reducing taxes) when private business investment is low, and cooling down the economy (by reducing spending and/or raising taxes) when excessive investment is creating inflation. As well, because the poor tend to spend rather than save their money, government programs that put money into the hands of the poor can help to ensure that there is sufficient demand for the goods and services that business can supply. This in turn can result in full or nearly full employment. In general, Keynesian economic policies reflect the view that government can have a positive role in ensuring the smooth functioning of the free-market capitalist system without directly intervening in business decisions.

Keynesian economic policies were adopted to varying extents by most of the advanced capitalist countries during and after the Second World War. They were successful in providing for three decades of sustained growth and prosperity. However, Keynesian economic policies fell out of favour among economists and government policy-makers in the mid 1970s when economies suffered from a simultaneous combination of inflation and economic stagnation ("stagflation").

Instead of the Keynesian emphasis on the need for government to manage the economy by maintaining sufficient demand for the products of the economy, traditional ideas that the free-market economy will stabilize itself without government intervention have been influential in recent decades. In particular, the ideas of Milton Friedman have had considerable importance.

Friedman's perspective, known as monetarism, is based on the view that government's role in the economy should be largely restricted to that of controlling the supply of money. Keynesian policies led governments to increase the supply of money, which caused inflation, in order to cover the debts caused by government spending. Friedman argued instead that each year, governments should have a "balanced budget" (that is, spending should not exceed revenues), even though this means that government will reduce its spending in recessionary times as tax revenues decline. In addition, in the monetarist view, autonomous central banks such as the Bank of Canada (or in the United States, the Federal Reserve) should fight inflation by limiting the growth of the money supply and keeping interest rates high when inflationary pressures occur. By keeping government out of direct involvement in managing the economy, autonomous central banks could administer the bitter medicine needed to prevent inflation.

Friedman also argued that the role of government in the economy should be substantially reduced. With less regulation and lower taxes, there will be greater incentives for investment and production. Economic problems will be resolved by the free market rather than by government. In practice, however, major tax cuts have often not been matched by significant cuts in government spending, even by governments strongly committed to the free market. For example, the substantial tax cuts instituted in the United States after the 2000 election of President George W. Bush led to large government deficits and mounting government debt as government spending rose—due, in part, to increased spending on security and defence.

SOCIALIST ECONOMIC SYSTEMS

SOCIALIST ECONOMIC SYSTEM
An economic system based on social (usually state) ownership and control of the economy.

A **socialist economic system** is one in which there is social rather than private ownership and control of the economy. Usually, a socialist economic system is thought of as one in which the state owns the major industries and resources of a country. However, there are other possible versions of a socialist economy, such as ones based on communes or co-operatives whose members collectively own their enterprises. Socialist economic systems are based on the socialist ideology (discussed in Chapter 5), which seeks a more equitable distribution of income and wealth and a society based more on co-operation than the selfish pursuit of wealth.

CENTRALLY PLANNED STATE SOCIALIST ECONOMIC SYSTEM
An economic system involving state ownership of almost all enterprises and centralized planning by state officials.

Communist-led governments in the former Soviet Union, China, Eastern Europe, North Korea, Cuba, and Vietnam established **centrally planned state socialist economic systems** (also referred to as a "command economy").[1] These systems featured state ownership of almost all enterprises and centralized planning by state officials. As they tried to carry out five-year plans, state officials made decisions as to what goods would be produced, the quantities to be produced, and where and how they would be produced, along with decisions about how consumer goods would be priced.[2]

Communist-led governments were often successful in mobilizing their countries to industrialize and in achieving key objectives set by the political leadership—for example, the Soviet Union was the first country to put a satellite into orbit. As well, the communist-led countries generally provided a wide variety of social services to their population, including child care, education, subsidized housing, health care, and pensions. Unemployment was almost unknown, and workers were essentially guaranteed their jobs for life.

Problems

The centrally planned state socialist economies had serious difficulties. It is very difficult to plan all details of a complex economy. Making the task more difficult was inadequate information. Information that reflected negatively on the government and the performance of the economy was routinely suppressed because of the dictatorial nature of communist-led governments. Thus, planners did not have the data needed to direct the economy. The outcome was that the centrally planned economies were inefficient. Planners were often unable to match supply and demand, resulting in a surplus of some goods and shortages of others. Heavily subsidized prices for basic necessities, such as bread and housing, resulted in shortages as demand exceeded supply. Consumers often had to wait in long

---

[1] There are also a number of Third World countries that have a high level of state ownership of business without necessarily sharing the socialist objective of an equalitarian society. These economic systems are often described as statist.

[2] The communist-led government of the former Yugoslavia established a system of market socialism, in which state-owned industries controlled by their workers produced goods and services that were sold in a basically free marketplace.

◄ Heavily subsidized prices for basic necessities, such as bread, sometimes result in shortages as demand exceeds supply.

lines to obtain the limited amount of goods available. Because factory managers were generally expected to meet quotas based on the quantity of goods to be produced, shoddy merchandise was often the result. With strict bureaucratic controls in place, there was not much incentive to innovate and take risks. As well, in their efforts to achieve rapid industrial growth, the communist-led countries often ignored environmental concerns, and thus suffered severe pollution problems.

The communist-led countries were committed to creating a classless society. However, those with political power, such as the Communist Party elite, often were, in effect, a privileged class. For example, many goods were frequently only available at special stores for the party elite. Likewise, certain holiday resorts were only open to a privileged few.

With the collapse of communism in the Soviet Union and Eastern Europe at the end of the 1980s and in the early 1990s, only North Korea and Cuba continue to have state socialist economies. The People's Republic of China, although still governed by the Communist Party, has been moving away from state ownership and central planning.

MIXED ECONOMIES

No contemporary economic system can be considered as purely free-market capitalist, as governments are involved in affecting economic decisions and the distribution of wealth. In Canada, for example, the generation and distribution of electricity is in the hands of a Crown (state-owned) corporation in many provinces. Most cities run public transit systems and the Canadian government owns VIA Rail, the national passenger rail service. Nevertheless, a large majority of business enterprises are in private hands, and Canadian governments play only a minor role in planning and directing the economy. Thus we would consider countries such as Canada, the United States, and the United Kingdom to have basically free-market capitalist systems.

However, a number of countries have **mixed economies** in which there is substantial state ownership or control of major elements of the economy along with a substantial degree of private ownership and some ability of private businesses to make their own decisions. For example, in rebuilding and modernizing its economy in the decades after the Second World War, the French government established national plans for economic development through a system of voluntary co-operation with business and labour. The French government had considerable power to persuade business to follow its economic plans, as many important sectors of the economy—including banking, insurance, energy, transportation and communications, and automobile production—were at least in part state-owned. As well, the French government used its controls over prices, lending rates, and investment funds to influence business to follow its economic plans (Roth, Warwick, & Paul, 1989). State direction was successful in creating a modern, prosperous economy, although in recent decades the French economy has suffered from weak economic growth and high unemployment (Hauss & Smith, 2000). Nevertheless, France provides its population with a high level of public services and social benefits.

Similarly, as will be discussed in Chapter 18, substantial government economic involvement in collaboration with major business interests has been successful in pursuing rapid economic development in newly industrialized countries such as South Korea and Taiwan. On the other hand, there are a number of poorer countries with substantial state economic involvement that have not succeeded in developing their economies. Having a large proportion of the economy state owned or directed can be associated with problems of corruption, inefficiency, and stagnation.

THE WELFARE STATE

Thus far we have been considering government involvement in the economy primarily in terms of the ownership, control, planning, and regulation of economic activity by comparing capitalist, socialist, and mixed economic systems. However, it is important to analyze the role of government not only in how goods are produced, but also in how the goods produced are distributed. Governments are involved, to varying degrees, in providing for the well-being of their populations. In particular, many modern governments have developed a **welfare state** in which "government-protected minimum standards of

MIXED ECONOMY
An economic system in which there is substantial state ownership or control of major elements of the economy along with a substantial degree of private ownership and some ability of private business to make their own decisions.

WELFARE STATE
A term used to describe countries in which government ensures that all people have a minimum standard of living and are provided some protection from hardships resulting from unemployment, sickness, disability, and old age.

income, nutrition, health, housing, and education [are] assured to every citizen as a political right, not as a 'charity'" (Wilensky, 1975, p. 1).

In the past, there was generally an expectation that individuals should be self-reliant. The failure to provide for oneself and one's family was seen as a result of personal irresponsibility rather than a general failure of the economy. This view was challenged by the Depression of the 1930s, when millions of people were unable to find work. The Depression also demonstrated the inability of private charities and local governments to deal with the problems faced by the needy. The successful mobilization of society and the economy by governments for the Second World War increased the capabilities of government and created more positive attitudes toward an active role for government. There were expectations that governments should take responsibility for the well-being of returning soldiers and the families of those who had sacrificed their lives. As well, the threat of communism and the growing strength of labour and socialist parties created a political climate favourable to the development of the welfare state as a way of protecting the free-market capitalist system from challenges.

The welfare state has been the subject of considerable debate in recent decades, as discussed in Box 3-4, Criticism of the Welfare State. While some welfare state programs, such as medicare in Canada and old age pensions, are popular among the public at large, there is less support for social assistance (welfare) and employment insurance. Since the mid 1990s, the Canadian government has substantially reduced the proportion of unemployed persons who are eligible to collect employment insurance, and most provincial governments have reduced social assistance payments. In addition, some provinces have required that the able-bodied work for their social assistance payments. Ontario requires some welfare recipients to take basic education and receive addictions treatment, if needed. British Columbia limits, with some exceptions, social assistance for the employable to two years within any five-year period. In the United States since 1996, welfare has been limited to five years in one's lifetime.

INEQUALITY AND POLITICS

Differences in income, wealth, and economic opportunities are often the basis of social and political divisions. A major source of political controversy is the question of whether and to what extent government should be involved in ensuring the material well-being of the population and taking action to reduce economic inequalities. Some argue that the free-market capitalist system rewards individuals fairly in terms of their contribution to the economy. Others argue that the inequalities generated by the economic system are

Criticism of the Welfare State

Critics view the welfare state as substantially increasing the tax burden that people face, and contributing to government deficits and debt. Increases in government spending and borrowing are seen as crowding out private investment and activity. The welfare state interferes with the "discipline" of the marketplace, particularly by reducing the incentive for people to work if welfare or unemployment benefits are too generous. Instead, the welfare state encourages people to become dependent upon government and less likely to take responsibility for their own lives.

Are these criticisms of the welfare state valid? The provision by the Canadian government of basic health care, education, and various social services has contributed to the high quality of life of Canadians. Furthermore, the welfare state does not necessarily reduce the competitiveness of an economy. It can allow people to take greater risks, such as finding new jobs, knowing that they have security to fall back on. As well, various social programs help people to adjust as economies change in response to globalization (Atkinson, 2000). In the contemporary knowledge-based economies of the advanced countries, an efficient welfare state combined with major government investments in education, health, and culture can be helpful in developing a highly productive workforce (Castells, 2004).

Welfare state programs contributed to the long period of social peace and economic growth in the decades after the Second World War by helping to achieve a compromise between the demands of workers and the pursuit of profit by business. Welfare state policies may help to legitimate the free-market capitalist system in the eyes of the public by removing some of the harshness of an economic system that would otherwise lead to challenges and criticisms. Indeed, the dismantling of many of the welfare state programs of the former Communist-led regimes in Russia and Eastern Europe has caused considerable dissatisfaction among the population.

Cutbacks in social assistance and employment insurance have increased the number of people in dire poverty and overburdened charitable organizations in Canada that provide food banks, housing for the homeless, and other basic services. The lack of political power of the poor has often made them targets for reductions in government services while the rich have benefited from tax cuts.

A basic question underlies the debate over the welfare state: Do all citizens have the right to a basic standard of living regardless of their circumstances?

unfair and that large disparities in wealth and income are potentially harmful to the political community and should be reduced through government action.

Class Divisions

SOCIAL CLASS

A grouping of people who have a similar position in the economy and related social status.

Many theorists have postulated that as societies modernize and industrialize, class divisions would become the most important basis of political conflict. A **social class** is a grouping of people who have a similar position in the economy and related social status. As discussed in Chapter 5, Marxists see modern capitalist societies as fundamentally divided between the working class, who sell their labour power, and the capitalist class, who own the means of production. The capitalist class, through its economic power, is able to dominate and exploit the working class. Other theorists view social class in terms of a combination of differences based on income, occupation, education, and social status, and thus see a more complex pattern of class divisions.

Class divisions in countries with modern capitalist systems are not generally as rigid as the social and economic divisions in pre-modern times, such as the division between lords and serfs in feudal times or India's caste system (which still exists despite being formally outlawed). There is some mobility between classes, and some very wealthy individuals come from ordinary backgrounds. However, there is a tendency for people to stay in the same social class for life and, to some extent, for class positions to be passed on to the next generation. The growth of middle-class occupations and the availability of higher education to middle- and working-class families have reduced the sharpness of class divisions. Although inequalities in income and wealth have not significantly decreased in the richer countries, and in some cases have increased in recent times, the development of the welfare state has served to blunt the conflict between social classes. Nevertheless, even in richer countries there is an underclass of persons who struggle to make ends meet, working in low-wage and part-time positions or unemployed.

The political significance of social class depends, to a considerable extent, on the level of **class consciousness**—that is, the extent to which people see themselves as members of a particular social class. Where unions and working-class-oriented political parties are strong, workers are more likely to view themselves as members of the working class and act politically in solidarity with their social class. In countries where other divisions are strong, such as those based on ethnicity, religion, or region, people are less likely to identify with a particular social class and less likely to act in accordance with their class interests.

A number of analysts argue that class divisions are declining in importance in post-industrial societies, where a high proportion of the workforce is engaged in information and technology-based enterprises and in service occupations, rather than in manufacturing or resource-based industries. The increasing availability of post-secondary education to a substantial proportion of the population may have also reduced the significance of education-based differences in the perspectives of different classes. Other analysts argue that economic globalization will result in new forms of class differences. The movement of manufacturing and information technology jobs from wealthier countries to low-wage countries may result in a heightened division in post-industrial countries between a minority with high-paying jobs and the majority with low-paying, insecure service jobs.

CLASS CONSCIOUSNESS
The extent to which people see themselves as members of a particular social class.

Regional Divisions

Conflict concerning the distribution of income and role of government in the economy does not only involve social classes. Economic development in many countries has occurred in an uneven fashion, and prosperity often varies considerably from one part of a country to another. In Canada, for example, the Atlantic provinces are poorer and less economically developed than Ontario and Alberta. Likewise, southern England is more prosperous than the north, and northern Italy is more economically developed than the south. Areas with high unemployment, lower incomes, and a weak economic base may feel that they have been treated unfairly by government and businesses in the economically powerful regions. Furthermore, as societies modernize, there is typically a large migration of people from rural areas and smaller communities to large urban centres. This creates practical problems for those remaining in rural areas as institutions such as schools and hospitals become less viable and subject to closure. People living in poorer regions and rural areas will often demand special assistance from the central government. This may, in turn, cause some resentment in the richer regions that feel that their wealth is unfairly being taken away from them.

Women and Minorities

Women and ethnic or racial minority groups often face discrimination in seeking employment and have lower-paying jobs and fewer opportunities for promotion. In Canada, for example, there are exceptionally high rates of poverty and unemployment among Aboriginals, and many recent immigrants have difficulty finding employment that matches their qualifications. In some countries, the situation is reversed, with many wealthy business people being members of a minority group. This can cause resentment among the members of the majority ethnic group. In Uganda, for example, the East Indian minority (many of whom were brought by the British as indentured servants to build a railway) played a major role in business life until their expulsion in 1972. Similarly, many French Quebecers have been resentful of the wealth and economic power traditionally concentrated in the hands of some members of the English-speaking minority in Quebec. However, actions by the Quebec government since the 1960s have promoted the development of a French-speaking business and managerial class.

AFFIRMATIVE ACTION
The adoption of programs designed to make the workplace, universities, legislatures, or other institutions more representative of disadvantaged groups and groups that have suffered from discrimination.

In theory, employers in a free-market economy hire those individuals best able to contribute to the profitability of their companies regardless of the characteristics of those individuals. Discrimination against persons of a particular group would make the firm less competitive by depriving it of the best individuals. In reality, discrimination can be hard to avoid because of subtle prejudices.

The entry of a large proportion of women into the paid workforce has highlighted issues related to gender-based economic inequalities in recent decades. Although laws in Canada and many other countries require that employers pay women and men equally for work that is substantially the same, women on average earn significantly less than men. As well, a relatively small proportion of women reach the highest positions in either private or public employment or work in non-traditional occupations such as mining or engineering. As discussed in Box 3-5, Rectifying Gender Inequality, women's groups argue that governments need to take active measures such as **affirmative action** and **pay equity** policies to ensure a fairer distribution of income and employment opportunities between women and men.

PAY EQUITY

A policy that requires employers to provide equal pay for work of equal value; for example, by raising the pay of persons in occupations that are largely staffed by women to the same pay as persons in comparable occupations that are largely staffed by men.

BOX 3-5

Rectifying Gender Inequality

The measures often advocated to rectify gender inequality in the workplace include affirmative action programs, pay equity laws, and subsidized child care. Affirmative action (also known as employment equity) involves the adoption of programs designed to result in the hiring and promotion of a higher proportion of women and disadvantaged minorities. Such programs are designed to create a more representative and diverse workforce and to overcome subtle forms of discrimination. For example, affirmative action programs have been established in the Canadian public service with targets for increasing the proportion of women, Aboriginals, persons with disabilities, and visible minorities in each occupational category. Employers with sizable Canadian government contracts are also required to establish affirmative action programs.

Pay equity legislation requires that employers provide equal pay for work of *equal value*. In particular, this involves raising the pay of persons in occupations that are largely staffed by women to the same pay as persons in comparable occupations (in terms of a combination of skill, effort, responsibility, and working conditions) that are largely staffed by men.

For example, an employer might be required to bring the pay of secretaries up to the level of pay of janitors after an assessment of the two occupations. Pay equity legislation applies to public servants at the national and provincial levels in Canada, to many workers in the broader public sector such as schools and hospitals, to most private-sector employees in several provinces, and to nationally incorporated companies such as banks.

In addition, the provision of government-subsidized, quality child care would help to overcome the obstacles that working women with young children often face. Critics argue that affirmative action programs constitute reverse discrimination against white males and lead to an undesirable emphasis in hiring and promotion on one's personal characteristics rather than qualifications and performance. The backlash against affirmative action is particularly strong in the United States, where quotas for black Americans in employment and education have been highly controversial. The business community has generally been opposed to pay equity legislation, believing that the market should determine salaries. As well, since pay equity involves raising salaries, it is an additional cost to business.

Summary and Conclusion

Politics often revolves around questions related to how the wealth of society should be produced and distributed. A major topic of political controversy is the extent to which government should involve itself in the economy. The free-market capitalist economy is typically viewed by economists as the most efficient way to produce goods and services. Government involvement beyond the minimum needed for the capitalist system to function reduces the overall wealth of society. The pursuit of individual interests in the free marketplace results in the maximization of the total wealth of the community.

Others argue that more substantial government activity is needed to achieve the common good. In the pursuit of profit, business may exploit its workers, mislead consumers, and despoil the environment. Government action is needed to regulate business activity to direct it toward the common good. The highly uneven distribution of wealth created by the free-market capitalist system should be modified through government action so as to reduce inequalities and ensure that all persons have an adequate standard of living.

Supporters of the free-market system point out that competition in the marketplace determines what is produced and how wealth is distributed. This, they argue, avoids the arbitrary use of power, which leads to privileges for some and discrimination for others. People are rewarded according to their contribution to the wealth of society regardless of their personal characteristics. The free-market system provides incentives for hard work, initiative, and innovation.

Critics of the free-market capitalist system argue that in reality it is often characterized by a concentration of power in the hands of business interests, a power that has been enhanced by economic globalization. This gives business considerable ability to influence governments. The result is that governments may be more interested in promoting the interests of business than in seeking the common good of society as a whole.

Placing ownership and control of the economy in the hands of the state may eliminate the power of private business, but does not necessarily result in the common good, as the experience of socialist economic systems indicates. Instead, as Robert Paehlke (2003, p. 122) suggests, we should consider how the "dynamic productive power of capitalism" can be harnessed to enhance the quality of social life and protect the environment. The common good, in this perspective, requires balancing the "bottom line" of efficiency and economic growth provided by a free-market system with the social and environmental health of the community.

Overall, the exercise of power in political life is often directed at gaining a larger or fairer share of the economic pie for particular groups. Perceptions of inequalities and their significance in politics are affected by ideas, ideologies, and the ways in which various political organizations seek to mobilize support. The feminist ideology and women's movement, for example, have helped to focus attention on gender inequalities that were often not seen as politically relevant in the past. Similarly, it has been argued that the focus of the major Canadian political parties on ethnic, linguistic, and regional divisions has reduced the political significance of class divisions in Canada (Brodie & Jenson, 1988).

Key Terms

Discussion Questions

1. Should Canada move toward a purer free-market capitalist economic system?

2. Are business corporations too powerful in Canada? Should corporations be accountable for their actions?

3. Should the welfare state be reduced or expanded? Should welfare recipients be required to work for welfare? Should a maximum time limit be placed on one's right to collect welfare payments?

4. How important are class divisions in Canada? Do you think that class divisions will have a greater or lesser impact on politics in the future?

5. Are affirmative action programs desirable? As a student about to enter the workforce, do you believe that pay equity legislation should be applied to private business?

Further Reading

Brown, M.B. *Models in political economy: A guide to the arguments*, 2nd ed. London: Penguin, 1995.

Friedman, M. *Capitalism and freedom*. Chicago: University of Chicago Press, 1981.

Geider, W. *One world, ready or not: The manic logic of global capitalism*. New York: Simon and Schuster, 1997.

Held, D., & Kaya, A. (Eds.). *Global inequality: Patterns and explanation*. Cambridge, UK: Polity Press, 2007.

Korten, D.C. *When corporations rule the world*, 2nd. ed. West Hartford, CT: Kumarian Press, 2001.

Lindblom, C.E. *The market system: What it is, how it works and what to make of it*. New Haven, CT: Yale University Press, 2001.

Pierson, C., & Castles, F.G. (Eds.). *The welfare state: A reader*. Cambridge, UK: Polity Press, 2000.

Rae, B. *The three questions: Prosperity and the public good*. Toronto: Viking, 1998.

PART II

IDEALS AND IDEOLOGIES

Chapter 4

THE DEMOCRATIC IDEAL

PHOTO ABOVE: Arnold Schwarzenegger, former bodybuilder and Hollywood icon, drew international attention when he was sworn in as governor of California in November 2003.

1. discuss the advantages and disadvantages of democracy

2. distinguish between direct democracy and representative democracy

3. explain the meaning of liberal democracy and discuss the possible tensions between liberal and democratic ideals

4. evaluate the desirability of referendums, initiatives, and recall elections

5. discuss the concept of deliberative democracy

6. consider the problems that globalization may create for democracy

Arnold Schwarzenegger drew international attention when he was sworn in as governor of California in November 2003. Thousands watched live and millions more were able to tune in to the televised version as the former bodybuilder and star of such films as *The Terminator* and *Total Recall* took political control of the most populous American state. Exercising their right to recall elected politicians, voters had sacked Governor Gray Davis—who had been re-elected governor just a year earlier—and put their political futures in the hands of a Hollywood icon.

The right to recall politicians before their term is up is allowed in only a few democratic systems. Some American states and municipalities provide for the recall of state and local politicians, voters in Venezuela can recall any elected politician including the president, and British Columbia in 1994 adopted procedures for the recall of members of the provincial legislature.

California uses an unusual version of recall elections. Elected public officials can be recalled if signatures equal to at least 12 percent of the votes cast for the position in the previous election are obtained. This results in a recall election in which a question placed on the ballot asks whether the official should be immediately recalled. A second question on the same ballot asks voters who should replace that official if the first question passes. In 2003, a Republican congressman spent more than US$1 million of his own money hiring a professional petition-gathering company to launch a recall campaign against the Democratic governor, who was blamed for the large state deficit and a proposal to raise taxes. After more than a million signatures were obtained in the allotted time, a recall election was held. Fifty-five percent voted to recall Governor Davis. Schwarzenegger was elected by just less than 50 percent of those

answering the second ballot question, which had a list of 135 candidates for the governor's position. Gray Davis was the first California governor recalled since the recall legislation was adopted in 1911.

No representatives in British Columbia have thus far been recalled, as the requirement that 40 percent of eligible voters sign a petition makes recall more difficult than in California. However, one member of the provincial legislature who had engaged in unscrupulous behaviour (including writing letters to the editor using phony names, praising his own accomplishments) resigned rather than face a recall election.

Some people argue that simply electing a representative every few years is insufficient to make a political system truly democratic. Through mechanisms such as recall elections, people can have more control over the decisions for their political community. In particular, representatives who do not act on the wishes of their constituents or who engage in corrupt practices can be removed from office. Others argue that recall elections can make it difficult for representatives to act for the common good because they make it easier for particular interests to pressure elected representatives and give added power to those with the money or organization needed to mount a recall campaign.

A POPULAR IDEAL

Democracy is one of the most popular political ideals in the contemporary world. Almost all government leaders proclaim their belief in democracy, and claim that their country is democratic or on the path to democracy. Wars have been fought in the name of democracy and those seeking democracy have often had to struggle against dictatorial governments.

The term *democracy* comes from ancient Greek words that can be translated as rule by the people. The democratic ideal is that all adult citizens should have an equal and effective voice in the decisions of the political communities to which they belong.

Despite the popularity of democracy, the ideal of rule by the people is difficult to implement fully. Even though we normally think of countries like Canada, the United States, the United Kingdom, India, and Germany as democratic, the question can be raised as to whether the people really rule in these countries. As we will examine in this chapter, there are different views as to what makes a political system democratic and whether a fuller application of democratic ideals would be feasible and desirable.

IS DEMOCRACY DESIRABLE?

Democracy has often been subject to criticism and ridicule, as indicated by some of the quotations in Box 4-1, Some Views of Democracy. Even those who support democracy have often been less than enthusiastic. Until about a century and a half ago, most political thinkers were critical of the democratic ideal and were skeptical about whether democracy could work in practice. It was only in the past century that a significant number of countries became democratic and only in recent decades that the majority of the world's countries could be considered democratic. Even so, many of the newer democracies are fragile and are only democratic to a limited extent.

Arguments in Favour

Those who promote the democratic ideal argue that it is the best way to achieve the common good. By involving the population as a whole in governing, the interests and values of different parts of the population are more likely to be reflected in decisions than if control of decision making is in the hands of a single individual or a particular group. As well, by encouraging people to be freely involved in making governing decisions, those decisions can potentially benefit from the discussion and deliberation of persons with a wide variety of different viewpoints. Even if the public as a whole is not directly involved in governing, democratic procedures such as elections can help to ensure that those holding governing positions are held accountable to the people and serve the good of the population as a whole.

Some Views of Democracy

What is democracy? Many writers, politicians, and thinkers have offered their thoughts on the topic:

- "The art and science of running the circus from the monkey cage." (American journalist H.L. Mencken)
- "The bludgeoning of the people, by the people, for the people." (Irish writer Oscar Wilde)
- "It substitutes election by the incompetent many for appointment by the corrupt few." (Irish playwright George Bernard Shaw)
- "The worst form of government except all those others that have been tried from time to time." (British Prime Minister Sir Winston Churchill)

- "Democracy means choosing your dictators, after they've told you what it is you want to hear." (American writer Alan Coren)
- "Democracy is not perfect, but it is the only form of government that respects the dignity of the individual and protects the individual's human rights." (American political scientist James David Barber)
- "Man's capacity for justice makes democracy possible, but man's inclination to injustice makes democracy necessary." (German theologian Reinhold Niebuhr)

Governments that have been chosen by the people are more likely to be accepted as legitimate by their populations. Because the people have a role in the governing process, they are more likely to accept what government does, even if they happen to disagree with particular decisions. Thus, democratic governments may be more effective than non-democratic ones, even though the processes of democratic decision making are often complex. As well, democracies have the positive feature of allowing for a peaceful transition of power. Citizens can remove a government with which they are dissatisfied without having to resort to violence. Democracy may also encourage people to be more civic minded. Through involvement in governing, people may feel a greater attachment to the political community and be more likely to assume a sense of responsibility to their fellow citizens. Citizens may derive a sense of fulfillment and meaning through sharing in the governing of their community.

Finally, democracy is often associated with the value of equality. Although the adoption of democratic procedures does not necessarily result in greater social or economic equality, democracy has the potential to give some influence to those who would otherwise be powerless. This influence may encourage elected politicians to develop policies to aid the disadvantaged.

Arguments Against

Critics of democracy often question whether ordinary citizens have the time and knowledge to make intelligent decisions concerning the governing of their society. Classic political philosophers such as Plato (c. 428–347 BCE) and Aristotle (384–322 BCE) argued that demagogues (persuasive speakers) would sway the citizenry, leading to decisions that were not for the common good. Modern critics worry about the masses being swayed by emotional appeals in the mass media. Similarly, critics of democracy argue that undesirable policies result from politicians pandering to the wishes and prejudices of the mass public. For example, politicians often offer "goodies" to the public in order to gain its support in an election—and frequently the public fails to pay due attention to the costs of what is being promised.

Although democracy is often promoted as an alternative to the tyranny of dictators, some political thinkers have worried about whether democracy can degenerate into the "tyranny of the majority." The majority, particularly if aroused by a sensational issue, may be inclined to demand that the rights and freedoms of unpopular minorities or individuals be removed. A democratic system may result in decisions that reflect the wishes of the majority, but there is a danger that minorities could be consistently ignored.

Democracy is also sometimes criticized for being "all talk, no action," involving endless debate and rules that often seem designed to prevent government from acting. Because a variety of interests and viewpoints are taken into account, the democratic decision-making process can be slow. To satisfy different interests, democratic decisions often involve compromises rather than adherence to principles. Non-democratic systems, it is argued, are better able to take the strong measures that may be needed to deal with serious problems.

Finally, there are those who argue that democracy is an impossible ideal to achieve. Power will always be in the hands of a few people. In this view, democracy is a sham—window dressing to hide the realities of politics and add a facade of legitimacy to those who really hold power. Elections are exercises in manipulation, and those in positions of power, even if elected, serve their own interests, rather than the interests of the population.

THE MANY VERSIONS OF DEMOCRACY

Direct Democracy

DIRECT DEMOCRACY
A system in which citizens make the governing decisions.

About 2500 years ago, the important Greek city-state of Athens adopted a system of **direct democracy**, that is, a system in which citizens make the governing decisions. The citizens of Athens met in an open assembly about ten times a year and, after discussion in which all citizens could participate, the decisions governing this powerful state were made by a vote of those present. The ideal of the citizenry involved in actively discussing and deliberating about public issues was defended by the fourth century BCE Athenian statesman Pericles, who argued that "instead of looking on discussion as a stumbling-block in the way of action, we think it an indispensable preliminary to any wise action at all" (Thucydides, *The Peloponnesian War*, II, 40; quoted in Warren, 2002, p. 174).

By today's standards, ancient Athens would not be considered highly democratic: only a minority of Athenians had the rights of citizens. Women, slaves, and those not born in Athens were excluded from political life. In other ways, however, ancient Athens was highly democratic. Not only were citizens directly involved in deliberating about and deciding on the major issues for their state, but many of the officials who administered the decisions of the Assembly were chosen by lottery. Because administrators held their positions for only a relatively short period of office, many citizens, at some point in their lives, would serve as state officials. By keeping terms of offices short, the democrats of ancient Athens hoped to prevent powerful individuals or groups from controlling the political system and exercising tyrannical power.

The influential Greek philosophers Plato and Aristotle criticized Athenian democracy, arguing that the common people ruled in their own selfish interests. In particular, they argued that the majority of people, being poor, would use their political power to take the wealth of the rich, rather than acting for the common good of all.

Better than democracy, in Aristotle's view, was a system he called polity, which involved a mixture of rule by the few and rule by the many. The ancient Roman Republic, where a few consuls implemented laws passed by the Senate (composed of aristocrats) and the Assembly (composed of ordinary citizens), could be considered an example of mixed rule. The ideal of mixed rule also influenced the founders of the United States, who adopted a system in which the different branches of government each check the powers of the others (as discussed in Chapter 16).

Canadians for Direct Democracy
www.npsnet.com/cdd

The direct democracy of ancient Athens lasted about 250 years, but the idea of direct democracy has not completely disappeared. Citizen meetings make decisions in a few New England towns and small Swiss cantons (provinces). As well, the random selection of citizens to serve on juries bears a resemblance to the practices of ancient Athens. However, the idea of citizens assembling to make governing decisions became impractical as larger states developed. Thus, democracy in the modern era is generally associated with the concept of elected representation of the citizenry. Nevertheless, some have suggested that contemporary technology, such as interactive television and the Internet, could be used to recreate the decision making by citizens' forums that is characteristic of direct democracy.

Representative Democracy

REPRESENTATIVE DEMOCRACY
A form of democracy in which citizens elect representatives to the legislature to make decisions on their behalf.

Representative democracy involves citizens electing representatives to the **legislature**, a body that is responsible for the formal approval of legislation and the raising and spending of funds by the government. As well, in parliamentary systems (see Chapter 15), elected legislatures (such as the Canadian House of Commons) are the key source of political authority for government. The prime minister and Cabinet (the political executive that oversees the

LEGISLATURE
A body that is responsible for the formal approval of legislation and the raising and spending of funds by the government.

FIGURE 4-1

VOTING RIGHTS TIMELINE, CANADA

1867—1917
Women, and generally those without substantial property or income, most Indians, and in some provinces those of Chinese or Asiatic origin not allowed to vote.

1918
All Canadian women 21 years or older provided they were not alien-born and met property requirements could vote federally.

1917
Female military nurses allowed to vote. Persons born in an enemy country as well as Mennonites and Doukhobours deprived of vote.

1920
Property requirements eliminated.

SOURCES: From "Electoral facts" by W. Brown, 1999, *Electoral insight, 1*(2), pp. 28–36; and *A history of the vote in Canada* by Elections Canada (1997), Ottawa: Minister of Public Works and Government Services.

government) are usually members of the elected legislative body and must retain the support of the majority of elected representatives. Representatives must seek re-election after a limited period of time. In presidential systems, such as the United States, both the president and the members of Congress (the legislative body) are elected representatives of the people. Representative democracy is an indirect form of democracy in the sense that the people do not directly make the governing decisions, but rather through an election determine who makes such decisions on their behalf.

Representative legislatures originated in meetings called by monarchs when they needed to gain the support of persons from different parts of their realm for new taxes. Eventually in Britain and elsewhere, legislatures challenged the power of the monarch and gained control of governing. Later still (generally in the early twentieth century), pressure from various sections of the public that did not have the right to vote resulted in representative bodies becoming democratic in the sense that all citizens could participate in the election of representatives. As Figure 4-1 illustrates, the right to vote was only gradually extended to all adult citizens in Canada.

Extending the right to vote and hold office to all citizens does not, however, ensure that legislatures will be representative in the sense of accurately reflecting all characteristics of the population. For example, women are underrepresented to varying extents in all legislatures, as Table 4-1 indicates.

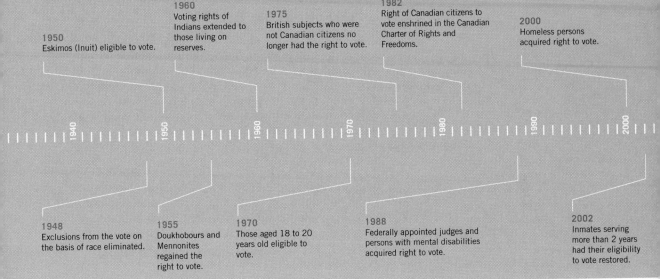

1950
Eskimos (Inuit) eligible to vote.

1960
Voting rights of Indians extended to those living on reserves.

1975
British subjects who were not Canadian citizens no longer had the right to vote.

1982
Right of Canadian citizens to vote enshrined in the Canadian Charter of Rights and Freedoms.

2000
Homeless persons acquired right to vote.

1948
Exclusions from the vote on the basis of race eliminated.

1955
Doukhobours and Mennonites regained the right to vote.

1970
Those aged 18 to 20 years old eligible to vote.

1988
Federally appointed judges and persons with mental disabilities acquired right to vote.

2002
Inmates serving more than 2 years had their eligibility to vote restored.

In most contemporary parliamentary democracies, elected representatives, other than those who are in the Cabinet, usually have a limited involvement in developing governing decisions. It is the political executive (in Canada, the prime minister and Cabinet), along with public servants, who have a key role in the development of laws and policies. The general role of Parliament is to debate

Democracy Watch
www.dwatch.ca

TABLE 4-1
WOMEN IN NATIONAL LEGISLATURES

Note: Figures are for the lower house (such as the Canadian House of Commons) in countries with two legislative chambers. The figure for Canada reflects the results of the 2008 election.

COUNTRY	% WOMEN IN LEGISLATURE	COUNTRY	% WOMEN IN LEGISLATURE
Rwanda	48.8%	United Kingdom	19.7%
Sweden	47.3%	Italy	17.3%
Finland	42.0%	United States	16.3%
Costa Rica	38.6%	Bangladesh	15.1%
Cuba	36.0%	Indonesia	11.3%
Spain	36.0%	Russia	9.8%
Argentina	35.0%	Japan	9.4%
Germany	31.6%	Brazil	8.8%
Australia	24.7%	India	8.3%
Mexico	22.6%	Egypt	2.0%
Canada	22.1%	Saudi Arabia	0.0%
Poland	20.4%	**World Average**	**15.6%**

SOURCE: *Adapted from* Women in national parliaments *by Inter-Parliamentary Union (IPU) (2007). Retrieved May 20, 2007, from www.ipu.org/wne-e/classif.htm.*

and approve proposed laws that are presented to it by the prime minister and Cabinet. Representatives are almost always members of a political party, and elections focus on the competition among political parties to determine which party (or parties) will form the government. Elected representatives are generally expected to vote along party lines. This means that they do not necessarily vote in accordance with the views of the majority in the constituency they represent. Representation, then, is more by party than by individual representatives.

Liberal Democracy

The version of representative democracy that developed in modern Western societies is often described as **liberal democracy**. Liberal democracy, as the term suggests, combines the ideology of **liberalism** (discussed in Chapter 5), which advocates a high level of individual freedom, with a democratic system of governing based on the election of representatives. The power and scope of government should be limited, government should abide by the rule of law, and the rights of the people should be protected. In this view, democracy should be based on a vibrant **civil society** in which citizens are free to discuss,

LIBERAL DEMOCRACY
A political system that combines the liberal ideas of limited government, individual freedom, and the rule of law with a democratic system of governing based on the election of representatives.

LIBERALISM
An ideological perspective advocating a high level of individual freedom, based on a belief in the inherent dignity and worth of each individual.

▶ Elections Canada has recently made it possible for the homeless to vote.

organize, and act, particularly through a diversity of voluntary groups and organizations that are not controlled by the state.

Liberal democracy is generally accepted not only by liberals, but also (sometimes with qualifications) by contemporary conservatives and democratic socialists.

Liberal democracy is based on the belief that power, even the power of a government that is supported by the majority of the people, is liable to be abused. Liberal democracy includes the following principles:

- Limits should be placed on what governments can do. Those in positions of political authority should not be able to rule in an arbitrary manner; rather, decisions should be taken according to established laws and procedures.
- All persons should have the freedom to express their views, including the freedom to criticize government, and the freedom to organize themselves for political action.
- The communications media should be free of government control so that diverse sources of information and ideas are easily available to the public.
- Political parties should be able to freely compete for political power.

To some extent, the liberal ideal of individual freedom fits nicely with the democratic ideal of rule by the people. If government is overbearing and exercises too much control over society and individuals, the ideal of rule by the people will be undermined. On the other hand, some view liberal democracy as a combination of two different and potentially inconsistent ideas. The democratic ideal is based on the view that the political equality of all citizens is desirable. Each citizen should count equally in making the governing decisions for the political community. However, the liberal ideal, particularly in its classic form of favouring the free marketplace, does not necessarily challenge the concentration of economic and social power in the hands of a few. The wealthy, and those who control large business corporations, have the potential to use their economic power to gain a much larger voice in affecting political decisions than the ordinary citizen. For those who favour **social democracy** (see Chapter 5), liberal democracy is a limited form of democracy. In this view, democracy involves more than establishing procedures to elect representatives and protecting the rights and freedoms of citizens. A meaningful democracy also requires that government act so as to ensure that there is a substantial degree of social and economic equality.

Plebiscitary Democracy

Plebiscitary democracy involves giving citizens greater control than in a representative democracy through the use of such devices as referendums, initiatives, and recall elections. This version of democracy is often associated with the perspective of **populism**, which is based on the idea that

CIVIL SOCIETY
The voluntary groups and organizations that are not controlled by the state.

SOCIAL DEMOCRACY
The belief that the capitalist economy should be reformed to ensure that it works for the common good of all and that greater social and economic equality is desirable to achieve a meaningful democracy.

PLEBISCITARY DEMOCRACY
A form of democracy in which citizens have greater control than in representative democracy through the use of such devices as referendums, initiatives, and recall elections.

POPULISM
A perspective that advocates putting power in the hands of the people rather than the elites who control politics and society.

fundamental differences exist between ordinary people and the elites who control politics and society (Laycock, 2002). Ordinary people, in the populist perspective, possess common sense. Politicians, government bureaucrats, political parties, intellectuals and leading cultural figures, and the owners of banks and other big businesses are often viewed by populists as immoral, corrupt, or out of touch with common people. Elites and "special interests" control the community and take advantage of the hard-working majority. Representative democracy, populists argue, places power in the hands of politicians who may be more interested in their own political careers, in acting in accordance with the views of their party, and in promoting special interests than in taking direction from the people whom they are supposed to represent. In practice, however, populist political parties have often concentrated power in the hands of a persuasive leader who claims to speak for ordinary people.

REFERENDUM
A vote by citizens on a particular issue or law.

REFERENDUMS   A **referendum** gives people the opportunity to vote on a particular issue or proposed law.[1] A number of countries require that changes to their constitution be approved by a referendum. Referendums can also be used in some countries to repeal a law that has been passed by a legislative body. Many American states and municipalities make frequent use of referendums, although there has never been a national referendum in the United States. In Canada (as discussed in Box 4-2, The Use of Referendums in Canada) referendums have been used occasionally.

Although referendums involve a vote by the people, the decision to hold a referendum and the wording of a referendum are generally set by those in control of the government or the legislature. Thus, there is a possibility that a referendum can be used to manipulate the people through misleading wording. Indeed, many non-democratic governments have used referendums to try to legitimate their rule. For example, some dictators have held referendums asking for approval of their continued rule without allowing a choice among alternative candidates and without providing an opportunity for public criticism of the leader.

INITIATIVE
A procedure that gives citizens the right, by obtaining a sizable number of signatures on a petition, to have a proposition that they have drafted put to a vote by the electorate for approval.

INITIATIVES   A stronger means of giving the public a direct voice in decision making is the **initiative**. This procedure gives citizens the right, by obtaining a sizable number of signatures on a petition, to have a proposition that they have drafted put to a vote by the electorate for approval (see Box 4-3, The Initiative and Stockwell Day). This right for laws to be proposed and approved by the people has been established in Switzerland, Italy, twenty-four

---

[1] A distinction can be made between referendums whose results are binding on government and those that are only advisory (the latter sometimes referred to as plebiscites). However, even if a referendum is not legally binding, governments will often accept its results.

BOX 4-2

The Use of Referendums in Canada

There have been only three referendums at the national level in Canada. They concerned the prohibition of liquor (1898), conscription during the Second World War, and the package of constitutional changes known as the Charlottetown Accord (1992).

Referendums have been somewhat more common at the provincial and local levels. The Quebec government has held two referendums concerning independence. In 1980, 40.5 percent of Quebecers voted in favour of giving the Quebec government a mandate to negotiate "sovereignty-association" (a politically independent Quebec in an economic association with Canada) with the Canadian government. In 1995, 49.3 percent of Quebec voters supported giving the Quebec government a mandate to negotiate Quebec sovereignty. In response to a challenge to the 1995 referendum, the Supreme Court of Canada provided an opinion in 1998 that only if there was a clear majority on a clear question could a province negotiate its independence with the other Canadian governments. The Canadian Parliament reinforced this ruling by passing the Clarity Act (2000). This Act states that the Canadian government will only enter into negotiations regarding the secession (separation) of a province if the Canadian House of Commons determines that a clear majority of the population of that province has voted in favour of secession on the basis of a clear question.

The Clarity Act raises important issues. Should referendums on important questions require the approval of more than 50 percent of those voting to be passed? How can we ensure that a referendum question is clear? If a referendum is necessary to allow a province to secede, does this suggest that referendums should be required for other important issues?

Although referendums involve a vote by the people, the decision to hold a referendum and the wording of a referendum are generally set by those in control of the government or the legislature, as was the case in Canada in 1995. Debate raged over whether the wording was misleading.

American states, and British Columbia. For example, in 1978, a California initiative (Proposition 13) requiring major tax cuts was passed. This led to major cutbacks in government programs because of the reduced tax revenues. Similar measures were subsequently adopted through the initiative procedure in several other states.

Initiative & Referendum Institute
www.iandrinstitute.org

The Initiative & Referendum Institute Europe
www.iri-europe.org

The Initiative and Stockwell Day

One of the policy positions of the Canadian Alliance party, which merged with the Progressive Conservative party in 2003, was a proposal to allow citizen initiatives at the national level if signatures were obtained from 3 percent of voters. Stockwell Day, the Alliance's leader at the time of the 2000 Canadian election, was ambiguous during the campaign about his position on this proposal. On the comedy show *This Hour Has 22 Minutes,* Rick Mercer satirized the issue by conducting a mock initiative campaign. His proposed law to force Stockwell Day to change his name to Doris Day was supported by millions of email votes!

Although there is a possibility that initiatives could be used for frivolous purposes, as Mercer demonstrated, setting a high threshold for petitions can limit the number of initiatives that come to a general vote. For example, no initiatives in British Columbia have thus far gained enough support to come to a vote. The requirement that at least 10 percent of eligible voters in each provincial electoral district must sign the initiative petition within a ninety-day period has discouraged initiative efforts.

RECALL
A procedure that allows citizens to remove representatives from office. By gaining a sufficient number of signatures on a petition, citizens can require that their representative seek re-election before the representative's term is over.

RECALL As discussed in the opening vignette, **recall** procedures allow citizens to remove representatives from office. Although California includes the choice of a new representative on the same ballot as the question about whether the current representative should be recalled, other jurisdictions that allow the recall of representatives hold another election to choose a new representative after a majority has voted to recall the current representative. The adoption of recall elections is often viewed as incompatible with a parliamentary system of government, since the recall of representatives from a small number of constituencies could result in the defeat of the governing party.

PROBLEMS WITH PLEBISCITARY DEMOCRACY There are some practical problems with referendums, initiatives, and recall elections. Citizens are not always prepared to vote on long and difficult proposals. When faced with a number of complex referendum and initiative questions on the ballot, voters may find it difficult to make informed decisions. This is particularly the case if referendums or initiatives are worded in a manipulative fashion. Concerns have been expressed that voters may be swayed by the expensive advertising efforts of interest groups that present the issues simplistically or unfairly, or by businesses that may stand to profit by the vote. For example, various businesses spent $700 000 in order to obtain a "yes" vote in a 2001 New Brunswick referendum regarding the establishment of video lottery terminals in that province. In California, more than $100 million was spent on the 2006 campaign for Proposition 87, which would tax the producers of oil extracted in that state to fund programs to reduce oil consumption and provide incentives for alternative energy. The large oil companies that spent the majority of funds were successful in defeating the initiative by a 55 to 45 percent margin. As in regular elections, it takes money and organization to win votes.

Referendums, initiatives, and recall may stimulate some public discussion of important issues, encourage representatives to be more responsive to voters, and result in laws that reflect the wishes of the majority. However, like regular elections, there are possibilities for manipulation and the exertion of one-sided influence. Voting is not necessarily the product of informed discussion and deliberation. As well, although some referendums have had a high rate of turnout, such as when 93.5 percent of Quebecers voted in the 1995 referendum, frequent use of referendums, initiatives, and recall may result in low turnout rates. This is particularly the case when voters have to deal with multiple, complex questions.

Deliberative Democracy

In recent years, there has been considerable discussion among political theorists about the possibility of a **deliberative democracy** in which decisions are made based on discussion by free and equal citizens (Elster, 1998). Through involvement in deliberative processes, it is hoped that people will become better informed, more active citizens. Through dialogue, people will come to understand the viewpoints of others and then, ideally, work together constructively to propose policies that are in the common good. Unlike representative and plebiscitary versions of democracy, deliberative democracy brings citizens into decision making through discussion, rather than primarily through voting.

In theory, representative democracy involves thorough discussion and deliberation about political issues by the elected representatives of the people who have the time, knowledge, and experience to devote to this important task. However, the reality is that thorough discussion and deliberation rarely occur in bodies such as the Canadian House of Commons that consist of elected representatives. Instead, it is behind the closed doors of Cabinet and among senior government officials and advisers to the Cabinet that almost all laws and policies are developed. Debate in the Canadian House of Commons typically involves the governing party defending its actions and proposals and the opposition parties criticizing the government. Debate is often related more to the struggle among parties for power than to an effort to seek the common good through discussion.

To some extent, contemporary governments have been encouraging increased public participation in the decision-making process through various forms of public consultation, such as public hearings and forums on various issues. Although this is useful in allowing a variety of viewpoints to be heard, there is a tendency for public hearings to be dominated by spokespersons for particular interests. Further, governments often do not feel obliged to explain and justify why they are not following the advice given to them.

DELIBERATIVE DEMOCRACY
A political system in which decisions are made based on discussion by citizens rather than by elected representatives alone.

Deliberative Democracy Consortium
www.deliberative-democracy.net

▶ The British Columbia Citizens' Assembly discusses its recommendations for changing the province's electoral system.

CITIZENS' JURY

A group of randomly selected persons that deliberate about and make recommendations concerning particular issues.

Advocates of deliberative democracy often envision it as operating primarily among citizens at the local level, where face-to-face dialogue is possible and the issues being discussed may have direct relevance for the lives of those involved. Giving people in local communities responsibility for the management of their resources, such as rivers, forests, or coastal fisheries, or establishing community Parliaments (Resnick, 1997) may encourage deliberative decision making.

Citizens' juries are another way to involve ordinary citizens in deliberation and decision making. They have been used in a variety of countries (including the United Kingdom, the United States, Germany, Spain, Australia, Bulgaria, and Brazil) in recent years. The citizens' jury brings together a group of randomly selected citizens. Like the juries used to determine the outcome of some court trials, citizens' juries are composed of persons without any special knowledge of the topic under consideration. Trained facilitators are used to guide the deliberation, jurors are provided with information, and witnesses are called to explain and justify different viewpoints. The jurors then make recommendations that are passed on to a governmental body (or, as discussed in Box 4-4, Choosing an Electoral System, put to all citizens in a referendum) for possible action.

Citizens' juries directly involve only a tiny proportion of the public in deliberation. However, if combined with public hearings or referendums, they may stimulate broader public discussion of particular issues. For such a process to be meaningful, the recommendations of the citizens' jury must have some significance in the policy-making process (Smith & Wales, 2002).

Choosing an Electoral System

In 2003, British Columbia's government introduced what it termed a Citizens' Assembly to make a recommendation as to whether a new system should be used to elect provincial legislators. Two citizens were randomly selected from each provincial district to form, along with an appointed chair (a former university president), an assembly of 159 members. The random selection procedure was adjusted to ensure that equal numbers of males and females were chosen and that the assembly reflected the age distribution of the population. Service on the assembly was voluntary and members received $150 a day. In addition to obtaining expert advice on different electoral systems, the assembly was required to hold public hearings across the province before making its recommendations. According to the participants, the deliberations were serious and meaningful.

The recommendation for a new system of elections (single-transferable vote) was put to the voters of the province in a binding 2005 referendum. Although 57.7 percent voted in favour of the new system, this was short of the approval by 60 percent of voters and by majorities in 60 percent of the province's electoral districts that was required for the adoption of the new system. Given the closeness of the vote, a second referendum on the proposal is planned for 2009.

A similar process was subsequently used in Ontario, which also resulted in a recommendation to change the province's electoral system (to a mixed-member proportional system, as discussed in Chapter 10). The proposal was put to citizens in a referendum in October 2007, but only 37 percent of those voting supported the change.

A study of a citizens' jury in Denmark (which they termed a deliberative poll) found that ordinary citizens were willing to engage in reasoned deliberation about the complex issue of whether Denmark should adopt the common European currency (the euro). Participants not only increased their knowledge of the issue, but also gained a better understanding of different viewpoints as well as becoming more interested in the issue. In the deliberations, participants mainly used arguments involving general principles and appeals to the common good, although self-interested arguments were also used and some participants tended to dominate the discussion.

The deliberations were televised and extensively reported in the mass media. In the end, however, voters in Denmark rejected the adoption of the euro even though a majority of those involved in the deliberations favoured it (Andersen & Hansen, 2007).

DEMOCRACY AND THE NATION-STATE

Democracy is often thought to work best in a political community where there is a common identity, common culture, and common values and ideals. When one has a sense of partnership with other citizens, it is easier to consider the common good of the community. It is not surprising, therefore, that modern democracy often developed alongside the development of the nation-state.

In countries that are divided by language, it may be difficult for a common dialogue about political issues to develop among those speaking different languages. In countries with sharp cultural, regional, class, or other divisions, there may be insufficient trust and respect to sustain a dialogue about the good of the community as a whole. Nevertheless, viable democracies have been built in countries such as Canada, Belgium, and Switzerland despite the challenges posed by linguistic, cultural, and regional divisions. Indeed, some argue that diversity helps to create a more vibrant democracy because a variety of different perspectives can be brought into political discussion.

One way that democracy can be sustained in countries with sharp divisions is by avoiding a strict application of the principle of majority rule. By trying to ensure that there is a broad consensus among different groups about major issues, and by trying to ensure that different groups are represented in government, minority groups may be less likely to feel dominated by the majority. Indeed, politics in some continental European democracies leans in the direction of finding a consensus rather than majority rule (Lijphart, 1999). Another way to try to accommodate different cultural groups that are geographically concentrated is to adopt a **federal system** in which some important decisions are made at the provincial level (see Chapter 14). In this way, different groups can have a degree of democratic self-government.

FEDERAL SYSTEM
A system of governing in which sovereign authority is divided or shared between the central government and regional governments, with each deriving its authority from the constitution.

GLOBALIZATION AND DEMOCRACY

Democracy is based on the idea that the members of a political community should make the decisions that determine the direction and well-being of their community. Of course, there are always limits to the ability of even a small community to control its own destiny. Our understanding of the consequences of our actions is often limited, such that we may have trouble determining what actions are in our community's best interests. Unexpected events—whether a crop failure, a severe storm, an environmental disaster, or the development of a new source of wealth—can throw plans off course.

Globalization is sometimes seen as a threat to democracy. Economic globalization tends to increase the extent to which countries are affected by events that are beyond their direct control. As a country's economy becomes more and more intertwined with those of other countries and the rest of the world, its government may be less able to independently manage the national economy. Our well-being as individuals and as a community becomes increasingly affected by what is happening beyond the borders of our country. Global markets, financial institutions, and business corporations become increasingly important. As well, economic globalization may create pressures for governments to focus on economic competitiveness at the expense of policies that seek to achieve greater equality among citizens.

Globalization also tends to foster multiple identities. As the globalization of culture develops, there may be increased tendencies for identification with the nation-state to decline in intensity while other identities develop. For example, citizens of France and Germany may be slowly developing a European identity while at the same time increasing their identification with their particular region as the nation-state declines in significance. Feminists, environmentalists, and executives of multinational corporations may develop some degree of identification with their counterparts around the world. Ethnic minorities may develop increasing ties with those of similar ancestry in other parts of the world. Although these multiple identities are very positive in some ways, they have the potential to reduce the feeling of being involved in a common endeavour for the good of the national community.

Globalization also tends to create multiple sources of governing to deal with the growing number of problems, such as climate change, the HIV/AIDS epidemic, global financial problems, and international terrorism, which require international action. In addition to being governed by several levels of government within the state, political globalization involves new regional and global organizations beyond the state that also have an effect on our lives. International organizations such as the World Bank, International Monetary Fund, World Trade Organization, and the United Nations are not particularly democratic. Such organizations, although directed by representatives of member governments, are not generally accountable to the people affected by their actions. The decisions of many international organizations are made behind closed doors with little public input. The principle of political equality does not generally apply to international organizations, and their rules and decisions often seem to be based more on power than on fairness (Coleman, 2002).

A sense of common citizenship among the members of a political community is often thought to be a necessary basis for a stable democracy. As discussed in Box 4-5, Cosmopolitan Citizenship, a sense of "cosmopolitan citizenship" may need to grow among the people of the world if the democratic ideal is to be meaningful in an era of globalization. Dialogue among people in different countries about the common good of the world is currently very limited. Nevertheless, recent years have seen the development of various global political movements (for example, feminist, environmentalist, and human rights movements) that seek to raise various issues and demands and propose solutions to problems at the international level.

Cosmopolitan Citizenship

David Held (2000, p. 57), a professor of political science and sociology at Britain's Open University, argues that the concept of citizenship needs to be broadened to include cosmopolitan citizenship if the increasingly important systems of power that exist beyond the level of the state are to be democratically controlled:

> If many contemporary forms of power are to become accountable and if many of the complex issues that affect us all—locally, nationally, regionally and globally—are to be democratically regulated, people must have access to, and membership in, diverse political communities. . . . democracy for the new millennium should describe a world where citizens enjoy multiple citizenships. They should be citizens of their own communities, of the wider regions in which they live, and of a cosmopolitan, transnational community.

Several questions arise when we consider just how realistic Held's ideal of cosmopolitan citizenship is:

- Can people put aside, at least to some extent, the interests of their nation-state to consider the good of the world as a whole?
- Can fundamental cultural differences, such as the differences between the West and other parts of the world, be overcome to create a cosmopolitan citizenship?
- Are the divisions between the rich and poor countries so great as to prevent the development of trust among the peoples of the world?

Nevertheless, as systems of power beyond the state become increasingly important, people may need to develop a sense of cosmopolitan citizenship if democracy is to remain meaningful.

Summary and Conclusion

The democratic ideal is that of rule by the people. By placing political power in the hands of the people, those who hold the democratic ideal believe that the common good is more likely to be achieved than in non-democratic systems, in which decisions are made by rulers who are not held accountable to the people they govern.

While the democratic ideal appears very popular in the contemporary world, many political thinkers over the centuries have had serious concerns about democracy. Even if, in general, democratic countries tend to function better than non-democratic ones, this does not mean that every democracy functions well,

nor does it mean that every non-democratic country is corrupt or tyrannical.

Representative democracy has generally been the system used to implement the democratic ideal. Through the competitive election of representatives and political parties, it allows citizens the opportunity to hold government accountable for its actions. Representatives and governing parties, it is assumed, will be sensitive to the interests and wishes of voters because of their desire to be re-elected.

Representative democracy could, however, be considered a limited version of democracy, as the people elect others to make decisions on their behalf rather than directly participate in decision making. As well, questions often arise as to whether the decisions of elected representatives really reflect the interests, values, and opinions of the citizenry. There has, therefore, been a continuing interest in supplementing representative democracy with aspects of direct democracy. Plebiscitary democracy involves making greater use of voting, in the forms of referendums, initiatives, and recall elections, to determine issues by a majority vote and to try to ensure that representatives act in accordance with the wishes of those who elected them. Deliberative democracy seeks to involve citizens in the discussion and resolution of problems.

Supporters of representative democracy argue that politicians are best suited to seek the common good by using their experience, knowledge, and judgment to make decisions subject to being held accountable periodically to the electorate. Those who advocate plebiscitary democracy argue that governing decisions should reflect the wishes of the majority. Advocates of deliberative democracy assume that dialogue among citizens having a variety of perspectives will lead to a search for the common good, or will make possible acceptable compromises among different views of the common good (Warren, 2002).

Associated with the democratic ideal are the values of freedom and equality. Liberal democracy combines representative democracy that focuses on adopting procedures for citizens to elect those who make governing decisions with the liberal view that people should be able to freely express their opinions and organize to make their voices heard by government. As well, advocates of liberal democracy argue that there should be limits on the power of government and that governmental power be dispersed rather than concentrated. A vibrant opposition, a vigilant mass media, and an independent judiciary are viewed as essential to prevent arbitrary government actions. Social democratic views of democracy focus more on egalitarian values. Establishing political rights for citizens to vote and express their views are important but, they argue, insufficient for a meaningful democracy. Powerful groups, such as large corporations, are able to exercise a dominant influence on government. Inequalities in the distribution of social and economic power need to be reduced and the basic needs of all the population fulfilled in order to allow all citizens to have an equal voice in the decisions taken by the political community.

Although the ideal of democracy has gained widespread acceptance in the modern world, it faces continuing challenges. In states with substantial divisions, the mechanisms of majority rule can result in the heightening of tensions among different groups. Further, democracy may become less meaningful as international and global institutions become more important. Developing a reasonable level of democracy is more difficult in international and global political communities than in those states where a common sense of citizenship exists.

Key Terms

Discussion Questions

1. Is democracy the best form of government?

2. Should Canada move in the direction of becoming more democratic? If so, how could this best be achieved?

3. Is it important that representative bodies reflect the characteristics of the population?

4. Should representatives do what they think is best or what the majority of people want them to do?

5. Is democracy possible for governing organizations beyond the state?

Further Reading

Barber, B. *Strong democracy: Participatory democracy for a new age.* Berkeley, CA: University of California Press, 1984.

Carter, A., & Stokes, G. (Eds.). *Democratic theory today: Challenges for the 21st century.* Cambridge, UK: Polity Press, 2002.

Cronin, T. *Direct democracy: The politics of initiative, referendum, and recall.* Cambridge, MA: Harvard University Press, 1989.

Dahl, R.A. *On democracy.* New Haven, CT: Yale University Press, 1998.

Dryzek, J. *Deliberative democracy and beyond: Liberals, critics, contestation.* Oxford: Oxford University Press, 2000.

Gutmann, A., & Thompson, D. *Why deliberative democracy?* Princeton, NJ: Princeton University Press, 2004.

Held, D. *Models of democracy,* 3rd ed. Cambridge, UK: Polity Press, 2006.

LeDuc, L. *The politics of direct democracy: Referendums in global perspective.* Peterborough, ON: Broadview Press, 2003.

Mansbridge, J. *Beyond adversary democracy.* New York: Basic Books, 1980.

Paehlke, R.C. *Democracy's dilemma: Environment, social equity, and the global economy.* Cambridge, MA: MIT Press, 2003.

Resnick, P. *Twenty-first century democracy.* Montreal: McGill–Queen's University Press, 1997.

Chapter 5

LIBERALISM, CONSERVATISM, SOCIALISM, AND FASCISM

PHOTO ABOVE: Vladimir Lenin's brother was arrested and then hanged for plotting to assassinate Tsar Alexander III. On learning of the execution, Vladimir promised to "make them pay for this!" Soon thereafter, he began studying the works of revolutionary thinkers Karl Marx and Frederick Engels and later, as the leader of the Bolsheviks, advocated revolutionary action.

CHAPTER OBJECTIVES

After reading this chapter you should be able to:

1. explain the meaning and significance of political ideology

2. discuss the ideas of liberalism, conservatism, socialism, and fascism

3. outline the development and major variations of each ideology

4. apply the terms "left" and "right" to the analysis of political perspectives

After his brother was arrested for concealing a bomb in a medical encyclopedia, Vladimir Ilych Ulyanov—and ultimately world politics—underwent a profound change. Vladimir was still a teenager when his older brother Alexander was hanged for planning to assassinate Russia's Tsar Alexander III. On learning of the execution, Vladimir proclaimed, "I'll make them pay for this! I swear it!" (Shub, 1966, p. 16).

Expelled from university for supporting student demands, Vladimir began studying the works of revolutionary thinkers Karl Marx and Frederick Engels and passed the examinations needed to become a lawyer. Later, in exile in Switzerland, he adopted the name Lenin. He became the leader of the Bolshevik party (later known as the Communist party), which advocated revolutionary action.

With Russia suffering extreme hardships and military defeats in the First World War, Tsar Nicholas II was forced to abdicate in March 1917. A provisional government continued the devastating war and did little to alleviate the dire circumstances faced by much of the population. Using the slogan "peace, bread, land," the Bolsheviks led a successful attack on the seat of government in Petrograd (now St. Petersburg). After a bitter civil war, Lenin was able to gain control of Russia, which was renamed the Union of Soviet Socialist Republics.

In many ways, the communist regimes of Lenin and his successor Stalin were even more oppressive than the tsarist governments that had ruled Russia for centuries. Dissent of any kind was brutally repressed. Forced labour camps were set up in remote regions of Russia. Whole populations were exiled from their homelands. And millions of peasants died of starvation as a result of the policies adopted by the Communist government.

Strongly held ideas and beliefs, whether religious or political, can have a profound effect on the world and on our lives. They can, for example, shape the way that we understand the world. In this chapter and the next chapter, we will examine various basic perspectives on the world, termed political ideologies.

POLITICAL IDEOLOGIES

A **political ideology** is a package of interrelated ideas and beliefs about government, society, the economy, and human nature that inspire and affect political action. Each ideology provides a different perspective that is used to understand and evaluate how the world actually works (Sunderlin, 2003). Marxism, for example, looks at the world through the lens of class conflict, feminism sees the world in terms of male dominance, and liberalism views historical development as involving the struggle for individual liberty.

Most political ideologies also provide a vision of what the world should be like and how it should work. Usually, ideologies propose a means of political action to achieve their objectives. Some ideologies challenge and seek to transform the existing basic power arrangements; other ideologies provide justifications for the existing order. Ideologies are often associated with social movements and political parties. For example, democratic socialism has been closely associated with the labour movement and with political parties such as the New Democratic Party in Canada and Social Democratic parties in Europe.

Political ideologies often borrow from the works of leading political philosophers. However, ideologies involve simplifications of political philosophy because the goal of political ideology is to motivate political action by large numbers of people. Rather than carefully assessing different sets of ideas, ideological thinking typically involves a dedication to developing a particular perspective.

The development of political ideologies is associated with the ideas of the European **Enlightenment** and with the economic and social upheavals associated with the development of capitalism and the Industrial Revolution. The mid-eighteenth-century Enlightenment involved a major shift from traditional religious beliefs toward an optimistic belief in the power of human reason to make the world better. Setting the tone for the modern world, Enlightenment thinkers argued that through reason and science, people could understand the world. Progress could be achieved by consciously shaping the world and its institutions. Human beings could create a better society on earth, rather than waiting for the life after death promised by religion. The French Revolution of 1789, influenced in part by Enlightenment ideas, involved a fundamental challenge to the traditional bases of authority—the monarchy, the aristocracy, and the Catholic Church. New and competing sets of ideas developed about how society and the state should be organized and run. Likewise, the rise of capitalism and the Industrial Revolution disrupted previous patterns of economic and social life, leading to intense disputes over the desirability of the capitalist system. The political ideologies that developed in Europe spread to the rest of the world, although they were often modified by different cultures and circumstances.

POLITICAL IDEOLOGY
A package of interrelated ideas and beliefs about government, society, the economy, and human nature that affect political action. Each ideology provides a different perspective that is used to understand and evaluate how the world actually works. Most ideologies present a vision of what the world should be like and how political action can be used to achieve that vision.

ENLIGHTENMENT
An intellectual movement that developed in the mid eighteenth century, emphasizing the power of human reason to understand and improve the world.

Ideological conflict has been at the centre of political life for the past two centuries. Intellectuals, politicians, journalists, and political activists often have a particular ideological perspective. Controversies over a variety of specific public policy issues often reflect differences among those who have different ideological perspectives. Many people do not consciously hold an ideological perspective, but nonetheless are affected in their thinking by elements of one or more ideologies. Whether in a subtle or explicit manner, ideological perspectives are often conveyed to the public by governments, various political and social groups, the educational system, and the mass media.

The Negative Side of Ideology

The term *ideology* is sometimes used in a negative sense to describe viewpoints that are inflexible, designed to persuade the public in a deceptive manner, and extreme. There is some truth to this negative characterization. There are those who treat the leading texts of their ideology as if they were the word of God. Some adherents of an ideology are closed-minded persons who refuse to seriously consider any criticisms of their perspective. Ideological thinking can be simplistic, and ideological adherents may provide distorted depictions of reality to fit their mental model of the world. More importantly, ideologies have been used to justify the unjustifiable, such as the extermination of the European Jewish population by the Nazis and the mass murder of educated city residents in Cambodia in the 1970s.

However, ideologies are not only the belief systems of fanatics, extremists, and simplistic thinkers. An ideology can provide some coherence, consistency, and direction to a person's political thinking and actions. Even those who consider themselves pragmatic or practical are often influenced by an ideological perspective. As Boris DeWeil argues, the ongoing debate among different ideologies is an inherent and desirable aspect of democratic politics, resulting from the

▶ Ideologies have been used to justify the unjustifiable, such as the death of about one-fifth of the population of Cambodia from 1975 to 1979. In an attempt to create an agrarian communist utopia, Pol Pot's Khmer Rouge regime evacuated the cities and undertook a deliberate campaign of destroying the educated part of the population through starvation, slave labour, and executions. Some Western intellectuals, blinded by the regime's ideology, tried to deny the reality of the Cambodian "killing fields."

fact that people have different value priorities (for example, whether equality or freedom is more important). Ideologies provide us with different ideas about the common good and how it may be achieved. "Without ideology, politics becomes the pursuit of power as its own reward" (DeWeil, 2000, p. 5).

Examining Ideologies

In examining ideologies, we should keep in mind that each ideology is a broad perspective containing many variations and changing over time. It is not always easy to distinguish clearly between one ideology and another because differences between them may be subtle. However, each of the major ideologies does have some distinguishing themes (see Table 5-1).

Political parties with ideological names, such as the Liberal or Conservative parties, do not *necessarily* reflect the ideology corresponding to their name. Political parties are often, but not always, founded on a set of ideological

TABLE 5-1
IDEOLOGIES: KEY THEMES

Note: These are only broad characterizations that do not capture the diversity and evolution of each ideology.

LIBERALISM	CONSERVATISM	SOCIALISM	FASCISM
Human nature Individuals able to think and act according to reason	Humans imperfect with capacity for evil	Humans co-operative and social	People motivated by emotion rather than reason
Key value Individual freedom	Order, stability, social harmony	Equality	Loyalty to nation-state
Political system Liberal representative democracy	Traditional institutions	Egalitarian democracy	Authoritarian leadership
Rights Protect individual rights	Rights balanced by duties	Provide universal social and economic rights	Subordinate individual to the state
Morality State should not impose morality	Maintain traditional moral values	Promote equalitarian values	Promote heroic virtues
Economy Free-market with equality of opportunity	Free-market with social harmony	Planned economy	Corporate state
Political analysis Struggle for freedom	Radical changes undesirable	Class conflict and struggle for equality	Racial or national conflict

FIGURE 5-1

POLITICAL IDEOLOGIES ON THE LEFT–RIGHT DIMENSION

principles. However, in the pursuit of electoral success, they may find it desirable to modify or ignore those principles.

Left and Right

A simple way of depicting ideological positions is in terms of left and right, as illustrated in Figure 5.1. In contemporary usage, the **left** is associated with the pursuit of greater social and economic equality, while those on the **right** generally see inequality as a natural feature of human society.[1] A secondary meaning is that those on the right believe that traditional (religious-based) moral values should be reflected in laws and supported by community institutions, while those on the left generally oppose state support for religious institutions and favour laws based on universal human rights rather than traditional morality.

Although the left–right dimension is useful, it has its limitations. For example, the depiction of communism as extreme left and fascism as extreme right ignores the reality that there are some similarities between these two perspectives, particularly in the **totalitarian** practices of communist and fascist states. Portraying political perspectives along a single dimension can be misleading, as the differences among the ideologies are multidimensional. For example, ideologies differ along an authoritarian–libertarian dimension, which focuses on the proper relationship of the individual to the state or other authorities, as well as on an equality–inequality dimension.

LEFT
The general ideological position associated with advocacy of greater social and economic equality, laws based on human rights rather than traditional morality, and opposition to state support for religious institutions.

RIGHT
The general ideological position associated with opposition to imposing greater social and economic equality and with maintaining traditional (religious-based) moral values and institutions.

TOTALITARIAN
A type of state that attempts to control all aspects of life.

Your ideological position: an easy, anonymous, five-minute quiz
www.politicalcompass.org

LIBERALISM

The ideology of liberalism emphasizes the desirability of a high level of individual freedom, based on a belief in the inherent dignity and worth of each individual. Individuals are assumed to be capable of using reason and taking rational actions in pursuit of their interests. Thus, individuals should take responsibility for their own lives with as little interference from others as possible (see Box 5-1, John Stuart Mill: A Liberal Perspective, for a classic statement of this point of view). Establishing a set of basic rights for all individuals allows people to live their lives as they see fit (Barry, 1996).

---

[1] The terms *left* and *right* originated in the seating arrangements of the French National Assembly established after the French Revolution of 1789. Those who favoured the old order sat to the right of the chairman of the Assembly. Those who opposed the absolute authority of the monarch, demanded that the power and privileges of the Catholic Church be reduced or eliminated, and favoured redistributing the property and wealth of the nobility sat on the left (Needler, 1996).

John Stuart Mill: A Liberal Perspective

In his influential essay *On Liberty*, English liberal thinker John Stuart Mill made the case that individuals should be free to pursue their own good in their own way:

> The only purpose for which power can be rightfully exercised over any member of a civilised community, against his will, is to prevent harm to others. His own good, either physical or moral, is not a sufficient warrant. He cannot rightfully be compelled to do or forbear because it will be better for him to do so, because it will make him happier, because, in the opinions of others, to do so would be wise, or even right. These are good reasons for remonstrating with him, or reasoning with him, or persuading him, or entreating him, but not for compelling him, or visiting him with any evil in case he do otherwise. . . . Over himself, over his own body and mind, the individual is sovereign (Mill, 1859/ 1912, p. 15).

Although Mill was a passionate advocate of individual liberty and *On Liberty* is regarded as a definitive defence of individual human liberty, Mill, like other liberals and conservatives of his time, did not believe that the conquered peoples who were ruled by the British Empire were ready for self-rule. Liberty, it seems, was suitable for the British. Like children, people in India and elsewhere needed paternalistic guidance and control.

Historically, liberalism developed out of the struggles against the arbitrary power of absolute monarchs, restrictions on free business activity, the imposition of one set of religious values on the population of a country, and the granting of special privileges to particular groups—whether churches, aristocrats, or business monopolies.

Although liberals see a need for government, they are concerned that government will abuse its power. Thus, a central goal of liberalism is to ensure that the rights of individuals are firmly protected so they cannot be taken away by government. Liberals strongly advocate the **rule of law**. Government should act only in accordance with established laws rather than in an arbitrary fashion, and all persons should be equally subject to the law.

Liberals also want to limit the scope of government activity. This involves distinguishing a substantial area of private activity, where government should not be involved, from matters of public concern, in which government may be involved. As former Canadian Liberal Prime Minister Pierre Trudeau argued, "The state has no place in the nation's bedrooms." What goes on between consenting adults, in this perspective, should be left to their own moral judgment.

Religion, in the liberal view, is a private matter based on the conscience of the individual. A policy of tolerance should be adopted concerning those holding different beliefs. Government should not require or promote adherence to any particular religion, and laws should not be based on any one particular religious perspective. Government, in the view of most liberals, is not a creation of God to promote moral values, but rather a human creation for more limited purposes.

RULE OF LAW
The idea that we should be subject to known, predictable, and impartial rules of conduct, rather than to the arbitrary orders of particular individuals. Both the rulers and the ruled should be equally subject to the law.

Liberalism is also associated with the view that government should be based on the consent of the governed. Historically, however, many liberals were reluctant to support the right to vote for all citizens, fearing that the uneducated masses were not sufficiently committed to the value of individual liberty. Contemporary liberals are strongly committed to the principles of liberal democracy, and generally prefer representative democracy to the plebiscitary forms of democracy discussed in Chapter 4.

Classical Liberalism

CLASSICAL LIBERALISM
A form of liberalism that emphasizes the desirability of limited government and the free marketplace.

Classical liberalism places great importance on limited government and the free marketplace. John Locke (1632–1704), a key figure in the development of classical liberalism, argued that individuals had been free and equal in the state of nature (that is, before the establishment of government), but lacked the means to settle disputes fairly. Therefore, through what he termed the "social contract," people agreed to establish government for limited purposes—namely, the protection of life, liberty, and property. Government should be limited in its powers, acting as a trustee to protect the rights of the people, and removable by the people, by force if necessary, if it infringes on the liberties that it is supposed to protect.

LAISSEZ-FAIRE SYSTEM
A system in which privately owned businesses, workers, and consumers freely interact in the marketplace without government interference. The role of government is limited to such activities as maintaining order, enforcing contracts, and settling disputes.

Classical liberals also advocate the adoption of a **laissez-faire system** in which workers, consumers, and privately owned businesses freely interact in the marketplace without government interference. Economic freedom, including the freedom to produce and trade, to sell one's labour, and to own and enjoy one's property, is seen as a basic human freedom. Individual property rights are also viewed as important in protecting liberty against the power of the state by dispersing power and resources among the population. The proper role for government in economic matters is only to protect property, prevent fraud, and impartially settle disputes.

Reform Liberalism

REFORM LIBERALISM
A version of liberalism that combines support for individual freedom with a belief that government action may be needed to help remove obstacles to individual development.

Reform liberalism (sometimes referred to as welfare liberalism, social liberalism, or modern liberalism) combines support for individual freedom with a belief that government action may be needed to help remove obstacles to individual development. Reform liberalism developed in the latter part of the nineteenth century as many liberals became concerned that the laissez-faire system established in countries such as Britain seemed to offer little to develop the capabilities of workers and disadvantaged sectors of society. Life was harsh for the majority of the population, who worked long hours in unsafe conditions to eke out a living with no protection against sickness, disability, unemployment, or old age. Freedom was of little benefit for those who had to worry about where their next meal was coming from.

English philosopher T.H. Green (1836–1882) laid some of the foundation for reform liberalism by arguing that government action is not necessarily the enemy of freedom, but can provide the basis for people to be free to develop their individuality. The absence of physical and legal restraints on our actions ("negative freedom") does not necessarily make us free. If we think of freedom as a "positive power or capacity of doing something worth doing or enjoying," then individuals in a primitive society with little or no government are less free than modern citizens, who are subject to the many laws and regulations of governments (quoted in Qualter, 1986, p. 98). Although modern society presents greater opportunities to be free, in Green's positive sense there are many obstacles, such as poverty, ill health, a deadening environment, and long hours of work, that can prevent people from fully developing themselves. Government, by helping to ensure that individuals have the means to live a life of dignity and self-respect, can help to make freedom meaningful for all rather than a special privilege for a few.

Therefore, Green argued, government has a responsibility to remove the social and economic obstacles that can hinder individual development in order to establish a meaningful right to freedom. A somewhat active government is needed in order to establish the conditions in which individuals can freely develop their capabilities. While individuals should be responsible for their own development, government, by helping to ensure that individuals have the means to live a life of dignity and self-respect, can aid individuals in the pursuit of freedom. Fighting poverty, protecting the health and safety of workers, improving the quality of cities, and ensuring that everyone has adequate housing are proper activities of government.

Reform liberals argue that government should play a role in assisting the disadvantaged through such measures as unemployment insurance, old age pensions, health care, and subsidized education. This creates a more meaningful freedom for the less fortunate members of society by ensuring that a minimum standard of living is available to all.

Reform liberals generally share with classical liberals a belief in the virtues of a free-enterprise system. However, reform liberals argue that property rights may need to be limited, to some extent, in order to advance the rights and freedoms of others. For example, the freedom of a factory owner may need to be limited by government regulations in order to protect labourers from unsafe working conditions, consumers from harmful products, and the environment from the discharge of pollutants.

Reform liberals also generally accept the view of British economist John Maynard Keynes that a laissez-faire system based on the pursuit of self-interest does not necessarily lead to the common good. Government needs to use its powers to help make the economy run more smoothly, particularly by adopting policies that foster full employment, while leaving private businesses unhindered in their individual operations. Reform liberals also favour a role for government in regulating business activities so that large business corporations do not stifle competition.

Although both classical and reform liberals believe that individuals are naturally equal, classical liberals focus on *equal rights*—the right of all individuals to be treated the same in terms of the law. Reform liberals go beyond equal legal rights to advocate government policies that are designed to create *equal opportunities*. For example, reform liberals argue that government should ensure that young persons, whether their parents are rich or poor, have the opportunity to receive a good education. This might involve providing special assistance in obtaining education to members of groups that have suffered from discrimination.

Liberal International
www.liberal-international.org

Neo-liberalism

Contemporary liberalism, particularly in North America, is often associated with reform liberalism. However, the ideas of classical liberalism continue to be important, particularly in the form of **neo-liberalism**, a perspective based on a strong belief in the free marketplace and opposition to government intervention in the economy.

NEO-LIBERALISM
A perspective based on a strong belief in the free marketplace and opposition to government intervention in the economy.

For advocates of neo-liberalism, the marketplace provides a just system of incentives for hard work and initiative. Government economic planning, business regulation, redistributive taxes, and social welfare are seen as illegitimate infringements on fundamental property rights. Human beings are motivated by self-interest, particularly material self-interest. The competitive marketplace responds to the wishes of consumers and ensures that the economy operates at maximum efficiency.

Government and its agencies, being in a monopolistic position, are inevitably inefficient and concerned with advancing the power and privileges of bureaucrats and politicians. State-run services such as health, education, and welfare lack the efficiency created by competition and restrict the ability of consumers to choose the kinds of services that they want. Welfare, neo-liberals argue, takes away the incentive to work and creates dependency upon government. High taxes to support government services reduce the incentives for entrepreneurs to invest and create jobs. Subsidies to business, assistance to help the development of poorer regions, marketing boards for agricultural products, and other government projects serve to distort the marketplace, reducing efficiency and disrupting the natural processes of economic adjustment. The globalization of the economy is seen in a very positive light, and neo-liberals strive to remove barriers to a global free-market system.

The ideas of neo-liberalism are often associated with contemporary conservatism, discussed in the next section of this chapter. Although the terms *neo-liberalism* and *neo-conservatism* are often used interchangeably, neo-liberalism focuses on the desirability of a free-market economy while neo-conservatives focus more on cultural and moral values and a strong military.

CONSERVATISM

Conservatism, particularly in its traditional form, emphasizes the values of order and stability in the community. Conservatives are usually critical of those who advocate rapid and fundamental change. Although societies were generally conservative in nature and thought before the modern era, conservatism as a distinctive perspective or ideology developed particularly in response to liberal and radical ideas associated with the French Revolution (1789).

The French Revolution swept away the "old order," replacing the authority and privileges enjoyed by kings, nobles, and clergy with the Declaration of the Rights of Man. The revolutionaries attempted to rationally reorganize society and institute the principle of popular sovereignty. However, the revolution degenerated into terror directed at the opponents of the new regime, and eventually Napoleon seized power and crowned himself as Emperor. Although the ideas of the French Revolution were spread by Napoleon's conquest of much of continental Europe, his defeat resulted in efforts to restore the old order in Europe.

Some conservatives (labelled **reactionaries**) responded to the failures of the French Revolution by advocating a return to the values and institutions of the old order. Other conservatives, such as Edmund Burke, took a more moderate position, arguing that change, when necessary, should be slow, gradual, and consistent with the particular traditions of a country (see Box 5-2, Edmund Burke: Traditional Conservatism).

Conservative thinkers view humans as inherently imperfect, with a great potential for evil and a limited capacity to use their reasoning abilities. To maintain civilized values against the ever-present tendencies of evil, laws need to be respected and vigorously enforced by government, and respect for those in positions of authority must be maintained. Thus, conservatives have generally favoured a strong government able to protect order and stability and to pursue national interests. As well, conservatives often argue that traditional, religion-based moral values need to be maintained in order to prevent the collapse of civilized society.

Because of the individual's limited capabilities to reason and because of the complexity of society, conservatives argue that we should respect the wisdom that has been slowly built up over the ages. This wisdom, they argue, is reflected in traditional customs and practices. Conservatives tend to be very skeptical of attempts to improve society by deliberate political effort.

Conservatives are strong defenders of property although, unlike classical liberals, the owners of property are seen as having obligations to society. Property, along with religious institutions, marriage, and family, is viewed as a bulwark of the social order. Conservatives typically oppose government policies designed to move society in the direction of greater equality (for example, by redistributing income, wealth, and property from the rich to the poor). In the conservative perspective, people are naturally unequal.

CONSERVATISM

A perspective or ideology that emphasizes the values of order, stability, respect for authority, and tradition, based on a view that humans are inherently imperfect, with a limited capacity to reason.

REACTIONARY

A conservative who favours a return to the values and institutions of the past.

The Canadian Conservative Forum
www.conservativeforum.org

BOX 5-2

Edmund Burke: Traditional Conservatism

Edmund Burke (1729–1797), an Irish-born member of the British Parliament best known for his condemnation of the French Revolution, is often considered the founder of conservatism in the English-speaking world.

In his *Reflections on the Revolution in France* (1790), Burke predicted that the attempt to create a new society in France based on the application of abstract, universally applicable principles would fail. The French revolutionary ideology, if imported to Britain, would destroy the constitutional traditions that had served Britain well. Human beings, Burke argued, are naturally flawed in their character and limited in their reasoning abilities. Governing decisions should be based on the circumstances surrounding a particular issue, rather than on abstract principles based on reason. Civilized institutions have been built up over a long period of time and those institutions reflect the accumulated wisdom of many generations. Change, although necessary, should proceed slowly, building on the past rather than pursuing innovations that are disruptive of the gifts of the past.

The radical liberals who supported the French Revolution viewed society as a collection of independent individuals, each with a set of rights.

Instead, Burke argued, society should be viewed as a living organism in which the well-being of the individual is dependent on the well-being of the whole, or as a fabric composed of interwoven threads. Society and the state are not simply based on a temporary contract among individuals, but rather are a permanent partnership "between those who are living, those who are dead, and those who are to be born" (Burke 1790/1955, p. 110). Governments, along with an official, established religion are important features of human society that are needed to restrain the passions of individuals. Instead of proclaiming the universal rights of all humanity, Burke argued that the traditional liberties of particular countries should be defended. Government should not be viewed as an obstacle to freedom, as freedom is dependent on the order created by government. Political power should be in the hands of the "natural aristocracy" found largely among the nobility and gentry; men of law, science, and the arts; and some businessmen who had the virtues needed to represent the people as a whole. Rather than acting according to the opinions of voters, who may be uninformed, legislators should use their own judgment about the good of society.

Attempts to impose equality are disruptive and undermine the natural leadership of elite groups.

Traditional conservatives often have mixed feelings about the free-market capitalist system. In the past, some conservatives looked back fondly to the feudal order, where a landowning hereditary aristocracy preserved civilized values. The relentless pursuit of profit by entrepreneurs was often viewed with disdain. Although most contemporary conservatives are strong supporters of the free-market capitalist system, some traditional conservatives continue to be concerned that an unrestricted free-market capitalist system creates social divisions that can threaten national unity and social order. Further, some traditional conservatives have worried that the revolutionary impact of the modern free-market economy and associated global free trade could undermine the local values and particularisms that conservatives cherish. The individualistic and materialistic values associated with the capitalist system do not fit easily with the more organic and community-oriented values of many traditional conservatives.

The New Right

A reinvigorated version of conservatism, often termed the **New Right**, developed in the 1970s combining, in various ways, the promotion of free-market capitalism (neo-liberalism) and traditional cultural and moral values (sometimes referred to as social conservatism). In part, the New Right is a reaction to the development of the welfare state and the growth of government in the decades after the Second World War. Welfare state policies are viewed by the New Right as undermining individual responsibility and creating dependence on the state. Responsibility for welfare should be shifted, as much as possible, from government to faith-based charities and other voluntary organizations.

The New Right was also a reaction to the "New Left," a perspective that views the marginalized in society (such as ethnic and racial minorities, students, youth, women, and the poor) as oppressed groups whose liberation would lead to fundamental changes in society. For the conservative-minded, the New Left and radical criticism of the status quo posed a threat to Western values, while the "counterculture" of 1960s youth promoted immorality.

For the New Right, identity politics (discussed in Chapter 2) involves "special interests" seeking privileges. In particular, the New Right has been critical of affirmative action programs, arguing that legal equality and laws preventing discrimination are sufficient to provide equal opportunities for all. Attempting to ensure equal outcomes creates unrealistic expectations and an overly activist, coercive government (Medcalf & Dolbeare, 1985). In addition, government encouragement for groups to develop their distinctive cultures and identities is viewed by the New Right as weakening the nation-state by undermining the common interests and values of the nation (Whitaker, 1997).

In the New Right's view, Western civilization faces a cultural crisis because of the decline of traditional moral values. The overbearing nature of big government has undermined the ability of communities to maintain moral norms (Frum, 1996). Liberal social values have fostered a permissive society in which "anything goes" while moral principles are ignored.

The New Right (particularly the element known as the Christian Right) has often focused on the promotion of traditional family values, which it contends are threatened by abortion, homosexuality, premarital sex, divorce, and sexually explicit television, movies, and music. The traditional moral views of the New Right can also be seen in their views on crime. Unlike the liberally minded, who often see crime as a result of societal injustices and seek to rehabilitate criminals, the New Right argues that criminals need to take full

NEW RIGHT
A perspective that combines, in various ways, the promotion of free-market capitalism and traditional cultural and moral values.

responsibility for their crimes. Thus, they favour harsh punitive measures to deter criminal behaviour.

The New Right (particularly the element labelled "neo-conservative") is also associated with a taking a hardline approach in international relations. In the 1980s, key figures in the New Right advocated defeating communism rather than merely containing it. The New Right has advocated strong action against what American President George W. Bush in 2002 termed the "axis of evil" (Iran, Iraq, and North Korea). The United States and its allies should exercise global leadership and use its strength to promote Western values—including democracy, freedom, and the free-market capitalist system—world-wide. This involves ensuring that the United States has overwhelming military superiority and a willingness to take unilateral military action with its allies against "rogue regimes" and the supporters of terrorism, with or without the approval of the United Nations.

Understanding Neo-conservatism
www.publiceye.org/conservative/neo
cons/neocon.html

TENSIONS WITHIN THE NEW RIGHT   There are important tensions within the New Right perspective, which generally advocates a free economy in a strong state (Gamble, 1994). Those contemporary conservatives who have adopted the individualistic, market-oriented perspective of neo-liberalism typically want the role of government kept to a minimum. In particular, "economic" or "fiscal" conservatives focus on reducing government spending and eliminating government debt and deficit. Social conservatives tend to be critical of the individualism, freedom, and materialism of modern society and favour government action to help create a moral community.

Traditional Conservatism and the New Right

In some ways, the New Right is not entirely new. Conservatives have always been defenders of property rights and have supported the idea of limited government while favouring laws to punish "immoral" behaviour. Both traditional conservatives and the New Right have been strongly critical of socialism and the redistribution of wealth by government. Many traditional conservatives, however, do not accept the pure free-market and minimal-government perspective associated with some elements of the New Right. In addition, the activist approach of the New Right to foreign policy, particularly in exporting democratic values, tends to differ from traditional conservatism, which was typically concerned with maintaining a stable "balance of power" in international politics (discussed in Chapter 20) and, in the United States, sought to limit foreign involvements.

Traditional conservatism emphasizes the need to respect authority and thus, in modern times, tends to favour limited forms of democracy. In contrast, the New Right has a substantial element of populism that is critical of authority and believes that the common people should be in more direct control of decision making through such devices as referendums, initiatives, and recall. New Right populists claim that politicians, government officials, and judges have undermined traditional values, catered to what the New Right considers to be "special interests," and do not reflect the views of the majority. Plebiscitary democracy is viewed as a way of ensuring that political decisions reflect the views of the "silent majority" that holds traditional or conventional moral values.

More generally, traditional conservatives preach the virtues of moderation and gradual change. The New Right, by contrast, has tended to pursue its convictions with greater ideological zeal.

SOCIALISM

Socialism, like reform liberalism, developed as an important political ideology in reaction to the harshness of the early capitalist system, which was reinforced by the laissez-faire approach of some governments. However, unlike liberalism, socialism views human beings as basically social rather than self-interested. Socialists are critical of the capitalist system not only for what they see as its exploitative nature, but also for its emphasis on competition, which undermines the co-operative and community-oriented nature of humanity. Socialists view inequality as largely the result of the power relations in society and the economy rather than the inherent differences in the capabilities of individuals. A more equal society in terms of the distribution of wealth, income, and power will lead to a greater sense of community and solidarity and will facilitate co-operation rather than conflict (Heywood, 2003). Social justice can be achieved by reducing inequalities and ensuring that all persons have the rights and resources needed for a life of dignity.

Within the socialist ideology, there are a variety of views as to what an ideal society would be like and how such a society could be achieved. Generally, socialists favour some form of social rather than private ownership of the major means of production so that many of the decisions that affect the life of the community are no longer in the hands of the owners of business. Some have envisaged the establishment of small, self-sufficient communes in which property would be collectively owned, all would work co-operatively, and material goods would be shared equally (see Box 5-3, Utopian Socialism). Others have looked to the state to own the major means of production and operate them for the good of society as a whole. Still others envision a system of worker-run enterprises. Many contemporary socialists look to some form of mixed economy where government plays a substantial role in planning and regulating the economy as well as providing various free public services.

Marxism and Communism

The writings of Karl Marx (1818–1883) and Frederick Engels (1820–1895), often termed Marxism, were of great importance in the development of the socialist ideology. Their analysis, termed **historical materialism**, starts with

SOCIALISM
An ideological perspective based on the view that human beings are basically social in nature and that the capitalist system undermines the co-operative and community-oriented nature of humanity. Socialism advocates the establishment of an egalitarian society.

The Socialist International
www.socialistinternational.org

HISTORICAL MATERIALISM
The view that historical development and the dynamics of society and politics can be understood in terms of the way society is organized to produce material goods.

Utopian Socialism

In his classic book *Utopia*, English writer Thomas More (1478–1535) condemned the evils of pride, envy, and greed that result "wherever men have private property and money is the measure of everything" (1516/2004, p. 198).

In existing societies, More asserted, the rich "serve their own interests under the name of the common good" while in reality looking after only their private good. Instead of only a few being prosperous and happy "while all the rest live in misery and wretchedness," he imagined a society in which all things are owned in common, money is no longer used, and everyone is free to take from the common storehouses all the necessities that are needed to live a meaningful life. In such a society, people would be concerned with the "common affairs" of the society, rather than worrying about earning a livelihood (More, 1516/2004, pp. 198–202).

More did not intend *Utopia*, which literally means "nowhere," to be a blueprint for society. However, a number of socialists, particularly in the nineteenth century, developed elaborate models of an ideal communal society. These "utopian socialists" were criticized by other socialists, including Marx and Engels, for having the naive view that fundamental changes could occur by developing visionary schemes or establishing model communities instead of taking political action to transform the capitalist system.

Nevertheless, a number of small-scale communes of a religious or secular nature have been established at various times. Israel's kibbutzim are one of the few successful long-lasting communal societies. However, they involve only a very small proportion of the Israeli population.

the assumption that to understand historical development, we must examine the way society is organized to produce essential material goods such as food, clothing, and shelter. In every society except the most primitive, Marx and Engels argued, production involves the exploitation of a subordinate class by a smaller, dominant class. The leading ideas, beliefs, and morals of a society serve the interests of the dominant class, and thus help it in its struggle against challenges by the exploited subordinate class. However, each of the basic systems of production—slave-owning, feudal, and capitalist—has internal tensions ("contradictions") that eventually become irresolvable. This leads to an overthrow of that system and its replacement by a new system of production.

In their examination of the capitalist system of production, Marx and Engels argued that the profits obtained by the owners of capital (the bourgeoisie) were based on the exploitation of the workers (the proletariat). The capitalist system appeared to be free, as goods and labour could be freely bought and sold in the marketplace. It was, however, only the appearance of freedom. Workers, in reality, had little choice but to sell their labour power to survive. In addition, the emphasis on competition, profit, and selfishness in the capitalist free-market system violated what Marx and Engels viewed as the essentially social and creative nature of humanity.

This statue of Marx and Engels in the former East Berlin is a reminder of the importance of the communist ideology in the past century.

The capitalist system is an important, but not the final, stage of historical development. Conflict between the working class and the bourgeoisie will intensify because the two groups have incompatible interests. The large working class developing as a result of industrialization will eventually organize itself into a revolutionary force. Workers will come to see the need to overturn the capitalist system and replace it with a system based on social, rather than private, ownership of the means of production.

Marx and Engels argued that, because the state generally acts in the interests of the capitalist class, the working class will have to take control of the state and then use the state apparatus to transform the capitalist system into a socialist system. This will likely necessitate a revolution, as capitalists will be unlikely to give up their control voluntarily or peacefully. However, as workers in Europe began to gain the right to vote in the late nineteenth century, Marx and Engels saw a possibility that in some countries working class control of state power *might* be achieved through the election of socialist political parties, provided that police and military forces were not used to suppress the socialist movement.

In the perspective of Marx and Engels, the capitalist system faces inherent contradictions that will contribute to its eventual demise. Competition among capitalists will result in weaker capitalists being forced out of business. The remaining capitalists will then have monopoly control of the marketplace, undermining free competition. Marx and Engels also argued that the capitalist system was prone to ever-increasing crises of severe unemployment and depression because of the chaotic nature of capitalism.

Marxists Internet Archive
www.marxists.org

COMMUNISM   Marx and Engels were more concerned with analyzing the dynamics of the capitalist system than with setting blueprints for the future. But they did suggest that, after the revolution, the workers would control the state in the interests of the working class ("the dictatorship of the proletariat"), and would use the state to expropriate the property of the capitalists. *Eventually*, they argued, the selfishness that is characteristic of economic systems based on private ownership would disappear. The increased production of an economy devoted to human needs would lead to material abundance that could fulfill the basic needs of everyone. A further transition from socialism to **communism** would then occur. In a communist society, everyone would be free to take from society what they need. Although production would be highly organized, the need for a coercive state would diminish or disappear because, in the view of Marx and Engels, the need for a coercive state arises out of the need to use coercion to maintain private property and the inequality that it entails.

LENINISM   As Russian Communist party leader, Vladimir Lenin (1870–1924) modified the ideas of Marx and Engels. In Lenin's view, the capitalist system could only be overthrown by force—but the workers themselves could not spontaneously overthrow the system. What was needed was a tightly disciplined party firmly controlled by a revolutionary vanguard.

Because nineteenth-century Russia was largely a peasant society with a relatively small working class, the role of the party that was in the vanguard of the proletariat (that is, the Communist party) was particularly important in leading the revolution and directing the subsequent course of revolutionary change. Instead of putting power in the hands of councils of workers and peasants, as many of those involved in the Russian Revolution had hoped, Lenin, and even more so his successor, Joseph Stalin (1877–1953), established a tight grip on Soviet society and established a totalitarian regime dedicated to rapidly building an industrialized economy. Similarly, tight party control has been characteristic of government in China, where the Communist party under Mao Zedong (1893–1976) was successful in capturing power in 1949 after a lengthy guerrilla war.

THE COMMUNIST SYSTEM COLLAPSES   Communist party control of the Soviet Union and Eastern Europe collapsed at the end of the 1980s. A loosening of the tight control exercised by Communist leaders allowed the people to overthrow their governments with a minimum of violence. Although China is still controlled by the Communist party, it has abandoned efforts to create a communist society. Various versions of Marxism continue to provide important perspectives on the world. However, communism, as developed and implemented by Lenin, Stalin, and Mao, is no longer a powerful force in the contemporary world.

COMMUNISM

A system in which private property has been replaced by collective or communal ownership and in which everyone would be free to take from society what they need.

LENINISM

The version of Marxism that includes the belief that the capitalist system can only be overthrown through force by means of a tightly disciplined party controlled by a revolutionary vanguard.

Democratic Socialism

A key difference between **democratic socialism** and communism is that democratic socialists believe that only democratic methods should be used to work toward a socialist society. Democratic socialists reject the notion of the dictatorship of the proletariat, arguing instead that political rights and freedoms should be respected. Likewise, although they believe that an active government is needed to provide for the well-being of the citizenry, they share the view of liberals and conservatives that governments should abide by the rule of law and not act in an arbitrary manner.

Rather than complete state ownership of the means of production, democratic socialists have favoured measures such as public ownership of some key industries, encouragement for co-operative enterprises, requirements that workers have a voice in the decisions of the businesses where they work, and government planning and regulation of the economy. To achieve greater equality, democratic socialists advocate government provision and subsidization of various services, along with the redistribution of income and wealth from the rich to the poor through the tax system.

Social Democracy

Over time, democratic socialist parties have watered down or dropped their commitment to fundamentally transform the economic system. Ideas about nationalizing (having the government take over) the "commanding heights" of the economy, or about replacing the capitalist system, have generally moved to the fringes of democratic socialist parties. Indeed, many leading figures within democratic socialist parties prefer to call themselves social democrats[2] to indicate that they no longer believe in a socialist economic system (that is, one with a substantial level of state ownership or control).

Instead, contemporary social democracy generally includes the belief that the capitalist economy can be reformed to ensure that it works for the common good of all. Social democrats also advocate greater social and economic equality to achieve a meaningful democracy. As Ed Broadbent (2001), a former leader of Canada's New Democratic Party, puts it, market economies have "generated the wealth needed to provide effective social rights," but its unequal distribution of income and power "runs counter to the democratic goal of equal citizens." For Broadbent, democracy involves not only political and civil rights,

> **DEMOCRATIC SOCIALISM**
> The perspective that socialism should be achieved by democratic rather than revolutionary means, and that a socialist society should be democratic in nature with political rights and freedoms respected.

---

2 The term *social democracy* has had different meanings. In the nineteenth century, European socialist parties called themselves social democrats even though many adopted a Marxist approach. After the establishment of the Soviet Union, there was a split between Marxist-Leninists, who called themselves communists, and social democrats, who rejected the revolutionary path to socialism. In recent decades, the term *social democracy* has often been applied to those who no longer advocate the goal of a socialist economy.

but also entitlements that ensure that various social and economic rights such as health, education, employment, and child care are available to all persons. In other words, social democrats believe that the excesses of the free-market capitalist system can be curtailed by government action to provide a welfare state, greater equality, and regulation of the market economy.

Social democratic ideas provided much of the basis for the consensus concerning the welfare state and the relations between business and labour that developed in many of the countries of the Western world after the Second World War. However, globalization and neo-liberalism have created challenges for social democrats, who have generally looked to a strong nation-state to provide a variety of public services and a substantial degree of control of the market. In Western Europe, some social democrats played a key role in developing the European Union and ensuring that its free market policies were combined with guarantees of human rights and environmental protection. In the United Kingdom, former Prime Minister Tony Blair sought to modernize social democracy through the "Third Way," which involved greater acceptance of the free market, globalization, individualism, and personal responsibility. Other social democrats, while favouring global social justice and the development of democratic global institutions, are critical of economic globalization, emphasize the importance of social solidarity rather than individualism, and see a continuing need for the market economy to be controlled for the common good (Leggett, 2007).

Anarchism

ANARCHISM
An ideology that views the state as the key source of oppression and seeks to replace the state with a system based on voluntary co-operation.

Anarchism, which literally means "without rule," seeks to eliminate the state, which it views as a key source of oppression. Socialist anarchism (or anarcho-communism) advocates the elimination of both the state and private property. In its place, socialist anarchists advocate a co-operative or communal society based on what they see as the natural principle of mutual assistance. Instead of large and powerful states, they envision a world based on voluntary co-operation among a network of local communities.

Anarchists generally favour "direct action" such as demonstrations, civil disobedience, street theatre, and general strikes, rather than the establishment of political parties (which they view as an instrument of power) and voting to achieve their objectives. Although many anarchists oppose all forms of violence, including participation in wars, some anarchists have used violence and selected assassination of business and government leaders in the hope of encouraging a popular uprising to "smash the state."

Anarchy Archives
http://dwardmac.pitzer.edu/Anarchist_Archives/

Various forms of socialist anarchism were important in the international socialist movement in the latter part of the nineteenth century as well as in the Spanish Civil War (1936–1939). However, anarchism has generally been overshadowed by communism, democratic socialism, and social democracy in the past century. Nevertheless, anarchism continues to have some significance—for example, as an element of the anti-globalization movement.

FASCISM

The ideology of **fascism** developed in the period between the First and Second World Wars based, in part, on the views of various thinkers who were critical of the ideas of the Enlightenment. Fascism combines an aggressive form of nationalism with a strong belief in the naturalness of inequality and opposition to both liberal democracy and communism.

Nationalism and Racism

Loyalty to the nation-state is extremely important in fascist thought. In the fascist view, the well-being of the individual is based on the well-being of the nation-state to which the individual belongs. Individuals owe absolute loyalty to the state, and the state has the right to control all activities in order to promote its interests. Further, the state is seen by fascists as a cohesive or organic whole that is based on the bonds of a common culture or ancestry. Foreigners and those of minority cultures are typically viewed as a hindrance to the creation of a homogenous society based on the dominant nationality.

Related to the extreme nationalism of fascist ideology is a belief in the superiority of particular nationalities and races. This superiority is exhibited not only in cultural achievements, but also in such characteristics as bravery and heroism. War allows that superiority to be realized, and the conquest and subordination of "inferior" nations and races is justified.

NAZISM The ideas of racial superiority and racial conflict were particularly evident in **Nazism**. Building on some nineteenth-century theories that viewed racial differences as profound, the Nazis proclaimed their belief that the Germans and some related Nordic peoples were the heirs of an "Aryan master race" that could be restored through careful breeding. As a "culture-creating" master race, a revived Aryan race would exert dominance over other "inferior" races. The Nazis viewed the Jews as their key racial enemy and sought to rid Europe of the Jews. This resulted in the systematic genocide known as the **Holocaust** (see Box 5-4, The Holocaust).

Belief in a Natural Inequality

Fascists also believe that there is a natural inequality within society between the masses (ordinary people) and their natural leaders. The masses can be mobilized by skilful leaders through the use of slogans and symbols. Democratic leaders are seen as weak because they pander to the masses to gain their support. Instead, fascists often argue that a heroic leader with a creative "will to power" will arise above the masses in exceptional circumstances. Such an exceptional leader, fascists believe, embodies the will of the people. Fascism favours strong, authoritarian leadership, arguing that natural leaders should be allowed free rein to rule in the interests of the nation-state, enhancing its unity, culture, and power.

FASCISM
An ideology that combines an aggressive form of nationalism with a strong belief in the naturalness of inequality and opposition to both liberal democracy and communism.

NAZISM
A version of fascism associated with Adolf Hitler, the Nazi leader of Germany, emphasizing racial conflict and the superiority of the "Aryan race."

HOLOCAUST
The systematic extermination of six million European Jews by the Nazis during the Second World War.

The Holocaust History Project
www.holocaust-history.org

BOX 5-4

The Holocaust

The potential of ideological thought to lead to horrific consequences is clearly demonstrated by the outcome of the racist ideology of the Nazis.

Anti-Semitism (that is, hatred and persecution of Jews) has a very lengthy history throughout Europe. In the 1920s and 1930s, stirring up anti-Semitic prejudices was an important part of the Nazi appeal. After gaining power, the Nazis began taking away the rights of Jews, including their citizenship, and encouraged attacks on Jewish businesses and individuals. Many countries (including Canada) refused to take in more than a small number of Jews seeking to flee continental Europe. As the German armies conquered Eastern Europe in the Second World War, they began rounding up Jews and shooting them in mass pits or gassing them in mobile gas chambers. Eventually, Adolf Hitler and his top officials decided on what they termed the "final solution" to the "Jewish problem" (that is, the total elimination of the Jewish people). Persons of Jewish ancestry were transported to massive concentration camps for slave labour and systematic, industrial-style extermination.

In all, the Nazis organized the deliberate murder of about six million persons of Jewish ancestry, including about one and a half million children. In addition, about five million other persons were killed, deemed "unfit" because of their nationality, disabilities, sexual orientation, or political views. The Holocaust is particularly horrifying because of the systematic, determined, and state-directed nature of the "extermination." Further, it occurred in modern and so-called civilized societies, often with the acquiescence and involvement of people throughout Europe, despite some heroic exceptions.

Rejection of Enlightenment

Underlying the fascist ideology is a rejection of much of Enlightenment thought. Human beings, fascism assumes, are basically motivated by emotion rather than by reason. People are rooted in their ancestry and their territory, and can be mobilized into action through myths and propaganda. The liberal and socialist ideologies that are based on Enlightenment ideas about human progress are thus rejected. As well, fascism rejects the idea that we are all part of a common humanity (Eatwell, 1995). Instead of the liberal and socialist belief that a peaceful world can be created, fascism sees struggle and the use of force as inevitable.

Because fascists see the world as based on a struggle for dominance, they argue that constant preparation for war is necessary. The strength of one's nation-state must be developed to ensure its dominance. Divisions or disagreements within the nation-state cannot be tolerated because they might lead to weakness. Fascists believe that it is right and natural that the strong should dominate and subjugate the weak, and that humanitarian policies directed to aiding the disadvantaged lead to weakness. Adapting the **social Darwinist** ideas of English social theorist Herbert Spencer (1820–1903), fascists see war and conflict as a natural process allowing humanity to evolve through the "survival of the fittest."

SOCIAL DARWINISM
The use of Darwin's theory of evolution to argue that competition and conflict allow humanity to evolve through the "survival of the fittest."

Corporate State

Fascism is also critical of liberal and socialist systems of thought for their focus on achieving material well-being. Not surprisingly, then, the fascist ideology tends to be unclear about the economic organization of society other than seeking an alternative to both capitalism and communism. Benito Mussolini's Italian fascist regime adopted the idea of the **corporate state,** in which business and labour would work harmoniously to achieve goals established by the state to advance the good of the nation (Heywood, 2003). In practice, this involved the subordination of labour and business to the fascist regime and the suppression of the labour movement.

CORPORATE STATE
A system associated with fascist Italy in which business and labour work harmoniously to achieve goals established by the state to advance the good of the nation.

A New Order

Fascism is often depicted as a reactionary ideology. To some extent this is valid, as fascism rejects many aspects of modern society and politics, including individualism and materialism, which fascism views as a cause of moral decay. However, fascism embraces only selected myths from the past—such as the ideal of the heroic Teutonic warrior or the glories of the Roman Empire. Indeed, fascism tends to both glorify the ethnically homogenous rural communities of the past and celebrate modern technology with a vision of a technological future (Neocleous, 1997). Unlike reactionary conservatives, fascists view themselves as creating a new order rather than restoring the old order in Europe.

Fascism can be described as a radical right-wing ideology. The interwar fascist movement gained considerable support from nationalistic, authoritarian conservatives and other right-wing forces who shared with fascists a belief in order, leadership, and authority and who were anti-Semitic and anti-democratic. However, fascism tends to be distinct in its emphasis on conflict, militarism, total control of society, mobilization of the people behind a populist leader, and its rejection of most moral principles (Mann, 2004).

The Continuing Significance of Fascism

Fascism is often associated with the dictatorial regimes of the Italian fascist leader Benito Mussolini (1883–1945) and the German Nazi leader Adolf Hitler (1889–1945). However, fascist movements also had substantial followings in a variety of countries in the 1930s, and some leading non-fascist figures expressed admiration for Mussolini and Hitler. The decisive defeat of the militarist fascist regimes in the Second World War and the revelation of the horrors they perpetrated resulted in the discrediting of the fascist ideology. Nevertheless, there has been a revival of fascism, to some extent, in various countries in recent years.

NEO-FASCISM Contemporary fascism (**neo-fascism**) often tries to cultivate a more respectable and democratic image than the fascist movements of the interwar period. The second-place finish—albeit with only 18 percent of

NEO-FASCISM
A revival of fascism in contemporary times.

the vote—of French neo-fascist National Front leader Jean-Marie Le Pen in the 2002 presidential election shocked many people. (Le Pen is notorious for his dismissal of the Holocaust as "a detail of history.") Likewise, the Austrian Freedom Party, which was part of the governing conservative coalition from 2000 to 2004 after winning more than a quarter of the vote, is often viewed as leaning in a fascist direction, although it denies that it is fascist. The Italian National Alliance, originally a neo-fascist party, calls itself "post-fascist" and was a member of a governing conservative coalition from 1994 to 1996 and 2001 to 2006. Although neo-fascist political parties avoid the thoroughly racist doctrines of Hitler's Nazi party, they often appeal to nationalist values and express animosity toward immigrants, particularly darker-skinned immigrants.

NEO-NAZISM AND OTHER EXTREMIST GROUPS More extreme than the neo-fascist political parties are various neo-Nazi groups in Germany and some other European countries that have terrorized members of minority groups and immigrants. In the United States, groups like the Aryan Nation promote racism and the ideal of an all-white America. As well, various militia groups train for armed resistance to what they believe is a new world order conspiracy (by the United Nations and other international institutions, Zionists, banking institutions, the Illuminati, or Freemasons) to take over the United States. Individuals influenced by militia groups carried out the bombing that killed 168 people at the U.S. government building in Oklahoma City in 1995.

Summary and Conclusion

Political ideologies have had a major impact on politics in the modern era. Most ideologies have a vision of a better world and some ideas about the political actions needed to achieve their vision. Political ideologies provide not only basic sets of values and goals to those who engage in political activity, but also differing ways of analyzing and understanding the world.

Liberalism focuses on the ideal of individual liberty. The coercion of individuals, even to promote the values of the groups and communities to which the individual belongs, should be minimized. In the perspective of liberalism, the common good of society is best achieved by allowing individuals to pursue their own interests, develop their own capabilities and morality, and act on their own values. Those with power are likely to use that power for their own interests. Thus, limiting power, protecting individual rights and freedoms, and establishing the rule of law are important means to achieve the objectives of liberalism. A peaceful and prosperous world can be developed through the promotion of tolerance, adherence to laws, and the facilitation of global interactions through free trade and the free interaction of ideas. For classical liberals, the free market, equal legal rights, and limited government ensure that individuals are not subject to the arbitrary and oppressive power of government and other institutions.

Reform liberals are concerned with achieving meaningful freedom for all; thus, government can play a useful role in removing the obstacles to individual development, even if that means that some limitations may have to be placed on the free market.

Conservatism, because of its pessimistic view of human capabilities, does not generally present an ideal of a better world that can be achieved through conscious political action. The common good is best obtained in an orderly community in which traditional moral values and institutions are maintained. Traditional practices are seen as containing accumulated wisdom. The limitations of human reason suggest that change should be gradual in nature. Individuals should accept their place in society and be encouraged to work for the good of the community as a whole. Respect for those in positions of authority should be promoted, and those with wealth and privilege should be encouraged to look after the well-being of society as a whole. Because of human frailties and the human capacity for evil, restraints on individual actions are necessary to ensure the common good of the community.

The New Right version of conservatism views the welfare state and the undermining of traditional Western values as the cause of many contemporary problems. The New Right generally favours strengthening the state's ability to fight criminal and immoral behaviour and to promote Western values at home and abroad. As well, many New Right conservatives favour a global laissez-faire capitalist system with minimal government involvement in the economy.

Socialism promotes the ideal of a society based on co-operation and equality. The focus of the capitalist system on the pursuit of profit and individual wealth hinders the achievement of the common good. Eliminating oppression and inequalities and ensuring that the needs of all are fulfilled would allow humans, as social and co-operative beings, to pursue the common good of humanity. For communists, a revolution based on the working class is needed to destroy the oppressive power of capitalism and the capitalist-based state. This will allow for the creation of a classless socialist—and eventually communist—society. Democratic socialists, on the other hand, argue that socialism can be achieved through the election of a socialist party and the gradual evolution of society toward socialism. Contemporary social democrats suggest that the major ideals of socialism can be achieved by reforming capitalism, reducing inequalities, and guaranteeing social and economic rights to all.

Fascism seeks to build a powerful, united, militaristic nation-state that will provide strong leadership and direction to the masses. Order, leadership, and discipline are needed to be strong in a world characterized by conflict and the struggle for dominance. Fascists view the idea of the common good of humanity as a whole as unrealistic. Instead, the collective good of the state, nation, or race is emphasized in fascist thought.

Key Terms

Discussion Questions

1. How important are political ideologies in contemporary political life?

2. Is a particular ideological perspective prevalent at your university or college?

3. Is J.S. Mill's argument that individuals are the best judges of what is in their own interest valid? Are contemporary laws that require the use of seat belts and ban the use of "recreational" drugs unjustified?

4. Are socialism and communism still relevant in the contemporary world? Is fascism likely to become a significant political perspective again?

5. Which one of the ideologies has the best perspective on how the common good can be achieved?

Further Reading

Berlin, I. *Liberty*. Oxford: Oxford University Press, 2002.

Eatwell, R. *Fascism: A history*. New York: Penguin Books, 1995.

Gaus, G.F. *Contemporary theories of liberalism: Public reason as a post-Enlightenment project*. London: Sage, 2003.

Giddens, A. *The third way: The renewal of social democracy*. Cambridge, UK: Cambridge University Press, 1998.

Gray, J. *Liberalism*. Milton Keynes, UK: Open University Press, 1986.

Griffin, R. *The nature of fascism*. London: Routledge, 1993.

Harrington, M. *Socialism*. New York: Penguin Books, 1989.

King, P. (Ed.). *Socialism and the common good: New Fabian essays*. London: Frank Cass, 1996.

Kristol, I. *Neoconservatism: The autobiography of an idea*. New York: Free Press, 1995.

Laqueur, W. *Fascism: Past, present, future*. New York: Oxford University Press, 1996.

Laycock, D. *The New Right and democracy in Canada: Understanding Reform and the Canadian Alliance*. Don Mills, ON: Oxford University Press, 2002.

Mann, M. *Fascists*. New York: Cambridge University Press, 2004.

Manning, D.J. *Liberalism*. New York: St. Martin's Press, 1976.

McLellan, D. *Marxism after Marx*. London: Macmillan, 1983.

Nisbet, R. *Conservatism: Dream and reality*. Milton Keynes, UK: Open University Press, 1986.

Pierson, C. *Hard choices: Social democracy in the twenty-first century*. Cambridge, UK: Polity Press, 2001.

Roussopoulos, D. (Ed.). *The anarchist papers*, rev. ed. Montreal: Black Rose, 2002.

Scruton, R. *The meaning of conservatism*, 2nd ed. London: Macmillan, 1984.

Segal, H. *Beyond greed: A traditional conservative confronts neo-conservative excess*. Toronto: Stoddart, 1997.

Singer, P. *Marx*. Oxford: Oxford University Press, 1980.

Chapter 6

FEMINISM, ENVIRONMENTALISM, AND RELIGIOUS FUNDAMENTALISM

PHOTO ABOVE: During a highly publicized demonstration by feminists against the 1968 Miss America contest, protesters, who criticized the long-standing beauty contest for exploiting women's bodies for the satisfaction of men, nominated a sheep as the new Miss America. Women threw their high heels, girdles, and false eyelashes—but no bras—into a freedom trash can.

CHAPTER OBJECTIVES

After reading this chapter you should be able to:

1. discuss the feminist perspective and compare the different versions of feminism

2. explain the different views on equality within the feminist ideology

3. describe and discuss the distinctive features of environmentalism

4. analyze the perspective of religious fundamentalism

5. explain the significance of Islamic fundamentalism

The year is 1968. A sheep has just been nominated for the title of Miss America, and women are throwing their high heels, girdles, false eyelashes, and other symbols of oppression into a "freedom trash can." This is all part of a much-publicized demonstration against the Miss America Pageant by feminists who attack it as a beauty contest that exploits women. A young female reporter, seeking to link the Miss America demonstration to Vietnam War protests where draft cards and the American flag had been burned, described the women as burning their bras. Although no bras were actually burned, militant feminists will thenceforward be ridiculed by their critics as "bra burners."

The Miss America contest was one of the early targets of the women's liberation movement because it was viewed as a manifestation of how a male-dominated society dehumanizes women by treating them as sexual objects. Some of those involved in this movement developed the radical feminist perspective that holds that the oppression of women is the most basic feature of all societies. A fundamental transformation of society is needed to liberate women and achieve true equality.

Some prominent political commentators have argued that the age of ideologies has ended (Bell, 1998; Fukuyama, 1992). Now that communism has collapsed and the differences between liberals, conservatives, and social democrats have diminished, political controversy, they say, will involve the details of policy rather than the clash of sharply different perspectives.

However, the three perspectives examined in this chapter—feminism, environmentalism, and religious fundamentalism—each seek major changes in the values, institutions, and policies of the political community. Feminism and religious fundamentalism present sharply opposing views concerning the proper role of women in society. Environmentalism, particularly in its stronger versions, presents fundamental challenges to our ways of thinking about humanity and our relationship to nature, the way our institutions operate, and how we should live.

FEMINISM

Feminism is often thought of in terms of achieving equality for women. This involves not only establishing equal rights and opportunities for women and eliminating discriminatory practices, but also challenging the traditional views about women that have often had the effect of confining women to domestic life and restricting their freedom. Beyond seeking to achieve equality with men, many feminists argue that political decisions should give greater emphasis to the different experiences and values of women instead of being based primarily on male values.

In the view of most contemporary feminists, all societies are, to varying extents, characterized by **patriarchy**. As explained by Lorraine Code, "patriarchal societies are those in which men have more power than women, readier access than women to what is valued in the society and, in consequence, are in control over many, if not most aspects of women's lives" (1988, p. 18). Changing the patriarchal nature of society is a basic goal of feminism.

The *Declaration of the Rights of Man*, a product of the French Revolution of 1789, inspired one of the first statements of feminist ideas. In *A Vindication of the Rights of Woman* (1792), Mary Wollstonecraft (1759–1797) rejected the common notion that women's natural role was to please men and to bear and raise children. Wollstonecraft argued that women are human beings with the same capacity for rational thinking as men and should therefore have the same rights as men. If women appeared more emotional and less concerned about the good of the political community, it was a result of being deprived of adequate education and the opportunities to develop themselves, rather than being an inevitable product of their nature (Adams, 2001). Likewise, John Stuart Mill argued in *The Subjection of Women* (1869) that freeing women from being subordinate to men, providing equal educational opportunities, and establishing a full set of civil and political rights for women were justified because women had the same capacity for rational thought and action as men.

Although both Wollstonecraft and Mill advocated full equality for women, they assumed that women were more likely to choose domestic life rather than paid employment. By being educated and equal, women would be better equipped to raise their children, and marriages would be happier if wives could interact intelligently with their husbands. Other early feminists, particularly those involved in the revolutionary politics of Marxism and anarchism of the late nineteenth and early twentieth centuries, went further, to advocate the liberation of women from their domestic roles as well as to advocate liberation from traditional sexual constraints.

As with other ideological perspectives, there is a variety of different versions of feminism. This diversity is often discussed in terms of three basic categories:

1. liberal feminism
2. socialist feminism
3. radical feminism

FEMINISM
A perspective that views society as patriarchal and seeks to achieve full independence and equality for women.

PATRIARCHY
A system in which power is in the hands of men and in which many aspects of women's lives are controlled by men.

Feminist Collections
www.library.wisc.edu/libraries/
WomensStudies/fcmain.htm

Liberal Feminism

Liberal feminism extends the struggle of many early feminists for equal legal and political rights to the advocacy of equal opportunities for women in such areas as education and employment. As the influential American feminist Betty Friedan put it, "My definition of feminism is simply that women are people in the fullest sense of the word, who must be free to move in society with all the privileges and opportunities and responsibilities that are their human and American right" (Friedan, 1998, p. 317). In particular, she discussed the problems of women in American suburbs in the early 1960s and concluded that women suffered by being confined to the role of housewife. Pursuing a career and gaining economic independence would allow women to lead more fulfilling lives (Friedan, 1963).

For liberal feminists, the key problem is the discrimination against women that limits their opportunities. Ending unjust laws and adopting affirmative action programs will allow women to participate fully in the mainstream of society. Liberal feminism thus focuses on ensuring that women have the freedom and opportunity to engage in politics, business, careers, and employment on the same basis as men.

Socialist Feminism

Socialist feminism views women as oppressed both by the male-dominated character of society and by the capitalist system. Women's housework and child care are unpaid labour that is essential for the profitability of capitalism and for ensuring that there is a supply of labour for the future. Women also provide the capitalist system with a "reserve army" of low-cost labour that can be mobilized when needed to maintain the profitability of capitalist enterprises. Socialist feminists argue that male–female relations reflect the exploitative relationships of capitalists to workers. Just as the capitalist boss dominates and exploits workers, so too husbands are dominant in the home and exploit the labour of their wives.

Socialist feminists argue that the liberation of women involves both a struggle against patriarchy and the transformation of capitalism into a more co-operative and egalitarian socialist society. The free, public provision of child care and possibly other domestic services would help to create the conditions for the liberation of women. Overcoming the sexual division of labour, in which women have primary responsibility for most domestic duties, along with transforming the division of labour in the capitalist system, would also enable everyone to live more creative, fulfilling lives.

Both liberal and socialist feminism involve the application and modification of classic ideologies to the situation of women. Liberal feminism views the achievement of equal opportunities and participation of women in the workforce and politics, particularly in the higher positions traditionally occupied

by men, as the major way to change the patriarchal nature of society. A fundamental transformation of the organization of society is not needed to achieve the
objectives of liberal feminism. Socialist feminism generally sees the capitalist system as a major obstacle to equality for women. A society in which women and
men are truly equal would be organized on the principle of co-operation rather
than competition. For those influenced by the Marxist version of socialism, the
struggle of working-class women and men to overturn capitalism is the fundamental strategy needed to achieve women's liberation. However, most socialist
feminists do not accept the idea that the struggle of women should be subordi-
nated to the struggle of the working class. In their view, overturning capitalism
would not necessarily liberate women and end the sexual division of labour.

Radical Feminism

In the 1960s, a variety of protest movements (including Black Power,
American Indian, anti-war, and student movements) seeking major changes
in society and politics were formed. However, many women involved in
these movements found that they were male-dominated, and often did not
treat women and issues concerning women with equal respect. This led to
the development of the women's liberation movement and the associated
perspective of **radical feminism**.

In the radical feminist perspective, patriarchal values are deeply
embedded in culture and affect the way that women, as well as men, see
themselves (Millett, 1985). Institutions such as the state, the family, and
schools perpetuate male dominance and the subjugation of women. Male
supremacy is maintained through the dominant values, ideas, and practices
of society, which encourage women to be dependent upon and subservient to
men. Beauty contests, feminists argue, are just one example of how women
are treated as sexual objects whose role is to satisfy men. Male supremacy is
also maintained, according to radical feminists, by the use of force in the
form of violence against women, including the threat of rape, to keep women
under control and subordinate (Brownmiller, 1975).

Radical feminism views the oppression of women as the oldest, most perva-
sive, and most deeply entrenched form of oppression. As Robin Morgan, a leading feminist writer and organizer of the Miss America protest argued, "Sexism is
the root oppression, the one which, until and unless we uproot it, will continue to
put forth the branches of racism, class hatred, ageism, competition, ecological disaster, and economic exploitation" (Morgan, 1977, p. 9). The implication is that
the struggle of women against oppression is fundamentally revolutionary because
it has the potential to end various forms of domination and subordination.

LIBERATION The goal of radical feminism is **liberation**. Liberation, whether
used in feminist theory, Marxism, or the theories developed by those
challenging imperialist power in the Third World, goes beyond the concept of

RADICAL FEMINISM
A version of feminism that views
society as based fundamentally
on the oppression of women, and
seeks to liberate women through
the fundamental transformation
of social institutions, values, and
personal relationships.

Feminist Theory Website
www.cddc.vt.edu/feminism/enin.html

LIBERATION
Freeing the human potential that
has been stifled by the organization and values of society.

freedom that is at the core of the liberal ideology. Liberation involves freeing the human potential that has been stifled by the organization and values of society. Oppression warps the personality of the oppressed, particularly by forcing them to adopt the values of the oppressor. Indeed, from this point of view, those in the oppressor groups are also deprived of an authentic human existence by being expected to take the dominant role.

In other words, radical feminists argue that the way that society defines what it is to be female and male is restrictive to both women and men. Patriarchal values not only are oppressive to women, but also force men to adopt socially defined masculine values and behaviours, rather than developing a fully rounded character. For radical feminists, women as an oppressed class are the revolutionary force needed to bring about liberation by struggling against male dominance and the ideology of male supremacy. Liberation will ultimately be for the good of all.

Liberation, thus, is not simply a matter of ending male domination of positions of governing authority or of limiting the power of the state over women. Rather, radical feminism seeks a fundamental transformation of social institutions, values, and personal relationships. Because male power is exhibited in all aspects of life, radical feminists view their task as one of challenging male dominance in all of its manifestations. Thus, they are critical of the liberal feminist focus on achieving equal rights and opportunities in education, employment, and government. Removing barriers to women's participation in the public sphere is, in their view, insufficient to overturn the patriarchal nature of society. Likewise, they are often critical of Marxist feminists who focus on a transformation of capitalism rather than challenging male supremacy.

Instead, radical feminists argue that "the personal is political," suggesting that conventional personal and sexual relationships between women and men need to be challenged as part of their struggle against a patriarchal society. Indeed, many radical feminists view male dominance in the family as the root of male social, political, and economic domination. By making the personal political, radical feminists hope to expose and challenge what they view as a major basis of male power (Bryson, 2003).

Many radical feminists argue that women must organize separately from men in order to free themselves from oppression. Even though there are some men who are sympathetic to the cause of women's liberation, men who join women's organizations are likely to take a dominant position, and women will tend to be passive and subordinate. The prevalence of male power and values makes it necessary for women as an oppressed class to organize themselves collectively as women. Further, because those who are oppressed often do not realize that they are oppressed and have internalized the values of the male-dominated society, radical feminists argue that a key task is to raise women's consciousness (awareness) of their oppression and to encourage women to take pride in their identity as women.

Feminism and Male–Female Differences

From the feminist viewpoint, gender roles, such as the expectation that men will be breadwinners and women will look after domestic duties, are socially created and imposed, rather than reflecting inherent biological differences between men and women. Liberation involves being free of such socially created roles and thus able to adopt or experiment with different roles.

Nevertheless, many feminists believe that women tend to have different values and ways of thinking than men, based on their experiences as women (see Box 6-1, Do Women Think about Moral Values Differently than Men?). Female values such as nurturing, caring, co-operation, emotion, and spirituality are undervalued in male-dominated societies, which instead emphasize such values as competition, aggression, and rationality. Society, particularly in the radical feminist view, needs to be transformed so that female values are given greater importance, either because they are superior to male values (for example, more likely to lead to a peaceful and harmonious world), or because female and male values are complementary if given equal weight. As Barbara Ehrenreich and Deidre English argue (1979, p. 292),

> The human values that women were assigned to preserve [must] expand out of the confines of private life and become the organizing principle of society. The market . . . must be pushed back to the margins. And the "womanly" values of community and caring must rise to the centre as the only human principle.

BOX 6-1

Do Women Think about Moral Values Differently than Men?

Some classic thinkers (including Aristotle, Rousseau, and Freud) argued that women have a less developed sense of morality than men. However, based on studies of the moral development of men and women, American psychologist Carol Gilligan concluded in her book *In a Different Voice* (1982) that men and women tend to have a different, but equally valid, sense of morality.

Because women think of themselves more in terms of their relationships with others, they are more likely to base their moral judgments on an ethic of care and on the specific context and circumstances in which moral issues arise. In contrast, men tend to base their moral judgments more on abstract, universally applicable principles of "right" and "wrong."

In Gilligan's view, male conceptions of morality have been the standard by which morality has been judged. The "different voice" of women has not been heard (Freedman, 2001).

Traditionally, women were often viewed as more "natural" than men because of their role in reproduction and nurturing infants. This was used to justify their confinement to domestic activities and their exclusion from the public sphere, where the "higher" human qualities, such as the ability to reason, are desirable. Most feminists reject the idea that biological characteristics necessarily result in differences between women and men in values and behaviour. Instead, feminists typically argue that women's values are based primarily on the roles that society has prescribed for them, such as raising children and caring for sick and elderly family members.

The argument that male–female differences are a product of society rather than nature is sometimes questioned. For example, despite the best efforts of some parents to engage in gender-neutral child-raising, many young girls seem to prefer to play with dolls and young boys are more likely to want to play with guns. We are left without a definitive answer as to whether female tendencies to be caring and nurturing and male tendencies to be competitive and aggressive are socially created or a product of biological differences.

Promoting Women's Identity

Connected to the emphasis on women's values, feminists have sought to promote the identity of women. By celebrating women and their values, feminists hope to encourage women to be more independent and politically active. The development of a distinctive identity and culture of women is seen, particularly by radical feminists, as an important element in encouraging women to have the confidence to collectively liberate themselves from oppression. Instead of the view that all individuals should be treated the same, many feminists, particularly radical feminists, hold the view that women *as a group* should be treated equally to men with their distinctive identity recognized and fostered.

Some feminists, however, have been critical of the notion that women share a common identity arising out of their common experiences as women. Black feminists, for example, have argued that women of colour suffer double oppression based on their gender and their race. The characteristics of sisterhood proclaimed by the largely white, middle-class, educated, heterosexual spokespersons for the feminist movement do not, some feminists argue, adequately reflect the diversity of women's experiences (Code, 1988).

Is Feminism Still Relevant?

The feminist ideology and the women's movement have raised a variety of issues that were previously largely ignored in politics. There is, however, considerable disagreement about the extent to which the women's movement has succeeded in changing the position of women (see Box 6-2, "You've Come a Long Way, Baby"?). Table 6-1 gives an indication of the current circumstances of women in Canada.

BOX 6-2

"You've Come a Long Way, Baby"?

Some years ago, commercials for a brand of cigarette designed for women celebrated the advances made by women. It featured, in language that could be deemed sexist, the slogan "You've come a long way, baby." But there is still debate about whether feminism has achieved its objectives and whether contemporary Western societies are patriarchal and oppressive.

There is little doubt that women continue to suffer from brutal and oppressive treatment in many parts of the world. In a number of countries, women continue to be deprived of adequate education, limited in their employment opportunities, restricted in their personal life, treated as inferior in law, and subject to such cruelties as genital mutilation. However, in many countries there have been some major changes in the position of women, particularly in the past few decades:

- Discriminatory laws have generally been abolished.
- Women have entered the paid workforce in large numbers and mothers with young children are often employed outside the home.
- Females now form the majority of university students in Canada and the United States, and even high-status professional programs such as law, medicine, and business administration have, or will soon have, more female than male students.
- The tendency for the mass media to portray women in negative terms has diminished. Instead of "dumb blondes" and *Father Knows Best*, some television shows and movies treat males as a subject of ridicule.
- Publishers carefully vet textbooks to eliminate sexist language, many universities have established women's studies programs, affirmative action programs have been created to encourage the hiring and promotion of women, and sexual harassment officers have been hired by universities and some businesses to try to protect women from being abused by those in positions of power.
- Rights to divorce, contraception, and abortion have allowed women in many countries to free themselves from abusive relationships and to gain control over their bodies.

However, feminists argue that progress toward equality and liberation is still limited, even in Western societies. Women still have only a small share of political power. For example, in Canada only about one-fifth of legislators at the national and provincial levels are female. Likewise, the proportion of women in top positions in the business world is still small. Women tend to be employed in jobs that are perceived as "women's work" (such as secretary, nurse, and primary school teacher), with the average employment earnings of women still substantially below that of men. Women continue to have primary responsibility for raising children in many households, and also often have the task of caring for sick and elderly family members. Women are still often judged in terms of their physical attractiveness, and negative stereotypes of women are still quite prevalent.

Do women still have a long way to go to be fully equal? Will the current generation, which includes many highly educated and motivated young women, complete the feminist "revolution," or are obstacles still in their way? Even though the position of women in Western societies has changed considerably in recent decades, the under-representation of women in positions of power will undoubtedly continue to be an issue in both politics and the working world.

TABLE 6-1

THE CIRCUMSTANCES OF CANADIAN WOMEN

Note: A ratio of 1.0 indicates female–male equality. A value below 1.0 indicates that women have or do less than men, while a value above 1.0 indicates that women have or do more than men.

	FEMALE-TO-MALE RATIO
Total income before tax (2003)	0.62
Low income after tax (2003)	1.12
Total workload (1998)	1.04
– Paid work	0.62
– Unpaid work	1.56
Employed (2004)	0.85
Unemployment rate (2004)	0.91
Average hourly wage (2004)	0.82
University undergraduate enrolment (2004–2005)	1.39
University graduate enrolment (2004–2005)	1.00

SOURCE: *Adapted from* Economic gender equality indicators 2000, *by W. Clark, 2001, retrieved July 15, 2004, from www.swc-cfc.gc.ca/pubs/egei2000/egei2000_e.html;* Women in Canada: A gender-based statistical report, *5th ed. Ottawa: Ministry of Industry, 2006;* Average hourly wages of employees by selected characteristics, profession, and by province, *by Statistics Canada, 2007, retrieved July 19, 2007, from www40.statcan.ca/l01/cst01/labr69a.htm; and Statistics Canada data cited in* CAUT Almanac of post- secondary education in Canada, *by Canadian Association of University Teachers (2007), CAUT: Ottawa. Some calculations by authors.*

ENVIRONMENTALISM

The world faces numerous serious environmental problems. These include:

- Increasing emission of greenhouse gases, such as carbon dioxide and methane, resulting from fossil fuel burning, deforestation, and increased agricultural production. The resulting global climate changes could have profound consequences for all life forms.
- Depletion of many natural resources.
- Contamination and misuse of water supplies. A substantial proportion of the world's population lacks access to clean water, and water shortages may reduce food production in the future.
- Devastation of tropical rainforests, which contain much of the Earth's biological diversity, and the extinction of an unprecedented number of species of animals and plants. The decline in biodiversity may hamper the search for new medicines and hinder the world's capability to maintain agricultural production.
- Pollution of various forms, which is degrading the environment and harming the health of humans and other species.

In 1962, American biologist Rachel Carson's *Silent Spring* eloquently made the case that synthetic pesticides were silencing the voices of birds that heralded the coming of spring. More generally, Carson pointed out that the fragile ecology of the earth was threatened by the large-scale production and use of dangerous chemicals. A series of environmental disasters, including massive oil spills, further increased concern about environmental problems and led to the development of a large environmental movement. In conjunction with this movement, the ideology of **environmentalism** developed.

Environmentalism is not simply an expression of concern about various environmental problems and support for efforts to clean up the environment and reduce pollution. Rather, environmentalism *as an ideology* tries to provide a distinctive perspective on the fundamental causes of environmental problems and a vision of an environmentally friendly world.

Environmentalism includes the belief that humanity needs to fundamentally change its relationship with nature. Influenced by the science of ecology, which emphasizes the complex interrelatedness of the natural world, environmentalism argues that humanity needs to view itself as part of the intricate and fragile web of nature, and to understand our dependence upon nature so as to live in harmony with it. Instead of viewing humanity outside of nature with the right to control and dominate nature, we need to think of ourselves as part of nature and limit our impact on the earth (Schumacher, 1973).

As Petra Kelly (1947–1992), a founder of the German Green party, stated:

> We must learn to think and act from our hearts, to recognize the interconnectedness of all living creatures, and to respect the value of each thread in the vast web of life. . . . We have borrowed the Earth from our children. Green politics is about having just "enough" and not "more," and this runs counter to all of the economic assumptions of industrial society. . . . The industrialized countries must move from growth-oriented to sustainable economies, with conservation replacing consumption as the driving force (quoted in Ball & Dagger, 2004, pp. 442, 445).

Those who hold an environmentalist perspective argue that one of the basic causes of environmental problems is the idea that we can control nature and use it for our benefit without concern for the consequences. Instead of a focus on human well-being (termed **anthropocentrism**), environmentalism (particularly in its stronger versions) advocates the adoption of a more **ecocentric** philosophy that views nature as having its own intrinsic value—that is, value in and of itself, rather than its value for human use (Eckersley, 1992).

Limits to Growth

Environmentalism also views our obsession with economic growth as a basic cause of environmental problems. Since the Industrial Revolution, there has been a massive increase in the production and consumption of material goods. People in the developed countries have come to enjoy high levels of consumption, while the production and consumption of goods is increasing rapidly in newly industrialized countries such as China and India. Governments have often made the pursuit of economic growth their primary objective, and the success of different countries is usually measured in terms

ENVIRONMENTALISM
A perspective based on the idea that humanity needs to change its relationship to nature so as to protect the natural environment and ensure that it can sustain all forms of life.

ANTHROPOCENTRISM
The focus on human well-being that is at the centre of most political thought.

ECOCENTRISM
The view that nature has intrinsic value and should not be valued only in terms of its use for human beings.

of their gross national product (the monetary value of the goods and services produced).

The environmentalist perspective emphasizes that there are limits to growth (see Box 6-3, The Limits to Growth: A Famous Bet). The Earth has a limited carrying capacity—that is, there are inherent limits to the capacity of Earth's ecosystems to support increasing levels of consumption while absorbing waste. Studies of our "ecological footprint" suggest that if persons throughout the world had the same impact on the environment as the average person in the richer countries, we would need two or more Earths to sustain the existing population of the world (Rees & Wackernagel, 1996). Continuing growth in human use of the Earth's resources cannot go on endlessly. At some point, the Earth will reach the end of its ability to absorb our effluents and provide the resources for our ever-increasing production of material goods.

Ecological Footprint Quiz
www.ecofoot.org

SUSTAINABILITY
Maintaining the integrity of ecosystems by ensuring that renewable resources are not being used at a rate that exceeds the ability of ecosystems to regenerate them, developing renewable substitutes to replace the consumption of non-renewable resources, and ensuring that the emission of pollutants does not exceed the ability of the ecosystem to handle them without damage.

▶ Environmentalists raise basic questions about the relationship between human beings and the environment that have been largely ignored by other political ideologies. Environmentalists advocate a fundamental transformation of society and politics, as well as basic changes to our ways of thinking.

A Sustainable Society

A basic goal of environmentalism is that of **sustainability**, particularly in terms of maintaining the integrity of ecosystems. Specifically, renewable resources should not be used at a rate that exceeds the ability of ecosystems to regenerate them. Renewable substitutes should be developed to replace the consumption of non-renewable resources. The emission of pollutants should not exceed the ability of the ecosystem to handle them without damage (Korten, 1996). Instead of continual growth of production and consumption, some of those who hold the environmentalist perspective favour a steady-state (no growth) economy so as to live within the capacities of the Earth. This would ensure that future generations have the same enjoyment and benefit of the environment that we do.

BOX 6-3
The Limits to Growth: A Famous Bet

In 1972, a group of industrialists, politicians, and academics known as the Club of Rome predicted that within one hundred years there would be an uncontrollable and disastrous collapse of society when the limits to growth were exceeded (Meadows, Meadows, Randers, & Behrens, 1972).

The scenario appeared in a Club of Rome report called *The Limits to Growth,* which was based on a global computer model that attempted to project a variety of current trends into the future. The growth of the world's population and the accelerating use of non-renewable natural resources, particularly oil, caused by an expanding global economy would mean that the resources needed to provide materials and energy would become very costly and scarce.

The doomsday scenario of the Club of Rome has come under considerable criticism. Its computer model simplistically projected current trends into the future, assuming that the accelerating rate of increase in resources and population would continue indefinitely. In reality, the rate of increase in population growth and resource usage has slowed down. In 1980, economist Julian Simon publicly bet Paul Ehrlich, a biologist well known for his doomsday scenarios, a thousand dollars that the real price of any set of natural resources Ehrlich chose would be lower in the future. Ehrlich chose the prices of copper, chrome, nickel, tin, and tungsten as of 1990. As it turned out, the price of each of these minerals *was* lower in 1990, and Simon won the bet (Dryzek, 1997).

Simon argues that there are no limits to growth. Human ingenuity and the competitive marketplace will result in more resources being found, substitutes invented, and pollution problems resolved. The resourcefulness of humanity and the vast resources of the world will allow for indefinite economic growth, provided that governments do not take actions to restrict growth. However, some of the optimistic predictions Simon made in 1984—that by 2000 fish catches would increase and cheap nuclear power would be available while problems such as climate change, water scarcity, soil erosion, and pollution would diminish in significance (Simon & Kahn, 1984)—did not come true. For example, one study estimated that the world's oceans now contain only about one-tenth of the amount of large predatory fish, such as cod, that existed before the adoption of large-scale industrial fishing. The collapse of various fish stocks due to overfishing may in turn have significant but unknown impacts on ocean and planetary ecosystems (Myers & Worm, 2003).

Raising fears about the survival of humanity and life on earth has helped to increase awareness of environmental problems, although exaggerated claims of impending doom can also damage the credibility of some environmentalists. On the other hand, the view that human use of the environment can continue to grow and human ingenuity can deal with any problems that might arise ignores the ever-growing strain on the Earth's ecosystems created by increased production, consumption, and population.

How can a sustainable society be achieved? Encouraging individuals to change their attitudes concerning nature and adopting more environmentally friendly practices (as summarized by the slogan "reduce, reuse, recycle") can be useful. However, many of those who hold the environmentalist ideology argue that fundamental social, economic, and political changes are also needed to achieve a sustainable society. For example, British environmentalists Jonathon Porritt and Nicholas Winner argue that what is needed is "nothing less than a nonviolent revolution to overthrow our whole polluting, plundering and materialistic industrial society and, in its place, to create a new economic and social order which will allow human beings to live in harmony with the planet" (quoted in Dobson, 2000, p. 9).

For some environmentalists the ideal economic and social order would be based on local communities that are largely self-sufficient and self-governing. Greater self-sufficiency would reduce the amount of energy used for transportation and encourage communities to live within the ecological capabilities of their local area. Large global corporations would no longer be the basis of the economy. Smaller, locally based enterprises, co-operatives, and communes geared to local needs rather than the global marketplace might be the basis of production. Instead of remote, bureaucratic governing bodies, members of the local community would make decisions on a participatory basis. Their decisions would be sensitive to environmental concerns, it is assumed, because residents of the local community can see the direct effects of their decisions on the local environment. Generally, the local community, with its possibilities for face-to-face interaction, is seen as a more natural community than large states and global corporations. The need for coordination among local communities could, ideally, be achieved by a loose association of communities in a peaceful, global network.

Others who hold an environmentalist perspective see a need for strong states and even a world government with the power to develop and implement plans to deal with large-scale global environmental problems (Dobson, 2000). Self-sufficient local communities might have an unacceptably low standard of living and lack the knowledge and capability to deal with environmental problems. As well, the difficulties in achieving coordination among a large number of local communities could be immense, and there is no guarantee that local communities would act in a sustainable manner.

Sustainable Development

A major problem for environmentalism is that limiting economic growth on a global basis could deprive persons in the poorer countries of the opportunity to try to catch up to the standard of living of the richer countries, or even to ensure that their basic needs are satisfied. Many environmentalists (including Green parties) therefore try to combine the objective of sustainability with the idea of global social justice that involves a more equitable distribution of the world's wealth and a concerted effort to deal with global poverty. Some argue that consumption in the richer countries should be sharply reduced and major efforts be made to redistribute wealth from the richer countries to assist the poor.

Discussions of how to take action to deal with both environmental problems and global poverty have often focused on the concept of **sustainable development**. The World Commission on Environment and Development

SUSTAINABLE DEVELOPMENT
Meeting the needs of the present without compromising the ability of future generations to meet their own needs; it involves development to ensure that the needs of the poor are fulfilled and protecting the environment for the well-being of future generations.

(1987, p. 8), which popularized this concept, defined sustainable development as ensuring that development meets "the needs of the present without compromising the ability of future generations to meet their own needs." There are two elements to this definition:

- First, development is needed to ensure that the needs of the poor are fulfilled.
- Second, the sustainability of the environment needs to be protected for the well-being of future generations.

Although the Commission's report highlighted a number of serious environmental challenges and noted the necessity of maintaining the carrying capacity of the Earth, it did not accept the limits-to-growth argument. Instead, the Commission noted that economic growth was needed for much of the world to overcome poverty. However, the Commission argued that the quality of growth should be changed so as to put less stress on the environment. Economic growth should be more equitable, extreme rates of population growth limited, and the resource base of economies conserved and enhanced. Hope was placed on reorienting technology to deal with environmental problems, integrating environmental and economic objectives in political decision making, and increasing public participation in the decisions that affect their communities.

The Commission's report and subsequent discussions of sustainable development have been vague, allowing many businesses, governments, and environmentalists to adopt the general goal of sustainable development while often differing on the meaning of that goal and the actions needed to achieve it.

Varieties of Environmentalism

The idea of sustainable development as expressed, for example, by the World Commission on Environment and Development, could be considered a version of **reform environmentalism**. Reform environmentalism is less distinctive than the stronger versions of environmentalism that we have been discussing, and can be found in combination with other ideological perspectives such as liberalism, conservatism, and socialism. Unlike stronger versions of environmentalism that advocate fundamental changes, this perspective views the solution to environmental problems primarily in terms of better science, technology, and environmental management. Developing and using better pollution-control technology, encouraging more recycling efforts, promoting measures to assess and mitigate the negative potential effects of new developments, and taking more care to conserve natural resources are seen as resulting in environmental improvement.

REFORM ENVIRONMENTALISM
A perspective that views the solution to environmental problems primarily in terms of better science, technology, and environmental management.

BOX 6-4

Are We All Green Now?

British Prime Minister Margaret Thatcher once declared, "We're all green now." Politicians, government officials, and business leaders regularly proclaim their commitment to protecting the environment. But despite the passage of environmental laws, signing of international environmental agreements, and establishment of plans for sustainable development, many environmentalists claim that we are still headed toward environmental disaster. For example, although an international agreement that led to the drastic reduction in the use of ozone-depleting chlorofluorocarbons counts as a major success story, reduction in the greenhouse gas (GHG) emissions that can cause climate change continues to be an elusive goal.

Building on a commitment at the 1992 Earth Summit to prevent an increase in GHG emissions, representatives of 160 countries reached an agreement in 1997 (the Kyoto Protocol) to deal with the climate change problem. The Kyoto Protocol requires most of the wealthier industrialized countries to reduce their emission of the greenhouse gases responsible for climate change to a level below their 1990 levels (6 percent below for Canada) by 2012. Developing countries are not subject to the same requirements, but are encouraged to limit emissions voluntarily, and there are incentives for the richer countries to help the poorer countries control their emissions.

Although the United States government signed the Kyoto Protocol, it has refused to ratify it. President George W. Bush and the American Senate claimed that studies concerning climate change were not definitive. Further, they argued that because developing countries are not required to reduce their emissions, the Kyoto Protocol could make American industries uncompetitive.

The Canadian government ratified the protocol in 2002, despite objections from the Alberta government and the petroleum industry. However, emissions of greenhouse gases have increased substantially since 1990 in Canada (see Figure 6-1), thus making it very unlikely that Canada will be able to meet the Kyoto commitment to reduce emissions. Indeed, while not officially rejecting the Kyoto Protocol, the Conservative government led by Stephen Harper cut many of the programs that had been established to deal with the problem of climate change.

Despite mounting evidence that GHG emissions carry serious and potentially irreversible long-term risks to humanity, many governments have preferred talk to serious action. Worldwide, the rate of GHG emissions has increased from 1 percent per year prior to 2000 to 2.5 percent per year from 2000 to 2006 (Black, 2006). Many petroleum companies have tried to discredit the evidence of global climate change, and business-sponsored think tanks have raised fears about the costs of reducing emissions. However, a British government report prepared under the direction of Nicholas Stern, a former chief economist of the World Bank, estimated that *not* taking action to deal with climate change would cost the world economy US$7 trillion (Black, 2006). Meanwhile, people continue to buy gas-guzzling vehicles that contribute to the emissions. Environmentalists may have been successful in raising our environmental consciousness, but this does not mean that we act in a green fashion.

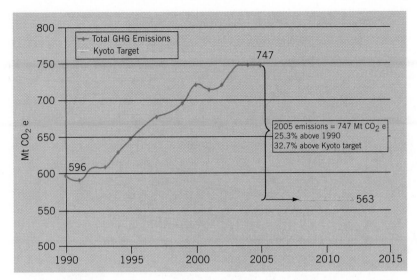

FIGURE 6-1

CANADA'S GREENHOUSE GAS EMISSIONS, 1990–2005

SOURCE: *Environment Canada,* Canada's 2005 greenhouse gas inventory: A summary of trends, *2007, Figure 1, retrieved July 9, 2007, from www.ec.gc.ca/pdb/ghg/inventory_report/2005/ images/fig1_3.gif.>. © Environment Canada 2005.

Reform environmentalism does not view economic growth and environmental protection as necessarily incompatible. Industry, it is argued, can become more efficient and profitable by incorporating environmental considerations into the production process and adopting more sophisticated, less polluting technologies (Weale, 1992). Indeed, in a number of countries, considerable progress has been made since the 1970s in adopting a variety of environmental policies, reducing some types of pollution, and using energy more efficiently. However, as Box 6-4, Are We All Green Now?, indicates, we continue to face serious environmental challenges.

Among the stronger and more distinctive versions of environmentalism are deep ecology, social ecology, and ecofeminism. **Deep ecology** views the anthropocentric beliefs that have been at the centre of Western thinking as the fundamental cause of environmental degradation, and advocates the cultivation of an environmental consciousness and a sense of oneness with the world that recognizes the unity of humans, plants, animals, and the Earth (Devall & Sessions, 1998). Deep ecology views all forms of life as being of intrinsic value, with humans having no right to reduce the richness and diversity of life forms except to satisfy vital needs. As well, deep ecology advocates a substantial decrease in the human population, the return to a simpler lifestyle in which human impact on the environment is greatly reduced, and the protection and expansion of areas of wilderness to allow other species to flourish (Naess & Sessions, 1993).

Social ecology views social, economic, and political relationships of hierarchy and domination as the cause of both human and environmental problems. Creating an egalitarian and co-operative society is needed to end domination within human societies and the exploitation of nature. Both social

DEEP ECOLOGY

An environmentalist perspective that views anthropocentrism as the fundamental cause of environmental degradation and advocates the cultivation of an environmental consciousness and a sense of oneness with the world that recognizes the unity of humans, plants, animals, and the Earth.

Foundation for Deep Ecology
www.deepecology.org

SOCIAL ECOLOGY

A perspective that views social, economic, and political relationships of hierarchy and domination as the cause of both human and environmental problems.

► California Governor Arnold Schwarzenegger visits Vancouver, British Columbia, to help fight global warming.

Institute for Social Ecology
www.social-ecology.org

ECOFEMINISM
A combination of environmentalism and feminism that views male dominance as the basic cause of the degradation of the Earth.

The Ecofeminism Web-ring
www.ecofem.org

ecology and deep ecology favour small-scale, self-sufficient communities in a decentralized world. Social ecology, however, views humans as active and creative stewards of the natural world, while deep ecology promotes a view of humans as being just one of numerous life forms.

Ecofeminism, a combination of environmentalism and feminism, views male dominance as the basic cause of the degradation of the Earth. Male domination and exploitation of nature is an extension of male domination of women; the "rape" of nature arises out of male desires for control and mastery in a patriarchal society. Women, it is argued, are more closely related to nature and are more likely to understand the world in terms of a network of interrelationships. Thus, giving greater importance to women's values, perspectives, and experiences is needed to restore harmony with nature.

In general, most major environmental groups and green parties lean in the direction of reform environmentalism as they seek to develop politically acceptable policies to deal with environmental problems. Nevertheless, stronger versions of environmentalism challenge the dominant world view that places the highest priority on economic growth, views the natural world as a resource to be used for human benefit, and believes that science and technology are capable of solving all environmental problems (Taylor, 1992).

RELIGIOUS FUNDAMENTALISM

Speaking at the national convention of the American Legion, President George W. Bush (2006) said, "The war we fight today is more than a military conflict; it is the decisive ideological struggle of the 21st century." Bush's comments were directed at Islamic extremists who engaged in terrorist attacks against the United States and other countries. In this view, the struggle against the ideology motivating Islamic extremism has replaced the struggle against communism that was a crucial feature of the twentieth century, particularly in the decades after the Second World War. But what ideology motivates Islamic extremism? Is it a perspective held only by a small number of fanatics, or is it part of a broader ideological perspective that plays a significant role in the politics of the fifty-seven countries that consider themselves Islamic and the 1.3 billion people of the Islamic faith (Lewis, 2004)? Are there parallels to perspectives held by those who believe in other religions?

The revival of Islam based on a strict, literal interpretation of the Quran and a belief that public and private life should be governed by the sharia (Islamic law) is often described (particularly by outside observers) as **Islamic fundamentalism**. The term **fundamentalism** originated in the United States in the early twentieth century to describe "conservative evangelical Protestants" who wanted "to preserve the 'fundamentals' of the Christian faith" from biblical critics and proponents of the theory of evolution (Almond, Appleby, & Sivan, 2003, pp. 1–2). Fundamentalists of various religions view their sacred scriptures (such as the Bible or the Quran) as the literal word of God, reject analyses that find inconsistencies in the scriptures, and are critical of efforts to interpret sacred scriptures in light of modern realities.

Fundamentalism is not simply a return to orthodox or traditional versions of religion. In an effort to create or revive a "purer" form of their religion, fundamentalists often interpret or emphasize certain aspects of sacred texts in ways that differ from established religious institutions and religious authorities (Almond, Appleby, & Sivan, 2003). This may involve rejecting some of the traditional interpretations of sacred texts and religious customs that they view as inconsistent with the word of God.

One common feature of various forms of fundamentalism is the view that religion is not simply a matter of private belief, but a way of life for the individual and the community as a whole. Thus, fundamentalists are critical of the separation of church and state that has become a basic principle in many Western societies.

Fundamentalists are particularly critical of **secular humanism**, the view that ethical principles and moral standards can be developed through human reason. Fundamentalists blame secular humanism for what they see as the ills of modern societies, in particular the decline in morality.

Generally, fundamentalists believe that society should be God-centred rather than human-centred (Zeidan, 2004). God's laws, as laid out in sacred

ISLAMIC FUNDAMENTALISM
The revival of Islam based on a strict, literal interpretation of the Quran and a belief that public and private life should be governed by the sharia (Islamic law).

FUNDAMENTALISM
The revival of strict religious beliefs seeking to promote the fundamental principles of the faith, including the belief that sacred scriptures are the word of God and should be strictly followed in all areas of life.

SECULAR HUMANISM
The view that ethical principles and moral standards can be developed through human reason.

scriptures, should be the basis for the laws proclaimed and enforced by governments. Immoral behaviour should be suppressed and religious belief encouraged throughout society. The view that all aspects of the political community, including individual beliefs and activities, should be required to conform to God's laws is particularly strong among Islamic fundamentalists.

The concern of fundamentalists with morality is evident in their views on sexual behaviour and the family. Fundamentalists view homosexuality, abortion, and sex outside marriage as evils. Likewise, they object to the portrayal of sexuality and nudity in the media and seek to encourage modesty in dress and behaviour. Islamic fundamentalists seek to prevent immoral behaviour by such measures as avoiding the mixing of sexes in schools and other public places, forbidding the use of alcohol, and, in the strongest versions, banning dances and music and requiring that women cover their faces as well as their bodies and be chaperoned when venturing outside of their homes. Most fundamentalists—whether Christian, Jewish, or Muslim—uphold a patriarchal vision of the family, viewing the husband as the head of the household and provider for the family and the wife as being responsible for the raising of children and other household duties.

Fundamentalists generally view the world in terms of the struggle between good and evil. This struggle against evil (referred to as jihad in Islam) is both an internal personal struggle against sin and temptation and, for many fundamentalists, an external struggle against the forces of evil in the world. Some fundamentalists seek to build an enclave that strictly follows the laws of their religion and shields the community of believers from the temptations of the outside world (Almond, Appleby, & Sivan, 2003). Others believe that they

▶ In the strongest version of Islamic fundamentalism, women are required to cover their entire bodies.

have a duty to spread God's message throughout the world by converting non-believers as well as persuading those of their own faith to return to the path of righteousness. Because of the belief that there is only one true faith, the long-term goal of some fundamentalists is to create a global political community adhering to God's laws that will unite all believers and replace existing states.

Importance

Fundamentalism has become an important political as well as religious doctrine. In the United States, fundamentalists associated with the Christian Right (through organizations such as the Christian Coalition) have been very active in the Republican party and played an important role in the election of President George W. Bush. Various groups associated with the Christian Right were also successful in preventing the Equal Rights Amendment that would have entrenched male–female equality in the American constitution from gaining the necessary approval. Prominent American fundamentalist preachers Jerry Falwell and Pat Robertson argued that the terrorist attacks on the United States in 2001 were God's punishment because America had strayed from the path of Christian morality. In Canada, fundamentalists have been active in the Reform and Canadian Alliance parties (now part of the Conservative party), the Christian Heritage party, and Ontario's Family Coalition party. Jewish fundamentalists helped to persuade Israeli governments to establish Jewish settlements in the occupied West Bank based on a belief that God gave the Jewish people all of their biblical territories.

Islamism

Militant versions of Islamic fundamentalism, which can be termed **radical Islamism**, advocating strong action to purge "degenerate" foreign elements from Muslim society and establish a "pure" Islamic state based on the sharia have become important in various parts of the Islamic world in recent decades. The revolution in Iran in 1979 against a Western-oriented regime resulted in the establishment of an Islamic Republic in which clerics play a dominant role. The Taliban applied an extremely harsh version of Islamic fundamentalism on most of Afghanistan from 1996 to 2001. Various militant Islamic fundamentalist movements and political parties continue to challenge and seek to overthrow governments throughout the Middle East, North Africa, and central Asia that are viewed as not conforming to Islamic law.

The development of various forms of radical Islamism is sometimes explained in terms of the sense of humiliation experienced as parts of the once powerful and culturally advanced Islamic world came under the control of Western powers in the late nineteenth century and the first half of the twentieth century. Direct foreign control of a number of Muslim countries ended in the

RADICAL ISLAMISM
The perspective often associated with those seeking to purge "degenerate" foreign elements from Muslim society and establish a "pure" Islamic state based strictly on the sharia (Islamic law).

period after the Second World War, although some Western powers continued at times to involve themselves in the affairs of Muslim countries (for example, British and American involvement in the overthrow of an elected government in Iran in 1953).

The adoption of the Western ideologies of nationalism and socialism by the rulers of many Muslim countries that sought to modernize and develop their countries was largely unsuccessful. These failures encouraged some to look to the creation of a religiously based political community (uniting all Muslims rather than dividing into nation-states) as an alternative to corrupt governments.

A return to the "straight path" of Islam in accordance with their interpretation of the Quran is seen not only as a solution to the problems faced by many Muslim countries, but also as a way of creating a positive sense of identity. By rejecting Western practices and lifestyles, a purer Islamic identity could be reasserted (Milton-Edwards, 2005).

Some Islamic fundamentalists seek to recreate the glories of historic Islamic civilizations, some of which made major contributions to the advancement of knowledge and culture. However, what is often ignored is that these contributions were facilitated by their openness, at the time, to learn from other cultures and by the willingness of some Islamic rulers to allow a degree of tolerance of religious minorities in their midst. For example, the Islamic Moors who conquered and ruled Andalusia (southern Spain) from the eighth to the thirteenth centuries established leading universities that revived the knowledge that had been developed by Greek and other civilizations. Islamic and Jewish scholars sometimes collaborated in the advancement of knowledge.

QUTB AND BIN LADEN During his stay in the United States in the late 1940s, Sayyid Qutb, a key figure in the development of the ideology of radical Islamism, was shocked by the American way of life, which he viewed as sinful, degenerate, sexually promiscuous, and materialistic (Lewis, 2004). This contributed to his hatred of Western societies. Qutb argued that Muslims needed to fight to revive Islam, which had been abandoned by the Westernizing rulers and elites of the Muslim world. Through a militant jihad, Muslims could ensure that the message of God would be heard throughout the world (Cook, 2005). This included using physical force to overthrow Muslim rulers who had departed from the ways of Islam. Qutb, an active member of the Muslim Brotherhood, was executed for alleged involvement in an attempted assassination of Egyptian President Nasser in 1966.

In extreme versions of Islamism, such as that espoused by al-Qaeda leader Osama bin Laden, Western "Crusaders" and Jews are viewed as conspiring to destroy Islam. Violence and self-sacrifice ("martyrdom") are required to defeat the enemy (including "infidel" Muslims), even though the Quran contains prohibitions against suicide and, in most circumstances, the killing of civilians. For bin Laden and some other radical Islamists, the global Islamic community they seek to create is based on the austere community led by Mohammed in Medina (Saudi Arabia) in the seventh century. However, they have become adept at using modern technology, such as the Internet and video, to spread their message and mobilize their followers.

Those committed to a violent global jihad constitute a small minority of Islamic fundamentalists. Indeed, questions have been raised as to whether the radical philosophy espoused by Qutb and bin Laden reflects the fundamentals of Islam. Nevertheless, small numbers of committed believers can have major political effects, particularly when large numbers of persons might be influenced in certain circumstances.

Summary and Conclusion

The goal of feminism is to achieve a society in which women enjoy independence and equality, with full control over their own lives and bodies. In addition to working toward removing obstacles to the full and equal participation of women in social, economic, and political life, many feminists have sought to affirm the distinct identity of women. Achieving equality and giving greater significance to female values are seen as being not only desirable for women, but also for the common good of humanity. As well, feminist scholars have challenged traditional ways of understanding the world that, they argue, ignore the importance of gender and the contribution of women.

The ideology of environmentalism raises important questions about the relationship between human beings and the environment. Environmentalism views human dominance and exploitation of nature as leading to disastrous consequences for the world. Humans need to recognize that they are a part of nature and should learn to live in harmony with it. This involves treading lightly on the Earth and ending the exponential growth in production, consumption, population, and waste. From an environmentalist point of view, the common good should refer not only to the good of

human beings, but also to the good of the world as a whole, of which we are an integral part. An important challenge facing environmentalism is the question of how to achieve sustainability while addressing the need to eliminate global poverty.

Religious beliefs have always been an important force in political life, affecting a variety of political ideas and ideologies. Religious fundamentalism, in recent years, has become an important political phenomenon. While religious fundamentalists promote a rigid interpretation of their faith's scriptures and typically seek to impose a strict moral code on society, other versions of religious faith have reinterpreted sacred scriptures to move in different directions.

Religious fundamentalism poses a profound challenge to the liberal, secular views that have come to dominate Western political thinking. Fundamentalists generally seek to undo the separation between religion and the state. Religion is seen as not just a matter of private belief, but the basis for a good society; the laws laid out in sacred scriptures are of enduring importance and should be the basis for any human-created laws. For some religious fundamentalists, a total belief in the righteousness of their cause serves to justify extreme actions to achieve their objectives. In particular, some groups associated with radical Islamism have had profound effects on contemporary politics through their terrorist actions and attempts to create an Islamic community based on the rule of God and the sharia.

Each perspective discussed in this chapter, particularly in its stronger versions, raises important, basic political questions. The intensity of the political controversies generated by these perspectives suggests that ideological disputes have not ended. Instead, these perspectives have tended to shift the focus of ideological debate to issues that were not generally the focus of the older ideological perspectives.

Key Terms

Discussion Questions

1. Why do some feminists view women as oppressed? Is this a valid depiction of the position of women in Canada? Are fundamental changes needed to improve the position of women?

2. Would a government that had female majority and female leadership act differently than governments dominated by men?

3. How can a sustainable society best be achieved?

4. Is Islamic fundamentalism a threat to Western civilization?

5. Should countries where most people identify with a particular religion base their laws on the sacred texts of that religion? Should government try to protect the moral basis of the community?

Further Reading

Almond, G.A., Appleby, R.S., & Sivan, E. *Strong religions: The rise of fundamentalisms around the world.* Chicago: University of Chicago Press, 2003.

Burke, J. *Al-Qaeda: The true story of radical Islam.* London: I.B. Taurus, 2004.

Davidson, L. *Islamic fundamentalism: An introduction,* revised ed. Westport, CT: Greenwood Press, 2003.

Dobson, A. *Green political thought,* 4th ed. New York: Routledge, 2007.

Donovan, J. *Feminist theory: The intellectual traditions,* 3rd ed. New York: Continuum, 2000.

Dryzek, J.S. *The politics of the earth: Environmental discourses,* 2nd ed. Oxford: Oxford University Press, 2005.

Freedman, J. *Feminism.* Buckingham, UK: Open University Press, 2001.

Lewis, B. *The crisis of Islam: Holy war and unholy terror.* New York, Random House, 2003.

McKenzie, J.I. *Environmental politics in Canada: Managing the commons into the twenty-first century.* Don Mills, ON: Oxford University Press, 2002.

Milton-Edwards, B. *Islamic fundamentalism since 1945.* London: Routledge, 2005.

Ruthven, M. *Fundamentalism: The search for meaning.* Oxford: Oxford University Press, 2004.

Tong, R. *Feminist thought: A comprehensive introduction,* 2nd ed. Boulder, CO: Westview Press, 1998.

Wright, L. *The looming tower: Al-Qaeda and the road to 9/11.* New York: Alfred A. Knopf, 2006.

PART III

POLITICAL ORGANIZATION, PERSUASION, AND ACTION

Chapter 7

POLITICAL CULTURE, POLITICAL PARTICIPATION, AND POLITICAL SOCIALIZATION

PHOTO ABOVE: Some people saw the destruction of New York's World Trade Center by al-Qaeda terrorists in 2001 as evidence that there was a "clash of civilizations" between Islam and the West.

1. explain the meaning and significance of political culture

2. discuss the differences between the Canadian and American political cultures

3. outline the level of political interest, knowledge, and participation in Western democracies

4. examine the decline of confidence and trust in politicians and governments

5. discuss the low level of voting by young people

6. define political socialization and discuss the agents of political socialization

7. explain the postmaterialist theory of change in political culture

The image of the twin towers of New York's World Trade Center collapsing after they were struck by jets hijacked by al-Qaeda terrorists is one that few people will forget.

The horrific events of September 11, 2001, seemed to confirm the argument of Harvard University political scientist Samuel P. Huntington (1993, 1996) that a "clash of civilizations," such as the clash between Islam and the West, will become the leading source of international conflict. Cultural conflicts, he suggests, have replaced the ideological conflict between communism and capitalism as the major potential source of world war. Huntington (1993) views the world as increasingly divided into seven or eight major civilizations—broad cultural groupings based on differences in history, language, traditions, and particularly religion (Western, Confucian, Japanese, Islamic, Hindu, Slavic-Orthodox, Latin American, and possibly African). In contrast to those who view globalization and modernization as resulting in increased homogenization or Westernization of the cultures of the world, Huntington argues that non-Western peoples are rejecting Western values and building on their own indigenous cultures. "The Western ideas of individualism, liberalism, constitutionalism, human rights, equality, liberty, the rule of law, free markets, the separation of church and state," he writes, "have little resonance in other cultures" (Huntington, 1993, p. 40).

Huntington's analysis has been criticized on a number of grounds. Although there are major differences between Western and non-Western societies on social and moral issues (such as divorce, abortion, gender equality, and homosexual rights), the adoption of tolerant liberal values by Western societies on such issues is a relatively recent phenomenon. As well, although authoritarian political institutions are firmly entrenched in some non-Western countries, such as most Arab countries, surveys have found that the majority of the population in some of these countries sees democracy as desirable (Inglehart & Norris, 2003; Tessler, 2002). In a number of cases, the problems of developing a democratic political culture can be attributed, in part, to the artificial boundaries imposed by Western powers, the support for dictatorial regimes that has been provided by some Western countries, and the vigorous suppression of democratic movements by some regimes (Bellini, 2004; Stephan & Robertson, 2003).

Huntington has also been criticized for exaggerating the similarities among the cultures within each broad civilization. The extreme zealots who wish to impose a strict interpretation of Islamic law and who support terrorism are not representative of the diversity of the Islamic world. Likewise, although there are broad similarities among the peoples of the Western world, there are also important differences in political culture both between and within particular countries.

In this chapter we will explore some aspects of political culture, focusing particularly on the political culture generally associated with Western democracies. We will also examine political participation, because a vibrant democratic political culture is often thought to be one in which citizens are actively involved in political life. Finally, we will look at the extent to which political values, attitudes, and beliefs are passed on from one generation to the next and whether important changes are occurring in the political values of contemporary societies.

POLITICAL CULTURE

POLITICAL CULTURE

The general political values, attitudes, and beliefs that are widely held within a political community.

The general political values, attitudes, and beliefs that are widely held within a political community are often referred to as its **political culture**. One way that political scientists examine political culture is through sample surveys that indicate what proportion of the public has various politically relevant attitudes.

Political culture can also be thought of as something more than the aggregate of individual views, that is, as a "collectivity's orientations and assumptions about politics" (Stewart, 2002, p. 24). Some analysts examine the literature, popular culture, symbols, myths, political institutions, constitution, and policies of a country to gain an understanding of its collective political culture (Bell, 2004). As well, political culture can be analyzed by looking at the nature of political discourse—that is, the language, meanings, and interpretations that are used in political life to discuss and make use of key terms such as democracy, freedom, and equality (Benedicto, 2004).

It is often assumed that each country has a particular political culture based on such factors as the characteristics of the population, its history, and its political experiences. However, in many countries there are different subcultures based on particular class, ethnic, linguistic, regional, gender, or generational groupings. In Canada, for example, not only are there differences between the political culture of the French-speaking people of Quebec and that of the rest of the country, but also such seemingly similar provinces as Saskatchewan and Alberta have somewhat different political cultures (Wiseman, 2001). Similarly, there are important regional differences in political culture in the United States, with the southern states, in particular, having a substantially different political culture than the rest of the country (Grabb & Curtis, 2005).

Further, as Huntington's analysis suggests, there may be general similarities among groupings of nations ("civilizations") with similar backgrounds, traditions, and religious beliefs. Others explain the general differences in political culture among the different regions of the world more in terms of different levels of socio-economic development, with more prosperous regions of the world developing the cultural values that emphasize such values as individual autonomy, self-expression, political freedom, and gender equality (Inglehart & Welzel, 2005). Finally, globalization may be fostering the development of universal values that are being adopted, to varying extents, by people throughout the world (Lane & Ersson, 2005).

Thus, while examining the political culture of particular countries is useful in helping to explain (along with other factors) the differences in politics, governing, and policies of different countries, it is worth keeping in mind that there are also important cultural similarities among various groupings of countries. As well, it is often suggested that in the contemporary world globalization and multiculturalism have resulted in both an increased spreading of certain values around the world and an increased diversity of values within many countries (Lane & Ersson, 2005).

Basic Political Values and Orientations

One way of describing the political culture of a political community is in terms of the ideological perspectives and basic values and orientations that affect the thinking and the policies of that political community. For example, some describe the political cultures of Canada and the United States as basically liberal while those of the Scandinavian countries are more social democratic. The political cultures of Western countries (particularly those influenced by Protestantism) are often described as tending to be individualistic and egalitarian while the political cultures of many Asian countries are said to be more communal or collectivist and accepting of hierarchy and authority.

FRAGMENT THEORY Louis Hartz (1964) developed an interesting theory to account for what he saw as the ideological differences between European societies and the countries colonized by the European powers. Hartz argued that as the societies of Western Europe developed from feudalism to capitalism, traditional conservative perspectives clashed with the liberal perspectives that arose among those seeking a freer society and a free-market economy. This clash between conservative and liberal views led to a synthesis in the form of socialism. The outcome, Hartz concluded, is that Western European political cultures are diverse, with conservative, liberal, and socialist perspectives all important elements of their political cultures. In countries colonized by European settlers, however, only the leading part of the mother country's political culture was carried to the new lands. In Hartz's view, the United States and Canada are basically liberal "fragments" where such values as individual freedom are predominant.

There has been considerable controversy about the application of Hartz's theory to Canada. Some point out that it ignores French Canada, which historically had a political culture that was very conservative in nature. Others suggest that the United Empire Loyalists (Americans who left the United States after its War of Independence because of their loyalty to the British Crown) brought to Canada some traditional conservative values (sometimes referred to as a "Tory touch") along with the liberal values characteristic of the American political culture.[1] This in turn made possible the later development and acceptance of an element of socialist values, which in Hartz's theory

---

[1] The majority of Americans today do not consider themselves to be "liberal." However, Hartz and others consider the American political culture to be liberal, particularly in the classical liberal sense of emphasizing individual rights and freedoms and favouring a free-market economy with a limited role for government.

require the presence of both liberal and conservative orientations (Horowitz, 1966). Thus, even though the individualistic values of liberalism are important in both Canada and the United States, liberalism is not the only significant ideological perspective in Canada. Needless to say, the idea that Canada has a "richer" political culture than the United States is popular among Canadian nationalists!

FORMATIVE EVENTS Seymour Martin Lipset (1990) used a somewhat different explanation for what he viewed as a persistent pattern of differences between the Canadian and American political cultures: the two societies were fundamentally shaped by their historical experiences. The United States was founded through revolution; while Canada's historical experience was counter-revolutionary. Canadians did not join Americans in overthrowing British rule, which resulted in a more conservative political culture in Canada.

Canadians, Lipset argued, are more concerned than Americans about maintaining law and order and are more deferential toward those in positions of authority. Canadians are also less individualistic than Americans and more willing to support collective action for the common good. Thus, he argued, Canadians are more willing to look to government to resolve problems and more willing to trust those in government. Canadian political culture also is characterized by a greater willingness than American political culture to accept and tolerate differences in society. Although Lipset viewed the Canadian political culture as more conservative than the American, he modified his analysis to note that Canadians had become more liberal than Americans in their views on social and moral issues such as abortion, homosexual rights, and decriminalization of marijuana usage. Lipset attributed this to the growing strength of conservative fundamentalist religious groups in the United States as compared to the more liberal direction taken by the major Canadian religions. Although he viewed the American political culture as including a strong belief in equality of opportunity so that individuals could advance based on their own merit, he noted that Canadians had become more willing than Americans to support government action to pursue egalitarian policies that redistribute wealth and income to the poor and disadvantaged (Lipset, 1990).

Although some aspects of Lipset's depiction of the differences between the two political cultures are valid, it is questionable whether Canadians are still generally more conservative than Americans. In addition to the changes noted by Lipset, survey research has also found that Canadians, on the whole, have become less deferential to authority than Americans (Nevitte, 1996). As well, the levels of trust and confidence in government have tended to become lower in Canada than in the United States in recent decades.

AMERICANIZATION? As this discussion indicates, political cultures can change over time. This has led to concerns that American influence, particularly through the mass media, will eventually erase the distinctiveness of Canadian

◀ Although both the Canadian and the American political cultures have changed substantially in recent decades, significant differences remain, especially where social and moral issues are concerned. For instance, the Canadian government (unlike the government of the United States) makes marijuana available for certain (very limited) medicinal purposes.

political culture. However, an analysis of changes in social and political attitudes between 1981 and 1990 found little evidence of the Americanization of Canadian values. While Canadians and Americans became somewhat more similar in their economic orientations, there was no overall pattern of convergence or divergence in political values (Nevitte, 1996). Indeed, the gap between Canadians and Americans on social values appears to be widening. For example, the proportion of Americans agreeing with the statement that "the father of the family must be master in his own house" increased from 42 percent in 1992 to 49 percent in 2000, while the proportion of Canadians agreeing with this traditional value decreased from 26 percent to 18 percent over the same period (Adams, 2003).

Democratic Political Culture

Although a democratic system requires democratic political institutions such as elections, political parties, and governments that are responsive to the people, it is most likely to be sustained if the country has a democratic political culture. Countries where democratic values are not widely held risk reverting to a non-democratic system.

At a minimum, there should be support for the basic principles of democracy. In addition to acceptance by the public and the political elites that an elected government is legitimate, the stability of a democratic system will likely be enhanced if the population has a high level of trust in government and other political institutions (Almond & Verba, 1963). A reasonable level of political interest and political knowledge could also be regarded as necessary so that citizens can participate meaningfully in political life and hold government accountable for its actions.

SUPPORT FOR DEMOCRACY A high proportion of the populations of the advanced democratic countries has a positive view of the principle of democracy. For example, about 90 percent of citizens in various advanced democracies agree that "democracy is better than other forms of government" (Dalton, 2006). However, satisfaction with the way in which democracy works in practice is not as strong. Sixty-two percent of Canadians and 64 percent of Americans said they were "very satisfied" or "somewhat satisfied" with the way that democracy works in their country, with lower levels of satisfaction in some other democratic countries (Nadeau, 2002).

Like other developed Western countries, Canada's political culture is based to a considerable extent on liberal democratic values. Most Canadians share a belief in the desirability of democracy, political freedom, individual rights, political equality, and government based on the rule of law. A consensus about general political values is, however, not always matched by a high level of support for the application of these values in practice. For example, although most Canadians support the principle of protecting civil liberties, the majority of people favour suspending civil liberties if there is a national emergency (Sniderman, Fletcher, Russell, & Tetlock, 1996). Likewise, despite a political culture based on individual rights and freedoms, few Americans opposed the stricter measures limiting rights and freedoms that were adopted after the 2001 terrorist attacks on the United States.

VIEWS OF GOVERNMENT AND POLITICIANS Public confidence and trust in government, representatives, political leaders, and political parties has declined in almost all of the advanced democratic countries in recent decades (Dalton, 2006). For example, the proportion of Canadians saying that you can trust the government in Ottawa to do what is right "most of the time" or "just about always" declined from 58 percent in 1965 to 33 percent in 1993 (Roese, 2002). A poll conducted by the Environics Research Group in 2004 found that 58 percent of Canadians had little or no confidence in their political leaders. Similarly, 59 percent of those polled said that they thought that most politicians are mainly in politics "because they want to advance their own ambitions" rather than "because they want to do something good for the country" (Canadian Broadcasting Corporation, 2004). While 93 percent of Canadians rated firefighters and 87 percent rated nurses as trustworthy, only 12 percent rated local politicians and 7 percent rated national politicians as trustworthy (IPSOS-Reid poll cited in *The Globe and Mail Online*, January 21, 2007). About three-quarters of Canadians give political leaders a low or very low rating on ethics and honesty, with a similar proportion feeling that political leaders do not tell the truth or keep their promises (Centre for Research and Information on Canada, 2002). Only about one-sixth of survey respondents in Germany, France, and Britain said that they had "a great deal" or "quite a lot" of confidence in political parties (Dalton, 2006).

The low levels of trust and confidence in government in many advanced democracies are matched by feelings that governments and politicians are not particularly responsive to the people. For example, about two-thirds of Canadians agreed with the statement that "government doesn't care what people like me think," with a similar proportion feeling they had "no say" in what government does (Clarke, Jenson, LeDuc, & Pammett, 1996; Marzolini, 2002). Nearly three-quarters of Canadians agreed that "those elected to Parliament soon lose touch with the people" (Marzolini, 2002).

What explains the general distrust of government and politicians? In some cases, political scandals and broken promises have created suspicion. However, the fact that increasing distrust is a feature of most advanced democracies suggests that other factors are also involved. Citizens have become better informed about the failures of government through the mass media and, as discussed in Chapter 8, the mass media have tended to become more critical of politicians. A more educated public has higher expectations of government, which leads to disappointment when those expectations are not fulfilled. Interestingly, it is among the more educated and younger parts of the public that the decline in trust has been greatest (Dalton, 2006). It has also been suggested that dissatisfaction is a result of the declining capacity of governments to satisfy the needs and desires of the citizenry because of the impact of globalization (Pharr, Putnam, & Dalton, 2000). In addition, the decline in trust and confidence in politicians and political institutions may be part of a general decline in deference toward authority in various forms.

Overall, although citizens have become more critical of government, political parties, and politicians, this does not seem to indicate dissatisfaction with democracy. It may, however, help to explain the increase in protest activity and an increased desire for a greater voice for citizens in decision making.

POLITICAL INTEREST AND KNOWLEDGE   Most citizens do not have a high level of interest in politics, although they pay some attention to politics, particularly during election campaigns. For example, in 2000 only 11.5 percent of Canadians said that they are "very interested" in politics and an additional 37 percent said that they were "somewhat interested." In 1999, nearly one-fifth of Germans and Americans indicated that they were "very interested" while less than one-tenth of persons in Britain, France, and Italy were very interested in politics (World Values Survey, www.worldvaluessurvey.org). About four-fifths of Canadians say that they often or sometimes discuss politics with others, read about elections in newspapers, watch television

Canadian Opinion Research Archive
www.queensu.ca/cora

World Values Survey
www.worldvaluessurvey.org

election programs, and are very or fairly interested in elections (Clarke, Jenson, LeDuc, & Pammett, 1996).

As an example of how knowledgeable people are about politics, consider that 84 percent of Canadians polled in 2004 could name Canada's prime minister. (Interestingly, 97 percent of Canadians knew who was president of the United States.) However, only 33 percent knew who the leader of the official opposition was and only 10 percent could name the minister of finance (Canadian Broadcasting Corporation, 2004). Sixty percent of Canadians would fail the test of basic knowledge about Canada that immigrants need to pass to become citizens, although 70 percent of a sample of first-generation Canadians passed (IPSOS Reid/Dominion Institute, 2007). The majority of Canadian voters do not know which party has taken a particular stand on most of the important issues during election campaigns (Fournier, 2002). Likewise, only one-third of Americans knew who their representative in the House of Representatives was and slightly more than half knew which of the two major parties was more conservative (Milner, 2002).

Take a short citizenship test
www.cbc.ca/cgi-
bin/quiz/quiz.cgi?quiz=quiz070701

Although the general level of political knowledge (and sophistication in understanding politics) may be low, most people are knowledgeable (and have a reasonably sophisticated understanding) about those political issues that they consider important to themselves personally (Elkins, 1993). Many citizens are not knowledgeable about the major political issues as defined by politicians, journalists, or academics, but rather focus on understanding the particular issues that interest or concern them. Parents, for example, will likely be more knowledgeable about the education issues that affect their children than about constitutional issues.

POLITICAL PARTICIPATION

Even though there has been increasing dissatisfaction with politicians and political parties, the majority of people generally participate in political life at least to the extent of voting in elections. On average, nearly three-quarters of adults in the established democracies vote in a national election (International Institute for Democracy and Electoral Assistance, 2007b).

Voting

Election turnouts have declined to varying extents in many democratic countries since peaking in the 1960s and 1970s (Dalton, 2006). For example, turnout in the United Kingdom dropped from 71 percent in the 1997 election to 59 percent in the 2001 election, the lowest turnout since 1918. Turnout has also declined in recent Canadian elections (see Figure 7-1). In particular, turnout in the 2008 election (58.8%) was the lowest in Canadian history. Recent elections in countries such as the United States, the United Kingdom, and France have, however, seen a reversal of this trend.

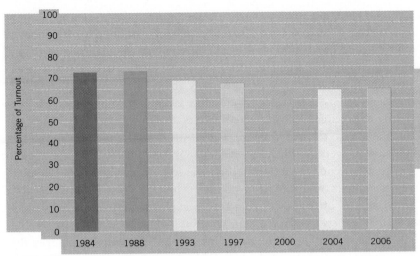

FIGURE 7-1
**TURNOUT IN RECENT
CANADIAN NATIONAL
ELECTIONS**

Notes: Turnout figures represent the total ballots cast as a percentage of electors on the voters' list. Changes in the way the voters' list is prepared and the conduct of elections make comparisons imperfect.

SOURCE: *Elections Canada,* Voter turnout at federal elections and referendums 1867–2006. *Adaptation rests with the authors. Retrieved May 27, 2007, from www.elections.ca.*

As Table 7-1 indicates, there is considerable variation among democratic countries in turnout for elections. The variation in turnout rates not only suggests that some countries have a more participatory democratic political culture, but also reflects differences in the rules governing elections and the nature of political party competition in particular countries.

TABLE 7-1
TURNOUT IN RECENT ELECTIONS, SELECTED COUNTRIES

COUNTRY	YEAR	% VOTER TURNOUT	COUNTRY	YEAR	% VOTER TURNOUT
Australia	2004	94.3	Spain	2004	75.7
Belgium	2007	91.0	Indonesia*	2004	75.2
Peru*	2006	87.7	Japan	2005	67.5
Denmark	2005	84.5	Canada	2006	64.7
Chile*	2006	84.4	Czech Republic	2006	64.5
France*	2007	84.0	Hungary	2006	64.4
Italy	2006	83.6	Russia*	2004	64.4
Brazil*	2006	83.2	United Kingdom	2005	61.4
Sweden	2006	82.0	United States*	2004	60.3
Netherlands	2006	80.4	Iran*	2005	59.8
Austria	2006	78.5	Mexico*	2006	58.6
Norway	2005	77.4	India	2004	57.7
Argentina*	2003	76.9	Nigeria*	2003	57.5
South Africa	2004	76.7	Poland*	2005	51.0
New Zealand	2005	76.6	Switzerland	2003	45.4
Greece	2004	76.6	Pakistan	2002	41.8

Notes: Turnout is in parliamentary elections, except for countries marked with an asterisk (*), where turnout is for presidential elections (second round where applicable). Several countries have compulsory voting, but only in Australia and Belgium is it strictly enforced. Turnout is calculated in terms of the proportion of registered voters, except in the United States where the calculation is based on potentially eligible voters. Some figures are unofficial.

SOURCES: *International Institute for Democracy and Electoral Assistance. Retrieved July 11, 2007, from www.idea.int/vt/index.cfm. IFES, Election guide, Retrieved July 11, 2007, from www.electionguide.org. M. McDonald, Voting age and voting-eligible population estimates and voting turnout. Retrieved from elections.gmu.edu/Voter_Turnout_2004.htm.*

EXPLANATIONS   Some countries, including Australia, Belgium, and Italy, require that all citizens vote. Where such rules are enforced through fines or other penalties, voter turnout is, not surprisingly, substantially higher than in other countries. The amount of time and effort that it takes to vote can also affect the turnout rate. For example, only about half of those of voting age cast their ballots in presidential elections in the United States. About one-quarter of potentially eligible voters are not able to vote because they do not take the time to register. Voter turnout in American elections is also substantially higher every fourth year, when there is a presidential election, than in "midterm" elections held every second year to elect members of the House of Representatives and one-third of the members of the Senate. As well, Americans are often faced with a long, complex ballot that includes candidates for a variety of national, state, and local offices, as well as various referendums and initiatives. Accessibility also affects voting rates: countries that make voting possible by mail and provide alternatives for those who will be absent on election day have substantially higher voter turnout (Blais, Massicotte, & Dobrzynska, 2003).

International Institute for Democracy and Electoral Assistance
www.idea.int

Countries using proportional representation systems of election (see Chapter 10) tend to have higher voter turnout because every vote counts in terms of determining how many representatives each party has in the legislature. In countries that use a single-member plurality system, such as Canada, many votes could be considered irrelevant, as it does not matter whether a candidate wins by one vote or twenty thousand votes. Thus, some people may not bother to vote if they think that their preferred candidate is well ahead of the other candidates or, alternatively, if they think that the candidate they support has no chance of winning.

Countries with well-organized political parties that can mobilize people to vote are also more likely to have high turnout rates. Being contacted by a party worker and persuaded to vote on election day by the party that you support increases the likelihood that you will cast a ballot. Likewise, countries where a high proportion of people have a strong attachment to a political party are more likely to have high turnout rates. The nature of party competition can also affect the level of voter turnout. If the major parties differ significantly in ideological terms or on major policy issues, a higher proportion of citizens will likely vote. Voter turnout tends to be higher in countries that feature a larger number of significant political parties because more voters may feel that there is a party that represents their particular interests or ideas. As well, voter turnout tends to be higher in elections that feature a close race among the leading parties or candidates.

Other Types of Political Participation

Only a small proportion of the public (3 percent in both Britain and the United States) is actively involved in politics through working for a party or candidate during an election (Dalton, 2006). Membership in political parties has been declining in most countries, with only about 1 to 2 percent of Canadians holding a party membership (Cross, 2004; Scarrow, 2000). However, citizen involvement in a wide variety of issue-oriented public interest groups has been increasing. For example, the proportion of Americans who said that they belonged to civic associations, environmental groups, women's groups, or peace groups increased from 6 percent in 1980 to 33 percent in 1999 (Dalton, 2006). Other countries have also seen a substantial increase in membership in such groups, although to a much lesser extent than the United States. By participating in public interest groups and social movements, citizens can try to affect government policies and promote social change. To some extent, involvement in political action groups is replacing involvement in non-political social organizations (see Box 7-1, Bowling Alone?).

Various forms of protest activity have also become more common in contemporary political life. For example, 43 percent of adults in France, 36 percent in the United States, 30 percent in Germany and Canada, and 25 percent in

BOX 7-1

Bowling Alone?

Political scientists have been concerned about the implications of an apparent decline of citizen involvement in the organizational life of their communities, but the trends are open to debate.

In his travels in the United States in the 1830s, French aristocrat Alexis de Tocqueville (1805–1859) found a high level of involvement of ordinary citizens in the direction of their communities. This, he concluded, provided a firm basis for American democracy (Tocqueville, 1835/2000). Likewise, contemporary political scientists often suggest that a vibrant civil society, in which citizens are involved in organizations that are not controlled by the state, is an important part of a democratic political culture.

In a study of the contemporary United States, Robert Putnam found that involvement in a variety of social organizations was declining. For example, membership in bowling leagues had declined sharply;

instead, people were bowling with friends or family. Putnam attributed the decline in the membership of social organizations, in part, to the individualizing effects of television viewing. Spending much of our free time watching television reduces the time available for involvement in social organizations. Declining involvement in social organizations, he argued, is leading to a decline in the vitality of democracy (Putnam, 2000).

However, there has been some dispute about whether civic involvement has declined. Even though involvement in organizations such as Scouts, parent–teacher associations, and bowling leagues has declined, membership in other organizations, such as conservation and environmental groups, has increased substantially (Dalton, 2006; Ladd, 1999). Likewise, in Canada, membership in most types of voluntary organizations has increased (Baer, Curtis, & Grabb, 2001).

Great Britain say that they have engaged in a demonstration, boycott, unofficial strike, or occupation of a building (Dalton, 2006).

Who Participates?

Young adults are less likely to vote and participate in election campaign activity than middle-aged or older voters. For example, in the 2004 Canadian election only about 39 percent of those aged eighteen to twenty-one and a half, and 35 percent of those twenty-one and a half to twenty-four voted, as compared to

BOX 7-2

Why Do So Few Young People Vote?

Studies of voting behaviour in a variety of countries have found that younger people are less likely to vote than older people.

Surveys conducted at the time of the 2000 Canadian election indicated that while most middle-aged and older people felt that they had a moral obligation to vote, this sense of duty was somewhat weaker among younger voters. Also, younger people pay less attention to elections, have less interest in politics, and have less political knowledge (Blais et al., 2002, 2004; Pammett & LeDuc, 2003). However, the lower level of voting among the young was *not* a result of a more cynical outlook on politics or a higher level of negative feelings concerning all the political parties. In fact, younger people were not more cynical than the rest of the population, and only a very small proportion of younger (and older) people had negative views about all parties (Blais et al., 2002).

To some extent, there is a tendency for people to be more likely to vote as they get older. Termed a life-cycle effect, this could be a result of becoming more connected to one's community through work, involvement in community organizations, and raising a family, as well as a result of increased interest and knowledge of politics. However, it has been found that each new group of young people reaching voting age has a lower rate of voting than did the previous group when they reached voting age. In other words, it is not just the young who are less likely to vote, but also recent generations. This generational effect suggests that as they grow older, today's younger people will still be less likely to vote than their parents and grandparents. Indeed, the generational effect is the leading factor in explaining why overall turnout rates have generally dropped in Canada, with this trend likely to continue (Blais et al., 2004).

Considerable concern has been expressed about the low level of voting among young people. Elections Canada has undertaken a variety of activities to inform young people about the process of elections and to encourage them to participate. Although the rules governing elections have been changed to make it easier for people to vote, many young people do not realize that they can vote on election day even if they are not on the official voters' list. There have also been suggestions that schools should provide more (and better) political education to encourage young people to engage in political activity and ensure that their viewpoints and interests are represented and respected in the political process.

about 75 percent of those aged fifty-eight to sixty-seven (Elections Canada, 2005).[2] Similarly 37 percent of those eighteen to twenty-four voted in the 2005 United Kingdom election compared to 75 percent of those sixty-five and older (Market and Opinion Research International poll, www.idea.int). As explained in Box 7-2, Why Do So Few Young People Vote?, both the **life cycle effect** and the **generational effect** contribute to this low level of voting. However, younger people are more likely than older people to engage in protest activities, and they participate in issue-oriented groups at almost the same rate as older persons (Dalton, 2006).

EDUCATION AND SOCIAL CLASS Political participation is also related to education and other indicators of social class such as income. That is, those with higher levels of education, higher incomes, and professional or managerial occupations are more likely to engage in various forms of political participation, including both electoral and protest activity (Dalton, 2006). However, in countries where there is a major party that represents the working class, differences in voting participation among those in different class positions are small (Verba, Nie, & Kim, 1978). One might expect that the large increase in post-secondary education enrolment in recent decades would have the effect of increasing the turnout in elections. In fact, the rate of voting participation among university graduates has declined slightly in recent elections. Voting by those with less education, however, has declined sharply, thus offsetting the increase that could be expected from the growth in post-secondary education (Blais et al., 2004).

GENDER Although politics has traditionally been thought of as a male activity, studies in Canada and other advanced democracies have found that differences between women and men in some forms of participation are quite small or non-existent (Dalton, 2006; Mishler & Clarke, 1995). For example, in both Canada and the United States, women have been very slightly more likely to vote than men in recent elections. It is in higher-level political activities, such as seeking and holding national or provincial political office (see Chapter 4, especially Table 4.1) or a top position in a political party or interest group, that women are much less likely to be involved than men.

ATTITUDES Political participation is also affected by various individual political attitudes. Those with a strong sense of attachment to a political party are more likely to vote and be involved in election campaign activities (Dalton, 2006). Those with a high level of **political efficacy**, political interest, and political knowledge are more likely to be active participants in politics.

LIFE CYCLE EFFECT
The effect on attitudes and behaviour of one's age. As a person grows older, his or her attitudes and behaviours may change due to changing circumstances (such as education, marriage, employment, and retirement) related to age.

GENERATIONAL EFFECT
The effect on attitudes and behaviour of the views of different generations that persist throughout the life cycle.

POLITICAL EFFICACY
The attitude that individuals can have an impact on politics and that government is responsive to what people want.

---

[2] Using a different methodology, one estimate is that only 22.4 percent of eighteen- to twenty-year-olds and 27.5 percent of twenty-one- to twenty-four-year-olds voted in the 2000 Canadian election (Pammett & LeDuc, 2003).

POLITICAL SOCIALIZATION AND CHANGING VALUES

Opinions about specific political issues and personalities can often change quickly. However, a person's basic political values, attitudes, and beliefs are more resistant to change. Therefore, **political socialization**, the processes by which the values, attitudes, and beliefs of the political culture are transmitted to members of the political community, is important. Socialization can provide for continuity as the values and beliefs of older generations are passed on to newer generations. As well, immigrants may want, or be encouraged, to adopt some of the values and beliefs that are prevalent in their new country.

Political socialization, however, is not always a process that ensures continuity in political thinking. Revolutionary regimes often attempt to change traditional values and beliefs by socializing young people with new values and resocializing older people. Even in non-revolutionary political systems, governments or other powerful forces may attempt to modify the political culture through deliberate socialization efforts so as to promote the legitimacy of government and other social and political institutions, develop a sense of national pride, or achieve other objectives.

Political socialization does not involve only deliberate efforts to indoctrinate people with particular values and beliefs. It often occurs in a more haphazard fashion—for example, when young people observe the discussions and actions of adults.

There are a variety of different agents of political socialization, including the family, peer groups, the educational system, the mass media, religious organizations, the military, unions, and the workplace. Although socialization is a lifelong process, it is generally assumed that many basic values and orientations are acquired at an early age. Thus, the family is likely to be a major agent of political socialization. In particular, parents are very important in shaping the religious, ethnic, and other group identities of their children. American studies in the 1950s and 1960s also found that children and young adults have a strong tendency to adopt the party identification of their parents, although later studies did not find quite as strong a tendency (Jennings & Niemi, 1968, 1981). The correspondence between parents and young adults in other political attitudes—such as political trust, political efficacy, orientations toward political participation, and opinions on public policy issues—is generally not particularly strong (Jennings, 1984; Jennings & Niemi, 1981; Mintz, 1993).

State-Directed Socialization

Countries vary in the extent to which state institutions make deliberate and vigorous efforts to promote particular political values. Revolutionary regimes such as the former Soviet Union, the People's Republic of China, and Nazi Germany devoted great efforts to socializing the young (as well as the population as a whole) into the new values associated with the revolutionary ideology. Schools,

the media, youth groups, and a variety of other organizations were required to promote "correct" values and criticize traditional values.

In liberal democracies, educational systems are often less explicitly political in terms of promoting a particular ideological perspective. Indeed, schools in many Canadian provinces provide only a limited amount of education concerning the political system. Nevertheless, schools often promote various politically relevant values and objectives.

The establishment of public educational systems in the nineteenth century was associated, in many countries, with the goal of creating a unified nation-state (Weber, 1976). In the United States, the school system was seen as a means of creating a common sense of being American among a diverse immigrant population. American values were promoted through required courses in "civics." Public education systems also served the needs of the emerging industrial system for a disciplined workforce through the practices enforced in the classroom.

In the 1960s and 1970s a more child-centred educational approach was adopted in many jurisdictions in the advanced democracies. This approach focused on developing the potential of each individual in a less structured environment. Values such as respect for differences and cultural diversity were promoted, thus coinciding with the political trend in various countries to recognize and promote multiculturalism.

In recent years this "liberal" approach to education has been challenged. Concerns about preparing for the challenges of a competitive global economy have led to a renewed emphasis on standards, testing, and basic skills such as mathematics and literacy. Concerns about "homegrown" terrorism and the integration of immigrant families with different cultural practices have led some countries such as the United Kingdom, the United States, and France to consider, and in some cases implement, educational policies that reverse the tolerant, multicultural approach of previous decades and instead promote dominant national values and patriotism (Mitchell, 2003). For example, some American states have reinstituted requirements concerning patriotic rituals such as reciting the pledge of allegiance. France, in a move directed at the large Muslim minority, has banned religious symbols and clothing including the hijab (head scarf) from schools.

The success of government-directed socialization efforts in many countries should not be exaggerated. Teachers do not necessarily follow the government-prescribed curriculum. Religious groups and the Western media brought Eastern Europeans messages that contradicted the socializing messages conveyed by the Communist party. As well, young people do not simply passively accept what they are told. When different socializing agencies provide different perspectives, young people may develop their values, attitudes, and beliefs in their own way. Thus, new generations are neither copies of older generations in their political thinking, nor do their ideas necessarily reflect the ideas of the dominant ruling groups.

Changing Value Priorities

Ronald Inglehart (1977, 1990) has suggested that modern societies are undergoing a fundamental change in value priorities. According to his **postmaterialist theory**, political socialization is affected by the conditions present when a person is young. The generations that grew up in the relative security and affluence of the Western world since the Second World War are more likely to give priority to **postmaterialist values** such as freedom of expression, participation, concern about the quality of life, and appreciation of a more beautiful environment. Earlier generations are more likely to have materialistic values such as a concern for economic growth, order, and physical security (see Box 7-3, Are You Materialist or Postmaterialist?). This is not simply a matter of being more concerned with material and security needs as one grows older. Rather, studies conducted by Inglehart and his associates have found that the increased tendency to give priority to postmaterialist values has persisted among recent generations as they grow older.

Postmaterialism, in combination with the development of a post-industrial, knowledge-based economy, greater access to higher education, and more effective means of mass communications, may be creating major changes in the

POSTMATERIALIST THEORY
A theory that modern societies are undergoing a fundamental change in value priorities because generations that grew up in the relative security and affluence of the Western world since the Second World War are more likely to give priority to postmaterialist values than to materialist values.

POSTMATERIALIST VALUES
Non-materialist values such as freedom of expression, participation, concern about the quality of life, and appreciation of a more beautiful environment.

Are You Materialist or Postmaterialist?

Read the following statement and answer the two questions to determine if you would be considered materialist or postmaterialist.

There is a lot of talk these days about what the aims of this country should be for the next ten years. Listed below are some of the goals to which different people would give top priority. If you had to choose, which one of these things would you say is the most important? Which would be the next most important?

1. Maintaining order in the nation.
2. Giving people more say in important government decisions.
3. Fighting rising prices.
4. Protecting freedom of speech.

If you chose items 1 and 3, you would be considered materialist; if you chose items 2 and 4, you would be considered postmaterialist; and if you chose a different combination, you would be categorized as mixed.

The four items on this quiz do not fully reflect all of the values associated with materialism and postmaterialism, but are often used instead of a twelve-item scale. The other postmaterialist values are: more say in work/community, more humane society, make cities/country more beautiful, and ideas count more than money. The other materialist values are: a high level of economic growth, a stable economy, fight against crime, and a strong defence (Dalton, 2006).

Adapted from the World Values Survey, www.worldvaluessurvey.com

political culture of the advanced democracies. These changes, argues Russell Dalton (2006), have resulted in a **new style of citizen politics**. This includes greater citizen activism, the questioning of authority, the development of new political parties and new social movements, the raising of new types of issues (such as issues related to the environment and gender equality), and the development of more liberal social values (for example, greater acceptance of homosexual rights). As well, the significance of traditional political divisions based on class, religion, and strength of attachments to political parties has been declining.

The extent of value change should not be exaggerated. Although an increasing proportion of people in the advanced democracies can now be considered postmaterialist in their value priorities while a smaller minority is basically materialist, the majority of the population has a mixture of materialist and postmaterialist value priorities (as indicated in Table 7-2). Materialist concerns about unemployment, economic prosperity, health care, and taxes are still often the leading political issues. Postmaterialist issues (such as concern for the environment) have been added to the political agenda, but have not transformed the conflicts and social divisions that typically affect political life. What makes postmaterialism potentially more significant is that postmaterialist priorities are particularly evident among younger generations and among those with more education.

NEW STYLE OF CITIZEN POLITICS
Changes in political culture related to postmaterialism, the development of a post-industrial, knowledge-based economy, greater access to higher education, and more effective means of mass communications. This new style includes greater activism, the questioning of authority, the development of new political parties and new social movements, the raising of new types of issues, and the development of more liberal social values.

TABLE 7-2
MATERIALIST AND POSTMATERIALIST VALUES, CANADA AND THE UNITED STATES

	CANADA			UNITED STATES	
	1982	1990	2000	1990	1999
Materialist	22.3%	11.9%	8.6%	16.4%	9.5%
Mixed	61.7	62.6	62.0	61.1	64.9
Postmaterialist	16.0	25.5	29.4	22.5	25.6
N (of respondents)	1186	1647	1882	1839	1179

SOURCE: *Calculated by the author from the World Values Surveys. Inglehart, Ronald et al. World Values Surveys 1982, 1990, 1999 and 2000 [computer file]: ICPSR version. Ann Arbor, MI: Institute for Social Research [producer], 1999. Ann Arbor, MI: Inter-university Consortium for Political and Social Research [distributor], 2003. Data retrieved from www.worldvaluessurvey. org/services/index.html on May 27, 2007. The classification is based on the questions and procedure outlined in Box 7-3, combining the first and second priorities of respondents. The questions were not asked in the 1982 United States survey.*

Summary and Conclusion

Understanding the political culture of a country can be helpful in understanding the politics and governing of a country. The dominant political values in a country will likely affect how people think and act in political life, how political institutions operate, and what kinds of policies its governments tend to adopt. The level of political participation by citizens may affect the degree to which governments are responsive to the wishes of the people. In particular, government policies are more likely to reflect the values and demands of those elements of society that are most politically active.

The political cultures of the advanced Western countries are often viewed as more liberal and individualistic than the political cultures of other parts of the world that are more collectivist and deferential to authority. Whether this is a persistent feature based on religious values (particularly Protestantism), a result of historical circumstances, or the level of socio-economic development is unclear. Within Western political cultures, there are significant differences—for example, Canada and Western Europe tend to be somewhat less individualistic and more liberal and secular in social and moral values than the United States.

Researchers have found that the democratic ideal of an interested, active, and well-informed citizenry is far from realization even in countries where democratic values and institutions have become solidly entrenched. Although there has been increasing interest in politics, a relatively small proportion of the population is highly interested in politics and follows politics closely. Despite increased education, the level of political knowledge of much of the population does not seem particularly high. Voting participation in some countries is lower than it was a couple of decades ago, although participation in citizens groups and protest activities has been increasing. Younger people, in particular, have a low (and generally declining) level of voting, which may mean that their viewpoints and interests are not given great attention in the process of political decision making. Although being active in politics does not necessarily mean that a group is influential, avoiding involvement tends to make a group invisible and politically irrelevant.

A high proportion of citizens in Western democracies say that they support democracy. However, the levels of trust and confidence in government and politicians have become rather low in a number of countries in recent times. Some analysts have argued that this indicates that there is a "crisis in democracy." Increasing demands from citizens have "overloaded" governments, in the sense that governments do not have the resources to meet all of the demands being placed on them by citizens. Dissatisfaction with government has grown, creating a potential problem of legitimacy for democratic governments (Crozier, Huntington, & Watanuki, 1975). Others argue that a more educated, postmaterialist citizenry has higher expectations of government. With increased information, citizens are more aware of what goes on in government. Citizens have become dissatisfied because of the slowness of governments to respond to their desire for more effective participation (Dalton, 2006).

Research concerning political culture and political participation raises some important issues concerning the ability of democratic countries to pursue the common good. On the one hand, the development of a more critical citizenry can be helpful in making government more responsive to the needs and preferences of citizens and in holding government accountable for its actions. The increase in active participation, particularly in citizens groups that seek the common good (or at least their version of the common good), can be viewed as a positive feature of modern, democratic politics. On the other hand, the rather low level of political knowledge among the citizenry raises questions about whether the common good can be effectively pursued through active citizen participation in politics. A tendency for voting participation to decline increases the likelihood that governments will be based on the electoral support of a minority of citizens. This may encourage politicians to be concerned with the good of only a limited part of society rather than all of the community. The low level of voting among young people is particularly troubling. If newer generations continue to find politics "boring" and pay little attention to politics (Blais et al., 2002), there may well be long-term implications for the pursuit of the common good and the quality of democracy.

Key Terms

Generational effect 163

Life cycle effect 163

New style of citizen politics 167

Political culture 152

Political efficacy 163

Political socialization 164

Postmaterialist theory 166

Postmaterialist values 166

Discussion Questions

1. Do you think that a "clash of civilizations" is inevitable?

2. Does Canada have a distinctive political culture? Are differences from American political culture likely to persist?

3. Why did you vote or not vote in the last election? Why do you think that younger voters are less likely to vote than older voters? Is voting a civic duty that all citizens have a responsibility to perform?

4. Do you have the same basic political values and beliefs as your parents, other family members, or your friends? How would you explain the similarities and differences?

5. Is a postmaterialist political culture developing? What are its implications for political life?

Further Reading

Adams, M. *Fire and ice: The United States, Canada and the myth of converging values.* Toronto: Penguin, 2003

Dalton, R.J. *Citizen politics: Public opinion and political parties in advanced industrial democracies,* 4th ed. Washington, DC: CQ Press, 2006.

Huntington, S.P. *The clash of civilizations and the remaking of world order.* New York: Simon & Schuster, 1996.

Inglehart, R., & Welzel, C. *Modernization, cultural change, and democracy: The human development sequence.* New York: Cambridge University Press, 2005.

Lipset, S.M. *Continental divide.* New York: Routledge, 1990.

Manzer, R., *Public schools and political ideas: Canadian educational policy in historical perspective.* Toronto: University of Toronto Press, 1994.

Milner, H. *Civic literacy: How informed citizens make democracy work.* Hanover, NH: University Press of New England, 2002.

Putnam, R. *Bowling alone: The collapse and revival of American community.* New York: Simon & Schuster, 2000.

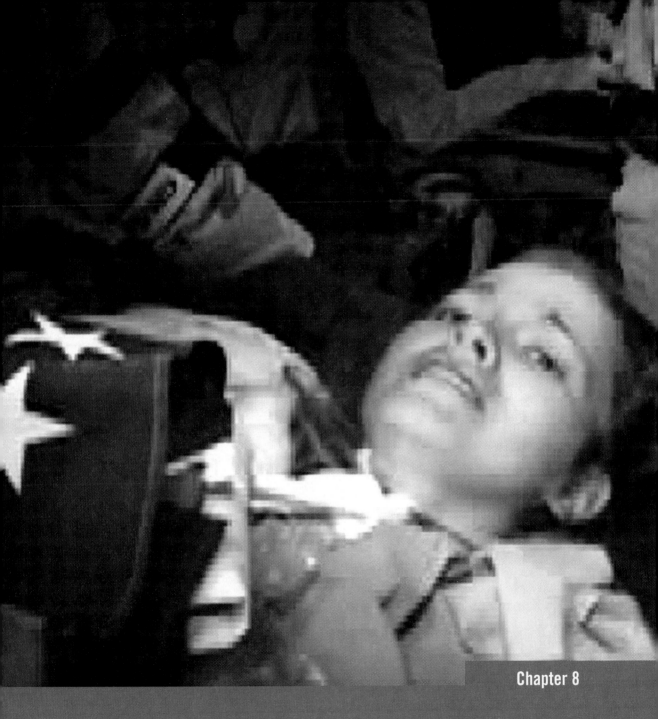

Chapter 8

POLITICS AND THE MEDIA

PHOTO ABOVE: Teenage American army supply clerk Jessica Lynch, pictured here in a video released by the Department of Defense, became a celebrity overnight when the American media set their sights on her in 2003.

Teenage American army supply clerk Jessica Lynch became a celebrity overnight when the U.S. media set their sights on her in 2003. According to reports, Lynch had resisted capture after being ambushed by Iraqi troops, had survived mistreatment in an Iraqi hospital, and then was freed in a daring rescue by American soldiers. The media showed dramatic film of the nighttime rescue, courtesy of the U.S. military. Massive media coverage turned Lynch into a heroine and reinforced the positive image of the American military. Apparently, however, there was considerable exaggeration in the story. Lynch had suffered her injuries in a vehicle accident rather than at the hands of Iraqis. She had been unable to fire at Iraqi soldiers because her rifle had jammed and was treated well in hospital. Iraqi soldiers had left the hospital before her "rescue" (Kampfner, 2003).

That was one of the highlights of media coverage during the American-led invasion of Iraq. From the initial "shock and awe" missile attacks on Baghdad to the toppling of Saddam Hussein's statue in that city twenty days later, the media provided extensive coverage of the invasion. Journalists embedded with military units reported live from the front lines. Retired military officers provided lengthy discussions of the strategies and weapons being used. The sights and sounds of war—although very little of the blood and gore—were broadcast to homes around the world.

There is an old saying that "truth is the first casualty of war." To mobilize the public to support the sacrifices of war, governments typically mount large-scale propaganda efforts trying to depict the enemy as evil. Controls are often placed on the media, not only to prevent the release of strategic details that could help the opposing forces militarily, but also to try to maintain enthusiasm at home for the war effort.

After the invasion of Iraq was officially declared to be over, the American and British media began to take a more critical stance, raising questions regarding whether they had been misled about the justification for the war. In April 2004, investigative reporter Seymour Hersh[1] published articles in New Yorker magazine documenting the abuse and torture of Iraqi prisoners by American soldiers. Although stories of abuse had been circulating for some time, they had been largely ignored by the mainstream media.

With graphic photos available and sentiment turning against continued involvement in Iraq, Hersh's story received widespread publicity. Thus, although most of the American and British mass media initially gave very little attention to critics of the invasion of Iraq and instead provided uncritical support for their governments' actions, the media did eventually adopt a more critical perspective.

In this chapter, we will examine whether the media provide us with an objective or a biased view of politics. We'll look at how effective the media are in providing the citizens with an understanding of political events, and whether the media have a major effect on the way that the public thinks about politics.

---

[1] Thirty years previously, Hersh had reported the story of an American massacre, covered up by the military, of 504 civilians at the village of My Lai during the Vietnam War.

THE COMMUNICATIONS MEDIA

Television, radio, and widely circulated newspapers are often referred to as the **mass media**. The mass media tend to reach a large audience that is not strongly differentiated by social characteristics such as class, education, gender, culture, and age. With its ability to attract even the young and the illiterate, television—particularly when there was little choice of programs—most fully exemplifies this aspect of the mass media. However, the proliferation of television channels made possible by cable and satellite television has meant that television viewership has become fragmented as new specialty channels erode the dominance of the major networks, which appeal to a general audience. Overall, just as there has been, over the past few decades, a substantial decline in daily newspaper readership, so too the proportion of people who regularly watch network news broadcasts has declined in recent times (Pfau, Houston, & Semmler, 2007).

Nevertheless, television news is still the leading source of political information for the public as a whole. For example, 52 percent of Canadians said that television was their main source of information about the 2000 election, compared to 23 percent who cited newspapers and 11 percent who mentioned radio (Blais, Gidengil, Nadeau, & Nevitte, 2002). Surveys have also found that the majority of the public rates television news as the most credible source of information (Ranney, 2001). However, the quantity of information supplied by television news is very small. A transcript of an hour-long news broadcast would fit easily on a single page of a newspaper.

A distinction can be made between the **elite media** and the mass media. The elite media consist primarily of the newspapers and magazines that are read by decision-makers in government, business, and leading social institutions as well as by those highly interested in public affairs. For example, *The Globe and Mail* and *Le Devoir* in Canada, *The New York Times* and *The Wall Street Journal* in the United States, *The Times* and the *Guardian* in Britain, and *Le Monde* in France could be considered elite media. The elite media are serious in tone, attempt to provide a comprehensive record of political and business news, and generally view themselves as speaking to a national (or occasionally an international) audience. They are more likely to influence political decision-makers than the mass media. Many newspapers imitate the authoritative tone of the elite media and are influenced by their coverage of politics, while giving more attention to the entertainment, sports, and lifestyle news needed to attract a mass audience. Tabloid newspapers like the *Toronto Sun* and sensationalist magazines like the *National Enquirer* appeal particularly to the less informed and less politically interested segment of mass population, focusing on crime, sports, celebrity gossip, and sexual titillation.

MASS MEDIA
Television, radio, and widely circulated newspapers that tend to reach a large audience that is not strongly differentiated by social characteristics.

ELITE MEDIA
The newspapers and magazines that are read by decision-makers in government, business, and leading social institutions, as well as by those highly interested in public affairs.

The Center for Media and Public Affairs
www.cmpa.com

In addition to providing news of current events, the media, to varying extents, provide in-depth treatment of selected topics. Magazines, in particular, provide feature articles that can explore the background and context of a topic. Television newsmagazine shows (for example, *60 Minutes, Dateline,* and *W5*) provide a lengthier presentation of selected topics than do news broadcasts. Newspaper columnists provide commentary on public affairs, and opinion ("op-ed") articles provide a forum for experts and advocates to state their views and proposals.

Although there are a variety of different media and media outlets, the sources of news are often quite limited. Much of what constitutes news comes from news services that collect and disseminate news stories largely from official sources such as government and police. Some newspapers and radio stations simply copy the story intact from the news service, which leads to uniformity of coverage. Canadian Press, a news service that is co-operatively owned by various media outlets, is a prime source for news in Canada, with most of its international news coming from American-based Associated Press.

Impact of the Internet

The development of the Internet has resulted in major changes in political communications. Through the Internet we are able to access easily a diversity of perspectives on politics and, through chat groups, discuss matters that interest us with people around the world. Non-governmental organizations have been able to mobilize large numbers of people for political actions through their websites and email messages. Governments and political parties can provide information to interested persons without having their message filtered through the critical lens of the mass media. The Internet has not, however, displaced the traditional media as a major source of political news—in fact, many people use their Internet connection to visit the websites of traditional media. Nevertheless, instead of the traditional pattern of reading a single newspaper or watching a particular news broadcast, those using the Internet will often access a variety of newspapers, magazines, and other media sources.

Although access to the Internet has grown rapidly, concerns have been expressed about the digital divide separating those with access from those without (Norris, 2001). People in some poorer countries have limited access to the Internet (see Table 8-1). As well, much of the content of the Internet is in English, making the Internet less useful to much of the world's population. In addition, although the Internet provides access to a wealth of political information and ideas, there are indications that it tends to be used for political information more by those who are already politically interested and knowledgeable than by those who are not, thus reinforcing the gap between those who are "information-rich" and the "information-poor" (Norris, 2000).

The Internet provides unregulated access to a diversity of perspectives. However, the Internet is used not only to inform, but also to spread lies and

TABLE 8-1
**INTERNET, TV,
AND NEWSPAPER USE,
SELECTED COUNTRIES**

COUNTRY	% INTERNET USERS (2005)	% HOUSEHOLDS WITH TELEVISION RECEIVERS (2005)	DAILY NEWSPAPER CIRCULATION (% OF POPULATION, 2000)
Bangladesh	0.3	12	N/A
Brazil	19.5	91	4.6
Canada	52.0	99	16.8
China	8.5	89	5.9
Czech Republic	47	N/A	N/A
Ethiopia	0.2	0.2	N/A
France	43.0	95	14.2
Germany	45.5	95	29.1
India	5.5	32	6.0
Indonesia	7.3	65	2.3
Italy	47.8	96	10.9
Japan	66.8	99	56.6
Mexico	18.1	93	9.4
Nigeria	3.8	26	2.5
Pakistan	6.7	47	3.9
Poland	26.2	91	10.2
Russia	15.2	98	N/A
South Korea	68.4	N/A	N/A
Sweden	76.4	94	41.0
Turkey	22.2	92	N/A
United Kingdom	62.8	N/A	32.6
United States	63.0	98	19.6

SOURCE: *This work, Table 5.11 The Information Age, was originally published by the World Bank in a volume entitled* World development indicators in 2007. *To purchase a copy of* World development indicators, *please visit www.worldbank.org/publications. Original data source: International Telecommunication Union's (ITU) World Telecommunication Development Report Database. Retrieved July 15, 2007, from http://siteresources. worldbank.org/DATASTATISTICS/RESOURCES/table5_11.pdf.*

hatred. Good journalistic practices such as checking facts and avoiding reliance on a single unverified source do not apply to the Internet. Indeed, in an attempt to stay on top of events, the mass media have sometimes reported Internet-based rumours. For example, during the American presidential primaries in 2004, the mass media gave considerable attention to the false story originating from the sleazy, Internet-based Drudge Report that Democratic candidate John Kerry had had an affair with an intern.

THE POLITICAL ROLE OF THE MASS MEDIA

In non-democratic countries, the media are generally expected to avoid any criticism of the ruling group. Publishers may be required to submit what they propose to print to government censors. Media outlets that are critical of government or spread "dangerous" ideas may be shut down and those responsible for "sedition" punished. The broadcast signals of foreign media

▶ The Internet is a communications medium that has, to a considerable extent, avoided both corporate and governmental control. Unfortunately, however, in comparison to the mainstream media, it falls short of the democratic ideal of informed discussion.

Index on Censorship
www.indexonline.org

may be jammed, Internet sites blocked, the sale of satellite dishes and short-wave radios prohibited, and those caught tuning in to foreign stations arrested. In totalitarian systems (see Chapter 19), the media are instruments of propaganda that are used systematically to promote the ideological perspective of those in control of the government and encourage the population to actively pursue ideological goals.

Ideally, in liberal democracies the media should play a major role in encouraging the free discussion of ideas, providing the information citizens need to make an informed choice in elections, and preventing abuses of power. There are, however, different perspectives concerning how well the media actually perform these roles (Siebert, Peterson, & Schramm, 1956).

Perspectives

LIBERTARIAN PERSPECTIVE ON THE MASS MEDIA
The idea that if the mass media are free from government control and regulation, individuals will be able to obtain and assess the information and ideas they want.

SOCIAL RESPONSIBILITY PERSPECTIVE ON THE MASS MEDIA
The view that the media have a responsibility to the public. Freeing the media from government regulation and control does not necessarily result in the public interest being served.

In the **libertarian perspective**, if the mass media are free from government control and regulation, individuals will be able to obtain and assess the information and ideas they want. With different ideas freely competing in the media, citizens can use their own judgment as to which ideas are good and which are bad. Freedom from government control also allows the media to hold government accountable for its actions.

The **social responsibility perspective** argues that a system of free media does not necessarily result in the public interest being served. In search of profitability, the media may resort to sensationalism rather than living up to its responsibility to be "truthful, accurate, fair, objective and relevant" and to provide a "forum for the exchange of comment and criticism" by the public (McQuail, 1994, p. 124). In this perspective, the media should be viewed as a "public trust." This does not necessarily require substantial government regulation or control, but might be achieved by such measures as adopting codes of journalistic ethics, encouraging professionalism among journalists, and establishing press councils to hear citizen complaints about the media (McQuail, 1994).

The **dominant ideology perspective** on the mass media is strongly critical. Those who hold this perspective argue that the major media in liberal democracies convey the values of the powerful and serve the interests of those who benefit from the status quo (see Box 8-1, Herman and Chomsky's Propaganda Model). Private ownership of the mass media is used to promote capitalist values and the global dominance of capitalist countries rather than to facilitate the free exchange of ideas. From the

DOMINANT IDEOLOGY PERSPECTIVE ON THE MASS MEDIA
The view that the major media convey the values of the powerful and serve the interests of those who benefit from the status quo.

BOX 8-1

Herman and Chomsky's Propaganda Model

A widely discussed version of the dominant ideology perspective is provided by Edward Herman and Noam Chomsky. They argue that "the media serve, and propagandize on behalf of, the powerful societal interests that control and finance them" (Herman & Chomsky, 2002, p. 5). Specifically, in their "propaganda model" of the mass media, they outline five filters that limit what American audiences receive (Herman & Chomsky, 2002):

- the ownership of the mass media by large media corporations
- the dependence of the mass media on advertisers
- the reliance of the mass media on government, business, and conservative think tanks for information and analysis
- the flak (negative responses or pressure) that the media receive if their presentations are received negatively by powerful groups and individuals
- the expectation that media take a strong stance against those deemed to be enemies of the United States and the American way of life

Although some of the specifics of Herman and Chomsky's analysis apply particularly to the United States, their general argument that the mass media do not challenge dominant ideological values has been applied to discussions of the media in other liberal democracies. The mass media's emphasis on conventional politics, including elections, party leadership races, and parliamentary debate, means that dissenting voices are often marginalized. Although some social movements, such as the feminist and environmental movements, have been skilful in obtaining media coverage, they do not receive the regular attention given to more conventional political organizations. As well, by focusing their attention on specific events (whether a murder, a hurricane, or the resignation of a Cabinet minister), the media often give little attention to ongoing problems such as poverty or the weak enforcement of environmental laws. The problems that the political community faces are portrayed more as a matter of individual defects or unusual circumstances, rather than as a result of the dominant values and structures of society.

dominant ideology perspective, public ownership of the mass media, guaranteed access of community groups to the media, or the development of alternative media are some possible ways in which the dominance of capitalist values might be challenged.

OWNERSHIP AND REGULATION

In liberal democracies, newspapers and other print media have usually been privately owned and free of government regulation, except for censorship related to wartime and national security. Early newspapers were often connected to a particular political party; today, a number of European newspapers continue to be associated with a party or with the Catholic Church. North American newspapers are commercially oriented operations that seek to appeal to a mass audience, although many do support a particular candidate or party on their editorial page and may exhibit an ideological tendency in the balance of opinion pieces they publish.

In many liberal democracies, there is a mixture of private and public ownership of the broadcast media (radio and television). Fears that privately owned American broadcast networks would move into Canada led to the establishment of the Canadian Broadcasting Corporation (CBC) in 1936. Although the CBC is a government-owned Crown corporation and the recipient of substantial funding from Parliament, this network is expected to be non-partisan and independent of government control. In the United States, government ownership has been avoided; television and radio are almost entirely privately owned and profit-oriented. However, in 1967 the American Congress established the non-profit, non-governmental Corporation for Public Broadcasting that is responsible for the Public Broadcasting Service (PBS) and National Public Radio (NPR). These small networks rely primarily on private and corporate donations rather than government for their funding.

Until the early 1980s, almost all television broadcasting systems in Europe were publicly owned. Since then, many countries have opened up their airwaves to privately owned stations (see Box 8-2, Italy: Television and Political Power, for one example). Nevertheless, public broadcasting is still important in almost all European countries. Generally, an independent board appointed by government controls public broadcasting. In several countries, including Germany, Sweden, and the Netherlands, broadcasting is controlled by boards representing different political parties along with business, labour, religious, women's, and other organizations (Norris, 2000).

Publicly owned broadcasting outlets tend to devote substantially more attention to public affairs than the privately owned media that focus on profitable mass entertainment (Gunther & Mughan, 2000). In some countries the state-owned media are instruments of government propaganda; in other

Italy: Television and Political Power

The Italian government used to have monopoly control of television. However, each of the three public networks was, in effect, under the control of different political parties. Oversight boards helped to ensure that the public networks were generally impartial.

A 1976 ruling by the country's Constitutional Court changed all that by opening the way for private broadcasters. By the end of the 1980s, billionaire Silvio Berlusconi had gained control of private television, with his holding company Fininvest owning the three major private networks. In 1994, as the leading Italian parties collapsed as the result of a major corruption scandal, Berlusconi led his newly formed Forza Italia party to electoral victory. While the public networks were more balanced in their coverage, Berlusconi's television networks devoted much of their campaign coverage to his party's candidates, thus contributing to the victory of Forza Italia and its allies.

Subsequently, the management of the public networks was purged and replaced by Berlusconi supporters (Marletti & Roncarolo, 2000). This did not, however, result in a consolidation of Berlusconi's power. In 1996, his centre–right coalition lost an election to a centre–left coalition. In 2001, Berlusconi returned to power and resumed efforts to influence the direction of the public television networks—while continuing to own and control the major private television networks. During the 2006 election year, Berlusconi's television network was fined four times by the independent communications authority for being biased in favour of Berlusconi's party. His coalition narrowly lost in the 2006 election but won in 2008.

Control of private television, along with expertise in media politics, undoubtedly helped Berlusconi's successful and rapid entry into politics. As well, it suggests that television may help to create a personality-oriented politics in which traditional party allegiances are of diminishing importance. However, control of the media and success in creating a popular image do not necessarily result in success in governing.

countries public broadcasters are not afraid to criticize government actions. By placing control of publicly owned media in the hands of more or less non-partisan boards, democratic countries generally avoid the heavy-handed government control of the mass media that is characteristic of most non-democratic countries.

Regulation of the Media

The broadcast media are regulated, to varying extents in different countries, by government or a government-appointed agency. The initiation of regulation of radio and television was necessitated by technical considerations. Limited bandwidth meant that regulation was needed to allocate valuable licences and prevent stations from attempting to drown out their competitors. As well, governments wanted to ensure that the news media would act in the public interest, and thus typically required that broadcasting stations allot a certain amount of time to news and public affairs programming. The broadcast media

Freedom Forum
www.freedomforum.org

have usually been required to be non-partisan and to provide balanced coverage of politics.

Despite being independent of government, the decisions of regulatory agencies can be controversial. In 2004, the decision of the Canadian Radio-television and Telecommunications Commission (CRTC) not to renew the licence of the most popular Quebec City radio station, CHOI-FM, led to a storm of protest, including a massive demonstration. The CRTC decision was prompted by complaints about the offensive comments of the morning show host (who was subsequently elected to the House of Commons as an independent) concerning women, the mentally ill, and African students. At the same time, the CRTC made a controversial decision to allow cable companies to carry Al Jazeera, the Qatar-based Arab-language television news network well known for broadcasting messages from al-Qaeda, while requiring these companies to modify or delete anything on Al Jazeera that could be considered abusive. Jewish organizations criticized Al Jazeera for propagating hatred against Jews; others worried about the precedent of requiring cable companies to act as censors. As it turned out, the CRTC requirements discouraged cable companies from carrying Al Jazeera.

There has been a trend toward reducing government regulation of the broadcast media. For example, the "Fairness Doctrine" in the United States, a policy that required broadcast outlets to devote time to important public issues and provide a "reasonable opportunity" for opposing positions to be aired, was repealed in 1987. President Ronald Reagan argued that with the large number of channels available on cable, regulation was no longer needed (Patterson, 2000).

The Internet has thus far generally avoided regulation (although some non-democratic countries including China, Iran, and Myanmar try to block access to many sites and prosecute those who post comments critical of the government). With an immense number of different sources of information and ideas, a highly decentralized structure, and the ability of any person to express and circulate his or her views, it could be viewed as the libertarian ideal.

Electronic Frontier Foundation
www.eff.org

Corporate Ownership

An important feature of the privately owned mass media is corporate ownership. Large corporations now own the majority of media outlets. There is a trend toward concentration and cross-media ownership, in which a few large corporations own a variety of different media and related industries. General Electric, Time Warner, Disney, National Amusements (through CBS and Viacom), News Corporation, Bertelsmann, and Vivendi have large holdings of television and radio networks and stations, cable TV outlets, Internet portals and websites, newspapers and magazines, as well as book publishers, music companies, film producers, theme parks, and professional sports teams. In

Canada, CTVglobemedia, CanWest Global, and Quebecor control a substantial proportion of the media.

Media outlets that are part of large corporate empires may be less likely to report on problems occurring with other firms in the corporation. As well, there may be expectations that the media will promote other products of their corporate owners. Ownership of different types of media by the same corporation reduces the diversity of the media, and may result in a reduction in the number of journalists if resources are shared among the different media owned by the same corporation.

BIAS AND OBJECTIVITY

The ownership of much of the mass media by large corporations may result in a bias toward defending and promoting the interests of big business and the values of the capitalist system. Media owners tend to be conservative and oriented to the dominant interests in society. Their choice of executives to run their media outlets will likely reflect, at least to some extent, their ideological orientation. On the other hand, as profit-oriented enterprises, media corporations will normally want to attract as large an audience as possible. This may involve avoiding taking political stances that offend segments of the public. As well, to attract large audiences, media outlets may find it necessary to allow the voices of different elements of the public to be heard.

The Campaign for Press and
Broadcasting Freedom
www.presscampaign.org

Nevertheless, a number of prominent newspaper owners have used their position to promote their political views. For example, one of the reasons that Conrad Black established the *National Post* and purchased the largest chain of newspapers in Canada was to give voice to his strongly conservative views. (Under financial pressure, he later sold most of his Canadian interests.) CanWest Global has required that its newspapers cover some news stories in a manner consistent with the views of its owners, the Asper family. As well, CanWest Global required its local newspapers to carry some editorials prepared by the head office. The company, however, backed off after considerable criticism of this directive. Fox News, part of the News Corporation's media empire, is well known for its strong right-wing bias.

Advertising Influence

The extent to which the mass media are affected by their dependence upon advertising revenue is not easy to determine. Certainly, there have been cases in which advertisers have attempted to pressure the media, particularly to avoid negative publicity. Indeed, democratic governments have, at times, used their large advertising budgets to try to stifle negative coverage. For example, in the 1980s the Newfoundland government withdrew its advertising from an independent weekly newspaper that had been strongly critical of the government's involvement in a costly, unsuccessful effort to make the foggy capital of the province a major producer of greenhouse cucumbers.

To their credit, various media outlets have, on occasion, refused to submit to advertising pressure. However, it is possible that the power of major advertisers is relevant in a more indirect way. A media outlet may think twice before investigating a story that portrays a major advertiser in a negative way. As well, television stations may shy away from producing or carrying controversial programs with which advertisers would not want to be associated. For example, in 2003 the CBS network backed off from its plan to air the docudrama *The Reagans* amid concerns that conservative groups would pressure corporations to withdraw their advertisements.

Views of Journalists

Journalists and reporters are, on the whole, less likely to be conservative than most of the owners and managers of the mass media, although the question of whether they tend to lean in a leftist or socially progressive direction is contentious (Alterman, 2003; Croteau, 1998; Miljan & Cooper, 2003). However, it should be noted that editors and producers review and sometimes change the material that journalists submit, choose what stories are to be followed, and decide what stories will appear.

Even if journalists as a whole may tend to be critical of those in positions of power, this does not necessarily apply to most prominent journalists, such as TV news anchors, who earn high salaries and are treated like celebrities. They hobnob with the rich and powerful, and are often invited to high-paying speaking engagements arranged by business leaders. This raises questions as to whether leading journalists tend to lose their detachment from power and wealth and are therefore less likely to raise the concerns of ordinary people or criticisms of the powerful.

Fairness & Accuracy in Reporting
www.fair.org

Objectivity

When an independent commercial press that appealed to the mass public was developed in North America in the late nineteenth century, journalists began to view themselves as professionals conveying the objective truth to the public. Editors expected writers to report only the facts without exaggeration, interpretation, or opinion (Hackett & Zhao, 1998). A sharp distinction was made between fact and opinion, with opinions relegated to the editorial page.

However, the "facts" do not necessarily speak for themselves. Without background and interpretation, the facts may be largely meaningless for much of the public. Indeed, since the "facts" often come from official sources, the attempt to appear objective has been viewed by some analysts as reflecting a bias in favour of the dominant political forces (Hackett & Zhao, 1998). As well, since reporting inevitably involves selectivity in deciding what to report, objectivity may be impossible to achieve fully.

Columbia Journalism Review
www.cjr.org

THE NEW OBJECTIVITY The ideal of objectivity has not disappeared but, as Robert Hackett and Yuezhi Zhao (1998) point out, it has tended to be treated in the broader sense of allowing background and interpretation, provided that reporters attempt to be impartial, fair, and balanced. For example, to achieve the appearance of fairness, reporters are expected to seek reaction to a statement by a government leader from opposition party spokespersons. When an issue is considered controversial, both sides are often presented. However, this means that complex issues may be simplified into a "pro/con" format, ignoring the reality that there may be more than two sides to an issue. The media may only find it necessary to provide balanced treatment to issues that are matters of dispute among contending political parties. And viewpoints and positions that reflect the leading values of society may go unquestioned.

The media make considerable use of experts to provide comments and some background on issues. However, because most experts come from established institutions and organizations, challenging perspectives are not likely to receive much coverage. In particular, business-supported think tanks, such as C.D. Howe Institute and the Fraser Institute in Canada, often supply many of the experts who comment on a variety of topics.

FRAMING Instead of the traditional emphasis on the facts characteristic of newspaper reporting, television news typically uses a "story" format in order to make the news more interesting. Treating a news item as a story introduces a subtle form of selectivity known as **framing**. Framing involves "selecting and highlighting some facets of events or issues, and making connections among them so as to promote a particular interpretation, evaluation, and/or solution" (Entman, 2004, p. 5). Typically, a problem is defined, the cause of the problem is identified, a moral judgment is conveyed or implied, and remedies are suggested or endorsed in order to tell a consistent story (Entman, 2004). For example, during the invasion of Iraq in 2003, the media in the United States framed the story in terms of an effort to liberate Iraqis from an evil dictator who possessed weapons of mass destruction. Alternative interpretations were largely ignored.

Not all news stories carry a complete frame, but the metaphors and images that are chosen to depict a news story affect the way the news is described by journalists and the way it is perceived by the public. For example, election campaigns are often described in terms of a horse race, with great attention being given to public opinion polls (see Box 8-3, Public Opinion Polls). Questions of which party or candidate is ahead or behind and who is gaining or dropping back are often the frame within which specific events—a speech, a debate, or a rally—are discussed. The media tend to analyze the content of a speech or party policy positions in terms of the strategies adopted by a party or candidate for gaining power, instead of examining the feasibility and implications of the party's proposals.

FRAMING
Selecting and highlighting some facets of events or issues, and making connections among them so as to promote a particular interpretation, evaluation, and/or solution.

BOX 8-3
Public Opinion Polls

"Polls [poles] are for dogs," former Prime Minister John Diefenbaker once said. Many Canadians had similar thoughts after media coverage of the 2004 election heavily featured public opinion polls that wrongly predicted a Conservative party victory.

Properly done, a poll based on a random sample (one in which each individual has an equal probability of being chosen) of one or two thousand people can usually reflect quite accurately the opinions of a large electorate. The statistical laws of probability tell us that random samples of one thousand people, for example, will be accurate within about three percentage points nineteen times out of twenty. In other words, if a poll shows the Liberal party with the support of 40 percent of the population, we can be 95 percent certain that the actual support for the party is between 37 percent and 43 percent. A larger poll will have a smaller margin of error, but there is always a slight possibility that a poll will inaccurately reflect the opinions of the population.

In the 2004 election, several polls, all commissioned by media outlets and conducted near the end of the campaign, found that the Liberal and Conservative parties were virtually tied in popular support. Projections based on these results suggested that the Conservatives would win significantly more seats than the Liberals.[*] The media highlighted this conclusion and speculated about the nature of a Conservative government. Instead, the Liberals beat the Conservatives 36.7 percent to 29.6 percent, winning one hundred and thirty-five seats versus ninety-nine for the Conservatives.

Were the polls wrong? Not necessarily. Polls only reflect opinions at a particular point in time. There are indications that in the several days between the time the polls were conducted and election day there was a shift toward the Liberal party. Indeed, the extensive reporting of the polls could have contributed to this shift: some voters, concerned that the Conservatives might win the election, might have switched their vote to the Liberals. Instead of punishing the Liberals for their perceived misdeeds in office, these voters may have decided that electing a Conservative government was too risky.

Using poll results to predict election outcomes always holds some risks. A significant proportion of survey respondents say that they are undecided or only leaning toward one party. An increasing proportion of people refuse to be interviewed for polls. Many of those who do respond to a poll end up not voting. Finally, seat projections based on poll results are prone to substantial errors because they are based on a variety of assumptions. Small changes in the popular vote, for example, can result in substantial changes in the number of seats each party wins.

It is important to be aware of the limitations of polls and how they are interpreted. Indeed, political parties have, at times, presented false or misleading reports of the polls that they have conducted. During the 1968 election campaign, for example, PC strategists circulated an imaginary set of poll results showing their party in the lead in a desperate attempt to stem the groundswell of support for the Liberal party. Although the media focus on poll results is often criticized, it has also been argued that the media attention to poll results can provide some useful information to voters. For example, by drawing attention to the possibility of a Conservative victory in 2004, the reporting of poll results may have encouraged voters to consider whether they really wanted to elect a Conservative government.

---

[*] Polls conducted by four polling firms from June 21 to 24, 2004, found the two leading parties either tied or with only an insignificant difference of 1 percent. A poll conducted by SES Research for the Parliamentary Channel did indicate a Liberal lead of 34 percent to 30 percent for the Conservatives, but little attention was given to this result.

The media typically frame politics in terms of the struggle among party leaders for power. In effect, a choice has been made to explain events and circumstances in terms of the qualities of leaders rather than in terms of broader social, economic, and political forces. This may exaggerate the power of a prime minister or president and create the impression that the leader is personally involved in all decisions. Further, the use of metaphors drawn from warfare and boxing, such as a candidate scoring a "knockout punch" in a debate, may tend to reinforce the image of politics as a male activity (Gidengil & Everitt, 2002).

THE MEDIA AND GOVERNMENT: WATCHDOG OR LAPDOG?

Watchdogs

In a liberal democracy, the media are often expected not only to provide the political information needed by the public to choose among the contending parties, but also to play a watchdog role. By bringing to public attention abuses of power or the failure of governments to deal with important problems, the media can help to check the power of government and assist citizens in pressuring government to correct problems. For example, the media played a role in helping to uncover the sponsorship scandal (involving wasteful and undocumented payments made to Liberal-connected advertising firms) that rocked the Canadian government in 2004 and 2005.

In some cases, the media dig out the abuses themselves; in others, they play the watchdog role by highlighting issues raised by the opposition parties, whistle-blowers (employees who go public when there has been wrongdoing within their organization), the Auditor General (an independent officer of Parliament), or anonymous sources within government who leak information.

Center for Investigative Reporting
www.muckraker.org

Early commercial newspapers, particularly in the United States, engaged in some sensationalist exposure of corruption (known as muckraking) in both business and government. The development of the modern watchdog role and associated investigative reporting is often associated with the Watergate scandal of the early 1970s, as discussed in Box 8-4, Watergate: An Investigative Reporting Success. The watchdog role of the media has been aided by the access-to-information laws passed by many governments in recent decades. However, investigative reporting is time-consuming and costly and thus is not generally a major feature of the media's coverage of politics.

Attack Dogs

Some critics of the mass media have argued that the contemporary mass media, particularly in the United States, have turned from watchdogs into attack dogs. The media have sometimes mounted sharp personal attacks on

BOX 8-4

Watergate: An Investigative Reporting Success

Before the 1972 American election, operatives working for Republican President Richard Nixon's re-election committee broke into the Democratic Party offices in Washington's Watergate complex. Subsequently, the president's senior staff tried to cover up these illegal activities. Investigative reporting by journalists Bob Woodward and Carl Bernstein at *The Washington Post,* aided by an anonymous high-level source nicknamed Deep Throat (the deputy director of the FBI, who revealed his identity in 2005), unravelled the story. Eventually Nixon resigned in disgrace rather than face an impeachment trial.

Although the case of Watergate shows the potential significance of the investigative role of the media, questions can be raised as to whether the media take on this role regularly and consistently. In the case of the Watergate scandal, the publisher of *The Washington Post* was willing to devote considerable resources to allow reporters to pursue the story for a lengthy period of time. President Nixon had never maintained good relations with the press and his administration's failed attempt to prevent *The New York Times* from publishing the Pentagon Papers (a secret study of the decision making that led to the Vietnam War) turned the elite media against Nixon. In other circumstances, such as in the climate of fear that followed the 2001 terrorist attacks on the United States, the media have been more reluctant to conduct investigations that might reflect negatively on government leaders.

politicians and other prominent persons. Political scientist Larry Sabato (1992) described American journalists as being like sharks, engaging in a "feeding frenzy" when they sense that a politician or a celebrity is in trouble. For example, massive media attention, national and international, was given to the arrest and trial of former football star O.J. Simpson for the alleged murder of his wife, to musician Michael Jackson for allegedly molesting children, and to celebrity Paris Hilton's jail time for alcohol-related reckless driving. Reporters competed furiously to find juicy bits of information, rumours, and gossip to embellish the stories. Similarly, the media were obsessed with American President Bill Clinton's relationship with Monica Lewinsky in the late 1990s, obscuring important national and international issues.

More generally, the media have a tendency to take an aggressive, confrontational approach to political personalities, perhaps as a reaction to the efforts of governments and political parties to try to manipulate the media (Nadeau & Giasson, 2003).

The media often scrutinize the words and actions of leading politicians, more to ridicule them than to analyze their ideas. Canadian party leaders have, for example, suffered considerable media ridicule for losing their luggage, dropping a football, wearing a wetsuit to an election campaign kickoff, and wearing a required hairnet while touring a cheese factory. The media (particularly in the

United States) have also often paid considerable attention to the personal lives of politicians: digging up or spreading gossip about their past marijuana usage, personal relationships, or sexual orientation.

Lapdogs

The prevalence of critical and negative journalism should not be exaggerated. The media can also be seen, to some extent, as lapdogs. There is often a cozy relationship between government and journalists, and much of what constitutes news originates from official sources. In the past, some politicians would hand out cash to journalists in order to encourage them to give favourable treatment to a press release. To this day, some journalists may be influenced by the hope of obtaining employment within government, receiving extra income through speech writing or ghostwriting a book for a politician, or gaining access to gather material for a popular biography of a prominent political figure.

More importantly, journalists who are viewed as sympathetic to the government are more likely to be given the inside story, an exclusive interview with a leading political figure, or a "leak" of an impending government

"I'm so glad the media keeps us informed about politics."

announcement. Even though contemporary journalists generally prefer to avoid too close a relationship with politicians, they rely on politicians and government officials for information to make sense of what is happening within government and to provide anecdotes and gossip for an interesting story. With pressure to report the news as quickly as possible and with the media trying to produce news at the lowest possible cost, journalists often lack the capability to properly research the news stories they are presenting.

Sleeping Dogs

Media watchdogs are sometimes asleep or muzzled. For example, the pattern of systematic physical, sexual, and cultural abuse of generations of Aboriginals forced to attend residential schools across Canada did not receive media scrutiny until long after the schools were closed. Likewise, in the case of physical and sexual abuse of boys by the Christian Brothers at the Mount Cashel Orphanage in St. John's, Newfoundland, the leading provincial newspaper apparently suppressed the story under influence from the hierarchy of the Catholic Church and other community leaders (Harris, 1991). American television networks have largely ignored the use of depleted uranium in U.S. military weaponry in the 2003 Iraq War, despite evidence of long-term, serious potential health consequences for both American soldiers and the Iraqi population.

Project Censored
www.projectcensored.org

Walking the Dog: News Management

Governments and politicians often try to manage the news so as to avoid gaining negative treatment. **News management**—controlling and shaping the presentation of information—includes such techniques as issuing news releases close to news deadlines so that journalists cannot check the facts or obtain critical comments. Information that reflects negatively on government is often released when a more dramatic news event is occurring, or during summer or on weekends, when many journalists are not working and audiences are small.

NEWS MANAGEMENT
The controlling and shaping of the presentation of news in order to affect the public's evaluation of news stories.

Politicians and their media advisers are often concerned with controlling the "spin" put on what they have said—that is, trying to ensure that a favourable interpretation is placed on information. For example, during a leaders' debate, "spin doctors" for each party will try to persuade journalists that their leader has won the debate and explain away any mistakes that their leader has made.

To avoid unfavourable framing of their proposals and actions, governments spend large sums of money on advertising to carry their message directly to the public. Although some government advertising is designed to increase awareness of government services and programs, governments

In April 2004, investigative reporter Seymour Hersh published articles in *The New Yorker* magazine that included pictures illustrating the abuse and torture of Iraqis in the Abu Ghraib prison. This brought to public attention the evidence of abuse that had been largely ignored by the mainstream media.

have also mounted substantial advertising campaigns to promote their perspective on particular issues, boast about their accomplishments, and present themselves in a positive light. Similarly, political parties, interest groups, public relations firms, and think tanks often supply press releases, prepared newspaper articles, and television and radio clips that are distributed to media outlets free of charge. Such stories are sometimes incorporated into the news with little or no editing—particularly by media outlets that have limited resources.

News management by government is most clearly seen in times of war and, more generally, in much of the coverage of international affairs. The mass media often see it as unpatriotic to question their government's decision to go to war and feel obliged to support their country's troops. Government officials and military leaders usually try to control the media tightly during a foreign conflict. In the case of the 2003 invasion of Iraq, discussed at the start of this chapter, only carefully selected embedded journalists were allowed into Iraq and they were restricted in what they could report. During the 1991 Gulf War (involving the United States and its allies after Iraq's conquest of Kuwait), journalists were generally confined to the American military's Central Command headquarters in Qatar, a considerable distance from the war, and thus had to rely on military briefings and images supplied by the military. Canadian government and military leaders have tried to suppress information about the alleged torture by some authorities in Afghanistan of captured insurgents handed over to them by Canadian troops.

THE MEDIA AND DEMOCRACY

Debate exists about whether the mass media provide the political information that is needed for people to participate meaningfully in political life, make intelligent choices among parties and candidates, and hold those in public office accountable for their actions. Citizens require not only a set of facts, but also sufficient background and explanations and diverse opinions about what should be done in order to make sense of political issues.

The growth of the communications media in recent decades has greatly increased the amount of political information that is potentially available to the public. Someone addicted to politics could spend every waking hour following politics in the media. However, criticisms are often raised about the quality of information that the ordinary person obtains, particularly through televised news broadcasts.

Infotainment

INFOTAINMENT
The merging of information and entertainment in news and public affairs programming of the mass media, particularly television.

The mass media need to attract large audiences to be profitable—or, in the case of publicly owned media, to justify the costs of government subsidies. This typically encourages the mass media, particularly television, to focus on providing entertainment to their audiences. Not only may this mean that news and public affairs programming is given limited resources, it can also result in the merging of information with entertainment. This combination, labelled **infotainment**, is particularly evident in television, in part because of the characteristics of the medium (Taras, 1990). Television newscasts often focus on stories that can be portrayed with dramatic images. As the cynical saying about television news puts it, "If it bleeds, it leads."

For example, Arthur Kent, the Canadian-born journalist who reported on the 1991 Gulf War for the American television network NBC, was critical of NBC and other networks for refusing to run serious stories about foreign affairs. Kent was fired as a result of his outspoken criticisms. However, during his successful lawsuit against NBC, network executives testified that news coverage was affected by a concern to broadcast entertaining stories (Kent, 1996).

Stories that can be portrayed in terms of conflict and controversy receive the most attention. News items have become increasingly short to discourage bored viewers from switching to a different channel. Statements and comments by politicians, experts, or ordinary people are edited to a single, snappy sound bite lasting a few seconds. It is obviously difficult, if not impossible, to explain an issue meaningfully in the sixty seconds that may be allotted for a television news story. Television news thus tends to be simplistic, and does not generally provide the context or historical background needed to understand the events that it portrays (Postman, 1985).

Are criticisms of the media exaggerated? There is little doubt that the media emphasize the immediate and the dramatic. Leaders, the competition for power, and public opinion polls are usually given greater attention during election campaigns than the analysis of issues and party platforms. Nevertheless, the media do often play a valuable role by pointing out the inconsistencies in the platforms of political parties and the exaggerations and distortions that are common in the rhetoric of those involved in politics. And by investigating important problems such as poverty, pollution, and the quality of the health care system, the media can draw attention to the need for action.

THE EFFECTS OF THE MEDIA ON THE PUBLIC

Do the mass media have a strong effect on the political attitudes, opinions, and behaviour of the public? Many early researchers viewed the media as having direct and strong effects on the mass public. This **hypodermic model** saw the public as gullible and at the mercy of the communications media. For example, the German Nazis were thought to have stirred up emotions and expanded their support through dramatic films such as Leni Riefenstahl's documentary of the Nazi rally at Nuremberg, *The Triumph of the Will* (1934).

HYPODERMIC MODEL
The view that the messages conveyed by the mass media have a direct effect on the attitudes, opinions, and behaviour of the public.

The first major systematic studies of media effects in the 1940s and 1950s, however, came to the opposite conclusion. Studies of voting behaviour in the United States found that exposure to election campaigns in the media had little effect on voters. Voters tended to vote in accordance with their social characteristics and long-standing ties to a political party rather than being affected by the mass media or the election campaign. Voters tended to pay attention to and remember only messages that came from the candidate or party that they supported. They also tended to misperceive any messages regarding their favoured party or candidate that were not consistent with their own viewpoints. Furthermore, the ideas and opinions presented in the media were often filtered through opinion leaders within each group rather than directly influencing the public as a whole.

Minimal Effects Model

A **minimal effects model** of media influence was developed to explain the lack of substantial media effects on the public. Through selective attention and selective perception, individuals filtered out messages that might cause them to change their attitudes and behaviour. The effect of messages conveyed through the media is primarily to reinforce existing attitudes. Messages carried through the media might have some success in mobilizing

MINIMAL EFFECTS MODEL
Through selective attention and selective perception, individuals filter out messages that might cause them to change their attitudes and behaviour. The effect of messages conveyed through the media is primarily to reinforce existing attitudes.

those who supported a candidate to vote, but would be unlikely to change a person's mind as to which candidate to support. Persons with little knowledge or interest in politics might be affected by persuasive communications. However, such persons are less likely to make use of the media to follow politics and less likely to vote.

Studies in the past few decades have suggested that the media can in some ways have important effects on the public. Because social characteristics and partisanship have generally been of declining significance in affecting voting behaviour, messages in support of different parties and candidates are more likely to receive attention and potentially have an effect on voters. Likewise, because an increased proportion of citizens make their voting decision during an election campaign, more people may be susceptible to the influence of the media during campaigns than in the past.

Agenda-Setting

AGENDA-SETTING EFFECT
The effect of the media on what the public thinks are the key issues or political priorities at a particular point in time.

Communications researchers suggest that the media may not necessarily be able to affect what people think (that is, their attitudes, beliefs, and opinions), but can affect what they think about (that is, what they consider important). In other words, the media have an important **agenda-setting effect**—they can affect what the public thinks are the key issues or political priorities at a particular point in time. By raising and emphasizing a particular issue, the media can make that issue important in the minds of the public. For example, although famines in Ethiopia are a regular occurrence, the considerable attention given by the mass media to the Ethiopian famine in 1984–85, particularly through pictures of starving children, temporarily made this issue, which few had been aware of, the subject of considerable public interest and concern (Bosso, 1989). Donations poured into relief agencies, and politicians were expected by the public to respond to the crisis. When media attention to the issue faded, famine relief dropped off the political agenda, even though the problem of famine remained.

There are limits to the agenda-setting effect of the media. For example, despite the massive attention the Canadian media gave to the constitutional "crisis" of the 1980s, it did not become a major issue for most Canadians. The agenda-setting effect is strongest when the media raise issues that directly touch the lives of people or are issues that people can relate to.

Although the media sometimes raise issues that would otherwise be ignored, the media often follow the political agenda set by politicians, political parties, and other authoritative sources. During election campaigns, for example, it is the issues and controversies raised by the leading parties that are typically the subject of media attention, even though they may not be the problems that the public is most concerned about. Those who have a critical perspective on the media point out that there are a variety of important issues that receive little or no attention from the media.

Judgment Criteria

The mass media also have the potential capability to affect the criteria by which people judge political events and personalities (termed **priming**). Topics that are emphasized in television news broadcasts can influence how voters decide which candidate or party to support (Iyengar & Kinder, 1987). If, for example, party A is viewed by most voters as the most competent to handle economic issues while party B is viewed as the most competent to handle social issues, a focus on social issues by the media may encourage people to base their evaluations of the parties more on social issues than on economic issues. This may in turn increase the electoral support for party B, even if the evaluations of each of the parties' competence to deal with economic and social issues did not change. Likewise, by drawing attention to particular character traits of political figures, the media can influence perceptions of politicians, particularly new political figures who have not developed a clear image in the minds of the public.

PRIMING
The potential capability of the media to affect the criteria by which people judge political events and personalities.

Other Effects

Finally, it should be noted that research supporting the minimal effects model often focuses on the effects of political communication in changing attitudes in the context of an election campaign. During an election campaign, the public is subject to a variety of conflicting messages and people are more likely to be skeptical of what they read, hear, or view. Some studies have suggested that messages not directly related to partisan politics can change the opinions, attitudes, beliefs, and values of the public. For example, an American study found that a specially designed thirty-minute television show was able to change public attitudes in an egalitarian and environmentalist direction (Ball-Rokeach, Rokeach, & Grube, 1984).

The mass media may also have subtle, long-term effects that are not easily detected by researchers. For example, a number of media critics have argued that the tendency of the mass media to treat politics in a negative way has led to cynicism and passivity on the part of citizens, a sense that politics is a nasty business that we can't do anything about. The increasingly negative tone of media coverage of politics in North America in recent decades has resulted, in this view, in the decline of trust in politicians and political parties and in a decline in voting participation (Cappella & Jamieson, 1997; Robinson, 1976). However, researchers have found that those who are heavier users of the political content of the media are more likely to have higher levels of political trust and to involve themselves in election campaigns than those who do not use the media to follow politics (Norris, 2000). Indeed, it may be argued that investigative reporting and the increased willingness of the media to question the actions of those with political power may have encouraged the public to analyze critically what goes on in political life and to act to try to rectify problems and injustices. In other words, a critical media can encourage citizen action while a media that is simply negative toward politics may result in passivity.

Summary and Conclusion

The communications media play a central role in modern politics. Political activity, whether an election campaign, a debate in the House of Commons, or a protest demonstration, is conducted with a concern for gaining favourable media coverage. Journalists raise or highlight many of the issues that become subjects of political discussion and action. Through their description and definition of political issues, the media may affect thinking about how issues should be resolved. The information and ideas that are used to make sense of politics often come to us from the media. Although empirical research has discounted the idea that the media have a powerful effect in changing political attitudes, it is possible that the media have a subtle, long-term influence on the way people think about politics.

The political information that we receive from the communications media is a result of a complex set of forces. The personal views and corporate interests of the owners of the media, the views and professional values of journalists, the influence of advertisers, the need to attract and maintain an audience, government regulations, the efforts of spin doctors to manage the news, and the characteristics of the different media all affect the presentation of political information.

The libertarian perspective holds that freedom of the communication media from government control and regulation results in the availability of a diversity of viewpoints. Through the competition of ideas, truth will tend to prevail over falsehood and thus the common good will be promoted. A free media system can also bring abuses of power and the problems in society to public attention, allowing people to hold government accountable and to make informed political decisions.

Governments in the advanced democracies have tended to move away from government ownership and regulation of the media. However, the concentration of corporate ownership reduces media diversity, and media freedom does not guarantee that all opinions are

fully and equally presented. As media commentator A.J. Liebling stated many years ago, "Freedom of the press belongs to the man who owns one."

Critics of the contemporary mass media often argue that citizens are not provided with the political information and diverse viewpoints needed in a meaningful democracy. To maximize profitability, the media tend to focus on entertainment and to trivialize politics. To promote the common good, the social responsibility perspective suggests that the media should view itself as a public trust with the responsibility to provide accurate information and the differing opinions that citizens need to be well-informed participants in a democracy.

The media do, to varying extents, try to inform the public, provide objective information, and present differing viewpoints on public issues. And the media in the advanced democracies have shown an interest in holding governments accountable by publicizing government mistakes and wrongdoing. To some extent, the media have accepted an obligation for social responsibility by adopting codes of journalistic ethics, encouraging professionalism among journalists, and establishing press councils to hear citizens' complaints. However, the average media consumer, particularly those dependent on television news for much of their political information, may not receive adequate information to make informed judgments.

The dilemma that the social responsibility perspective faces is that it may not be realistic to expect large media corporations to act in a socially responsible way if that interferes with the need to attract large audiences who may generally be more interested in entertainment than political analysis. However, the alternative of greater government regulation or control of the media may result in the stifling of the free expression of opinions and create pressure to conform to government's viewpoints.

The dominant ideology perspective views the media as presenting the viewpoints and serving the interests of the privileged and powerful. Corporate ownership of the major media tends to give a conservative orientation to the media that is favourable to the interests of big business and the capitalist state. However, even if the owners and top executives of many media outlets have a conservative orientation, many journalists have a different perspective than their bosses. Although the media do tend to reflect the basic orientation of their country's government to international politics, there are often limits to their "cheerleading" role. For example, the American media initially gave almost unquestioned support to their government's military involvement in Vietnam and Iraq, but gradually adopted a more critical stance.

Key Terms

Agenda-setting effect 192

Dominant ideology perspective on the mass media 177

Elite media 173

Framing 183

Hypodermic model 191

Infotainment 190

Libertarian perspective on the mass media 176

Mass media 173

Minimal effects model 191

News management 188

Priming 193

Social responsibility perspective on the mass media 176

Discussion Questions

1. Do the mass media provide you with a good, unbiased understanding of political events?

2. Should there be more or less government ownership and regulation of the mass media?

3. How would you rate the performance of the Canadian mass media in terms of helping to achieve democratic ideals?

4. Does the Internet provide a means to overcome the problems of the mass media?

5. Do you think that the mass media have a greater effect on the way that people think about politics than other influences?

Further Reading

Boehlert, E. *Lapdogs: How the press rolled over for Bush.* New York: Free Press, 2006.

Fox, B. *Spinwars: Politics and new media.* Toronto: Key Porter, 1999.

Hallin, D.C., & Mancini, P. *Comparing media systems: Three models of media and politics.* Cambridge, UK: Cambridge University Press, 2004.

Herman, E.S., & Chomsky, N. *Manufacturing consent,* updated ed. New York: Pantheon Books, 2002.

Kurtz, H. *Spin cycle: Inside the Clinton propaganda machine.* London: Pan, 1998.

Nesbitt-Larking, P. *Politics, society, and the media: Canadian perspectives.* Peterborough, ON: Broadview, 2001.

Pfau, M., Houston, J.B., & Semmler, S.M. *Mediating the vote: The changing media landscape in U.S. presidential campaigns.* Lanham, MD: Rowman & Littlefield, 2007.

Skinner, D., Compton, J.R., & Gasher, M. (Eds.). *Converging media, diverging politics: A political economy of news media in the United States and Canada.* Lanham, MD: Lexington Books, 2005.

Taras, D. *Power and betrayal in the Canadian media,* updated ed. Peterborough, ON: Broadview, 2001.

Chapter 9

POLITICAL PARTIES

PHOTO ABOVE: During the 2003 Progressive Conservative party leadership convention, Nova Scotia MP Peter McKay initially emerged as a front-runner, but after the third ballot he was still short of the votes needed to win. In exchange for a written promise from McKay that the PCs would not merge with the Canadian Alliance, third-place candidate David Orchard agreed to ask his followers to vote for McKay, who then easily won the fourth ballot.

CHAPTER OBJECTIVES

After reading this chapter you should be able to:

1. distinguish among different types of political parties
2. explain the significance of parties
3. evaluate the methods used for choosing party leaders
4. outline the characteristics of the major Canadian

parties and the changing nature of the Canadian party system

5. assess the argument that parties are in decline and discuss the implications of the changing role of political parties

The May 2003 leadership convention of the Progressive Conservative (PC) party of Canada would turn out to be its last. Nova Scotia MP Peter McKay was the front-runner, but after the third ballot he was still short of the 50 percent of votes needed to win. In exchange for a written promise from McKay that the PCs would not merge with the Canadian Alliance, third-place candidate David Orchard agreed to ask his followers to vote for McKay, who then easily won on the fourth ballot. Several months later, however, McKay, fearing that the PC party would be wiped out in an election, allowed merger talks with the Alliance to proceed. In December 2003, the PC party was dissolved and a new Conservative party—dominated by the Canadian Alliance—was established.

The PC party (known as the Conservative party before 1942) had a long-established history—it was founded by Canada's first prime minister, Sir John A. Macdonald. Macdonald's Conservatives dominated Canadian politics in the nineteenth century, but were less successful in the twentieth century, in part because of their difficulty in appealing to Quebecers. This changed in the 1980s, when PC leader Brian Mulroney achieved remarkable success in reversing the twentieth-century Liberal dominance of Quebec. However, regional tensions resulted in many Quebecers and Western Canadians switching to new parties (the Bloc Québécois and the Reform Party) that more strongly represented their particular interests and viewpoints. By the end of the 1993 election campaign, the PC party had just two seats in the House of Commons. The Reform party, which represented the New Right ideology as well as the concerns of Western Canada, was the second-largest party in the House by 1997. However, it had little success

in gaining representation outside of Western Canada. With the right-wing vote split between the Reformers and PCs, the Liberals regained their domination of national politics. In 2000, an attempt to unite the right under the Canadian Alliance banner foundered. Eventually, though, members of both parties voted in favour of a merger, though a number of prominent members of the PC party refused to join the new Conservative party. The new party, headed by former Alliance leader Stephen Harper, defeated the Liberal party in the 2006 election. Peter McKay was rewarded with the position of foreign affairs minister in the Conservative minority government. In 2007, he became national defence minister.

In this chapter, we examine the development of political parties and how they are organized. We will also discuss the importance of political parties and the extent to which joining a party provides the ordinary person with an opportunity to affect the governing of their political community.

THE IMPORTANCE OF POLITICAL PARTIES

Political parties play a crucial role in elections: they recruit candidates, organize election campaigns, and present alternatives to the electorate. In addition, parties in democratic and many non-democratic countries have a central role in legislative bodies, and in governing. In parliamentary systems, for example, members of one party (or a coalition of parties) comprise the political executive (prime minister and Cabinet) and control the legislature. By electing their members to leading public offices, political parties provide direction for the governing of a political community. Parties that are not involved in governing, the opposition parties, are important in voicing criticisms of the government, holding the government accountable for its actions, raising public concerns that have not been adequately dealt with by the government, and developing themselves as an alternative to the governing party.

Political parties are also important in representing the different interests or viewpoints of various groups of voters. By voting for or against the governing party, voters can hold the government accountable for its actions or inactions. In addition, parties can provide an important vehicle for citizens to involve themselves in various aspects of politics.

POLITICAL PARTIES
Organizations that have a central role in the competition for political power in legislative bodies, and in governing.

THE ORIGINS AND DEVELOPMENT OF POLITICAL PARTIES

Cadre Parties and Mass Parties

A classic study of political parties by Maurice Duverger (1964) made a distinction between two basic party types, cadre parties[1] and mass parties, based on their origins and organizational structures.

Legislative bodies have always had factions composed of individual members with similar interests and perspectives. **Cadre parties** generally emerged from these factions as the right to vote started to broaden and members of factions found it useful to develop some sort of organization to assist members in being elected and re-elected. These organizations involved local "notables" (that is, the local elite) who had the prestige and financial resources to support a party's candidate. Party organizations tended to be small, without much in the way of formal organizational structures. The party outside of Parliament typically consisted of a loose network of these elite-based constituency associations.

CADRE PARTY
A loosely organized party established by members of a legislative body with the support of local notables concerned with electing members of the party to legislative bodies, rather than building a strong, centralized, membership-based organization outside of the legislature.

---

[1] The term *cadre* may be confusing. As used by Duverger (1964), it refers to the control of the party by an elite group. Unlike a revolutionary cadre, cadre parties are not characterized by a strong ideological commitment. And unlike a military cadre, the leaders of a cadre party do not typically control a highly disciplined and highly centralized organization.

PARLIAMENTARY PARTY
The organization of a political party's members who have seats in Parliament.

MASS PARTY
A party that draws its support from a regular dues-paying membership and features a strong party organization outside of the legislature.

PARTY CONVENTION
A meeting of delegates from party constituency associations as well as the party's legislators and party officials.

EXTRAPARLIAMENTARY PARTY
A political party organization outside of Parliament.

IRON LAW OF OLIGARCHY
A generalization that claims that all organizations, even those that appear democratic, inevitably become dominated by a small group of leaders.

Cadre parties are concerned basically with electing members of the party to legislative bodies, rather than building a strong, centralized, membership-based organization outside of the legislature. This leaves the **parliamentary party** and its leadership relatively free to take positions in Parliament and government as they see fit. A cadre party thus provides a limited link between the people and the government.

The **mass party** developed around the end of the nineteenth century and the start of the twentieth century as a large proportion of the population gained the right to vote. Socialist and Labour parties were formed out of working-class movements seeking to challenge the elite domination of political life. Other mass parties were formed in some countries based on nationalist movements, farmers' movements, and religious movements. Unlike the cadre parties that were largely internally created within legislatures, the mass parties were generally externally created to represent major sections of the newly enfranchised population such as the working class. Because many of these parties did not have the support of the wealthy, they generally tried to develop a large membership base that supported the party by regularly paying a small membership fee.

Collecting fees from large numbers of people required a large organization based on a network of local branches with a central office. Democratic procedures were adopted, including regular meetings of elected delegates of the membership (**party conventions**) to approve party positions and to choose people for leadership positions in the party. Because mass parties generally developed outside of the legislature, members elected to the legislature were expected to follow the wishes of the **extraparliamentary party** (that is, the party organization outside of Parliament). As well, mass parties typically sought to penetrate and associate with various social groups such as unions and religious organizations (Gunther & Diamond, 2001). Generally, mass parties attempted to involve their members on a regular basis and to educate their members concerning their party's perspective (Ware, 1987). In some countries this involved running newspapers, sponsoring sports teams, and organizing the lives of their members through recreational and social activities.

Mass parties generally have a stronger link between citizens and political leaders than do cadre parties. Analysts of mass parties have noted, however, that power tends to be concentrated in the party officials (those with paid positions within the party organization) rather than in the ordinary members of the extraparliamentary party. Based on his observation in the early twentieth century of the German Social Democratic party (a classic example of a mass party), Robert Michels (1911/1962) developed what he termed the **iron law of oligarchy**. This generalization claims that all organizations, even those that appear democratic, inevitably become dominated by a small group of leaders.

CHANGES As mass parties in a number of countries succeeded in developing large, membership-based organizations, cadre parties eventually found it necessary to respond to this challenge by developing regular membership-based organizations and adopting some of the democratic procedures pioneered by mass parties. Nevertheless, traces of the difference still remain. Parties with cadre origins often consider the party leadership as the final determinant of party positions and tend to rely more than other parties on financing from business and the wealthy. In contrast, parties with mass origins typically place the authority to approve policy positions in the hands of a party convention and tend to involve their members more in policy development.

In recent decades, the development of modern election campaign techniques, such as the use of television advertising and the solicitation of funds through direct mail and the Internet, has reduced the necessity of building and maintaining a large membership organization. In many countries, including Canada, parties are now funded to a considerable extent by the state. Professionals skilled in the techniques of advertising, public relations, fundraising, campaign management, and public opinion research have become increasingly important to parties in their efforts to gain political power. Mass parties, like parties with cadre origins, eventually found it necessary to make use of campaign professionals to try to appeal to a broader electorate.

Contemporary Political Parties

Most major political parties today are often described as **electoral–professional parties** (Panebianco, 1988). Such parties are electoral in that their dominant concern is winning elections, and professional in their reliance on experts to market their party to the electorate. These parties will mobilize substantial numbers of supporters during an election campaign (and usually when leaders and candidates are being chosen), but will tend to shrink to a small number of active members at other times.

CATCH-ALL PARTIES Even if most significant contemporary political parties can be described as basically electoral–professional, distinctions can still be made among different types of political parties. **Catch-all parties** attempt to appeal to all or almost all of the electorate. This type of party will have only a vague ideological position and will tend to shift its policy positions in response to public opinion. Election campaigns may feature appeals to the interests of a wide variety of groups combined with a focus on the personal qualities of the party's leader and candidates (Gunther & Diamond, 2001; Kirchheimer, 1996).

The term *catch-all party* originated as a way of describing the changes in many Social Democratic parties from mass parties committed to achieving socialism through the mobilization of the working class to parties that sought broader support to gain or maintain political power. However the concept can also be applied to most contemporary liberal and conservative parties. Analysts of Canadian political parties have typically used the term **brokerage party** to describe the leading parties in the sense that they have attempted to

ELECTORAL–PROFESSIONAL PARTY
A political party whose dominant concern is winning elections and that relies on professional experts to market the party to voters.

CATCH-ALL PARTY
A party that tries to appeal to all segments of the population, particularly by downplaying or abandoning its ideology and emphasizing the qualities of its leaders.

BROKERAGE PARTY
A party that attempts to find compromises to accommodate a variety of interests (particularly regional and ethnic/cultural divisions) so as to try to build broad support across the country in a non-ideological manner.

find compromises to accommodate a variety of interests (particularly regional and ethnic/cultural divisions) so as to try to build broad support across the country in a non-ideological manner.

PROGRAMMATIC PARTIES Some parties have a distinct ideological perspective or a coherent set of policy goals that are consistently followed over time. These **programmatic parties** may try to appeal to voters by offering a clearer direction for governing and being more principled than a "catch-all" party. For example, most Green parties could be considered programmatic, although they have had to accept compromises in their positions when joining coalition governments.

PERSONALISTIC PARTIES A few parties have been formed to promote the election of a particular individual as prime minister or president, particularly a leader who can claim to represent the people as a whole. The classic case of a **personalistic party** is the Gaullist party (Union pour la Nouvelle République) formed to support General Charles de Gaulle, who led the "Free French" government-in-exile during the Second World War. De Gaulle was seen as a non-partisan leader who could end the turmoil of French politics that existed for many years after the end of the war. Likewise, in Argentina, the Partido Justicialiste was formed in 1945 to support the presidential candidacy of Juan Perón and continues to be the leading party long after his death in 1974. More recently, billionaire Italian businessman and football club owner Silvio Berlusconi created his own party, Forza Italia, which successfully supported his political ambition to become prime minister.

OTHER PARTY TYPES In addition to parties that seek to win elections and form the government, there are some parties that seek to represent the interests of a particular ethnic or cultural group, nationality, or region with no intention of seeking votes from outside their segment of society. For example, the Scottish Nationalist party (which favours independence for Scotland) participates in elections for the United Kingdom Parliament contesting seats only in Scotland.

Canadian Political Parties

THE CONSERVATIVE PARTY Canada's first organized political party, the Conservatives, originated as a cadre party based on the coalition of factions that supported the union of the British North American colonies in 1867. The Ontario Tory and Quebec *Bleu* factions, supported by business and religious leaders along with some moderate members of the Reform faction, were central elements in the development of the Conservative party. With the aid of the patronage resources of government, the Conservatives became a unified party in Parliament in the 1870s (Carty, 1988). The party added the label Progressive in 1942, when John Bracken, the Liberal-Progressive premier of

---

PROGRAMMATIC PARTY
A party that has a distinct ideological perspective or a coherent set of policy goals that are consistently followed over time.

PERSONALISTIC PARTY
A party established to promote the election of a particular individual as prime minister or president.

Conservative Party of Canada
www.conservative.ca

FIGURE 9-1

THE DEVELOPMENT OF CANADIAN POLITICAL PARTIES

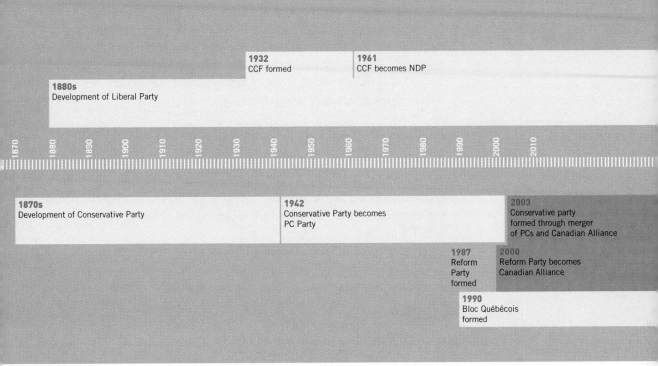

Manitoba, was selected as the party's leader.[2] As we saw at the start of the chapter, the Progressive Conservative (PC) party merged with the Canadian Alliance in 2003 to form the Conservative party (see Figure 9-1). The Canadian Alliance, in turn, was based on the Reform party founded in 1987 as a Western Canadian right-wing populist party.

The new version of the Conservative party (although less distinctive than the Reform party) favours smaller government, freer markets, closer relations with the United States, and increased provincial government power. It also advocates tax cuts and generally supports traditional social values.

THE LIBERAL PARTY The Liberal party developed out of a diverse set of factions, including Ontario Reformers (some known as the "Clear Grits"), who favoured greater democracy; the Quebec *Rouges,* who opposed the power of the Catholic Church; and Maritimers who had opposed joining Canada. By the latter part of the 1880s, the Liberal party had become a

Liberal Party of Canada
www.liberal.ca

---

[2] The Progressives, based on a farmers' protest movement, won the second-largest number of seats in the 1921 Canadian election and, under various labels, gained control of the government in several provinces. Many Progressives at the national level switched to the Liberal party, although some were involved in the formation of the Co-operative Commonwealth Federation (CCF).

unified party in Parliament. The Liberal party can be considered a cadre party in terms of its origins with an extraparliamentary party organization that was slow to develop.

Although the contemporary Liberal party can best be understood as a brokerage or catch-all party, it views itself as committed to the principles of liberalism and a defender of the 1982 Charter of Rights and Freedoms. It has also tended to distinguish itself from its key opponents in modern times by its defence of a strong central government.

THE NEW DEMOCRATIC PARTY The New Democratic Party (NDP) has its roots in the Co-operative Commonwealth Federation (CCF), which was established in 1932 by delegates from various farmer, labour, and socialist groups during the height of the Great Depression. Its limited support at the national level and weak finances led the CCF to join with the Canadian Labour Congress (the largest umbrella organization of labour unions) to form the NDP in 1961.

The NDP could be considered, at least to some extent, a programmatic party. Although the NDP has moderated its democratic socialist ideology, it tends to be distinctive in its advocacy of the welfare state and egalitarian policies. As well, it favours a higher level of government regulation of business activities and stronger environmental measures. It also generally opposes greater military involvement with the United States.

THE BLOC QUÉBÉCOIS The other major party at the national level, the Bloc Québécois, was founded in 1990 by some members of Parliament (mainly PC but also Liberal) who were upset by the opposition that had developed in English-speaking Canada to a proposed constitutional agreement, the Meech Lake Accord, that would have recognized Quebec as a distinct society. The Bloc contests seats only in Quebec and generally has a close relationship with the Parti Québécois, which represents the independence movement at the provincial level. The Bloc is a voice for Quebec nationalism and is primarily concerned with representing Quebec's interests in the Canadian House of Commons. Because the Bloc supports independence for Quebec, it has no interest in running candidates outside of the province. Like the NDP, it tends to favour social democratic policies and stronger environmental measures.

OTHER PARTIES There are also various smaller parties that regularly contest Canadian elections. These smaller parties receive very little attention and have little chance of electing members. However, by gaining more than 4 percent of the vote in the 2004 and 2006 elections and 6.8 percent of the vote in the 2008 Canadian election, the Green party could be considered a significant political party. Although distinctive in its focus on environmental issues, the Canadian Green party has become generally moderate in its policy positions.

PROVINCIAL PARTIES There are a number of different political parties at the provincial level. The creation of a new Conservative party in 2003 did not directly affect provincial politics, where Progressive Conservative parties continue to be significant in the majority of provinces. There are no formal links between the Conservative parties at the two levels. The Liberal party is a significant political party in most provinces. There are formal links between its federal and provincial wings in some provinces, but not in Quebec, Ontario, British Columbia, Alberta, and Manitoba. The NDP has close links between its federal and provincial wings except in Quebec, where the provincial party no longer exists. Among the major parties that exist exclusively at the provincial level are the Parti Québécois, the Action démocratique du Québec, the Saskatchewan Party, and the Yukon Party (the latter two replacing provincial and territorial PC parties). Elections and governing in the Northwest Territories and Nunavut do not involve political parties.

PARTY ORGANIZATION

Imagine that you decide to join a political party. Undoubtedly you would be asked to help the party elect its candidate in your constituency in the next election. As well, in addition to paying a small membership fee, you would likely be asked to make a regular donation to the party. But would your opinions and the opinions of other "ordinary" members of the party have a substantial effect on how the political community is governed? To discuss this question we need to examine the organization and operations of political parties. In particular, we need to look at the extent to which ordinary party members (those not sitting as part of a legislative or governing body) are influential in selecting the party leader and the candidates that represent the party in an election and in developing and deciding on the policy positions that the party takes.

Selecting the Party Leader

Choosing a party leader is a very important task for political parties. Not only is the leader the chief spokesperson for the party but, more importantly in a parliamentary system, the leader whose party gains the most representatives in an election usually becomes the head of government (see Chapter 15). In effect, parties choose the most powerful person in government.

Parties use several different methods to choose their leaders:

- *Selection by parliamentary party.* In the past, parties typically relied on the parliamentary party to select the leader. Such a system, unlike the alternatives discussed below, ensures that leaders have the support of their colleagues so that they can effectively lead their party in Parliament. Leaders chosen by the parliamentary party (as was the case in the Conservative party of the United Kingdom until recently) are likely to have considerable parliamentary experience, and candidates do not need financial backing to seek the leadership. Selection by the parliamentary party, however, does not provide a voice for ordinary citizens who are party members.

- *Selection at party conventions.* Party conventions allow various components of the party to participate in the election of the leader. Typically, delegates elected from each constituency, along with the party's legislators, party officials, and representatives of different associations within the party (for example, women, youth, student, and other groups), choose among leadership candidates at a convention. The standard procedure is to hold successive ballots. The candidate with the least number of votes or any candidate not receiving a certain number of votes is dropped from the ballot until one candidate has a majority of the votes cast.

  While party conventions are more representative of the party as a whole than is the parliamentary party, the choice of the convention will not necessarily reflect the choice of all party members. Delegates will tend to have a higher socio-economic position than the general membership (in part because of the costs of attending a convention), and the presence of substantial numbers of non-elected delegates may give party elites some ability to influence the results. On the positive side, delegates to a party convention are likely to be committed party members, and party conventions allow those choosing the leader to meet the candidates, hear their speeches, and discuss the merits of the candidates with other delegates. Party leadership conventions also attract considerable media attention, which can potentially boost the party's popularity.

- *Selection by direct membership vote.* In recent times, some parties have decided to choose their leader by a direct membership vote. That is, all party members have the opportunity to choose among the leadership candidates. In some ways, the direct membership vote is the most democratic way of choosing a leader. Not only does it allow each party member a direct voice in choosing a leader, but also it makes it easier for party members who cannot spend the money or devote the time to attend a leadership convention to participate in the choice. As well, the ability of candidates to perform well in an election campaign can be tested by their campaign for party leadership. On the negative side, direct membership vote systems can place the power to select a leader in the hands of those with little or no involvement or attachment to the party. During leadership campaigns, party membership often multiplies as each candidate's team aggressively tries to recruit large numbers of new party members—many of whom do not renew their membership after voting in the leadership contest. Although these problems are also evident in the election of delegates in the convention system, they can be more serious in direct membership vote systems.

COSTS   The choice of leaders by either the convention or membership vote system can be very costly for the candidates. For example, Paul Martin spent nearly $10 million to win the leadership of the Liberal party of Canada in 2003, while Sheila Copps, the only other contender to stay in the race until the end, spent about $900 000. The Conservative party in 2004 required candidates to pay a deposit of $100 000 to enter the leadership race (half was refundable). Stephen Harper, the successful Conservative candidate in 2004, reported spending of just over $2 million, while the second-place candidate, Belinda Stronach, spent about $2.5 million. The high cost of mounting a credible campaign has discouraged a number of potential candidates from contesting the leadership.

Canadian party financing law now strictly limits contributions to leadership candidates, as discussed in Box 9-1, Financing Leadership Campaigns. Although this may have the effect of reducing spending on leadership campaigns, it also means that potential candidates will have to devote considerable attention to raising funds from large numbers of donors.

BOX 9-1

Financing Leadership Campaigns

During the 2006 Liberal leadership race, reporters discovered that eleven-year-old twins had each donated $5400, the maximum individual contribution allowed under Canadian party financing law, to the campaign of Joe Volpe. The children presumably did not open their piggy banks in a demonstration of youthful political interest! Rather, because the law bans contributions by businesses and unions, the top executives of Apotex (a leading Canadian pharmaceutical company) along with their spouses and children had donated a total of $108 000 to Volpe's campaign. The embarrassed candidate returned the money to underage donors even though the donations were legal.

Other candidates (including Bob Rae, who borrowed $750 000 from his brother) were able to raise money through repayable loans that are not covered by the legislation. However, because Canadian law since 2004 has banned corporate contributions, none of the candidates raised enough money to spend the maximum of $3.4 million set by the Liberal party. Stéphane Dion reported spending $1.7 million, while second-place candidate Michael Ignatieff spent $2.2 million and Bob Rae, who ended up in third place, spent $2.3 million. Most of the candidates ended up with hundreds of thousands in outstanding loans and unpaid debts.

Changes to the law concerning party financing that came into effect in 2007 limit contributions to leadership campaigns to $1100 per person. The loophole allowing loans to candidates is being reconsidered.

▶ Not wanting to appear ageist, Joe Volpe gladly accepts donations from children too.

TRENDS Canadian parties adopted the party convention method of choosing a party leader in the first decades of the twentieth century. In recent years, many provincial parties have adopted direct membership vote systems. At the national level, recent methods of selecting a leader include the following:

- Jack Layton was chosen as the NDP leader in 2003 through votes that members could cast by mail, the Internet, or at a party convention. One-quarter of the votes were reserved for members of affiliated labour unions.
- The Liberal party used a combination of delegate convention and direct membership vote to choose Paul Martin as leader in 2003 and Stéphane Dion as leader in 2006 (see Box 9-2, The Victory of a "Dark Horse"). Party members in each constituency indicated their leadership preference. Based on this, delegates committed to supporting a particular candidate on the first ballot at the convention were selected, with requirements ensuring the selection of an equal number of female and male delegates and a certain number of young people. Delegates were also elected by Liberal student, women, seniors, and Aboriginal clubs and commissions. In addition, many persons could vote at the convention because of their executive position within the party or their role in representing the party in Parliament or as a candidate for election.

BOX 9-2

The Victory of a "Dark Horse"

Unlike the 2003 liberal leadership contest that saw Paul Martin defeat Sheila Copps with an overwhelming 94 percent of the vote, the 2006 race featured a dramatic contest among eight candidates with a surprise victory by Stéphane Dion. The front-runners in the campaign for leadership, Michael Ignatieff and Bob Rae, had the support of most of the prominent figures within the party and received most of the attention during the campaign. Interestingly, the choices of the party elites were outsiders (Ignatieff, who had been elected to Parliament earlier that year, had lived outside Canada for most of his adult life; Rae was a former NDP premier of Ontario who had only recently joined the Liberal party). By contrast, Dion, a political science professor, had served in the Liberal Cabinets of Jean Chrétien and Paul Martin, but was judged by the elite as less likely to win an election.

Ignatieff won the most votes cast by Liberal party members and led on the first ballot, with 1412 votes compared to Rae with 977 votes, Dion with 856, and Gerard Kennedy with 854 votes. Other candidates were well behind. On the second ballot, Dion increased his vote by more than Kennedy. As a result of an informal deal between these two candidates to support whichever of them was ahead, Kennedy withdrew his candidacy and publicly supported Dion. Although delegates were free to vote as they wished after the first ballot, a large majority of Kennedy's supporters voted for Dion on the third ballot, dropping Rae into third place. With Rae eliminated on the fourth ballot, Dion defeated Ignatieff by a 55 to 45 percent margin.

After the poor showing of the Liberal party in the 2008 election and the failure of Dion to replace the Harper government with a Liberal–NDP coalition government, Dion was pressured to resign immediately. Michael Ignatieff was chosen by the Liberal MPs in consultation with the party's national executive as interim leader. With no other contenders, Ignatieff was confirmed as party leader by a Liberal party convention held in spring 2009.

- The newly formed Conservative party chose Stephen Harper as leader in 2004 through a direct membership vote, with each constituency rather than each member having an equal voice in the decision.

The method chosen by the Conservatives and Liberals of giving each constituency an equal weight (either through the election of constituency delegates to a convention or through a direct membership vote system weighted by constituency) is intended to ensure that the winning leadership candidate has broad national support. However, in parts of the country where a party is weak, it can mean that a handful of party members in one constituency has the same effect on the outcome as thousands of members in a different part of the country.

A study of eighteen established democratic countries found that 44 percent of parties chose their leaders by a party convention, 24 percent by a vote of the parliamentary party, 23 percent by a vote of party members, and 10 percent by a national party committee (Scarrow, Webb, & Farrell, 2000). As in Canada, there appears to be a general tendency to include party members in the selection of a leader.

Candidate Selection

Political parties are also important in the selection of candidates for election. Very few candidates are successful in being elected unless they represent a political party. A variety of methods is used by parties in different countries to choose candidates. Some countries conduct a vote among party members or, in the case of the United States, a **primary election** involving registered voters (as discussed in Box 9-3, Primary Elections). Others have delegates representing party members make the selection. Still others appoint a candidate selection committee or rely on local or regional party officials. Generally, most of the advanced democracies involve the local or regional party organization in the selection process, with the party leader or party executive having the ability to veto the choice of candidates (Scarrow, Webb, & Farrell, 2000).

CANADIAN PROCEDURES In Canada, candidates are normally selected by a vote at a constituency party meeting or by ballot boxes set up in different locations in the rural constituencies. In a few cases, particularly where there are no formal party membership procedures, any resident of the constituency can vote. Occasionally, in some parts of the country, party executives rather than the constituency party members have chosen the candidates. In addition, the Liberal party has given its leader the power to appoint a

PRIMARY ELECTION
A state-run election in which American citizens select the candidates they want to represent their party in the general election.

BOX 9-3

Primary Elections

In the United States, primary elections are held to choose each party's candidates for election to almost all public offices. In some states only registered supporters of a party may vote in their party's primary, but other states allow voters to participate in whichever party's primary they choose. Primary elections are used in most states to choose delegates committed to support a presidential candidate at a national party convention.

The primary election system is less party-oriented than the process used in most other systems, as most citizens (whether or not they are party members) can vote to determine who the candidates will be. The adoption of this system in the United States reflected a distrust of parties and concern about the corrupt practices often associated with party "bosses." However, the primary system weakens political parties since they do not have much control over the selection of party candidates, and reinforces the tendency in American politics for legislators of each party to act independently rather than as members of a group. The primary election system provides an opportunity for those without a connection to a party to win a party's nomination if they can mount a strong public campaign. The system typically results in potential candidates having to raise large amounts of money to win a nomination, thus making successful candidates dependent on wealthy backers.

number of high-profile ("star") candidates without holding a nomination meeting. This can allow a party to improve its image by choosing respected persons from outside the party or by recruiting candidates from diverse backgrounds. However, it can cause problems within the party if the wishes of local constituency associations are ignored.

Canadian election law also gives party leaders the right to reject a candidate from representing the party—a power that has been used occasionally to overturn the choice of an embarrassing candidate by the constituency association. Nevertheless, constituency associations in Canada do generally have control of the process of nominating candidates, giving Canadian parties a more decentralized character than parties in many other countries (Carty, 2002). However, the Conservative party, like its Reform and Canadian Alliance predecessors, has adopted rigorous procedures for vetting the qualities of all potential candidates.

Although members of the constituency association usually play a key role in choosing their party's candidate, they do not generally exercise much influence over the candidate once he or she is elected. At times, party rules and procedures, written or informal, have ensured the renomination of the party's sitting members of Parliament without having to seek the support of party members in their constituency. For example, in December 2006, Liberal leader Stéphane Dion announced that all sitting Liberal MPs would be free from challenges to their renomination for the next election.

GENDER QUOTAS The constitutions or laws of fifty-seven countries (for example, France, Argentina, and Mexico) require that parties nominate a certain proportion of women as candidates. In addition, 168 political parties in 69 countries have voluntarily adopted gender quotas. However, such laws and party policies have fallen far short of achieving gender parity in parliamentary bodies (International Institute for Democracy and Electoral Assistance, 2007a).

In Canada, there are no legally established quotas for female candidates and the proportion of female candidates is rather low (see Table 9-1). Some political parties, however, have undertaken to try to ensure that more female candidates are nominated. The NDP has set an objective of having 60 percent

Bloc Québécois	26.7%
Conservative party	20.5%
Green party	29.7%
Liberal party	36.8%
New Democratic party	33.8%
Other parties/Independents	18.2%
Total	27.8%

TABLE 9-1

PERCENTAGE OF FEMALE CANDIDATES BY PARTY, 2008 CANADIAN ELECTION

SOURCE: *http://www.parl.gc.ca/information/about/process/house/hfer/ hfer.asp?Language-&Search-WomenElection.*

female candidates in "winnable" constituencies (excluding those where the incumbent is seeking re-election), and requires that constituencies prove that they have searched for one or more potential candidates who are female or from other under-represented groups before selecting a candidate. Liberal leader Stéphane Dion set an objective of having at least one-third female candidates. Such quotas or objectives, however, can reduce the ability of local party members to choose their preferred candidate.

Party Policy

As we have seen, parties with mass origins generally give formal authority to a party convention to approve the policy positions that the party is supposed to pursue, while parties with cadre origins typically view policies adopted at party conventions as only one source of advice for the leader and the party's parliamentary members. Indeed, until the 1960s, the Liberal and PC parties of Canada did not hold regular party conventions to discuss policy. Policy resolutions proposed at leadership conventions were not always thoroughly discussed, formally voted upon, carefully recorded, or made accessible. After being elected PC leader in 1956, John Diefenbaker apparently ordered the destruction of all copies of the policy resolutions adopted at the convention because they did not reflect the direction in which he wanted to take the party (Dyck, 2004).

In some parties there is vigorous debate over policy resolutions at party conventions, providing an opportunity for those active within the extra-parliamentary party organization to be involved in the discussion of party policy positions. However, the party leader and key party officials often exercise a considerable degree of control over the process of discussing and adopting resolutions at a party convention. Efforts may be made to modify or avoid a vote on resolutions that could harm a party in its attempts to gain public support. Furthermore, the election platforms of parties are typically developed by the party leader and the leader's advisers concerned with appealing to the electorate. In the legislature, the party leader and parliamentary party members often feel free to interpret party resolutions as they see fit. After their party is elected, the prime minister and Cabinet typically argue that they have to make decisions that are for the good of the political community as a whole, rather than acting in accordance with their party's policy resolutions.

Overall, then, party members are more likely to have an effective voice in candidate and leadership selection than in determining the policies that their party will pursue. Nevertheless, modern political parties do, to varying extents, involve their ordinary members in policy discussion even if control of party policy decisions rests largely in the hands of the party leadership (Scarrow, Webb, & Farrell, 2000).

Party Caucus and Party Government

Parliamentary parties are generally tightly organized. In parliamentary systems, as discussed in Chapter 15, there is a strong expectation that each party's members of Parliament will support the positions that the **party caucus** (a closed-door meeting of the party's parliamentary members) has decided to take. In particular, the party leader typically exercises considerable influence and control over the parliamentary party.

Political parties in modern parliamentary systems play a crucial role in governing. The prime minister and Cabinet are almost always members of a particular parliamentary party (or, in the case of coalition governments, members of the parties forming the coalition) and rely on the support of their parliamentary party to maintain their positions and to approve their legislative proposals. However, this does not necessarily mean that the governing party as a whole has a high level of influence on the decisions of the government. Not only are the prime minister and Cabinet crucial in making policy decisions, but they are also affected by the advice provided by the permanent employees of the government, the circumstances of their country, the pressure of interest groups, the constraints of external and global forces, and the desire to appeal to the public in order to win re-election. Nevertheless, a change in which party governs can make a difference in the actions that are taken by government.

PARTY CAUCUS
A meeting of the party's parliamentary members.

PARTY FINANCE

Parties need considerable amounts of money to finance their operations. In particular, modern election campaigns can be very costly. The financing of political parties and candidates has often been considered a major political problem. There are risks that donors will be able to buy influence through their financial support. In particular, donations may be made to a party in the hope of, or as a reward for, a government contract or other benefit. Even when such patronage is not involved, politicians may be more concerned about maintaining the support of their financial backers—often large corporations and wealthy individuals—than about acting in the public interest. As well, better-financed parties and candidates may have a strong advantage in attempting to gain the support of the electorate.

Many countries have established limits on election expenses, put restrictions on campaign advertising, provided public subsidies to parties and campaigns, and required public disclosure of significant donations. Generally, this allows for fairer competition among political parties, reduces the likelihood that undue influence will be placed on politicians, and reduces the taint of scandal and corruption that has often been associated with money in politics. Public financing systems, however, can be used to discriminate against smaller or new political parties and thus maintain the dominance of the larger, established parties. As well, the dependence of parties on public funds may reduce their incentive to maintain strong ties with their supporters (Katz & Mair, 1995).

Until 2004, there were no limits on contributions to political parties and candidates at the national level in Canada. The Liberal and PC parties relied heavily on contributions from business corporations to fund their parties and their election campaigns. The NDP derived a significant proportion of its funding from unions. Contributions by businesses and trade unions to political parties and leadership contenders were banned in 2004. In 2007, this ban was extended to candidates, nomination contestants, and constituency party associations. In addition, individuals are now limited to contributing a maximum of $1100 (indexed to inflation) per year to each of the following: political parties, other party entities (constituency associations, nomination contestants, and candidates), leadership contestants, and independent candidates.

The restrictions on contributions are offset, to a considerable extent, by payments to parties from public funds. Each year, registered political parties, except those that received a very small proportion of votes, now receive $1.75 (indexed to inflation) from the Canadian government for each vote they obtained in the previous election. As well, parties are reimbursed for 50 percent of eligible campaign expenses if they obtained 2 percent of the national vote or 5 percent in those constituencies in which they ran candidates. Candidates are reimbursed for 60 percent of their expenses if they obtain 10 percent of the vote in their constituency. There are also limits on the spending of candidates and parties in elections and nomination contests, public disclosure of contributors and expenditures, and tax credits for those who contribute to parties and candidates.

PARTY SYSTEMS

PARTY SYSTEM
The pattern of competition among political parties.

In many long-standing democratic systems, the basic pattern of competition among the major political parties—the **party system**—is relatively stable over time. We can examine the party system in two ways:

- the number of relevant political parties
- the pattern of ideological competition

Number of Relevant Parties

Every democratic country has a large number of parties, but many parties (for example, the Communist party of Canada and the Vegetarian party in the United States) have so little support that they have virtually no relevance to the competition among political parties to elect representatives and govern the country.

Determining which parties are relevant is not a simple matter. The Green party has become somewhat relevant in Canadian elections, but is still irrelevant in the House of Commons, where it has thus far had no representatives. The Bloc Québécois, on the other hand, has no intention of forming the government in Canada. However, its successes in winning seats in Quebec have affected the outcome of elections. When no party wins a majority of seats in the House of Commons, the Bloc can affect the decisions of government and its ability to remain in office. The relevance of a party thus can be considered in terms of its level of support from the electorate, its representation in a legislative body, and its significance in affecting the governing of a political community.

Party systems in democratic countries can be classified into four basic types in terms of the number of relevant parties:

- one-party dominant
- two-party
- two-plus party
- multiparty

A **one-party dominant system**[3] is one in which a single party rules for long periods of time and the opposition parties are not likely to gain the support needed to successfully challenge the dominant party for control of the government. For example, the Liberal Democratic party has governed Japan since the late 1940s, with only a temporary interruption between 1993 and 1996. The American southern states featured one-party dominance by the Democrats from the late 1870s until at least the 1960s. Alberta can be characterized as having a basically one-party dominant system at the provincial level (though with different dominant parties for lengthy periods of time) since its creation in 1905. Singapore and Botswana also have one-party dominant party systems. Typically, one party is able to be dominant in a democratic political system when the opposition to the governing party is divided among a number of parties representing different segments of the electorate.

ONE-PARTY DOMINANT SYSTEM
A party system in which a single party rules for long periods of time and the opposition parties are not likely to gain the support needed to successfully challenge the dominant party for control of the government.

◀ Japan has a one-party dominant system in which the Liberal Democratic party has governed for almost all of the time since the late 1940s. However, there have been frequent changes in the prime minister selected by the party. For example, Shinzo Abe, pictured above, resigned in September 2007 after less than one year in office.

---

[3] A one-party dominant system differs from the one-party rule characteristic of many non-democratic countries in that other parties are free to contest elections.

TWO-PARTY SYSTEM
A party system in which two major parties contend to control the government. Two-party systems are competitive in the sense that a single party does not govern for a lengthy period of time.

Two-party systems feature two major parties that contend for control of the government. Two-party systems are competitive in the sense that a single party does not govern for a lengthy period of time. Normally, one party is able to gain a clear majority of seats in the legislative body and is able to control the government. Parties other than the two major contenders for power are only of minor significance. The United States is a classic example of a two-party system, with the Democratic party, which leans somewhat in a liberal direction, and the Republican party, which leans in a conservative direction, dominating the national political scene for the past century and a half. Almost all presidents and members of Congress have been elected as Republicans or Democrats during this lengthy period of time. Other parties have challenged the dominance of the older parties, but the Democratic and Republican parties have been successful thus far in warding off these challengers.

Among the major advanced democracies there are few other examples of two-party systems. Australia, with a stable coalition between the Liberal and National parties in competition primarily with the Labour party, could be considered a two-party system. Several Canadian provinces (the Atlantic provinces other than Nova Scotia and the Western provinces other than Alberta) have basically two-party systems.

Britain is sometimes described as having a two-party system, as only the Conservative and Labour parties have formed the government since the 1920s. However, since the 1974 election, the Liberal Democratic party has gained the support of about one-sixth of the British electorate. Although its representation in the British House of Commons has been relatively small and it is not generally considered to be a serious contender for control of the government, the Liberal Democratic party plays a significant role in British politics. Thus, Britain could be considered to have a **two-plus party system**. Likewise Germany, where the major parties—the Christian Democrats and the Social Democrats—do not have sufficient representation to govern alone, can be classified as a two-plus system. At the provincial level, Ontario could be considered to have two-plus party system.

TWO-PLUS PARTY SYSTEM
A party system in which there are two major contenders for control of the government but other parties also have a significant amount of support, which may at times prevent either of the larger parties from gaining a majority of legislative seats.

MULTIPARTY SYSTEM
A political party system featuring several parties that are significant actors in the competition for political power.

Multiparty systems, the most common party system, feature several parties that are significant actors in the competition for political power. For example, almost all continental European countries have multiparty systems. Nova Scotia since 1998 has featured a close three-way contest for political power among the PCs, NDP, and Liberals. Although the 2007 Quebec election resulted in a close contest among three parties (Liberals, Parti Québécois, and Action démocratique), the 2008 Quebec election saw a sharp decline in support for the action démocratique.

Some simplification of extreme multiparty systems (that is, where a large number of parties are able to gain representation) may be obtained where parties agree to campaign and govern as a bloc. In Italy, where about twenty parties are represented in the Chamber of Deputies, most of the parties in recent times have joined either the House of Freedom coalition on the right or the L'Unione coalition on the left. This has helped to create a stable governing system by one or the other coalition. Multiparty systems typically involve coalition governments in which two or more parties agree to control the government because of the inability of any single party to regularly gain a majority of seats in the legislature.

THE CANADIAN PARTY SYSTEM Canada historically has had a two-party system; indeed, only the Liberal and Conservative (or Progressive Conservative) parties have ever held power at the national level. However, since 1921, various other parties have also been relevant in the competition for representation in the House of Commons. In eleven of the twenty-six elections from 1921 to 2008, no party was able to win a majority of seats in the House of Commons. Various parties, in addition to the Liberal and Conservative parties, have played an important role in the competition for votes and in minority government situations, thus affecting the governing of the country. The contemporary Canadian party can, therefore, be considered either a two-plus party system or a multiparty system[4] (see Figure 9-2).

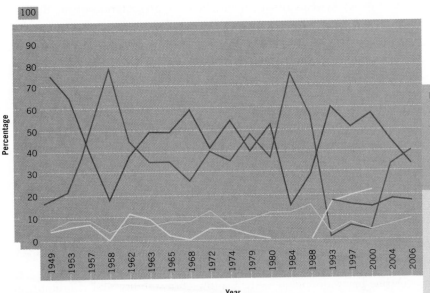

FIGURE 9-2

PARTY REPRESENTATION IN THE HOUSE OF COMMONS, 1949–2006

Legend
— Liberal
— PC and Conservative
— CCF and NDP
— Social Credit and Reform/Alliance
— Bloc Québécois

Notes: PC and Conservative was Progressive Conservative party, 1949–2000; Conservative party, 2004 and 2006. CCF and NDP was CCF, 1949–1958; NDP, 1962 onward. Social Credit and Reform/Alliance was Social Credit and Ralliement Créditiste, 1949–1980; Reform, 1988–1997; Canadian Alliance, 2000. Independents not shown.

SOURCES: *Calculated from* Party politics in Canada *(8th ed.), by H.G. Thorburn & A. Whitehorn (Eds), 2001, Toronto: Prentice-Hall; and Elections Canada (2004 and 2006), retrieved December 11, 2006, from www.elections.ca.*

[4] However, after the virtual collapse of the PC party in 1993, Canada had a one-party dominant system, as the Liberals faced no real contender for national power until the merger of the PC party and the Canadian Alliance a decade later.

STRENGTHS AND WEAKNESSES Two-party systems have the benefit of providing for stable government, as either of the major parties can usually gain a majority of seats in the legislature. This allows the winning party to implement its program and be held accountable for its actions in government. Voters can choose to keep the governing party in office or replace it with the other major party. However, in trying to gain the support of the majority of voters, the two dominant parties may end up becoming so similar in their policy positions that voters are left without a clear choice, and minority viewpoints may be poorly represented. Two-party systems tend to be highly adversarial, a struggle between the party that is in power and the party that is out of power, thus making attempts to find a consensus difficult.

Two-plus party systems can provide for greater diversity and innovation than two-party systems. Smaller parties can be a source of new ideas and different perspectives. Larger parties may adopt some of their ideas to avoid losing support to a smaller party. For example, the New Democratic party has helped to influence Liberal governments to adopt various social programs, particularly when the Liberals have been in a minority government situation. However, the power that may be exercised by a small party in a minority government situation might be considered undemocratic unless it pursues policies that are desired by the majority of the population.

Multiparty systems often provide better representation of the diverse interests and perspectives that exist within a political community than a two-party system. However, if parties only represent various particular interests, there is a danger that the common good of the political community will be ignored. As well, if a multiparty system contains a large number of parties, voters may have difficulty making an informed choice. The coalition governments that are often the product of multiparty systems can have the positive feature of being broadly representative and encouraging greater dialogue and consensus building within government. Coalition governments in countries such as Sweden, Germany, and Switzerland have been stable and effective. Voters may have difficulty holding a coalition government accountable for its actions if the different parties in the coalition try to blame each other for problems. Since governing coalitions are often formed after an election, voters may not know exactly what governing coalition they are getting with their vote. The choice of a government may be more in the hands of party leaders who negotiate the coalition than in the hands of voters.

A one-party dominant system allows for stability and continuity in government. However, without a strong alternative party that is potentially capable of forming a government, the dominant governing party cannot easily be held accountable for its actions. It may become unresponsive to the public, complacent, or corrupt. Moreover, when one party governs for a lengthy period of time, an overly close relationship between the governing party and public officials may develop (Whitaker, 1977).

Ideological Competition

Analyzing a party system in terms of the number of relevant political parties provides only a limited picture of the nature of the party system. To gain a fuller picture, the ideological positioning of the parties needs to be considered.

Although electoral–professional parties generally tend to downplay their ideological positioning, most party systems do feature at least some degree of ideological competition. Many countries outside North America feature competition between social democratic parties and conservative parties. In Canada and the United States, the ideological differences between the leading parties generally have not been consistent and clear. Nevertheless, a study of the attitudes of the members of different Canadian parties found that there were substantial differences in their perspectives, including, to some extent, differences between the members of the Liberal and the PC parties (Cross & Young, 2002). Of course, even if parties tend to attract members who have differing perspectives, this does not necessarily mean that parties will differ in the image they present to the public in an election campaign or in their actions if elected to govern.

It is often argued that political parties will tend to adopt similar positions as they seek to win elections (as discussed in Box 9-4, Do Parties Tend to Converge in Their Basic Positions?). Indeed, researchers have found a tendency for the leading parties to become less ideological as time passes and to drift to the centre of the ideological spectrum (Caul & Gray, 2000). As well, there has been a tendency for parties established to represent particular segments of society to move toward a broader appeal. For example, the British Labour party, under the leadership of Tony Blair, dropped its commitment to public ownership of industry and moved away from a focus on the interests of the working class. However, this was not simply a successful electoral strategy; it also reflected the ideological vision (termed the "Third Way") of Blair and his supporters.

However, this tendency for parties to move away from an ideological stance is not absolute and, in fact, there have been occasions when "catch-all" parties have moved in an ideological direction. For example, the moderate British Conservative party was turned into an ideological vehicle for the New Right under the determined leadership of Prime Minister Margaret Thatcher. Likewise, the Republican party in the United States has been strongly influenced by the New Right since the election of President Ronald Reagan in 1980. The provincial PC governments led by Michael Harris (premier of Ontario, 1995–2002) and Ralph Klein (premier of Alberta, 1992–2006) also implemented policies reflecting the New Right ideology rather than the more centrist policies pursued by previous PC governments in their provinces.

A focus on winning elections will often encourage a party's leadership to adopt moderate positions and downplay their ideological orientations during an election campaign. However, many of those active in a political party are concerned not only with winning elections, but also with implementing their views about what is best for the political community. Thus, some party

BOX 9-4

Do Parties Tend to Converge in Their Basic Positions?

In *An Economic Theory of Democracy* (1957), Anthony Downs argued that in a two-party system, parties will converge in the ideological centre, defined in terms of the ideological position held by the largest number of voters. Assuming that voters are aware of the positioning of the parties and will vote for the party that is closest to their own position, a left-wing party will find that it gains more votes as it moves toward the centre. Likewise, there is a strong electoral incentive for a right-wing party to move to the centre such that the two parties become indistinguishable in ideological terms. It should be noted that Downs's theory does not apply fully to situations where there are more than two parties. If, for example, there is a far-left party as well as a moderate leftist party, the moderate leftist party may lose votes to the far-left party if it moves too close to the centre.

Although Downs's theory provides a simple model of the dynamics of party competition, it has also been subject to considerable criticism among researchers. Party members may choose leaders and candidates whose policy positions most closely resemble their own position rather than that of the average voter (Adams & Merrill, 2005). Voters may be concerned with choosing the party that is closest to them not only in terms of the ideology and policies of the party, but also in terms of the credibility and competence of the party and the qualities of its leader and candidates. As well, many voters may be unclear about the positioning of the parties, particularly if parties are deceptive concerning their positions and that of their opponents (Grofman, 1996).

---

activists who are committed to a particular perspective may seek to move their party in a more ideological direction. Although taking a strong ideological position is often seen as harmful to a party's electoral fortunes, in certain circumstances it can lead to electoral success, as indicated by the examples of Thatcher and Reagan.

NEW PARTIES The establishment of new parties can also contribute to making the party system more ideological. In recent decades, Green parties promoting an environmentalist ideology along with advocacy concerning social justice, feminism, grassroots democracy, and peace have been established in about seventy countries.

Global Greens
www.globalgreens.info

Likewise, in recent decades, new right-wing populist parties favouring major tax cuts and reductions in government have at times been able to gain substantial support in several countries, including Canada, Denmark, and Norway. More extreme right-wing parties have developed significant support in countries such as France, Italy, and Austria. Thus, even if competition among the leading parties often tends to be more about gaining power than debating different ideological perspectives, new parties may inject different basic points of view into the party system. In some cases, this has encouraged other parties to adopt positions advocated by newer parties in order to avoid losing some of their supporters.

THE DECLINE OF PARTIES?

Some political scientists have argued that political parties are in decline (for a discussion, see Meisel & Mendelsohn, 2001). The membership of political parties in many countries has been dropping since the 1960s (Scarrow, 2000). Party membership in Canada has always been low, with only about 1 to 2 percent of Canadians being regular members of a political party (Cross, 2004). There has also been a substantial decline in many countries in the proportion of citizens who report that they have a strong sense of attachment to a particular party.

In addition, the public often has a negative view of political parties. For example, in 2004, a survey in European Union countries found that an average of only 18 percent of respondents stated that they had "a great deal" or "quite a lot" of confidence in political parties, significantly lower than the level of confidence in various other political and governmental institutions (Dalton, 2006). Likewise, a study found considerable "anti-partyism" in Canada (Gidengil, Blais, Nadeau, & Nevitte, 2002). To some extent, the distrust of parties is understandable. Some political parties have been instruments of corruption—using their political power for their own benefit. As well, there has been considerable criticism of political parties for their reliance on big business or labour unions for much of their funding. Tendencies to make extravagant promises and ambiguous pronouncements and to wage dirty, unfair campaigns against their opponents also help to create a negative image for parties.

The growing number of public interest groups and the development of new social movements (discussed in Chapter 11) have provided citizens with new means to take political action. Unlike working within a political party, where compromises are needed to reconcile the interests and values of a diversity of persons and groups, participation in an interest group or social movement may allow a more forthright pursuit of one's values and interests. As well, political parties have not generally reformed themselves sufficiently to satisfy the desire of many political activists for meaningful participation in policy deliberation. For example, a survey of Canadian party members found that there was considerable dissatisfaction with their limited influence in the development of party policy positions (Cross, 2004).

The decline of parties should not be exaggerated. Although parties in many countries have seen a decline in the number of dues-paying members, this may be offset by an increase in the involvement of members in some party activities, and increased communications between the national party organization and ordinary party members (Scarrow, 2000). Parties in most countries have also become better organized, more professional, able to carry out more activities, and able to hire more staff due to state financing (Webb, 2002).

Parties continue to be important in recruiting candidates for public office, providing choices for voters in elections, and governing. Although some of the sharp ideological conflicts between parties of the left and the right that existed in many countries in the past have declined, ideological and programmatic differences among parties do continue to exist in many countries and affect how different parties act in government (Webb, 2002). In addition, party discipline remains tight in the legislative bodies of most countries.

Summary and Conclusion

Political parties play a central role in the competition for political power and in the governing of modern democratic states. Some parties developed as a means to help legislators get elected as the right to vote began to expand. Other parties were created by groups outside the legislature to promote a particular ideological perspective and the interests of major sections of the population that were not adequately represented in the legislature. In pursuit of political power, parties have often moved away from representing particular perspectives or interests. Nevertheless, parties often reflect, sometimes in subtle ways, differing perspectives and interests.

Political parties have often been thought of as a crucial link between citizens and government. A competitive party system allows voters to choose which set of politicians should be responsible for governing and which party's platform they prefer. However, parties have often been criticized for being elitist organizations. The involvement of people who join political parties is often limited to canvassing on behalf of the party's candidates during an election campaign. In recent decades, political parties generally have become more democratic in the processes they use to select their leaders and candidates and in the holding of regular party policy conventions. Changes in the regulation of party finance in Canada

and a number of other countries have helped to reduce the influence on political parties of big business and wealthy donors. Nevertheless, parties still tend to be dominated by the leader and a small number of insiders.

Even though many citizens have negative views of political parties and have turned to other means of political involvement, parties are still crucial elements of modern democracies. By choosing among competing parties, voters may be able to hold the government accountable for its actions or inactions and select which program, direction, and vision for the political community they prefer. Competition among parties can help to prevent the abuse of power and allow ordinary citizens some ability to influence the direction of the political community.

By raising the concerns of those who might not otherwise be heard and developing policies to gain their support, political parties may also facilitate the development of a more inclusive and egalitarian political community. Where parties are strong and well organized, the poor, less educated, and disadvantaged elements of society are more likely to vote and thus, potentially, to be treated as a significant political force. Parties are also important in aggregating (putting together) the interests and perspectives of different sectors of society and trying to develop a coherent program for governing that will have wide support. Other organizations, such as interest groups, can be effective in *articulating* particular interests, but are less concerned about *aggregating* different interests. Thus, it has been argued that parties are essential "to bring interests together for the common good" (Dalton & Wattenburg, 2000, pp. 283–284). Nevertheless, the focus on broad, general appeals to the public often based on the qualities of the party's leader (aided and abetted by the treatment of politics by the mass media) can reduce the significance of parties in putting together a program that aggregates a variety of different interests.

The conflicts generated by parties in their competitive pursuit for power can divert attention from the real problems that a political community faces. Instead of debating possible solutions to problems, political parties may focus on trivial issues, mislead the public about the positions taken by the contending parties, or turn rational discussion into emotional arguments. On the other hand, by seeking the support of those whose problems would otherwise be ignored in political life and by creating platforms that appeal widely, parties may bridge societal divisions and mobilize those with little political power. Thus, in the pursuit of power, political parties can potentially serve the common good.

Key Terms

Brokerage party 201

Cadre party 199

Catch-all party 201

Electoral–professional party 201

Extraparliamentary party 200

Iron law of oligarchy 200

Mass party 200

Multiparty system 216

One-party dominant system 215

Parliamentary party 200

Party caucus 213

Party convention 200

Party system 214

Personalistic party 202

Political parties 199

Primary election 210

Programmatic party 202

Two-party system 216

Two-plus party system 216

Discussion Questions

1. Is there a particular party (or more than one party) that seems to reflect your viewpoints, interests, and identity, or do you feel that none of the major parties really represents you?

2. Are all of the major interests and viewpoints in Canada adequately represented by the major Canadian parties?

3. Is it important for political parties to be democratic in their organization?

4. How should parties choose their leaders?

5. Is the common good better served by two broad catch-all parties, or by a multiparty system in which a variety of different societal interests and ideological perspectives are represented?

6. Are political parties a necessary and desirable aspect of democratic politics?

Further Reading

Bickerton, J., Gagnon, A.-G., & Smith, P.J. *Ties that bind: Parties and voters in Canada.* Don Mills: Oxford University Press, 1999.

Campbell, C., & Christian, W. *Parties, leaders, and ideologies in Canada.* Toronto: McGraw-Hill Ryerson, 1996.

Carty, R.K., Cross, W., & Young, J. *Rebuilding Canadian party politics.* Vancouver: UBC Press, 2000.

Cross, W. *Political parties.* Vancouver: UBC Press, 2004.

Gagnon, A.-G., & Tanguay, A.B. *Canadian parties in transition,* 3rd ed. Peterborough, ON: Broadview Press, 2007.

Gunther, R., Montero, J.R., & Linz, J.J. (Eds.). *Political parties: Old concepts and new challenges.* Oxford, UK: Oxford University Press, 2002.

Thorburn, H.G., & Whitehorn, A. (Eds.). *Party politics in Canada,* 8th ed. Toronto: Pearson Education Canada, 2001.

Webb, P., Farrell, D., & Holliday, I. (Eds.). *Political parties in advanced industrial democracies.* Oxford: Oxford University Press, 2002.

Chapter 10

ELECTIONS, ELECTORAL SYSTEMS, AND VOTING BEHAVIOUR

PHOTO ABOVE: During the 2000 U.S. election, Republican George W. Bush beat the Democratic party candidate, Vice-President Al Gore, even though Bush received fewer votes than Gore, and despite irregularities in the Florida ballots and voting procedures. The U.S. Supreme Court rejected Gore's appeal for a recount—thus awarding the presidency to Bush.

CHAPTER OBJECTIVES

After reading this chapter you should be able to:

1. discuss what is needed for elections to be considered free and fair
2. explain and evaluate the different types of electoral systems
3. evaluate the usefulness of election campaigns in helping people decide how to vote
4. outline the different factors that explain voting behaviour

The 2000 U.S. presidential contest was so close that the outcome was in dispute for many weeks. In the end, Republican party candidate George W. Bush beat the Democratic party candidate, Vice-President Al Gore—despite receiving about 500 000 fewer votes.

When Americans cast their votes for their presidential choice, their votes do not directly result in the election of the president. Instead, the president is selected by members of an electoral college, who are committed to voting for the presidential candidate who has won the most votes in a particular state.* Even if one candidate wins a state by only a tiny margin, that candidate (in almost all states) will receive all of the electoral college votes for that state. The votes of the electoral college are, therefore, a distorted reflection of the votes cast by American voters. As a result of the 2000 election, Bush received 271 electoral college votes while Gore received 267. A few hundred votes in the state of Florida made the difference in the choice of Bush as president.

Afterwards, arguments raged concerning irregularities in the Florida vote, where the ballots were not properly designed and inconsistent procedures were used for counting ballots. State Republican politicians, led by Governor Jeb Bush, George W. Bush's brother, controlled the election procedures, but were unwilling to allow a full recount of votes. In the end, the U.S. Supreme Court, in a five-to-four decision, rejected Gore's appeal for a recount, thus in effect awarding the presidency to George Bush. Gore accepted the Supreme Court decision and encouraged Americans to support the president. An analysis of the Florida vote commissioned by some of the major media (although having no legal significance) later concluded that Gore should have received Florida's electoral college votes and therefore become president.

Elections are a central feature of democracies, providing citizens with the opportunity to choose their representatives and their government. However, as the Bush–Gore case illustrates, questions about the fairness of election procedures may arise. This chapter examines such questions, as well as issues such as whether election campaigns help voters to make informed decisions about the governing of their political community, why voters choose particular parties and candidates, and what influences the outcome of elections.

---

* The electoral college does not actually meet and has no function other than selecting the president and vice-president. Members of the electoral college send in their vote. Electoral college members, who are selected by each political party, almost always vote for the candidate who won the most votes in their state.

DEMOCRATIC ELECTIONS

Nearly all countries now hold elections. However, elections vary greatly, from those that can be considered democratic in terms of ensuring that voters have a free and fair choice to those that coerce or manipulate voters into endorsing a dictatorial ruler (see Box 10-1, An Undemocratic Election). The practice of elections in many countries, particularly newer democracies, falls between these two extremes. Even long-established democracies do not necessarily provide a completely fair election process. We will examine what constitutes a democratic election, and then consider the different electoral systems that translate votes into legislative representation.

BOX 10-1

An Undemocratic Election

In 2002, Iraqis were called on to vote as to whether Saddam Hussein should be given another seven-year term as president. According to an official spokesperson, all 11 445 638 eligible citizens voted, and every one of them voted *yes*. Saddam thus succeeded in surpassing the 99.95 percent support that he had received in the 1995 election.

Not surprisingly, outside observers cast doubt on the credibility of the results. There were no booths to provide privacy to voters. Ballots were numbered in such a way that voters' identities could be ascertained by government officials. Banners of Saddam were displayed inside and outside polling stations. People were observed stuffing multiple ballots into ballot boxes. The results of the election were announced before all of the votes had been counted. Although Saddam claimed he had the complete support of the people, there was no way of knowing whether that support was genuine.

Saddam's 100 percent victory? Outside observers cast doubt on the credibility of the results of the 2002 presidential election in Iraq. Although Saddam Hussein was awarded another seven-year term as president, and he claimed he had the complete support of every single voter, the results were highly suspect.

The Basic Principles

There are several basic features of democratic elections.[1] Voters should be able to choose freely among candidates and parties seeking office. To protect voters from intimidation, democratic countries use a secret ballot. To ensure meaningful competition, all citizens should have the right to run in elections, and all political parties should have the right to nominate candidates and campaign on their behalf. In other words, an election is undemocratic if only those candidates authorized by the state or other institutions are allowed to run, or if some parties are prevented from participating in an election campaign. Sometimes, however, even democratic countries have banned extremist political parties that are viewed as a threat to the democratic system. For example, in the past Canada banned the Communist party and Germany continues to ban Nazi parties.

Freedom House
www.freedomhouse.org

UNIVERSAL SUFFRAGE Democratic elections are based on the principle of "one person, one vote," with each vote having the same value. Thus, we usually only consider a system of elections fully democratic if there is **universal suffrage**—that is, all adult citizens have the right to vote regardless of such characteristics as gender, ethnicity, wealth, or education. Further, it should be easy for citizens to exercise their right to vote. For example, provisions should be made for students and others who are away from home on election day to vote, and the use of difficult registration requirements should be avoided. Ensuring that each vote has the same value can be controversial, as persons in rural and remote areas worry that their interests will not be given due attention because of the large numbers of voters in the major cities. As well, elected representatives will have a more difficult task in meeting their constituents in a large, sparsely populated region.

UNIVERSAL SUFFRAGE
The right of all adult citizens to vote regardless of such characteristics as gender, ethnicity, wealth, or education.

INFORMATION Voters need to be provided with useful information if their vote is to be meaningful. Parties and candidates must have the opportunity to get their message to voters. This may involve putting some limits on spending to ensure that one party or candidate does not dominate the campaign, and providing some subsidies to help parties and candidates that do not have the support of wealthy contributors. Extensive government advertising during an election campaign should be avoided, as it could give the governing party an unfair advantage. The media should provide fair and extensive coverage of the contending parties and candidates.

Elections Canada
www.elections.ca

In a number of countries, elections are often accompanied by violence. For example, as they registered voters in 2004 for Afghanistan's first election, officials faced numerous attacks by Taliban guerrillas seeking to disrupt and de-legitimize the election. Likewise, in countries with deep social divisions some groups may fear serious consequences if a party representing an opposing

---

[1] This discussion of democratic elections is based in part on the indicators used by Freedom House (n.d.), retrieved May 16, 2004, from www.freedomhouse.org.

section of society should win. Violence may be used to intimidate candidates from running and voters from casting their ballots.

INDEPENDENT COMMISSION To ensure that elections are conducted fairly, it is important that the process be overseen by an independent commission. Similarly, the drawing of constituency boundaries should be done by an independent body to prevent **gerrymandering**, the manipulation of the division of the country into constituencies in such a way that a particular party benefits. The contending parties and candidates should be able to observe the casting and counting of votes. Foreign observers have played a role in ascertaining whether elections have been properly conducted in newly democratic countries. If there is evidence that the election rules have not been properly followed, losing candidates should have the right to request a recount and to appeal to the courts or an independent body. The adoption of electronic voting systems in some parts of the United States is raising concerns about the possibility of electoral fraud by tampering with ballot software. Without physical ballots, recounts may be impossible and the accuracy of vote tabulations has been questioned.

Elections are only meaningful if those elected have real power. In some countries, elected legislative bodies simply legitimate the decisions of a monarch or dictator. In some other countries, the military will step in if it disagrees with decisions taken by elected officials.

A REGULAR VOTE To ensure that those elected to office are held accountable to the people, it is important that elections be held on a fairly regular basis. In most democratic countries, the election of representatives occurs at least once every four or five years, as in Canada. A small number of countries, including Australia and New Zealand, require elections be held within a three-year period. In presidential systems, the dates for elections are fixed by law. For example, the election of the president of the United States is always held on the Tuesday following the first Monday of November every fourth year.

In parliamentary systems, the prime minister and Cabinet have to retain the support of the majority of members of the elected House of Commons. Failure to maintain that support (as exhibited in a vote of non-confidence in the government or the defeat of a crucial aspect of the government's agenda such as the budget) usually results in an election. As well, the Canadian prime minister can at any time request that the governor general authorize the holding of an election. Except in unusual circumstances, the governor general will accept this request. This flexibility in the timing of elections potentially gives an advantage to the prime minister's party, as an election can be called when public opinion poll results are favourable and the governing party can plan its campaign in advance.

A number of countries with parliamentary systems have adopted fixed election dates to make elections fairer and the administration of elections

GERRYMANDERING
The manipulation of the division of the country into constituencies so as to benefit a particular party.

ACE Electoral Knowledge Network
www.aceproject.org

International Institute for Democracy and Electoral Assistance
www.idea.int

easier (Milner, 2005). A degree of flexibility is usually retained by allowing for an election if the governing party is defeated on a vote of non-confidence.[2] This system of holding elections on a fixed date was adopted in Canada at the national level in 2007 (although Prime Minister Harper requested an election in 2008 rather than waiting for the fixed election in 2009), and has in recent years been adopted at the provincial level by British Columbia, Ontario, Newfoundland and Labrador, Prince Edward Island, New Brunswick, and the Northwest Territories.

TYPES OF ELECTORAL SYSTEMS

ELECTORAL SYSTEM
The system used to translate the votes that people cast into the composition of the legislature and the selection of the government.

Beyond examining whether elections allow voters a free choice and are conducted fairly and honestly, it is important to understand the **electoral system** that is used to translate the votes that people cast into the composition of the legislature and the selection of the government. The choice of electoral system raises controversial questions about the fairness of elections as well as the effects of elections on politics and governing.

There are four basic types of electoral systems:

- single member plurality
- majoritarian (including runoff elections and preferential voting)
- proportional representation (including single transferable votes)
- mixed member proportional

As Table 10-1 indicates, the single member plurality (SMP) and the proportional representation (PR) systems are the most common, although the mixed member proportional system has also become quite common.

Single Member Plurality

SINGLE MEMBER PLURALITY (SMP) SYSTEM
An electoral system in which voters in each geographical constituency elect a single representative to the legislature. The candidate with the most votes is elected, regardless of whether that candidate received the majority of votes.

In a **single member plurality (SMP) system,** voters in each geographical constituency elect a single representative to the legislature. The candidate with the most votes is elected, regardless of whether that candidate received the majority of votes.

Canada, like many of the former British colonies, uses the SMP system.[3] The SMP system (sometimes referred to as a "first-past-the-post" system) provides a simple method for a representative to be chosen from a

---

[2] In Germany, the governing Social Democratic party was able to have an early election in 2005 despite fixed election dates. It arranged for its own party members to abstain from voting on a motion expressing confidence in the government, which was defeated. The German president then called an election, as the government no longer had the confidence of the German parliament.

[3] Historically in Canada, there were a small number of two-member constituencies at the national level and in some provinces. They were elected in a manner similar to single-member constituencies, with the candidates getting the most votes elected. British Columbia used a preferential voting system for the 1952 provincial election. Some Canadian cities have, in the past, used proportional representation systems.

SINGLE MEMBER PLURALITY	RUNOFF	PREFERENTIAL BALLOT VOTE	SINGLE TRANSFERABLE	MIXED MEMBER PROPORTIONAL	PROPORTIONAL REPRESENTATION
Bahamas	Egypt	Australia*	Australia*	Bolivia	Argentina
Bangladesh	France	Fiji	Ireland	Germany	Austria
Bermuda	Haiti	Papua NG	Malta	Hungary	Belgium
Botswana	Iran			Japan	Brazil
Canada				Mexico	Chile
Ghana				New Zealand	Czech Rep.
India				Philippines	Denmark
Jamaica				South Korea	Greece
Kenya				Thailand	Israel
Malaysia				Tunisia	Italy
Nigeria				Ukraine	Netherlands
Tanzania					Poland
United Kingdom					S. Africa
United States					Spain
					Sweden
					Switzerland
					Turkey

TABLE 10-1

ELECTRICAL SYSTEMS USED TO ELECT MEMBERS OF THE NATIONAL LEGISLATURE, SELECTED COUNTRIES

Note: Australia uses a preferential ballot for elections to its House of Representatives and single transferable vote for its Senate elections.

SOURCE: *Compiled from International Institute for Democracy and Electoral Assistance, retrieved June 2, 2007, from www.idea.int/esc/world.cfm.*

particular area. Elections, however, involve more than choosing a representative for a legislative body. They are also very important for choosing a party to form a government for the country, and thus involve choices among competing parties. The SMP system often inaccurately translates the votes a party receives across the country into the seats that it receives in the legislature (see Box 10-2, Distortion in the Single Member Plurality System). In particular, the SMP system usually gives an added boost in representation to the leading party. For example, in the 2005 election in the United Kingdom, the Labour party received 55 percent of the seats in Parliament based on only 35 percent of the vote. In the 1993, 1997, and 2000 Canadian elections, the Liberal party received a majority of seats in the House of Commons based on about two-fifths of the votes cast. However, as Table 10-2 indicates, the distorting effects of the SMP system are stronger in some elections than others and affect the representation of some parties more than others.

In some cases, the effect of the SMP system has been to allow the governing party to completely dominate the legislature, thus hindering the provision of effective opposition to the governing party. For example, the 1987 New Brunswick provincial election resulted in the Liberal party winning all of the

BOX 10-2

Distortion in the Single Member Plurality System

Imagine a very small legislature consisting of five seats. The hypothetical results of voting in each of the five constituencies are as follows:

Party A would win all of the seats despite having the support of only 40 percent of the voters,

while the substantial proportion of the population who voted for parties B or C would be unrepresented.

	CONSTITUENCY #1	CONSTITUENCY #2	CONSTITUENCY #3	CONSTITUENCY #4	CONSTITUENCY #5
Party A	40%	40%	40%	40%	40%
Party B	39%	39%	39%	39%	39%
Party C	21%	21%	21%	21%	21%

seats based on its 60 percent share of the vote. Similarly, in the 2001 British Columbia provincial election, the Liberals won seventy-seven of the seventy-nine seats based on 57.6 percent of the vote.

The SMP system generally favours the most popular party at the expense of smaller parties. However, parties that have their support concentrated in particular geographical areas tend to do much better than parties with modest support spread across the country. The Bloc Québécois has benefited from the workings of the SMP system while the NDP has received a substantially smaller proportion of seats than votes in every national election. Parties with relatively low levels of support are generally unable to gain representation in the legislature. The Green party did not elect any

TABLE 10-2

THE IMPACT OF THE SMP ELECTORAL SYSTEM: CANADA 2004, 2006, AND 2008

PARTY	2004 ELECTION			2006 ELECTION			2008 ELECTION		
	VOTES	SEATS	DIFFERENCE	VOTES	SEATS	DIFFERENCE	VOTES	SEATS	DIFFERENCE
Liberal	36.7%	43.8%	+7.1	30.2%	33.4%	+3.2	26.3%	25%	−1.3
Conservative	29.6%	32.1%	+2.5	36.3%	0.3%	+4.0	37.7%	46.4%	+8.7
NDP	15.7%	6.2%	−9.5	17.5%	9.4%	−8.1	18.2%	12.0%	−6.2
Bloc	12.4%	17.5%	+5.1	10.5%	16.6%	+6.1	10.0%	15.9%	+5.8
Green	4.3%	0.0%	−4.3	4.5%	0.0%	−4.5	6.8%	0.0%	−6.8
Others	1.3%	0.3%	−1.0	1.0%	0.3%	−0.7	1.0%	0.6%	−0.4

SOURCE: *Elections Canada, Calculations and adaptation rest with the authors. Retrieved March 21, 2009, from www.elections.ca.*

members to the House of Commons despite obtaining 664 668 votes in the 2006 election and 940 747 votes in the 2008 election.

The SMP system also tends to exaggerate the regional character of the parties in the legislature. For example, the Liberal party obtained the majority of its seats from Ontario in the 1993, 1997, and 2000 Canadian elections, even though the majority of its votes came from other parts of the country. The Conservative party obtained sixty-eight of its ninety-nine seats in the 2004 election from Western Canada, giving the party a strongly Western Canadian character, even though 56 percent of its votes came from other parts of Canada.

Occasionally, the distorting effects of the electoral system can result in the most popular party losing the election. The PC party won the 1979 Canadian election with close to a majority of seats based on 36 percent of the vote, even though the Liberal party obtained 40 percent of the vote. Similarly, in several provincial elections, including British Columbia (1996), Quebec (1966 and 1998), Newfoundland (1989), Saskatchewan (1999), and New Brunswick (2006), the party that received the second-highest number of votes won the election and formed the government. The 2000 American presidential election, discussed at the start of this chapter, illustrates the same basic principle: George W. Bush barely won the presidency, even though Al Gore gained slightly more of the popular vote, because of the "winner take all" basis of the **electoral college**.

Majoritarian Systems

Majoritarian electoral systems are designed to try to ensure that the winning candidate has the support of the majority of voters. For presidential elections, many countries, including France, Russia, and Chile, use a system of **runoff elections** (also known as two-round elections). If no candidate receives a majority of votes, another election is held in which only the top two candidates appear on the ballot. Runoff elections are also used for the election of representatives to the French Assembly. If no candidate obtains a majority of votes, a second election is held. Only the candidates who received at least one-eighth of the vote on the first ballot can remain on the second ballot. The candidate with the most votes on the second ballot wins. Usually the winning candidate obtains a majority as a result of deals made between parties so that only the top two candidates appear on the second ballot.

Another type of majoritarian electoral system is **preferential voting** (also known as the alternative vote). Instead of marking X beside the name of the candidate one prefers, voters can rank candidates in order of preference. If no candidate has a majority of first preferences, the candidate with the least votes is dropped and the second preferences of those who voted for that candidate are added to the votes of other candidates. This process continues until one candidate has a majority.

ELECTORAL COLLEGE
A body that elects the president of the United States. Members of the electoral college from each state are expected to vote for the presidential candidate who has won the most votes in their state.

MAJORITARIAN ELECTORAL SYSTEM
An electoral system designed to try to ensure that the winning candidate has the support of the majority of voters.

RUNOFF ELECTION
An election held if no candidate receives a majority of votes; generally, only the top two candidates appear on the ballot to ensure that the winning candidate has a majority of the votes cast.

PREFERENTIAL VOTING
An electoral system in which voters rank candidates in order of preference. If no candidate has a majority of first preferences, the candidate with the least votes is dropped and the second preferences of those who voted for that candidate are added to the votes of other candidates. This process continues until one candidate has a majority.

Proportional Representation

PROPORTIONAL REPRESENTA-
TION (PR) SYSTEM An electoral
system in which the proportion
of seats a party receives in
the legislature reflects the
proportion of votes it has
obtained.

Both the single member plurality and majoritarian electoral systems typically result in legislatures that do not reflect the overall distribution of support for political parties. To deal with this issue, many countries have adopted some form of **proportional representation (PR) system**, in which the proportion of seats a party receives in the legislature reflects the proportion of votes it has obtained.[4] If, for example, 40 percent of voters supported party A, 39 percent supported party B, and 21 percent supported party C, this would result (in a pure PR system) in 40 percent of the seats going to party A, 39 percent to party B, and 21 percent to party C.

A PR system requires that several representatives be elected from each electoral district. The larger the number of representatives for each district, the more closely the representation of the parties in the legislature will reflect the support each party has in the electorate. In a few cases—the Netherlands, Israel, and Slovakia—the country as a whole is treated as a single district, such that representatives do not represent a particular geographical area.

In some countries that use PR (for example, Spain, Norway, and South Africa), individual legislators are selected based on the order of their placement on a list of candidates drawn up by each party. In our hypothetical five-member legislature, the top two names on party A's list of five candidates would become legislators. Other PR systems (for example, Sweden, Poland, and Brazil) allow voters to indicate which candidate they prefer in the list of the party that they have chosen to vote for.

COALITION GOVERNMENT
A form of government in which
two or more parties jointly govern,
sharing the Cabinet positions.

A PR system, by quite accurately reflecting the support for parties by voters, almost always results in a situation where no single party has a majority of seats in the legislature. Thus, PR systems typically involve **coalition government**, where two or more parties share in governing. PR systems also often result in a substantial number of parties being represented in the legislature. To try to prevent an overly complex party system in the legislature and keep small extremist parties or parties representing very narrow interests from gaining a voice in legislature, many countries with a PR system require that parties obtain a certain percentage of the popular vote as a prerequisite for gaining legislative seats. For example, the minimum threshold to gain representation is 4 percent in Norway and 3 percent in Greece.

Although a PR system provides for more accurate representation of voter support for political parties than other electoral systems, it may reduce the strength of the link between a legislator and his or her constituency.

---

[4] For a description of the different formulas that are used to calculate how seats are distributed among parties, see Blais and Massicote (2002).

Multimember constituencies tend to be much larger than single-member constituencies, and PR systems tend to focus on representation by party rather than by individual legislators.

SINGLE TRANSFERABLE VOTE The **single transferable vote (STV) system** used in Ireland could be viewed as a variation on the proportional representation system. Voters mark their preferences for candidates in a multi-member constituency. Candidates receiving a certain proportion of the vote are declared elected. The second preferences of votes that are surplus to what the winning candidates need are then transferred to candidates who have not reached the quota. The process is continued until all seats in the constituency are filled (Blais & Massicotte, 2002). Unlike other proportional representation systems, STV focuses on the choice of candidates rather than parties. Indeed, it encourages competition for votes among the candidates of the same party, thus potentially contributing to tensions within a party. STV does not generally produce as accurate a translation of party votes into party representation as other PR systems, although the distorting effects are usually not large. For example, in the 2007 election in Ireland, the leading party (Fianna Fáil) received 46.4 percent of the seats based on 41.6 percent of the first-preference votes.

Mixed Member Proportional

To try to combine the benefits of a single member representing a particular constituency with an accurate translation of votes into seats, some countries have adopted a mixture of SMP and PR systems, termed a **mixed member proportional (MMP) system.** Those who advocate changing Canada's SMP system often propose an MMP system (see Box 10-3, Changing Canada's Electoral System).

In MMP systems, voters cast one vote for the party they prefer and one vote for the candidate they prefer. Some legislators are elected to represent particular constituencies, based on gaining the most votes in that constituency. Others (about one-half of the legislators in the case of Germany) are selected so as to make the overall representation of the parties in the legislature proportional to the votes received by each party in the election. In effect, the selection of representatives by PR in most MMP systems is used to compensate parties that were hurt by the workings of SMP (this is termed a compensatory system). In other MMP systems (such as the system used in Japan), part of their legislative body is elected by SMP and the other part by PR (referred to as a parallel system). The overall result for party representation in parallel systems is not as proportionate as in compensatory MMP systems.

SINGLE TRANSFERABLE VOTE (STV) SYSTEM
An electoral system in which voters mark their preferences for candidates in a multimember constituency. Candidates receiving a certain proportion of the vote are declared elected. The second preferences of voters that are surplus to what the winning candidates need are then transferred to candidates who have not reached the quota. The process is continued until all seats in the constituency are filled.

All about BC-STV
www.bc-stv.ca/allabout.htm

Fair Vote Canada
www.fairvotecanada.org

MIXED MEMBER PROPORTIONAL (MMP) SYSTEM
An electoral system in which voters cast one vote for the party they prefer and one vote for the candidate they prefer. Some legislators are elected to represent particular constituencies based on gaining the most votes in that constituency, while others are elected based on the popular vote received by their party.

Changing Canada's Electoral System

A number of Canadian political scientists and other observers of Canadian politics have advocated modifying or changing Canada's single member plurality (SMP) electoral system. Concerns have often focused on the effects of SMP in heightening regional divisions (Cairns, 1968) as well as distorting the wishes of the electorate.

Adopting proportional representation or mixed member proportional systems has also been seen as a way of encouraging parties to provide for greater representation for women and minority groups. In countries with such systems, parties are often more likely to make their candidate lists more representative of different social groups than in countries with SMP systems, where constituency party associations are usually responsible for choosing candidates.

The leading political parties have had limited interest in electoral system change because the SMP system works to their political advantage. As well, until recently there was relatively little public pressure for change. However, there has been growing interest in electoral reform. As we saw in Chapter 4, the Citizens' Assembly in British Columbia proposed the adoption of a single transferable vote system for that province, while the Ontario Citizens' Assembly recommended a mixed member proportional system. Other provinces have also considered changes to their electoral system in recent times. At the national level, a report of the Law Commission of Canada (2004) tabled in the House of Commons recommended that an MMP system similar to that of Scotland be adopted.* In this proposal, two-thirds of the seats in the House of Commons would be filled by the candidates who had received the most votes in their single member constituencies, while votes for the parties would be used to select the other members, who would represent provinces (or regions within Ontario and Quebec) on a compensatory basis.

Another Commonwealth country, New Zealand, switched from a single member plurality system to MMP in 1993 after two consecutive elections in which the party with the most votes did not win the elections. Changing the electoral system had major effects on politics and government. Since adopting MMP, New Zealand has had coalition governments and there has been greater diversity in the legislature as more parties have been able to gain representation.

---

* See the Law Commission of Canada's report on electoral reform at www.lcc.gc.ca/en/themes/gr/er/er_report/er_report_toc.asp.

ELECTION CAMPAIGNS

Parties, leaders, and candidates have many potential ways of appealing to voters for support. Pippa Norris (2002) distinguishes between three basic types of campaigns:

- premodern campaigns
- modern campaigns
- postmodern campaigns

Premodern Campaigns

Premodern campaigns were characteristic of the advanced democratic countries until the 1960s or early 1970s. These campaigns involved considerable personal contact with the voters and campaigning was largely localized. Party volunteers canvassed their neighbourhoods, seeking to determine who supported their candidate so they could ensure that their supporters voted on election day. Leaflets were dropped in mailboxes and supporters were encouraged to put up signs. National leaders traversed the country by train, greeting supporters at the railway stations in small communities and holding rallies in the larger centres. National campaign organizations were small, with the leader and some experienced party advisers establishing the general direction of the campaign.

Despite the localized nature of campaigning, premodern campaigns in the mid twentieth century were oriented, in many countries, to carrying the party's message to voters throughout the country (in some countries through newspapers that were connected to a particular party), particularly by appealing to members of groups that supported that party (Plasser & Plasser, 2002).

Modern Election Campaigns

Modern election campaigns are more sophisticated. Public opinion polling is used to provide the basic information needed to develop campaign strategies. Professional consultants, including experts in advertising and marketing, largely determine how the campaign will be conducted and the kinds of appeals that will be made to the voters. Modern campaigns are more centrally coordinated or controlled than premodern campaigns.

The development of television has contributed to the emphasis in modern campaigns on managing the image of the party leader (or, in the United States, candidate). Creating favourable "photo ops" of the leader that will be picked up by the national television news broadcasts is of great importance. As well, short, attention-getting television advertisements are a central feature of modern election campaigns. The typical campaign strategy is to focus on simple, basic themes (Plasser & Plasser, 2002).

Modern campaigns often tend to downplay political party affiliations. Instead of appealing primarily to the party faithful to mobilize them to vote on election day, the goal of the modern campaign is to appeal to a broader, national audience. The more localized and personalized techniques of the premodern campaign continue to be used, but are not of central importance in the modern campaign (Norris, 2002).

Waging a modern election campaign requires substantial amounts of money and access to professional expertise. Particularly in the United States, an industry of professional campaign consultants has developed. American-based campaign professionals have been hired by parties in many countries to assist in running their campaigns. However, in some countries, legal regulations prevent the full adoption of modern campaign techniques. For example, a number of countries, including the United Kingdom, France, and Belgium, do not allow paid political advertising on television. Instead, many countries provide longer, free-time television broadcasts to the parties (Norris, 2002). In addition, various institutional characteristics (including the nature of the electoral, party, media, and governing systems) and cultural factors affect the ways in which American-developed modern campaign techniques are applied in other countries.

Postmodern Campaigns

Norris suggests that a new postmodern style of campaigning is currently developing. New forms of communication such as the Internet allow a return to more interactive and personalized styles of political communication. Specialized television channels, computerized direct mail and telemarketing techniques, and the use of email allow campaigners to direct specific messages to targeted groups and individuals. In addition to public opinion surveys, postmodern campaigns make extensive use of focus groups to develop their messages to targeted voters and to design effective television commercials. Even more than in the modern campaign, there is a focus on strictly controlling the message and developing the capability to instantly rebut the arguments of opponents (Plasser & Plasser, 2002).

Norris (2000, p. 147) also argues that we are moving toward "the permanent campaign, in which the techniques of electioneering become intertwined with those of governing." The techniques developed to market the party during an election campaign may also be used by the governing party to try to control the message the government presents to the public. In addition, parties are increasingly using campaign-style advertising, even if an election is not imminent, using television and Internet video media such as YouTube™.

Postmodern campaigning may help the public to become more informed and help parties to be more responsive to specific segments of the public. However, postmodern campaigning that focuses on professional marketing of a political "product" could also be considered manipulative and detrimental to the quality of democratic discussion.

Election Campaigns and Informed Choice

Ideally, elections allow people to choose among parties offering different platforms or directions for the country, and thus affect the way the country is governed. Candidates try to meet as many of their constituents as possible during the election campaign. The mass media provide extensive coverage of election campaigns. Parties carry their basic message to the public through extensive advertising. As well, party platforms and other campaign materials are now accessible online.

However, political parties do not always clearly state their views on major issues during election campaigns. Because parties want to appeal to a diverse set of voters, they are often reluctant to take clear positions that might be viewed negatively by a significant group of voters. Instead, vague statements about how they are going to make the political community great are often combined with sharp attacks on their opponents. Much of the 2004 Canadian election campaign, for example, consisted of each party attacking one or more of the other parties rather than explaining what their party would do if elected.

PROMISES Parties usually make a variety of specific promises during an election campaign. However, voters cannot be certain that the promises will actually be carried out. For example, during the 2003 Ontario election, Liberal leader Dalton McGuinty signed a written promise not to raise taxes. After the party was elected, the Liberals claimed that the provincial government's finances were much worse than had been portrayed by the defeated PC government. The Ontario government's 2004 budget included an increase in taxes in the form of health care premiums. Legal action against Premier McGuinty was dismissed by Judge Paul Rouleau, who wrote that "anyone who believes a campaign promise is naive about the democratic system" (*Globe and Mail Online*, January 29, 2005).

◄ Do campaigning politicians tell us what they will really do if elected?

ADVERTISING   The short (often thirty-second) television advertisements that have become a major feature of modern election campaigns do not provide detailed information. Rather, they often rely on repeating a simple slogan or playing on people's fears (see Box 10-4, Negative Campaign Ads). The emphasis in modern campaigns on the party leaders can mean that consideration of the policy directions proposed by the parties is limited. The televised leaders' debates that have become a regular feature of election campaigns in most countries do potentially provide an opportunity for the voters to compare the arguments of the different parties as well as some of the qualities of the leaders. However, leaders' debates in Canada have sometimes degenerated into shouting matches. Finally, as discussed in Chapter 8, coverage of election campaigns in the mass media has often been criticized for avoiding serious discussion of the issues, focusing more on the horse-race aspect of the election.

GLEANING USEFUL INFORMATION   Although election campaigns can be criticized for being exercises in manipulation, obfuscation, and dishonesty, those who follow a campaign carefully can often gain useful information about the parties' positions on specific issues and their general values. For example, in the 2006 Canadian election campaign, the Conservatives promised a cut in the goods and service tax while the Liberals emphasized their tax cut for the poor. The Conservatives promised parents with young children $1200 a year while the Liberals and NDP promised to create more child-care spaces. The Conservatives promised more money to provincial governments to correct the "fiscal imbalance" between the two levels of government while the Liberals and NDP argued that there

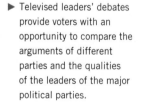

▶ Televised leaders' debates provide voters with an opportunity to compare the arguments of different parties and the qualities of the leaders of the major political parties.

BOX 10-4

Negative Campaign Ads

Negative advertising plays on voters' fears—but its success is unclear.

In the 2004 American presidential election campaign, the Swift Boat Veterans for Truth ran a number of strongly worded television ads. They claimed that Democratic candidate John Kerry was unfit to serve as president because he had exaggerated his record as leader of a swift boat unit in the Vietnam War, did not deserve the combat medals he had received, and had betrayed the trust of those in his unit by criticizing the war after his service was completed. However, almost all of the veterans involved in the ad campaign had not served in his unit; most of those who served under him praised his war record. Nevertheless, the smear campaign severely damaged his reputation. In the 2006 U.S. Congressional election campaign, the Republican party ran a television ad showing al-Qaeda leaders and gun-bearing militants making threatening statements with the sound of a ticking bomb in the background. The short commercial ended with the statement "These are the stakes. Vote November 7." Another ad accused a member of the state Congress of calling a phone-sex line and leaving taxpayers with the bill. In reality, the call lasted one minute at a cost of $1.25 and was followed by a call to a government department, which has an almost identical phone number.

Negative advertising has also been present in Canadian election campaigns. For example, Liberal party ads in 2004 featured strong attacks on Conservative leader Stephen Harper, such as one that quoted Harper saying, "When we're through with Canada, you won't recognize it," against a backdrop of a Canadian flag disintegrating. In 2006, the Liberals ran attack ads using close-ups of Harper accompanied by the sound of beating war drums. One of the ads (quickly withdrawn) stated that Harper wanted "soldiers with guns in our cities." Another accused him of speaking to "a secret, ultra right-wing American think tank." In 2007, in anticipation of a possible election, the Conservative party ran a number of negative advertisements stating that Stéphane Dion "is not a leader."

Overall, negative campaign advertising along with the frequent use of personal attacks on those in opposing parties has become a major feature of election campaigns in many countries (Plasser & Plasser, 2002). Negative advertising is not necessarily more effective in persuading voters than positive ads that focus on the reasons to vote for a particular party or candidate (Lau, Sigelman, Heldman, & Babbitt, 1999). However, viewers are more likely to remember an attack ad than a positive advertisement. Researchers have also found that negative attack ads reduce voting turnout, while positive ads slightly increase turnout (Ansolabehere, Iyengar, Simon, & Valentino, 1997). The increasing use of negative advertising may be a contributing factor to the general decline in voter turnout as well as to the increasing distrust of politicians and political parties.

was no fiscal imbalance. The Conservatives argued that the Kyoto Protocol on global climate change was fatally flawed while the Liberals promised to accelerate progress toward the Kyoto target and the NDP promised to meet those targets by 2010. The 2008 campaign focused on Conservative criticism of the Liberal "Green Shift" plan to impose a carbon tax and reduce other taxes.

Canada Votes 2006
www.cbc.ca/canadavotes/index.html

Of course, we have to be careful in interpreting the meaningfulness of the parties' campaign rhetoric. Although parties that are elected to govern may feel it necessary to fulfill or partly fulfill many of their specific promises, the general impression given by vague statements may be misleading. Promises to fix the health care system, reduce pollution, or operate government more efficiently are not very helpful unless there are clear indications as to how such objectives are to be achieved. Likewise, attacks on another party for its proposals, actions, or inactions are not very meaningful unless alternative strategies are laid out.

VOTING BEHAVIOUR

Why do people vote the way they do? Who tends to vote for which party? What affects the outcome of elections? Political scientists have devoted much research effort to such questions, particularly by using survey research techniques. However, the answers tend to be complex because a large number of factors can affect voting behaviour.[5] These factors can be divided into two categories (Miller & Niemi, 2002):

- long-term predispositions of voters based on their interests, social characteristics, values, and sense of identification with a particular political party.
- short-term factors related to the circumstances of a particular election such as the leaders, candidates, and campaign issues.

Canadian Election Study
www.ces-eec.umontreal.ca

Long-Term Predispositions

SOCIAL CHARACTERISTICS Members of a social grouping, based on such characteristics as class, religion, culture, region, or gender, may tend to support a particular party that they associate with the interests or the identity of their group. Thus, one or more major social divisions often affect the long-term patterns of support for different political parties.

Class   In most countries, there is a tendency for class divisions (divisions based on position in the economy or a combination of income, education, and social status) to affect voting behaviour. Most democratic countries have one or more social democratic parties, allied formally or informally to the labour movement, that are able to gain the votes of a substantial proportion of unionized workers. As well, most democratic countries have one or more conservative parties, often informally allied to business interests, that are able to gain the votes of a substantial proportion of the more affluent and business-oriented

[5] The discussion of voting behaviour in the following sections is based on the model of Blais, Gidengil, Nadeau, and Nevitte (2002).

segments of society. However, there has been a tendency for such differences in voting by class to decline over time as class distinctions have become blurred, the traditional industrial working class has shrunk, and many workers in the richer countries have gained the ability to attain more middle-class lifestyles in times of prosperity.

In the case of Canada, class voting has not been strong at the national level, although class differences are significant in affecting voting behaviour in provincial elections in several provinces. Many Canadians think of themselves more in terms of provincial and ethnic identities than in class terms, and political parties (except, to some extent, the NDP) have not been viewed by the majority of voters as connected to particular classes. Nevertheless, the 1999 to 2002 World Values and European Values Surveys found that the level of class voting in Canada was about the same as most other advanced democracies (Dalton, 2006). A study of the 2004 Canadian election found that the NDP did better (other things being equal) among those in union households than among those who were not, with the reverse being the case for the Conservatives. Differences based on income level, however, were fairly small (Gidengil et al., 2006a).

Religion In a number of countries, there is a relationship between religion and voting choice, both in the sense that persons of different religious denominations may tend to support different parties and in the sense that those who are religious are generally less likely to vote for parties on the "left" than those who are not religious. For example, in the United States, Catholics Jews, and those with no religion are more likely than Protestants to vote for the Democratic party. As well, in the 2004 presidential election, Republican George W. Bush received 61.5 percent of the vote of those who regularly attended church compared to only 44.3 percent of those who did not (Olson & Green, 2006). In Britain, Catholics are more likely than Presbyterians and Anglicans to vote for the Labour party. In France, those who are not religious are more likely than those who are religious to vote for one of the parties of the left (Dalton, 2006).

In Canada, Catholics (along with non-Christians) are generally more likely than Protestants (particularly evangelical and fundamental Protestants) to vote Liberal, although the reverse is true in Newfoundland and Labrador. The Conservatives (and their Reform/Alliance predecessors) tend to do well among Christian fundamentalists, while the NDP tends to do better among those with no religion (Gidengil et al., 2006a). Explaining the continuing significance of religious differences (particularly between English-speaking Catholics and Protestants) in Canadian voting behaviour has been a puzzle for political science researchers (Blais, 2005).

Generally, while there is a tendency in various countries for voting differences between different denominations to decline in significance, differences between religious and other voters often continue to be important. This may be the result of the rise of fundamentalism in some countries along with the attention given to controversial moral issues such as abortion and same-sex marriage (Dalton, 2006).

Cultural Groups Ethnic, racial, cultural, and linguistic differences in voting behaviour are apparent in countries that have minority groups with a distinctive identity. For example, 92 percent of black Americans voted for the Democratic Congressional candidates in 2004, compared to 71 percent of Hispanics and 44 percent of whites (Dalton, 2006). Likewise, a large majority of Canadians of non-European ancestry vote for the Liberal party (Blais, Gidengil, Nadeau, & Nevitte, 2002).

Region In some countries, such as Canada, there are important regional differences in voting behaviour. Support for different parties often varies substantially across Canada, reflecting not only differences in the culture and economy of different parts of the country, but also a tendency to evaluate governments and political parties in terms of how good or bad they are for the interests of one's province or region. In some countries, regional parties (such as the Bloc Québécois, the Basque Nationalist party in Spain, and the Lega Nord in Italy) have developed to represent particular regional (often combined with ethnic and linguistic) identities.

Gender The differences in voting behaviour between women and men have attracted considerable interest in recent years. However, gender differences in voting behaviour are generally quite small. In some countries, there is a tendency for women to be more likely than men to vote for conservative (or religious) parties. In other countries, women, particularly younger women, are slightly more likely to vote for leftist parties (Dalton, 2006).

In the United States, women are somewhat more likely to vote for the Democratic party than the Republican party. For example, in the 2004 American presidential election, 55.5 percent of men voted to re-elect Republican president George W. Bush, compared to 48.2 percent of women (Olson & Green, 2006). In Canada, women have generally been slightly more likely than men to vote for the Liberal party. In recent Canadian elections, women have been more likely than men to vote for the NDP, while men have been more likely than women to vote for conservative parties (Blais, Gidengil, Nadeau, & Nevitte, 2002; Gidengil et al., 2006b).

Some analysts have suggested that the gender gap will widen, in part because of the tendency of women to hold different (more liberal or leftist) values on such topics as social programs, free enterprise, military action, and the treatment of criminals (Gidengil, Blais, Nadeau, & Nevitte, 2003; O'Neill, 2002).

Other Characteristics Various other social characteristics are related to differences in voting behaviour in some countries. For example, although age is not usually related to the choices voters make, Green parties have tended to receive greater support from younger voters. In the 2004 Canadian election, senior citizens were more likely than young and middle-aged voters to support the Liberal and Conservative parties. Conversely, the NDP, Bloc, and Green parties drew less support from older voters (Ekos, 2004). In the 2008 U.S. Presidential election, Democratic Party canadiate Barack Obama drew strong support from younger voters.

Rural voters are often more likely to be supportive of conservative parties than urban voters. For example, in the 2004 and 2006 Canadian elections, the Conservative party did not win a single seat in Canada's three largest cities, but did well among rural residents.

Importance Although social divisions have generally been of declining importance in affecting voting choice in the advanced democracies, there are still some important differences in the voting patterns of different social groupings. In the case of Canada, region, culture (including ethnicity), and religion continue to be related to voters' party choices.

VALUES Studies in a number of countries have found that general values such as egalitarianism and libertarianism, along with how people view themselves in left/right terms, are related to their voting choices (Miller & Niemi, 2002). In Canada, a study of voting in the 2004 election found that those who favoured free-enterprise values were more likely to vote Conservative and less likely to vote NDP. Likewise, those with social conservative values (that is, traditional values on such issues as the rights of gays and lesbians and the role of women) were more likely to vote Conservative and less likely to vote Liberal or NDP (Gidengil et al., 2006a).[6] In Quebec, support for Quebec sovereignty clearly distinguished those who vote for the Bloc Québécois from those who vote for the Liberal party (Blais, Gidengil, Nadeau, & Nevitte, 2002).

Thus, regardless of whether voters consciously evaluate the parties in terms of left and right and whether or not different values are emphasized in election campaigns, views on basic political values are often related to the choices made by voters (Nevitte, Blais, Gidengil, & Nadeau, 2000).

PARTY IDENTIFICATION Political scientists often use party identification as a major explanation for why people vote the way that they do. **Party identification** can be thought of as a long-term psychological attachment to a particular political party. It is not simply an agreement with the positions that a party is currently taking, or a preference for a particular leader or candidate representing the party. Rather, it is a long-term feeling of closeness to a party that may be developed at quite an early age similar to one's attachment to a particular religious or ethnic group.

PARTY IDENTIFICATION
A long-term psychological attachment to a particular political party.

---

6 These conclusions are drawn from an analysis of voters outside Quebec.

Those who identify with a particular political party will tend to develop a positive view of the party's leader and candidates, prefer that party's position on the issues of the day, and believe that their party is most competent to handle the tasks of governing. Thus, even though voters typically vote in accordance with their evaluation of the leaders, candidates, and issue positions of the parties, the long-term influence of party identification may lie behind voters' evaluations of the particular features of an election.

The theory of party identification is not meant to suggest that an individual's vote is completely determined by long-term party ties. Voters with weak or non-existent ties to a party will frequently shift their votes from election to election, resulting in changing election outcomes. A particularly unpopular party personality or party issue position may alienate or turn off even some strong party supporters. However, the theory suggests that deviations from voting for one's party will be only temporary. Party identifiers may occasionally vote for another party while still retaining their original party identification.

Although the theory of party identification is useful in understanding voting behaviour and long-term patterns of support for different parties, party identification has been declining in importance in many countries. Fewer people now view themselves as strong party identifiers, and the proportion of people who view themselves as independent or without a party identification has been increasing in recent decades in the advanced democracies (Dalton, 2000, 2006).

In Canada, 56 percent of eligible voters at the time of the 2000 election considered themselves as fairly strong or very strong identifiers with a particular party at the national level (Blais, Gidengil, Nadeau, & Nevitte, 2002). In a 2006 survey, only 22 percent did not identify with any political party. Those who said that they were very strong identifiers usually identified with the same party when interviewed on four occasions during and after the 2004 and 2006 election campaigns. By contrast, close to one-half of those who described themselves as "not very strong" identifiers changed to another party or to having no identification in at least one of the surveys (Gidengil et al., 2006c). Although a substantial proportion of Liberal identifiers faced with the Liberal "sponsorship scandal" and an uninspiring performance by the Liberal leader voted for a different party in 2006, few Liberals changed their party identification (Gidengil et al., 2006c). Thus, party identification continues to be significant for a substantial proportion of the Canadian electorate.

Short-Term Influences

If some long-term influences on the vote are tending to decline in significance, short-term factors such as the personalities and issues of an election campaign could hold increasing significance. A substantial proportion of voters now claim that they make their voting choice during the election campaign, and a significant proportion changes their vote intention during the campaign. Surveys conducted during the 2000 Canadian election campaign found that about one-third of the voters could be considered to have been affected by the campaign (Blais, Gidengil, Nadeau, & Nevitte, 2002). A poll conducted at the end of the 2004 Canadian election found that about one-quarter of respondents said they made up their minds in the twenty-four hours before they voted (Compas, 2004). In 2006, a poll conducted between one and three days before the election found that 14 percent of respondents said they had not yet made up their minds on how to vote, although 45 percent said they had decided before the election was called. As well, 21 percent said they had changed their minds during the campaign (Environics/CBC 2006 Federal Election Survey).

It is not easy to determine the relative importance of such factors as the quality of leaders and candidates, the issue positions of the parties, and general perceptions of the quality and competence of the parties, as each factor will tend to influence the others. For example, those who trust a particular party leader may come to agree with the positions that leader's party takes on certain issues, while those who agree with a party's positions may be more inclined to develop a favourable impression of that party's leader and candidates. As well, the importance of different short-term factors may differ from election to election and from country to country, depending upon how the parties appeal to the voters and what the mass media emphasize in their coverage of a particular election.

LEADERS Evaluations of the leaders can have a significant effect (independent of party identification) on which party a voter chooses to support in an election (Blais, Gidengil, Nadeau, & Nevitte, 2002; Clarke, Kornberg, Scotto, & Twyman, 2006). However, the evaluations of different party leaders often do not vary widely, thus limiting their effect on the *outcome* of an election (Gidengil et al., 2006a). Having a popular leader will not necessarily overcome other disadvantages a party faces. For example, although Joe Clark was the best-regarded leader by the end of the 2000 election campaign (Turcotte, 2001), his PC party only managed a fifth-place finish in terms of House of Commons seats.

CANDIDATES Constituency candidates tend to be less important than leaders in affecting voting behaviour and election outcomes. However, in a closely contested constituency, a strong candidate may make a difference. In American elections, candidates can have very important effects because candidates often distance themselves from their party. Thus, they gain or lose support based, to a considerable extent, on their own characteristics, campaign, and positions. Incumbent members of the U.S. Congress have a very strong ability to win re-election even if their party has become unpopular. Although incumbency can help Canadian MPs in their fight for re-election, it is insufficient to save them if their party has become unpopular—as almost all PC MPs found in 1993, when the party was reduced to two seats in Parliament.

ISSUES Although many voters cite issues as the most important reason for their vote choice, the leading parties often do not clearly stake out different positions on what should be done about important problems. Instead, **valence issues**—those on which there is a general consensus—have often been the most important issues in election campaigns (Clarke, Kornberg, Scotto, & Twyman, 2006). For example, health care was the leading issue in both the 2000 and 2004 Canadian elections (and a major issue in the 2006 election). However, there was little difference among the parties, as each party proclaimed its commitment to improve the public health care system and to spend more money on health care. Liberal accusations that the Alliance (2000) and the Conservatives (2004) favoured privatization of public health care were met with denials of that claim. Likewise, issues concerning government mismanagement and corruption (such as the sponsorship scandal in the 2004 and 2006 Canadian elections) could be considered a valence issue because no party is going to take the position of favouring corruption.

Valence issues may have an impact if voters feel that one party is more competent to handle the problem or if they assign blame or credit for the handling of the problem in the past. For example, the "sponsorship scandal" clearly hurt the Liberal party in the 2004 and 2006 Canadian elections. However, in many cases (such as the economic problems of unemployment and inflation), voters may feel that "their" party is best able to handle the problem, thus reducing the impact of the issue on the election outcome.

Do voters hold the governing party accountable for its actions in office? An analysis of the 2000 Canadian election found that voters' evaluations of the Liberal government's performance did generally have a significant effect on their electoral choice. (In Quebec, however, voters made their choice primarily based on their views about Quebec sovereignty.) Interestingly, though, the Liberal party was re-elected despite considerable voter dissatisfaction with its record on such key issues as health, taxes, and corruption. Those who were dissatisfied with the Liberal government's record divided their votes among the various opposition parties, thus limiting the negative impact of their dissatisfaction. A complicating factor was the tendency of many voters to blame their provincial government as well as the federal government for problems with the health care system (Blais, Gidengil, Nadeau, & Nevitte, 2002). In the case of the 2004 Canadian election, the Liberal party's ability to raise fears about the consequences of electing what they described as an extreme right-wing, Harper-led Conservative government may have swung support away from the Conservative party late in the election campaign. In the 2006 election, Conservative leader Stephen Harper made substantial efforts to have his party appear moderate, and efforts by the Liberal party to raise fears about a Harper government were less successful. This example suggests that holding a governing party accountable for its actions is difficult if voters are not comfortable with voting for an alternative party.

Summary and Conclusion

Elections are often viewed as the central feature of democratic politics. Elections allow voters to choose who will represent them in the legislature. More importantly, elections can provide an opportunity for voters to maintain or remove a government. If parties take different ideological positions, voters can shift the general direction of the government by their choice of which party to support. Although election campaigns feature manipulation of the voters by the competing parties and politicians, elections also tend to bring politicians into closer contact with voters. In anticipation of an election, parties and politicians ask themselves, "What do voters want?" Appealing to the public may have to be modified, however, to ensure the support of the party's financial backers and party activists.

A basic problem with elections is that we are asked to convey a lot of information by our vote. We may use our vote to express which of the competing platforms we prefer, which candidates and leaders we think are most competent, which party we think is best, what our evaluation is of the current governing party, and so on. However, placing a single X on a ballot cannot really convey our views on a variety of matters.

Voters often express a variety of different attitudes, values, preferences, and judgments when they cast their vote. This can make the interpretation of the result of a particular election difficult and controversial. The messages being sent by voters to politicians through an election are often unclear. Statements by a governing party that it has a mandate to carry out particular policies because it won an election can be misleading.

The electoral system can distort the choices made by voters. The single member plurality (SMP) electoral system tends to give a boost to the leading party at the expense of the smaller parties. Thus, the governing party often does not have the support of the majority of the voters for the direction in which it plans to take the political community, even if it has the majority of elected representatives on its side. Representation of diverse viewpoints and interests tends to be inhibited because of the discrimination suffered by smaller parties. Systems of proportional representation (PR), although providing fairer representation, typically result in coalition governments that may be difficult to hold accountable for their actions. Elections often result in only small changes in party representation, and major changes in government are less common than in SMP systems. Furthermore, some PR systems do not give voters the opportunity to get rid of undesirable representatives.

When we consider whether elections serve the common good, we should remember that elections are the culmination of the struggle for political power within a democracy. So it should not be surprising that election campaigns are designed to manipulate rather than to enlighten voters. The contending parties in an election are not engaged in deliberation about what is best for the community, but rather are engaged in a competitive struggle for support. In societies with deep social divisions, election campaigns can inflame those divisions, and thus violence sometimes accompanies elections. This is particularly the case for elections that are conducted on a winner-takes-all basis (for example, elections using the SMP system or presidential elections) in countries where some groups fear serious consequences if a party representing an opposing section of society wins. Finally, in the competitive struggle for votes, parties may try to outbid each other in making costly promises to voters. Hasty promises made in the heat of an election campaign may not result in the common good.

Despite their limitations, elections are important in enabling voters to hold a government accountable for its actions and to have some ability to affect the direction taken by the political community. In democratic systems, voters do sometimes use the opportunity provided by elections to remove governing parties that have become corrupt, incompetent, unresponsive, or lacking in new ideas. If elections are viewed by citizens as free and fair, those elected to govern will normally be viewed as legitimate authorities. Transitions of political power from one group to another can be accomplished smoothly. Overall, then, the common good is served by a system of free and fair elections. Establishing a legitimate government, providing an incentive for governments to be responsive to those they govern, and providing a peaceful mechanism to remove governments that do not deserve to continue to be in power is good for all members of the political community.

Key Terms

Coalition government 234

Electoral college 233

Electoral system 230

Gerrymandering 229

Majoritarian electoral system 233

Mixed member proportional (MMP) system 235

Party identification 245

Preferential voting 233

Proportional representation (PR) system 234

Runoff election 233

Single member plurality (SMP) system 230

Single transferable vote (STV) system 235

Universal suffrage 228

Valence issues 248

Discussion Questions

1. Are Canadian elections free and fair?

2. Should Canada change its electoral system?

3. Should politicians be expected to keep the promises they make in an election campaign? What should happen if they do not?

4. How would you interpret the outcome of the last national, provincial, or local election? Did voters send a message as to the direction that they want their government to follow?

5. What criteria have you used, or do you think you should use, in deciding how to vote? Should you vote for the best leader, the best party, or the best local candidate?

6. Do voters generally make intelligent choices in elections?

Further Reading

Baumgartner, J.C. *Modern presidential electioneering: An organizational and comparative approach.* Westport, CT: Praeger, 2000.

Clarke, H.D., Jenson, J., LeDuc, L., & Pammett, J. *Absent mandate,* 3rd ed. Toronto: Gage, 1996.

Courtney, J.C. *Elections.* Vancouver: UBC Press, 2004.

Duffy, J. *Fights of our lives: Elections, leadership and the making of Canada.* Toronto: HarperCollins, 2002.

Farrell, D.M., & Schmitt-Beck, R. (Eds.). *Do political campaigns matter? Campaign effects in elections and referendums.* London: Routledge, 2002.

Hyde, H. *Promises, promises: Breaking faith in Canadian politics.* Toronto: Penguin, 1997.

Milner, H. (Ed.). *Steps toward making every vote count: Electoral system reform in Canada and its provinces.* Peterborough, ON: Broadview, 2004.

Pammett, J.H., & Dornan, C. (Eds.). *The Canadian general election of 2006.* Toronto: Dundurn Press, 2006.

Plasser, F., & Plasser, G. *Global political campaigning: A worldwide analysis of campaign professionals and their practices.* Westport, CT: Praeger, 2002.

Chapter 11

TAKING COLLECTIVE ACTION: INTEREST GROUPS AND SOCIAL MOVEMENTS

PHOTO ABOVE: They are gas guzzlers, polluters, and far more prone to flipping and rolling over than cars—but because they meet fuel efficiency and safety regulations set for light trucks more than three decades ago, SUVs are perfectly legal. Automakers and auto worker unions have fiercely resisted attempts to make streets and highways safer by bringing SUVs under the same standards that apply to cars.

CHAPTER OBJECTIVES

After reading this chapter you should be able to:

1. discuss the nature and significance of interest groups and social movements
2. examine the organization of interest groups and social movements
3. distinguish between lobbying and other types of political action
4. discuss the extent to which interest groups and social movements help or hinder the achievement of the common good of the political community

Today it seems as if half the vehicles on the road in North America are either pickup trucks or SUVs— sport-utility vehicles. It wasn't always that way. Thirty years ago, pickups were working vehicles and SUVs didn't exist. What happened to change this picture was not just the changing tastes of the North American automobile buyer, but also politics.

In the 1970s, North America experienced its first round of rapidly rising fuel prices. This led governments, especially the United States, to set fuel economy standards for vehicles, but they applied only to passenger cars. Trucks, even light trucks like pickups and what would become SUVs, were excluded. The argument was that these were working vehicles and that government should not add unnecessarily to their price by mandating the same fuel efficiency standards that applied to cars. This logic was also extended to safety regulations.

Then automakers created the SUV. The success of Chrysler's 1984 Jeep Cherokee spurred other companies to turn out their own models. SUVs are very profitable for automakers because they are built on existing truck frames, which are also simpler and cheaper to build than passenger car frames. However, SUVs use more gas and are far more prone to flipping and rolling over than cars. Accidents involving SUVs produce a high rate of fatalities, particularly among the passengers of the other vehicle in a collision. Yet SUVs are perfectly legal because they meet the fuel efficiency and safety regulations set for light trucks. Attempts to bring SUVs under the guidelines that apply to cars are met with fierce resistance by automakers, who don't want to see their most profitable lines affected, and auto worker unions, who are happy to see some of their members making more than US$100 000 yearly thanks to the overtime they get building enough SUVs to meet demand.

So a political decision made almost three decades ago to give a break to the tradesmen and farmers, who were then the usual owners of pickups and four-wheel drives, has prevented governments from setting regulations that would make our streets and highways safer. And despite technological advances that can make automobiles more fuel efficient and less polluting, overall motor vehicle fuel efficiency has not improved in North America—in fact, SUVs are a major contributor to the increase in greenhouse gases that cause global climate change. The interest group representing the auto industry has been successful in ensuring that U.S. fuel efficiency standards have not been raised since 1985 and that the SUV loophole remains.

Meanwhile, in Canada, the auto industry successfully pressured the Canadian government not to impose fuel efficiency regulations in 1982. In return, it agreed to voluntarily follow the American regulations. Early in 2004, former Environment Minister David Anderson demanded that the auto industry move to increase fuel efficiency by 25 percent within six years. The Canadian Vehicle Manufacturers Association (CVMA) claimed that this was too great a challenge and pressured members of Parliament from Ontario, where most of the auto industry is located, to help it resist such policies. However, the environmental movement, which has helped to publicize the problem of global climate change, eventually succeeded in encouraging governments to establish stricter fuel economy standards. In 2007, the Canadian government announced plans for mandatory fuel economy regulations beginning with new vehicles in the 2011 model year. Likewise, new fuel economy regulations for SUVs and light trucks in the United States will be in effect by 2011.

This chapter explores interest groups like the CVMA and the ways in which they influence the making and implementation of government policies and laws. As well, this chapter examines social movements like the environmental movement that promote major changes in politics, society, and individual behaviour.

INTEREST GROUPS

An **interest group** is a group of people who have joined together to pursue common interests. Unlike political parties, whose major objective is to elect members to the legislature and, if possible, form the government, the political activity of interest groups is generally focused on trying to influence the making and implementation of the laws and policies of a political community.

Many interest groups do not exist exclusively or primarily for political purposes. However, in representing the interests of a particular segment of society, interest groups often find political action necessary or desirable to protect or promote the interests of the group (see Box 11-1, Are You a Member of an Interest Group?). For example, the major activities of the Canadian Medical Association include the exchange of medical information and the certification of doctors. However, because the interests of doctors are strongly affected by government policy, the Canadian Medical Association is also active in developing and promoting a variety of policy positions concerning the medical system. The Canadian Automobile Association is well known for the roadside assistance and travel planning that it provides to its motoring members. However, it also involves itself in political action—for example, by urging that the Canadian government establish stricter regulations concerning automobile fuel efficiency.

Types of Interest Groups

The many thousands of interest groups in modern democracies vary greatly in their characteristics, their ability to influence the political process, and the strategies they use to achieve their objectives. One way to make sense of the great variety of groups is to consider the different types of interests and goals that interest groups pursue.

Many groups have been formed by specific economic and occupational interests. Groups to promote various business, agricultural, and labour interests were among the first to be established in many countries. Most professions have also developed well-organized interest groups. Other groups have been formed to develop, express, and promote the identity, rights, and interests of a particular segment of society—consider the variety of interest

BOX 11-1

Are You a Member of an Interest Group?

Many people are members of interest groups, even if they did not deliberately join a group to undertake political action.

Sometimes people are not even aware that they are represented by an interest group. For example, at many universities, students are required to support the Canadian Federation of Students through their student fees. This organization takes action on such issues as student loans and government financing of post-secondary education. It also supports a variety of national and international causes, such as the protests in Quebec City in 2001 discussed in Chapter 1.

Many workers belong to a labour union affiliated with the Canadian Labour Congress, which promotes the interests of workers and the cause of equality. Many small business owners are members of a local branch of the Canadian Chamber of Commerce and/or the Canadian Federation of Independent Business, organizations that regularly lobby government on issues such as taxes. If you are a member of a religious organization, you may be interested in knowing that all major religious organizations have some political involvement. For example, the Canadian Council of Churches, representing the major Christian denominations, has expressed support for the rights of Aboriginal peoples and advocates "just trade" rather than "free trade."

Even if your only organized activity is sports, you may belong to an organization that is involved in political action to try to persuade governments to provide better sports facilities or more assistance to athletes. Women who join the YWCA for its athletic facilities may be surprised to learn that this indirectly makes them members of the National Action Committee on the Status of Women, which has been prominent in pursuing feminist causes.

One final example: The Consumers' Association of Canada claims to speak on behalf of all consumers in Canada, despite its relatively small formal membership. So even if you are not a formal member of an interest group, there may be an interest group that claims to represent you!

Canadian Federation of Students
http://cfs-fcee.ca

Canadian Ethnocultural Council
www.ethnocultural.ca

SELF-INTEREST GROUP
An interest group whose primary objective is to promote the interests of the group and its members and to seek benefits that are primarily or exclusively for their members.

PUBLIC INTEREST GROUP
A group that seeks to achieve goals that the group views as being for the good of the community as a whole rather than specific benefits for their members.

groups representing different ethnic groups (for example, the Chinese Canadian National Council). Groups formed to organize recreational activities occasionally undertake political action, particularly to gain government assistance: for example, a softball association may try to persuade a city council to improve the condition of ball fields in public parks.

A distinction is sometimes made between different types of interest groups, depending on whether they are primarily concerned with advancing their own interests or the good of the community as a whole.

SELF-INTEREST GROUPS Interest groups whose primary objective is to promote the interests of the group and its members are often referred to as **self-interest groups** (see Table 11-1). In particular, self-interest groups seek benefits from governments (such as a subsidy or a tax break for their industry) that are primarily or exclusively for their own benefit.

PUBLIC INTEREST GROUPS Other groups, often referred to as **public interest groups** or citizens' groups, do not generally seek specific benefits for

SELF-INTEREST GROUPS	PUBLIC INTEREST GROUPS
Canadian Manufacturers & Exporters	Council of Canadians
Canadian Bankers Association	World Wildlife Fund
Canadian Petroleum Association	Amnesty International
Canadian Vehicle Manufacturers Association	Ontario Public Interest Research Group
Canadian Auto Workers	John Howard Society
Fisheries Council of Canada	Canadian Civil Liberties Association
Canadian Polish Congress	Sierra Club
Canadian Association for the Fifty-Plus	Canadian Nature Federation

TABLE 11-1

SELF-INTEREST AND PUBLIC INTEREST GROUPS

their members, but rather seek to achieve goals that the group views as being for the good of the community as a whole (see Table 11-1).

Some public interest groups have been formed to promote a particular perspective, which they believe to be in the public interest, on a single issue. For example, pro-choice and pro-life groups are active in promoting their viewpoints on the issue of whether abortions should be legal. Mothers Against Drunk Driving seeks tougher laws concerning drinking and driving.

Other public interest groups have a broader focus in seeking to promote a general perspective and to affect public policy on a variety of issues. For example, the National Citizens Coalition (once headed by Stephen Harper, before he became prime minister) takes a strong free-enterprise perspective, promotes tax cuts, and advocates a reduction of government activity. Democracy Watch terms itself a "citizens' advocacy group" and campaigns for democratic reforms, government accountability, and corporate responsibility.

PROBLEMS WITH THE DISTINCTION The distinction between self-interest groups and public interest groups is often not clear. Self-interest groups usually argue that the policies they hope to obtain will benefit the whole community. For example, business groups seeking lower taxes claim that such policies will help to create jobs and prosperity. Ethnic groups may claim that government support for maintaining their culture helps Canada to be a more diverse and interesting country. Recreational groups will point to the benefits of better facilities for the health and well-being of the population. As well, groups that were established to promote a particular interest may combine self-interest with support for broader causes that do not provide exclusive benefits to their members. For example, the Canadian Federation of Students has involved itself not only in pursuing lower tuition fees and more government support for higher education but also, at various times, in pursuing various national and international causes it believes to be in the general public interest.

However, claims that particular issue positions, general perspectives, or causes are in the interest of the public as a whole are often controversial and

Canadian Council of Chief Executives
http://ceocouncil.ca

Sierra Club of Canada
www.sierraclub.ca

Greenpeace Canada
www.greenpeace.ca

The National Citizens Coalition
www.morefreedom.org

The Council of Canadians
www.canadians.org

may reflect the interests of a particular part of society. As well, some public interest groups have been accused of using their campaign for a public interest to hide the pursuit of private interests. Raising funds for a popular cause might be used, in some cases, primarily to provide generous salaries and benefits to the leaders and staff of the organization.

There is a great deal of variation in interest groups, not only in their goals and whom they represent, but also in terms of their organizational development. A distinction is often made between issue-oriented interest groups and institutionalized interest groups (Pross, 1993).

ISSUE-ORIENTED INTEREST GROUP An interest group that spontaneously develops to express the views of people on a particular issue, concern, or grievance.

ISSUE-ORIENTED INTEREST GROUPS Some **issue-oriented interest groups** spontaneously develop to express the views of people on a particular issue, concern, or grievance. For example, in many rural communities, groups have formed from time to time to demand better roads. Likewise, the Anti-Adams Mine Coalition that fought a plan to send Toronto's garbage to an abandoned mine in Kirkland Lake, Ontario, could be considered an issue-oriented group. Some issue-oriented groups have only a temporary existence and are not concerned about developing a formal organization. When the issue is resolved or passions concerning the issue dissipate, such groups may fold or fade away.

INSTITUTIONALIZED INTEREST GROUPS Many other interest groups have developed a formal organization, including such features as a well-established membership base, paid professional staff, permanent offices, and a capability to keep their members and the public aware of their views and

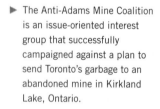

▶ The Anti-Adams Mine Coalition is an issue-oriented interest group that successfully campaigned against a plan to send Toronto's garbage to an abandoned mine in Kirkland Lake, Ontario.

activities. Such groups, termed **institutionalized interest groups**, typically develop and promote positions on a variety of issues, monitor the activities of government, and try to develop close working relationships with key government officials (Pross, 1993). Groups such as the Canadian Chamber of Commerce, the Canadian Federation of Agriculture, and the Assembly of First Nations are regular and long-lasting organizations that are important features of political life.

Temporary issue-oriented interest groups with little organization and permanent, well-organized institutionalized interest groups could be considered as extremes on a continuum of organizational development, with many groups falling somewhere between these two types. Some issue-oriented interest groups try to develop a more professional, structured organization so as to have a more permanent and effective vehicle for their concerns. For example, some of the groups involved with the abortion issue, such as Campaign Life and the Canadian Abortion Rights Action League, have maintained their existence over a considerable length of time, built an organization to carry out the objectives of the group, and developed expertise in promoting their goals. However, most institutionalized interest groups represent economic and professional interests or groups with a particular identity rather than specific issue concerns.

INSTITUTIONALIZED INTEREST GROUP A group that has developed a formal organization, including such features as a well-established membership base, paid professional staff, permanent offices, and the capability to keep its members and the public aware of its views and activities.

Democratic Organizations?

Many interest groups have democratic organizational structures. Institutionalized interest groups typically have some regular method for electing their chairperson and board of directors, who oversee the operations of staff members and set the direction for the organization.

However, the "iron law of oligarchy" discussed in Chapter 9 applies, to a considerable extent, to many interest group organizations. Although some interest groups do provide for active participation by their members in the group's decision making, there is often not a strong relationship between the members of an interest group and those who act on its behalf. Some of the large national interest groups devote most of their energies to influencing government policy-makers, leaving the "grassroots" members largely uninvolved in the organization (Shaiko, 1999).

Even though some interest groups do not provide a strong vehicle for the voices of their members, there will usually be some shared perspectives between the spokespersons for the group and its members. A group that deviates strongly from the views of its grassroots supporters or members may find that its funds, membership, and ability to mobilize members in support of its cause fade. Groups whose strategies to influence government policy include petition signing, demonstrations, and other forms of collective action by their members will be more likely to try to maintain links with their members than groups that rely on presenting policy briefs and sitting on government advisory committees. Organizations that have compulsory membership, provide useful services to their members, or—as in the case of cultural, religious, and recreational groups—were not formed to pursue a particular political issue or cause may be able to retain their members even if the political positions they pursue are not fully in tune with the views of the membership. However, a group is more likely to be influential if it can make a credible claim to represent a substantial membership and, when necessary, to mobilize those members to indicate the membership's commitment to the positions being pursued by the group's leaders.

Membership in Interest Groups

Organized collective action gives individuals a chance to be influential, which is usually why people join and support interest groups. Modern governments are large and the policy-making process is complex. Few individuals have the contacts and expertise needed to influence decisions. Although your member of Parliament may be willing to listen to your request, and a letter or email to a Cabinet minister or the prime minister may result in a computer-generated response, it is highly unlikely that an individual's demands or opinions will affect government decisions. Most individuals are much more likely to be able to influence political decisions through membership in an organization than by trying to influence politicians and government officials themselves.

THE FREE RIDER PROBLEM   Mancur Olson (1965) has questioned whether it is rational for individuals to join and support groups to pursue their political interests. In what he describes as the *free rider problem,* an individual can often enjoy the benefits of the successes of an interest group whether or not that individual is a member or financial supporter. If, for example, an environmental group is successful in a campaign to reduce air pollution, we all take advantage of that action whether or not we supported the group. Rational, calculating individuals may figure that it is to their advantage to let others contribute time and money to the campaign. Of course, if enough people think this way, an interest group will not be able to survive.

The free rider problem is particularly serious for public interest groups because their goals can benefit the political community as a whole. Self-interest groups that seek a specific benefit for their members find it easier to gain and maintain the support of those who will potentially benefit. For example, the Forest Products Association of Canada may have little difficulty in gaining the support of the few large paper manufacturers in order to fund its efforts to promote the interests of that particular industrial sector. Individual companies can anticipate a direct and substantial impact on their profitability if the organization is successful in persuading government to adopt certain policies that benefit their industry.

In some cases, the free rider problem is largely irrelevant because membership in a group is compulsory. For example, in unionized workplaces, union dues are automatically deducted from paycheques. Likewise, student unions, after obtaining a majority vote of students, have convinced university administrations to require that all students pay union dues. Similarly, if one wants to practise as a professional (such as a doctor, engineer, or pharmacist) one has to be a member of the appropriate professional association.

REASONS FOR JOINING To some degree, public interest groups can try to avoid the free rider problem by offering some particular benefits (termed **selective incentives**) to their members. Some groups provide a glossy magazine, offer merchandise at reduced rates, and arrange for reduced insurance rates and discounts on car rentals and hotel accommodations. Professional associations provide useful information to their members, arrange conferences, and offer continuing professional education.

Many public interest groups that provide few selective incentives have developed in recent decades, with some attracting very large numbers of members and supporters. For example, some environmental groups have millions of members and supporters. People often join or support public interest groups because of the satisfaction that can be achieved by expressing one's values and contributing to the good of the community. Some people also join interest groups for social reasons, that is, because they enjoy interacting and working with like-minded persons. More generally, an increasingly educated population with greater skills and more leisure time is more likely to pursue various causes through political action. Public interest groups are seen by many people as the most effective way to pursue the causes that they believe in. As well, modern communications and transportation technologies have made it easier for groups to organize people across the country and around the world.

Thus, just as many individuals do not join a political party in the hopes of gaining some particular benefit for themselves if their party is elected, so too the lure of individual material benefits does not explain the growth of public interest group membership. Nevertheless, many public interest groups experience a high turnover in membership and face large swings in membership and financial support as different causes become more popular. Therefore, they often have to devote considerable effort and resources to motivate volunteers and maintain financial solvency.

Support for Interest Groups

The development of many interest groups is the result not only of the willingness of individuals to join or support the group. Governments and philanthropic organizations have often provided some financial support and encouragement for the formation and development of interest groups. For

SELECTIVE INCENTIVE
A particular benefit that is made available to members of an interest group but is not available to the public as a whole.

example, since the 1960s, Canadian governments have encouraged and helped to finance the development of groups representing segments of the population that were largely unrepresented by well-organized interest groups, including Aboriginals, women, and poor people (Pal, 1993).

Why would governments fund groups representing disadvantaged segments of the population when such groups are often critical of government policies and government's lack of action to deal with their problems? Some governments have hoped to offset the heavy influence that groups representing business and other privileged elements of society are often able to exert on government. This may allow politicians and government officials greater flexibility to act in accordance with their own interests and values.

Particular government departments and agencies often find it useful to have active and vocal interest groups in their policy area so as to assist their struggle with other departments or agencies of government for more funds or new programs. Strong and active environmental groups, for example, may help Environment Canada to convince the rest of government to treat environmental issues more seriously, thus allowing Environment Canada employees to gain the resources and policies they feel are needed for their programs. More recently, as the scope of government has been reduced, government has found it useful and cost-effective to support interest groups that can take on some of the tasks that formerly were carried out by government departments and agencies. Some environmental groups, for example, undertake environmental monitoring, organize cleanups of streams, and conduct public awareness campaigns to promote pollution prevention.

FUNDING AND CRITICISM   It is sometimes thought that interest groups that receive assistance from government will become tame supporters of government. This is not always the case. For example, feminist, Aboriginal, and poor people's groups that have received funding from the Canadian government have at times been sharply critical of the policies of the governments that helped to fund them. In response, governments have sometimes reduced their funding of groups that are critical of government policies and actions. For example, the Assembly of First Nations (AFN) found its funding reduced after it chose a leader who was strongly critical of the government's Aboriginal policies. This, in turn, contributed to the AFN's 2003 election of a new leader, Phil Fontaine, who promised to rebuild good relations with the Canadian government in order to try to secure a substantial increase in funding.

Assembly of First Nations
www.afn.ca

Government funding of public interest groups has been criticized particularly by those who feel that some of the groups are too radical or represent only "special interests." Often ignored is the fact that business-oriented interest groups are, in effect, subsidized by government. In calculating their taxes, businesses can deduct contributions to interest groups and other expenses they incur in trying to influence government. In contrast, individuals can only receive a tax credit for contributing to organizations that are deemed to be charitable, which generally excludes organizations that devote significant resources (more than 10 percent of their revenues) to political action.

Faced with criticism of the funding of interest groups, the Canadian government has shifted much of its funding toward indirect assistance, such as paying groups for specific projects, providing assistance for research and participation at public hearings on particular issues, and funding conferences. Such piecemeal support creates uncertainty for groups that are dependent upon government funding, as they have no assurance that they will have the money needed to continue to pay their staff and rent their offices. It also means that their staff has to devote much time to preparing proposals for specific grants.

Interest Group Activities

In analyzing how interest groups go about trying to influence public policy, a distinction may be made between inside and outside strategies (Walker, 1991). **Inside strategies** involve interest group leaders developing close contacts with key decision-makers in government and the public service so that influence can be exerted in a quiet fashion. **Outside strategies** involve appealing to the public for support (for example, through the mass media and advertising) and mobilizing members and supporters to put pressure on decision-makers (for example, through petitions, emails, and demonstrations).

Inside strategies have the advantage of directly influencing those responsible for developing government policies. They are less likely to stimulate opposition and criticism than outside strategies. However, developing a very close relationship with the government may result in interest group leaders becoming influenced by, and associated with, the policy direction and concerns of the government. Outside strategies, if successful in mobilizing the support of the public, may be useful in pressuring politicians who are worried about their chances for re-election. Outside strategies may also be useful in building and maintaining an active membership-based organization. However, governments are often reluctant to be seen as backing down under pressure, and thus outside strategies can have difficulty exerting influence once government has publicly committed to a particular course of action.

CHOICE OF STRATEGIES   Different types of interest groups tend to use different mixtures of strategies. Business and professional associations are more likely to use inside strategies, although they may devote some attention to outside strategies if they find government unsympathetic to their concerns or if other groups mount strong public campaigns against their interests. Unions, public interest groups, issue-oriented groups, and groups that have developed out of social movements (discussed later in the chapter) are more likely to use outside strategies, although they may find that combining these with inside strategies is useful in persuading government to adopt specific policies (see Box 11-2, Campaigning for a Clean Harbour).

INSIDE STRATEGIES
Strategies in which interest group leaders develop close contacts with key policy-makers in government and the public service in order to influence public policies.

OUTSIDE STRATEGIES
Strategies in which interest group leaders appeal to the public for support in order to put pressure on decision-makers concerning public policies.

BOX 11-2

Campaigning for a Clean Harbour

Trying to clean up the St. John's harbour has meant dredging up support from far and wide.

The Newfoundland capital is just one of several Canadian cities that continue to dump untreated sewage into their harbours. Not only is raw sewage toxic to marine life, it also interferes with the development of the tourist industry and the enjoyment of the harbour. But in the case of St. John's, the substantial cost of building sewage treatment facilities, estimated at $93 million in 1997, was beyond the capability of the city government.

An arrangement to share the costs among the national, provincial, and local governments was worked out in the early 1980s. However, a dispute between the Canadian and Newfoundland governments in 1982 over an unrelated issue (the control of offshore oil) led to the suspension of plans to build a sewage treatment facility. The St. John's city government was subsequently unable to persuade the senior levels of government to carry out their commitments to provide funding.

In 1991, the Canadian government decided as part of its Green Plan to establish the Atlantic Canada Action Program (ACAP) to encourage community initiatives, particularly those that would deal with the environmental problems of harbours and coastlines. Based on this, the St. John's Harbour ACAP organization was formed by a group of local citizens. It built on a citizens' group, the Friends of St. John's Harbour, and included representatives of the three levels of government. Partial funding for the organization was provided by Environment Canada.

In addition to carrying out scientific research to document the environmental problems of the harbour, the St. John's ACAP decided that it needed to take political action to clean up the harbour. Its approach involved an outside strategy of mobilizing public support and an inside strategy of collaborating with governments to design the appropriate facilities and negotiate suitable financial arrangements. The group raised the issue in federal, provincial, and municipal elections and kept the public informed of the issue. It lobbied governments and gained the support of local businesses, especially the tourist and convention industries, for its goal.

In 1996, pressure from the St. John's ACAP helped persuade the three municipal governments in the St. John's area to commit themselves to the project and begin some preliminary work. It was another four years before the provincial government, worried that the Canadian government would not contribute, was persuaded to commit to sharing the costs of the project. The Canadian government was reluctant to commit to the project, fearing that it would be seen as a special handout to one area of the country. Finally, in 2002, as part of a national infrastructure-building program, the Canadian government agreed to provide one-third of the funding.

Although the experience of the St. John's ACAP suggests that a combined inside/outside strategy is desirable, it has its difficulties. Putting outside pressure on government may result in an antagonistic relationship that may impede efforts to collaborate with government. Interestingly, although the Canadian government (through Environment Canada) was involved with the formation and activities of the St. John's ACAP, the group had a difficult time persuading the Canadian government to act. On the other hand, an inside strategy of collaborating with government may detract from efforts to mobilize the public support that is often needed to convince governments to act. In this case, over time the two dedicated part-time staff members of the St. John's ACAP were able to learn the skills of successful interest group activity. They patiently pursued their goal despite years of frustration (Close & Mintz, 2005).

The results to date? Preliminary work on the harbour cleanup project began in 2003. And the primary sewage treatment plant is scheduled to begin operations in Fall 2008!

The political activities and strategies of interest groups will also be affected by the nature of government. Interest groups in the United States, for example, devote considerable effort to trying to influence individual elected representatives in Congress and members of the committees of Congress because of the substantial involvement of Congress in the development of public policies. Canadian interest groups, particularly institutionalized interest groups, tend to direct much of their activity toward influencing those public servants who are important in developing public policy and the particular Cabinet minister whose government department is most relevant to the concerns of the interest group. For example, interest groups representing farmers devote much of their efforts to trying to influence those involved in policy development within the Department of Agriculture and meet regularly with the minister to inform him or her of their concerns and proposals. Canadian members of Parliament do not normally receive the same level of attention from the major Canadian interest groups as senior officials in government departments because of their limited role in developing policy.

In several Western European countries (including, to varying extents, Austria, Germany, Sweden, and the Netherlands), the state actively collaborates with selected major interests (particularly the national organizations of business and labour) to seek a consensus concerning the country's major economic and social policies. State officials guide the development of a consensus among the leading interests. In turn, the leaders of these interests persuade those they represent to accept the agreements that have been reached (such as agreements concerning wage and price increases). In such systems (termed **corporatism**) the activities of the leading interest groups and their relationship to government are quite different than in Canada, the United States, or the United Kingdom.

CORPORATISM

A political system in which the state actively collaborates with selected major interests (particularly the national organizations of business and labour) to seek a consensus concerning the country's major economic and social policies.

LOBBYING The inside strategy is often associated with the activity of lobbying. The term **lobbying** arose from the practice of those seeking favours from government or seeking to influence the passage of legislation to congregate in the lobby of the British House of Commons to make their case to members of Parliament as they left the legislative chamber. In contemporary usage, lobbying refers to efforts to influence not only legislators, but also those involved in the executive and administrative aspects of government. In particular, lobbying refers to efforts to persuade policy-makers to adopt and implement certain policies or decisions, particularly through direct personal contact.

LOBBYING

An effort to persuade legislators, executives, or public officials, particularly through direct personal contact, to adopt and implement policies or decisions favoured by an individual, business, or group.

Lobbying has increasingly become a professionalized activity. In addition to individuals within corporations and interest groups who have developed expertise in lobbying government, a number of consulting firms specialize in lobbying on behalf of a variety of clients, particularly businesses.

Many professional lobbyists are persons who have had high-level experience in government as senior administrators, Cabinet ministers, or political assistants to Cabinet ministers. Their inside knowledge of the workings of government and the thinking of policy-makers, as well as their extensive contacts within government and administration, can make them valuable assets to their clients. However, the revolving door between working in government and working as a lobbyist, as well as the government's hiring of lobbying firms for research and public relations, often leads to ethical questions being raised about whether the relationship between government and lobbyists is too close.

Lobbying often has a very negative image, as it raises the possibility of special deals being worked out in secret to provide benefits, at public expense, to particular individuals, businesses, or groups. Governments in Canada, the United States, and elsewhere have adopted legislation to regulate the activities of lobbyists and to require public disclosure of some of their activities. It is difficult, however, to ensure that particular interests do not receive unjustified special benefits due to influence exerted behind closed doors.

INVOLVEMENT IN THE POLICY-MAKING PROCESS Lobbying is not the only type of "inside" activity engaged in by interest groups. In their interactions with government, many institutionalized interest groups do not simply put forward their demands and pressure government to give them what they want. Interest groups often supply information that government policy-makers need, and work with policy-makers to try to find effective solutions to problems (Montpetit, 2004). The development of government policies is often a product of the discussions among government officials, various interest groups, and experts in a particular policy field. In this situation, interest groups will represent the interest of their members, but as well they will often be involved in trying to find solutions that are acceptable to other interests and to government. For example, the environmentalist group Greenpeace, which is well known for its confrontations with government and business, increasingly relies "on high-level scientists and sophisticated policy-relevant knowledge" to "find, in cooperation with state and other non-state actors, innovative solutions to environmental problems" (Montpetit, 2004, p. 310).

The involvement of interest groups in the policy-making process is often facilitated through the use of "think tanks," non-profit organizations that do policy research and develop policy proposals from a particular perspective. For example, the C.D. Howe Institute and the Fraser Institute, both of which receive financial support from the business community, have considerable influence on policy discussion and development in Canada. The Canadian Centre for Policy Alternatives, which is supported by labour unions and individual members, provides policy advice of a "progressive" (leftist) nature.

MOBILIZING PUBLIC SUPPORT Most interest groups pay some attention to gaining support from the public for their concerns and proposals. For issue-oriented interest groups that have not developed close connections with policy-makers, the "outside" strategy of taking their case to the public may be the only way of effectively influencing public policy. Institutionalized interest groups may want to create or maintain a good public image for their organization and counteract any potential public campaign by those with differing views.

Mobilizing public support may involve getting the group's message to the public in the hope that a change in public opinion will affect the thinking of policy-makers. In a more active way, interest groups may encourage their members to sign petitions, email their elected representatives, vote for candidates and parties that support their cause, or participate in public demonstrations.

As well, interest groups often try to build coalitions with other interest groups in order to add weight to their claim to speak on behalf of a large number of people on a particular issue. For example, to bolster its campaign for stronger lobbying and ethics rules, Democracy Watch has built a coalition of thirty-one groups, ranging from the Canadian Labour Congress and the National Action Committee on the Status of Women to the Canadian Friends of Burma.

Democracy Watch
www.dwatch.ca

LEGAL ACTION Interest groups often make use of the judicial system to advance their interests. For example, environmental groups have had some successes in the courts in forcing the Canadian government to undertake environmental assessments of proposed projects that have potentially negative effects on fish habitats. However, using the court system to pursue interests can be costly. In the past, the Canadian government financed the Court Challenges program to assist equality-seeking groups, particularly women's groups and groups representing linguistic minorities, in challenging laws and policies that are viewed as discriminatory under the provisions of the Canadian Charter of Rights and Freedoms. This program was cancelled by the Conservative government in 2006.

The use of the legal system to pursue interest group objectives is particularly common in the United States, where laws often contain highly specific obligations for government action, and thus provide scope for legal action if the obligations are not fulfilled. In contrast, laws in Canada and elsewhere typically provide considerable discretion to government and administrators in determining when and how to carry out the general objectives contained in the law. For example, most environmental laws enable provincial governments or the Canadian government to take action to protect the environment, but do not require that they do so (Boyd, 2003). However, some legislation, such as the Canadian Environmental Protection Act, 1999, does contain mandatory requirements, and opens up the possibility that citizens could take legal action if government does not live up to its obligations (Valiante, 2002).

ESTABLISHING AND SUPPORTING POLITICAL PARTIES Interest groups have sometimes viewed involvement with a political party as a useful means of pursuing their goals. For example, the Canadian Labour Congress (an organization representing the majority of labour unions in Canada) played a key role in the establishment of the New Democratic party and has

Canadian Labour Congress
http://clc-ctc.ca

continued to be a supporter of that party, with members of various affiliated unions having a direct voice in the party. The Catholic Church and various Catholic organizations have been involved in Christian Democratic parties in a number of countries including Italy, where that party was at the centre of governments from 1945 until its collapse in 1994 as a result of patronage scandals. In the United States, groups reflecting fundamentalist religious beliefs, such as the Christian Coalition, have closely allied themselves with the Republican party in recent decades.

In general, the relationship between interest groups and political parties is often an uneasy one. Although interest groups are, in some cases, an important source of support for a political party, the goals of the two types of organizations often differ. The support of a particular interest group may be detrimental to the attempts of a party to expand its base of popular support or to form a coalition with other parties. For example, the close connection between the New Democratic party and its affiliated unions has been both an element of financial and organizational strength for the party and a potential detriment to its electoral fortunes because of the negative attitudes many people have toward labour unions.

The relationship between business interests and political parties tends to be of an informal nature. Businesses often support conservative and liberal parties, but this does not generally take the form of the direct involvement of business interest groups in the affairs of a particular party. For example, although individual businesses have in the past been major financial contributors to Canadian political parties, business interest groups have rarely contributed to political parties. Many interest groups want to avoid direct involvement with political parties so that they can maintain or develop good relationships with government leaders regardless of which party happens to be in power.

Influence Potential

Interest groups vary in their capabilities to influence public policy. Several factors contribute to the amount of influence that a group can exert:

- The size of the group's membership may affect the willingness of politicians to take the group seriously. However, a well-organized and cohesive smaller group may be better able to exert influence than a disunited large group.
- The ability of a group to mobilize its members and supporters and its ability to establish coalitions with other groups to advance its causes are important.
- Financial resources help in maintaining an effective organization, hiring professional lobbyists and political consultants who understand the workings of power and have good contacts with key officials, and conducting research and advertising on behalf of the group's concerns.

- Groups that are able to develop close ties with key government officials are more likely to be influential. This can allow them to get in on the "ground floor" in influencing government as it is developing a policy.
- Groups that are seen by government and the public as having expertise and credibility, such as the Canadian Medical Association and the Canadian Bar Association, have a strong influence potential.
- Groups whose ideas and proposals coincide with the general thinking of government, the media, or the public are more likely to be successful than groups whose ideas are out of favour or controversial.
- The ability to make credible threats about the adverse consequences of failing to act as the group recommends can be useful.
- A group is more likely to be influential if it does not face competing interest groups in a particular policy area.

Although a large number of interest groups have been established in modern liberal democracies where individuals enjoy the freedom to establish and join groups, some groups are more influential than others. In particular, it is often argued that business interests have a privileged position from which to influence many aspects of government policy. Business groups possess considerable financial resources, sources of information, and expertise, and often have close relationships with government that give them considerable influence potential. More fundamentally, the government's desire to retain the confidence of the business community in order to maintain the material well-being of the community means that the interests and policy preferences of business are likely to be highly influential in the development of a wide variety of government policies that affect the activities and profitability of business (Lindblom, 1977). By contrast, the poor and various disadvantaged groups in society often do not have strong and effective interest groups to represent their interests, and their concerns may not be taken as seriously by policy-makers as the interests of business.

SOCIAL MOVEMENTS

Social movements seek major social and political changes, particularly by acting outside of established political institutions (Martell, 1994). Groups based on social movements may, like interest groups, seek to change various laws and public policies. However, movements also have broader goals, such as challenging and transforming the values, power relationships, and institutions of society and politics. A social movement can be thought of as a network of groups and individuals who share a common cause and, generally, a common perspective. As well, movements are often based on, or seek to develop, a sense of collective identity among a substantial segment of society and seek to inspire collective action by this segment of society. For example, the women's movement has sought to raise the consciousness of women not only to

SOCIAL MOVEMENT
A network of groups and individuals that seeks major social and political changes, particularly by acting outside of established political institutions.

increase awareness of the problems women face, but also to create a sense of solidarity among women and to encourage collective action to promote women's values and identity in politics and society.

The distinction between social movements and interest groups can be unclear because many public interest groups originated in, and are associated with, social movements. There are, for example, many environmental interest groups that focus on influencing public policy concerning particular problems, but view themselves as part of a broader environmental movement that believes that major social, economic, and political changes are needed to deal with environmental problems. The National Action Committee on the Status of Women (NAC) could be viewed as representing the women's movement in Canada, but NAC and its affiliated member organizations also act as interest groups in trying to influence a variety of government policies.

The National Action Committee
on the Status of Women
nac-cca.ca

Social Movements & Culture:
A Resource Site
www.wsu.edu/~amerstu/smc/
smcframe.html

Old and New Social Movements

Social movements have a lengthy political history going back at least to the beginning of the industrial age in Europe (Heberle, 1951). One of the earliest movements was for the abolition of slavery in Britain in the late eighteenth century (Coupland, 1964). Another early British movement, the Chartists, pressed for the expansion of democratic rights in the 1830s, including the right to vote for all men (Thompson, 1984). Other nineteenth-century movements in various countries sought basic democratic rights for ordinary people (especially the emerging industrial working class), national independence (for example, in Greece and Hungary), and voting and legal rights for women (the suffragette movement).

A wave of protest and discontent that reached its peak in the late 1960s was associated with the development of a variety of new social movements, including the American civil rights movement, the women's movement, the environmental movement, Aboriginal movements, the anti-war movement, and various new nationalist movements (including a Quebec nationalist movement). Somewhat later the gay and lesbian rights movement developed. Many of those involved in these movements shared the view that "elitist" Western democracies should be transformed into "participatory" democracies, that major changes in values and institutions were needed to "liberate" oppressed groups, and that new lifestyles were desirable to create a more co-operative society that was in harmony with nature.

Some of those active in the new social movements had a vision of a "new politics" that differed from conventional politics (Dalton, 2006). In particular, they were critical of the hierarchy and power politics of conventional political organizations and sought to create informal unstructured organizations or networks based on grassroots participation. Likewise, direct action by participants (such as demonstrations, sit-ins, and blockades) was seen as more effective in bringing about substantial change than working through existing political parties and interest groups. By using

◀ Some Canadian Aboriginal groups have blockaded railways and highways to draw attention to their grievances.

dramatic actions, activists in the new social movements were able to gain television coverage for their causes.

The more flexible structures adopted by the new social movements give them real advantages because a broad framework allows a movement to grow and encompass as many of those as possible who share its broad objectives. However, this very breadth can harm movements by presenting a confused picture of who they are and what they want. For example, the objectives of the movement labelled as "anti-globalization" are often unclear because of the wide variety of groups that it attracts.

Changes in Movements

Over time, there is a tendency for organizations based on social movements to become more conventional in nature. The labour and socialist movements that developed in the latter part of the nineteenth century are no longer seen as challenging, unconventional forces in many countries. Likewise, many of the organizations that developed out of the women's and environmental movements have, to a considerable extent, become conventional in their structures and activities. When this happens we speak of the *demobilization, routinization,* or *institutionalization* of a movement (Wilson, 2002). It loses some of its spontaneity and becomes less confrontational in its relations with government. For example, a number of the large environmental organizations in the United States (sometimes referred to as the "Big Ten") became highly institutionalized organizations concerned primarily with fundraising and lobbying government officials. Foundations set up by wealthy business people provided an important base of financial support, allowing these organizations to hire professional managers to play leading roles in the organizations. The executives of large business corporations, including some whose corporations were major causes of pollution, were appointed to the boards of some of the national environmental organizations, and the leaders of the organizations came to prefer quiet negotiation and compromise with government and business to confrontation. Grassroots activists and local organizations that preferred a tougher stance in defence of the environment tended to be bypassed (Dowie, 1995). Nevertheless, like other public interest advocacy groups, most environmental groups continue to pursue their goals not only through "inside" strategies, but also through other means including legal actions, media publicity aimed at influencing the general public, boycotts, and demonstrations.

Some view the adoption of conventional interest group strategies as the "selling out" of a movement and its ideals. Others argue that it has increased the possibility of achieving success by influencing the policies of government and business through realistic proposals and by becoming an accepted participant in policy discussions. Nevertheless, it may still be appropriate to speak of the movement as a movement, as we do with the women's and environmental movements. Not only may there still be specific groups that remain on the fringes of "normal politics" (the usual and expected actors, issues, and methods that define most of what a political system does), but a substantial part of a movement's influence lies in its continuing ability to mobilize those who share its goals.

In the case of the environmental movement, the pronounced tendency of the large environmental groups to act like conventional interest groups has resulted, in some instances, in activists forming new groups more oriented to protest activities. For example, Friends of the Earth was started by a Sierra Club activist who had become critical of that organization's unwillingness to use confrontational tactics (although over time, Friends of the Earth has also become a professional, moderate organization). The Sea Shepherd Conservation Society was started by a founder of Greenpeace who favoured more vigorous direct action, and the radical group Earth First! was started by a former Sierra Club employee.

Overall, the continued existence of more "radical" elements within a movement can be useful in keeping the more moderate institutionalized groups from making excessive compromises of the movement's goals and principles. While institutionalized groups may become effective in the policy-making process, it is the more militant thinkers and activists who usually "generate the ideas that ultimately shape political discourse and shift the tides of history" (Bosso, 2005, p. 154). As well, the existence of groups that can mobilize activists in support of a cause can help to provide leverage for the more conventional groups to persuade government to accept their moderate proposals so as to avoid being confronted with more extreme demands and disruptive actions.

Transnational Social Movements

Social movements often migrate across borders and thus can be considered transnational. Older political movements such as the anti-slavery and labour movements were influential in many countries. Some newer social movements such as the women's and environmental movements have global reach, influencing politics, in varying ways, in many countries in almost all parts of the world as well as seeking to influence various international institutions. For example, organizations associated with the environmental movement such as Greenpeace International, Friends of the Earth International, and the World Wide Fund for Nature have offices and undertake activities in many countries. Although based in the richer countries, they also have a substantial presence in a number of less developed countries. The processes of globalization, particularly advances in communications and transportation, have facilitated the global reach of a number of social movements.

Peoples' Global Action
www.nadir.org/nadir/initiativ/agp/en/
index.htm

Activities

Those active in social movements often are involved in protest activities because their group has not been successful in achieving its goals through more conventional forms of political activity (see Chapter 12). Nevertheless, those associated with a social movement often establish public interest groups to pursue particular policy objectives related to the vision and perspective of the movement.

MOVEMENT PARTIES Those wishing to advance the cause of a social movement have occasionally established new political parties. As we saw in Chapter 9, social democratic and labour parties were formed in many countries by those involved in the labour and socialist movements. These mass parties initially operated in quite a different manner than the existing cadre parties. In recent decades, Green political parties have been established in about seventy countries to pursue the goals of the environmental movement (see Box 11-3, The German Greens).

The decision of those active in a social movement to establish a new political party to advance their cause, and the success of such a party, is affected, in part, by some basic features of a country's political system. Germany's electoral system, which provides representation to any party receiving more than 5 percent of the popular vote, encouraged activists from various movements to join together to form the Green party. That party has been able to gain representation and play a significant role in the legislature since 1983, despite its modest level of voting support. It also benefited early on from the financial support given by the German state to almost all political parties. Canada's single member plurality system, by contrast, makes it extremely difficult for smaller parties to elect representatives unless their support is concentrated in a particular geographical area (as is the case with the Bloc Québécois and the former Reform party, which reflected Quebec nationalist and Western right-wing populist movements, respectively). Thus, the Green party in Canada has, at least until recently, been a "fringe party" with little likelihood of gaining legislative representation. However, changes to election financing law have given the party the funds to

BOX 11-3

The German Greens

Although the first environmentalist parties were formed in Tasmania (Australia) and New Zealand in 1972, the German Green party (*die Grünen*) has been the most notable and influential environmentalist party. The German Greens developed not only from those involved in the environmental movement, but also from those in the other new social movements, including the feminist, peace, and anti-nuclear power movements, along with members of various radical left-wing groups opposed to the established mainstream political parties.

The German Greens considered themselves a "non-party party." Reflecting their new social movement origins, they established a highly decentralized organization and tried to avoid developing a professional party organization. For example, party officers received no salaries and members elected to the legislature were expected to donate a large portion of their salaries to eco-funds and to resign halfway through their terms of office so that legislative positions could be rotated. As well, at least one-half of the party's candidates for public office were to be female, party decisions were supposed to be made by consensus, and activists from various movements were given the right to be candidates even if not members of the Green party. Finally, the party avoided the selection of a leader, instead usually designating one woman and one man as spokespersons.

Twenty-seven Greens were elected to the West German legislature in the 1983 election (based on 5.6 percent of the vote). The Greens entered the very staid legislature carrying a symbolic tree with at least one Green, Joschka Fischer, wearing jeans and soiled sneakers. In his introductory speech he described the legislature as "an unbelievable gathering of alcoholics" and described the president (speaker) of the legislature as an "asshole."

The Greens, however, divided into two factions: the *realos,* who wanted to engage in normal party politics so as to increase their political power, and the *fundis,* who wanted to avoid compromises, retain the radical movement character of the party, and be more involved in extraparliamentary activity such as demonstrations and other forms of direct action rather than parliamentary action. A temporary electoral setback for the party in 1990 resulted in the *realos* gaining control of the party and working toward establishing a coalition with the Social Democratic party. This coalition came to power in 1998, with the Greens obtaining three Cabinet positions. Joschka Fischer, who had many years earlier beaten a policeman with a baseball bat during an anti-war demonstration and had associated with terrorists, became foreign affairs minister and quickly flew to Washington to reassure the American president that his government would remain a stable ally (Berman, 2001). Indeed, Fischer agreed to Germany's participation in the North Atlantic Treaty Organization's bombing of Serbia and its military intervention in Afghanistan. Fischer had to be protected by police when faced with bitter opposition by disgruntled party members who did not support the use of military force.

Although the German Green party retains some traces of its movement origins, it is no longer a radical challenger to conventional politics. Well before his retirement in 2005, Fischer had become a highly respected member of the legislative body he once detested.

Joschka Fischer, a prominent member of the Green party who entered the German Parliament in 1983 wearing jeans, retired in 2005 as a highly respected member of the institution he once despised.

carry its message to the public. And although the environmental movement in Canada has, until recently, largely ignored the Green party, the selection of Elizabeth May, former executive director of the Sierra Club, as leader in 2007 helped to gain support from the movement for the Green party.

As well, the federal system can facilitate the development of movement-based political parties. It is easier to mount a campaign that can have an impact in a single province, particularly if that province is relatively homogenous in its makeup, than to mount a successful campaign across a large and diverse country. The combination of the electoral system and the federal system contributed to the capture of provincial political power by the Social Credit movement party in Alberta in 1935 and the farmer-labour Co-operative Commonwealth Federation in Saskatchewan in 1943. More recently, the Parti Québécois, based on the independence movement in Quebec, has been a major provincial political force since 1976. The parliamentary system, which combines legislative and executive power, allows movement-based parties to enact their programs by winning a majority of legislative seats (even if they do not have the majority of votes). It also means that they do not have to divide their often limited resources by fighting elections for both legislative and executive offices, as is the case in presidential systems.

These facilitating factors of the electoral and governing institutions do not necessarily result in movements establishing new parties to take up their causes. Although the women's movement, like the environmental movement, has considerable popular support, efforts to establish a women's party in various countries have thus far been largely unsuccessful (with the partial exception of Iceland). Connections of movement activists to different mainstream political parties, beliefs that movement objectives might be better achieved through non-partisan action, a reluctance to expend a movement's energies on electoral politics, and a belief that engagement in party politics will lead to a compromise of the movement's principles often contribute to a reluctance to form a movement-based political party.

Summary and Conclusion

The freedom to organize into groups to express one's views and try to affect the decisions of the political community is a crucial element of liberal democracy. Interest groups potentially allow people to participate in the political process on a day-to-day basis, not just on the infrequent occasions when elections occur. They convey the views, opinions, and problems of various elements of society to government and to other citizens on a regular basis. As well, interest groups often supply government with useful information and advice, and some interest groups are directly involved with government in developing public policies.

However, interest groups have sometimes been criticized as threats to the common good and as undemocratic. Many interest groups seek special privileges for their members or for particular segments of society—privileges that may work against the interests of society as a whole. With a wide variety of groups seeking special privileges, who is concerned about the well-being of the country as a whole? For example, many business groups seek tax breaks or subsidies for their particular sector of the economy. However, if government satisfies these demands, it may mean that the population as a whole will have to pay higher taxes or suffer reduced government services.

Finally, although all are free in a liberal democracy to form groups to represent their interests, some elements of society are better represented than others by interest groups. In general, the well-off elements of society are better represented by interest groups than those who are poor, uneducated, or otherwise disadvantaged. Business groups are often considered to be highly influential in the making of public policy. Further, individual business corporations may be able to influence the political process through their public affairs staff by hiring lobbyists, making large contributions to political parties where this is not prohibited, and funding influential policy research institutes. Nevertheless, there has been a proliferation of public interest groups in recent decades promoting causes that can be considered to be for the common good of society. Such groups have often been able to get their message across through the skilful use of their resources, particularly if they have sympathetic supporters in the media, universities, philanthropic organizations, and government to help them convey their message. Social movements have often developed among segments of society that have been treated unfairly and ignored by government and conventional political institutions, and among those who believe that major changes in society and politics are needed. Even in democratic countries, the conventional channels for achieving desired goals are not always effective, and thus social movements often feel the need to use unconventional means to carry their message to the public and to government.

Does the development of social movements and interest groups make political parties as a means of representing the public irrelevant? Despite the criticisms that are often raised about political parties, they tend to be more likely than interest groups to develop broad platforms of general popular appeal and to have a vision of where the political community should be headed. Interest groups and social movements concerned with promoting a particular interest or cause tend to have a narrower vision and may be less concerned about developing positions with broad appeal.

Key Terms

Discussion Questions

1. What interest groups are you a member of? Do you think that they reflect your views?

2. Is the distinction between self-interested and public interest groups meaningful?

3. Are interest groups a threat to democracy and the common good?

4. Do you feel a connection to any social movement? Are there any social movements whose goals you strongly agree or disagree with?

5. Have social movements made a major contribution to Canada and the world?

6. Do you think that establishing a women's party would be beneficial or detrimental to the women's movement?

Further Reading

Berry, J.M. *The new liberalism: The rising power of citizen groups.* Washington, DC: Brookings Institution Press, 1999.

Carroll, W. (Ed). *Organizing dissent: Contemporary social movements in theory and practice,* 2nd ed. Toronto: Garamond Press, 1997.

Dowie, M. *Losing ground: American environmentalism at the close of the twentieth century.* Cambridge, MA: MIT Press, 1995.

Grant, W. *Pressure groups and British politics.* Houndmills, Basingstoke, Hampshire, UK: Macmillan, 2000.

Hochschild, A., *Bury the chains: The British struggle to abolish slavery.* London: Macmillan, 2005.

Pal, L.A. *Interests of state: The politics of language, multiculturalism and feminism in Canada.* Montreal: McGill-Queen's University Press, 1993.

Pross, A.P. *Group politics and public policies,* 2nd ed. Toronto: Oxford University Press, 1993.

Schier, S.E. *By invitation only: The rise of exclusive politics in the United States.* Pittsburgh, PA: University of Pittsburgh Press, 2000.

Shaiko, R.G. *Voices and echoes for the environment: Public interest representation in the 1990s and beyond.* New York: Columbia University Press, 1999.

Smith, J., & Johnston, H. (Eds.). *Globalization and resistance: Transnational dimensions of social movements.* Lanham, MD: Rowman & Littlefield, 2002.

Smith, M., *A civil society? Collective actors in Canadian political life.* Peterborough, ON: Broadview Press, 2005.

Vickers, J., Appelle, C., & Rankin, P. *Politics as if women mattered: A political analysis of the National Action Committee on the Status of Women.* Toronto: University of Toronto Press, 1993.

Young, L., & Everitt, J. *Advocacy groups.* Vancouver: UBC Press, 2004.

Chapter 12

UNCONVENTIONAL AND HIGHLY CONFLICTIVE POLITICS: FROM PROTEST TO REVOLUTION

PHOTO ABOVE: Lois Gibbs turned political activist extraordinaire when her children fell seriously ill and she realized that the Love Canal toxic dump she lived on top of was to blame.

CHAPTER OBJECTIVES

After reading this chapter you should be able to:

1. describe what political protest is and why people use protest as a political tool
2. discuss why not all political protest is democratic
3. understand why protest is an integral part of democratic politics
4. distinguish between insurgency and counter-insurgency
5. list and describe the characteristics of terrorism
6. discuss whether political violence is ever justifiable

Lois Gibbs was a housewife who became a political activist when her children fell ill. In 1976, Gibbs learned that the blue-collar subdivision in Niagara Falls, New York, where she lived with her husband and two small children was built on the Love Canal—an unfinished canal that had been used as a chemical disposal site. Over the years, the Hooker Chemical Company, later bought by oil giant Occidental Petroleum, had dumped twenty thousand tons (more than twenty million kilograms) of highly toxic chemical waste into the never-completed canal. It was covered over and the land was sold to the municipality of Niagara Falls for one dollar.

In 1978, Gibbs's children became very sick. Her son developed epilepsy and her daughter almost died of a rare blood disease. Gibbs went around to her neighbours with a petition, asking them if they were as upset as she was. They were, and soon they had formed the Love Canal Homeowners Association. Over the next two years, Gibbs led the association in legal and political battle against Occidental Petroleum and all three levels of government—city, state, and federal. Although the company and the governments all argued that the toxic wastes under Love Canal did not cause the residents' health problems, the community eventually won a settlement of US$120 million and more than eight hundred families were relocated to safe, healthy homes. President Jimmy Carter later declared the Love Canal a national disaster area.

The protest that Lois Gibbs organized and led has left two important legacies. One is the United States Environmental Protection Agency's Superfund, monies used to find and clean up toxic sites throughout the United States. The other is the Center for Health, Environment, and Justice (CHEJ), which Gibbs founded and heads. The CHEJ works with community groups across the United States to protect neighbourhoods from the hazards of toxic wastes.

The Love Canal incident sparked thousands of other grassroots campaigns against toxic sites. By being brave enough to stand up to the powerful and resourceful enough to found and lead a successful political protest, Lois Gibbs showed that even ordinary people can wield a lot of political power when they organize and refuse to take no for an answer.

POLITICAL CONFLICT
A state of opposition, usually involving groups and the state, over something government is doing or proposes to do.

POLITICAL PROTEST
Oppositional political action that takes place outside formal channels, generally seeking to have government make significant changes in its policies.

CIVIL DISOBEDIENCE
Deliberate lawbreaking that accepts punishment by state authorities as part of the action.

GUERRILLA WARFARE
A form of highly political warfare built around lightly armed irregulars who oppose a government and use hit-and-run tactics and political work to take power.

INSURGENCY
A rebellion or revolt, especially one employing the tools of guerrilla warfare.

REVOLUTION
The use of violence to overthrow a government, especially when the overthrow is followed by rapid and thorough social, economic, and political restructuring.

TERRORISM
The deliberate use of violence designed to induce fear in a population in order to achieve a political objective.

FIGURE 12-1
THE CONTINUUM OF PROTEST

POLITICAL CONFLICT: PROTEST TO REVOLUTION

To Canadians, **political conflict** means Question Period or a candidates' debate during an election campaign, and those *are* both forms of conflict. At its broadest, political conflict refers to a state of opposition: someone objects to what someone else is doing or proposes to do. The "someone else" is often the government but can also be groups or individuals holding positions on public issues different from one's own. Political conflict in Canada frequently takes place within formal governmental institutions, staying within the limits of the law, and is almost always peaceful. However, in other settings, political conflict can be violent, involving resort to arms. This chapter discusses political conflict that goes on outside formal governmental institutions. That type of conflict is often disruptive and sometimes violent, but it *is* a form of political participation. We will examine political protest, insurgency and guerrilla war, terrorism, and revolution.

The term **political protest** might conjure up images of helmeted police and rock-throwing demonstrators, but it can also suggest people picketing peacefully in front of city hall or organizing a petition. Political protest takes many forms (see Figure 12-1). The most moderate include petitions, legally approved demonstrations, and voluntary boycotts of certain products or firms. Nonviolent direct action—for example, civil disobedience, illegal demonstrations, or peaceful occupation of a building or office—is a stronger form of protest. It involves illegal activities but is not violent, as is best exemplified by **civil disobedience**—deliberate lawbreaking that accepts punishment by state authorities as part of the action. This was the strategy chosen by Gandhi in India from the 1920s to the 1940s, and by Martin Luther King in the United States in the 1950s and 1960s.

Very different is protest that involves violence. Sometimes violence is an unintended consequence of a march or boycott, but it can also be used intentionally as a provocation. In other instances, violence is chosen as the best way to secure a political objective. Assassinations, **guerrilla warfare**, **insurgencies**, **revolutions**, and **terrorism** fall into this category.

INSTITUTIONAL	MODERATE PROTEST	DIRECT ACTION	VIOLENCE
Voting	Petitions	Unofficial strikes	Unintentional
Lobbying	Legal demonstrations	Illegal demonstrations	Throw rocks,
Interest groups	Boycotts	Peaceful occupations	break windows
		Civil disobedience	Guerrilla warfare
			Assassination
			Terrorism

SOURCE: *Adapted with modifications from R.J. Dalton,* Citizen politics, *4th ed., p. 65. Washington, DC: CQ Press, 2006.*

Seeking Change

People do not protest, let alone turn to political violence, for no reason. Protest is a means to seek political change. It usually is employed only after conventional approaches, such as lobbying, have failed. In non-democratic systems, though, it may be the only way to achieve change. This does not mean that people involved in a protest or **protest movement** have personally tried other means, or would even support trying them. Rather, it points to the most common sequence of events.

ANALYZING PROTEST

To most people, seeking the common good suggests reasoned deliberation and debate, which are hallmarks of democratic politics. However, democracy did not grow just through the use of reason and polite persuasion. Those who hold power, the elite, are rarely keen to see their power diminished. Thus logic has often needed to be supplemented by more **contentious politics**—that is, protest involving ordinary citizens, often joined by more influential citizens, uniting to confront "elites, authorities, and opponents" (Tarrow, 1999, p. 2).

Political protest is political action because it aims to affect how public issues are treated. It is oppositional political action because those who protest want government to change its policies. This can mean that a government starts to do something it does not do now, stops doing something it now does, or takes action instead of doing nothing. However, oppositional activity is immensely varied and does not always include protest. We reserve the label *protest* for political actions with the following characteristics:

1. Actions take place outside of formal channels.
2. They are usually carried out by individuals or groups who are not ordinarily important political actors.
3. Protest politics generally aims to have government make significant changes in the policies it pursues.

We will look at each of these three traits separately.

Politics outside Formal Channels

Whether in dictatorships or democracies, politics works in set patterns. There are rules you are expected to follow to get something done. They may not always be formal, written rules, but rather norms or unofficial standards. In either case, being politically effective and getting what you want usually requires following those rules and working within channels.

Playing by the rules benefits both governments and the groups and individuals that regularly deal with government. It obviously helps governments because they set the rules. However, keeping within formal channels also works well for those who deal regularly with government because they master

PROTEST MOVEMENT
A group of people who mount a continuing challenge in opposition to some government policy or action by a private firm or individual.

CONTENTIOUS POLITICS
Protest involving ordinary citizens, often joined by more influential citizens, uniting to confront elites, authorities, and opponents.

the rules and can use them to their own benefit. But what if going through formal channels does not produce any results? In that case, there are two options: accept your fate or go outside formal channels.

When people have an issue that is very important to them, they are not likely to be satisfied with accepting defeat graciously. This is true even when the defeat comes as a result of a democratic process and reflects the will of the majority. Such an outcome is especially likely where the claimants belong to a permanent minority (for example, an ethnic or religious group) that the majority or government has consciously marginalized. Ordinary democracy may not work for those who can never become a majority.

"Unimportant" Actors or Issues

Protest is sometimes called the tool of the marginalized—people without the resources needed to gain political influence. We usually think of political influence as the ability to shape decisions, the ability to control large blocks of votes, or having a lot of money or particularly valuable information. Having these resources makes an individual or group valuable to government, and governments often accommodate those who are valuable to them. Prospects are bleak for those groups or individuals with scarce resources unless they too make themselves important to government.

Beginning in the 1960s, political scientists began to see protest as a political resource (Lipsky, 1968). Protest disrupts government's routines, making the authorities at least see that something is happening. Although government officials often characterize protest as lawlessness, they still know that some part of their community feels strongly enough about an issue to take to the streets. In reality, the marginalized may have little option but to use protest. Largely invisible to those in power before they begin to protest, those on the outside frequently find that the rules of the game do not work for them. However, once a protest movement has caught the authorities' attention, perhaps through a high media profile, it can then mobilize other resources, including the support of some politicians, and further enhance its status.

MARGINALIZATION
Exclusion from the mainstream.

Marginalization does not refer only to the dispossessed and literally disenfranchised. Issues, too, can be marginalized and only appear on the government's agenda after supporters take extraordinary measures. This explains the apparently contradictory phenomenon of the well-educated, middle-class-or-higher protester (Dalton, 2006) whose activity has been notable from the anti–Vietnam War movement of the 1960s to today's anti-globalization demonstrations. Although these individuals may have other resources that they can use to influence government, those resources may not work for a given issue. Thus, protest is another resource that the politically active can add to their arsenals (Opp, 1989). Yet even if protest is often the only tool of the marginalized, sometimes the well-placed use it as a tactic to get what they want (as discussed in Box 12-1, Premier Williams and the Canadian Flag).

Premier Williams and the Canadian Flag

In December 2004, Newfoundland and Labrador Premier Danny Williams ordered the Canadian flag removed from all provincial public buildings as part of a dispute with the federal government over the province's share of offshore oil revenues. The Maple Leaf stayed down from December 24, 2004, until January 28, 2005, when a deal was reached that brought Newfoundland and Labrador an additional $2.6 billion in revenues. Alongside Williams' protest, a website called Fair Deal for Newfoundland got twenty-five thousand Newfoundlanders and Labradorians to email Ottawa supporting the premier's position.

Some interpreted the premier's actions as petulant headline-grabbing, arguing that while Newfoundland and Labrador may be a small, poor province it is hardly a marginalized actor unable to get a hearing. However, months of working through channels, in the form of talks between the finance ministers from St. John's and Ottawa, had proven fruitless. So while we cannot say that Premier Williams' gesture got Newfoundland and Labrador the extra revenues, it is plausible that the shock of his move unblocked a stalled process.

Whatever actually achieved those results, this case makes us take a second look at conventional thinking about protest politics. Obviously, protest is not just an instrument for outsiders. However, the Newfoundland and Labrador premier used his protest not to gain entry to the political system or fight for a long-denied basic human right but to move negotiations in a favourable direction. Protest may occasionally be a resource for the relatively powerful, but it is more often the only resource available to the relatively powerless.

CHALLENGES AND BENEFITS OF ORGANIZING We should not think, however, that mobilizing people to undertake political protest is the easiest way to enter politics. There is, first, the problem of organizing people to act collectively. Mancur Olson (1965) argues that the rational thing for a person to do is not to join a movement, but rather to wait on the sidelines to see what it accomplishes. These *free riders* share the benefits of the organization's labour without having to do any work or take any risks.

Beyond the matter of getting people to join, movements cannot know how government will respond to their demands. There is no guarantee that the time and energy invested in building a movement and organizing protest actions will change the status quo and advance a group's vision of the common good. Nevertheless, over the years, Canadians have seen workers, farmers, women, fishers, Quebec nationalists, Aboriginals, gays and lesbians, and anti-abortion activists use political protest to put themselves and their causes on the public agenda. Many of these groups became regular parts of the political process, and today governments, whether federal or provincial, generally do not question the right of these groups to have a voice in policy-making. Whether events would have turned out the same way had the groups not protested is impossible to determine. What we do know is that protest advanced their causes substantially.

Gay and Lesbian Emergence: Out in Canada (CBC Archives)
http://archives.cbc.ca/IDD-1-69-599/life_society/gay_lesbian/

Riseup.net (contemporary progressive movements)
http://lists.riseup.net

Seeking Significant Change

Protesters usually believe that there is something terribly wrong that only government action can correct. Yet they also believe that the ordinary mechanisms of political pressure have failed, leaving protest as their last chance to be heard. This is why protest has been used to gain political rights for the excluded, to try to end wars, and to make absolutely clear the opposition of some part of the citizenry to some government policy. Protest is about changing what government does, and people have organized themselves into movements that seek political change for a very long time.

Protest and Political Change

In general, then, people protest because they perceive what Clark, Grayson, and Grayson (1976, p. 3) call "institutional deficiencies"—they think that something is not working right and has to be fixed. Those who decide to protest may risk imprisonment and still not gain their objective. Nevertheless, political protest has secured some dramatic results and contributed greatly to strengthening democracy in Canada. For example:

- *Women's right to vote.* Until the late 1800s, women everywhere were denied basic political rights. It was only in the twentieth century that political equality between men and women became a generally accepted principle of democratic life. The first step toward equality for women was winning the right to vote. Although we now find it unthinkable that women did not have the same political rights as men, it took Canadian women more than fifty years to gain the right to vote in all provinces. Along the way, the proponents of women's suffrage (women's right to vote) lobbied governments and used various forms of protest, such as staging mock parliamentary debates, to demonstrate that they could argue as persuasively and as rationally as men (Cleverdon, 1974).

- *Making farmers' voices heard.* Farmers in Canada in the late nineteenth and early twentieth centuries felt excluded from power and sought to change the political system to better reflect their needs (Lipset, 1950; Macpherson, 1954; Morton, 1950). Unlike the movement for women's suffrage, farmers' movements decided that they needed to form new political parties. Although farmers were then the largest occupational group in the country, they had little influence. Farmers felt that the parties that existed at the time, the Conservatives and Liberals, ignored their views and listened only to the demands of big business. The parties the farmers' movements founded (United Farmers, Progressives, Co-operative Commonwealth Federation [CCF]) or supported (Social Credit) sought to represent the views of not just farmers but all ordinary working people against the concentrated power of corporate interests. Although none of these parties ever won power federally, several of them governed provinces. Moreover, a number of them created Crown corporations (government-owned enterprises) that brought electricity and telephone service to many parts of rural Canada. One, the CCF, set up the country's first medicare system in Saskatchewan.

Votes for women and more political power for farmers were issues that Canada's political establishment of a century past would not put on the public agenda. For these two marginalized groups to have their demands heard, they had to move outside the usual political channels. The mechanisms of ordinary democracy had served them poorly, but political protest benefited them and democracy well. However, we should recall that it took more than three decades of hard work for women to win the vote and that the CCF's election as Saskatchewan's government in 1944 came twelve years after the party's founding. Protest is not a magic potion that confers immediate success on those who use it.

In fact, there are many cases where protest fails. Canada's peace movement has been active for years but it could not halt the testing of cruise missiles in Alberta in the 1980s and has had similarly little impact on decisions to send troops to Afghanistan. Outside of Canada, the record is similar. A study of attempts by poor black citizens of Newark, New Jersey, to use protest to claim their rights and gain power showed how those in power frustrated the protesters at every turn (Parenti, 1970). Similarly, women fighting for the vote in Britain in the early 1900s turned to violence after being consistently rebuffed by government. They smashed the windows of elegant shops along London's Regent Street and, when arrested, began hunger strikes. The authorities responded with force-feeding and eventually used the "Cat and Mouse Law": a woman was allowed to starve herself until her health deteriorated. She was then released but would be jailed again on regaining her health. In the end, British women won the vote not due to their protest but rather because of their contributions to Britain's efforts in the First World War, and even then they did not have the same voting rights as men until 1928 (Castle, 1987).

PROTEST IN DEMOCRACY

Some argue that political protest does not have a place in a democracy. They hold that people have the right to make their feelings known in elections, to work through their elected representatives, and to pressure government. Not everyone gets what they want, but that is not cause to go outside fair, well-known rules and procedures. If you fail to get what you want by working through regular democratic processes, it indicates that you are simply too weak or are pursuing goals that the majority rejects. Rather than protest, you should change your objectives and build a broader base.

The crux of this argument is the belief that democratic politics does not contain any biases. Although this view underlies our most basic beliefs about democracy, it is not entirely accurate. There are certainly many instances in which following established democratic procedures did not help the weak and marginalized. This was the case for black Americans who turned to protest to challenge the discriminatory system of **segregation** (see Box 12-2, The Civil Rights Movement).

Opportunity Structures

What allowed the protests in Canada and the United States to work was the ability of the movements' leaders to use the opportunities offered by their political systems. **Political opportunity structures (POS)** refer to the openings that political institutions and processes offer to or withhold from movements (Kitschelt, 1986; Tarrow, 1999). For example, the farmers' movement in Canada was able to build political parties and win power because our electoral system and system of parliamentary government, as well as the fact that farmers formed a majority of voters in several provinces, made this a workable option. More recently, **secessionists** in Quebec have used the same strategy with some success because supporters of Quebec's independence could unite behind a single separatist party and gain control of the Quebec government. Because they are less likely to vote as a bloc, women have not developed a specific women's political party to advance their causes.

TRANSNATIONAL POLITICAL PROTEST

Social movements and political protest have often migrated across borders. Nineteenth-century examples of transnational movements include the anti-slavery and labour movements. Later, the student movement of the 1960s and the women's rights movement of the 1970s were also international in scope. As well, protestors in a single country, such as the Zapatistas in Mexico, increasingly seek support for their cause from sympathizers around the world. Ironically, it is the anti-globalization movement that best exemplifies globalized political protest.

The anti-globalization movement, which often refers to itself as the global social justice movement, has focused on specific elements of globalization, particularly international finance and its effects on the world's economy. This has led the movement to target meetings of the World Trade Organization (WTO) and other forums promoting increased economic integration—such as the G8 summits of the leaders of the major industrialized countries, meetings of the International Monetary Fund and World Bank, and the European Union summits—for its protests. Since the movement's first major operation in 1998, in which it brought to the public's view a hitherto secret draft of a proposed Multilateral Agreement on Investment (Clarke & Barlow, 1997), it has moved more fully into contentious direct actions. Following the protests in Seattle in 1999, there were many big demonstrations (see Table 12-1), most of them

SEGREGATION
The legal separation of blacks and whites, particularly in the southern United States.

POLITICAL OPPORTUNITY STRUCTURES (POS)
The openings that political institutions and processes offer to (or withhold from) movements.

SECESSIONIST
A person who favours separation of a territory from an existing state.

Peoples' Global Action
www.nadir.org/nadir/initiativ/agp/en/index.htm

BOX 12-2

The Civil Rights Movement

The U.S. civil rights movement is one of the most famous examples of how people without power were failed by the democratic process.

Although Abraham Lincoln declared the abolition of slavery in 1863, for the next century black Americans suffered systemic discrimination. Conditions were worst in the southern states where segregation, the legal separation of races, was in force. This meant that black children and white children went to different schools, that blacks and whites could not use the same restrooms or drinking fountains, and that blacks even had to give up their seats on buses to whites.

Throughout the first half of the twentieth century, black Americans worked patiently through their country's courts to have segregation legislation declared unconstitutional. Although they had some significant victories, such as *Brown v. Board of Education,* 1954, which declared segregated education unconstitutional, actually getting states to change their laws proved difficult. Despite a constitutional provision adopted in 1870 establishing that the right to vote cannot be denied on account of race or colour, various means such as literacy tests were used to prevent most black Americans from voting.

Clearly, the normal channels of influence were of little use in trying to change discriminatory laws and policies. Protest action by the civil rights movement was needed to pressure governments to treat black Americans fairly. They then would appeal their convictions to a higher court, arguing that the law they broke actually violated the constitution and should have no force.

The greatest American proponent of civil disobedience was Dr. Martin Luther King (1929–1968), a Baptist minister who lived in the South.

Sit-ins were one of the most effective tactics used by the civil rights movement. Black students would sit in the section of a restaurant or lunch counter that was reserved for whites. They would be refused service and told to leave, but would stay until arrested. Eventually this practice mobilized public opinion in the United States behind the civil rights movement, and legislation outlawing segregation followed.

Had black Americans tried to keep working within the rules, as they had for many years, segregation might have continued much longer. Politicians were hesitant to change the law, fearing that white voters would not re-elect them. Dramatic action like sit-ins focused the country's attention on the abuses of segregation and hastened that system's demise.

---

involving clashes with police. One, in Genoa, Italy, saw three demonstrators killed, several hundred injured, and charges of torture levelled against the Italian police. The pace of protest slowed after 2003 but appears to have begun again at the 2007 G-8 summit in Heilingendam, Germany. The largest global protest demonstrations, however, have been held to protest the invasion of Iraq, attracting more than ten million demonstrators worldwide in March 2003, including one million or more in London, Rome, Madrid, and Barcelona.

► In 2003, more than one million people in Madrid marched as part of a global protest against the invasion of Iraq.

The anti-globalization movement is particularly adept at making use of modern communications technology. Of special importance is its use of email and the World Wide Web. These instruments, themselves part of the phenomenon of globalization, allow the anti-globalization movement to organize effectively without needing complex permanent structures. However, this flexibility also brings costs to the movement. Because there really is no central core institution, any group can adhere to the movement and participate in its demonstrations. As a result, violent anti-capitalist groups who wish to destroy the entire capitalist system mix with far less confrontational groups concerned about social justice on a global scale, which focus on what they see as the unfair system of international trade rules. The anti-capitalist and anarchist groups, a small minority within the anti-globalization movement

TABLE 12-1

PARTICIPATION IN ANTI-GLOBALIZATION PROTEST ACTIONS

Note: Estimates of the number of demonstrators varies widely.

PLACE	DATE	ESTIMATED NUMBER OF PARTICIPANTS
Seattle	September 1999	100 000
Washington	April 2000	10 000
Prague, Czech Republic	September 2000	12 000
Quebec City	April 2001	30 000
Genoa, Italy	September 2001	100 000
Barcelona, Spain	March 2002	250 000
Miami	November 2003	10 000
Heilingendam, Germany	June 2007	80 000

SOURCE: *Compiled by authors from press estimates, 1999–2007.*

but the part most likely to seek violent confrontations with the authorities, give the entire movement a far more radical appearance than many of its members desire.

POLITICAL VIOLENCE: TERRORISM, GUERRILLA INSURGENCY, AND REVOLUTION

Political violence can be defined as the use of physical force with a political objective. Violence can enter politics in several different ways (see Box 12-3, Violence and Politics):

1. *Violence can be a tactic chosen by an organization, be it a protest movement or a guerrilla army, to advance its aims.* Although this is more common in countries that are not democracies and consequently do not allow an open political opposition, even long-established constitutional democracies such as Canada or the United States can harbour groups that feel they must use violence to achieve their goals.

2. *Governments can also use violence against their citizens.* Sometimes this resort to physical coercion is circumstantial, responding to a specific situation. For example, governments may want protests stopped and may even order the police or military to use force against protesters. While such tactics are common in non-democratic countries, democratic governments sometimes react in the same way. Far less common among democratic governments, though unfortunately not unknown, is using violence systematically as a regular instrument to repress dissent and maintain order. This is called **regime violence**.

3. *Finally, violence can be an unplanned and undesired side effect of an otherwise peaceful political action, such as a protest march.* Due to some unpredictable event, either protestors or the police become aggressive and the two sides clash.

Canadians are generally repelled by political violence. A movement that regularly uses violence, as did the Front de libération du Québec (FLQ), a revolutionary separatist group that kidnapped and murdered a Quebec Cabinet minister in 1970 (as discussed later in this chapter), is likely to lose public support. This revulsion also occurs when the police react with excessive force, as happened at the 1997 APEC summit in Vancouver.[1] Canadians, like people in most democratic countries, usually draw the line at premeditated violence.

POLITICAL VIOLENCE
The use of physical force with a political objective.

REGIME VIOLENCE
Political violence used by a government against its citizens, generally as a way to repress dissent and maintain order.

The American Political Science Association, Task Force on Political Violence and Terrorism
www.apsanet.org/section_571.cfm

---

[1] RCMP officers and Vancouver riot police used violence against students who were peacefully protesting the presence of the Indonesian dictator Suharto at a meeting of the Asia–Pacific Economic Cooperation (APEC) being held at the University of British Columbia in 1997. Although there were suspicions that the prime minister's office had ordered the demonstrators to be forcefully dispersed, a later inquiry found no direct links.

BOX 12-3

Violence and Politics

British political scientist Bernard Crick argued that politics, which he termed the political method of rule, is built on negotiation and the reconciliation of differences. As such, it effectively excludes the use of violence as a governing instrument (Crick, 1993).

Nonetheless, we see violence used for political ends every day, both by governments and by groups challenging government's authority. Two questions arise from this: Why do people use violence for political ends? And how can we distinguish political violence from simple criminality?

States may use violence legitimately, either to defend themselves and their citizens or to preserve order. Sometimes, however, dictatorships and other non-democratic governments use violence simply to suppress their opponents and repress dissent. Although democratic governments may do the same, it is far less common than in dictatorships.

In such cases, violence may be the only instrument that citizens can use to protect themselves against the state or to try to change their government's behaviour. Many would consider this a legitimate use of political violence.

Violence becomes political when it is used to influence, defend, or overthrow government. That seems clear, even if no government would ever say that any use of violence against it was anything but criminal. However, revolutionaries committed to toppling a government often resort to ordinary criminal methods such as robbery or kidnapping to finance their operations or simply to display their strength. In these cases, the line between political and criminal action seems to disappear. A further complication arises when peaceful protest turns violent unexpectedly, or when violent elements, even criminal ones, use ordinary protest as a cover for their illegitimate intentions.

While political protest has included violence in Canada's past, such as the Rebellions of 1837–38, it is relatively rare and we are quick to forget how easily it can happen. Ted Robert Gurr's frustration–aggression hypothesis (Gurr, 1970) addresses the question of what triggers violent protest. Gurr argued that where levels of frustration are high within a population and have lasted for a long time, these feelings can readily find violent expression. This certainly seems to be what occurred at Oka, Ipperwash, and Burnt Church (see Box 12-4, Aboriginal Protest in Canada). However, this theory does little to explain why people sometimes direct their energies into violence and not other forms of political action.

The frustration–aggression hypothesis also does not address the question of why and when governments regularly use violence against their own citizens, what we have called regime violence. When we think of regime violence we usually think of a police state, one in which the security forces—police, military, secret police, intelligence services—have free rein to harass citizens. Their repertoire includes **disappearances**, detaining people without charge, brutality, and torture (see Box 12-5, The Mothers of the Plaza de Mayo). There are too many examples of political systems that have used violence systematically against their own people to list, but examples include Saddam Hussein's Iraq, the

DISAPPEARANCE
The kidnapping by security forces of an individual who is never heard from again.

BOX 12-4

Aboriginal Protest in Canada

In recent years, Canada's indigenous people, of whom there are more than one million, have made some important gains in negotiations over land claims and have seen Aboriginal rights enshrined in the constitution. Yet it has been violent confrontations between Aboriginal communities and federal or provincial authorities that most captured public attention. Three of these were especially important:

- *Oka.* In 1990, plans by the town of Oka in Quebec to expand a golf course involved expropriating land that held a local Mohawk cemetery. An armed standoff between Quebec Provincial Police (QPP) and the Mohawk Warriors' Society led to the shooting of a QPP officer. A seventy-eight-day stand-off with the Canadian army then followed.

- *Ipperwash.* In 1995, Ojibway from the Stony Point First Nation claimed that Ipperwash Provincial Park in Ontario belonged to them. A violent confrontation between the Aboriginals and the Ontario Provincial Police resulted in the death of protester Dudley George. The government of the day refused to order an inquiry into George's death, but after a change of government in 2003, a commission of inquiry was established. The inquiry uncovered evidence of racist and culturally insensitive behaviour by the authorities. Its report in 2007 recommended that the land be turned over to the Ojibway.

- *Burnt Church.* In 1999, a confrontation at Burnt Church, New Brunswick, brought Aboriginal and non-Aboriginal fishermen into conflict. A month before this episode, a Supreme Court decision held that treaties from the 1760s exempted Aboriginals in the Maritimes and eastern Quebec from current fisheries regulations. Non-Aboriginal fishermen objected, fearing that uncontrolled fishing would destroy the resource. The two sides clashed violently at Burnt Church, leading to the destruction of much of the Aboriginals' gear and the burning of three fish-processing plants.

Taliban's Afghanistan, the Soviet Union under Stalin, Germany under Hitler, and Argentina during the "Dirty War," 1976–1982.

Project Disappeared
www.desaparecidos.org/arg/eng.html

The former examples were all dictatorships, but sometimes democracies also resort to using regime violence. This most often occurs as a response to political protest. For example, in the 1960s, police forces in American states where the segregation of the races was legal used violence against citizens engaged in peaceful protests demanding that black Americans receive their full constitutional rights. It can also happen that the authorities turn a blind eye to private citizens who use violence against protesters or other dissidents. Again, the American South offers an example: for many years the Ku Klux Klan terrorized black citizens who sought to exercise their legal rights.

There are several reasons why states might use violence as an instrument of government against their own citizens. One is to instill so much fear in the population that it will not dare to act against the government. Another is to

The Mothers of the Plaza de Mayo

Argentina has had many military dictatorships but none as violent as the regime that ruled the country from 1976 to 1983. Seizing power after an elected government proved unable to contain a wave of violence generated by urban guerrillas, the military waged a "Dirty War" against those it considered subversives and dissidents. Suspects were swept from the streets, taken to interrogation centres, and never heard from again. These were the Disappeared, and there were between ten thousand and thirty thousand of them.

In 1977, the mothers, wives, sisters, etc., of the Disappeared, frustrated by government refusals to release any information regarding the whereabouts of their family members, began to protest. Although the military regime ended in 1983, even now the Mothers of the Disappeared still gather every Thursday afternoon in the Plaza de Mayo, a park in downtown Buenos Aires that faces the presidential residence on one side and the Ministry of Defence on another. There they march quietly, partly in memory of their loved ones, partly to press the now democratically elected government to prosecute the architects of the Dirty War and their accomplices.

Their struggle has continued long enough that the Mothers have begun searching for their stolen grandchildren, who were born in captivity and turned over to the families of military officers. Reynaldo Bignone, the last president under the military regime (1982–1983), was arrested in March 2007 and charged with the theft of the babies of the Disappeared. As Hebe de Bonafini, the president of the Association of the Mothers of the Plaza de Mayo, has said, the struggle will never end.

The Mothers of the Disappeared have held a silent march in the Plaza de Mayo, which faces the presidential palace, every Thursday since 1977 to protest the disappearance of as many as thirty thousand women, men, and children during the military dictatorship that lasted from 1976 to 1983. Some of their family members are still missing.

maintain in power an individual or group (which can be defined by class, colour, religion, ethnicity, or ideology) that would otherwise be thrown out. In fact, these two reasons often go together.

TYPES OF POLITICAL VIOLENCE

We will analyze three types of political violence. They are either important today or have been prominent during the last century. The first is guerrilla warfare (also called guerrilla insurgency) and its counterpart, counter-insurgency. The second is terrorism and the third is revolution.

Guerrilla Warfare or Guerrilla Insurgency

Like political protest, guerrilla warfare is principally an instrument of the weak. Also called guerrilla insurgency, it is a familiar form of violent political action. This kind of political violence has been practised from time immemorial; we find references to it that date back 3500 years, and it is mentioned in the Bible. Nevertheless, it only received its current name early in the nineteenth century, when it was applied to the Spanish resistance to Napoleon's invasion and occupation (*guerrilla* is Spanish for "little war"). Some guerrilla wars are obviously political, because they are waged as part of a revolutionary struggle. Anthony Joes, an expert on guerrilla warfare, holds that "guerrilla insurgency is quintessentially a *political* phenomenon" (Joes, 2004, p. 7; emphasis in original), even if those who fight guerrillas often portray them as bandits.

All guerrilla insurgencies share five traits (Beckett, 2001; Joes, 1992; Joes, 2004; Laquer, 1977). First, the guerrillas are highly mobile and use hit-and-run tactics rather than set-piece battles. Second, they are fewer in number and less well armed than their adversaries. Third, guerrillas operate in familiar, often difficult terrain, which can be rural or urban (see Box 12-6, Urban Guerrillas), where their enemy loses its edge in technology and numbers. Fourth, the guerrillas know their locale and often have local support, which simplifies the task of gathering intelligence and securing supplies. Finally, guerrilla war is protracted war; if it ends quickly, the guerrillas have probably lost.

Although guerrilla warfare has existed for a long time, it became especially well known in the twentieth century (see Table 12.2). Not only did a great number of exceptional guerrilla commanders emerge—for example, Mao Zedong in China, Augusto Cesar Sandino in Nicaragua (discussed in Box 12-7, Guerrilla Violence), Ho Chi Minh in Vietnam, and Fidel Castro in Cuba—but also guerrilla insurgency came to be identified with revolutionary struggle. The question we must ask is why revolutionaries would turn to guerrilla warfare. Although all of the characteristics of guerrilla operations noted above apply in general, there are two additional reasons that apply with special force to revolutionaries.

One of these is that revolutionaries—who could be Marxists, independence fighters, or motivated by religion—generally are persecuted by governments. To survive they must find methods that both let them mount a successful resistance and give them an opportunity to win adherents. Guerrilla operations do both. By emphasizing the use of small units, light arms, and brief engagements, guerrilla tactics allow insurgents to turn their usual liabilities—small size and poor equipment—into advantages. Further, having to operate clandestinely means that the insurgents must mix with the ordinary people for whom they claim to fight. This allows the revolutionaries to do the slow, painstaking work of convincing people to turn against the government

BOX 12-6

Urban Guerrillas

When we think of guerrillas, we imagine men and women in camouflage trekking through a jungle or scrambling over a mountain pass. We do so for two reasons. One is that the successes of rural guerrillas, such as Mao Zedong in China in the 1930s and 1940s and Fidel Castro in Cuba in the 1950s, have shaped our image of insurgent warfare. The other is that most guerrillas have operated mainly in rural areas. Doing so puts distance between them and the government's soldiers that they fight, gives them the advantage of operating in difficult terrain that they know better than their enemy, and puts them in touch with the rural poor, who are often among those guerrillas claim to defend. However, guerrillas can also operate effectively in urban areas.

We have seen this in Iraq, where most action against the U.S.-led coalition has taken place in the cities. In general, operating in urban areas offers certain advantages to irregulars, another name for guerrillas. They have access to a large base of potential recruits, supplies are easier to gain, urban home turf can be just as difficult as any jungle for a counter-insurgent to penetrate, and the counter-insurgent runs a very high risk of killing civilians, thus raising the insurgents' legitimacy.

Iraq is not the first case of urban guerrilla struggle. In the late 1960s and early 1970s, such groups were very active in Uruguay and Argentina. They were quite violent, robbing banks and kidnapping people for ransom to finance themselves, and provoked military coups in both countries, creating governments that eventually destroyed the guerrillas. The violence in Iraq is even worse. In early 2007, the Iraqi government estimated that more than a hundred thousand Iraqis had perished in the conflict that grew from the U.S.-led invasion of the country in 2003. Many of those deaths, although we do not know exactly how many, were caused by suicide bombers who have become the main weapon in this particular guerrilla war.

TABLE 12-2

GUERRILLA MOVEMENTS OF THE TWENTIETH AND TWENTY-FIRST CENTURIES

WHERE	WHEN	LEADER OR COMBATANTS
China	1920s–1949	Mao Zedong
Nicaragua	1927–1934	Augosto Cesar Sandino
Various	1939–1945	Second World War partisans
Algeria	1940s–1958	Independence fighters
Vietnam	1940s–1975	Ho Chi Minh
Malaya	1946–1954	Communists
Mozambique and Angola	1950s–1974	Independence fighters
Cuba	1956–1959	Fidel Castro
Afghanistan	1979–1989	Mujahedeen
Iraq	2003–present	Insurgents

Guerrilla Violence

Because they fight foreign occupiers or domestic dictators, we often lionize guerrillas, treating them as ideal democratic heroes. However, they are waging a struggle that has a brutal side and therefore must sometimes use brutality.

Augusto Cesar Sandino became famous for leading a guerrilla war against the U.S. troops who occupied Nicaragua in the late 1920s. His Ejército Defensor de la Soberania Nacional (Defending Army of National Sovereignty) worked patiently with peasants to win their allegiance but administered rough justice to those who took the government's side. Using machetes, the guerrillas would lop off an offender's head, or slice off his arms, causing him to bleed to death. These methods were used because, as Sandino said, "Liberty is not won with flowers" (Macaulay, 1986, p. 212).

(always a dangerous choice) and back the guerrillas. The guerrillas can fail militarily and still continue to exist if their political work succeeds. If they fail politically, though, military success will not suffice.

Just how do guerrilla revolutionaries do their political work? One objective is to show people that the government cannot protect them, so the guerrillas attack government installations, blow up power lines and bridges, and often kill government officials—police, military, mayors, etc. In general, guerrillas seek to limit the violence used against ordinary citizens, because the insurgents need their aid and it is these people whom the revolutionaries claim to defend. Some groups, however, have chosen to terrorize civilian populations. Among these are the Shining Path (Sendero Luminoso) guerrillas of Peru (Palmer, 1994; Rochlin, 2003) and the Contras or Nicaraguan Resistance, an insurgent group formed and armed by the United States government to attack the revolutionary government of Nicaragua in the 1980s (Grandin, 2006).

COUNTER-INSURGENCY C.E. Callwell, a nineteenth-century student of guerrilla warfare, said that "when [guerrilla warfare] is directed by a leader with a genius for war, an effective [**counter-insurgency**] campaign becomes well-nigh impossible" (quoted in Joes, 2004, p. 1). Yet guerrillas do not always win. Among the more famous counter-insurgent victories are two by the United States in the Philippines (1899–1902 and 1946–1954) and one by the British in Malaya (1948–1960). On the other hand, even more famous losses were suffered by the United States in Vietnam and by the Soviet Union in Afghanistan. Similarly, after 2003, U.S. forces in Iraq and, perhaps, Canadian troops in Afghanistan found themselves in a quagmire. What does it take to make a counter-insurgency work?

The answer is brief and seemingly simple: repress and reform. Government must control the guerrilla militarily at the same time that it addresses the

COUNTER-INSURGENCY
A blend of military and political action taken by a government to defeat an insurgency. The tactics are usually described as a mixture of repression and reform.

complaints of those who support the insurgents. Counter-insurgency thus has a political dimension just as insurgency does. This political dimension even slides over into the military side, because government forces have to find a level of violence that is high enough to stop the guerrillas but not so fierce as to alienate the general population.

Despite the centrality of politics in counter-insurgency, governments fighting guerrillas often overlook this element, preferring to rely on their superiority of force (Beckett, 2001; Hoffman, 2004; Joes, 2004). The latest U.S. Army field manual on counter-insurgency (U.S. Army, 2006) stresses political operations. Yet the United States' experience in Iraq suggests how difficult it is for governments and their militaries to adopt a strategy that would maximize their effectiveness against guerrilla insurgents and construct a political system better able to seek the common good.

Terror

What particularly sets terrorism apart from other forms of political violence such as war, rebellion, coup d'état, and revolution, is its conscious targeting of the innocent (as discussed in Box 12-8, Terrorism Today). Terrorists use this

BOX 12-8

Terrorism Today

Even before al-Qaeda's terrorist attacks on the United States on September 11, 2001, democracies were acquainted with terrorism. For example:

- North Americans have witnessed terrorist attacks by those who bomb abortion clinics, the bombing of an Air India flight in 1985, the right-wing extremists who blew up the Murrah Building in Oklahoma City in 1995, and Theodore Kaczynski (the "Unabomber"), who sent package bombs to unwitting victims.

- In Ireland and Britain, the Irish Republican Army (IRA) and its various factions used violence in their quest to bring Northern Ireland (Ulster) into the Irish Republic. The same applies to Spain, where the ETA (Euzkadi Ta Askatasuna, Basque Homeland and Freedom)

has waged a decades-long armed struggle to separate the Basque provinces from Spain.

- In the 1970s and 1980s, Germany faced serious episodes of terror by the Baader–Meinhof Gang (which called itself the Red Army Faction), while Italy suffered terrorist attacks from both the Red Brigades on the extreme left and fascists on the extreme right.

- Continuing into the twenty-first century, Israelis live perpetually with terror, as organizations such as Hamas and Hezbollah have turned to suicide bombers as a regular political tool to press for rights for Palestinians. These tactics provoke strong responses from the Israelis, leaving the Palestinians themselves in a state of terror.

tactic to sow fear among the population, either simply to demonstrate their power or in the hope that citizens will pressure their governments to meet the terrorists' demands.

Those who defend the use of terror usually assert that when fighting the strong, the weak must use any instrument that advances their cause, including not just violence but the use of violence against any target. This is the logic of total war. It is not surprising, therefore, that terrorists also contend that there are no innocent victims. Anyone who is not on the terrorists' side, fully supporting their cause, is an enemy—and in total war, whatever can be done to defeat the enemy must be done.

Consortium for Research on Terrorology and Political Violence (CRTPV)
www.publicinterest.ac.uk/content/view/40/37/

SUICIDE TERRORISM
A form of terrorist violence in which the attacker intends to die as well as killing the intended targets.

Of particular concern today is **suicide terrorism**: an attack in which the attacker's object is to kill her- or himself as well as the target. Nearly every day there is news of suicide attacks in Iraq, Afghanistan, and sometimes Sri Lanka that kill dozens. Although these have come to be identified with Muslim extremists, until the wave of suicide bombings began in Iraq in 2003 it was the Tamil Tigers of Sri Lanka, a Marxist organization seeking an independent Tamil state in the country's north, that had claimed the greatest number of victims. Further, political scientist Robert Pape (2005) concluded that the best predictor of a country having suicide terrorists was not religion but the presence of an outside force the terrorists could paint as an occupier.

Terrorism is not only a form of violence used by groups fighting against established states.[2] Some states also use terror against their own citizens. Campaigns of ethnic cleansing—systematic attempts to remove all people of a particular ethnicity from a region, often by killing them (for example, as carried out in Rwanda and Yugoslavia in the 1990s)—qualify as terror.

Police states and totalitarian regimes often resort to indiscriminate arrests, torture, and even murder to intimidate the population they govern. In many Latin American countries, particularly in the 1980s, "death squads" associated with repressive governments terrorized the population. As well, states sometimes sponsor terrorism to achieve international objectives. For example, Libyan intelligence agents were involved in the bombing of Pan-Am Flight 103 over Lockerbie, Scotland, in 1988, killing all on board (Coombes, 2003)—presumably as retaliation for an American attack against Libya's leader.

Terrorism is not unknown in Canada. Between 1963 and 1970, members of the Front de libération du Québec (FLQ) planted bombs, held up banks, and caused at least five deaths by bombs and gunfire. In October 1970, the FLQ kidnapped James Cross, the British trade commissioner in Montreal, and Pierre Laporte, labour minister in the Quebec government. Although Cross was released, Laporte was murdered by the terrorists.

---

[2] The designation of actions as terrorism is often highly controversial. For example, the Russian government condemns Chechen separatists who have bombed buildings and taken hostages as terrorists. Supporters of the Chechen rebels view the Russian government and military as terrorists for their brutal suppression of the breakaway Chechen Republic.

Canada's worst terrorist attack occurred on June 22, 1985, when bombs were planted by terrorists on board Air India Flight 182 before it left Vancouver. The bombing apparently was in retaliation for the Indian government's attack on the Golden Temple at Amritsar, the most important Sikh shrine. The bombs exploded while the 747 was over the North Atlantic and killed all 329 passengers and crew, the great majority of whom were Canadians.

Why is terror used to achieve political objectives? Is it because people see the stakes as being so high that the most extreme measures are justified? Or is it because terror works? Whatever the cause, terrorism is an ever-present concern.

Revolution

Revolution implies radical, far-reaching change. It is a concept that has always fascinated political scientists. We want to know why revolutions happen, why they succeed or fail, and what revolutionaries do once in power. Political science has two related but distinct definitions of revolution. The broader of these classifies any armed overthrow of a government as a revolution. These are political revolutions that change rulers. The narrower of these reserves the label of revolution for armed overthrows that bring in fundamental economic, political, and social changes. These are **social revolutions**.

SOCIAL REVOLUTION
A revolution that changes not just who governs but how a state, society, and economy are structured.

We find the best examples of social revolutions among the great revolutions of the modern age, an era that reaches back to the latter part of the eighteenth century. These events reshaped both how people think about the political world and how that world works. They defined new ways to govern, opened new political horizons for large, previously excluded sectors of society, and recast hierarchies of power and prestige. We usually include the following in this pantheon of revolutions:

- The American, 1776–1783, with its entirely new model of government
- The French, 1789, which began the end of aristocratic rule in Europe
- The Mexican, 1910–1920, the first social revolution in what we now call the Third World
- The Russian or Bolshevik, 1917, the first communist revolution
- The Chinese, 1949, a guerrilla-led communist revolution in the world's most populous country
- The Cuban, 1959, a guerrilla-led communist revolution in the Americas
- The Iranian, 1979, a revolution linked to religion
- The Eastern European, 1989, revolutions against communism

Other revolutions had important consequences for their countries but were of less historic significance. Some were wars of independence, as in Greece (1821–1829), while others emerged from systematic restructurings of state and society that followed military coups, as happened in Chile between

1973 and 1989.[3] Even failed revolutions, like the wave that swept Europe in 1848, can be important because they open the way to later reforms. Finally, there have been revolutions that were nearly non-violent, such as the 1989 Velvet Revolution in Czechoslovakia that brought the downfall of the country's communist regime (Wheaton & Kavan, 1992).

THEORIES OF REVOLUTION In everyday language, we often separate fact from theory, but in political science we use facts to build theories that we then use to interpret other facts. More formally, a "theory is a systematic explanation for observations that refer to a particular aspect of life" (Babbie, 1995, p. 49). Thus, a theory of revolution takes empirical observations about specific revolutions and derives from them an explanation about revolution in general. It considers why revolutions occur, what influences their evolution, and what results they produce.

The most famous theory of revolution comes from Karl Marx (1818-1883). He argued that fundamental changes in the structure of a country's economy, the means of production, lead to conflict between the class that controls the old means of production and the class based on the rising one. Concretely, he predicted that capitalism would generate conflict between the capitalists (the bourgeoisie) who owned and directed the economy and the working class (the proletariat) whose labour made the economy function. The outcome he foresaw had the proletariat winning and setting humanity on the road to communism, a society without systematic conflicts because it would abolish classes. His prediction has proven wrong.

More recent theorists have taken a more modest tack. Some have described specific revolutions in detail, searching for general patterns (Brinton, 1965). Others have hypothesized that key structural elements exist in all successful revolutions and have examined the record of revolutions to test their hypotheses (Skocpol, 1979). All search for a general theory of revolutions that will allow us to predict whether a revolution will happen in a particular setting and how it will develop. Some theorists argue that prediction is impossible. Focusing on the Iranian revolution of 1979, on which she is an expert, Keddie (1995) notes that the structural characteristics visible in Iran before the revolution also existed in other countries where no upheaval occurred. Goldstone (1995), however, believes that careful attention to trends as well as structures allows us to identify situations that will produce revolutions unless significant countermeasures are taken. What we know for certain is that there will be more revolutions, but we are unsure if we can predict where and when.

---

[3] Although the political, economic, and social changes in Chilean society were brought about by the political right, they can still be classed as revolutionary. There is no reason why revolutions have to bring greater liberty and equality.

Summary and Conclusion

Political protest attempts to influence government—it is a form of political participation. It can be the best, or only, political tool available to the excluded. Even in democracies, normal channels can prove ineffective for the weak and marginalized. Yet political protest poses difficult questions for democratic citizens. Most of us usually play by the established rules of politics. We believe that these rules are basically fair or, if not, that they can be changed by normally available methods. However, we also know that some of our fellow citizens cannot make those rules work for them. We may or may not endorse their aims, but we wonder why our democratic rules make effective political action impossible for some people. We are witnessing a perennial problem of democratic politics.

Very few who live in democratic states accept violence for political ends. At times we may sympathize with guerrilla rebels who wage wars to overthrow brutal dictators and with revolutions that promise people a better future. Where reasonable channels of political expression exist, though, it is difficult to justify the use of force. It is even more difficult for citizens of Canada or other well-functioning democracies to countenance the use of terror as a means of protest. While terror unfortunately is used in war (although we should question whether the indiscriminate killing of civilians and the use of chemical, biological, and nuclear weapons are ever justified), we are loath to consider it a legitimate instrument of politics. Likewise, we find it troubling that some democratic states have supported and provided assistance to governments, security forces, or rebels that use terrorist tactics.

Key Terms

Discussion Questions

1. Have you ever been involved in a political protest? In what circumstances do you think that you would get involved in protest activity? Would you engage in civil disobedience?

2. Is terrorism ever justified? Are terrorists irrational?

3. What are political opportunity structures and why are they important in understanding political protest?

4. Why do you think political violence has had a relatively limited role in Canadian protest politics?

5. What contemporary cases of political protest can you name? How are they different from older instances? How are they the same?

6. Why do revolutions occur? Why do you think Canada has never had a revolution?

Further Reading

Asprey, R. *War in the shadows.* New York: W. Morrow, 1994.

Bouvard, M. *Revolutionary motherhood: The Mothers of the Plaza de Mayo.* Wilmington, DE: SR Books, 1994.

Debray, R. *Revolution in the revolution.* New York: Grove Press, 1967.

Galula, D. *Counterinsurgency warfare: Theory and practice.* New York: Praeger Publishers, 1964.

Goldstone, J. (Ed.). *Revolutions: Theoretical, comparative, and historical studies,* 3rd ed. Belmont, CA: Wadsworth/Thompson Learning, 2003.

Guevara, C. *Guerrilla warfare.* Wilmington, DE: SR Books, 1997.

Irvin, C. *Militant nationalism.* Minneapolis, MN: University of Minnesota Press, 1999.

Katz, M. (Ed.). *Revolution: International dimensions.* Washington, DC: CQ Press, 2001.

Mao Zedong. *On guerrilla warfare.* New York: Praeger, 1961.

Pape, R. *Dying to win: The strategic logic of suicide terrorism.* New York: Random House, 2005.

Sanderson, S. *Revolutions: A worldwide introduction to political and social change.* Boulder, CO: Paradigm Publishers, 2005.

Smith, J., & Johnston, H. (Eds.). *Globalization and resistance: Transnational dimensions of social movements.* Lanham, MD: Rowman & Littlefield, 2002.

Tilly, C., & Tarrow, S. *Contentious politics.* Boulder, CO: Paradigm Publishers, 2007.

PART IV

GOVERNING

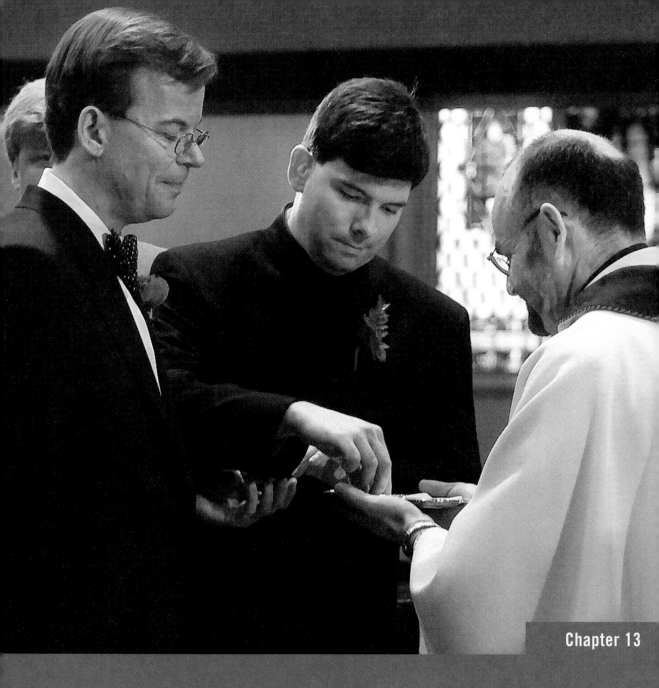

Chapter 13

THE CONSTITUTION, RIGHTS AND FREEDOMS, AND THE RULE OF LAW

PHOTO ABOVE: When Kevin Bourassa and Joe Varnell exchanged wedding vows in Toronto's Metropolitan Community Church in 2001, attendees included Ontario's NDP leader and journalists from around the world. Outside, protesters wore devil masks.

CHAPTER OBJECTIVES

After reading this chapter you should be able to:

1. explain the significance of a constitution and constitutional government
2. describe the major characteristics of the Canadian constitution and how it differs from the constitution of the United Kingdom
3. outline the provisions of the Canadian Charter of Rights and Freedoms
4. discuss the political importance of the courts
5. explain the meaning of the rule of law

When Kevin Bourassa and Joe Varnell exchanged wedding vows in Toronto's Metropolitan Community Church on January 14, 2001, Ontario's NDP leader attended, along with journalists from around the world. Governor General Adrienne Clarkson sent a congratulatory telegram. Outside, protestors wore devil masks.

The Ontario government of the time refused to register the couple's wedding licence and a legal battle over same-sex marriage ensued. Within a few years, courts in several provinces ruled that the traditional legal definition of marriage—a union of one man and one woman—was discriminatory and violated the equality rights provisions of the Charter of Rights and Freedoms in Canada's constitution. Bourassa and Varnell's marriage was officially registered on June 11, 2003, and since then many gay and lesbian couples have been legally married. However, Alberta Premier Ralph Klein indicated that, if necessary, he would use the "notwithstanding clause," a clause in the Charter that allows the passing of legislation that infringes on rights, in order to prevent the legalization of same-sex marriages in Alberta.

In 1999, the Liberals had supported a Reform party motion in the House of Commons upholding the traditional definition of marriage. However, following the provincial court decisions, Liberal Prime Minister Jean Chrétien decided to introduce legislation to define marriage as involving two persons. Calgary's Catholic bishop said that Chrétien risked burning in hell, and the Pope reminded Catholic politicians of their obligation to vote according to their faith. Upon becoming prime minister, Paul Martin tried to downplay the issue, hoping that a decision could be delayed until after an election. Toward the end of the 2004 election campaign, however, Martin was facing a possible Liberal defeat and decided to use the issue to attack the Conservatives.

The Conservatives, Martin argued, would take away people's rights by using the Charter's "notwithstanding clause." Conservative leader Stephen Harper said that he opposed same-sex marriage and, if his party formed the government, he would hold a free vote (one in which MPs were not expected to vote with their party) in the House of Commons to decide the issue. Although he avoided the question of whether the notwithstanding clause should be used to protect a ban on same-sex marriages from court challenges, other Conservatives were more forthright. MP Randy White proclaimed, "To heck with the courts . . . the politicians make the laws" (Hume, 2004). The Civil Marriage Act, which makes same-sex marriages legal in all parts of Canada, was passed by Parliament in July 2005. With the election of a Conservative government in 2006, the issue was reopened by a motion in the House of Commons asking the government to introduce legislation that would restore the traditional definition of marriage. The motion was defeated 175–123. As a result, the question of whether the Conservatives would try to use the notwithstanding clause to overrule the interpretation of the Charter by the courts that legalized same-sex marriages was avoided. Prime Minister Harper indicated that he didn't plan to reopen the controversial issue.

The issue of same-sex marriage raises questions not only about the definition of marriage, but also about how rights should be protected. Should the courts or legislative bodies have the final say in determining how general constitutional rights such as equality rights should be applied to particular issues?

In this chapter, we focus on the significance of constitutions, including their role in protecting rights and freedoms and limiting the arbitrary power of government.

WHAT IS A CONSTITUTION?

A **constitution** establishes the fundamental rules and principles by which a state is governed. It determines which institutions have the authority to make laws and governing decisions. A constitution also indicates what procedures must be followed in selecting the government and in passing laws, and what rights and freedoms are guaranteed to the population. In effect, a constitution places some restrictions on the power of governments. As well, constitutional documents often contain a general statement of the values and goals of the political community.

A constitution is generally considered to be the supreme or basic law of a country. Governments are expected to follow its provisions, and the laws passed by legislative bodies are expected to conform to the provisions of the constitution. However, non-democratic governments, and occasionally democratic ones, sometimes ignore their constitution when it suits their purposes. Although most countries have some form of constitution, many do not have a **constitutional government**—that is, a government that consistently acts in accordance with the rules and principles established in the constitution.

"Unwritten" Constitutions

The United Kingdom, which could be considered the first country to adopt a constitutional government, is sometimes described as having an unwritten constitution. Much of the British constitution consists of **constitutional conventions**—fundamental principles that are consistently followed, even though they are not contained in a legal document and are not enforceable in the courts. For example, by convention, the British monarch will always give the assent needed for a bill (proposed legislation) to become an Act (also known as a statute) if a majority in Parliament has passed it.

The British constitution is not entirely unwritten. A number of important statutes have been passed by the British Parliament concerning various aspects of the system of government. For example, the Scotland Act, 1998 established a Parliament for Scotland, and the Constitutional Reform Act, 2005 provided for the establishment of a Supreme Court of the United Kingdom (scheduled to be created by 2009). There is, however, no single constitutional document or clearly defined set of constitutional documents that could be defined as the British constitution. Thus, it is better described as an uncodified, rather than an unwritten, constitution. There has been discussion in recent years about codifying the main elements of the British constitution.

In addition, **parliamentary sovereignty** (also termed parliamentary supremacy) has been a basic principle of the British system of governing. In the traditional British system, Parliament is the supreme law-making body

---

CONSTITUTION
The fundamental rules and principles by which a state is governed.

CONSTITUTIONAL GOVERNMENT
A government that consistently acts in accordance with the rules and principles established in its constitution.

CONSTITUTIONAL CONVENTION
A fundamental principle that is consistently followed even though it is not contained in a legal document and is not generally enforceable in the courts.

PARLIAMENTARY SOVEREIGNTY
A basic principle of the British system of governing, recognizing Parliament as the supreme law-making body.

able to pass a law on any topic. As an old saying goes, "Parliament can do anything except turn a man into a woman and a woman into a man"—and today Parliament could presumably do that! Thus, a majority in Parliament can change the constitution through an Act of Parliament. Further, the principle of parliamentary sovereignty means that the courts cannot invalidate an Act of Parliament. The only limitation on the authority of Parliament is that it cannot bind future parliaments. In reality, however, basic constitutional principles (such as the rule of law discussed below) are deeply entrenched in the British political culture and thus are generally respected by the government.

The principle of parliamentary sovereignty (which is also a basic element of New Zealand's system of governing) has been modified in the United Kingdom, particularly by its membership in the European Union. The United Kingdom is committed to abide by the laws of the European Union—although parliamentary sovereignty could be reasserted by withdrawing from the Union.

Constitution Finder
http://confinder.richmond.edu

Formal Constitutions

The United States (1787) and France (1789) pioneered the use of a formal, written, codified constitution. As Heather MacIvor (2006) points out, those who developed the American constitution believed that legitimate authority should be based on the consent of the governed. A written constitution would limit the power of government and allow the courts to ensure that government acted in accordance with the will of the people that was expressed (it was assumed) in the constitution. However, the assumption that a written constitution necessarily reflects the will of the people, rather than the views of those who drafted it, can be questioned.

Almost all countries today have a formal constitution or a set of constitutional documents that establishes their major constitutional provisions. Special procedures usually have to be followed if the formal constitution is to be changed.

The distinction between a written, codified constitution and an unwritten, uncodified constitution should not be exaggerated. Formal constitutional documents typically do not provide a comprehensive set of provisions concerning how a country is to be governed. Various laws, conventions, customs, and judicial interpretations are also an important part of any constitution.

Canadian Constitutional Documents.
A Legal History
www.solon.org/Constitutions/Canada/
English

CONSTITUTION ACT, 1867
An Act of the United Kingdom Parliament that established Canada by uniting the colonies of Canada (Ontario and Quebec), Nova Scotia, and New Brunswick. It also set out many of the features of Canada's system of governing.

The Canadian Constitution

Like the constitutions of other countries, the Canadian constitution can be considered a combination of a variety of elements:

The **Constitution Act, 1867** (originally known as the British North America Act) is the core, written element of the constitution. This Act of the United

Kingdom Parliament established Canada by uniting the colonies of Canada (Ontario and Quebec), Nova Scotia, and New Brunswick. It also set out many of the features of Canada's system of governing. Over the years, there have been a number of amendments to the Constitution Act (see Figure 13.1). As well, various other historic British statutes and orders-in-council (Cabinet decisions) such as the Terms of Union by which British Columbia (1871) and Prince Edward Island (1873) joined Canada are part of the formal Canadian constitution.

CONSTITUTION ACT, 1982
The Act that made the constitution fully Canadian, added the Charter of Rights and Freedoms to the constitution, and established procedures for amending the constitution.

The **Constitution Act, 1982**, an amendment to the Constitution Act, 1867, made the constitution a fully Canadian document. The Constitution Act, 1982 made it clear that the formal constitution is the supreme law of Canada, and specifically indicated which documents are to be considered part of the codified constitution. As discussed below, it also added the Charter of Rights and Freedoms to the formal constitution and established procedures for amending the constitution.

There are a variety of ordinary legislative statutes, such as the Supreme Court Act and the Canada Elections Act, that can be considered constitutional because of their fundamental importance.

Constitutional conventions, many of which were inherited from Britain, establish many of the principles that determine the functioning of the system of governing. Judicial bodies such as the Supreme Court of Canada have made many important decisions that determine how the constitution is interpreted. For example, judicial bodies have had a major role in determining the legal powers of the national and provincial governments and in interpreting

▶ In 1982, Queen Elizabeth II signed the documents that made the constitution entirely Canadian.

(and in some cases expanding) the general provisions of the Charter of Rights and Freedoms.

AMENDING THE CONSTITUTION

Constitutional amendments are needed from time to time because of changing circumstances and the changing values of a country's citizens. Experiences with the constitution may also lead to a desire to improve it. However, to try to ensure that a government does not use constitutional changes to gain excessive powers or to take away constitutionally protected rights, most countries require a higher level of support to change their formal, written constitution than is needed to pass or change an ordinary law. For example, amendments to the American constitution require approval by a two-thirds majority in each of the two Houses of Congress and ratification by three-quarters of the state legislatures. Only twenty-seven amendments to the American constitution have been passed in more than two hundred years. Some countries (such as Sweden, Denmark, and the Netherlands) require that amendments be passed by parliamentary bodies twice—once before and once after an election. Other countries (including Australia, Switzerland, and Japan) require approval in a referendum as well as by legislative bodies (Rasch & Congleton, 2006).

CONSTITUTIONAL AMENDMENT
A formal change to the constitution.

Amending Canada's Constitution

Some aspects of the Canadian constitution can be changed without any procedural difficulties. The unwritten aspects of the Canadian constitution—conventions and judicial interpretations—typically evolve over time. Ordinary laws that are of constitutional significance can be changed by the adoption of a new law by a simple majority in Parliament or a provincial legislature.

The procedures adopted in 1982 for amending the Constitution Act are more complex:

- A few provisions of the Constitution Act, such as the offices of the monarch, governor general, and lieutenant-governors, and the composition of the Supreme Court of Canada, are only amendable by the resolution of a majority in Parliament[1] and in all of the provincial legislatures.

- Most of the Constitution Act (including the division of law-making authority between Parliament and provincial legislatures) can be changed with the agreement of majorities in the House of Commons and the Senate and majorities in at least two-thirds of the provincial legislatures,

---

[1] A majority in each of the chambers of Parliament (that is, the House of Commons and the Senate) is needed for any amendments to the constitution. However, if the Senate does not pass the resolution for the amendment, after one hundred and eighty days the House of Commons can repass the resolution, in which case the approval of the Senate is not needed for the amendment.

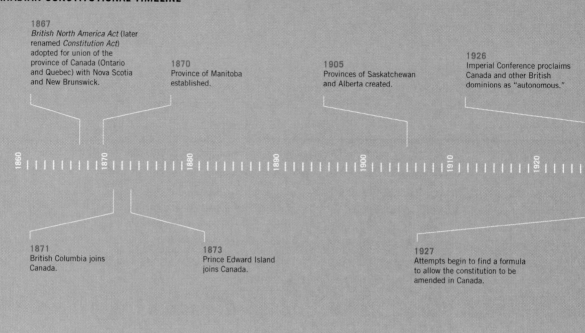

FIGURE 13-1
CANADIAN CONSTITUTIONAL TIMELINE

1867
British North America Act (later renamed *Constitution Act*) adopted for union of the province of Canada (Ontario and Quebec) with Nova Scotia and New Brunswick.

1870
Province of Manitoba established.

1905
Provinces of Saskatchewan and Alberta created.

1926
Imperial Conference proclaims Canada and other British dominions as "autonomous."

1871
British Columbia joins Canada.

1873
Prince Edward Island joins Canada.

1927
Attempts begin to find a formula to allow the constitution to be amended in Canada.

provided those legislatures represent provinces containing at least one-half of the population of all the provinces.[2] A province has the right to "opt out" of a constitutional amendment that reduces the powers of its legislature.

- Although a referendum is not required to approve constitutional changes, the use of a referendum in 1992 to seek approval for a major package of changes suggests that there is a political expectation that a referendum be held to approve major changes. British Columbia and Alberta require that a referendum be held before their legislatures approve a constitutional amendment.

- Changes to constitutional provisions that only affect certain provinces (such as the change of the name of the province of Newfoundland to Newfoundland and Labrador) only require the approval of Parliament and the affected provincial legislatures.

---

[2] Although this is still the procedure in the Constitution Act, the Canadian Parliament passed legislation in 1996 requiring that proposed constitutional changes introduced into the Canadian Parliament must also have the support of Ontario, Quebec, British Columbia, the Prairies (in effect, Alberta plus either Saskatchewan or Manitoba), and Atlantic Canada (at least two provinces containing at least one-half of the region's population).

1931
Statute of Westminster confirms that Canada is a sovereign country.

1960-1966
Quebec governments seek constitutional changes.

1976
Parti Québécois elected.

1982
Constitution Act, 1982 adopted making the constitution fully amendable in Canada and adding the Charter of Rights and Freedoms to the *Constitution Act.*

1990
Meech Lake Accord fails to pass in Newfoundland and Manitoba legislatures.

1995
Quebec referendum on sovereignty narrowly defeated.

1949
Most aspects of constitution can be amended in Canada. Supreme Court of Canada replaces the Judicial Committee of the British Privy Council as the highest court of appeal. Newfoundland joins Canada.

1967-1971
Constitutional negotiations end in failure.

1980
Quebec government request for a mandate to negotiate sovereignty-association defeated in a Quebec referendum.

1987
Prime minister and premiers reach agreement on the Meech Lake Accord.

1992
Prime minister, premiers, and Aboriginal leaders reach agreement on Charlottetown Accord. Accord defeated in a national referendum.

2000
Clarity Act setting out conditions for a province to become independent passed by Parliament.

Major amendments to the formal constitution have proven difficult to achieve, as witnessed by the failures of the **Meech Lake Accord** and the **Charlottetown Accord** (see Box 13-1, The Politics of Canadian Constitutional Change). Instead, modifications to the system of government have been achieved at times without changing the formal constitution.

RIGHTS AND FREEDOMS

Nearly all constitutions contain provisions concerning the rights and freedoms of individuals. In the United States, for example, the Bill of Rights has been part of the constitution since 1791. As a result, American governments are prohibited from passing laws that infringe upon those rights. Typically, constitutionally protected rights and freedoms include the right of all citizens to participate in political life through such means as voting and running for public office, provide for such freedoms as that of expression, religion, and association, and establish such legal rights as the right to a fair trial. Many countries also include **positive rights** in their constitutions—rights to services or benefits such as the right to education, health care, and employment. Such rights, however, are often not enforceable through the legal system, but rather are statements of goals and principles that are implemented through the

MEECH LAKE ACCORD
A 1987 package of constitutional changes that was not passed. It contained controversial provisions, including the recognition of Quebec as a distinct society.

CHARLOTTETOWN ACCORD
A package of constitutional changes, including recognition of the inherent right of Aboriginals to self-government and major changes to the Senate to provide for equal representation by each province regardless of population size. It was defeated in a referendum in 1992.

POSITIVE RIGHTS
A right to services or benefits such as the right to education, health care, and employment.

BOX 13-1

The Politics of Canadian Constitutional Change

The constitution has often been a flashpoint for political controversy in Canada.

Starting in 1927, national and provincial leaders met on and off in an attempt to reach agreement on a formula for amending the constitution in Canada. The formula that was finally adopted in 1982 was reached only after a bitter set of negotiations between the federal and provincial governments.

In addition to disagreement over the choice of an amending formula, there have been serious disagreements over the content of the constitution. Beginning in the early 1960s, Quebec governments sought constitutional changes to give them greater power to lead the social and economic development of their province. Other provincial governments, including Alberta and Newfoundland, have sought greater powers over their natural resources, as well as a stronger voice for the less populated provinces in Parliament through changes to the Senate.

The Constitution Act, 1982 was put into effect over objections by the Quebec government and many Aboriginal leaders. Quebec provincial politicians claimed that constitutional convention necessitated the agreement of all provincial legislatures for constitutional changes that affected the powers of the provinces. As well, the Quebec government was disappointed that promises of constitutional changes to enhance the position of Quebec were not fulfilled. Aboriginal leaders argued that treaties that had been signed with the British Crown were being transferred to Canada without their agreement.

Although challenges to the Constitution Act, 1982 in the courts proved unsuccessful, Quebec governments have questioned the legitimacy of Canada's written constitution. To try to resolve this issue, Prime Minister Brian Mulroney and all ten premiers agreed on a package of constitutional changes in 1987, termed the Meech Lake Accord. However, there was widespread opposition to the accord among English-speaking Canadians, particularly to the proposal that Quebec be recognized in the constitution as a distinct society. Aboriginal Canadians were disappointed that the Meech Lake Accord did not include recognition of their inherent right to self-government. The Accord, which required the agreement of all legislatures, failed to pass in the Manitoba and Newfoundland legislatures and thus died in 1990.

A second package of constitutional changes, the Charlottetown Accord, was agreed to by the prime minister, ten premiers, two territorial leaders, and leaders of the four major Aboriginal organizations in 1992. Its centrepiece was the recognition of the inherent right of Aboriginals to self-government. It also proposed major changes to the Senate to provide for equal representation by each province regardless of population size, and recognition of a variety of characteristics of Canada, including a somewhat more specific definition of Quebec's distinctiveness than presented in the Meech Lake Accord.

The Charlottetown Accord was defeated in a national referendum by a vote of 55 percent to 45 percent. The majority of English-speaking Canadians felt that it gave too much to Quebec, the majority of French-speaking Quebecers felt that it gave too little to Quebec, and the majority of Aboriginals felt that the self-government provisions were too limited.

Overall, the different views on the nature of Canada held by many English-speaking Canadians, French-speaking Quebecers, and Aboriginals have made major changes to Canada's formal constitution very contentious. With a high level of agreement needed for constitutional change, it is not surprising that major changes have been difficult to achieve.

ordinary processes of governing (Glendon, 1995). Many countries, including Canada, are signatories to the International Covenant on Economic, Social and Cultural Rights, which includes various positive rights. However, the International Covenant does not have the enforcement mechanisms that are generally included in constitutional protection of rights.

International Covenant on Economic, Social and Cultural Rights
www.unhchr.ch/html/menu3/b/a_ cescr.htm

Canadian Civil Liberties Association
www.ccla.org

Protecting Rights in Canada

The original Canadian constitution, the Constitution Act, 1867, did not explicitly protect rights and freedoms, with the exception of the right to use English or French in Parliament, the Quebec legislature, and certain courts, as well as the rights of denominational schools to receive public funding in some provinces. Instead, following British practice, it was assumed that Parliament and provincial legislatures would not infringe upon traditional liberties, and that judicial bodies would interpret laws in a manner consistent with those liberties.

The tradition of respecting rights and freedoms was generally followed. However, there were important exceptions, such as the treatment of Aboriginal peoples and the incarceration of Canadian citizens of Japanese descent during the Second World War. In the 1960s, the Canadian government and many provincial governments adopted Bills of Rights, although these did not have the weight of a constitutional provision. In 1982, the **Charter of Rights and Freedoms** was added to Canada's formal, written constitution (see Box 13-2, The Canadian Charter of Rights and Freedoms: Basic Provisions). The Charter is superior to ordinary legislation, and thus all legislation is expected to be consistent with its provisions. It explicitly allows the courts to invalidate legislation that is inconsistent with the Charter, and applies to the actions of all governments and organizations under the control of government.[3]

CHARTER OF RIGHTS AND FREEDOMS
As part of the Constitution Act, 1982, the Charter protects a variety of rights and freedoms. It is superior to ordinary legislation, explicitly allows the courts to invalidate legislation, and applies to the actions of all governments and organizations under the control of government.

Canadian Charter of Rights and Freedoms
laws.justice.gc.ca/en/charter

Limits to Rights and Freedoms

Rights and freedoms are not absolute. For example, freedom of expression is an important right, but it does not give a person the right to yell "Fire!" in a crowded theatre when there is no fire. Many countries have laws that prohibit the possession, production, and distribution of pornography, prohibit the expression of hatred directed at various groups, and place limits on advertising directed at children. Although certain limitations to freedoms are necessary to avoid harm, the question of how far governments should go in limiting freedoms to protect people from potential harm is often controversial. Generally, when rights and

---

[3] Human rights codes adopted by provincial and national governments provide for various human rights, including protection against various forms of discrimination by private employers and other organizations and individuals. These codes, however, are not part of the constitution.

BOX 13-2

The Canadian Charter of Rights and Freedoms: Basic Provisions

The basic provisions of the Canadian Charter of Rights and Freedoms include the following:

- *Fundamental freedoms* (Section 2) protect freedom of conscience and religion, and freedom of opinion and expression, including freedom of the media, freedom of peaceful assembly, and freedom of association.
- *Democratic rights* (Sections 3 to 5) include the right of all citizens to vote and hold elected office. The maximum term of Parliament and provincial legislatures is limited to five years.
- *Mobility rights* (Section 6) include the right to move and to pursue a livelihood in any province. However, provinces are allowed to adopt policies that give preference to their own residents for such matters as employment if the province has a below-average rate of employment.
- A variety of *legal rights* (Sections 7 to 14), including the right to life, liberty, and security of the person, the right to be secure against unreasonable search or arbitrary detention, the right to a trial within a reasonable period of time, the right to be presumed innocent until proven guilty, and the right not to be subject to any cruel and unusual punishment.
- The *equality rights* clause (Section 15) provides that every person is equal under the law and has the right to the equal protection and equal benefit of the law without discrimination on such grounds as race, origin, colour, religion, sex, age, or mental or physical disability. However, *affirmative action* laws or programs designed to help disadvantaged individuals or groups are permitted.
- *Language rights* (Sections 16 to 23) include the declaration that English and French are the official languages of Canada and New Brunswick and are given equal status in the operations of the Canadian and New Brunswick governments. Canadian citizens whose mother tongue is either English or French have the right to have their children educated in their own language where numbers warrant. In Quebec, this right only applies to parents who received their schooling in Canada.

In general, the Charter includes quite a comprehensive set of individual rights and freedoms. The affirmative action provision allows governments to help disadvantaged groups. Some group rights are also established by another section of the Constitution Act, 1982 that recognizes and affirms the rights of Aboriginal peoples and rights that Aboriginal peoples have obtained through treaties and land claim agreements in the past or in the future.

However, some—particularly the more conservative-minded—argue that property rights should be explicitly protected in the Charter. Others, particularly social democrats, have advocated that various positive rights such as the right to employment and education should be included in the Charter.

freedoms are entrenched in the constitution, the courts may be called upon to determine whether laws limiting rights and freedoms are justified or excessive.

The **reasonable limits clause** of the Canadian Charter of Rights and Freedoms explicitly allows for laws to place reasonable limits on rights and freedoms, provided that the limits can be "demonstrably justified in a free and democratic

PROVISIONS THAT CANNOT BE OVERRIDDEN	NOTWITHSTANDING CLAUSE APPLIES TO
Democratic rights	Fundamental freedoms
Mobility rights	Legal rights
Language rights	Equality rights
Male–female equality rights	

TABLE 13-1

THE CHARTER AND THE NOTWITHSTANDING CLAUSE

society" (Section 1). For example, the Supreme Court of Canada has upheld laws prohibiting hate literature and possession of child pornography as reasonable limits on freedom of expression.

OVERRIDING THE CHARTER: THE NOTWITHSTANDING CLAUSE

The Canadian Charter of Rights and Freedoms was opposed by some who argued that Parliament rather than the courts should have the final say in determining what should be the appropriate extent of rights and freedoms. As a compromise, Section 33 of the Charter allows Parliament or a provincial legislature to override some rights by the use of the **notwithstanding clause** (see Table 13-1). This involves a legislative body explicitly declaring that a particular law shall operate *notwithstanding* the provisions of the Charter. Such a declaration is only effective for five years, although it can be re-enacted as often as is desired. Box 13-3, The Use of the Notwithstanding Clause, provides an example of how this clause has been used.

JUDICIAL REVIEW

In some countries, the courts have the authority to strike down legislation or governmental actions that are deemed to be in violation of the constitution. For example, even though the power of **judicial review** is not explicitly stated in the American constitution, the courts have assumed this power since 1803. In the United Kingdom, the courts can, if possible, interpret laws in ways that protect rights and can declare an Act of Parliament as incompatible with the Human Rights Act. However, they cannot invalidate an Act of Parliament.

In a number of European countries, including Germany and Austria, judicial review is carried out by a special constitutional court rather than by the regular court system. Many countries do not provide for judicial review, or only have a weak version of it (Lane & Ersson, 2000). Rather than determining whether legislation is constitutional, the courts may interpret laws in ways that emphasize individual rights and procedural fairness.

Judicial Activism

Even in countries where judicial review is available, there is considerable variation in the degree to which the courts are active in invalidating legislation and government actions that are inconsistent with the constitution. The

REASONABLE LIMITS CLAUSE A provision of the Canadian Charter of Rights and Freedoms that allows for "reasonable limits" to be placed on rights and freedoms provided that the limits can be "demonstrably justified in a free and democratic society."

NOTWITHSTANDING CLAUSE A provision in the Charter of Rights and Freedoms that allows a legislative body to explicitly declare that a particular law (related to some parts of the Charter) shall operate *notwithstanding* the provisions of the Charter. Such a declaration is only effective for five years, although it can be re-enacted as often as is desired.

JUDICIAL REVIEW The authority of the courts to strike down legislation or governmental actions that the courts deem to be in violation of the constitution.

The Use of the Notwithstanding Clause

The notwithstanding clause in Canada's Charter of Rights and Freedoms has stirred much controversy. Some view it as an unfortunate compromise between the supporters and opponents of the Charter that results in important rights being vulnerable to the whims of the governing party in Parliament or a provincial legislature and to the pressure of public opinion. Others argue that the clause allows flexibility and protects the democratic principle by ensuring that responsibility for some political decisions ultimately lies with the elected representatives of the people (Petter, 1990).

The notwithstanding clause has been invoked very rarely. Considerable attention was given to its use to protect the French character of Quebec. In 1988, the Supreme Court of Canada struck down the provision in Quebec's Charter of the French Language (Bill 101) that required most public signs in that province to be exclusively in French. The Quebec government then invoked the notwithstanding clause and passed a sign law permitting only French on signs outside stores while allowing French and English on signs inside stores. However, the Quebec government did not renew its use of the notwithstanding clause when the five-year limit ran out. Instead, it passed a new sign law in 1993, consistent with the Supreme Court's ruling, that required that French be given a prominent position on signs in Quebec.

The requirement that legislation must explicitly state that the Charter is being overridden makes it politically risky for a government to use the notwithstanding clause. As we saw in the opening vignette, those who advocate the use of the clause (for example, to pass legislation to circumvent court rulings allowing same-sex marriage) are often accused of seeking to trample on individual rights and freedoms.

JUDICIAL ACTIVISM
The term used when the courts are active in invalidating legislation and government actions that are inconsistent with the constitution.

United States is often viewed as the best example of **judicial activism**. For example, since the 1950s, the American Supreme Court has made important political decisions by overturning state laws that provided for racial segregation and ordering that children be bused from one neighbourhood to another to try to achieve racial integration in public schools.

In Canada, the courts have always had some ability to invalidate the laws passed by Parliament and provincial legislatures if those laws exceed the authority granted by the constitution to that level of government. The authority to invalidate legislation was expanded by the Charter of Rights and Freedoms in 1982. Since then, the courts have exhibited a degree of judicial activism by invalidating some laws and regulations. For example, in 1988 the Supreme Court struck down a law that (with certain exceptions) made abortion a criminal offence, ruling that the law violated the Charter right to "life, liberty and security of the person." A subsequent attempt to pass a new law specifying the conditions under which abortion would be allowed failed to be approved by Parliament. Similarly, the courts have struck down various laws that discriminate against gays and lesbians by interpreting the equality rights provision in the Charter so as to prohibit discrimination on the basis of sexual orientation even though sexual orientation is not explicitly mentioned in the Charter.

Is Judicial Activism Desirable?

Some commentators have argued that judicial activism has made Canadian courts too powerful. Instead of the elected representatives of the people making decisions about controversial issues, appointed judges who are unaccountable are, in effect, making important decisions concerning issues such as abortion, same-sex marriage, and the legalization of the medical use of marijuana. Because governments have been very reluctant to use the Charter's notwithstanding clause, there is no check on what some view as the excessive activism of the courts (Morton, 2003). As well, the courts (unlike governments) generally do not have the capability to monitor and assess the consequences of their decisions.

Other commentators argue that by actively using the Charter, the courts have helped to protect the rights of minorities. When it adopted the Charter of Rights and Freedoms, Canada established itself as a true constitutional democracy in which an independent judiciary sets limits to the power of government (Potter, 2003). The courts are more likely to be concerned about the rights of unpopular minorities than elected officials, who may be pressured by majority opinion.

In assessing each argument, it should be noted that the courts have been more active in invalidating legislation at some points in time and more deferential to the wishes of legislative bodies at other points in time, depending on the issues involved and the judges who are hearing the cases. As well, governments and legislative bodies have sometimes preferred to leave some controversial moral issues to the courts to decide.

As discussed in Box 13-4, Is Judicial Activism Desirable?, there has been considerable controversy about the role of judicial activism in Canada's courts.

The courts generally only consider the validity of laws and regulations when faced with a particular case. Given the costs of pursuing cases through the court system, many laws and government actions are not reviewed by the courts. Canadian governments can refer a proposed law to the Supreme Court for an advisory opinion (as the Canadian government did concerning same-sex marriages), although this use of the courts is not very common. Nevertheless, governments will usually try to ensure that new legislation is "Charter proof" to avoid the possibility that it will be struck down when a case comes before the courts.

THE RULE OF LAW

Closely connected to the idea of constitutional government is the concept of the **rule of law**. The rule of law is often defined as the idea that all persons should be subject to *known, predictable,* and *impartial* rules of conduct, rather than to the arbitrary orders of particular individuals. Those entrusted with governing authority have a responsibility to act in accordance with the legal rules and procedures established in the constitution.

RULE OF LAW
The idea that all persons should be subject to *known, predictable,* and *impartial* rules of conduct, rather than to the arbitrary orders of particular individuals.

An important aspect of the rule of law is that both the rulers and the ruled should be equally subject to the law. It also carries with it the idea that the state should not be able to use its coercive powers against an individual unless that person has violated a specific, known law, as judged by an impartial institution (that is, an institution that is not influenced by the government). Further, for the rule of law to be meaningful, laws should only be made by known and accepted procedures.

Generally, in liberal democracies the principle of the rule of law is well established, although, as with all principles, some exceptions do occur. Security forces in many countries have violated the law, at times, to deal with those that they consider threats to order and security. To deal with terrorism, governments have, on occasion, modified, suspended, or ignored constitutional rights and freedoms (see Box 13-5, Terrorism and the Rule of Law).

Overall, the rule of law does *not* simply mean that everyone should obey the law, and that laws should be enforced. Dictators can pass laws or decrees that give them absolute powers and then punish people for disobeying the arbitrary laws they have established. But this does not constitute what is usually meant by the rule of law. Instead, the rule of law exists where there are limits on the powers of government and those who act in the name of the state, laws are not arbitrary and unfair, and procedures are followed to ensure that every person accused of violating a law is given a fair and impartial hearing.

The Independence of the Judiciary

To ensure that the rule of law is upheld, we expect the courts to be independent of government and other influences. Where there is no independent court system, governments and their agents can intimidate the population, and the principle that all persons should be treated fairly and equally by the law is likely to be undermined.

To protect their independence, judges in Canada and many other constitutional democracies are given a high level of job security, such that they cannot be removed from their position by the government. For federally appointed judges in Canada, removal can only occur through the agreement of a majority in both Houses of Parliament, and this action will only be taken after the Canadian Judicial Council, which is composed of the chief justices and associate chief justices of Canada's superior courts, conducts an inquiry.

In addition, it is considered improper for politicians to try to influence a judge, for example, by calling a judge to discuss a case. Judges are expected to refrain from political activity once appointed to the bench.

SELECTION PROCESS Although judges are supposed to be completely non-political and non-partisan once appointed, the selection of judges is often in the hands of political leaders.

BOX 13-5

Terrorism and the Rule of Law

Terrorism and the rule of law: several hundred foreigners were held for very lengthy periods of time at Guantanamo Bay, a U.S. military base leased from Cuba, without being charged. Allegations of ill treatment and torture of prisoners later surfaced.

In the wake of the terrorist attacks on the United States in 2001, the governments of many democratic countries took strong measures to deal with terrorism. Some of these measures have been criticized for violating the rule of law and individual rights and freedoms.

For example, the Parliament of the United Kingdom passed legislation in 2001 that allowed resident foreigners suspected of terrorism to be interned without trial, if they did not want to be deported to their home country where they might be subject to torture or the death penalty. After this Act was ruled to be in conflict with the Human Rights Act, the UK Parliament passed the Prevention of Terrorism Act, 2005, which allowed judges to authorize house arrest and other control measures for both citizens and foreign nationals suspected of involvement with terrorism. Critics argued that this violated the legal principle of habeas corpus (the right to a court hearing to determine whether a person is detained lawfully), which dates back to the Magna Carta of 1215.

The United States has gone further in its "war against terrorism." Several hundred foreigners, including juveniles, captured during the conflict in

Afghanistan were held for very lengthy periods of time at Guantanamo Bay, a U.S. military base leased from Cuba where American law does not apply, without being charged. As well, prisoners were denied access to their families and to legal counsel. They have been subjected to ill treatment and some "enemy combatants" have been transported to foreign countries, where allegedly they have been tortured. A few American citizens (such as José Padilla, who was arrested at a Chicago airport in 2002 after returning from Pakistan) have also been deprived of traditional rights because of suspected involvement with terrorism. Designated an "enemy combatant" by President Bush, Padilla was held for more than three years in a military jail (much of the time in solitary confinement and allegedly tortured) without charges being filed, access to legal counsel, or the right to challenge his detention. He finally went on trial in 2007 and was found guilty of conspiracy to murder, kidnap, and maim and of providing material support for terrorism. President Obama has ordered Guantanamo closed and the "enemy combatant" designation ended. The fate of those shipped to other countries is not yet known.

Canada's anti-terrorism legislation adopted in 2001 allows individuals suspected of involvement in terrorism to be held for seventy-two hours without a charge being laid, and potentially to be imprisoned for up to twelve months if they do not abide by certain restrictive conditions. Through security certificates endorsed by a federal judge, non-citizens could be held indefinitely without charge based on secret evidence unless they decided to return immediately to their home country. This provision (which was only used in a few cases) was struck down by the Supreme Court of Canada in 2007.

The Canadian anti-terrorism legislation also provides that those called before an investigative hearing can be compelled to testify, requires

(continued)

(continued)

lawyers to report in secret to government authorities if they believe their clients are engaged in suspicious transactions, makes it a serious offence to give money or financial or other related services to groups or individuals that the Canadian government declares to be terrorist, and allows the Canadian Security Establishment to intercept private international communications by Canadians without judicial authorization.

We are left to consider the question of how to reconcile concern with security in the face of the threat of terrorism with a commitment to individual rights and freedoms. For some, the threat of terrorism justifies extraordinary measures; others argue that terrorism should be fought without substantial changes to our rights and freedoms.

Although the laws and constitutions of many countries allow for the temporary suspension of liberties in emergency situations, there is no indication that the threat of terrorism will be a short-lived phenomenon. For Canada, there is an additional economic dimension to this issue. If the United States feels that Canada is not taking adequate measures to prevent terrorists from using Canada as a base for their operations, they may impose very strict border controls that would cause immense damage to Canada's economy because of our reliance on exports to the United States.

The prime minister recommends the appointment of the justices of the Supreme Court of Canada and the chief justices of the provincial Supreme Courts. In recent years, an advisory committee including MPs from each political party has been appointed. This committee generates an unranked short list of three from the candidates selected by the prime minister and the minister of justice after consultations with leading members of the legal community. (This process was not followed in 2008 because the Opposition parties objected to the inclusion of two cabinet ministers on the committee.) An ad hoc parliamentary committee then questions the nominee chosen by the prime minister in a televised hearing (although told not to ask personal questions or questions about how the prospective judge would rule on particular issues). The decision to recommend the nominee continues to rest with the prime minister, as the parliamentary committee does not have veto power.

For other federally appointed judges, the minister of justice makes recommendations to the Cabinet after applicants are assessed by a regional Judicial Advisory Committee. In 2006, a change in the makeup of these committees occurred such that a majority of the members are appointed by the Canadian government and include a representative of the police. This change was criticized by the country's top judges for compromising the independence of the committees (*Globe and Mail Online*, November 10, 2006). A provincial Cabinet minister, the attorney general, makes recommendations to the provincial Cabinet concerning the appointment of judges to the lower provincial courts.

Generally, the appointment of judges, particularly at the Supreme Court level, will tend to reflect the perspective of the prime minister. Some provincial premiers have argued that the appointment of Supreme Court judges on the recommendation of the Canadian prime minister jeopardizes the ability of the Supreme Court of Canada to fairly adjudicate disputes between the Canadian government and provincial governments.

In the United States, the president's nominees for the Supreme Court and all other federal judges must face hearings conducted by the Senate Judiciary Committee before the Senate decides whether to confirm the nomination. Some of these hearings have involved extensive investigations into the lives and beliefs of the nominees. Presidents often choose nominees based on their ideological orientations, and the Senate has rejected nominees whose views differ substantially from that of the Senate majority.

In some American states, judges are elected by voters rather than appointed, and are subject to re-election at regular intervals. While this provides for some democratic accountability of judges, it may also reduce the willingness of judges to act fairly and impartially when the public is incensed about a particular crime or issue.

In Canada and the United States, judges typically are selected after being members of the legal profession for a number of years. As well, Canadian Supreme Court judges often have experience as judges in a lower court. By contrast, in a number of Western European countries, judges are selected after completing law school and receive specialized training before beginning their judicial career. In many countries, a judicial appointments commission (often consisting of judges, lawyers, and parliamentary appointees) is responsible for recommending promotion to higher levels of the court system.

In recent times, to varying extents, efforts have been made to appoint judges with more diverse characteristics than in the past. At the time this textbook was written, four of the nine Supreme Court of Canada judges were female, including Chief Justice Beverley McLachlin. In contrast, only one of the nine members of the United States Supreme Court was female.

◀ Canadian prime ministers have tried to make the Supreme Court of Canada more representative by appointing women to this important body. Beverley McLachlin is Canada's first female Chief Justice.

Summary and Conclusion

The basic legal framework for governing is provided by the constitution. Ideally, constitutions reflect a fundamental consensus among citizens about the governing of their country. Where the constitution is widely accepted, the power of those in governing positions becomes legitimate authority as long as constitutional rules and procedures are followed. However, as the case of Canada indicates, it can be difficult to reach a consensus about some of the provisions of a constitution.

The constitutions of many countries potentially limit the power of government by establishing various rights and freedoms for the population. Constitutional protections of rights and freedoms have the effect of increasing the importance of the courts in the political process. This is the case particularly where the constitution gives the courts the power to invalidate legislation that interferes with rights and freedoms and where the courts are active in exercising that power.

The protection of rights and freedoms may be considered desirable for the promotion of the common good. A free society in which people do not fear arbitrary action by government and have the right to participate in political life will be more likely to foster the good of all than a society controlled by a dictatorial government. Establishing rights to education, housing, employment, social security, and a clean environment may also work to the benefit of the community as a whole. However, this raises the question of how such positive rights should be provided if they are to be more than rhetorical promises.

Some commentators argue that too much emphasis is placed on individual rights, in countries such as the United States, the United Kingdom, and Canada, without a corresponding concern for the responsibility of individuals to each other and to their community. For example, it can be argued that the right to vote carries with it a responsibility to make an informed judgment about what is good for the community when voting. Similarly, the freedom of the media should be used to provide fair and honest reporting to the public.

Others argue that if freedoms are only granted to those who act "responsibly," then the freedoms may be so limited as to be meaningless. The point of political freedoms is to allow a diversity of opinions to be expressed so that through discussion the best course of action can emerge. Developing a sense of responsibility in all citizens is undoubtedly desirable, but it is best achieved through encouragement and education rather than by legal requirements.

Critics of our "rights culture" also argue that by focusing attention on individual rights, discussion about the common good may be neglected. Going to court to pursue one's rights is not only expensive, and thus more available to the wealthier elements of society, but also detracts from the democratic political activity of trying to convince others that a particular course of action is for the common good. Taking legal action can be a useful way to get government, public agencies, or private businesses to live up to their responsibilities. However, frivolous lawsuits can be costly to society as a whole.

The provision of law is a basic and essential function of government. Laws are necessary if we are to enjoy freedom. Without laws, some people would use fear and intimidation to limit the freedom of others. Our freedoms can also be limited if government and its agencies do not feel bound by the rule of law. Preventing the abuse of power by government and its agencies is not an easy task given the power resources available to governments. The great powers that governments possess make it important that government and its officials as well as the general population be equally subject to known, predictable, and impartial laws. The rule of law is more likely than the arbitrary rule of powerful individuals to provide stability, fairness, and justice for the political community. However, heightened concerns about terrorism in recent times have raised difficult questions about how to reconcile a desire for greater security with the rule of law and the rights of individuals.

The courts are important not only in ensuring that people accused of violating the law receive a fair trial, but also in interpreting and, in some countries, reviewing laws and government actions to ensure that they are compatible with the constitution. To ensure that the judicial system works for the common good and protects the rights of individuals and minorities, it should be independent of government, impartial, and fair.

Key Terms

Discussion Questions

1. Should efforts be made to overcome the opposition of Quebec governments to the adoption of the Constitution Act, 1982? Should Quebec be recognized in the constitution as a distinct society?

2. Should positive rights be added to the Canadian Charter of Rights and Freedoms?

3. Should the notwithstanding clause be eliminated from the Canadian constitution?

4. Should the rule of law and civil liberties be suspended when a country is faced with terrorist threats?

5. How should judges be chosen?

6. Is judicial activism desirable?

Further Reading

Coyne, D. *Roll of the dice.* Toronto: James Lorimer, 1992.

Knopff, R., & Morton, F.L. *Charter politics.* Scarborough, ON: Nelson Canada, 1992.

Malleson, K., & Russell, P.H. (Eds.). *Appointing judges in an age of judicial power: Critical perspectives from around the world.* Toronto: University of Toronto Press, 2006.

Mandel, M. *The charter of rights and the legalization of politics in Canada,* rev. ed. Toronto: Wall and Thompson, 1989.

MacIvor, H. *Canadian government and politics in the Charter era.* Toronto: Nelson Thomson, 2005.

McRoberts, K. *Misconceiving Canada: The struggle for national unity.* Toronto: Oxford University Press, 1997.

Russell, P. *Constitutional odyssey,* 3rd ed. Toronto: University of Toronto Press, 2004.

Webber, J. *Reimagining Canada: Language, culture, community, and the Canadian constitution.* Montreal: McGill–Queen's University Press, 1994.

Chapter 14

MULTIPLE GOVERNMENTS

PHOTO ABOVE: On May 16, 2007, Alex Salmond, leader of a party that is committed to holding a referendum on independence for Scotland, became head of the Scottish government.

CHAPTER OBJECTIVES

After reading this chapter you should be able to:

1. describe and assess unitary, federal, and confederal systems
2. define the meaning of devolution and discuss how it has been applied
3. compare the Canadian federal system to other federal systems
4. outline the basic features of the European Union
5. discuss the significance of local government

On May 16, 2007, Alex Salmond, the leader of the Scottish National Party, which is committed to an independent Scotland within the European Union, was sworn in as First Minister of the Scottish government.

The United Kingdom has often been thought of as a highly centralized country. The concept of parliamentary sovereignty, which has been a basic principle of the British constitution, meant that the British prime minister and Cabinet with the support of the majority party in Parliament has had virtually unlimited powers. For example, although there are a large number of local governments, Prime Minister Margaret Thatcher didn't hesitate to eliminate the Greater London Council in 1986 because she viewed the government of Metropolitan London led by "Red Ken" Livingstone as too radical. Nevertheless, the United Kingdom can be considered a multinational country in which England, Scotland, Wales, and Northern Ireland each retain a distinctive identity (Gamble, 2006). Although political authority has been concentrated in London, some laws and policies have reflected the differences among the component units of the country.

As in a number of other countries, there has been a move away from centralized political authority in the United Kingdom in recent times. The rise of nationalism, particularly in Scotland in the 1970s, created pressure for change. The governing Conservative party under Thatcher was perceived as pursuing a centralization of power. This contributed to the Conservative party losing all of its seats in Scotland and Wales. The Labour party, which had considerable support in those areas, adopted the cause of establishing Scottish and Welsh Parliaments. Upon being elected in 1997, the party proceeded to hold a referendum in Scotland and Wales that endorsed (narrowly, in Wales) the idea of a Parliament for Scotland and an Assembly for Wales. This did not, however, fully satisfy many in Scotland who felt that the powers granted were too limited. Others in the United Kingdom, however, worried that the creation of Scottish and Welsh governments could eventually lead to the breakup of the United Kingdom.

The Scottish National Party narrowly won the election to the Scottish Parliament in 2007, winning 47 of the 129 seats. Because it leads a minority government with the support of only the two Green party members, its ability to achieve its objectives is very limited, although it has promised to hold a referendum on independence by 2010. As is the case with Quebec and Canada, the majority of Scots favour more powers for the Scottish Parliament rather than independence for Scotland.

The devolution of powers to regional parliaments has caused some grumbling in England. Members elected from Scotland, Wales, and Northern Ireland vote on matters in the Parliament of the United Kingdom that affect only England (such as education), but members from England do not have a voice on these matters for other regions. A plan to establish a series of regional assemblies in England was scuttled when voters in northeast England defeated a proposal for a regional assembly in 2004.

Not only are there multiple governments within the United Kingdom, but that country is also a member of the European Union (EU). The laws and regulations adopted by the governing bodies of the EU affect the governing of the United Kingdom.

In this chapter, we examine the different patterns of multiple governments that affect our lives.

MULTIPLE GOVERNMENTS

Virtually every country has more than one government. In addition to the central government, often termed the national government, there are usually a variety of local governments. Many countries also have regional (subnational) governments or regional administrative units. This raises several important questions:

- How do governments within a country relate to one another?
- Is the central government the supreme authority, or is authority shared between central and regional governments?
- Do different governments within a country co-operate for the common good of the country, or are the relations between governments characterized by conflict and power struggles?

To understand the relations among governments within a country, a distinction is usually made between unitary systems and federal systems. In a **unitary system**, sovereign authority rests with the central government. In a federal system, sovereign authority is divided or shared between the central government (often termed the federal government) and regional governments, termed provincial governments in Canada and state governments in the United States, India, and Australia.

UNITARY SYSTEMS

Many countries have unitary systems of government (see Table 14-1 for examples). The constitutional relationship among different governments is hierarchical, with regional and local governments subordinate to the central government. Even though the central government typically delegates some powers to other levels of government or to regional and local administrative authorities, the central government is superior to other governments.

Unitary systems generally provide uniformity across the country in terms of common laws and policies. However, the central government may make some adjustments in its laws and policies for the circumstances of different parts of the country. As well, it may rely on regional or local authorities to carry out some of its policies.

Devolution

The governments of some countries with unitary systems have granted some legislative (law-making) powers as well as administrative responsibilities to one or more regional bodies—a process termed **devolution**. For example, France and Italy have established regional governments with elected assemblies that have significant powers in their region of the country. As discussed in the introductory vignette, the United Kingdom

UNITARY SYSTEM
A system of governing in which sovereign authority rests with the central government; regional and local governments are subordinate.

DEVOLUTION
A system of governing in which the central government grants some legislative (law-making) powers as well as administrative responsibilities to one or more regional bodies.

TABLE 14-1
**UNITARY AND
FEDERAL SYSTEMS**

BASICALLY UNITARY	BASICALLY FEDERAL
Bangladesh	Argentina
Bolivia	Australia
Chile	Austria
Czech Republic	Belgium
Denmark	Brazil
Finland	Canada
France	Ethiopia
Greece	Germany
Hungary	India
Ireland	Malaysia
Japan	Mexico
Netherlands	Nigeria
New Zealand	Russia
Poland	South Africa
South Korea	Spain
Sweden	Switzerland
Turkey	United States
United Kingdom	Venezuela

has established regional governments and legislatures for Scotland, Wales, and Northern Ireland, though not for England, which has a large majority of seats in the UK Parliament. These governments are able to legislate on such matters as health, education, law and order, and transportation. However, the powers of these governments concerning taxation are very limited in the case of Scotland and non-existent in the case of Wales and Northern Ireland.

Devolution does not involve sharing sovereignty with regional governments. The Parliament of the United Kingdom could revoke the devolution of powers regardless of the wishes of the regional legislature. Indeed, the Parliament of the United Kingdom suspended the Parliament of Northern Ireland in 1972 (reinstated in 2007) because of the violent conflicts in that territory. Nevertheless, many see Scotland as becoming increasingly self-governing within the United Kingdom. It is very unlikely that the British government would try to take away the powers that have been granted to the Scottish Parliament, particularly because they were supported by a substantial majority of Scottish voters in a referendum.

Generally, there has been a tendency in recent decades for central governments in unitary systems to devolve powers to regional authorities. In part, devolution has allowed for greater responsiveness to the needs, cultures, and circumstances of different parts of the country and for greater participation of citizens in governing. As well, devolution can be a response to nationalist movements seeking self-government or independence.

▶ Bitter opponents Protestant Unionist leader Ian Paisley and Catholic Sinn Fein leader Gerry Adams sit together after agreeing on a historic power-sharing agreement that allowed the reopening of the Northern Ireland Assembly in 2007.

FEDERAL SYSTEMS

In a federal system, regional governments—such as provincial governments in Canada and state governments in the United States—are not subordinate to the central (national or federal) government. The federal and provincial governments each derive their authority from the constitution. Provincial governments cannot be abolished by the national government, nor can the federal government be abolished by provincial governments. Constitutional changes, particularly those that affect the powers of the two levels of government, require the agreement of both levels of government. Both the central and the regional governments interact directly with those they govern. That is, citizens directly elect representatives to both their regional government and the central government, and the laws and policies of each of these governments directly affect the people and territory they govern.

Reasons for Adoption

In some cases, federal systems have been established as a way of creating or holding together large countries. Federal systems have also been adopted in some countries to provide regionally based language, ethnic, or cultural groups with a degree of self-government.

The first modern federal system was established in the United States in 1789 when the thirteen states that had fought for their independence from Britain agreed to establish a central government. The founders of the United

States believed in the virtues of limited government and wanted the states to continue to be self-governing in many respects (Lyons, Scheb, & Richardson, 1995). Thus, they developed a federal system in which necessary governing powers would be divided between the two levels of government. Subsequently, a variety of other countries (listed in Table 14-1) adopted federal systems.

Canada adopted a federal system because the idea of uniting the British North American colonies that was proposed in the 1860s met with considerable opposition in both Quebec and the Maritimes, where many people feared being dominated by the central government. Maritimers wanted to retain the legislatures they had developed. Quebecers, fearful of the potential consequences of becoming a minority in the new country, wanted to retain control over their own culture.

Division of Powers

Federal systems typically involve a division of powers between national and provincial governments, with the constitution giving some responsibilities to the national government and other responsibilities to provincial governments (see Table 14-2). To varying extents, the constitutions of federal countries also

TABLE 14-2

THE CONSTITUTIONAL DIVISION OF POWERS IN CANADA

SOME AREAS OF LAW-MAKING THAT ARE THE EXCLUSIVE RESPONSIBILITY OF THE PARLIAMENT OF CANADA	SOME AREAS OF LAW-MAKING THAT ARE THE RESPONSIBILITY OF THE PROVINCIAL LEGISLATURES	AREAS IN WHICH BOTH PARLIAMENT AND PROVINCIAL LEGISLATURES HAVE LAW-MAKING AUTHORITY
Regulation of trade and commerce (interprovincial and international) Unemployment insurance Postal service Defence Fisheries Currency Banking Indian affairs Criminal law Marriage and divorce The "peace, order, and good government of Canada" Foreign affairs	Management of public lands Hospitals Municipal institutions Education Most "local works and undertakings" Laws concerning property rights and the relations among individuals Administration of justice within a province "Generally all Matters of a merely local or private nature in the Province" Non-renewable natural resources, forest resources, and electrical energy	Agriculture Immigration Public pensions

provide for some concurrent policy areas (such as agriculture and immigration in Canada) where both levels of government can pass legislation.

It is virtually impossible to divide legislative authority neatly between the national and provincial governments, and thus there is inevitably some overlap in the responsibilities of each level of government. Through their interpretation of constitutional provisions, the courts or other judicial bodies have often played a significant role in determining the powers of each level of government. For example, the "peace, order, and good government" clause in the Canadian constitution has been interpreted quite narrowly, rather than giving the Canadian government a general power to act in the interests of the country as a whole. In some countries, such as Germany, Belgium, and Spain, there are special constitutional courts that interpret the constitutional division of powers; in others, including Canada and the United States, the general court system, headed by the Supreme Court, settles disputes concerning which level of government is constitutionally responsible for particular matters (Galligan, 2006).

SHARED DECISION MAKING   Some federal systems are characterized primarily by shared decision making. For example, in the German federal system, the national Parliament is responsible for legislation in most fields, although this may involve negotiations between the representatives of the national governing coalition parties and the representatives of the Land (state) governments that sit in Parliament. The Land governments have responsibility for administering most of the legislation passed by the national Parliament, although much of the actual provision is, in turn, carried out by local governments (Courchene, 2007; Swenden, 2006).

Intergovernmental Relations

CLASSICAL FEDERALISM
A version of federalism in which the federal and provincial governments each concern themselves with their own areas of constitutional authority without infringing upon the areas of authority of the other level of government.

In what is often termed **classical federalism**, the federal and provincial governments each concern themselves with their own areas of constitutional authority without infringing upon the areas of authority of the other level of government. Thus, classical federalism, which in Canada lasted from the mid-1890s until 1939 (with the exception of the period around the First World War), involved a low level of interaction between the two levels of government.

As the activities of governments expanded, particularly with the development of the modern welfare state, the need to coordinate the policies of the central and provincial governments became more important. Contemporary federal systems typically feature both levels of government involved in many of the same areas of activity, often jointly involved in developing and administering important services. As well, large amounts of financial resources often need to be transferred from the central to the regional governments to carry out their programs. For example, the Canadian government contributes to the financing of many programs that are the constitutional responsibility of provincial governments, as discussed in Box 14-1, Health, Education, and Social Programs in Canada.

BOX 14-1

Health, Education, and Social Programs in Canada

The Canadian constitution places the responsibility for education, health care, and most social programs in the hands of the provincial level of government, but the federal government has been involved in all of these programs to varying extents through its ability to spend money as it sees fit.

Through the Canada Health Transfer and the Canada Social Transfer, the Canadian government provides some of the money needed by provincial governments, on a per capita basis, to fund post-secondary education, medical and hospital insurance, and social assistance (welfare).

In the case of health care funding, the Canada Health Act requires that provincial and territorial governments adhere to five basic principles in order to receive the federal government's contribution to the cost of the program. The provinces must ensure that:

- all persons are covered
- all medically necessary hospital and physician services are covered
- health care is publicly administered
- persons moving from one province to another are covered
- all persons have reasonable access to insured services without cost

Provinces that do not adhere to the principles may have the Canadian government's contribution reduced.

In the case of social assistance, provincial governments cannot impose minimum residency requirements. Within these qualifications, provincial governments are free to spend the money they receive from the Canadian government as they see fit.

The Canadian government, however, is often interested in becoming directly involved and gaining the political credit for its spending, even though its contribution to the costs of these programs is much smaller than that of provincial governments. In the area of post-secondary education, for example, the Canadian government has become directly involved—despite the objections of some provincial governments—in such areas as research funding and the Millennium Scholarships.

In the health care field, the Canadian government has earmarked new federal health care spending for new programs, new equipment, and new technologies. Although provincial governments have been demanding substantially more money from the Canadian government for health care, some provincial governments are unhappy that additional money often comes with stipulations as to how it should be spent.

As the costs of providing important services continue to escalate, conflicts over the sharing of costs and control of the programs will likely continue to be a major feature of politics in Canada.

CO-OPERATIVE FEDERALISM Modern federal systems involve a high level of interaction between the two levels of government—often described as **co-operative federalism.** This interaction primarily involves the executives (prime minister and Cabinet and premiers and their Cabinets) as well as senior officials rather than Parliament and provincial legislatures.

Despite the substantial level of co-operation among the two levels of government in developing, financing, and administering many programs, this

CO-OPERATIVE FEDERALISM
A federal system in which the two levels of government are jointly involved in developing, financing, and administering many government services.

does not necessarily mean that the relationships between the two levels of government are harmonious. There can be serious power struggles if the central government tries to impose national standards on programs run by provincial or state governments. Each level of government typically wants a larger share of total government revenues so that it can provide popular programs and services or lower taxes. The interests of particular states or provinces may differ from the interests of the country as a whole. The competition between different political parties that may be in control of each level of government can also create tensions in intergovernmental relations.

The Canadian federal system, in particular, often features considerable conflict between national and provincial governments. A number of provincial governments have resented the "interference" of the national government in areas of provincial authority and have wanted increased powers for provincial governments along with a larger share of tax revenues. Many provincial premiers have found that being strong defenders of provincial interests is useful in winning re-election, even if that means challenging a Canadian government of the same political party. Likewise, some Canadian governments have found it useful to take an adversarial relationship with some provincial governments so as to be seen as a strong defender of the national interest. Co-operative federalism is not really all that co-operative!

Attempts to coordinate the activities of the two levels of government typically involve difficult negotiations between the Canadian and provincial governments. Nevertheless, there has been an increasing level of collaboration among Canadian governments in recent years (Simeon & Cameron, 2002). For example, environmental policy is, to a considerable extent, the product of a consensus among provincial, territorial, and Canadian ministers of the environment and their officials. This was formalized with the adoption of the Canada-wide Accord on Environmental Harmonization in 1998.[1]

Regional Representation

In most federal countries, the interests of states or their equivalent are represented in the upper chamber (such as the Senate) of the national Parliament. In some cases (such as the United States, Brazil, and Australia), each state has the same number of representatives. In other countries (including Canada and Switzerland), each province or canton does not have the same number of representatives, but less populated areas receive more representation than they would if representation was in proportion to population.

In many cases, the members of the upper chamber are elected by voters in each state. Because of the importance of political parties in most

---

[1] The Quebec government has not signed the Accord. It has, however, worked out a co-operation agreement with the Canadian government on environmental assessment.

◀ We can keep dumping in this river for now . . . it will take years until the federal and provincial governments agree on who should legislate a ban.

countries, this means that representatives of each state will tend to vote in accordance with the national perspective of their party rather than the particular interests of their state. In the United States, however, party discipline is weaker, allowing senators more opportunity to represent the interests of their state. In Germany, the head of government and several Cabinet ministers from each Land (state) are members of the Bundesrat (Federal Council, the upper chamber of the national Parliament). This gives Land governments the ability to be involved in national decision-making, as about one-half of German legislation requires the approval of the Bundesrat (Oeter, 2006).

The Canadian Senate was intended to represent regional interests. However, its members are appointees of present and past prime ministers. Thus (pending proposed changes), it does not effectively represent provincial interests. To some extent, provincial interests are represented in the Canadian government through the practice of including persons from all or almost all provinces in the Canadian Cabinet. However, the ability of Cabinet ministers to represent provincial interests is limited by Cabinet solidarity and Cabinet secrecy (as discussed in Chapter 15).

Federalism and Multi-Level Governance
www.unc.edu/depts/europe/conferences/mlg

Centralization and Decentralization

There are considerable differences among federal systems in the extent to which governing is decentralized. In some federal systems (such as that of Australia), the national government can be considered the major government, with considerable control over government finances and with the ability to take a leading role in a wide variety of policy areas. The Canadian federal system, on the other hand, can be viewed as decentralized, as it features strong provincial governments whose decisions have a major impact on the lives of citizens. Provincial governments in Canada have unconditional control of a larger share of government revenue than in most, if not all, other federal systems.

The extent to which a federal system is centralized or decentralized is affected not only by the provisions concerning the division of powers in the constitution and how the constitutional division has been interpreted by judicial bodies, but also by various political, social, and economic factors. Individual countries have moved in the direction of centralization or decentralization depending on the circumstances of a particular time. Despite being established as a quite decentralized federal system, the central government in the United States has come to play a leading role in American politics, although state governments continue to have important constitutional powers. Many Americans look to the central government to solve economic, social, and security problems. The international role of the United States helps to enhance the power of the central government. Despite the rhetoric of national politicians in favour of enhancing the powers of state governments, legislation such as the Homeland Security Act and the No Child Left Behind Act has reduced the power of state governments in recent times (Albritton, 2006).

Institute of Intergovernmental Relations
www.iigr.ca/iigr.php

The Canadian federal system, in contrast to the American system, initially concentrated considerable power in the hands of the Canadian government. A number of provincial governments have been assertive in using their powers and have, at times, resisted efforts by the federal government to get involved in matters under provincial jurisdiction. Judicial decisions in the late nineteenth and early twentieth centuries also contributed to decentralization by interpreting the constitution in ways that limited some of the general powers of the Canadian government. In recent decades, the threat of Quebec independence has helped to move the Canadian federal system further toward decentralization. Resource-rich provinces such as Alberta, along with the large and powerful province of Ontario, have also at times created strong pressures in favour of decentralization.

MODERNIZATION AND GLOBALIZATION   In the past, it was often thought that as countries modernized, they would become more centralized. Regional differences would decline as transportation and communication links tied a country closer together. The increased mobility of people would make ties to a particular place of residence less important. A strong central government would be needed to manage the national economy effectively and provide a variety of social services to the population. However, the trend in recent decades has often been in the opposite direction. In both unitary and federal systems, there has been a tendency to disperse power from the central government to regional and local governments (Hooghe & Marks, 2001).

Some analysts have suggested that globalization encourages decentralization (Courchene, 1992). In a more globalized economy, the ability of central government to manage the national economy is reduced. Regions and important cities can develop international and global links. For example, the North American Free Trade Agreement has, to some extent, increased economic links between Canadian provinces and neighbouring American states at the expense of economic links across Canada. However, the impact of globalization appears to be mixed: in some cases it has encouraged a trend toward centralization, in others toward decentralization, and in still others has had no apparent effect. One set of studies found that the effects of globalization have not, at least not yet, been powerful enough to change the balance between centralization and decentralization in various federal systems. Changes in the direction of centralization or decentralization appear to be affected more by domestic factors than by external factors such as globalization (Lazar, Telford, & Watts, 2003).

Asymmetrical Federalism

In some federal systems, such as the United States, there is uniformity among the regional governments in that each has the same legislative powers. In others, such as India, Russia, Malaysia, and Belgium, some regional governments have a greater degree of self-government than other regional governments, a system described as **asymmetrical federalism** (Watts, 1999). In some cases, the constitution establishes different powers for different regional governments (as discussed in Box 14-2, Asymmetrical Federalism in Spain and Canada). Asymmetry can also result when the central government delegates certain powers or the administration of some programs to particular regional governments (or particular regional governments delegate some powers to the central government).[2]

ASYMMETRICAL FEDERALISM
A version of federalism in which some provincial or state governments have a greater degree of self-government than others.

The Canadian federal system has generally been symmetrical even though the Constitution Act, 1867 provided for a different system of private law for Quebec (the *Code Civil*) and for guarantees of denominational education in some provinces. Through legislative and administrative arrangements, various asymmetrical features have developed. For example, Quebec has its own

---

[2] Many unitary systems also feature asymmetry in that certain regional governments have more powers than others.

Asymmetrical Federalism in Spain and Canada

In the past, Spain was highly centralized. Since it moved from dictatorship to democracy, it has become quite decentralized, although it does not formally call itself a federation. Its constitution adopted in 1978 lists the areas in which its seventeen Autonomous Communities (called *autonomías* in Spanish, equivalent to provinces or states) may elect to exercise their jurisdiction. Each of these Communities proposes an autonomy statute, effectively its constitution, where it lays out the powers it wishes to exercise and which it must negotiate with the national government. Thus, one Autonomous Community, such as the Basque Country, may decide to assume more control over its health care system than does another, such as Castilla y Leon.

In Canada, the question of whether Quebec should be recognized as a distinct society, which could provide a justification for greater powers than the other provinces, has been very controversial.

For many Canadians outside Quebec, the principle of the equality of the provinces is fundamental. Each provincial government should have the same powers and Quebec should not have any form of different or special status. More powers for the Quebec government, it is argued, would undermine national unity and lead eventually to Quebec independence. Many French-speaking Quebecers, on the other hand, view the Quebec government as representing one of the major founding peoples of Canada and support the desire of the Quebec government to lead the social and economic development of the province.

Asymmetrical federalism can make a federal system more flexible by responding to the different characteristics and viewpoints of different areas of the country. However, it tends to reduce the uniformity of programs and policies across the country and increase the complexity of the federal system.

public pension plan, which is similar to the Canada Pension Plan but controlled by the Quebec government. In 2006, it established the Quebec Parental Insurance Plan, which provides more generous maternity, paternity, parental, and adoption benefits than are available through the Employment Insurance program in the rest of Canada.

Community Self-government

Federalism usually involves a division of authority between the central government and a number of regional governments. However, federalism can also involve linguistic, ethnic, or religious communities having a degree of self-government. For example, the federal system in Belgium involves three communities (corresponding to the Dutch-, French-, and German-speaking groups) that have responsibility for linguistic and cultural matters, as well as three regional governments. In Canada, the gradual movement toward Aboriginal self-government could result in a "third order" of government, with substantial authority based on membership in particular Aboriginal communities.

Such governments might not be confined to Aboriginal lands, but could have some ability to provide education and social services to Aboriginals living in cities. Recent treaty and land claim settlements have provided some Aboriginal nations with quite extensive constitutionally protected governing authority.

ASSESSING UNITARY AND FEDERAL SYSTEMS

Benefits of the Unitary System

There are several reasons why a unitary system might be the best way to provide for the common good. In a unitary system:

- The governing authorities may be more likely to work for the common good of the whole country, as there are no strong subnational governments promoting the particular interests of their region at the expense of the country as a whole.
- National unity may be promoted because greater attention is likely to be given to national issues and problems. In a federal system, provincial governments may find it politically advantageous to highlight and exaggerate regional grievances so that they can be perceived by voters as defenders of their province.
- The central government can be more easily held accountable by citizens as it cannot easily shift blame for problems to other governments.
- People will be more likely to have the same level of government services available in all regions. Uniform standards for education, health care, and environmental quality are likely to be adopted.

   In a federal system, provincial governments competing to attract investment might lower environmental and labour standards or offer subsidies and tax breaks to companies. Unless adequate **equalization payments** are provided, people in poorer provinces would likely receive a lower level of services from their provincial government than people in the richer provinces (see Box 14-3, Equalization Payments). Thus, the sense of everyone being equal citizens may be weaker in a federal system than in a unitary system.

- Greater efficiencies in governing are possible. With a central government in control, policies can be consistently directed toward certain objectives without different governments pursuing different and possibly inconsistent goals. Costly duplication of services by different governments may be avoided. Total administrative costs will likely be lower if many of the activities of government are centralized.
- People may find it easier to have their professional, technical, and educational qualifications recognized, find employment, and conduct business in different parts of the country.

EQUALIZATION PAYMENTS
Payment made by the federal government to try to ensure that different provincial governments are able to provide an equivalent level of services to their populations without resorting to excessive levels of taxation.

BOX 14-3

Equalization Payments

Most federal systems, other than the United States, provide some form of equalization payments to try to ensure that different regional governments are able to provide an equivalent level of services to their populations without resorting to excessive levels of taxation.

The Canadian government, for example, provides equalization payments to the governments of the less prosperous provinces (as of 2009–2010, all provinces except British Columbia, Alberta, Saskatchewan and Newfoundland and Labrador) to give them the same financial capability (ability to raise money through taxes) as an "average" province (see Figure 14-1). Nevertheless, this may be insufficient to provide equivalent services in provinces where needs are greater or the costs of

providing services are higher as a result of a more geographically dispersed population or a higher proportion of people needing social services. There have also been serious controversies concerning the treatment of non-renewable natural resources (particularly oil and gas). Fifty percent of the revenues from non-renewable resources are now included in the equalization formula. Poorer provinces argue that their revenues from these resources should not be included (as was promised by the Conservative party in the 2006 election) because they are one-time sources of revenue. In 2008, the Canadian government announced its intention to limit the increases in equalization payments to the rate of growth of the Canadian economy.

FIGURE 14-1
EQUALIZATION PAYMENTS PER CAPITA, 2007–08

Note: Payments are estimates based on projections concerning provincial government revenues.

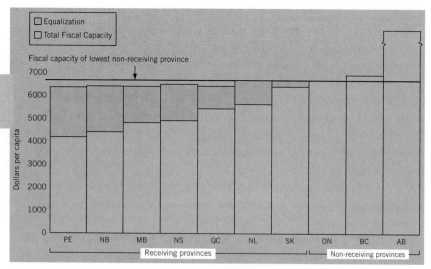

SOURCE: *"Seven provinces to receive over $12.7 billion in Equalization payments in 2007–08" retrieved June 15, 2007, from www.fin.gc.ca/fedprov/eqpe.html. Reproduced with the permission of the Minister of Public Works and Government Services Canada, 2007.*

Benefits of the Federal System

Federal systems also have a variety of positive features:

- Provincial or state governments may be more sensitive to the needs and desires of people in particular areas of the country. The flexibility of a federal system enables provincial governments to adopt policies that reflect the circumstances of their region and the values of the people in that region.
- Less populated and remote areas of the country might be ignored in a unitary system, but can find a voice in their own provincial government.
- Citizens may find it easier to participate in the policy-making process in their own province than in the processes of a distant central government.
- A federal system allows for greater diversity than a unitary state. Minorities that are concentrated within a particular province can use their provincial government to develop their culture. For example, the French language and culture in Canada has been preserved and developed in part because of the powers of the Quebec government. In this case, a group that is a minority in the country as a whole constitutes a large majority in a particular province, and thus is able to achieve a degree of self-government.
- Conflicts between cultural groups can be reduced through the adoption of a federal system. For example, Belgium, faced with continuing tensions between the Dutch-speaking Flemish community and the French-speaking community in Flanders, gradually moved away from a unitary system and in 1993 adopted a federal system to reduce these tensions. However, the federal systems of the former communist regimes of the Soviet Union, Yugoslavia, and Czechoslovakia broke up primarily because of the tensions between different cultural groups. Where differences between regionally based groups are too intense and a sense of identity with the country as a whole is weak, a federal system may be unable to survive (Galligan, 2006).
- A federal system helps to limit the concentration of power. Consistent with the ideal of liberal democracy, a federal system places constitutional limits on the powers of each government. Competition between central and provincial governments may serve to check the power of each level of government.
- A federal system can allow for experimentation with different policies and approaches by different governments. For example, the government of Saskatchewan initiated the system of free medical care that was subsequently adopted by other provinces and then turned into a nationwide program funded, in part, by the Canadian government. Because of the array of forces opposed to public health care (doctors, private insurance companies, and conservative governments), medicare might not have been adopted across the country without the successful example set by a determined provincial government.

CONFEDERAL SYSTEMS

Independent states generally retain their sovereignty when they interact with each other on the international stage. In some cases, however, sovereign states have agreed to delegate some of their authority to a joint government with limited authority while retaining their sovereignty. In this arrangement, known as a **confederal system**, the institutions of the confederation only have those powers that have been delegated to it by the governments of the sovereign states.[3] Because the member-states retain their sovereignty, they could withdraw from the confederation without necessarily seeking the approval of other member-states. In a pure confederal system, the institutions of the confederation do not directly interact with citizens. Instead, they rely on the member-states to implement the agreements (Swenden, 2006).

Confederal systems are not very common. Switzerland, until 1848, was a confederation of cantons. A loose German confederation of thirty-nine states existed between 1815 and 1866. After the War of Independence, the independent American states established a confederal system in 1781. The Congress of the United States (controlled by representatives of state governments) had very limited powers and there was no head of government or head of state for the country. Congress could declare war and conduct foreign relations, but it did not have the power to levy taxes or prevent states from levying tariffs on goods coming in from other states. Within a few years, agreement was reached to establish a federal system to create "a more perfect union" of the states.

CONFEDERAL SYSTEM
A system of governing in which sovereign states have agreed to delegate some of their authority to a joint government with limited authority while retaining their sovereignty.

THE EUROPEAN UNION

The **European Union** (EU) is a unique system of governing in which many European countries have pooled some of their sovereignty while retaining their independence. The EU combines features of confederal and federal systems. Some of the institutions of the EU are supranational (that is, they provide governing above the state) while others are intergovernmental (that is, they are based on agreements between the governments of sovereign states).

The origins of the EU can be traced to the commitment of some European leaders to avoid the repetition of the wars that had devastated the continent. In 1951, six countries formed the European Coal and Steel Community to manage these materials that are important for warfare. This was followed in 1957 by the establishment of the European Economic Community (later termed European Community), which led to the creation of a common market. It also developed a common agricultural (and fisheries) policy and programs to aid the poorer EU members.

EUROPEAN UNION (EU)
The European Union (EU) is a unique system of governing in which many European countries have pooled some of their sovereignty while retaining their independence.

---

[3] Although the formation of Canada in 1867 is often described as Confederation, Canada has never had a confederal system. Likewise, Switzerland is officially named the Swiss Confederation, but has a federal system of governing.

◀ The European Union is an important set of governing bodies for most countries in Europe.

In 1992, the Treaty on the European Union (often referred to as the Maastricht Treaty) proclaimed the goal of "creating an ever closer union among the peoples of Europe." The EU has expanded from twelve members to include, as of 2009, twenty-seven European countries along with three official candidate and five potential candidate participating member-states.

Pillars

The EU is based on three pillars. The first pillar, the European Community, makes all citizens of the member-states also citizens of the EU, with various rights including the right to freely move and reside within the EU. It established an economic and monetary union, with the euro (the European currency) replacing national currencies.[4] The adoption of the euro along with the establishment of the European Central Bank involved requirements that member-states adopt certain fiscal policies, including a maximum level of government debt and annual deficit and a relatively low rate of inflation. The European Community has established institutions that are responsible for common policies in a variety of areas, including agriculture and fisheries, environment, education and culture, and social policy.

The second pillar involves co-operation in the adoption of common foreign and security policies. The third pillar is police and judicial cooperation in criminal matters, including organized crime, terrorism, and drug trafficking.

Europa: The European Union Online
http://europa.eu.int

---

[4] The UK, Sweden, and Denmark have not adopted the euro. The adoption of the euro by newer members of the EU will be phased in over a number of years provided they meet certain conditions.

Institutions and Decision-Making

The major institutions of the EU are:

- *The European Council.* Although technically not an EU institution, the presidents or prime ministers of the member-states usually meet four times a year to recommend general guidelines for the EU.[5]
- *The Council of the European Union* (also known as the Council of Ministers). The major decision-making body of the EU, the Council is composed of ministers from each of the member-states. Different ministers sit on the Council, depending upon the policy area being considered. The presidency of the Council is rotated among the member-states every six months.
- *The European Parliament.* Voters in the EU countries directly elect the European Parliament. Originally it was only a consultative body, but it now has joint legislative and budgetary powers with the Council of the EU. It can censure the European Commission and conduct independent inquiries. It does not, however, initiate legislative proposals.
- *The European Commission.* Appointed by the governments of the member-states subject to acceptance by the EU Parliament, the Commission initiates legislative proposals, oversees the implementation of common EU policies (either by the civil service of the EU or by member-states), and acts as guardian of the EU treaties. The president of the European Commission along with one commissioner from each member-state (who are approved as a group by the EU Parliament) are appointed for a fixed five-year term. Members of the Commission are expected to act independently of the government of the state that selected them.
- *The Court of Justice of the European Union.* Composed of one independent judge from each member-state, the Court interprets and applies European Community laws (termed regulations and directives).

Confederal or Federal?

Unlike federal systems, the EU has not yet established a constitution (see Box 14-4, A Constitution for the European Union?). Instead, the EU was established and has been modified by treaties ratified by all of its member-states. Some of the decisions of the EU, particularly those in the second and third pillars, have to be approved by the governments of all member-states. As well, although the EU has established a substantial bureaucracy, the member-states are largely responsible for implementing and administering EU laws and regulations.

---

[5] The European Council should not be confused with the Council of Europe, a larger organization that deals particularly with the protection of human rights.

A Constitution for the European Union?

There has often been controversy concerning the future of the EU. For some, such as former German Foreign Minister Joschka Fischer, the EU should work toward becoming a fully federal state. Others, such as former British Prime Minister Margaret Thatcher, fear that moves toward greater European integration will result in the loss of national sovereignty, domination by the leading powers such as Germany, and excessive regulation by Brussels-based EU officials. Criticism of the EU has also come from the anti-globalization movement.

Differing views about the EU contributed to the problems it has faced in adopting a constitution. In 2004, after lengthy and difficult negotiations, the governments of the member-states unanimously supported adopting a treaty that would establish a formal constitution for the EU. The constitution would consolidate the various treaties upon which the EU is based, simplify some of the complex procedures of the EU (for example, by combining the three pillars), make it somewhat easier for the EU to adopt new laws, and codify uniform human rights provisions.

Although a number of national legislatures ratified the treaty, it was rejected by voters in referendums in France and the Netherlands (and would likely have been defeated by voters in the UK). Without sufficient popular support to obtain ratification in all member-states, the constitutional proposal was shelved.

In June 2007, a summit of EU leaders reached agreement on a mandate to draft a Reform Treaty (rather than a constitution) with the objective of achieving ratification by 2009. The agreement includes proposals that the EU president be selected for a two-and-a-half-year term, that the EU Charter of Fundamental Rights be legally binding (with the UK exempted), that a smaller qualified majority be used to make decisions, and that would somewhat strengthen the ability of the EU to speak with a unified voice in foreign affairs.

In 2008, voters in Ireland rejected the Treaty. It is unlikely that the Treaty will be ratified in its present form. Concerns that the EU will become a "super-state" appear unfounded, as the EU lacks the support needed to gain acceptance of all of the characteristics of a modern state.

However, the EU differs from a pure confederal system in several ways: Most of the decisions of the first pillar do not require agreement by all member-states, but rather by a qualified majority (nearly three-quarters of Council members plus a majority, or in some cases two-thirds, of the member-states).

The EU has the ability to make some decisions that can be binding not only on its member-states but also directly on the public and on business enterprises.

The European Parliament is directly elected by individual voters and has gradually become more significant.

The Court of Justice of the EU can make decisions based on EU law that take precedence over the laws of member-states on those matters that the member-states have allowed the EU to legislate.

Challenges

Public support for the EU is limited and national identities continue to be much stronger than a European identity. There is considerable reluctance in many countries (for example, the United Kingdom) about transferring more sovereignty from their own state to the EU and resentment when EU laws challenge national laws. The EU also faces considerable challenges as it becomes more culturally diverse, a result of its recent expansion to include many of the former communist countries of Eastern Europe. The potential inclusion of Turkey (officially secular but with a population that is primarily Islamic) is particularly controversial. The inclusion of countries in Eastern Europe creates substantial financial costs in terms of aid to the poorer countries. The right of persons in the poorer countries to move to the richer Western European countries to obtain employment provides economic benefits to the richer countries that face labour shortages as a result of low birth rates, but can cause animosity among those who dislike changes to the ethnic and cultural makeup of their country.

INTERNATIONAL GOVERNMENTAL ORGANIZATIONS (IGOs)

INTERNATIONAL GOVERNMENTAL ORGANIZATIONS
Associations of states created to facilitate co-operation among themselves.

The contemporary world has seen the development of a large number of **international governmental organizations** (also termed intergovernmental organizations)—associations of states created to facilitate co-operation among themselves. For example, the North American Free Trade Agreement (NAFTA), the Association of Southeast Asian Nations, the Caribbean Community, and, in South America, the Andean Pact and Mercosur have important effects on the trade, investment, and some other policies of their members. The North Atlantic Treaty Organization (whose members include Canada, the United States, many European states, and Turkey) involves common defence and military policies. The African Union (and the proposed Union of South American Nations) seeks broader regional integration that might, some time in the future, create organizations similar to that of the European Union.

Some IGOs are simply agreements among states to co-operate, coordinate actions, or adopt some specific policies. Other IGOs set up mechanisms to settle disputes among their members and establish organizations to facilitate co-operation, propose new measures, provide research, and monitor performance.

Overall, IGOs are not supranational governments that create a political union among their member-states. Nevertheless, they can have important effects on governments, businesses, and individuals. For example, NAFTA requires that the policies its members adopt generally should not result in restrictions that reduce trade or harm the profitability of potential investors. Further, by contributing to the creation of an integrated North American market, NAFTA may enhance the pressure for members to adopt similar economic, social, and environmental policies so as to ensure that their businesses are competitive within the region.

LOCAL GOVERNMENTS

Although attention in political life is often focused on politics and governing at the national and international level, it is the local communities we live in that are particularly important to our quality of life. The friendliness and safety of our neighbourhoods, the availability of parks, playgrounds, and public places, our ability to commute to work or school within a reasonable period of time, the accessibility of recreational and cultural activities, and the opportunities for involvement in community life are important determinants of our happiness.

United Cities and Local Governments
www.iula.org

Local (municipal) governments are typically responsible for many of the services that affect the quality of life in our communities, such as water, sewage treatment, garbage disposal, road maintenance, public transportation, fire and police protection, land development and zoning, parks, and recreational facilities. Some local governments have responsibilities for administering welfare and other social services. Local governments are also usually involved in promoting the economic development of their community.

Local governments often only have whatever authority the central government—or, in the case of federal systems, provincial or state governments—decides to delegate to them. Thus, despite their importance, local governments are generally subordinate to higher levels of government. The actual degree of autonomy of local governments may vary over time depending upon the thinking of the higher levels of government. For example, in Great Britain, which has a long tradition of strong local self-government, both Conservative and Labour governments have moved in recent decades toward greater regulation by the British government. By contrast, France, which has a long tradition of central control, has moved to allow greater autonomy to local and regional communities (Stoker, 2006).

A few countries (for example, Germany, India, and Switzerland) provide constitutional protection for the powers of local governments (Watts, 1999). Likewise, in the United States, many state constitutions provide some protection for the powers of municipal governments, with the larger cities often provided with some form of "home rule" that protects their powers and structures from being changed without their consent (Sancton, 2002).

The Canadian Version

In Canada, local governments are the responsibility of provincial governments. Although local governments make important decisions affecting their communities, they generally have to carry out their activities in accordance with the rules and regulations adopted by their provincial government and have to seek provincial approval for some decisions. Indeed, provincial governments can alter the boundaries of municipal governments as they see fit. For example, in 1998, the government of Ontario decided to

Federation of Canadian Municipalities
www.fcm.ca

amalgamate the six municipalities of the metropolitan Toronto area despite opposition from local political leaders and 73 percent of those who voted in a referendum.

Local governments in Canada (unlike those of American cities) do not have the authority to raise revenues from income or sales taxes. Instead, they depend largely on property taxes and, to a lesser extent, provincial government grants (which are often tied to conditions or purposes set by the provincial government) and various user fees. Although the Canadian government does not have any direct constitutional authority over local governments, it has from time to time provided funding to help pay for special projects such as the development of public mass transit systems. Since 2005, the Canadian government has given local governments a share of gasoline tax revenues for environmentally sustainable municipal infrastructure.

Overall, local governments receive only about 8 percent of the taxes raised by governments (Federation of Canadian Municipalities, 2006). This is often inadequate to provide for municipal services. This problem has worsened in recent times as provincial and national governments have downloaded some programs onto municipal governments without providing sufficient financing.

As cities have grown, demands have been made that city governments should have greater political and financial power. Major cities (and their surrounding regions) have become leading forces of national and global economic growth in the knowledge-based economies of the advanced countries. However, they lack sufficient powers and finances to carry

▶ The City of Toronto has been seeking greater legislative and financial powers so that it can more effectively carry out its role as a leading force in the national and global economy.

out this role effectively (Courchene, 2007). Former Toronto Mayor Mel Lastman suggested that Toronto, which has a greater population than all of the Atlantic provinces plus two of the Prairie provinces combined, should be given provincial government status. Through Ontario's City of Toronto Act, 2006, Canada's largest city has been given broader legislative powers, a greater ability to manage its own financial affairs, and recognition of its right to enter into agreements with the Canadian government.

Complex Governing Authorities

There are often complex sets of governing authorities at the local level. Schools are generally run by elected school boards that may be responsible for all of the schools in a city or in a region of a province. Likewise, there may be library boards, police boards, community centre boards, health boards, hospital boards, transit authorities, conservation authorities, parks boards, public utilities commissions, and water and sewage authorities. Such agencies, boards, and commissions are often independent of the municipal government and may service a broader geographical area than a municipal government. This fragmentation of decision-making power at the local level can make it difficult for city politicians and administrators to pursue a coherent set of objectives or respond to the wishes of city residents (Leo & Mulligan, 2006). As well, various local authorities (such as school and hospital boards) have been increasingly subject to control by provincial governments rather than by the local community.

Democracy and Local Government

Are local governments more likely to foster the participation of citizens than more distant central or provincial governments? Given the direct effect of local governments on the people they govern, one might expect citizens to be more likely to participate at the local level. Indeed, some democratic theorists have argued that democracy at the local level is an essential building block of a democratic political system. It may be easier for citizens at the local level (particularly in smaller cities and towns) to develop connections to other citizens, engage in meaningful discussion, learn about the issues that affect them, and actively participate in political life (McAllister, 2004).

Turnout in local elections, however, is almost always lower than in national or provincial elections. Although this generalization is valid for a variety of countries for which information is available, the lower level of voting in local elections is particularly evident in Canada (see Table 14-3), where average turnout is about 35 percent (McAllister, 2004).

TABLE 14-3

VOTER TURNOUT IN RECENT MUNICIPAL ELECTIONS, SELECTED CANADIAN CITIES

Note: Figures derived from media reports are unofficial and may not be calculated on a strictly comparable basis.

CITY	YEAR OF ELECTION	TURNOUT
Ottawa	2006	54%
Toronto	2006	41%
Montreal	2005	39%
Winnipeg	2006	38%
Vancouver	2005	32%
Victoria	2005	26%
Calgary	2004	18%

The low voter turnout is particularly evident in larger cities. For example, turnout in Ontario local elections averaged 54 percent in places with less than ten thousand people compared to 37 percent in cities with more than one hundred thousand people (Kushner, Siegel, & Stanwick, 1997).

Political parties, which can make voting easier by highlighting issues and mobilizing voters, are not generally involved in local politics in Canada.[6] In some cases, the lack of credible challengers to an incumbent mayor can make a local election uninteresting. Where the Republican and Democratic parties involve themselves in local politics in the United States, voter turnout is higher than in cities that feature non-partisan elections, but still usually substantially lower than in national and state elections. In Western Europe, higher voter turnout in local elections may reflect the ability of political parties to mobilize voters in local elections on the basis of national political issues and long-standing ideological and social divisions. In such countries there is often not a sharp distinction between national and local politics (Milner, 1997; Morlan, 1984).

The low level of participation in municipal elections in Canada does not necessarily mean that citizens are uninterested in the decisions that affect their local community. Many cities have active community and neighbourhood organizations involved in improving the quality of life in the city. Issue-oriented groups and civic movements have attracted considerable support for such efforts as challenging freeway construction that would go through quiet neighbourhoods, preserving the character of neighbourhoods that are threatened by development projects, protecting green spaces, and promoting the provision of low-cost housing for the poor.

---

[6] Civic parties exist in some cities, including Montreal and Vancouver, and at times the NDP has involved itself in local politics in some cities.

Summary and Conclusion

Almost all countries have multiple governments. The existence of multiple governments adds complexity to political life and makes an understanding of the relationships among governments essential for an understanding of governing processes.

Unitary systems feature a hierarchical relationship among governments, with the central government superior to other governments, although some distinctive parts of the country may be granted a significant level of autonomy and local or regional authorities may have responsibility for delivering many government services. Federal systems feature a substantial level of self-government for provinces or their equivalent and, generally, a shared involvement in a number of policy areas between central and provincial governments. Each citizen is directly affected by both national and provincial governments, and citizens elect both a national and a provincial government. Confederal systems result when sovereign states join together to establish a central governing agency with limited powers delegated from the member-states. The European Union features a unique combination of confederal and federal features in its evolving system of governing.

Although local governments deliver a variety of important services to their communities, they are often restricted in their capabilities because of controls by "higher" levels of government and limited financial resources. Despite the development of many groups seeking to improve the quality of life in their community, local politics often falls short of the democratic ideal of an active, engaged citizenry.

The existence of multiple governments has important political implications. Coordination and co-operation among different governments within a country are important requirements for effective governing. However, power struggles between national and provincial governments, as well as their different interests and values, can make co-operation difficult to achieve, as is often evident in the Canadian federal system.

Globalization will likely lead to more complex patterns of governing, in which a variety of governing bodies affect our lives. Globalization does not only tend to involve the development of institutions above the level of the state, but also tends to make urban and regional governments more important. Ensuring that multiple governments work toward the common good and are responsive and accountable to those they govern presents difficult challenges.

Key Terms

Discussion Questions

1. What are the advantages and disadvantages of a federal system?

2. Why has the Canadian federal system tended to become more decentralized?

3. Do you think that the Canadian government should continue to set conditions for provincial health care systems?

4. Should Canada move further in the direction of asymmetrical federalism?

5. Why might the European Union be considered a combination of confederal and federal systems?

6. Do you think that local governments should have greater authority?

Further Reading

Bakvis, H., & Skogstad, G. (Eds.). *Canadian federalism: Performance, effectiveness, and legitimacy.* Don Mills, ON: Oxford University Press, 2002.

Burgess, M. *Comparative federalism: Theory and practice.* London: Routledge, 2006.

Cini, M. (Ed.). *European Union politics,* 2nd ed. Oxford: Oxford University Press, 2007.

Heuglin, T.O., & Fenna, A. *Comparative federalism: A systematic inquiry.* Peterborough, ON: Broadview Press, 2006.

Lightbody, J. *City politics, Canada.* Peterborough, ON: Broadview Press, 2006.

Magnette, P. *What is the European Union? Nature and prospects.* Houndmills, Basingstoke, Hampshire, UK: Palgrave Macmillan, 2005.

McAllister, M.L. *Governing ourselves: The politics of local communities.* Vancouver: UBC Press, 2004.

McCormick, J. *Understanding the European Union: A concise introduction,* 2nd ed. Houndmills, Basingstoke, Hampshire, UK: Palgrave, 2002.

Rocher, F., & Smith, M. (Eds.). *New trends in Canadian federalism,* 2nd ed. Peterborough, ON: Broadview Press, 2003.

Smith, J. Federalism. Vancouver: UBC Press, 2004.

Tindal, C. R., & Tindal, S.N. *Local government in Canada,* 6th ed. Toronto, ON: Nelson Canada, 2004.

Watts, R.L. *Comparing federal systems,* 2nd ed. Montreal: McGill–Queen's University Press, 1999.

Chapter 15

PARLIAMENTARY SYSTEMS

PHOTO ABOVE: On May 19, 2005, Independent MP Chuck Cadman stood to cast the deciding vote that allowed the minority Liberal government to remain in office.

1. outline the basic characteristics of the parliamentary system
2. describe how the prime minister and Cabinet are chosen in Canada
3. discuss whether there is too great a concentration of power in the Canadian governing system
4. define the meaning of majority, minority, and coalition governments
5. discuss the significance of party discipline in a parliamentary system

In the Canadian election held on June 28, 2004, the Liberal party won the most seats in the House of Commons, but their 135 seats were well short of a majority of the 308 seats in the House. Liberal leader Paul Martin chose to stay on as prime minister and formed a minority government—that is, a Cabinet composed entirely of members of his own party. The Liberal government needed the support of one or more other parties to stay in office.

The Conservative party and the Bloc Québécois were eager to defeat the Liberal government. Faced with the need to pass a budget, Martin agreed to the demands by NDP leader Jack Layton to amend the budget by adding $4.6 billion for social programs and delaying a reduction in the corporation income tax rate. With the support of the NDP for the amended budget, the Liberals had almost enough votes to avoid being defeated in the House, particularly when Conservative MP Belinda Stronach crossed the floor to join the Liberals and received an appointment to the Cabinet. When the budget amendment came to a vote on May 19, 2005, the fate of the government depended on which way an Independent MP, Chuck Cadman (who had failed to be nominated as a Conservative candidate in the 2004 election), would vote. Suspense mounted as each MP rose to vote until Cadman, to the cheers of Liberals, stood to vote in favour. The result was a tie, 152–152, with the Speaker of the House, Liberal MP Peter Milliken, then casting the deciding vote in favour. The Liberal government remained in office until the NDP withdrew its support and the three opposition parties passed a motion of non-confidence in the government on November 28, 2005. This led to an election early in 2006, which resulted in a minority Conservative government.

As we will discuss in this chapter, a parliamentary system of government, such as Canada has, requires that the prime minister and Cabinet ("the government") retain the support ("confidence") of the elected legislative body, the House of Commons. This is most easily achieved when one party has a majority of seats. But where there are several political parties with significant levels of support, gaining a majority may be difficult, leading to either a minority government or a government by a coalition of two or more parties that jointly share the responsibilities of governing ("coalition government").

Minority governments are sometimes seen as inevitably unstable and unproductive. This is not necessarily the case, however. In the 1960s, Liberal Prime Minister Lester Pearson led two minority governments that were highly productive. With the support of the NDP, the Liberals were able to pass legislation establishing medicare, the Canada Pension Plan, and the new Canadian flag. When the governing party does not have a majority, it has to take into account the wishes of other parties. This sometimes results in a governing party adopting policies that it might otherwise be reluctant to support.

THE PARLIAMENTARY SYSTEM

Many democratic countries—including Canada, the United Kingdom, most other countries of the Commonwealth, many European countries, and Japan—have **parliamentary systems** of government. Presidential systems (such as that of the United States) and semi-presidential systems (such as that of France) will be examined in Chapter 16.

A basic feature of parliamentary systems is the close interrelationship of Parliament (the legislative body) and the political executive (the prime minister and Cabinet). The members of the political executive are themselves members of Parliament, usually from the elected part of Parliament (in Canada, the House of Commons). The close interrelationship of the legislative and executive aspects of the parliamentary system is often described as creating a "fusion of powers." The authority of the political executive is based on its ability to maintain the support of the majority of elected members of Parliament. If that support is withdrawn, the executive is generally expected to resign.[1]

Although Parliament has to approve new laws, it is normally the political executive that proposes the laws passed by Parliament. The political executive also presents the government's spending and taxing plans for Parliament's approval. As well, the political executive is responsible for overseeing the implementation and administration of the laws passed by Parliament and for making the day-to-day governing decisions. However, while the political executive is the governing body, it is expected to be responsible (that is, accountable) to Parliament for its actions. Thus, a parliamentary system is often referred to as **responsible government** because those with governing authority are responsible to Parliament.

The Head of State

Parliamentary systems have different individuals as head of state and head of government. The **head of state** is an important but largely ceremonial position in a parliamentary system of government. The head of state carries out a variety of official functions, but is expected to be "above" politics and thus is not usually involved in making governing decisions. Having a non-political head of state can provide a symbol of unity for a country (see Box 15-1, Should Canada Have Its Own Head of State?). The head of state will not be tarnished by government incompetence or scandal because the head of state is not involved in politics and governing. This provides the legitimacy needed for the

PARLIAMENTARY SYSTEM
A system of governing in which there is a close interrelationship between the political executive (prime minister and Cabinet) and Parliament (the legislative or law-making body). The executive is generally composed of members of the House of Commons (the elected parliamentary body) and must maintain the support of the House of Commons.

RESPONSIBLE GOVERNMENT
A governing system in which the political executive (the prime minister and Cabinet) is accountable to Parliament for its actions based on the principle that the political executive must retain the support of the elected members of Parliament to remain in office.

HEAD OF STATE
A largely ceremonial position as the official representative of the state. In a parliamentary system, the head of state is not usually involved in making governing decisions, but has the responsibility to ensure that a legitimate government is in place.

---

[1] In Germany, Spain, and Israel, a motion of non-confidence presented by a member of an opposition party can only be passed if a majority is able to agree on another person to be prime minister. This provision, termed a "constructive vote of confidence," makes it less likely that the government will be forced out of office.

BOX 15-1

Should Canada Have Its Own Head of State?

Canada's use of the British monarch as head of state emphasizes Canada's historic ties to Britain and continuing membership in the Commonwealth, of which the Queen is the ceremonial head. However, for a significant proportion of Canada's population, the use of a foreign monarch as the formal head of state is an outdated relic of the country's colonial past.

The issue of the monarchy has occasionally generated political debate, as for example in 2002, when former Foreign Affairs Minister John Manley suggested that Canada should have an elected head of state. Generally, though, other constitutional issues have tended to overshadow differences of opinion concerning the monarchy. In Australia there has been serious discussion about replacing the British monarch with an Australian head of state. However, despite considerable popular support for replacing the monarch, disagreements about how to choose an Australian head of state have thus far prevented this change from occurring. Whatever method of selection might eventually be agreed upon, it would not likely have a significant effect on the parliamentary system.

Commonwealth Parliamentary
Association
www.cpahq.org

CONSTITUTIONAL MONARCHY
A governing system in which the powers of the monarch are greatly restricted by formal constitutional provisions or "unwritten" constitutional conventions. The monarch is primarily a symbolic figure rather than an active participant in the governing processes.

GOVERNOR GENERAL
The person who carries out the duties and responsibilities of the monarch at the national level in Canada.

LIEUTENANT-GOVERNOR
The person who carries out the duties and responsibilities of the monarch at the provincial level in Canada.

head of state to act, if necessary, in some unusual circumstances, to ensure that a government is in place or to dismiss a government that is acting unconstitutionally.

In some countries with parliamentary systems, the head of state is a president with a limited term of office. The president may be directly elected by the country's citizens (as for example in Austria, Ireland, and Israel) or selected by a vote of members of the national Parliament along with, in some cases, regional representatives (as for example in Germany, Greece, and Italy). In a number of countries with parliamentary systems (including the United Kingdom, Sweden, Denmark, and the Netherlands), a hereditary monarch is the head of state. The powers of the monarch in such countries have, however, been greatly restricted by formal constitutional provisions or "unwritten" constitutional conventions. Democratic countries that retain a monarch as head of state are, therefore, sometimes referred to as **constitutional monarchies**.

Canada (like some other former British colonies that are members of the Commonwealth) can be considered a constitutional monarchy. National and provincial governments act in the name of the Crown. However, the duties and responsibilities of the monarch, Queen Elizabeth II (who is technically the Queen of Canada as well of the United Kingdom), have been delegated to the **governor general** at the national level and to **lieutenant-governors** at the provincial level. The governor general and lieutenant-governors are appointed by the monarch on the recommendation of the Canadian prime minister for a five-year term (which is sometimes extended for a year or two).

The governor general has the important responsibility of ensuring that a government (prime minister and Cabinet) is in place at all times. Usually, the choice of prime minister is merely a formality: The governor general is expected to choose the leader of the party that has the support of the House of Commons. In the event of the death, retirement, or resignation of the prime minister, the governing political party will recommend a replacement. The governor general must also approve all legislation, a variety of appointments, and various executive decisions, such as the ratification of treaties and a declaration of war. However, in these matters, the governor general always acts on the advice of the prime minister and Cabinet. Only if the prime minister and Cabinet were ignoring the constitution or lacked the support of the House of Commons would the governor general be justified in acting independently. Lieutenant-governors have essentially the same powers and responsibilities at the provincial level.

About Government
www.gc.ca/howgoc/howind_e.html

The Prime Minister and Cabinet

The **head of government**, the prime minister, is responsible for selecting the members of the **Cabinet**. Together, the prime minister and Cabinet ministers are the political executive with responsibility for governing. The prime minister is normally a member of the House of Commons and thus not directly elected by voters in the country as a whole. Instead, the prime minister is the leader of the party that is able to maintain the support of the majority of the members of the House of Commons. In some countries such as Germany, the chancellor (prime minister) is elected by the members of the Bundestag (the equivalent of the Canadian House of Commons). In others where it is uncommon for one party to win a majority of seats, the head of state may hold discussions with various party leaders after a parliamentary election to determine who has sufficient support to head the government. In Canada, a prime minister whose party was defeated in an election is expected to resign, allowing the governor general to choose the party leader that is most likely to have the support of a majority of members in the House of Commons.[2] Regardless of the precise procedure used for selecting the head of government in different countries, the prime minister is usually the leader of one of the largest parties.

HEAD OF GOVERNMENT
The person who heads the executive side of government and is usually responsible for choosing the Cabinet. In Canada, the prime minister is the head of the Canadian government while the heads of provincial governments are known as premiers (in Quebec, *premier ministre*).

CABINET
The members of the political executive. The Cabinet is led by the prime minister, with many or most Cabinet ministers having the responsibility of heading a government department.

Majority, Minority, and Coalition Governments

To understand the composition of the Cabinet and the relationship between the Cabinet and Parliament, it is important to make a distinction among majority, minority, and coalition governments. A **majority government** is one where the prime minister's party has a majority of members of the House of

MAJORITY GOVERNMENT
The government formed when the prime minister's party has a majority of the members of the House of Commons; thus, a single party forms the government.

---

[2] If one party has a majority of seats in the House of Commons, that party's leader will be the prime minister. If no one party has a majority of seats, it will usually, but not always, be the leader of the party with the most seats in the House of Commons. For example, in the 1985 Ontario election, the Progressive Conservative party won the most seats, but after the NDP agreed to support a Liberal government (although not establishing a formal coalition), the Liberal leader was selected as premier.

Commons (or an equivalent body in other countries). In this situation, the prime minister will choose Cabinet ministers from among his or her party's members of Parliament (almost all from the House of Commons). A single party led by the prime minister forms the Cabinet and through its majority in the House of Commons is able to exercise considerable control over that body.

MINORITY GOVERNMENT
A single party governs, but that party does not have a majority of members in the House of Commons; thus, a minority government needs to gain the support of one or more other parties to pass legislation and to stay in office.

If no single party has elected its members to a majority of seats in the House of Commons, one party may, nevertheless, form a **minority government**. As with a majority government, the prime minister chooses the Cabinet from among his or her party's members of Parliament. To pass legislation, gain approval for government's spending and taxing plans, and avoid being defeated on a vote of non-confidence, the prime minister and Cabinet need to gain the support of one or more other parties (unless an opposition party decides to abstain from voting). This support may be on an issue-by-issue basis or be part of a general agreement between the governing party and another party. The ability of the political executive to control the House of Commons will thus be limited, and negotiations with other parties will usually be necessary.

COALITION GOVERNMENT
A government in which two or more political parties jointly govern, sharing the Cabinet positions.

Alternatively, if no one party has a majority of seats, a **coalition government** consisting of two or more political parties may be formed.[3] In this situation, there will be negotiations among the coalition partners to determine which Cabinet positions each party will receive and the policies the government will pursue. In some cases (as in contemporary Italy), coalitions among parties will be formed before the election such that the winning coalition will form the government. In other cases, such as Germany, the negotiations among parties seeking to form a coalition government may occur after the results of an election are known (See Box 15-2, Coalition Governments in Germany). Shifts in the parties joining or leaving the coalition may also occur without an election being held, as has been the case in Israel.

Typically, coalition governments involve parties that are closest to each other in ideological terms. In a number of countries, coalition governments are stable such that the coalition remains in office for its full term and is able to govern effectively. In some countries, however, coalition governments have been undermined by disputes among the coalition partners. Italy, for example, was characterized by political instability, with sixty-one coalition governments formed since 1945 (although until 1984 all were dominated by the Christian Democratic party). The establishment of two broad coalitions of parties, one leaning left and the other leaning right, has brought greater stability to Italian politics since 1996.

In general, majority and minority governments tend to be predominant in countries that use single member plurality systems. Such systems tend to result in a smaller number of parties gaining significant representation in Parliament.

---

[3] In times of war or serious political crisis, a national unity coalition government may be formed even if one party has a majority. This occurred in Canada during the First World War as most Liberals outside Quebec joined a Union government led by the Conservatives.

Coalition Governments in Germany

Ever since democracy was restored to West Germany in 1949, the country has been governed by a series of coalitions. Usually these stable coalitions have involved the small liberal Free Democratic party (FDP) in coalition with either the Christian Democrats (CDU/CSU) or Social Democrats (SPD), although from 1966 to 1969 West Germany was governed by a grand coalition of the CDU/CSU and SPD, the two largest parties. From 1998 to 2005, a Social Democratic–Green coalition governed Germany.

The 2005 election result was very close, with the CDU/CSU winning 226 seats, the SPD 222, the FDP 61, the Left party 54, and the Greens 50. The leaders of both the SPD and the CDU/CSU claimed that they should be chancellor. With neither of the leading parties wanting to negotiate with the Left party (composed of former communists and a breakaway faction of the SPD), the CDU/CSU and SPD were able to put aside their differences and in a less than a month agreed to form a coalition. Angela Merkel, the leader of the CDU/CSU, became chancellor and each party received eight of the sixteen Cabinet positions.

This, along with the overrepresentation of the leading party that usually occurs, increases the likelihood that one party will gain a majority of seats. Although minority governments do occur, as they have in Canada, the leading political parties typically hope to form a majority government, and thus will view a minority government as a temporary departure from the majority government norm. By contrast, countries with proportional representation systems tend to give significant representation to a larger number of parties. It is rare in a country with proportional representation for one party to gain a majority of parliamentary seats. Thus, parties are more likely to accept the need for a coalition government (although in some cases the coalition may not control a majority of seats).

Types of Parliamentary Systems

Arend Lijphart (1999) has distinguished between two basic models of democratic governing systems that we can use to examine the workings of parliamentary systems in different countries.[4] The **Westminster model** (named after the Palace of Westminster, where the Parliament of the United Kingdom meets) is characteristic of the United Kingdom and, to varying extents, many of the former British colonies, including Canada. Among its features are the concentration of power in the hands of prime minister and Cabinet and an adversarial relationship between the governing party and the opposition party or parties. It is sometimes referred

WESTMINSTER MODEL
A model of governing that developed in Britain, featuring majority rule, executive dominance, and an adversarial relationship between the government party and the opposition parties.

[4] The following description of Lijphart's models focuses on the features most relevant to our discussion of parliamentary systems. Lijphart includes other features such as whether the governing system is unitary and federal, the pattern of interest group relations with government, and whether the society being governed is homogeneous or multiethnic.

▶ The Palace of Westminster, where the Parliament of the United Kingdom meets.

The UK Parliament: An Introduction to Parliament
www.parliament.uk/works/index.cfm

CONSENSUS MODEL OF DEMOCRACY
A model of governing featuring the sharing of governing power and a balance of power between the political executive and Parliament.

as a majoritarian system, in the sense that the party with a majority of elected members in the House of Commons is able to make the governing decisions regardless of the views of other parties. The primary role of the opposition parties is to criticize the policies and actions of government so as to hold the government accountable, rather than be involved in the development of laws and policies.

In contrast, some continental European countries such as Belgium and Switzerland[5] can be characterized in terms of a **consensus model of democracy**. Among the characteristics of this model is the sharing of governing power, including involvement in decision making by a variety of different political parties representing diverse segments of the population. The consensus model is associated with broad-based coalition governments and is more likely to feature a balance of power between the political executive and Parliament rather than executive dominance.

[5] Switzerland has a unique system in which the government is headed by a collegial seven-person executive (Federal Council) representing the major political parties, elected by the Swiss Assembly for a fixed four-year term of office. Nunavut and the Northwest Territories could also be considered consensus based, as their Legislative Assemblies are elected on a non-party basis with the members of the government elected by the Legislative Assembly.

The majoritarian model is particularly relevant in countries with a two-party or, less clearly, a two-plus party system. In such systems, one or the other of the dominant parties will usually be able to form a majority government and implement its program. The system can be considered democratic if there is, from time to time, a change of the party in power. Thus, even if minority views and interests are ignored by the governing party, those in the minority may eventually become part of the governing majority. In contrast, the consensus model tends to be associated with countries that have multiparty systems. Such a party system usually leads to coalition governments that have to take into account the varied views and interests represented by different members of the governing coalition.

Although it is often thought that Westminster-style majoritarian systems provide more effective governing than consensus democracies, Lijphart's analysis of government performance in thirty-six countries concluded that majoritarian democracies are "not superior to consensus democracies in terms of managing the economy and in maintaining civil peace" (Lijphart, 1999, p. 274). Consensus democracies were more likely to be "kinder and gentler" in terms of government provision of welfare, environmental protection, the punishment of criminal behaviour, and the provision of aid to developing countries (Lijphart, 1999). As well, consensus democracies tend to be better at representing the diversity of the population, have higher rates of participation in elections, and have higher levels of popular satisfaction with government.

THE CANADIAN PARLIAMENTARY SYSTEM

The Canadian parliamentary system of government, reflecting the country's British political heritage, basically follows the Westminster model. However, the federal system, the Charter of Rights and Freedoms, and the power of judicial review exercised by the courts place limits on what the Canadian government backed by a majority in Parliament can do. Nevertheless, the

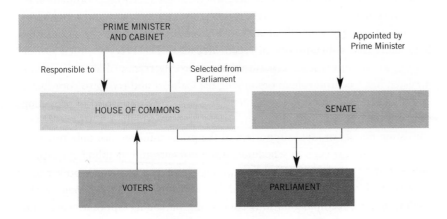

FIGURE 15-1

A SIMPLIFIED DEPICTION OF THE CANADIAN PARLIAMENTARY SYSTEM

prime minister and Cabinet are at the centre of the governing process at the national level in Canada. Although the prime minister and Cabinet are expected to be responsible and accountable to Parliament for their actions, in reality the prime minister and Cabinet normally control the dominant party in the House of Commons. Thus, the Canadian parliamentary system (like those of other countries that basically follow the Westminster model) can be described as a system of **executive dominance**, as it places considerable power in the hands of the prime minister and Cabinet.

The Prime Minister

The prime minister is the leading figure within the Canadian Cabinet. The prime minister determines who will be appointed to the Cabinet and what their responsibilities will be. At any time, the prime minister may change the responsibilities of any Cabinet minister or demand a Cabinet minister's resignation. The prime minister is also responsible for organizing the Cabinet, and thus determines what Cabinet committees there will be and who will sit on those committees. The prime minister chairs Cabinet meetings, sets the agenda for those meetings, and, since votes are not held in the Cabinet, determines the consensus of the Cabinet. In addition to playing a leading role in Cabinet, prime ministers are party leaders. They take on responsibility for their party's election campaigns and play a leading role in defending the government in the House of Commons. The mass media and the public pay far more attention to the prime minister than to any other political figure. Prime ministers make a substantial number of prestigious appointments and thus can reward loyal supporters. Although modern prime ministers do not run a particular department of government, they normally play a leading role in representing the country in international meetings, in federal–provincial relations, and in constitutional negotiations with provincial governments.

A prime minister cannot govern alone. Nevertheless, prime ministers have tended to become less dependent upon their Cabinets for advice and more concerned with providing central direction or, at least, central coordination to the government. To help to achieve this, the size, importance, and activities of the offices that provide advice and assistance directly to the prime minister have increased substantially in recent decades. The **Privy Council Office (PCO)**, an administrative structure that is directly responsible to the prime minister, has a central role in organizing the Cabinet and trying to coordinate and direct the activities of government. It is also very important in providing policy advice to the prime minister. The **Prime Minister's Office (PMO)**, consisting mainly of loyal supporters of the prime minister, not only provides secretarial support such as scheduling appointments and handling correspondence, but also is involved in maintaining the prime minister's power and popularity by providing partisan advice, writing speeches, managing the media, making recommendations concerning patronage appointments, and

EXECUTIVE DOMINANCE
A descriptive term applied to the Canadian parliamentary system (and other countries that follow the Westminster model) because it places considerable power in the hands of the prime minister and Cabinet through their ability to control the House of Commons, particularly in a majority government situation.

PRIVY COUNCIL OFFICE (PCO)
An administrative structure, directly responsible to the Canadian prime minister, that has a key role in coordinating and directing the activities of government and in providing policy advice to the prime minister.

PRIME MINISTER'S OFFICE (PMO)
The office that provides support and political advice to the prime minister.

trying to maintain party unity and loyalty to its leader. Together, the PCO and PMO provide the prime minister with a dedicated source of advice and a capability to direct and coordinate the activities of government. The concentration of power has led some analysts to characterize the governing system in Canada (and various other parliamentary systems such as the United Kingdom and Australia) as **prime ministerial government,** as discussed in Box 15-3, Prime Ministerial Government.

PRIME MINISTERIAL GOVERNMENT
The view that the prime minister has become the dominant member of the political executive, rather than the "first among equals" in the Cabinet.

BOX 15-3

Prime Ministerial Government

Has Canada has developed a prime ministerial government? Have prime ministers become the equivalent of American presidents in the sense that they are the chief executive, rather than occupying the traditional position as "first among equals" in the Cabinet?

In his study of governing in Canada, Donald Savoie (1999, pp. 7, 362) concluded that

power has shifted to the prime minister and his senior advisers at both the political and public service levels and away from Cabinet and Cabinet Committees. . . . Cabinet has now joined Parliament as an institution being bypassed. . . . The Canadian prime minister has little in the way of institutional check, at least inside government, to inhibit his ability to have his way.

Indeed, Jeffrey Simpson (2001) has argued that Canada has evolved into a "friendly dictatorship." Others, however, argue that the idea that there has been an almost dictatorial concentration of power in the hands of the prime minister and his senior advisers is a myth. The prime minister sets the overall tone and priorities of government and makes

some critical decisions, but typically leaves the implementation of policy priorities to individual Cabinet ministers and their staff (Goldenberg, 2006). Some prime ministers, however, are more likely to involve themselves as much as possible in all aspects of governing, while others focus on a few key priorities.

Although some prime ministers and premiers have dominated their Cabinets and set the direction for their governments, it should be kept in mind that some Cabinet ministers are also very important in government policy-making because of the departments they control and their popularity within the party or the country. For example, through most of the decade that Jean Chrétien was prime minister, he had to contend with the considerable power wielded by his popular rival, Paul Martin, who held the important position of finance minister. Despite the intense competition for power between Chrétien and Martin, they were usually able to agree on important budget priorities (Goldenberg, 2006).

The power of the Canadian prime minister is also limited by the nature of the federal system. Prime ministers often face serious difficulties in their

(continued)

(continued)

Former British Prime Minister Margaret Thatcher's political career was ended by her failure to maintain the support of her party caucus.

relationships with provincial governments, and may have to compromise to achieve objectives that require the involvement of provincial governments. Prime ministers usually have less difficulty maintaining the support of their party and party caucus. However, that support cannot be taken for granted. For example, Prime Minister Chrétien was eventually pressured to retire by his party's caucus.

The concentration of power in the hands of the prime minister and an inner circle is not unique to Canada. The United Kingdom and other countries that follow the Westminster model have also tended to move from Cabinet government to prime ministerial government (Weller, 1985). Margaret Thatcher, British prime minister from 1979 to 1990, governed with single-minded determination and changed the direction of British politics, overriding opposition within Cabinet and her party's caucus. In the end, however, she failed to maintain sufficient support of her caucus and resigned. Tony Blair, British prime minister from 1997 to 2007, also was a dominant figure within the British government, often ignoring the views of Cabinet and caucus and adopting a presidential style. Like Jean Chrétien, however, his rival and successor, Gordon Brown, Chancellor of the Exchequer (the equivalent of finance minister), had considerable power and independence in determining the financial policies of the government. In the end, like Margaret Thatcher, Blair was pressured by his party to resign despite winning three successive elections.

The Cabinet

Although in most parliamentary systems it is the prime minister who decides who will be appointed to the Cabinet, there are often political considerations that affect the prime minister's choice. Canadian prime ministers devote considerable attention to ensuring that their Cabinets are geographically representative. There is almost always at least one Cabinet minister from each province (except, occasionally, Prince Edward Island), with more Cabinet ministers from the provinces with greater populations. The proportion of French Canadians in the Cabinet has generally been in proportion to their share of Canada's population. There is also an expectation that French Canadians outside Quebec and English-speaking Quebecers will each have their own representative in the Cabinet.

Before 1957, Cabinets were exclusively composed of men of British, Irish, or French ancestry. In recent times, prime ministers have made an effort to appoint more women and persons of different ethnic and racial backgrounds to the Cabinet. Nevertheless, the Cabinet, like Parliament, is not fully representative of the diversity of Canadian society. For example, the twenty-six Cabinet ministers appointed by Prime Minister Stephen Harper after the election of the Conservative party in 2006 only included six women. A problem with selecting a representative Cabinet is that a prime minister is generally limited by the extent to which the party's members of Parliament reflect the diversity of the country. This, in turn, is affected by the party's nomination processes and whether a party makes deliberate efforts to try to ensure that persons with various characteristics are nominated and elected. After the 2008 electon, eleven women (of the twenty-three female Conservative MPs) were appointed to Harper's thirty-eight member cabinet.

DEPARTMENTS Many of the activities of government are divided among a number of departments (such as justice, health, and national defence), each of which is headed by a Cabinet minister who is expected to take responsibility for the actions of his or her department. Other Cabinet ministers, currently termed **Ministers of State** in Canada, may be given responsibilities for policy areas such as sport, public health, multiculturalism, and families and caregivers, but have no department to oversee.

> **MINISTERS OF STATE**
> Cabinet ministers who are not responsible for a particular government department.

Because each department is concerned with a particular policy area and the particular set of interests associated with that policy area, there is often some tension among the different departments. For example, the agriculture department has had a more favourable view of the use of certain pesticides than the department of the environment. Further, each department will typically seek more money and employees for its programs, while the

◀ Prime Minister Stephen Harper chose twenty-six MPs for his first Cabinet, but only six of these were women.

TREASURY BOARD
A permanent Cabinet committee with its own staff and minister that plays a central role in governing in Canada because of its responsibility for the expenditures and management practices of government.

CABINET SOLIDARITY
The convention in a parliamentary system that each member of the Cabinet is expected to fully support and defend the decisions and actions that the Cabinet takes.

Institute on Governance
www.iog.ca

CENTRAL AGENCY
An organization that tries to provide direction and coordination to government. In Canada, the key central agencies are the Privy Council Office, the Prime Minister's Office, the Treasury Board, and the Department of Finance.

typically seek more money and employees for its programs, while the Department of Finance and the **Treasury Board,** a Cabinet committee responsible for the government's expenditures, will normally try to limit spending.

CABINET ORGANIZATION The Cabinet has traditionally been viewed as a body that collectively makes governing decisions. Because each member of the Cabinet is expected to maintain **Cabinet solidarity** (that is, fully support and defend the decisions and actions that Cabinet takes), there is an expectation that the Cabinet as a whole will discuss and deliberate on the key governing decisions. In reality, however, modern Cabinets are too large and Cabinet ministers often have too little time to fully consider all of the decisions that government makes.

Thus, discussion of specific Cabinet decisions is typically done in one of the committees of Cabinet. Some prime ministers, including Stephen Harper, have used a select group of Cabinet ministers, the Priorities and Planning Committee that Harper currently chairs, to set the strategic direction of the government and make many decisions on behalf of the Cabinet as a whole.

COORDINATION Although many individual Cabinet ministers are responsible for overseeing a department of government, in recent decades considerable attention has been devoted to trying to coordinate the diverse activities of government. In Canada, this coordination and direction for the government is provided by what are termed **central agencies.** These include the Privy Council Office, the Prime Minister's Office, the Treasury Board, and the Department of Finance (which develops the government's budget and assesses the impact of government activity on the economy).

POWERS The prime minister and Cabinet are responsible for the executive powers of government. This includes the conduct of relations with provincial and foreign governments, the issuing of a large number of regulations, the making of a substantial number of important appointments, and oversight of the administrative apparatus of government. The prime minister and Cabinet play a key role in the legislative process. Almost all legislation passed by the Canadian Parliament is proposed to Parliament by the Cabinet. Although Parliament has to approve proposals for raising and spending money by government, such proposals can only be made by the Cabinet.

CABINET RESPONSIBILITY The prime minister and Cabinet are accountable for their actions in governing through their responsibility to the House of Commons. Because the prime minister and Cabinet hold their positions only as long as they have the support of the majority of members of the House of Commons, there is an expectation that the Cabinet as a group will defend, explain, and take responsibility for the actions of the government in Parliament. In a majority government situation, where the governing party has a majority of seats in the House of Commons, it is highly unlikely that the House of Commons would pass a motion of non-confidence in the government or defeat important legislative and financial proposals presented by the Cabinet.

Nevertheless, the rules of the House of Commons provide opportunities for the opposition parties to raise questions about and criticisms of the actions and performance of the government. In particular, Canada's daily Question Period provides for lively, if not always informative, exchanges between the opposition and governing parties.

In addition to the **collective responsibility** of the Cabinet to the House of Commons, there is an expectation that individual Cabinet ministers will take responsibility for the activities of the department they administer. If there are serious problems within a department, opposition party members typically call for the minister to resign from the Cabinet. However, Cabinet ministers in Canada have not resigned for the errors of officials in the departments they administer. Instead, Cabinet ministers are more likely to promise to look into a problem.

COLLECTIVE RESPONSIBILITY
The convention that the Cabinet as a group will defend, explain, and take responsibility for the actions of the government in Parliament.

SECRECY The accountability of the government is also limited by **Cabinet secrecy**. The Cabinet meets behind closed doors, Cabinet documents normally remain secret for twenty years, and the advice given to the Cabinet is not usually released publicly. Cabinet secrecy helps to maintain Cabinet solidarity and ensure that the Cabinet is seen as a united team, regardless of the disagreements that undoubtedly exist among individual Cabinet ministers. Cabinet discussions can be full and frank because participants know that word of disagreement will not get out to the media or opposition parties. As well, it helps to shield public servants who advise the Cabinet from public criticism (public servants, being politically neutral, do not normally respond to criticisms). However, the principle of Cabinet secrecy can be used to avoid releasing research conducted by the government that would aid in public discussion of an issue and assist the opposition parties and the public in holding the government accountable for its actions.

CABINET SECRECY
The convention that the Cabinet meets behind closed doors, Cabinet documents normally remain secret for a lengthy period of time, and the advice given to the Cabinet is not usually released publicly.

Access to Information and Privacy
http://canada.justice.gc.ca/en/ps/atip

In recent times, the Access to Information Act has allowed journalists, interest groups, opposition parties, and concerned citizens the ability to obtain information that previously remained secret. Although such laws have made government more transparent, various types of information can be withheld from the public, and officials have frequently been slow to respond to requests for information. The 2000 Report of the Information Commissioner, for example, stated that the Canadian government had a penchant for secrecy that undermined the democratic process and that the government had failed to live up to the spirit of its access-to-information legislation. The Commissioner also alleged that his staff members had been threatened by the PMO. In overturning the government's attempt to keep some documents secret, Madam Justice Eleanor Dawson ruled that limitations to access to information should be "limited and specific" so that "citizens can participate meaningfully in the democratic process" and ensure "that politicians and bureaucrats remain accountable to citizens" (quoted in Sallot, 2004).

Parliament

Parliament is responsible for passing laws and approving the spending and taxing plans of government (see Figure 15-2). In addition, Parliament, particularly the House of Commons, is expected to hold the government accountable for its actions. In this regard, Parliament provides a visible forum in which the opposition can criticize the actions or inactions of government and the governing party can defend what it is doing. This not only helps to keep the government "on its toes," but also may help voters to make up their minds as to which party to support in the next election. In addition, although the Cabinet oversees the development of most new laws, Parliament can play a useful role by carefully examining proposed legislation and suggesting modifications of some details of proposed legislation to make it more effective. Finally, individual members of Parliament frequently raise issues and concerns of those they represent.

FIGURE 15-2

THE GENERAL PROCEDURE FOR PASSING LEGISLATION IN CANADA

Notes: A few bills are presented first to the Senate and then proceed to the House of Commons. Where the second chamber proposes amendments to a bill that has been passed by the first chamber, it is returned to the first chamber for further consideration.

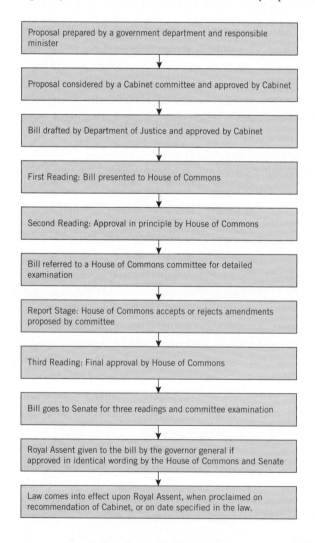

Proposal prepared by a government department and responsible minister

Proposal considered by a Cabinet committee and approved by Cabinet

Bill drafted by Department of Justice and approved by Cabinet

First Reading: Bill presented to House of Commons

Second Reading: Approval in principle by House of Commons

Bill referred to a House of Commons committee for detailed examination

Report Stage: House of Commons accepts or rejects amendments proposed by committee

Third Reading: Final approval by House of Commons

Bill goes to Senate for three readings and committee examination

Royal Assent given to the bill by the governor general if approved in identical wording by the House of Commons and Senate

Law comes into effect upon Royal Assent, when proclaimed on recommendation of Cabinet, or on date specified in the law.

Many countries have two separate chambers (often termed "houses") involved in the legislative process (termed bicameral legislatures). In some cases, this is a carry-over from the non-democratic past, when a body representing privileged interests was seen as necessary to check the power of a body representing the people. In most federal systems, the second or upper chamber represents the interests of provinces or states.

The Parliament of Canada consists of two chambers: the House of Commons and the Senate. Provincial legislatures have only a single chamber of elected representatives (that is, a unicameral legislature).

The Parliament of Canada
www.parl.gc.ca

The House of Commons

The Canadian **House of Commons** is the elected chamber of Parliament, with each member representing a particular geographical constituency. Representation is by population, with constituency boundaries drawn so that, in most cases, each member of the House of Commons represents approximately the same number of people. However, there are constitutional guarantees to maintain a minimum level of representation from the smaller provinces and territories. Thus, even though Ontario and Quebec have the majority of seats in the House of Commons, there is a slight overrepresentation, in terms of population, of the smaller provinces and territories.

On the surface, the House of Commons controls the executive because the prime minister and Cabinet have to maintain the confidence (support) of the House of Commons. If a majority of members of the House of Commons pass a motion of non-confidence in the government, or if a major proposal made by the Cabinet, such as a budget proposal, is defeated, the prime minister must either request that an election be held or resign. However, in reality it is the prime minister and Cabinet who normally control the House of Commons. **Party discipline** is the basic operating principle of the House of Commons (see Box 15-4, Should Party Discipline Be Relaxed?). That is, members of each party normally vote in accordance with the position that the party has adopted in caucus. The prime minister and Cabinet are usually able to convince their party's members in the House of Commons to support them and their legislative proposals. Thus, as long as their party elected a majority of members to the House of Commons, the prime minister and Cabinet do not have to worry about losing the confidence of the House of Commons. Party discipline ensures that the political executive will remain in power. Nevertheless, the opposition parties can sometimes persuade the government to change or withdraw a legislative proposal, particularly if the opposition can mobilize public opinion to its side or if the proposal is not a high priority for the government.

HOUSE OF COMMONS
The elected chamber of Parliament, with each member of the House representing a particular geographical constituency.

PARTY DISCIPLINE
The expectation that legislators will vote in accordance with the position that the party has adopted in caucus.

PRIVATE MEMBERS Ordinary members of the House of Commons who are not in the Cabinet (termed **private members**) have generally played a limited role in the development of new legislation. Private members cannot propose laws that

PRIVATE MEMBERS
Ordinary members of the House of Commons who are not in the Cabinet.

BOX 15-4

Should Party Discipline Be Relaxed?

Party discipline has generally been tighter in Canada than in other countries such as the United Kingdom, where strict party discipline is only maintained for votes of non-confidence, votes on the government's budget, and votes on certain issues deemed to be crucial to the government's program.

In the United Kingdom, unlike in Canada, it is not unusual for legislative proposals coming from Cabinet to be defeated in the House of Commons. Votes in the British House of Commons are designated according to three classifications: one-line whip,* in which MPs, including Cabinet ministers, are free from party discipline; two-line whip, in which party members are encouraged and Cabinet ministers are expected to vote in accordance with their party's position; and three-line whip, in which party discipline is imposed on all members.

In Canada, there have been only a few free votes for which party discipline has been withdrawn—usually on controversial moral issues such as capital punishment and abortion—so that members can follow their consciences.

The tightness of party discipline in Canada has often been criticized. Party discipline reduces the significance of ordinary members of Parliament, who are expected to toe the party line. Members may be expected to vote against the wishes or interests of their constituents. Provincial and regional interests may not be adequately represented in Parliament because parties and their leaders may be concerned about the dominant interests of the country as a whole or those areas viewed as crucial to electoral success.

There are, however, some positive features to party discipline. It helps to ensure that the positions taken by different parties are clear. This makes it easier for voters to choose among competing parties and to hold the governing party accountable for its actions. As well, it means that individual members of Parliament are less subject to pressure from lobbyists and special interests. Further, it means that the government can focus on doing what it considers to be for the common good of the whole country without having to contend with individual members of Parliament seeking special benefits for their constituency in return for their voting support.

A number of party leaders have promised to loosen party discipline, but have been reluctant to do so after becoming prime minister. Nevertheless, in recent years there has been an increasing number of votes in which some party members have not supported the position of their party. This was particularly evident between 2000 and 2003 as a result of feuding within the governing Liberal party between the supporters of Prime Minister Jean Chrétien and those who wanted him replaced by Paul Martin.

In his campaign for the leadership of the Liberal party, Paul Martin promised to eliminate what he termed the "democratic deficit" by increasing the role and independence of members of Parliament. Included in his reform proposals was the adoption of the British system of classifying votes, with the intention that only a few matters would be subject to a three-line vote. This could give members of Parliament who are not in the Cabinet a greater ability to influence ordinary legislative proposals. However, in the minority government situations that followed the 2004 election, party discipline generally remained tight.

---

* The Whip is the enforcer of party discipline.

involve the imposition of taxes or the spending of money for a new and distinct purpose without the approval of Cabinet. Only a few bills, usually of a minor nature, proposed by private members have been passed by Parliament. However, in 2007, the opposition parties succeeded in proposing and passing a law requiring the government to respect Canada's commitments under the Kyoto Protocol by preparing a plan to reduce greenhouse gas emissions. Nevertheless, Prime Minister Harper stated that the government would be unable to implement this law. More frequently, ordinary members of Parliament have been successful in making minor modifications to legislation proposed by the Cabinet.

COMMITTEES **House of Commons committees,** composed of government and opposition party members in proportion to their party's strength in the House, provide detailed examination of proposed legislation, and often suggest modifications to the legislation. At times they investigate or hold public hearings on particular policy issues, thus making some contribution to the development of new policies.

OPPOSITION The House of Commons is particularly important in providing a public forum for the criticism and defence of the actions of the executive and its legislative proposals. The party with the second-highest number of seats is designated as the **official opposition** and leads off the questioning or criticism of government every day that the House is sitting. Other parties with at least twelve seats in the House of Commons have official party status, which, along with other privileges, gives them a budget for hiring research and support staff.

Various opportunities are provided for opposition members to propose **non-confidence motions** in the government. Although non-confidence motions are usually unsuccessful, they provide an opportunity to focus attention on what the opposition parties see as the failings of the governing party.

Although the House of Commons provides a forum for debating proposed legislation, the governing party quite often uses motions of **closure** and time allocation to cut off or limit debate in the House, sometimes in response to a **filibuster**—the term for delaying tactics by the opposition. For example, the Liberal government of Jean Chrétien used closure to end debate on anti-terrorism legislation in 2001 and on ratification of the Kyoto Protocol on global climate change in 2002. The increasing use of motions to limit debate by governing parties, both national and provincial, has been criticized by many political observers.

The Senate

Canada's **Senate,** the other chamber of Parliament, was established, in part, to provide a body of "sober second thought" to check the democratic tendencies of the House of Commons. Although the government does not need to maintain the confidence of the Senate, legislation needs the approval of the Senate as well as the House of Commons.[6] As in the House of Commons, senators examine legislative

HOUSE OF COMMONS COMMITTEES
Committees composed of government and opposition party members in proportion to their party's strength in the House of Commons; they provide detailed examination of proposed legislation, and often suggest modifications to the proposed legislation.

OFFICIAL OPPOSITION
The party with the second-highest number of seats in the House of Commons is designated as the official opposition and leads off the questioning or criticism of government every day that the House is sitting.

NON-CONFIDENCE MOTION
A motion put forward by the opposition members in a legislature expressing a lack of confidence in the government. If passed, the prime minister is expected to either resign or request that an election be held.

CLOSURE
A procedure in a legislative body that cuts off debate if approved by a majority vote.

FILIBUSTER
The use of various delaying tactics by those opposed to the passage of a particular piece of legislation.

SENATE (CANADA)
The upper chamber of Parliament, appointed on the recommendation of the prime minister. Senators hold their positions until age seventy-five.

---

6 Only in the case of resolutions to approve constitutional changes can the Canadian House of Commons override the opposition of the Senate.

proposals and introduce modifications that are, on occasion, accepted by the government and the House of Commons. Senators usually have been reluctant to block the passage of legislation approved by the House of Commons. However, when Brian Mulroney was prime minister (1984–1993), the Liberal majority in the Senate engaged in confrontation with the Progressive Conservative majority in the House of Commons on such important legislation as the Canada–United States Free Trade Agreement and the imposition of the goods and services tax.

Generally, the Senate does not receive as much media and public attention as the House of Commons. Because of the expertise of many senators, the greater amount of time available for deliberation, and the somewhat less partisan nature of the Senate, this second chamber (particularly through its committees) often makes useful suggestions for improving legislative proposals. Over the years, the Senate has also prepared important reports on such topics as poverty, the mass media, science policy, free trade, terrorism, and aging.

REPRESENTATION The Senate is designed to provide equal regional representation to offset the representation by population in the House of Commons. There are twenty-four senators from each of Ontario, Quebec, the Maritimes (ten each from Nova Scotia and New Brunswick; four from Prince Edward Island), and the West (six each from Manitoba, Saskatchewan, Alberta, and British Columbia), plus six from Newfoundland and Labrador and one from each of the three territories. However, since senators are not elected by provincial voters nor appointed by their provincial legislature or provincial government, it is questionable whether senators "represent," in a meaningful way, the province for which they are appointed.

APPOINTMENTS Senators are appointed by the prime minister and hold their positions until age seventy-five. A senator can only be removed from office for failing to attend two consecutive sessions of Parliament, becoming bankrupt, or being convicted of treason, a felony, or other "infamous crime." Most senators are appointed because of their loyalty to the party and the prime minister that is in power. When former hockey star Frank Mahovlich was appointed to the Senate, he told reporters, "I guess it's because I kept my mouth shut and didn't cause any trouble. I'm not familiar with the Senate and policies" (quoted in Bercuson & Cooper, 1998).

Because prime ministers appoint mostly party loyalists to the Senate, when another party is elected it will typically find that the outgoing party continues to control the Senate. For example, despite losing the 2006 Canadian election, the Liberal party continued to hold a substantial majority in the Senate.

Reform of the Senate has been a staple of Canadian political discussion for many decades with some, such as the New Democratic party and Ontario Liberal premier Dalton McGuinty, advocating its abolition (see Box 15-5, Reforming the Canadian Senate). The ability of an appointed body to reject legislation passed by an elected, representative body is often viewed as a relic of the non-democratic past. In the United Kingdom since 1911, the House of Lords, the equivalent of the Canadian Senate, can only delay the passage of legislation. Efforts are underway to make the House of Lords an elected body.

It is also often argued that in a federal system, the Senate should represent provincial interests. In Germany, for example, the Upper House consists of representatives of the *land* (provincial) governments.

BOX 15-5

Reforming the Canadian Senate

Reform of the Senate has been a perennial topic of Canadian politics, but thus far there has been limited progress.

In the 1980s, a movement based in Alberta developed to promote the idea of a "Triple-E" Senate (one that is *elected*, *effective*, and based on an *equal* number of representatives from each province). A Triple-E Senate would give a stronger voice to the smaller provinces. As we will see in the next chapter, the United States has a powerful elected Senate based on equal representation from each state. To promote the idea of an elected Senate, the Alberta government has held province-wide elections since 1989 to choose potential senators.

An elected Senate with equal representation from each province would probably quite frequently be controlled by a different party than the House of Commons. Being elected, senators would be less likely to back off from a confrontation with the House of Commons. Thus, there would be a need for negotiation and compromise between the governing party and the Senate to avoid a deadlock in Parliament. In Australia, a deadlock occurred in 1975 between an elected Senate based on equal state representation and the House of Representatives (equivalent to the House of Commons) controlled by different parties, when the Senate refused to approve the appropriations of funds needed to run the government. This resulted in a very controversial decision by the governor general to dismiss the prime minister (who retained the confidence of the House) and appoint the opposition leader as interim prime minister until elections for both houses of Parliament were called.

What is the likelihood of the Triple-E proposal being adopted? Changing the number of representatives from each province to create a Triple-E Senate would involve the difficult process of constitutional amendment. It is unlikely that Quebec and Ontario would agree to the reduction in power that would result from the election of an equal number of representatives from each province in an effective Senate. As well, it is likely that various groups, such as women and Aboriginals, would insist on guaranteed representation in a reconstituted Senate.

One of the promises Conservative leader Stephen Harper made in the 2006 election campaign was that he would only appoint Senators who were elected by voters in their province. Despite this promise, he appointed Michael Fortier to the Senate (and to the Cabinet) shortly after becoming prime minister. However, in 2007, Prime Minister Harper appointed Bert Brown, who had been elected in Alberta, to the Senate. Brown, a leader in the movement for an elected Senate, had once ploughed his neighbour's field with a large "Triple E or else" slogan.

In 2006, the Conservative government proposed legislation to limit the term of newly appointed senators to eight years and to consult voters before recommending an appointment to the Senate. However, the Liberal majority in the Senate stalled passage of the legislation, arguing that the Supreme Court should be asked for an opinion on the constitutionality of modifying the Senate without seeking the agreement of provincial legislatures. The legislative proposal died with the end of the parliamentary session in September 2007, but will likely be reintroduced.

Summary and Conclusion

Parliamentary systems are often described as having a fusion (close interrelationship) of legislative and executive powers. Despite the label *parliamentary system*, very considerable power rests with the prime minister and Cabinet, particularly in a majority government situation. Although the prime minister and Cabinet must retain the support of the House of Commons, this is largely a formality in a majority government situation. Nevertheless, they are expected to be responsible to the House of Commons for their actions.

The Westminster version of parliamentary system, in which majority government is the norm, facilitates decisive action by the government. By maintaining tight party discipline, the governing party can act in ways that it believes will be for the good of the country as a whole or, at least, for the re-election of the governing party. It also can facilitate the accountability of the government to the people, as praise or blame for the actions of the government and the laws passed by Parliament can be attributed to the governing party.

However, the concentration of power can have negative consequences. A majority government, elected by a minority of voters, may ignore different sections of the population or different viewpoints. Because of strict party discipline, the task of holding the government accountable for its actions rests with the opposition parties in the House of Commons. Although the parliamentary system does provide an opportunity for the opposition parties to question and criticize the prime minister and Cabinet, this does not often lead the government to modify its policies. Further, the secrecy within which government tries to operate and the large number of activities conducted by modern governments can make it difficult for the opposition parties to investigate the activities of government. Effective access to information legislation; independent officers of Parliament able to scrutinize government spending, pursue public complaints, and ensure that those entrusted with power are acting ethically; an independent judiciary; vigilant media; and an attentive public are important in ensuring that government does not abuse its power.

Parliamentary systems feature collective decision-making by the prime minister and Cabinet, with Cabinet ministers often chosen to be representative of some of the important segments of society. In theory, then, government decisions are based on discussion and deliberation by experienced persons, most of whom have the expertise of their departments of government to provide them with advice. Power has, however, tended to drift from the Cabinet as a whole to the prime minister and a small group of aides, officials, and ministers at the centre. Prime ministerial government may result in a clear direction for a government run by a decisive leader, but it carries the risk of wrong-headed or insensitive decisions made by the head of government without adequate deliberation among those with different ideas.

The Westminster model of parliamentary government has often been viewed as the ideal form of democratic government. However, despite its virtues of simplicity, stability, and decisiveness, critics have argued that governing systems oriented to finding a consensus not only are more representative and inclusive, but also can provide good government.

Overall, the parliamentary system of government, particularly in its Westminster version (as used in Canada), usually provides the opportunity for a governing party to implement its program and facilitates the accountability of government. The Canadian parliamentary system, however, tends to pay less attention to the representation of diverse interests and to the role of ordinary members of Parliament in the development of laws and policies than is the case with the American presidential system, discussed in the next chapter.

Key Terms

Discussion Questions

1. Does the parliamentary system tend to give too much power to the prime minister?

2. Should party discipline in Parliament be loosened?

3. Should the Canadian Senate be maintained as is, changed, or abolished?

4. Should Canada replace the monarchy with an elected head of state?

5. Is a coalition government preferable to a minority government? What coalitions would be most likely to form in Canada?

6. Is the Westminster model preferable to the consensus model of democracy?

Further Reading

Docherty, D.C. *Legislatures*. Vancouver: UBC Press, 2005.

Docherty, D.C. *Mr. Smith goes to Ottawa: Life in the House of Commons*. Vancouver: UBC Press, 1997.

Franks, C.E.S. *The Parliament of Canada*. Toronto: University of Toronto Press. 1987.

Lijphart, A. *Patterns of democracy: Government forms and performance in thirty-six countries*. New Haven: Yale University Press, 1999.

Savoie, D.J. *Governing from the centre: The concentration of power in Canadian politics*. Toronto: University of Toronto Press, 1999.

Seidle, F.L., & Docherty, D.C. (Eds.). *Reforming parliamentary democracy*. Montreal & Kingston: McGill-Queen's University Press, 2003.

White, G. *Cabinets and first ministers*. Vancouver: UBC Press, 2005.

Chapter 1

PRESIDENTIAL AND SEMI-PRESIDENTIAL SYSTEMS

PHOTO ABOVE: On November 14, 1995, the government of the United States shut down when the president and Congress were unable to agree on the government's budget.

After reading this chapter you should be able to:

1. outline the basic differences between parliamentary and presidential systems of government
2. discuss the relationship between the president and Congress in the United States
3. compare the strengths and weakness of presidential and parliamentary systems
4. explain the basic features of semi-presidential systems
5. evaluate semi-presidential systems

On November 14, 1995, the government of the United States shut down. More than 14.8 million non-essential federal government employees were sent home and many government offices were closed.

The American system of government occasionally suffers from "gridlock" (difficulty getting things done), particularly because of tension between the executive and legislative branches. In 1994, the Republican party, which had become dominated by right-wing conservatives with strong ideological commitments, won a majority in the House of Representatives. They sought to eliminate major federal health and welfare programs by rejecting the government budget proposed by Democratic President Bill Clinton. While the November shutdown lasted only five days, the continuing inability to reach an agreement resulted in another shutdown from December 15 to January 6. Eventually, with the majority of the public blaming the Republicans in Congress for the crisis and with Clinton able to convince a substantial proportion of the public that the Republican proposals went too far, a modified version of Clinton's budget was passed. Existing programs were maintained, cuts to government spending were smaller than the Republicans had demanded, and Clinton vetoed the more radical proposals that the Republican Congress passed (Brady & Volden, 2006). Clinton was easily re-elected president in 1996; the Republicans continued to have a majority in both Houses of Congress, losing eight seats in the House and gaining two in the Senate in the 1996 election.

Despite the continuation of "divided government" (a situation where the majority in Congress and the president represent different political parties), agreement on subsequent budgets between the president and Congress were successful in producing a balanced budget and budgetary surpluses (Burden & Kimball, 2004).

The events of 1995–1996 are an extreme example of the gridlock that can make substantial changes difficult to achieve in the American political system. In part, gridlock can be the result of the "divided government" that has frequently occurred in the American presidential system in the past several decades. Even when the president's party has a majority in Congress, gridlock can still occur because individual members of Congress are often more interested in voting in accordance with the wishes and interests of their district or state rather than voting along party lines. Bargaining and compromise are typically needed to make the system work.

In this chapter we will examine presidential forms of governments using the United States as our primary example. We will also discuss semi-presidential governing systems (such as that of France), which combine some features of presidential and parliamentary government.

THE PRESIDENTIAL SYSTEM

The **presidential system** of government was developed in the United States. The founders of that country, having for years clashed with the powerful British-appointed royal governor of each colony, were concerned about concentrating powers in the hands of a single person. Concentration of power, they felt, would threaten individual liberty—a key value for the revolutionaries. However, many of the founders also recognized the need for strong leadership. Thus, they devised a system of **checks and balances** in which each of the three branches of government—the executive led by the president, the legislative (**Congress**), and the judicial (headed by the Supreme Court)—would be able to check the power of the other branches so that no one individual or institution could become too powerful.

To ensure that each branch could check the power of the other branches, a system of **separation of powers** was established. The president and Congress have separate bases of authority. Unlike in a parliamentary system, those holding executive positions cannot be members of the legislative branch.

A presidential system also differs from a parliamentary system in that the executive does not need to maintain the support of the legislature to remain in office. Both the president and the members of Congress have fixed terms of office. The president cannot dissolve Congress and order an election in the hope that this will result in a Congress that is more willing to support the executive. Even though the executive and legislative branches are independent of each other, actions often involve both branches

The presidential system has been adopted (with some modifications) by almost all countries in Central and South America as well as by some in other parts of the world, including Indonesia, the Philippines, Cyprus, Nigeria, Ghana, and Malawi (Shugart, 2006).

The President

In a presidential system, the president is both head of state and head of government. That is, the president carries out the ceremonial duties associated with the head of state, but also heads the executive branch of government. As chief executive, the president is commander-in-chief of the armed forces, exercises considerable control over foreign policy, helps to shape domestic policy, and exercises some control over the public service. Although the president heads the executive branch of government and thus is responsible for the implementation of laws, the president is also involved in the legislative activity of passing laws. Not only are the president and the executive branch active in proposing some legislation to Congress, but the president's ability to veto laws passed by Congress (discussed below) means that Congress has to take into account the president's views in passing legislation.

PRESIDENTIAL SYSTEM
A system of governing in which the president and Congress each separately derive their authority from being elected by the people and have a fixed term of office. The president is both head of government and head of state.

CHECKS AND BALANCES
A basic principle of the American presidential system in which each of the three branches of government is able to check the actions of the others so that no individual or institution becomes too powerful.

CONGRESS
The legislative branch of the American government.

SEPARATION OF POWERS
A basic feature of presidential systems in which the executive, legislative, and judicial branches of government are separate from each other with each having different personnel and different bases of authority.

The president nominates a variety of senior officials and Supreme Court and other federal judges. However, to check the power of the president, many presidential nominations (including Cabinet and senior departmental officials, ambassadors, federal and Supreme Court judges, members of regulatory agencies and advisory boards, and military officers) must be approved by the Senate (the upper chamber of Congress). Likewise, although the president has the authority to make treaties, they must be approved by a two-thirds majority in the Senate.

The American President
www.whitehouse.gov

Cabinet and Executive Offices

The Cabinet secretaries who are appointed by the president and confirmed by the Senate head up the various departments of government. However, the American Cabinet as a whole is not a key decision-making body. Some presidents have avoided holding regular Cabinet meetings, and the president does not necessarily follow the advice of Cabinet. Although some individual Cabinet secretaries are important advisers to the president, much of the advice given to the president comes from the White House staff—usually individuals with strong personal loyalties to the president. Nevertheless, individual Cabinet secretaries are important in running their departments and drafting proposals and regulations. The president also controls various executive offices (referred to as the Executive Office of the President), including the Office of Management and Budget and the Council of Economic Advisers, which gives the president important sources of advice. Of particular importance is the National Security Council, chaired by the president and including the chair of the Joint Chiefs of (Military) Staff and the Director of National Intelligence, which plays a central role in national security and foreign policy decisions.

Although Congress is responsible for legislation, the president can issue executive orders concerning how laws and policies are to be carried out. Further, by appointing top officials, the president can try to affect how the laws passed by Congress are implemented. For example, President Ronald Reagan tried to eliminate many environmental regulations by appointing like-minded persons to head the Environmental Protection Agency and cutting the funding for the Agency. However, two of his anti-environment appointees to head the Agency resigned in disgrace. Subsequently, Congress passed stronger, more enforceable environmental legislation (Kraft, 2004).

Presidential Selection and Term

The president, along with a vice-presidential running mate, is elected by the American people. Although voters in the United States choose among the competing presidential candidates, technically they are voting for members of the Electoral College committed to casting their ballot for a particular presidential candidate. A majority of Electoral College votes is needed to elect a president (see Chapter 10). If no candidate has a majority of Electoral College votes, the president would be elected by the House of Representatives, the lower house of Congress, with each state delegation casting a single vote. Because the United States has developed a two-party system, this has not occurred since 1824.

Other countries with presidential systems directly elect their president rather than using an electoral college. In many countries (such as Brazil, Chile, and Argentina) a runoff election is held if no candidate has a majority (or in some countries, a large plurality) of votes. In Mexico and the Philippines, however, the candidate with the most votes on a single ballot wins. For example, in the 2006 Mexican election, the winning candidate (Felipe Calderón) obtained 36.38 percent of the vote compared to 36.34 percent for the second-place candidate.

Because of concerns that excessive power may accumulate in the hands of a long-serving president, presidential systems limit the amount of time that presidents can hold the office. For example, Mexico limits its president to a single six-year term. The president of the United States has a fixed term in office of four years and can be elected to a maximum of two terms. Unlike the prime minister in a parliamentary system, the president holds office even if the president lacks the support of Congress.

IMPEACHMENT Although presidents have a fixed term of office, Congress does have the ability to remove a president who has engaged in illegal behaviour. The process, known as **impeachment**, is difficult and lengthy. In the United States, the president, other top officials, and judges can only be removed from office if convicted of "treason, bribery or other high crimes and misdemeanours." After an investigation by the Judiciary Committee of the House of Representatives, a majority in the House has to pass articles of impeachment stating the offence(s). Then, after holding a trial, a two-thirds majority in the Senate has to find the president guilty in order to remove the president (see Box 16-1, Presidential Impeachment).

IMPEACHMENT
A process by which a president and other public officials can be removed from office after being accused of criminal behaviour and convicted by a legislative body.

The Vice-President

A candidate for vice-president in the United States is handpicked by a presidential candidate to serve as an election running mate, sometimes providing balance in the sense of appealing to different regions and to persons with a somewhat different ideological perspective than the president. The vice-president has the constitutional right to preside over the Senate, although only occasionally does so, and can only vote in the case of a tie. Otherwise, the major constitutional role of the vice-president is to be available to take over the presidency in case the president dies or is unable to

Presidential Impeachment

Although a number of American presidents have faced impeachment proceedings, no president has ever been removed by this process. Richard Nixon resigned in 1974 before he could be impeached for participating in the cover-up of illegal activities (including breaking into Democratic party offices in Washington's Watergate building). In 1999, Bill Clinton was accused of false testimony and obstructing justice when he stated that he had not had sexual relations with his intern, Monica Lewinsky, in a deposition to a grand jury as part of a sexual harassment civil lawsuit. Although a small majority of the House voted to impeach the president, only one-half of senators voted for conviction, and thus Clinton was able to complete his term. Voting was almost entirely along party lines, indicating the political nature of the impeachment procedure.

The power of impeachment has been successfully used in several other countries to remove a president, particularly for corruption. For example, President Collor of Brazil was removed from office in 1992 as a result of allegations by his younger brother that Collor was benefiting from illegal deals engaged in by a friend of the president. The "gifts" from his friend included two ranches, renovations of his apartments in Brazil and Paris, expensive cars for his children, and cash to various family members. Pressure from the public to impeach the president helped to ensure that representatives in Congress voted to impeach despite attempts by the president's friends to bribe representatives (Kara, 2005).

In contrast, President Samper of Columbia was able to survive credible allegations that his presidential campaign was funded by the Cali cocaine cartel. Efforts to impeach him were voted down by Columbia's House of Representatives, which also prohibited further investigations. In this case, the popularity of the president discouraged representatives from voting for impeachment (Hinojosa & Pérez-Liñán, 2005).

continue in office (see Box 16-2, The Significance of the Vice-President). Depending on the president, some special tasks may be assigned to the vice-president.

The American Congress

The American Congress is a legislative body composed of two separate bodies:

- The **House of Representatives**, which is elected every two years from districts of approximately equal population size.
- The **Senate**, which is composed of persons elected for six-year terms on a two-per-state basis.

The president does not have the power to dissolve Congress and thus has to live with a Congress that has a different political perspective (see Figure 16-1). Because the president does not need the support of Congress to remain in office, Congress can feel free to reject legislative or budgetary proposals from the president, knowing that it will not lead to a new election. To protect the independence of Congress, the president and the Cabinet secretaries are not allowed to be members of Congress.

HOUSE OF REPRESENTATIVES
The lower chamber of the American Congress, elected for a two-year term from districts of approximately equal population size.

SENATE (UNITED STATES)
The upper chamber of Congress. Two senators are elected by voters in each state for a six-year term.

The Significance of the Vice-President

The office of vice-president has not attracted the most flattering commendations:

- "The most insignificant office that ever the invention of man contrived." (President John Adams)
- "It's not worth a bucket of warm piss; it doesn't amount to a hill of beans." (Vice-President John Nance Garner)
- "About as useful as a cow's fifth teat." (President Lyndon B. Johnson)
- "The only thing the job calls for is waiting: waiting for the president to die or be impeached; waiting for the Senate to wind up in a tie so the vice-president can break it. That's all the vice-presidency is about: waiting. Everything else is make-work." (Lynn Cheney, wife of Vice-President Richard Cheney, in a 1988 novel)

But is the insignificance of the vice-president exaggerated? In recent decades, vice-presidents have provided advice to the president and been members of the important National Security Council. Although the importance of the vice-president varies from one presidential administration to the next, Vice-President Richard (Dick) Cheney had a major influence on government policies in George W. Bush's administration. Unlike other vice-presidents in recent decades, however, Cheney, because of his age and health, did not seek to become president at the end of Bush's two terms in office.

Thus, although the significance of the vice-president depends primarily upon the wishes of the president, the vice-presidency has tended to become an important executive institution.

Both the Senate and the House of Representatives are active bodies. Because the Senate is smaller, contains elected representatives of states rather than smaller districts, has a longer term of office, and has the authority to approve treaties and reject presidential nominees, the Senate is considered to be the more important of the two chambers. Many members of the House of Representatives are interested in seeking to become senators when the opportunity arises. Nevertheless, both chambers are active in the legislative process. Proposed legislation often contains different provisions when passed by each chamber. A joint conference committee is then established to find a compromise between the two bills. Bills must be passed in identical form in the two chambers before being presented to the president (see Figure 16-2). "Revenue bills"

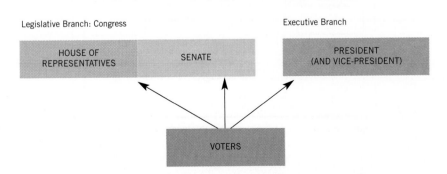

Legislative Branch: Congress

Executive Branch

HOUSE OF REPRESENTATIVES | SENATE

PRESIDENT (AND VICE-PRESIDENT)

VOTERS

FIGURE 16-1
A SIMPLIFIED DEPICTION OF THE AMERICAN PRESIDENTIAL SYSTEM

FIGURE 16-2

HOW A BILL BECOMES A LAW IN THE UNITED STATES

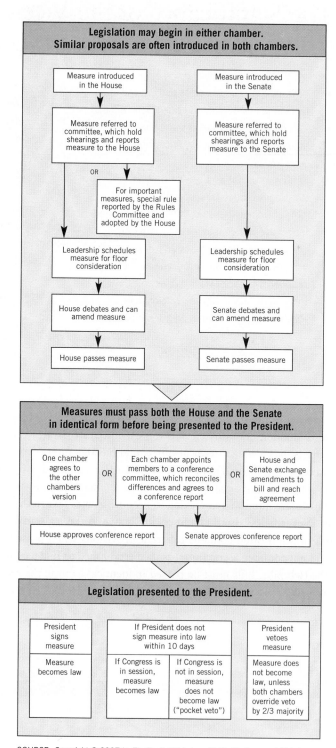

SOURCE: *Copyright © 2007 by TheCapitol.Net, Inc. All Rights Reserved. This image, section 8.01 from the Congressional Deskbook, by Michael Koempel and Judy Schneider, is reprinted with permission. www.CongressionalDeskbook.com.*

(those involving taxes and, in practice, government spending) have to be initiated in the lower chamber, the House of Representatives, although the Senate can propose amendments.

The American president does not attend Congress except to present the annual State of the Union address. Proposals for legislation must be presented by a member of Congress.[1] Although the executive branch prepares many of the legislative proposals that Congress considers, Congress is very active in modifying or rejecting the executive's proposals. Members of the American Congress have sizable staffs that are often involved in drafting and modifying legislative proposals. Congress is therefore active not only in approving legislation, but also in the development of legislation.

PRESIDENTIAL VETO As a check on the legislative power of Congress, the president has the authority to veto any law passed by Congress. Congress can override the **presidential veto,** but this requires a two-thirds majority in each body of Congress, and thus is quite rare.

The veto power of the president, although important, has limitations. The president can only veto a bill in its entirety, rather than approving some aspects and rejecting others.[2] Thus, if Congress is passing a bill that the president opposes, members of Congress will often include some provisions that the president wants in order to reduce the likelihood of a veto. Even if the president does not use the veto frequently, the anticipation of a veto will often lead Congress to modify its proposals to try to satisfy the president.

CONGRESS'S OVERSIGHT ROLE Congress exercises oversight of the activities of the public service because of its powers to investigate government activity. Public servants are frequently called to testify before Congressional committees. Both Congress and the president take an active role in determining the government's spending plans (unlike the system in Canada, where parliamentary approval is normally a formality).

PARTY DISCIPLINE Party discipline in the American Congress has traditionally not been very tight. Each of the two major American political parties usually contains quite a broad spectrum of persons with differing perspectives. As well, since the president and Cabinet do not need the support of a majority in Congress to stay in power, there is less pressure to maintain party discipline than in a parliamentary system.

Individual members of the U.S. Congress frequently vote as they see fit, or in the interests of the constituency they represent, rather than as members of a

United States House of Representatives
www.house.gov

United States Senate
www.senate.gov

PRESIDENTIAL VETO
The ability to prevent the passage of a bill. For example, the president of the U.S. has the authority to veto laws passed by Congress, although this veto can be overridden by a two-thirds majority in each House of Congress.

---

[1] In other countries, the president usually has the authority to introduce legislation to Congress and may be able to limit the ability of Congress to amend the proposed legislation.

[2] If the president simply does not sign a bill, it automatically becomes law within ten days. However, if Congress has adjourned within that time period, the bill does not become law (termed a "pocket veto"). In some American states, the governor possesses a line-item veto, allowing the governor to reject parts of the proposed legislation. Some countries give their president this powerful tool.

party team. This means that the president may not be able to get Congress to support his policies even when the president's party controls Congress. For example, after being elected in 1992, President Bill Clinton, a Democrat, was unable to persuade Congress to vote for legislation establishing a universal medical care system, even though the Democratic party had a majority in the House of Representatives and the Senate for his first two years in office. Similarly, when the Republicans controlled Congress from 2002 to 2006, Republican President George W. Bush was unable to get Congress to pass many of his proposals without major modifications, particularly concerning domestic political issues (Brady & Volden, 2006).

Conversely, a president faced with a Congress that has a majority of opposing party members has some ability to influence individual members of Congress regardless of their party affiliation. For example, in the early 1980s, Republican President Ronald Reagan was able to get much of his program adopted despite the control of Congress by the Democratic party. Reagan persuaded some conservative-minded Democrats of the virtues of his proposals. As well, by making his case directly to the American public, he created a favourable climate of opinion for his proposals, thus putting pressure on members of Congress to pass them.

Although party discipline is not as tight in the United States as in most parliamentary systems, it should not be concluded that parties are irrelevant. Members of a party do tend to vote the same way as the other members of their party. The parties in Congress have become somewhat more cohesive in the past few decades as the Democrats have become more consistently liberal or centrist and the Republicans more conservative. For example, an analysis of the voting records of the Senate from 2000 to 2002 found that all but one of the fifty Democratic senators took leftist (liberal) positions on the majority of issues while all but one of the fifty Republican senators took rightist (conservative) positions on the majority of issues. Nevertheless, some moderate Democrats voted with the Republicans when they took relatively moderate positions, and some moderate Republicans voted with the Democrats on other issues (Brady & Volden, 2006).

COMMITTEES A final major feature of the U.S. Congress is the importance of congressional committees. It is in the hundreds of committees and subcommittees of the House and Senate that legislative proposals are most thoroughly debated, modified, or eliminated. In some cases, legislation is drafted by a congressional committee. The chairs of these powerful committees are chosen by the majority party in each House; the chair is often the party member who has served on that committee the longest. The committee chairs are often quite independent-minded and thus do not always feel the need to adhere to their party's positions.

In general, the passing of legislation in the American system is a very difficult process. There are a large number of obstacles to overcome. Presidents have to use all of their persuasive capabilities and negotiating skills in order to have their proposals accepted. As President George H.W. Bush said, perhaps with some exaggeration, it was easier to deal with Iraqi dictator Saddam Hussein than with the U.S. Congress. Within Congress, proposed legislation has to pass a variety of hurdles. For example, a committee chair may refuse to allocate time to discuss a bill. In the Senate, filibusters[3] are quite common, as each senator can speak on a proposal for as long as he or she wants. Senators are quite willing to use this power to express their opposition to a particular piece of legislation. A motion of cloture to limit debate must be passed by a 60 percent majority. Through the use of a filibuster, forty-one of the one hundred senators can prevent legislation from coming to a vote. Thus, controversial legislation will not likely be voted on in the Senate unless some support can be found in both political parties. To surmount the obstacles, a proposed bill, whether initiated in Congress or prepared by the president's staff, will typically be changed considerably as compromises and additions are made to gain the support of various persons and interests.

The Balance between Executive and Legislative Power

Does the presidential system in the United States provide a suitable balance of powers between the executive and legislative branches so that each is able to check the power of the other? At times, the balance has shifted in favour of Congress such that the system might be best described as a congressional system. At other times, the president has been dominant such that some have described the system as having an "imperial presidency," with the president becoming like a powerful monarch. In particular, as the United States became heavily involved militarily in global affairs and as concerns about national security increased, presidents have tended to assume greater powers, as discussed in Box 16-3, War Powers.

Is a Presidential System Preferable
to a Parliamentary System?

Evaluating governing systems is complex. A variety of criteria can be used, and different people are likely to have different views as to which criteria are most important. There is considerable variation in how any particular system of governing operates, not only as a result of different specific constitutional provisions, but also as a result of differences in the party system, the electoral system, and political culture as well as the broader circumstances and distribution of power that exists in any particular country. There are not only variations in how a particular system operates in particular countries, but also

---

3 Filibusters are not allowed for some budgetary and trade bills.

BOX 16-3

War Powers

There is an inherent tension in the American governing system concerning the use of military force. The president is commander-in-chief of the Armed Forces, and there is an expectation that the president will take a leading role in international affairs and matters relating to national security. However, it is the constitutional responsibility of Congress to decide whether to declare war and to provide the funds needed by the military. To circumvent the constitutional requirement concerning a declaration of war by Congress, presidents have, on a number of occasions, ordered military actions without a formal declaration of war.

In 1964, after alleged attacks on U.S. naval vessels by North Vietnam, President Johnson convinced almost all members of Congress to pass the Gulf of Tonkin Resolution, authorizing the president to take "all necessary actions to protect our Armed Forces." War was never declared, but this resolution was used to justify sending more than one-half million troops to fight in Vietnam and to engage in the bombing and invasion of Cambodia. As the lengthy conflict continued and the Senate Foreign Relations Committee found that they had been deceived about some of the attacks on American military vessels, strong opposition to the war effort grew among the public and many members of Congress.

With President Nixon discredited by the "Watergate" scandal and the attempts of his administration to stifle legitimate dissent, Congress decided to restrict the powers of the president by passing the War Powers Act in 1973. This Act (which was passed by overriding President Nixon's veto) requires that the president notify Congress when troops are to be sent into foreign combat and that troops be brought home within sixty days (or ninety days, if necessary) unless Congress declares war or extends the length of troop involvement. As well, the president is required to answer any questions about the conflict that are raised by Congress and to submit periodic reports.

The War Powers Act, while viewed by the executive as an infringement on its constitutional powers, has not been a serious obstacle to presidents deciding to engage in various foreign conflicts. By raising fears about a threat to national security (real or artificial), presidents have not had difficulty winning support from Congress to take whatever actions the president deems necessary, thus circumventing the power of Congress to declare war (Hess, 2005). For example, in 2002, Congress voted by a large margin to authorize the use of the Armed Forces against Iraq, "to defend the national security of the United States against the continuing threat posed by Iraq." An attempt by the majority in Congress in April 2007 to pass legislation requiring that the president start withdrawing troops from Iraq later that year was vetoed by President Bush. Although Congress could end a conflict by not approving the funds needed for troop engagement, this would be politically risky, as it would be portrayed as not supporting the troops.

differences over time within a particular country. Nevertheless, we can discuss some potential strengths and weaknesses in the presidential system by comparing it to the parliamentary system discussed in Chapter 15.

LEADERSHIP AND DECISIVE ACTION Those who prefer a presidential system often view it as providing strong leadership. The president leads the executive branch of government and is secure in office. Being elected, the

◄ American presidents have found ways to avoid the constitutional provision that only Congress has the authority to declare war.

president can claim to speak for the people of the country as a whole. As head of state, a president can usually count on the respect and support of the people (although some presidents have lost the respect of the majority of people during their term in office). However, given the independence of Congress, it is difficult for a president to ensure that a coherent set of policies are adopted.

In a parliamentary system, the prime minister and Cabinet are capable of decisive action in a majority government situation because of their domination of the legislative branch. However, where no party has a majority, bargaining and negotiating among parties is required to gain majority support for legislative proposals. In some countries, the parliamentary system has been characterized by series of weak and unstable governments because of a highly fragmented party system in which stable coalitions cannot be formed.

DEMOCRATIC ELECTION The presidential system is sometimes viewed as more democratic than the parliamentary system, as the president is elected by the people. However, Cabinet secretaries do not hold elected public office. In parliamentary systems, it is the party that chooses a leader to become prime minister depending upon the success of that party in an election.

REPRESENTATIVENESS Members of Congress have greater independence than members of Parliament to represent the population and interests of their district or state, as they are not as tightly bound by party discipline as is the case in most parliamentary systems. In contrast, the party discipline characteristic of parliamentary systems limits the ability of members of the House of Commons to represent their constituents. However, the Cabinet as a collective decision-making body is more important in parliamentary systems than in presidential systems, and prime ministers usually try to make their Cabinets representative of what they consider to be the most important sectors of the population.

RESPONSIVENESS Individual members of Congress are often very responsive to the voters or important interests in the districts or states they represent. However, the difficulties in passing legislation can make the governing system slow to respond to the wishes of the electorate as a whole. Although the American president may be responsive to the public in order to gain re-election, the term limit means that the president does not have to be responsive to public opinion in the second term. In parliamentary systems, the prime minister and the governing party have an incentive to be responsive to the voters to secure re-election and, in a majority government situation, have the ability to respond quickly to the views and demands of the citizenry.

ACCOUNTABILITY The president and Cabinet do not sit in Congress and are not accountable to Congress. Although the U.S. Congress can investigate executive actions, presidents and other executive officials may invoke "executive privilege" to try to avoid questioning of their actions. With authority split between the executive and the legislative branches in a presidential system, each branch can try to shift blame to the other for any problems, making it difficult for voters to hold the government accountable.

A parliamentary system makes government responsible to the House of Commons for its actions. However, in a majority government situation, the governing party doesn't normally need to worry about maintaining the necessary support of the House of Commons. Nevertheless, because the prime minister and Cabinet actively participate in the House of Commons, the public has an opportunity to assess the performance of the government through the ongoing debate between government and the opposition in the House. For example, Canada's Question Period allows the opposition parties to put the prime minister and Cabinet "on the spot" concerning what they claim are serious problems in governing.

OPENNESS The presidential system tends to be more open than the parliamentary system. Rather than policy choices being made in the secrecy of Cabinet, Congress plays an active and more public role in developing and modifying policy proposals. Policy differences between Congress and the president are often publicly aired. This transparency may facilitate greater public participation in the policy-making process and make the process more inclusive of differing interests and viewpoints. However, the openness of the American political system makes the system more susceptible to influence by groups with specific interests that may be able to prevent laws for the common good from being passed.

FLEXIBILITY Presidential systems tend to be less flexible than parliamentary systems (Linz, 1994). The fixed terms of office in presidential systems can make it difficult to resolve impasses between the executive and legislative branches, as an election cannot be held before the end of the term of each elected politician. In parliamentary systems, a government that is unable to retain the confidence of the majority in the House of Commons can be removed from office. Likewise, prime ministers that lose the support of their party or caucus can be forced or pressured to step down.

EXPERIENCE The American presidential system often features "outsiders" being elected as president. Former military leaders and popular personalities are sometimes able to appeal to the public at large even if they do not have a strong connection to a particular party. Although this may bring a fresh perspective to national politics, it means that the president may have very limited experience in national politics and government. For example, although Bill Clinton and George W. Bush had political experience as state governors, neither had experience in national politics before becoming president. As well, since a president is unrestricted in the choice of Cabinet secretaries, some of those chosen have had little or no political experience. Prime ministers usually have extensive political experience. However, some Canadian prime ministers (for example, Brian Mulroney) have come to office with little or no experience as an elected politician. Unlike parliamentary systems, in which a potential prime minister can gain experience and knowledge by serving as leader of an opposition party, presidential systems offer no formal role for losing presidential candidates.[4]

SEMI-PRESIDENTIAL SYSTEMS

A number of countries have adopted systems of governing involving a mixture of parliamentary and presidential features, which are often referred to as **semi-presidential systems**.[5] France, which adopted this system in 1958, is the best-known example. A number of other European countries, including Russia, Austria, Poland, Portugal, Slovakia, Bulgaria, Croatia, Romania, and Ukraine, have also adopted this system. The same is true of a number of

SEMI-PRESIDENTIAL SYSTEM
A governmental system in which an elected president shares power with a prime minister and Cabinet, which usually need to retain the support of the elected legislature.

---

[4] An exception is Nicaragua, where the runner-up in the presidential election automatically receives a seat in the National Assembly.

[5] They are also referred to as "mixed," "hybrid," "parliamentary-presidential," or "premier-presidential" systems.

countries in other parts of the world, including Peru, Sri Lanka, Taiwan, Madagascar, Mozambique, Senegal, and Niger (Shugart, 2006).[6] In these systems, an elected president shares executive power with a prime minister. As in a presidential system, the president has a fixed term in office and can only be removed through an impeachment procedure. Unlike the head of state in a parliamentary system, the president wields substantial powers, including the power to appoint (and, in some countries, dismiss) the prime minister (see Box 16-4, a Family Affair). As well, the president generally has the power (in some cases with limitations) to dissolve the elected legislature and require that an election be held. As in a parliamentary system, the prime minister and Cabinet (the government) are responsible to an elected legislative body and usually need to maintain the support of that body.

BOX 16-4

A Family Affair

In July 2006, Poland became governed by identical twins who held the offices of president and prime minister.

In the September 2005 parliamentary election, Jaroslaw Kaczynski led the Law and Justice party to a narrow victory. However, he did not want to assume the position of prime minister, so as to avoid affecting the December 2005 presidential election in which his brother, Lech, was a candidate for the same party. When the prime minister resigned in July 2006, President Lech Kaczynski appointed his brother as prime minister, a choice that was ratified by the Polish Parliament.

Although the twins campaigned to restore morality, they reportedly switched identities in high school to take exams for each other (Easton, 2005).

Jaroslaw Kaczynski resigned in October 2007 after his party lost a parliamentary election.

In July 2006, Polish President Lech Kaczyński appointed his identical twin brother as prime minister.

---

6 Some consider Ireland and Finland semi-presidential while others classify these countries as parliamentary because of the limited power of the president. South Korea and Sri Lanka are considered by some to be semi-presidential rather than presidential, although their prime ministers are not accountable to Parliament (Siaroff, 2003).

The French System

In France, the president is elected for a fixed five-year term. Unlike presidential and most semi-presidential systems, there is no formal limit to the number of terms that can be served.[7] The president appoints the prime minister, normally from the majority party or a coalition of parties that has the majority in the elected National Assembly. The president, with advice from the prime minister, appoints the members of the Council of Ministers (Cabinet), as well as top public, military, and judicial officials. The president chairs the meetings of the Council of Ministers. As in presidential systems, ministers do not sit in the Assembly. The Assembly, elected for a maximum five-year term, can censure the prime minister and Council of Ministers and force them to resign, but cannot censure the president or force a presidential election. However, unlike the American presidential system, the French president can dissolve the Assembly and have a new Assembly election conducted (although another election cannot be held for at least one year). The French president cannot veto laws passed by the Assembly, but can refer a proposed law back to the Assembly one time for reconsideration and can also refer the law to the Constitutional Court.

The French president can call national referendums, determine when the National Assembly meets and what its agenda will be, assume emergency powers, and propose constitutional amendments. As well, the president has a leading role in foreign affairs, is responsible for negotiating and ratifying foreign treaties, and is commander-in-chief of the armed forces (Elgie, 2005).

The French system was set up with the intention of making the president a powerful figure. Indeed, when the Assembly has a majority of members from the same party as the president (or parties that support the president), the president tends to be the dominant figure in the French government. The prime minister, in this situation, is usually someone who has personal loyalty to the president. Although the president does not have the constitutional authority to dismiss a prime minister, presidents have been able to encourage prime ministers of their own party to resign (in some cases, by requiring them to sign an undated letter of resignation before taking office).

However, if the majority in the Assembly represents a party that has a different perspective than the president, the president will find it necessary to choose the leader of that party as prime minister, as the government must have the support of the majority in the Assembly. The president can dissolve the Assembly and call an election, but if the election leads to a similar result the president will have to live with a government that has a different political perspective. In this situation, termed **cohabitation**, the president is forced to share power with the prime minister and Cabinet. From 1986 to 1988 and 1993 to 1995, Socialist President François Mitterand shared power with the conservative parties that

COHABITATION
The sharing of power between the French president and prime minister that occurs when the Assembly is controlled by a party opposed to the president.

---

[7] This may change, as President Sarkozy has indicated that he favours a limit to the number of terms a president can serve.

controlled the Assembly, while from 1997 to 2002, President Jacques Chirac, a conservative, shared power with Socialist Prime Minister Lionel Jospin.[8] In this situation, the prime minister has a strong ability to determine the domestic policies that will be adopted, regardless of the views of the president (Elgie, 2005).

The Russian System

Russia also has a semi-presidential system in which the president, elected for a fixed four-year term and a maximum of two terms, has considerable power to issue decrees that have the effect of laws without the approval of Parliament, and can also call referendums. The president is responsible for appointing the Cabinet, chairs the Cabinet, and has an unrestricted power to dismiss the government. The president also has developed a large administrative staff to provide the president with considerable governing capability. The president's nomination of a prime minister has to be approved by Parliament. If the president's choice is rejected three times by Parliament, Parliament is dissolved and a parliamentary election results.

President Boris Yeltsin (1991–1999) at times faced considerable opposition from Parliament. President Vladimir Putin (2000–2008)—with the support of the leading party in parliament, United Russia, and a high level of popular support—became a very powerful president. Indeed, under Putin, Russia reverted, to a considerable extent, to an authoritarian dictatorship with substantial control of the media and suppression of dissent. Putin has continued to be powerful by being appointed prime minister by his hand-picked presidential successor, and may seek to become president again.

Evaluation of Semi-Presidential Systems

Do semi-presidential systems combine the best features of the parliamentary and presidential systems? Or is the dual executive, each with significant powers, a recipe for instability? An early version of this system, Germany's Weimar Republic (established after the First World War), had difficulty dealing with the serious problems the country faced. This difficulty contributed to the coming to power of Adolf Hitler and the Nazi party (Linz, 1994). Unlike most contemporary semi-presidential systems, the Weimar constitution gave unlimited power to the president to dissolve Parliament. This allowed the president to ignore the views of Parliament (Morgan-Jones & Schleiter, 2004).

France, which changed in 1958 from a parliamentary system to a semi-presidential system after decades of political instability, is typically viewed as a success story, even though its government has functioned in quite different

---

[8] The likelihood of this occurring again has been reduced by a change that schedules the regular election of the Assembly shortly after the election of the president. In 2007, for example, the election of president Sarkozy was followed several weeks later by the election of a majority of his party and its allies to the Assembly.

ways depending upon whether the president has the support of the majority in the Assembly. Nevertheless, the French system is sometimes criticized for giving the president excessive power. Russia is a clearer case of a semi-presidential system that can allow excessive power to the president. However, in this case, the lack of a strong democratic culture along with the specific features of the governing system and the popularity of the president facilitate the exercise of strong presidential powers. On the other hand, in countries such as Portugal, Poland, Romania, Bulgaria, and Taiwan, the powers of the president are quite limited and thus the semi-presidential system leans in a parliamentary direction (Siaroff, 2003).

The governing responsibility of both the elected president and the prime minister and Cabinet that have the support of the Assembly can lead to tension and gridlock. However, there is flexibility in that the president can govern (for example, by appointing a non-partisan Cabinet) when the legislature is fragmented among different parties, and thus unable to provide majority support to the government. This has been found to be useful in a number of the newer democracies, particularly those in Eastern Europe, that have adopted this system (Schleiter & Morgan-Jones, 2005).

Summary and Conclusion

The term *presidential system* can be misleading. The president controls the executive branch of government and serves as both head of state and head of government. However, the separation of powers allows each of the three branches of government to check the powers of the other branches. At times, in the United States the president has tended to be more powerful than Congress. At other times, Congress has asserted its powers and limited the power of the president. Generally, however, although presidents typically dominate in terms of foreign and military policy, power is more diffused in a presidential system than in a Westminster-style parliamentary system where majority governments are common. The sharing of powers between the president and Congress usually makes bargaining and compromises between the president and Congress necessary in order to make governing decisions. Thus, some political scientists have suggested that it would be more accurate to describe the American system of government as a presidential–congressional system rather than a presidential system.

To a considerable extent the power of a president is dependent on the president's ability to persuade the public and individual members of Congress of the merits of a particular policy. As head of state as well as head of government, a president can successfully claim to speak on behalf of the national interest, as long as the president retains the respect of the people. Because individual members of Congress tend to represent state or district interests, it can be difficult for Congress to take coherent action for the common good of the country as a whole.

Semi-presidential systems have both a democratically elected president with significant powers and a prime minister and Cabinet that are responsible to an elected legislature. Because the elected legislature can be dissolved before its term is up, there is somewhat greater flexibility than in a pure presidential system, where both the president and the Congress have fixed terms in office.

There is considerable variability in semi-presidential systems in terms of the constitutional provisions of different countries; how these provisions operate in practice; and, within individual countries, whether the president has the support of the majority in Parliament. As with all systems of governing, the actual functioning of semi-parliamentary systems is dependent on such factors as the nature of the political party system, the context within which the governing system was established, and the personalities of the leading political figures (Elgie, 1999).

Key Terms

Checks and balances 375

Cohabitation 389

Congress 375

House of Representatives 378

Impeachment 377

Presidential system 375

Presidential veto 381

Semi-presidential system 387

Senate (United States) 378

Separation of powers 375

Discussion Questions

1. Do you think it would be best for a new democracy to adopt a parliamentary, presidential, or semi-presidential system?

2. What criteria are most important in evaluating different systems of governing?

3. Is Canada's parliamentary system preferable to an American-style presidential system?

4. Is there an appropriate balance between legislative and executive power in the United States?

5. Does the semi-presidential system create a hybrid that contains the best or the worst of the parliamentary and presidential systems?

Further Reading

Aberbach, J.D., & Peterson, M.A. (Eds.). *The executive branch.* Oxford: Oxford University Press, 2005.

Brady, D.W., & Volden, C. *Revolving gridlock: Politics and policy from Jimmy Carter to George W. Bush,* 2nd ed. Boulder, CO: Westview Press, 2006.

Cohen, R.E. *Washington at work: Back rooms and clean air,* 2nd ed. Needham Heights, MA: Allyn and Bacon, 1995.

Elgie, R. (Ed.). *Semi-presidentialism in Europe.* Oxford: Oxford University Press, 1999.

Fiorina, M. *Divided government,* 2nd ed. Boston: Allyn & Bacon, 1996.

Fisher, L. *The politics of shared power: Congress and the executive,* 4th ed. College Station, TX: A & M University Press, 1998.

Kelley, D.R. (Ed.). *Divided power: The presidency, Congress, and the formation of American foreign policy.* Fayetteville, AK: The University of Arkansas Press, 2005.

Lijphart, A. (Ed.). *Parliamentary versus presidential government.* Oxford: Oxford University Press, 1992.

Linz, J.J., & Valenzuela, A. (Eds.). *The failure of presidential democracy.* Baltimore, MD: Johns Hopkins University Press, 1994.

Reich, R. *Locked in the Cabinet.* New York: Vintage, 1998.

Shugart, M.S., & Carey, J.M. *Presidents and assemblies: Constitutional design and electoral dynamics.* New York: Cambridge University, 1992.

Chapter 17

PUBLIC POLICY AND PUBLIC ADMINISTRATION

PHOTO ABOVE: Tommy Douglas, the man who fought to get Canada a free public medical care plan, would have lost a leg as a boy had it not been for the compassion of a visiting doctor.

1. discuss general perspectives on public policy
2. analyze the policy process
3. describe the characteristics of bureaucracies
4. evaluate public administration reforms

As a young boy growing up in the first decades of the twentieth century, Tommy Douglas was diagnosed with osteomyelitis in his right leg. Because his family was not wealthy and could not pay for proper treatment, he would have lost his leg if not for the compassion of a visiting doctor. This inspired Douglas's lifelong fight for a free, public medical care plan that would cover all Canadians, rich or poor.

As the Co-operative Commonwealth Federation (CCF) premier of Saskatchewan, Douglas instituted universal hospital insurance in 1946. His government brought in a public medical care insurance system in 1962, despite opposition from the North American medical profession that culminated in a strike by doctors. Later, as leader of the New Democratic Party (NDP), Douglas campaigned for a national medicare system. With the support of the NDP, the Liberal minority government of Lester Pearson agreed in 1966 to provide federal funding for provinces that established medicare programs under federal guidelines, despite the opposition of some provincial governments. Douglas's dream was fulfilled in 1971, when all provinces had joined the program and all residents of Canada were covered by medicare.

The medicare system has become a symbol of national pride and identity for many Canadians. Medicare is seen as the leading example of how Canada is a more caring and egalitarian society than the United States, where about one-sixth of the population is not covered by a medical insurance plan and thus has trouble paying for costly medical treatment. Although many Americans are dissatisfied with their medical system, attempts to move toward universal health care coverage in the U.S. have been resisted by the powerful health insurance industry's campaign against "socialized medicine." Reform proposals developed by Hillary Rodham Clinton and put forward by Democratic President Bill Clinton failed to come to a vote in Congress despite his party's majority in that body.

This chapter introduces the study of public policy and public administration by examining several basic perspectives that attempt to explain the general patterns of public policy, particularly in terms of the distribution of power. We then look at the details of the policy process, focusing particularly on the Canadian case. Finally, the administrative structure of government that plays an important part in both the policy-making process and in implementing the policies that are adopted is examined in the last part of this chapter.

PUBLIC POLICY

Making public policy is a key aspect of governing. **Public policy** has been defined as "a course of action or inaction chosen by public authorities to address a given problem or interrelated set of problems" (Pal, 1992, p. 2). A public policy generally involves a series of decisions or actions to try to achieve a particular objective.

Although policies may be intended to deal with a problem, we should not assume that they will be successful in achieving their objective. For example, many cities have dealt with the problem of traffic congestion by building freeways. Building freeways, however, encourages people to become more dependent on cars, often leads to greater automobile usage, and may eventually result in increasing congestion.

In some cases, government may deliberately choose inaction to avoid controversy. For example, Canadian governments have often been reluctant to deal with difficult moral issues such as abortion and homosexual rights, preferring to let the courts deal with such issues by using the Charter of Rights and Freedoms.

Understanding what government does and how it affects our lives involves both looking at the broad set of forces that set the context for public policy and examining the details of the processes that lead to the adoption of specific policies. Among the broad set of forces are the ideas and ideologies that affect how those involved in policy-making think about public policy problems and the general approaches they take in dealing with those problems. The ideological perspectives we examined in chapters 5 and 6 play an important role in affecting how the various individuals and groups that are involved in policy-making decide what problems to address, how those problems are defined, and what general patterns of policies can be found in any political system. Further, since various individuals and groups have different, often competing views about what government should do, we need to consider the distribution of power and the way that different groups attempt to influence the general direction of public policy. Developing public policy is not only a process by which government officials try to determine which policy is "best" in some technical way, but also a political process that reflects the contending views and interests of different groups in society and different governmental institutions.

GENERAL PERSPECTIVES

There are a variety of widely differing general perspectives concerning the policy-making process and the outcomes of the policy process in democratic countries. Each of the approaches gives a different answer to why government acts the way it does and who tends to benefit from the actions of government (Brooks, 1998).

As discussed in Chapter 1, the *pluralist perspective* views government policies as the outcome of competition among a wide variety of organized groups that seek to protect and promote the interests of their members. Some groups may be more influential than others on particular issues, but no group has a dominant influence on a wide range of policies. Business interests have many resources that they can use to exert influence, but, pluralist theory argues, a variety of other groups and interests have some resources they can use to influence policy if they use those resources skilfully (Graefe, 2007). Further, the pluralist perspective views government as not systematically biased in favour of any particular group or interest. Politicians, it is argued, try to develop policies that satisfy a wide variety of groups.

Public choice theory assumes that all individuals involved in politics (including politicians, government employees, interest group leaders, and voters) are rationally attempting to maximize their own individual interests or preferences. Parties and politicians wanting to maximize their power by winning elections will adopt policy positions preferred by the majority of voters or those voters who are crucial to the outcome of an election. Public policies, in this view, generally reflect the choices made by voters. Public choice theorists often argue that this leads to excessive government spending as politicians and parties compete with one another by making expensive promises to gain votes.

Neo-Marxist theory views politics as reflecting the conflicts that result from the way society is organized to produce goods. Capitalist societies are viewed as fundamentally divided along class lines. Based on the unequal power of different classes over how wealth is produced and distributed, people organize themselves to challenge or maintain the capitalist system and the policies that sustain it. Some contemporary neo-Marxists extend this analysis to argue that capitalism also creates relations of inequality among individuals based on gender, race, ethnicity, and sexual orientation (Graefe, 2007).

The state in neo-Marxist theory can be viewed as a space in which the struggle of different social forces occurs, with the policies that are adopted by government reflecting the unequal power relations between the dominant capitalist forces and subordinate groups.[1] Economic globalization further enhances the dominance of capitalist interests and increases the pressure for policies that favour capitalist interests based on the argument that such policies are needed if a country is to be competitive in the global economy (Graefe, 2007).

State-centred theory views public policies as reflecting, to a considerable extent, the preferences and priorities of those in important positions of authority within various state institutions. Disputes over policies, in this view, often

PUBLIC CHOICE THEORY
A perspective based on the assumption that all political actors rationally pursue their own individual interests or preferences. Public policies will generally reflect the choices made by voters.

NEO-MARXIST THEORY
A perspective that views politics as reflecting the conflicts that result from the way society is organized to produce goods. Public policies in a capitalist society will reflect the unequal power relations between the dominant capitalist forces and subordinate groups.

STATE-CENTRED THEORY
This perspective views public policies as reflecting, to a considerable extent, the preferences and priorities of those in important positions of authority within various state institutions.

---

[1] In traditional Marxist theory as developed by Marx and Engels, the state is often described as an instrument of the "ruling class" of capitalists to defend their property and interests.

arise out of the internal struggles and conflicts among different state institutions. In contrast to pluralist, public choice, and neo-Marxist perspectives, state officials are seen as having considerable autonomy from social forces and an ability to gain support for the policies they prefer. The state-centred perspective tends to view senior public servants as being of particular importance because of their permanence and expertise.

Finally, the *elitist perspective* (discussed in Chapter 1) sees policies as made by, and reflecting the interests of, those who hold the top positions in powerful institutions. Depending on the country, this power elite may include one or more of the leaders of government, the economy, religion, and the military. For example, G.W. Domhoff (2006) argues that the leaders of large corporations rule the United States through their influence on government and their appointment to key government positions. In the elitist perspective, citizens do not have much effective power, even in democratic countries, as elites manipulate voters to protect their power and use the state for their own interests.

Evaluation

There is no consensus among political scientists as to which of the general perspectives (and numerous variants) is most useful for understanding public policy. The pluralist perspective has been modified by those who argue that business interests have a "privileged position" from which to influence policy because of the importance to government of maintaining the confidence of the business community to create jobs and economic prosperity (Lindblom, 1977).[2] As well, it has been pointed out that the pluralist perspective was developed to provide a description (perhaps idealized) of the American political system and thus is less applicable in other countries. For example, in a number of democratic countries (such as Austria, Sweden, and Germany) there is, to varying extents, active collaboration between the state and selected major interests (usually national representatives of business and labour) to set the direction of the political community, particularly in terms of economic and social policies. In such **corporatist systems**, the state attempts to provide direction for the major interests and only selected interests have a major influence on public policy.

Public choice theory can be criticized for its assumption that citizens determine the policies of government through their voting choices. Political parties often do not adopt clear policy positions in election campaigns. Many voters do not carefully examine the positions of parties in deciding how to vote. And, governments do not always act in accordance with their election promises.

Neo-Marxism can be criticized for paying insufficient attention to the effects on public policy of factors other than those that relate to the conflicts

CORPORATIST SYSTEM
A political system in which the state actively collaborates with selected major interests to set the direction for the political community, particularly in terms of economic and social policies.

---

[2] This modification is often labelled "neo-pluralism."

generated by the capitalist system. As well, like the pluralist perspective and public choice theory, it generally does not pay sufficient attention to the importance of actors within the state in affecting public policy. State-centred theory has the opposite problem: it tends to downplay the influence of social forces on the policies adopted by government. Likewise, the elitist perspective tends to ignore the significance of elections, parties, interest groups, and social movements. Further, the elitist perspective tends to overemphasize the cohesiveness of elite groups, thus giving insufficient attention to the disagreements and bargaining that goes on between different elite groups.

Overall, none of the theoretical approaches, while useful, seems to fully account for the general patterns of public policy. The best explanations of policy may differ from one policy area to another, from one country to another, and from one time to another. For example, foreign and defence policy might be best understood in terms of state-centred theory, while the pluralist, public choice, and neo-Marxist theories may be more useful in understanding economic and social welfare policies.

Other Factors

The general perspectives focus on who is powerful in affecting public policy and obtaining the outcomes that are in their interests. However, understanding public policy also requires attention to the role of ideas, ideologies, and the ways in which policy problems are defined and discussed.

For example, in the area of social policy, the problems of the disadvantaged were historically viewed as primarily matters of charity, and thus were often not thought of as matters needing substantial government action. As was noted in Chapter 3, the Great Depression of the 1930s led many to think about inequalities in terms of the defects of the capitalist system. Government came to be seen as responsible for rectifying these defects by providing minimum standards of living and protection against economic hardships. The welfare state approach, which often took the form of providing benefits to all citizens, was challenged by the ideology of neo-liberalism (discussed in Chapter 5), which focuses on the virtues of markets. Neo-liberalism views various government social programs as interfering with the free-market economy, particularly by reducing the incentive to work. The problems of the poor are seen as a result of their personal irresponsibility and dependence on the state.

Although neo-liberal ideas are still influential, there has been a tendency in recent years to view government social spending as "social investment." That is, child-care programs, parental leave, education, and health care investments are seen as helping to prepare individuals for employment or entrepreneurial activity in a globalized, knowledge-based economy. Instead of viewing social programs as redistributing wealth or as a drain on the economy, different types of social programs are often proposed and justified in terms of investments in future prosperity (Saint-Martin, 2007). Although these different orientations to social policy reflect, in part, the interests of different groups in society, they have also become, at various times, the dominant way of thinking about policy, affecting both policy-makers and the public.

International agreements play an increasingly important role in affecting the policies adopted by individual countries. International environmental agreements, for example, require that governments phase out the use of ozone-depleting chemicals and prohibit trade in products made from endangered species.

Trade agreements are particularly controversial because people hold different ideological views about free trade (see Box 17-1, Turtles and Trade). From the

BOX 17-1

Turtles and Trade

Protesters dressed up as sea turtles were an incongruous sight at the 1999 anti-globalization demonstrations that shut down a meeting of the World Trade Organization (WTO) in Seattle. But the flamboyant costumes were a vivid symbol of protesters' concern for an endangered species.

The WTO oversees a set of agreements that create legally binding rules and obligations on most of the countries of the world to achieve the objective of global free trade. The rules prevent countries from discriminating against the goods and services of other member countries. Dispute settlement panels can penalize offending countries for non-compliance with the rules.

In 1997, India, Malaysia, Pakistan, and Thailand took a complaint to the WTO concerning an American law banning the import of shrimp caught by trawlers that did not use devices to prevent harm to sea turtles, an endangered species. A dispute settlement panel of the WTO upheld the complaint, ruling that the American law resulted in a discriminatory trade practice that worked to the advantage of American fishers.*

The North American Free Trade Agreement, involving Canada, the United States, and Mexico, goes further by allowing businesses to sue the governments of any of the three countries if they adopt trade-restrictive policies that cause them to

lose business opportunities or future profitability. For example, Ohio-based S.D. Myers Corporation, a hazardous waste disposal firm, successfully sued the Canadian government to compensate it for the Canadian policy banning the export of PCBs, a potentially toxic chemical. By banning the export of PCBs, the Canadian government reduced the potential profits that S.D. Myers would obtain by processing Canadian PCBs at its American plant. Likewise, the Vancouver-based Methanex Corporation sued the American government for nearly one billion dollars because California banned the fuel additive MTBE, which is made from methanol that Methanex produces. California claimed that MTBE contaminates groundwater and soil through leaking storage tanks.

The cases of sea turtles and toxic chemicals illustrate an important issue: trade agreements can make it more difficult for governments to adopt such policies as strict environmental measures if they are deemed to be undue limitations on trade.

The original ruling stated that "like goods" (similar foreign or domestic products) have to be treated the same, regardless of whether or not the good was produced in an environmentally friendly manner. An appeal panel upheld the original ruling on the grounds that the United States had discriminated against Asian countries by providing only Caribbean countries with assistance to deal with the sea turtle problem.

neo-liberal perspective, trade agreements are for the common good of the world as a whole. They allow the poorer countries to have access to the markets of the richer countries and thus assist the poorer countries in developing their economies—as well as giving businesses in the richer countries access to new markets.

Those who are critical of the neo-liberal perspective argue that trade agreements limit the ability of governments to regulate business for the common good (for example, by making it more difficult to adopt environmental regulations or by restricting the import of goods produced in sweatshops). As well, by protecting the rights of corporations, some trade agreements can make it difficult for governments to use public provision of services as a policy instrument if such services are already provided by private business.

THE POLICY PROCESS

Moving from broad-scale generalizations about public policy, we can examine the details of the policy process, which is often analyzed in terms of a sequence of steps such as the following:

1. agenda setting
2. policy formulation
3. decision making
4. policy legitimation
5. policy implementation
6. policy evaluation

Agenda Setting

In any sizable political community, innumerable problems and concerns could potentially become a subject for public policy. However, only a small number of problems can be dealt with at any time. **Agenda setting** refers to the process by which potential problems come to the attention of policy-makers.

There are a variety of potential influences on agenda setting, including political parties, interest groups, social movements, and the mass media. Crises, particularly crises emphasized by the mass media, can also affect the level of attention given to different problems. For example, the deaths caused by contaminated drinking water in Walkerton, Ontario, in 2000 turned the problem of water safety into a major political issue.

Not all issues on the government's policy agenda originate from the demands of various groups and individuals in society. Various departments and agencies of government may initiate the policy process by raising issues that the public may not necessarily view as serious problems. Individual politicians may act as **policy entrepreneurs** by trying to promote a particular issue or cause to advance their political career. In such cases of "inside initiation,"

AGENDA SETTING
The process by which potential problems come to the attention of policy-makers.

POLICY ENTREPRENEUR
Someone who is ready to push a pet policy proposal whenever an opportunity arises.

efforts may be made by the department, agency, or individual politician to persuade the public, as well as the government as a whole, that a particular problem should be given priority in the policy process (Hessing, Howlett, & Summerville, 2005).

PUBLIC VERSUS GOVERNMENT AGENDA A distinction is sometimes made between the issues that are considered important by the public—the public agenda—and the issues that are considered important by the government—the governmental agenda. There is usually some relationship between the public agenda and the governmental agenda, as political leaders want to be seen as dealing with issues that are deemed important by the public. Governments make extensive use of public opinion polling to keep track of public concerns.

However, the relationship between the two agendas is not always a close one. Governments may place a high priority on issues that are of little concern to the public at large—such as constitutional issues in Canada—but are of particular importance to the processes of governing. Political leaders may also give high priority to problems that can be easily labelled and have solutions that can work to their political advantage. Complex problems with no easy and uncontroversial solution may be ignored or downplayed.

Furthermore, politicians may give symbolic recognition to a problem or concern of the public without developing a substantial policy. For example, some political leaders have viewed the provision of subsidized child care as a low-priority issue. Although claiming that they fully support such a policy, many years were spent in "studying" the issue and providing limited funding.

Policy Formulation

POLICY FORMULATION
Developing and evaluating different courses of action to deal with a problem.

C.D. Howe Institute
www.cdhowe.org

The Fraser Institute
www.fraserinstitute.ca

Canadian Centre for Policy Alternatives
www.policyalternatives.ca

Canadian Policy Research Networks
www.cprn.org

Institute for Research on Public Policy
www.irpp.org

The **policy formulation** stage of the policy process involves developing and evaluating different courses of action to deal with a problem (Adolini & Blake, 2001). A variety of individuals and groups are typically involved at this point. Inside government, public servants in policy-oriented positions often play a leading role in developing possible policy options. Governments also often commission outside experts such as consultants, pollsters, and academics to help in the formulation of policy. Reports of Parliamentary Committees sometimes provide recommendations that are useful in policy formulation.

Interest groups concerned about a particular policy area often provide policy advice to government policy-makers. Think tanks (policy research organizations) such as the C.D. Howe Institute, the Fraser Institute, and the Canadian Centre for Policy Alternatives provide analyses of problems and make policy recommendations based on a particular ideological perspective or a particular set of interests. Other research organizations such as the Canadian Policy Research Networks and the Institute for Research on Public Policy attempt to provide a balanced treatment of policy issues.

OPENING THE PROCESS The policy formulation process in advanced democracies has generally moved toward the involvement of a larger number of participants. Rather than a tight and closed relationship between a government department or agency and a small number of leading interest groups, analysts now often characterize the involvement of governmental and non-governmental actors in the development of policies in particular policy areas as a **policy network**.[3] The membership in the policy network may change from issue to issue, and no one set of actors or interests is in complete control of the policy area (Heclo, 1978). The extent to which governmental actors play a leading or dominant role in policy formulation and the extent to which a variety of different interests have a significant role in policy formulation varies considerably from policy area to policy area and from one country to another (Howlett & Ramesh, 1995). Overall, there has been an increasing interest in having greater public involvement in the policy-making process, particularly by consulting with all "stakeholders" (those affected by a policy decision in the issue area).

DEFINING THE PROBLEM The problem that needs solving has to be defined before policies are developed, and the way the problem is defined is very important. Different definitions of a problem can lead to very different types of policies. Problems may be defined, sometimes in competing ways, at the agenda-setting stage. However, those involved in formulation may modify or transform the way the problem is defined as they develop policy options.

The formulation of policies often involves the development of different options to deal with the problem being addressed. Those developing policy then have to analyze the pros and cons of the different options. A tool that is often used to assess policy proposals is **cost–benefit analysis** (see Box 17-2, Sizing Things Up: Cost–Benefit Analysis).

POLICY INSTRUMENTS In formulating policy, government must consider a variety of different policy instruments (for example, taxes, subsidies, and regulations) in order to assess which instrument or set of instruments will be most likely to achieve the desired results. For example, in dealing with the problem of industrial pollution, a government may establish regulations that limit the amount of discharge allowed, provide subsidies to help companies pay for pollution control equipment, levy a tax on each unit of harmful emission that is released, or encourage industry to adopt voluntary guidelines on

POLICY NETWORK
The governmental and non-governmental actors that participate in the development of policies in a particular policy field.

Centre for Cyber Citizenship
www.policy.ca

Public Policy Forum
www.ppforum.ca

COST–BENEFIT ANALYSIS
An economic technique that determines whether, and to what extent, the benefits of a policy exceed the costs.

---

[3] A distinction is often made between a policy network, consisting of those actors who have a direct interest or involvement in a policy area, and a broader policy community, which also includes all groups and individuals who have a more general interest in a policy area. The assumption is that members of the policy network will tend to be more influential in policy formulation than other members of the policy community (Hessing, Howlett, & Summerville, 2005).

Sizing Things Up: Cost–Benefit Analysis

Cost–benefit analysis provides a means of comparing differing policy options and helps to ensure that a particular policy actually has a net benefit, particularly in monetary terms.

Cost–benefit analysis is an economic technique that determines whether, and to what extent, the benefits of a policy exceed the costs. Because it involves putting a monetary value on all of the consequences of the policy, there are limitations to the approach. Assigning a monetary value to all costs and benefits can be difficult or arbitrary. If, for example, the policy option being considered involves allowing forest companies to cut trees in an area of natural beauty, how does one value natural beauty? Is it something more than the number of tourist dollars that might be lost? Likewise, in deciding on a new highway speed-limit policy, what value does one put on the lives that might be saved by a lower speed limit? Is it something more than the expected lifetime earnings of crash victims?

It is also often difficult to predict the consequences of a policy. For example, rent control is designed to ensure that housing is affordable, but it may have the unintended effect of reducing apartment construction and increasing the conversion of rental units into individually owned condos. If insufficient rental units are then available, people looking to rent may have to pay large bribes to landlords in order to find accommodation.

Another complication of cost–benefit analysis is that the costs or benefits of a policy often fall unevenly among different groups of people. Consolidating waste disposal in one location may bring cost savings that benefit the political community as a whole—but for the people who live next to the dump, the negative impact may far outweigh the benefits.

Cost–benefit analysis is sometimes criticized for ignoring the ethical dimension of policy-making. Is it always right to take a particular course of action just because the calculation indicates that the benefits outweigh the costs? Should financial considerations be the only measure of what is the best policy option?

Finally, although cost–benefit analysis can apparently analyze policy options in a rational or scientific way while avoiding political considerations, this is often a false hope. Different analysts using different assumptions often come up with widely differing assessments of costs and benefits. For example, in discussions of whether or not Canada should ratify the Kyoto Protocol to reduce greenhouse gas emissions related to global climate change, there were massive differences in assessments of the costs and benefits of that policy. Not surprisingly, analyses commissioned by environmental groups determined that there would be net benefits if Canada reduced greenhouse gas emissions, while analyses conducted by petroleum producers determined that there would be massive costs to the Canadian economy. Similarly, policy analysts working for the government in Alberta, where limitations on greenhouse gas emissions would have the greatest negative economic effect, calculated that the costs would be much greater than did the policy analysts working for the Canadian government.

Although cost–benefit analysis can be a useful tool in policy-making, its limitations should be kept in mind as options are discussed and evaluated.

emission reductions. Regulations have been the major approach used by Canadian governments to deal with pollution, although in recent times voluntary guidelines have increasingly been used. Emission taxes have been a more important policy instrument in some European countries than in North America. A newer policy instrument is the use of tradeable emission permits.

◀ A variety of policy instruments can be used to deal with the problem of industrial pollution.

Permits to emit a certain quantity of pollutants are issued by government, but industrial facilities that do not use the full amount of their permits can trade or sell their unused allotment. Pollution is reduced by issuing a smaller number of permits to each facility each year. This instrument is viewed as a cost-effective method of dealing with pollution, as each company can calculate whether it is financially better to adopt pollution-reducing measures or buy permits from other companies.

The choice of policy instrument is affected by the nature of the problem that the policy is seeking to address. Some types of policy instruments are more effective in dealing with certain types of problems. As well, the choice of instruments may be affected by the ideological perspective of those in governing positions and in the electorate. Neo-liberals are more likely to favour instruments that provide the least government intervention and distortion of the free market. Social democrats are more likely to favour regulation of business activity. In addition, the choice of instruments may be affected by the ability of different interest groups to influence government. Business interests are more likely to favour voluntary guidelines, while environmental groups are more likely to favour strict government regulations and emission taxes to deal with pollution problems.

Decision Making

The decision-making stage involves choosing among a small number of different options or deciding to postpone the adoption of any policy. In parliamentary systems, policy decisions are generally made at the executive level—particularly by the prime minister and Cabinet or a Cabinet committee.

Traditionally, the advice of senior public servants strongly influenced the decision-making process. However, outside consultants have increasingly been used as an alternative source of policy advice. The political effects of different courses of action, such as the effects on the government's popularity, relationships with other governments, and overall goals, as well as their effects on power relationships within the governing party, are important factors in the minds of government decision-makers and their political advisers. Pressure from interest groups and the opinions of the public also have an influence on decision making.

Policy Legitimation

Although in a parliamentary system the prime minister and Cabinet have a key role in overseeing policy formulation and making policy decisions, laws and authorization for government spending and taxing have to be approved by Parliament. This approval not only fulfills important legal requirements, but also can be a form of **policy legitimation** (that is, it adds legitimacy to the policy).

Discussion of a proposed policy in a legislature may help to increase awareness of the policy, and the public may be reassured that there has been an airing of different views before the policy was adopted. As well, the process of legislative approval sometimes results in changes in the legislation needed to put the policy into effect. This may have the effect of appeasing some groups who are opposed to the legislation.

Policy Implementation

The formal adoption of a policy is not the end of the process. **Policy implementation** is a very important part of the policy process. The passage of a law or regulation to deal with a problem does not necessarily mean that the action is carried out. Typically, programs need to be designed and money, staff, and expertise must be provided. As well, regulations need to be adopted to establish the rules needed to implement and administer the law.

Bureaucratic discretion is often necessary because of the complex, technical nature of policies. Rather than simply applying the words of a law or regulation, public servants often need to apply specialized knowledge to figure out the most appropriate means to achieve the general objective. To help with implementation, government officials may strike compromises and work with the groups affected. For example, regulators often reach agreements with industries being regulated to allow the industry time to adjust its operations to comply with a new regulation.

The implementation of policies does not simply involve senior public servants under the supervision of a Cabinet minister designing a program and providing instructions to public servants to carry it out. To be effective, those responsible for carrying out a policy must be motivated to carry out the policy. Issuing commands and having subordinates carry them out may not

POLICY LEGITIMATION
Gaining acceptance of a policy proposal; for example, through formal approval by a legislative body.

POLICY IMPLEMENTATION
Taking measures to put a policy into effect, such as developing rules and regulations and establishing an administrative structure.

work when those providing government services are professionals who believe that they should use their own judgment. For example, a government policy intended to increase the literacy and numeracy of students is only likely to succeed if teachers are committed to the policy.

Enforcement is an important aspect of the implementation of many policies. Although some policies offer encouragement to act in a certain way or provide for voluntary compliance, effective policies often require enforcement of their provisions. For example, it would be naive to expect an industry to voluntarily reduce its emissions of pollutants simply because the government asks it to, if such reductions are costly.

However, strict enforcement is sometimes undesirable or unworkable. For example, strict enforcement of pollution regulations may result in a major industry closing down because the costs of compliance are too high. Thus, government officials are often willing to give considerable leeway to companies that claim difficulty in meeting emission standards.

As well, enforcement of a policy may involve difficult and costly monitoring. For example, monitoring fish catches to ensure that quotas are not being exceeded is often difficult and evasion is common. Further, where a law is widely violated (for example, the law prohibiting the possession of cannabis), some police forces may decide that their limited resources are better spent on other offences.

Finally, policy implementation may be difficult if the co-operation and coordination of other levels of government needs to be obtained. For example, the Canadian government has at times faced difficulties in implementing its national health care policy because provincial governments are responsible for the health care system.

Overall, then, policy implementation is not simply a matter of administration—that is, of putting a policy into effect. There can be a considerable difference between the policy as envisioned by decision-makers and the policy that is actually put into effect. The implementation stage thus involves a combination of administrative and political decisions.

Policy Evaluation

The evaluation of policy is important, but it is an aspect of the policy process that may receive little or no attention, for a variety of reasons. **Policy evaluation** involves determining the extent to which a policy is achieving its objectives and how it can be made more effective. Such evaluation can potentially lead to policy change, whether by scrapping an unsuccessful policy or by making modifications to improve a policy's effectiveness.

Policy evaluation is important because few policies are completely successful in solving the problems for which they were designed. However, despite increased attention being given to evaluation, policies do not always receive systematic evaluation by government. Not only is the evaluation of policy often

POLICY EVALUATION
Determining the extent to which a policy is achieving its objectives and how it can be made more effective.

difficult, but governments may be reluctant to fully evaluate policies to which they have become politically committed for fear that the evaluation will reflect badly on them or because they do not want to reopen a controversial issue. Senior public servants may have a tendency to defend the programs that they are responsible for and be reluctant to conduct thorough evaluations that could lead to reductions in the budgets and staff associated with the programs they administer.

WHO EVALUATES? Some evaluation is performed by those involved in carrying out programs, the auditor general, interest groups, and government agencies or other groups through the statistics they gather. Some laws require that government undertake a review within a certain period of time. For example, the Canadian Environmental Assessment Act must be reviewed after five years. Health care agreements between the national and provincial governments in Canada require that each government issue a report on the quality of health care in its jurisdiction according to a standard set of indicators, although there have been problems in achieving this objective.

Various interest groups conduct evaluations of the successes and failures of government policies. For example, to make their case clearly to the public, some environmental groups issue report cards on government environmental performance. Businesses and business-oriented think tanks typically evaluate policies in terms of their effects on business profitability and competitiveness. Some international agencies provide a comparative analysis of the performances of different countries in various policy areas.

Policy evaluation is not simply a technical procedure. It can also be highly political as different groups evaluate policy from their particular perspective or for their particular purposes. The business-supported Conference Board of Canada is likely to come to a different evaluation of policies than the union-backed Canadian Centre for Policy Alternatives.

The Conference Board of Canada
www.conferenceboard.ca

The Policy Cycle

POLICY CYCLE
The analysis of the policy process as a continuous cycle of stages, with policies continually undergoing modification in response to evaluations of the policy.

The policy process is often described as a **policy cycle** (see Figure 17-1). This assumes that policies are continually undergoing modification in response to evaluations of the policies. Evaluations of existing policies may have an agenda-setting effect. Unsuccessful programs will likely lead to demands for change and place a particular problem back on the public and/or governmental agenda. This can potentially make the policy process a continuous, cyclical process.

However, the depiction of the policy process as a smooth, continuous cycle can be misleading. Policy evaluations that would, ideally, lead to policy changes are not always done. Unsuccessful programs have to compete with other policy problems for attention at the agenda-setting stage. If action is taken on a problem, the general public may believe that the problem has been

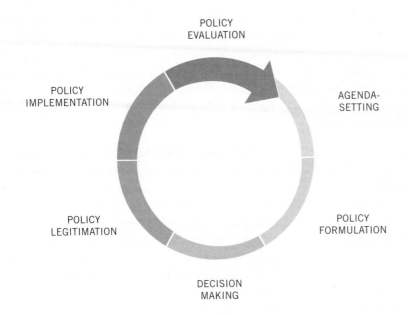

FIGURE 17-1
THE POLICY CYCLE

resolved, thereby reducing demands for further actions. Nevertheless, the policy process is dynamic and never-ending. New policy actors, new data and arguments, new ways of looking at problems, new expectations, changing circumstances, and new solutions mean that the policy process is a continuous one, with recurring debate over what should be done (Kraft, 2004).

The Policy Process in Practice

RATIONAL-COMPREHENSIVE MODEL It is often thought that the ideal policy process (termed the **rational-comprehensive model**) is one in which policy-makers establish clear goals to deal with a problem, examine all alternatives for dealing with the problem in terms of measuring the consequences (costs and benefits) of each alternative, and choose the best alternative (the one that maximizes the attainment of the goals at the lowest cost). This alternative is implemented, then monitored and evaluated to assess whether the goals have been achieved, and changed if necessary (Anderson, 1979). Even if this model does not perfectly describe the actual policy-making process, governments have devoted considerable efforts to try to create a more rational policy process.

Critics, however, argue that the rational-comprehensive model of the policy process is unrealistic, and that attempts to apply this model have often been unsuccessful. Governments often have ambiguous or conflicting goals. Policy-makers may not have the information they need for fully rational decision making, and the information that is available is often biased in favour of the interests that are supplying the information. Governing decisions are often

RATIONAL-COMPREHENSIVE MODEL OF THE POLICY PROCESS
A policy-making model that involves establishing clear goals to deal with a problem, examining all possible alternatives, and choosing the best alternative. The policy is then monitored and evaluated to assess whether the goals have been achieved, and changed if necessary.

made in a hurry, or even in an atmosphere of crisis, because governments tend to react to problems rather than anticipating them. Because policy-makers lack the resources, time, information, and capabilities to fully examine all possible options and their potential effects, Simon (1957) argues that they will likely choose the first acceptable policy alternative presented to them—one that looks as if it will work and meet their goals—rather than the best possible solution to a problem.

INCREMENTAL MODEL   Some suggest that the policy process generally involves making minor changes to existing practices (termed the **incremental model**). Rather than searching for the best solution to a problem, decision-makers tend to "muddle through" (Lindblom, 1959), trying to cope with problems through a limited response. Policy-makers typically only examine a small number of fairly similar alternatives based on past experience, and do not try to evaluate all possible consequences of each alternative. Rather, by making only minor adjustments to existing policies, policy-makers can rely on past experience to assess the policy options being considered (Doyle & Kellow, 1995).

Because policy-making typically involves reaching compromises among a variety of views and interests, both inside and outside of government, policy-makers tend to avoid the risks involved in taking a new policy direction. Instead, they hope to accommodate different interests by making small adjustments to existing policies.

STREAMS AND WINDOWS MODEL   Even if the outcome of the policy process is often only minor, incremental changes to existing policies, there are occasions when major new policies are adopted. The **streams and windows model** depicts the policy process as fluid, rather than a process involving an overall plan or a series of limited steps. Policy, problem, and politics "streams" move independently of each other. The problem stream involves the processes by which "various problems come to capture the attention of people in and around government" (Kingdon, 1995, p. 87). The policy stream refers to the proposals that a variety of individuals and groups interested in a policy area are continually developing. The politics stream includes the campaigns of interest groups and political parties, election outcomes and changes in government, and shifts in the national mood and public opinion. At times, the streams meet, resulting in "windows of opportunity" in which policy entrepreneurs—whether interest group leaders, academics, journalists, politicians, or bureaucrats—can successfully push their pet proposals (Kingdon, 1995). Health care policy discussed in Box 17-3, Universal Medicare: The United States and Canada, illustrates this analysis.

INCREMENTAL MODEL OF THE POLICY PROCESS
A policy-making model that suggests the policy process usually involves making minor changes to existing practices.

STREAMS AND WINDOWS MODEL OF THE POLICY PROCESS
A policy-making model that views the policy process as fluid. Changes in the identification of problems, policy proposals, and political circumstances create windows of opportunity in which policy entrepreneurs may successfully push their pet proposals.

BOX 17-3

Universal Medicare: The United States and Canada

In the early 1990s, the need to change the health care system in the United States became identified as a major problem. The election of a Democratic Congress and president favourable to change seemed to create a window of opportunity for health care reform. However, the other stream, policy, did not meet up with the problem and politics streams. Various proposals for reform were floated, but there was no consensus among those pushing for reform as to which policy proposal was best (Kingdon, 1995). The potential opportunity was missed. Even though the problems of health care remained, subsequent elections brought to power conservatives who opposed increased government involvement in the health care system.

In Canada, as mentioned in the introductory vignette, the election of a socially minded Liberal minority government supported by the NDP (which pushed for universal medicare) provided a favourable political circumstance for Canadian government action, even if some provincial governments were opposed. In terms of the policy stream, there was a consensus among those favouring reform, reinforced by the recommendations of a Royal Commission, that a universal, public medicare system was the best solution to the problem of access to health care in Canada. The positive experience of the Saskatchewan government, which had pioneered medicare and successfully withstood the opposition of doctors (including a doctors' strike), also helped to facilitate the adoption of a national medicare program in 1966.

The streams and windows model does not provide a complete explanation of the different directions in health care policy pursued by the United States and Canada, as other factors such as differences in political culture and political institutions are also relevant. Nevertheless, it does suggest that policy decisions are affected by particular circumstances.

Policy-making might best be understood in terms of a mixture of the three models. Some policies result from a lengthy and rather comprehensive process of examining and assessing various alternatives. Many government actions involve only minor adjustments to existing policies and programs. Occasionally, however, major shifts in public policy occur. Sometimes these shifts occur with a change of government, particularly when a party with a different ideological perspective comes to power (for example, the "Common Sense Revolution" instituted by Mike Harris's Progressive Conservative government in Ontario in the 1990s). At other times, a perceived crisis may lead to major changes in policy direction. For example, the terrorist attacks on the United States in 2001 resulted in many countries quickly adopting national security laws that limited the application of policies protecting civil liberties that these countries had pursued in previous decades.

PUBLIC ADMINISTRATION

Over the past century, governments have become more active in carrying out numerous programs, providing a variety of services to the public, and regulating the activities of business. Governments have required a large number of permanent employees (usually termed public servants) to carry out these activities.

Bureaucratic Organization

BUREAUCRACY

An organization in which people are hired and promoted based on their qualifications and merit, work is organized in terms of specialized positions, detailed rules and procedures are followed by all members of the organization, and there is a hierarchical chain of command so that those at the top can direct and supervise large numbers of people.

Public Service Commission of Canada
www.psc-cfp.gc.ca

Given the complex nature of many of the tasks, the public service has needed a high level of professional expertise and a specialized form of organization referred to as a **bureaucracy** (as discussed in Box 17-4, Bureaucratic Organization: A Threat to Democracy?). Instead of government employees being hired largely on the basis of political patronage (hiring based on ties to the governing party), hiring and promotion in the modern public service is based primarily on merit (such as qualifications and competitive examinations). The United States has a merit-based public service that was established after President James Garfield was assassinated in 1881, apparently by a disgruntled job seeker. However, the president appoints a number of top officials that are considered political in nature, and thus those officials are typically replaced when a new president is elected.

BOX 17-4

Bureaucratic Organization: A Threat to Democracy?

The organization of the modern public service is often termed a bureaucracy (a term that literally means "rule by offices"). In the view of Max Weber, bureaucratic organizations are a key characteristic of modern societies, reflecting the capitalist system's concern with efficiency and the modern political system's concern for legal–rational forms of rule. Thus, bureaucracy is an attribute of all large organizations, whether governmental or in the private sector. A pure bureaucratic organization is one in which people are hired and promoted based on their qualifications and merit, work is organized in terms of specialized positions (offices), detailed

rules and procedures are followed by all members of the organization, and there is a hierarchical chain of command so that those at the top can direct and supervise large numbers of people.

Although Weber viewed bureaucratic organizations as efficient, their adherence to rules and regulations can make bureaucratic organizations inflexible and impersonal. Weber also thought that the powerful bureaucratic organizations controlled by senior officials would dominate the governments of modern societies and limit the applicability of the democratic ideal of rule by the people (Heywood, 2002).

REPRESENTATIVE BUREAUCRACY Staffing the public service strictly based on merit can, however, make the public service unrepresentative of the characteristics of the society as a whole. An emphasis on formal qualifications, such as a university degree and scores on public service examinations, may result in hiring practices that favour people from some parts of society more than others. In Canada, efforts began in the 1960s to increase the relatively small proportion of French-speaking persons in the public service in order to create a public service that could operate in both official languages and increase French Quebecers' attachment to the Canadian government. Since then, efforts have been made to create a more **representative bureaucracy** by establishing targets for hiring and promoting more women, Aboriginals, visible minorities, and disabled people in the public service.

Politics and Administration

Public administration is often thought of in terms of the carrying out of the policies adopted by the government. As we saw in Chapter 15, each department of government is headed by a Cabinet minister who is expected to oversee and take responsibility for the actions of the department. In Canada, the day-to-day running of a department is in the hands of a **deputy minister**, usually a senior public servant appointed by the prime minister in consultation with the Clerk (head) of the Privy Council Office. The Privy Council Office also plays a major role in providing coordination and direction to the work of the deputy ministers and senior public servants.

Because public servants are a key source of information and advice for Cabinet ministers, they often play a major role in the policy-making process. As well, once a law is passed by Parliament and a program needs to be established, it is typically the public servants within a particular department that play a major role in how implementation is going to be conducted. Since laws are often fairly general in nature, this leaves considerable room for discretion. Likewise, the regulations needed to determine how the law is to be applied are often drafted by public servants with formal approval by Cabinet.

Overall, although the public service is expected to be non-partisan, its advice and actions nevertheless are political in the sense that they have an important effect on how the country is governed.

Criticisms of the Government Bureaucracy

The government bureaucracy has come under considerable criticism in recent decades for several reasons:

- Bureaucratic organization is often viewed as slow moving, rigid, and inflexible rather than efficient.
- The commitment of public servants to the public interest is sometimes questioned.
- Users of government services sometimes receive insufficient attention and respect.

REPRESENTATIVE BUREAUCRACY
A bureaucracy that reflects the characteristics of society, particularly by trying to ensure that all levels of the public service have a proportion of women and various disadvantaged minority groups similar to that of the population as a whole.

DEPUTY MINISTER
The executive head of a department of government appointed by the prime minister in consultation with the clerk of the Privy Council Office. The deputy minister runs the department with oversight by the Cabinet minister who is the political head of the department.

In particular, public choice theory, based on the assumption that individuals always pursue their own self-interest, has been used to argue that public servants seek to expand the programs and expenditures of government so as to enhance their own position, privileges, and power. The effect, compounded by the efforts of government to try to satisfy the demands of interest groups, is that government has become much larger than necessary. This, in the view of many public choice theorists, has stifled the growth of the more dynamic and efficient private sector.

Thinking about government administration has also been influenced by the popular book *Reinventing Government,* which argues that governing should involve "steering" rather than "rowing." In other words, setting the direction for government through the development of policy, which is the proper role of governing, should be separated from the delivery of services, which should be contracted out to private business as much as possible (Osborne & Gaebler, 1993).

Generally, then, concerns about administrative inefficiencies, the stifling of entrepreneurial initiatives by government "red tape," and excessive rules and regulations have led many governments to undertake major reforms of their administrative structures and practices. These changes are part of a broader movement to shrink the size of government, privatize state-owned enterprises, reduce regulation of business, and focus on being competitive in the global marketplace. As well, these changes are related to efforts to decentralize government by handing over various responsibilities to provincial, regional, and local governments.

New Public Management

NEW PUBLIC MANAGEMENT
The adoption of the practices of private business in the administrative activities of government.

The adoption of the practices of private business is a major feature of **new public management,** an idea that has influenced changes to government administration in many countries since the 1980s (see Box 17-5, Changing Administration in the United Kingdom). In particular, this approach emphasizes efficiency by reducing the size of the public service, providing performance incentives to employees, and encouraging competition to provide public services between private and public organizations so that services are provided at the lowest cost. Instead of the hierarchical structure and rules and procedures of the traditional bureaucracy, the emphasis is on decentralized structures in which managers have the autonomy to make managerial decisions and to create a leaner, more flexible operation. Further, like private business, the focus should be on satisfying the customers of public services. Finally, the new public management approach tends to see the public service as a provider or manager of services rather than a provider of policy advice to government. Thus, governments have increasingly called upon the political staff of Cabinet ministers, outside consultants, research institutes, and interest groups for policy advice.

Changing Administration in the United Kingdom

The influential British television series *Yes Minister* featured a negative depiction of the relationship between Cabinet ministers and senior public servants. This coincided with the real-world perspective of Margaret Thatcher, Conservative prime minister from 1979 to 1990. Thatcher viewed the public service as a serious obstacle to implementing her free-market ideological vision.

In *Yes Minister,* a savvy senior public servant manipulated a hapless, inexperienced Cabinet minister. The minister was dependent on the public servant, who really ran the department and ensured that any of the minister's proposals for changes that might be inconsistent with the department's interests were not acted upon (Savoie, 2003).

During the Thatcher years, the government, facing serious economic problems, instituted major changes in the traditional British administration. Many state-owned enterprises were privatized, regulation of private business was reduced, the expenditures of government departments were scrutinized, and public service staff numbers were substantially reduced.

Thatcher's reforms included the establishment of one hundred and thirty-eight independent executive agencies that employ about three-quarters of the public service. These agencies, each headed by a chief executive officer, are provided with performance targets by a Cabinet minister, but are given a considerable level of autonomy to achieve those targets. A Citizen's Charter requires that departments and agencies establish standards for their services and publicly disclose whether these standards are being met. Finally, a system of market testing allows private companies to compete against government agencies and departments for contracts to provide various public services (Borins, 2002).

As for *Yes Minister*, the program ended in the 1980s, a relic of a bygone era in the British civil service. However, Margaret Thatcher made sure the show's writer was awarded with a knighthood!

ALTERNATIVE SERVICE DELIVERY One aspect of the new public management is the development of new methods of delivering government programs, termed **alternative service delivery.** This may involve establishing government service agencies that have considerable autonomy from the normal departmental structures and rules, for example, Passport Canada, the Canada Revenue Agency, the Canadian Food Inspection Agency, and Parks Canada. In some cases, these agencies are expected to be self-financing.

Another form of alternative service delivery involves establishing partnerships with business (sometimes referred to as public–private partnerships), other levels of government, and voluntary organizations to deliver services. For example, the Career Edge internship program involves a partnership of the Canadian government with the YMCA and private businesses (Zussman, 2002). Alternative service delivery can also involve contracting out government activities to private business or to groups of former public

ALTERNATIVE SERVICE DELIVERY
New methods of delivering government programs, such as the establishment of service agencies that have considerable autonomy from the normal departmental structures and rules and establishing partnerships with business, other levels of government, and voluntary organizations to deliver services.

"Wouldn't it be great if government no longer ran the parks?"

servants. This approach is particularly common in the United States, where private businesses have been contracted not only by a number of cities to manage garbage collection and road maintenance, but also by state and national governments to run prisons and carry out a variety of military functions. For example, in 2006 there were about 100 000 civilians working under contract to the United States government as part of its military and reconstruction efforts in Iraq—not far short of the 140 000 U.S. troops then in that country (*Washington Post*, December 5, 2006, p. D01)

PROBLEMS A key problem with the efforts to make government more businesslike is that there are inherent differences between government and business. Business is concerned with making a profit; government should be concerned with the common good, even if this means undertaking activities that are costly. The objectives of government are more complex than the simple bottom line of profitability that drives business activity. Indeed, a focus on profitability may conflict with the interests of the public in such goals as environmental protection and social well-being (Paehlke, 2003).

The idea that the public service should be primarily involved in managing programs rather than developing policies is also controversial. Based on its experience in administering programs, the public service is able to provide useful advice in developing new policies and modifying existing ones. Further, a knowledgeable, professional public service protected by a high level of job security may be more likely to provide honest, forthright advice than consulting firms and partisan advisers who may tend to tell Cabinet ministers what they want to hear (Savoie, 2003).

The adoption of private sector methods does not necessarily lead to the most desirable results. Focusing on efficiency and competitiveness may undermine the sense of public service that has been developed among the employees of government in countries such as Canada and the United Kingdom. Although many large state-owned enterprises have a reputation for inefficiency, these problems do not necessarily apply to well-managed government public services.

For example, the Ontario government conducted a performance review of a large maximum security prison whose operations had been contracted out to a major American prison management corporation. It found that an equivalent government-run prison had better security, health care, and reduced repeat offender rates. Thus, the government decided to take over the running of the prison (CBC News, November 10, 2006). Likewise, an academic study of the privatization of the prison system in Mississippi found that the presumed advantage of greater efficiency was questionable and that privatization can create problems in achieving the public good (Morris, 2007).

Treating citizens as customers may encourage people to look after their own interests rather than working collectively to try to create a more just society. Likewise, it has been argued that treating citizens as individual customers results in the state "satisfying the sum of . . . private interests without a real concern for the public interest or common good" (Fortier, 2003, p. 8).

Finally, the idea that much of the work of the public service should be done by autonomous agencies, each responsible for a particular program, has been questioned. In looking at Britain and New Zealand, analysts have found that adopting this approach can make it more difficult for governments to deal with complex problems that require coordination among a variety of departments and agencies (Aucoin, 2002). For example, in the small country of New Zealand, a pioneer in the adoption of new public management, the establishment of three hundred separate agencies increased administrative costs and made coordination of public services difficult (Dunleavy et al., 2006).

Summary and Conclusion

The policies adopted by governments are typically the result of a complex process involving a variety of different political actors. Interest groups, social movements, political parties, think tanks, and journalists seek to influence the choice of issues that will be the subject of policy-making, as well as try to affect how policy-makers think about those issues.

Policy-making is not simply a matter of problem solving, or trying to determine the best policy to achieve the common good. Rather, it is a matter of choice in which resources are limited and the goals and objectives of those interested or involved in policy-making differ and cannot easily be weighed against each other. Most public policies have an effect on the distribution of well-being in society—the benefits and costs of a policy may not be evenly shared.

In other words, the policy process is a *political* process in which different goals, interests, and values are involved (Simeon, 1976). Because the policy process is a political process, the distribution of power in a society and the dominant ideological perspectives will likely affect which problems are addressed, how problems are defined, and what policies are adopted and implemented. The policies that are adopted and implemented do not necessarily reflect the common good, but rather tend to reflect the political interests of the government, the values and ideologies of those involved in the policy process, and the ability of various groups and individuals to exert influence. There are, however, a variety of different basic perspectives concerning who influences and who generally benefits from government policies.

The idea that the government bureaucracy is efficient and dedicated to the public interest has been challenged by those who contend that public servants pursue their own interests by seeking to expand the activities of government. The public service has also been criticized as being too rule-bound, slow to act, and prone to act in established ways. Attempts have been made to adopt a more businesslike approach to administration through the techniques of the new public management. Providing greater autonomy and flexibility for administrative managers may be useful in reducing inefficiency and cutting red tape. However, despite the criticisms often levelled at the bureaucracy, a strong, professional public service is important in the effort to pursue the common good of a political community. Good public administration involves not only the efficient delivery of services, but also the provision of quality advice to government. Even though there are now a variety of sources of advice used by government in developing its policies, the assessment of that advice and the coordination of the variety of governmental programs is necessary for good governing (Aucoin, 2002).

More generally, there has been a growing tendency for policy-making and administration to move away from the direct control of national governments. This tendency involves upward shifts to international bodies such as the World Trade Organization and the North American Free Trade Agreement, downward shifts to regional and local bodies, and horizontal shifts to the courts and a variety of autonomous agencies, public–private partnerships, and private contractors (Van Kersbergen & Van Waarden, 2004). Assuming that these shifts continue, developing mechanisms of accountability will be needed so that the common good is protected.

Key Terms

Discussion Questions

1. Can the best public policies be chosen scientifically?

2. Which of the five general perspectives do you think is most applicable to understanding public policy in Canada?

3. Which model of the policy process is the most realistic? Which would be the most desirable?

4. Is greater public participation in the policy process desirable? How can it best be achieved?

5. Is bureaucratic organization undesirable? What are the advantages and disadvantages of new public management reforms?

Further Reading

Adolini, J.R., & Blake, C.H. *Comparing policies: Issues and choices in six industrialized countries.* Washington, DC: CQ Press, 2001.

Boyd, D.R. *Unnatural law: Rethinking Canadian environmental law and policy.* Vancouver: UBC Press, 2003.

Brooks, S. *Public policy in Canada,* 3rd ed. Toronto: Oxford University Press, 1998.

Dunn, C. (Ed.). *The handbook of Canadian public administration.* Don Mills, ON: Oxford University Press, 2002.

Heidenheimer, A.J., Heclo, H., & Adams, C.T. *Comparative public policy: The politics of social choice in Europe and America,* 3rd ed. New York: St. Martin's Press, 1990.

Johnson, A.F., & Stritch, A. (Eds.). *Canadian public policy: Globalization and political parties.* Toronto: Copp Clark, 1997.

Kettl, D.F. *The global public management revolution: A report on the transformation of governance.* Washington, DC: Brookings Institution Press, 2000.

Osborne, D., & Gaebler, T. *Reinventing government: How the entrepreneurial spirit is transforming the public sector.* Reading, MA: Addison-Wesley, 1992.

Orsini, M., & Smith, M. (Eds.). *Critical policy studies.* Vancouver: UBC Press, 2007.

Pal, L.A. *Beyond policy analysis: Public issue management in turbulent times,* 3rd ed. Scarborough, ON: Nelson Thomson, 2005.

Savoie, D.J. *Breaking the bargain: Public servants, ministers, and Parliament.* Toronto: University of Toronto Press, 2003.

PART V

DEVELOPMENT, DEMOCRATIZATION, AND INTERNATIONAL POLITICS

Chapter 18

POLITICS AND GOVERNMENT IN THE WORLD'S POORER COUNTRIES

PHOTO ABOVE: The clients of the Grameen Bank in Bangladesh are among the world's poorest people—and the bank's pride and joy. Muhammad Yunus, an economist, believed the country needed a bank that would extend credit to Bangladesh's millions of landless men and women, thereby letting them create their own jobs and look after their families better.

CHAPTER OBJECTIVES

After reading this chapter you should be able to:

1. identify the terms that are used to depict the poorer countries
2. outline the extent of global inequality
3. discuss the meaning of development and the different development strategies
4. evaluate Canada's foreign aid policies
5. examine the political problems of the Third World

The clients of the Grameen Bank in Bangladesh are among the world's poorest people—and the bank's pride and joy. Ordinary commercial banks would not touch them because they have no collateral to pledge. The difference is that Dr. Muhammad Yunus, the 2006 Nobel Peace Prize winner and creator of the Grameen, believed the country needed a bank that would extend credit to Bangladesh's millions of landless men and women, thereby letting them create their own jobs and look after their families better. The bank, whose name means rural in Bangala, the language of Bangladesh, was founded in 1983 and has now lent to more than three million borrowers.

The Grameen Bank believes that credit for self-employment is a basic human right. It makes small loans, limited to about US$400 for business start-ups and US$650 for home building (Bangladesh has a per capita annual income of US$500, so the sums are not trivial). To help assure repayment and the proper use of loans, the bank organizes its customers to use peer pressure. The result has been a default rate of less than 0.5 percent and an on-time repayment record of 98 percent.

Perhaps the most striking thing about the Grameen Bank is its clientele, 94 percent of whom are women. The bank makes women its priority for three reasons. First, they are the society's poorest, thus the least likely to get help from a regular credit institution. Second, when extra cash enters a home, women are more likely to use the money for the family's good, whereas men tend to spend it on themselves. Finally, it is not uncommon for a man to desert his family, leaving a woman as the sole breadwinner.

The Grameen Bank has become a model for other countries. It does not solve all of the problems of underdevelopment, but is a partial response to one set of the many issues facing poor countries. However, by showing that mixing a lot of local initiative with creative thinking produces better lives for many people, the Grameen Bank has an importance that stretches far beyond Bangladesh.

To many Canadians, "development" means giving a poor country a standard of living that approaches Canada's, complete with personal computers and a car for everyone. In the very poor, extremely underdeveloped countries of the Third World, that kind of development, which has long been the goal of foreign aid programs, can miss the poorest. Even the most entrepreneurial and energetic of the poor find it almost impossible to get ahead under conventional development projects. That is why the Grameen Bank is so important.*

---

* For information about the Grameen Bank, see Wood and Sharit (1997), Yunus (1999), and the bank's website at www.grameen-info.org.

THE DEVELOPMENT GAP

Less than one-sixth of the people in the world live in high-income countries like Canada and the United States. The remaining five-sixths have a per capita income less than half that of Canada (see Table 18-1). Canadian governments have trouble funding all of the services that people need, so the situation is obviously worse where the money per person available to fund education, health care, roads, and other important services is far less than that of Canada. We live in a world where the average income of the 971 million people living in high-income countries is sixty-three times that of the 2.31 billion people living in low-income countries, although the difference falls to fourteen times greater if we use **purchasing power parity (PPP)** adjusted income figures (World Bank, 2005). Is it meaningful to talk about achieving the common good in the poorest countries? Should Canadians be concerned about the problem of global inequality? How can poor countries develop?

Over the years, social scientists have applied a variety of names to the world's poor countries. Among them have been **Third World**, developing, less developed, **underdeveloped,** and the **South** (terms discussed in Box 18-1, Evolution of the Term "Third World"). Political science prefers Third World (Green & Luehrmann, 2003; Handelman, 2003), but uses all of the terms noted above. Whatever name is used, it is the mix of the economic and social characteristics of poor states, on the one hand, and how their political systems function, on the other, that has drawn the attention of political scientists, policy-makers, and the politically informed public in the wealthy (or developed) countries of what some call the **North**.

PURCHASING POWER PARITY (PPP) A measure of per capita income that shows the purchasing power of an income, instead of its worth at current exchange rates.

THIRD WORLD
Less developed countries.

UNDERDEVELOPED COUNTRIES
A term often used to describe Third World countries.

SOUTH
Less developed, poorer countries.

NORTH
The rich, developed countries.

WHAT IS DEVELOPMENT?

Terms such as **"developing countries,"** "less developed countries," or "underdeveloped countries" are often used to describe Third World countries, but they raise several questions: What exactly does "development" mean? In what ways are poorer countries "less developed" than the richer countries? Are the poorer countries "developing"? Does that mean that they will become just like the richer "developed" countries?

DEVELOPING COUNTRIES
Countries that have not reached the same level of development as the richer, advanced countries.

TABLE 18-1
THE WEALTH OF THE WORLD

Note: Canadians, with an average annual income of US $23 930, account for 2.2 percent of the world's income but only 0.5 percent of the world's population.

INCOME GROUP	ANNUAL INCOME RANGE	% WORLD'S INCOME	% WORLD'S POPULATION
High	> US $9 386	80.4%	15.5%
Upper Middle	US $3 036–9 385	5.2%	5.3%
Lower Middle	US $766–3 035	11.4%	42.3%
Low	< US $765	3.0%	36.8%

SOURCE: *Calculated from World Development Report, by the World Bank (2006), Washington: The World Bank.*

BOX 18-1

Evolution of the Term "Third World"

A host of names has developed over the years to refer to the world's poorest countries.

The Third World was political scientists' first choice. That name was introduced in the late 1940s, to distinguish what was then a small number of independent countries in Africa, Asia, and Latin America from the blocs linked to the two great powers of the day: the United States and the Soviet Union. The United States and its allies among the wealthier industrialized countries (for example, Canada and Britain) formed the First World and the Soviet Union and its allies (for example, Bulgaria and Mongolia) were termed the Second World. Other countries constituted the "Third World."

Although many of these countries later banded together to form the Non-Aligned Movement, the Third World soon came to symbolize poverty and political instability far more than symbolizing an independent line in foreign policy.

The South is another label political scientists have used. This emphasizes the fact that most poor countries lie in the tropics, to the south of the rich states of the northern hemisphere. Of course, the name is not literally accurate, because the southern hemisphere includes developed countries such as Australia and New Zealand.

Underdeveloped, developing, and *less developed* are variations on a final theme used to categorize the poor states of the world. The focus here is the low levels of economic well-being that characterize the countries in this group. Nevertheless, there is the implicit assumption that development is possible and that someday all of the world's countries will do a better job of meeting their citizens' needs.

These countries tend to be new democracies, if they are democratic at all. The nations that broadly fit this description include all of Latin America and the Caribbean; Africa; the Middle East, except Israel; and Asia, except Japan, Singapore, Taiwan (Republic of China), and South Korea. Interestingly, the last three states were considered Third World countries until the 1980s. Now they are labelled *newly industrialized countries* to indicate that they are no longer poor, underdeveloped countries.

The less developed countries are often compared to the more developed countries in terms of per capita **gross domestic product (GDP)** (the amount of goods and services produced) and in terms of average income (see Table 18-1). Such measures are available for nearly all countries and give us a sense of the economic disparities between rich and poor nations. If countries increase their GDP, we can say that economic growth is occurring. Economic growth, however, does not always result in **development**. For example, economic growth need not lead to a reduction of poverty. Indeed, in some cases, increased poverty has accompanied increased growth (United Nations Development Programme [UNDP], 2003). Because of the great inequalities in wealth and power in many less developed countries, additional wealth often ends up in the pockets of the rich. New oil wells, mines, factories, stores, and dams may result in the dislocation of peasant farmers, urban workers, and indigenous peoples, reducing their ability to eke out a living. The

GROSS DOMESTIC PRODUCT (GDP)
The market value of goods and services produced in a country, excluding transactions with other countries.

DEVELOPMENT
A condition that involves the satisfaction of the basic needs of all of the people as well as the means for them to live fulfilling and productive lives based on the creation of a more diversified, sophisticated, and sustainable economy.

Development versus Growth

Imagine living in a country whose economy is based on mining diamonds.

If we mine and sell more diamonds, the economy's GDP will *grow*. But the country has not necessarily developed. Increased diamond mining might simply let the mine owners buy more imported luxury items or invest their profits abroad. However, processing the diamonds into jewellery or using the profits from diamond mining to develop new industries would lead to a more broadly based economy that would rely less on one commodity. It would also encourage people to develop more skills.

Generally, if more of the profits from increased mining activity remained in the country to buy locally produced goods and services, the economic *development* of the country would rise. Likewise, if government used increased tax revenues to improve roads, schools, and health care, there would be a stronger foundation for future development.

distinction between growth and development is discussed further in Box 18-2, Development versus Growth.

Development may be thought of in terms of three goals:

United Nations Development
Programme
www.undp.org

1. It involves satisfying the basic needs of all of the people, such as food, housing, clothing, and clean water, as well as the means to live fulfilling and productive lives, such as education, health care, employment, and security against severe hardships. For example, the United Nations Development Programme has as its objectives the elimination of extreme poverty, currently defined as subsisting on less than US$1 per day (UNDP, 2002), and improving the status of women. Improving the status of women, especially ensuring that young women receive an education, tends to result in a healthier population, slower population growth, and a more skilled workforce.

2. It builds a more diversified and sophisticated economy. This second goal demands moving from an economy centred on the production of unprocessed natural resources to one that turns them into finished goods. As well, it develops the scientific, technological, and managerial capabilities needed to compete with the developed countries. Further, it requires moving from being a supplier of low-cost labour to multinational corporations based in the rich countries to developing local entrepreneurial capacity and the banking, legal, and other services needed to support domestic businesses.

3. Development needs to be environmentally sustainable. Economic growth has often come through unrestrained exploitation of natural resources. Indiscriminate logging and fishing may bring short-term economic growth, but they harm long-term development. Indeed, one of the major dilemmas of development is that industrialization and increased wealth often create a heavy burden on the environment. Although the rich countries use a high proportion of the world's resources and produce a substantial share of global pollution, increases in the wealth in heavily populated Third World countries have the potential to place great

stresses on the world's environment. For example, shifting from bicycles to cars as a major means of transportation is creating serious problems of congestion and air pollution in many Third World cities and also contributes to global warming. From an environmental perspective, Third World economic growth that brings consumption levels like those of the richer countries would be disastrous. Both richer and poorer countries need to develop in a more sustainable fashion.

Center for Global Development
www.cgdev.org

Measuring Development

Rather than simply measuring a country's wealth, the United Nations Development Programme uses an index based on literacy and education, life expectancy, and per capita GDP to get a broader picture of how well countries are doing in their pursuit of development (see Table 18-2). On this **Human Development Index (HDI)**, rankings do not always correspond exactly to GDP.

Cuba, for instance, ranks 40 places higher on HDI than it does on GDP, indicating that it produces very good human development results for its level of economic activity. At the other extreme, Equatorial Guinea, a small African state, has HDI levels 93 places below its income rank. Equatorial Guinea

HUMAN DEVELOPMENT INDEX (HDI)
An annual index for most countries, calculated by the United Nations Development Programme and based on literacy and education, life expectancy, and per capita GDP.

TABLE 18-2
HUMAN DEVELOPMENT INDEX, SELECTED COUNTRIES, 2005

Note: Gross Domestic Product per capita is calculated in terms of purchasing power parity.

HDI RANK	COUNTRY	GDP PER CAPITA (US$)	% CHILDREN UNDERWEIGHT	% ADULT LITERACY	LIFE EXPECTANCY (YEARS)
5	Canada	30 677	—	100%	80
10	United States	37 562	—	100%	77.4
11	Japan	27 967	—	100%	82
52	Cuba	5 400	4%	96.9%	77.3
53	Mexico	9 168	8%	90.3%	75.1
63	Brazil	7 790	6%	88.4%	70.5
78	Ukraine	5 491	N/A	99.4%	66.1
85	China (PRC)	5 003	10%	90.0%	71.6
110	Indonesia	3 361	26%	87.9%	66.8
119	Egypt	3 950	9%	55.6%	69.8
121	Equatorial Guinea	19 780	19%	84.2%	43.3
127	India	2 892	47%	61%	63.3
135	Pakistan	2 097	38%	48.7%	63.0
153	Haiti	1 742	17%	50.9%	51.6
158	Nigeria	1 050	29%	66.8%	43.4
167	Congo (Dem. Rep.)	697	31%	65.3%	43.1
170	Ethiopia	711	47%	41.5%	47.6
176	Sierra Leone	548	27%	29.6%	40.8

SOURCE: *Adapted from United Nations Development Program, Human Development Report, 2005. New York: Oxford University Press.*

produces and exports oil, so it has a high national income that has not produced benefits for its people (UNDP, 2005).[1]

The good news is that, however it is measured, development has clearly occurred throughout the Third World. Compared to 1960, life expectancy has increased substantially, literacy rates and school enrolment at all levels have jumped, and women in particular have made great gains (UNDP, 1995). The percentage of those living in extreme poverty has fallen from 30 percent in 1990 to 23 percent today (UNDP, 2003). However, these global figures hide disturbing facts.

First, although a smaller percentage of the world's population qualifies as "extremely poor," more than one billion people still fall into that category. Further, some parts of the world—notably sub-Saharan Africa—are doing far worse than others and have even lost ground in the last twenty-five years. The rapid growth of the Chinese and Indian economies over the last decade has reduced poverty there. Since these two countries make up three-eighths of the world's population, improvements there cause global poverty figures to drop, even though poverty has worsened throughout Africa. Statistics reveal, but they also conceal.

Clearly, individual countries have made great strides. Forty years ago the countries of Southeast and East Asia were extremely poor, with a short life expectancy and high levels of illiteracy and infant mortality. From China to Thailand, however, conditions are much improved. In fact, aside from North Korea, the region's experience demonstrates that development is not just possible, but can be achieved in a generation.

However, just as there are development success stories, there are also failures. The most dramatic cases of failed development are found in sub-Saharan Africa, followed by the Middle East and parts of Latin America. Recognizing these problems, in 2000, the UN set out eight Millennium Development Goals (MDG), to be achieved by 2015: 1) eradicate extreme poverty and hunger; 2) achieve universal primary education; 3) empower women and advance gender equality; 4) reduce child mortality; 5) improve maternal health; 6) combat HIV/AIDS, malaria, and other diseases; 7) ensure environmental stability; and 8) develop a global partnership for development (UNMDG, 2005, 2006). However, the United Nations Development Programme's *Human Development Report* for 2005 (UNDP, 2005) reports that progress has been very slow due to the failure of wealthy countries like Canada and the United States to offer sufficient material support.

Despite the disappointing progress toward meeting the MDG, we should not forget that living standards throughout the poor world have improved over the past fifty years. We also need to recall that some countries have reached the ranks of developed nations. However, there are also states that have seen earlier movement toward development reversed and others where development simply has not occurred. Box 18-3, Three Development Scenarios, presents some cases of successful and failed development.

---

[1] HDI says nothing about a country's political system. Both Cuba and Equatorial Guinea are dictatorships. The difference in their HDIs shows clearly that not all dictatorships are the same.

BOX 18-3
Three Development Scenarios

The Third World presents us with cases of failed development and reversed development as well as successful development:

1. *Failed development.* When the Belgian Congo became independent in 1960, Belgium had not prepared its colony for independence, so there were few well-educated Congolese to exercise power. The new country plunged into civil war, with the Americans backing one faction and the Soviets another. The eventual winner of the conflict was Joseph Mobutu. Later he changed his name to Mobutu Sese Seko and the country's name to Zaire. From 1965 to 1997 he exercised dictatorial rule, becoming Africa's most corrupt leader. Things did not improve for the Congolese after Laurent Kabila ousted Mobutu and renamed the country the Democratic Republic of the Congo. It soon was swept up in warfare, and in 2001 Kabila was assassinated. His son then seized power, but in 2006 won the country's first ever multiparty election.

   The country's fifty-five million inhabitants have annual per capita incomes of only US$100, but their land is rich in natural resources. The Congolese, however, will not benefit from their gold, silver, and oil until they get political stability and honest rulers.

2. *Reversed development.* Early in the twentieth century, Argentina had a per capita income similar to Canada's. By 2003, it was less than 30 percent of ours. Argentina is a big country, with thirty-eight million well-educated people. It has significant natural resources (agricultural and mineral), a once large but now declining manufacturing base, and modern service industries. However, between 1930 and 1983 the country was almost always ruled by dictatorships, all of which pursued bad policies. Since 1983, the country has been democratic, but this has not solved its problems. In December 2001, Argentina's economy nearly collapsed and sparked a political crisis that saw five presidents governing within two weeks. Argentina should be rich, but it needs more stable democratic politics, plus sound and sustainable economic programs, to achieve this.

3. *Successful development.* South Korea (officially, the Republic of Korea) is a developed country today. It is not a large country, but has a population of thirty-eight million. At its founding in 1946, the country's prospects were poor. Formerly a Japanese colony, Korea was divided into a communist north (the Korean Democratic Republic) and a non-communist south. Over the next four decades, while North Korea stagnated, South Korea prospered by using a form of government-managed capitalism (Wade, 1990). It currently has a sophisticated economy based principally on manufacturing. South Korean firms like Samsung and Hyundai are household names in Canada. Until 1988, South Korea was ruled by a series of dictatorships, most of them military. It is now such a sufficiently stable democracy that it weathered a severe economic crisis from 1997 to 1998 without incident.

▶ Argentina should be rich, but it needs more stable democratic politics, as well as a sound and sustainable economic program, to achieve this.

HOW CAN COUNTRIES DEVELOP?

There is no simple solution to the problem of development. Those who study the issue often differ sharply on the causes of underdevelopment and on how best to achieve development. We will focus on the free-market approach, dependency theory, import substitution industrialization, and export-led industrialization.

The Free Market

Since at least the 1950s, the dominant model (called a paradigm) in discussions about development has emphasized the free market. The advice that the Third World gets from international agencies such as the International Monetary Fund and the World Bank, as well as from many economists, typically is based on the assumption that government involvement in the economy is undesirable. The free-market capitalist economic system, free trade, and unrestricted foreign investment, it is argued, lead to prosperity.

Free-market approaches to development have come in two packages that offer broadly similar advice: modernization theory and the Washington Consensus.

International Monetary Fund
www.imf.org

The World Bank
www.worldbank.org

MODERNIZATION THEORY
A development model that views the traditional values, practices, and institutions of Third World countries as the basic cause of underdevelopment. To develop, poor countries should change their cultural outlook, social structure, economic organization, and political system based on the model of the advanced Western societies.

MODERNIZATION THEORY Modernization theory was important from about 1950 to 1975. This theory viewed the traditional values, practices, and institutions of Third World countries as the basic cause of underdevelopment. More bluntly, the implication was that poor countries were "backward." To develop, poor countries had to change their cultural outlooks, social structure, economic organization, and political system. The rich Western societies, especially the United States, were the model that Third World countries should copy. This would not be difficult because modernization theorists argued that the right economic policies would set everything else moving. Once governments had taken the first steps, their role would be much reduced.

The prescription called for bringing in the most modern firms from abroad, the ones with the newest technology and best management. They would open a plant in a developing country, hire locals, and show other businesses the best way to do things. These local businesses would adopt the practices of the foreign firm and further diffuse the ideas of the developed world through society. Before long, a new middle class and a modern working class would emerge, free from the biases of their old society. These modern sectors would challenge the old elites, come to control government, and build a democracy. Unfortunately, things did not work like that. Foreign firms spun off fewer benefits than expected, so the modern, democratic middle and working classes did not grow much. Thus, the old elites retained power and democracy gained little ground. Overall, the economy did improve, but not as much as modernization's promoters had promised.

THE WASHINGTON CONSENSUS The free-market prescription got a second chance in the early 1980s and is still important today. Between 1973 and 1980, world oil prices skyrocketed. This began a chain of events that resulted in many Third World countries accumulating huge debts with foreign lenders. Because interest rates were also rising throughout that period and sales of Third World exports to the First World were slumping, many countries found themselves unable to meet their debt payments. To solve this problem and ensure that the debtor countries kept paying, the wealthy countries, led by the United States and the two most important **international financial institutions (IFIs)**—the World Bank (WB) and the International Monetary Fund (IMF)—put together a series of policies that became known as the **Washington Consensus.**

At the heart of the Washington Consensus are calls for countries to generate more revenue for debt repayment by cutting government expenditures—especially on health, education, and other social programs—to balance their budgets, selling off government-owned enterprises (privatization), and fully opening their countries to foreign goods and investments. These prescriptions form the heart of **structural adjustment programs (SAPs)**. SAPs were administered by international financial institutions that offer governments loans at very low interest rates ("soft loans") if their countries enact the programs endorsed by the Washington Consensus. Were a country to refuse to agree to a SAP, it could easily find that it had no access at all to international credit because private banks will not lend to clients, even sovereign states, that have proven unwilling or unable to pay their debts. Without such loans, countries might be unable to import such necessary items as light

INTERNATIONAL FINANCIAL INSTITUTION (IFI)
An organization that has some ability to affect the global economic system; for example, the International Monetary Fund and the World Bank.

WASHINGTON CONSENSUS
A series of policies put together by the International Monetary Fund and the World Bank that encourages developing countries to generate more revenue for debt repayment by cutting government expenditures to balance their budgets, selling off government-owned enterprises (privatization), and fully opening their countries to foreign goods and investments.

STRUCTURAL ADJUSTMENT PROGRAM (SAP)
A program administered by international financial institutions, which offer loans at very favourable interest rates to governments facing problems paying their debt if they adopt the programs espoused by the Washington Consensus.

bulbs or spare parts for cars and trucks, since exporters want to be paid in a major international currency, particularly U.S. dollars.

SAPs gave little heed to the social consequences of the economic policies they prescribed. Since 1999, SAPs have been replaced by programs that give more attention to the plight of the poor. One of these, the Enhanced HIPC initiative, focuses on highly indebted poor countries and can substantially reduce a nation's foreign debt. Another new program requires any country seeking assistance from the IFIs to consult with citizens' groups in preparing Poverty Reduction Strategy Papers (PRSP), which map an anti-poverty strategy. Nevertheless, the IFIs and the donor countries that give aid to the Third World are still setting conditions similar to those used under SAPs that the recipients must meet to receive funds. This might be acceptable if the programs produced development, but they seldom do.

As a result, some conclude that these multilateral initiatives are more about protecting the wealthy countries of the North (for example, by ensuring that countries do not default on their loans and destabilize the global banking system) than developing the South. Although the World Bank and the International Monetary Fund are mandated to assist the poorer countries, control of these organizations rests with the governments of the rich countries, who have a majority of the votes.

SUCCESS? Overall, free-market approaches have not been dramatically more successful than others in achieving development. Indeed, no country in the world has ever developed using a *purely* free-market framework. Governments have always taken an active role in shaping the economies of successful developing countries.

Dependency Theory

DEPENDENCY THEORY
A development model that views underdevelopment as a result of unequal power relations between the centre (dominant, capitalist countries) and the periphery (poor, dependent countries).

Dependency theory (Cardoso & Falletto, 1979; Frank, 1979) argues that underdevelopment results from unequal power relations between the dominant capitalist countries ("the centre") and the poor, dependent countries ("the periphery").[2]

In particular, Andre Gunder Frank argues that underdevelopment was a result of colonization of the periphery by the European powers. Over time, the centre developed at the expense of the periphery, which became underdeveloped (Frank, 1972). The periphery provides the raw materials and cheap labour needed to keep the capitalist system based in the rich centre profitable. However, the dependence of the periphery on the centre for markets in which to sell its goods and for capital to keep its economy running ensures that the periphery remains underdeveloped.

---

[2] The centre is also referred to by dependency theorists as *the core* or *metropolitan countries* and the periphery as *satellites*.

Dependency theorists also claim that the centre supports non-democratic governments in the periphery because these are more likely to maintain the system of dependency. In particular, non-democratic governments have often been based on local business elites that benefit from their connections to the corporations based in the rich countries.

A DIFFERENT FOCUS Most conventional theories see the causes of underdevelopment and poverty in the culture and politics of Third World countries or view the Third World as simply at an earlier stage of development than the First World. However, dependency theory believes that the global economic and political system prevents the development of the periphery, thus that North–South relations benefit the North.

CRITICISMS Dependency theory has often been criticized for not offering practical solutions to the problem of development. Some dependency theorists suggest that underdeveloped countries leave the global capitalist system (perhaps after a revolutionary overthrow of the local capitalist-oriented state) and become self-reliant. As well, some dependency theorists have suggested that peripheral countries work together to create an alternative to the global capitalist system.

However, countries that isolate themselves from the global economic system (for example, North Korea) generally pay a heavy economic price. The People's Republic of China undertook determined measures to become self-sufficient but eventually abandoned this strategy and has become a major exporting country and a member of the World Trade Organization. The creation of an alternative to the global capitalist system appears unlikely, particularly since the collapse of communism.

Two Practical Approaches: ISI and ELI

One practical approach to the problem of achieving development grew out of work done in the 1940s by the United Nations Economic Commission on Latin America (ECLA), which developed the centre–periphery distinction that dependency analysts use. ECLA theorists noted that countries of the centre had diversified economies, sound financial systems, and stable democratic governments, all of which peripheral countries lacked. To change this, they offered a recipe known as **import substitution industrialization (ISI)**.

IMPORT SUBSTITUTION INDUSTRIALIZATION ISI called for creating an industrial sector that would make many of the products a country was importing. Locally produced goods would then have a market as a substitute for imported goods. **Tariffs** (taxes on imports) would protect the domestic industries from foreign competition while they grew. Once grown, they would have transformed their countries by creating a new class of industrialists, a larger middle class, and a modern working class. This policy worked in

IMPORT SUBSTITUTION INDUSTRIALIZATION (ISI)
An economic development model that involves creating an industrial sector by placing tariffs on imported industrial products.

TARIFF
A tax on imports.

Canada and the United States in the nineteenth century, so it seemed likely to work in the Third World in the twentieth century.

For a while, ISI produced good results in countries such as Mexico, Brazil, and Argentina. However, after about thirty years it failed because of problems inherent in the policy. Many countries applying ISI did build new industries, but these industries never flourished. They kept making expensive goods of poor quality. If governments talked about reducing tariffs to make these firms become more efficient, their owners warned of foreign takeovers, while their workers staged demonstrations to protect their jobs. Governments got the message and backed down.

EXPORT-LED INDUSTRIALIZATION   Another practical approach to development is **export-led industrialization (ELI)**, now often called the **Asian model** because Asian countries have used it most effectively. It is slightly newer than ISI but has had a longer run of success, only encountering difficulties after about fifty very good years.

Sometimes called "the governed economy" (Wade, 1990), this model builds export industries. It features a capitalist system in which government and the biggest businesses work closely together. Government influences investments, provides incentives for exports, and even decides whether firms are allowed to export products. Like ISI, parts of the domestic market are typically protected from foreign competition. Conditions are often placed on the involvement of foreign companies, such as requiring them to create partnerships with local companies, transfer technology, and leave some of their profits in the country. As well, by keeping the value of their currency artificially low and by paying very low wages (often by suppressing unions and not enforcing labour laws), the newly industrialized countries can sell goods at very low prices (Martin & Schumann, 1997).

The objective of ELI is to build the strongest economy possible in the shortest time possible. Japan did this twice: in the nineteenth century when it first industrialized, and then when it rebuilt after the Second World War. South Korea and Taiwan (the Republic of China) followed Japan's lead. The latter two countries created their own variants of the Asian model to develop rapidly and better defend themselves against their communist neighbours (North Korea and the People's Republic of China, respectively) when U.S. economic assistance was reduced in the 1970s. Other countries that have followed this path more or less successfully include Singapore, Malaysia, Thailand, Indonesia, and more recently and spectacularly, the People's Republic of China.

The Asian Model has two striking features:

1. *It works with both non-democratic and democratic governments.* South Korea, Taiwan, and Indonesia were all dictatorships when they began their spectacular development, but now have democratic governments.

EXPORT-LED INDUSTRIALIZATION (ELI)
A model of economic development with a capitalist system in which government and the biggest businesses work very closely together to develop export industries. Government influences investments, provides incentives for exports, and can decide whether firms are allowed to export products.

ASIAN MODEL
The economic model of export-led industrialization associated with a number of Asian countries.

Association of Southeast Asian Nations
www.aseansec.org

Similarly, although Japan and Singapore are formally democracies, each is governed by a party that seldom loses elections.

2. *It has worked best in Asia.* Some commentators feel this success reflects cultural factors (called Asian values), including a strong work ethic, family and moral values, thrift, discipline, and an emphasis on social cohesion rather than individualism. Others point to the fact that the Asian countries that grew strong and prosperous using this model were particularly adept at using government to lead the way to development, both by managing their economies and by emphasizing education. Finally, some commentators hold that the Asian model has not spread because the international trade rules now in place discriminate against countries that use government to build their economies. Indeed, export-led industrialization was particularly successful in Japan, Taiwan, and South Korea, in part because the United States provided them with billions of dollars in aid and, prior to the 1990s, offered them favourable trading terms as part of a strategy of building a defence against communist countries.

BOTH APPROACHES HAVE WORKED The two practical approaches, ISI and ELI, have each worked well for a while, in some countries. This suggests that specific policies, even broad approaches to development, may work better in some places and at some times than in others. Intuitively, this makes sense: Canada did not follow the same path to development as the United States or Britain, yet all became developed democracies. Nevertheless, there is still a tendency to search for the magic bullet that solves everyone's economic and even political problems.

International Development Studies Network
www.idsnet.org

◀ Export-led industrialization was particularly successful in Asian countries such as Taiwan. Reasons for this success include the support of the U.S., which provided them with billions of dollars in aid and, prior to the 1990s, offered them favourable trading terms as part of a strategy of building a defence against communist countries.

DEVELOPMENT ASSISTANCE AND TRADING RELATIONSHIPS

Less developed countries often need considerable help from the richer countries if they are to supply the basic needs of their populations. They also need access to the skills and technology of the richer countries if they are to compete successfully in global markets. Various charitable organizations provide humanitarian assistance and supply volunteers to assist in development projects. However, it is the governments of the richer countries that have the financial resources to provide substantial development assistance to the poorer countries.

OFFICIAL DEVELOPMENT ASSISTANCE (ODA)
Aid to the poorer countries given by the governments of the richer countries.

Canada's foreign aid to poor countries, formally called **Official Development Assistance (ODA)**, is sometimes purely altruistic, as with disaster relief or humanitarian assistance. Often, however, wealthy countries use ODA to secure multiple objectives. In the case of Canada, it seems that the most important objective is helping Canadian business: more than two-thirds of Canadian aid is "tied" (World Bank, 2004), meaning that the money has to be spent in Canada, on Canadian goods and services, even if these are more expensive or less suited to the needs of the developing countries. Similarly, American law requires the U.S. government to buy food for aid from U.S. farmers, ship it on American boats, and use U.S.-based organizations to deliver the food to famine-stricken regions, even though food could be bought from farmers just outside the stricken area for far less (*Foreign Policy*, 2006).

Canada gives less aid than many Canadians think it does. In 1969, former Canadian Prime Minister Lester Pearson proposed that the wealthy countries dedicate 0.7 percent of their GDP to foreign aid. This goal has been accepted by the richer countries and adopted by the United Nations. However, only a few countries have met or exceeded this goal. Canadian governments have continued to be committed to that goal, but in reality, assistance as a proportion of GDP has been declining until recently. In 2005, Canada's ODA was about 0.34 percent of GDP, below the average of 0.47 percent for the world's developed countries.

Although aid does not seem to be especially generous, since the end of the Second World War in 1945 more than US$2 trillion has been spent on foreign aid. Supporters of ODA point to increased literacy, longer lives, and greater opportunities throughout the poor world. Further, Jeffery Sachs (2005), an economist and proponent of increased aid, argues that without significant external assistance many countries will be unable to break free from what he calls "the poverty trap" and attain a measure of economic prosperity.

Critics, however, note that 2.5 billion people, some 40 percent of the world's population, subsist on US$2 daily, thus that $2 trillion isn't working as intended. Robert Calderisi (2006), a Canadian who worked for many years with the World Bank in Africa, holds that aid to individual countries should be cut by half to make recipient governments manage the funds more carefully. William Easterly (2006), another economist, criticizes ODA programs for being paternalistic and unaccountable. He would like to give groups of poor people, not countries, development vouchers that they could use to contract the services of any aid agency or **non-governmental organization** (NGO). *New York Times'* columnist Nicholas Kristof (2006) takes an intermediate position, observing that while foreign aid has a poor record in economic development, it has contributed greatly to humanitarian issues. His colleague Tina Rosenberg (2006) endorses anti-poverty programs that get money and services directly to the poor, instead of going through governments. Programs like the Grameen Bank look like more effective ways to fight poverty and advance development than do the lavishly funded plans of the ODA bureaucracies.

One point that both sides agree on is that no country should receive ODA unless its government meets certain standards of **transparency** and **accountability**. Part of ODA's bad reputation comes from the period of the Cold War (1945–1990), when both the West (the United States, Canada, and their allies) and the Communist bloc (the Soviet Union and its allies) gave foreign aid to dictatorships to win their allegiance, rather than focusing directly on the poor.

Economic Discrimination

Seen from the perspective of the South, the reluctance of the North to send more aid is only part of the problem. Equally serious is the reluctance of the rich countries to open their markets fully to the Third World and to accept fair global trading rules.

Canada and its wealthy colleagues in the G8 (the world's seven largest economies, plus Russia)[3] and the Organisation for Economic Co-operation and Development (thirty countries with a commitment to capitalist economics and democratic politics) talk about free trade and levelling the international economic playing field. But when it comes to trading with poor countries, the richer countries find ways to discriminate against the products that poor countries produce more cheaply, mostly foodstuffs and textiles, in order to protect their own producers. As well, the richer countries heavily subsidize many exports, which then have a major competitive

NON-GOVERNMENTAL ORGANIZATION (NGO)
Private organizations that often deliver public services but are independent of government. NGOs have been very active in international development activities.

TRANSPARENCY
The visibility to the public of the governmental decision-making processes.

ACCOUNTABILITY
Having to be responsible for one's actions and having to accept the consequences of failure to perform as expected.

---

[3] Originally, in 1975, the organization was the G6: the United States, Great Britain, the Federal Republic of Germany, Italy, Japan, and France. Canada joined in 1976. Russia received partial membership in 1994 and full membership in 1998. Were the G8 to include the world's eight largest economies, Russia would have to be dropped in favour of the People's Republic of China, the fourth-biggest economy in the world.

advantage over Third World products. However, we insist that Third World countries must not protect their producers from our products. We can do this because we are stronger and the poorer countries need to trade with us so desperately that they often accept an unfair deal.

Trade Pacts

There are numerous trade agreements involving both rich and poor countries. One hundred and fifty countries plus the European Union (as of July 2007) are members of the World Trade Organization (WTO), an international organization dealing with the rules of trade between countries and the only international organization concerned with economics that does not assign member countries votes based on the size of their economies. There are also regional free-trade agreements such as the North American Free Trade Agreement (involving Canada, the United States, and Mexico), and bilateral agreements such as the Canada–Chile Free Trade Agreement.

Free-trade agreements establish binding trade rules and set up impartial panels to settle trade disputes. In theory, this helps weaker countries, as the arbitrary power of stronger countries can be constrained by the rules. The products of the poor countries can potentially gain access to the large, rich markets of the world's developed countries without facing discriminatory tariffs and quotas. However, many poor countries argue that trade agreements are biased toward the richer countries and do not lead to fair trade relations. For example, agriculture is the major economic activity in many less developed countries, with a large proportion of the population often engaged in farming. However, agriculture in the less developed countries faces severe challenges that the WTO, whose task is to facilitate international trade, has had trouble addressing.

The rich countries provide US$1 billion a day in subsidies to their own farmers. Agricultural products are then exported at very low prices, making it difficult for farmers in poorer countries to sell their products. Indeed, it has been estimated that the rich, developed countries spend six times more on subsidizing their agricultural production than they spend on development assistance (Oxfam, 2003).

Because poor countries are dependent upon access to the markets of rich countries, they are vulnerable to pressure to accept rules that may be more beneficial to the rich. In a major meeting at Doha, Qatar, in 2001, the WTO launched a round of trade negotiations aimed at phasing out agricultural export subsidies and eliminating most tariffs. However, by 2006, talks to achieve these objectives had broken down. The rich countries wanted new trading rules on international investment, competition, and government purchasing policies that would benefit the multinational corporations based in the rich countries, but would not compromise on agricultural subsidies.

POLITICS IN THE THIRD WORLD

Few Third World countries have been able to develop effective democratic systems. Politics in most of these states has been characterized by instability, military rule, violence, and corruption. These traits have contributed to the problems of development.

In the last quarter of the twentieth century, many less developed countries embraced democratic government in the "third wave of democracy" (Huntington, 1991).[4] Yet only a minority of countries have succeeded in forming strong, stable democracies (termed **consolidated democracies**). We shall consider the process of democratization in greater detail in Chapter 19.

In one sense, politics in the Third World is no different from politics anywhere. People want to control the state, to make rules that they think are good, and to enforce those rules as they think best. However, Third World politics diverges from politics in consolidated democracies, such as Canada, in three important ways:

1. Liberal democracies have been rare in the Third World.
2. Third World countries have weak governmental institutions.
3. Violence plays a much bigger part in Third World politics than in developed, consolidated democracies.

CONSOLIDATED DEMOCRACIES
Countries with democratic governments that are stable, well accepted by both ordinary citizens and political elites, and unlikely to be overthrown.

Organization of American States
www.oas.org

Few Liberal Democracies

Liberal democracies are political systems in which the government has to obey the law, just as any citizen does. In such systems, all citizens are assured that their rights and freedoms are recognized and protected, and they have a voice in how their government is run. Although these principles are well established in Canada and in most other First World countries, this has only rarely been the case in the Third World.

Had we looked at the governments of the Third World in 1980, we would have found only a handful of liberal democracies, including India in Asia, Botswana in Africa, Costa Rica in Latin America, and Barbados in the Caribbean. There were also countries that were semi-democracies or marginal cases, such as Singapore and Sri Lanka, but most Third World countries would not have been considered democratic.

Over the last quarter-century, many countries have made transitions to democracy and now the majority of countries, North and South, are considered

---

[4] Samuel Huntington identifies three great historic waves in which countries became democratic. The first wave lasted from the late eighteenth century until the 1920s. It produced the world's historic democracies: for example, the United States, Canada, the United Kingdom, and much of Western Europe. A second wave, associated with decolonization, began in 1945 and crested in the early 1960s. The latest wave started in 1974 when dictatorships fell in Portugal and Greece and still continues. Its greatest success was the fall of the Soviet bloc between 1989 and 1991. Waves of democracy are treated in greater depth in Chapter 19.

democratic. **Authoritarian governments** (another name for non-democratic states) failed and were replaced by democratically elected governments. Some of the failures resulted from the authoritarian government's mismanagement, others from the breakdown of communism, which left some Third World dictatorships without patrons. A few transitions came from external pressure by the United States and the international financial institutions. Most of the transitions were completed by the early 1990s.

However, it takes more than dismantling an authoritarian state and holding elections to build a strong, stable democracy. The transition to democracy has been difficult for many countries. A number of countries have the form but not the substance of democracy. In particular, there are often very few institutional limits on the executive's power. Once elected, a president or prime minister often has the power to govern without restraint until the next election.

Weak Institutions

Strong, **personalistic leaders** have historically dominated politics in poor countries. Almost always men, they are called *caudillos* in Latin America, *big men* in Africa, and *bosses* just about everywhere. Giving one leader too much power can be a problem anywhere, even in the United States (Schlesinger, 1973), Britain (Weir & Beetham, 1999), and Canada (Simpson, 2001). Consolidated democracies, however, generally have counterweights to executive power that seldom exist in new democracies.

These counterweights include **political institutions** inside and outside of government, such as legislatures, courts, the public service, the media, organized interests, political parties, and groups independent of government known as civil society. Democracies need to have both sets of institutions working well. Having strong political institutions lessens the risk that one person, group, or organization will become too powerful in two different ways. A multiplicity of robust institutions disperses power among many centres, each having some ability to counter the actions of the others. Further, having several powerful institutions in a political system gives citizens more chances to present their views to government.

Almost all countries have at least one strong governmental institution: the executive. In Canada, the executive refers to the prime minister or premier, the Cabinet, and the public service. In much of the Third World, however, the president or prime minister monopolizes executive power. As a result, there is little accountability and corruption is a very serious problem in some countries (as described in Box 18-4, Political Corruption: Nicaragua).

The Role of Force and Violence

Violence has always characterized politics in the developing world (as it once did in developed countries, too). Even countries with long histories of democratic

Political Corruption: Nicaragua

Alberto Alemán was elected president of the Central American country of Nicaragua in 1996, six years after entering public life as mayor of the country's capital, Managua. In 1990, Alemán had declared his personal wealth at US$30 000, good for a country where the per capita income was US$500 per year, but not exorbitant. When he left the presidency in 2001, the media estimated his wealth at US$250 million.

Investigations that began after Alemán stepped down unearthed evidence that made the quarter-billion-dollar figure believable. The former president was charged with embezzling more than US$100 million directly from government accounts while in office. He had even used a government credit card to pay for his engagement party and honeymoon (Close & Deonandan, 2004).

Though a corrupt leader, Alemán stood out from most Third World strong men in two ways. Instead of seizing power in a coup or by a rigged vote, he won an open election. Equally important, although he seldom gave his opponents a break, Alemán did not resort to violence to get his way.

rule, such as Costa Rica, have experienced coups, revolutions, and insurgencies in the past. Other democracies, such as Jamaica, still have a great deal of political violence, especially during election campaigns. And the non-democratic countries face even graver challenges, as violence is often a standard instrument of rule.

The clearest contemporary instances of political violence and its devastating effects on a country are found in a number of sub-Saharan African states. In the continent's east, Rwanda and Burundi have been racked by ethnic warfare that spilled over their borders and affected neighbouring states. Governments in the West African states of Sierra Leone and Liberia collapsed, leaving their citizens to be plundered and murdered by marauding armed bands; even now that the civil wars in those countries have ended, both face continuing hardship. Development is obviously impossible in these settings. Why, though, has violence been so common throughout the Third World?

In part, it is due to weak political institutions that cannot protect the public. It is also a sign that politics is a winner-take-all game, with no place left for opponents. Making matters worse is a failure of legitimacy. Citizens do not trust government because government excludes many interests and concentrates control in the hands of the already powerful. Governments then use force to repress their opponents, and those opponents use force to try to change the government. Although this oversimplifies the situation, it does give us a sense of the dynamics that produce political violence in the Third World.

CHANGING TIMES The main agent of political violence in the Third World has been a politically active military. Recently, however, those militaries have taken a less prominent role, thus there are fewer *coups d'état* (forcible seizures

COUP D'ÉTAT
A forcible seizure of power by the armed forces or occasionally the police.

▶ Sierra Leone suffered horribly when its corrupt government collapsed and armed rebel bands that forced youngsters to fight brutally terrorized the country.

DEMOCRATIC TRANSITION
A process of change involving abandoning authoritarian government for democratic rule.

of power by the armed forces or occasionally the police). Militaries in poor countries have long been politicized; that is, they have regularly taken clear political stances and often seized government to run it themselves. They have done this because they have the guns, but also because they are commonly the best organized institution in a country, with the highest concentration of technically skilled, well-trained personnel. Accordingly, when civilian politicians have been corrupt or incompetent, or have gone against the military's wishes, the soldiers would step in and take over (see Box 18-5, Military Coups).

Through the 1980s, it seemed as if there was no general solution to the problem of politically active militaries. However, the wave of **democratic transitions** that began then has coincided with a sharp fall in the frequency of coups. This may reflect a heightened democratic consciousness among soldiers, but there are several other explanations to consider.

One explanation is that citizens in many countries have become dissatisfied with military governments. This is especially true of four southern South American countries (Argentina, Brazil, Chile, and Uruguay) that saw particularly brutal and long-lasting military regimes in the late twentieth century. Another is that militaries around the world have recognized their nearly uniform failure as governors. Militaries can impose order and throw out inept rulers, but with only a handful of exceptions they have not presided over extended periods of development. Finally, the international community no longer tolerates military governments. International financial institutions now are very reluctant to make loans to military regimes and often demand that civilian governments cut military budgets to qualify for loans.

BOX 18-5

Military Coups

Military takeovers of government do not just happen. Studies of coups and how they work help us to understand this phenomenon (Farcau, 1994; Fitch, 1977; Luttwak, 1969).

- First, the army will almost certainly be involved because, of all the armed services, it has the resources that are best suited to toppling a government: armed troops, tanks, and other armour. The air force can strafe buildings and opposing troops, while the navy can shell shorelines and block harbours, but the army secures the area.

- Second, although some coups have been led by sergeants and generals, many coups are led by majors and colonels because they are in direct command of large numbers of soldiers.

- Third, coups succeed or fail based on whether key figures oppose or support them. For example, in 1981, an attempted coup in Spain failed because the king opposed it publicly, causing military commanders to fall in line behind him.

- Fourth, successful coups capture not only government leaders, but also the communications media. When a coup succeeds, it often forms a governing committee or junta (a Spanish word meaning "board" or "committee"). The junta contains all of the key players in coups.

- Finally, some coups are bloodless, because they are essentially unopposed, but others spur civil wars or lead to cruel dictatorships.

◀ On September 11, 1973, the Chilean military (with U.S. support) surrounded and bombed the presidential palace. The democratically elected Marxist president, Salvador Allende, committed suicide and the coup resulted in the establishment of a military dictatorship that tortured and killed thousands of leftists.

The military will always be a political actor and there will likely always be some military regimes. However, current trends suggest that there will be many fewer governments run by generals than in the past.

HISTORICAL PERSPECTIVE   Why do the political conditions just described apply to the Third World? The fact that today's wealthy democracies have pasts as unsavoury and unpromising as what we find in today's developing world tells us that improvement is possible. We often forget that democratization—in its social and economic manifestations of less rigid class barriers and a more equal distribution of wealth as well as in its political form—has been under way for more than two hundred years in the historic democracies of northwestern Europe and North America. To expect Africa, Asia, and Latin America to cover the same distance in a decade or even a generation is unrealistic. Nevertheless, ever more countries are offering their citizens increasingly accountable, honest, and efficient government. This signifies progress toward building a state that can pursue the common good.

"The president says that if we export more oil, we can buy more weapons so that our country will be stronger."

We must recognize, however, that poverty makes good government difficult. In poor countries, controlling the state may offer the surest road to wealth. Where that is the case, keeping the power to govern may seem too important to risk by submitting to elections, allowing a free press, and encouraging citizens to organize freely and make their demands on government. Such conditions also work against building strong state institutions other than the presidency and the security forces because strong organizations can become independent and work toward the common good instead of the ruler's interests. In addition, poor countries often have difficulty establishing an honest, efficient, and knowledgeable staff for government and its agencies. Because government may not be able to pay adequate salaries, public servants may look to other sources of income, such as soliciting bribes or holding multiple jobs, to make a decent living.

Foreign Intervention

The political problems that many Third World countries face are not all of their own making. To a considerable extent, they are a product of a history of domination and exploitation.[5]

The control and colonization of most of the world by the European powers often left Third World countries ill-prepared for governing after becoming independent. In a number of cases, the boundaries of the new countries made little sense, as they combined groups of people of different ancestries, cultures, languages, and religions. To make matters worse, the imperial powers frequently stimulated ethnic divisions within their colonies as part of a divide-and-rule strategy. In other cases, the descendants of the European colonists tried to maintain their economic and political power after independence against the challenges of indigenous peoples.

POST-INDEPENDENCE Further, although most of the Third World was able to achieve independence in the decades following the Second World War, this did not end foreign intervention in their affairs. During the Cold War, the Western and Soviet blocs struggled to gain the support of Third World governments. This involved not only giving their supporters economic and military aid, but also overthrowing unfriendly governments; supporting repressive regimes, revolutionary movements, and terrorist groups; and even encouraging wars among Third World countries.

The end of the Cold War reduced these negative forms of foreign intervention that disrupted the political development of Third World countries. However, concerns about international terrorism, the rise of radical Islamism,

---

[5] We should be careful to note that domination and exploitation have not been associated only with Western powers. Imperialism, colonization, slavery, forced religious conversion, and the massacre of conquered people have been carried out at various times by the powerful, whether Western or non-Western.

security of oil supplies, and the international trade in illegal drugs keep powerful countries intervening in the politics of the Third World.

OTHER FORMS OF POLITICAL INTERVENTION   Three other forms of political intervention have become important in recent times:

1. humanitarian intervention in failed states
2. democracy strengthening and promotion
3. politically conditioned aid

The first primarily involves international organizations such as the United Nations. The second is carried out mainly by individual countries, mostly the United States. International financial institutions and governmental development assistance agencies are responsible for the last.

Failed states are those that no longer have the capacity to maintain order. This is not a new phenomenon, but political scientists have only recently given it a name. Examples of failed states in recent years include Sierra Leone, Liberia, Somalia, and Haiti. In all of these cases, troops from several countries were dispatched under United Nations authority to restore order. One hundred years ago, either the disorder in a country whose government had ceased functioning would have been ignored or, more likely, a powerful state such as Britain, France, or the United States would have taken over.

Neither democratic strengthening nor political conditions for aid require sending troops. Both, though, make a country change its policies to conform to standards set by outsiders. In democratic strengthening, discussed further in Chapter 19, a foreign government or an NGO contracted by a foreign government offers assistance to a recipient country to make its political system more democratic. Usually the advice reflects the practices and interests of the government paying for the program. Although the recipient does not have to follow that advice, its government knows that keeping good relations with the donor demands enacting at least some of the proposed reforms. The world's leading promoter of democratic strengthening is far and away the United States (Carothers, 1999). Canada does rather less of this kind of work, generally limiting its involvement to assistance with the technical aspects of elections.

Aid is politically conditioned when countries must adopt specific economic policies, usually involving reduced government spending and greater openness to foreign investment and imports, in order to receive loans from the World Bank or the International Monetary Fund. Being able to withhold funds from countries in need gives these institutions leverage to get their favoured policies enacted. In the early twentieth century, great powers often imposed economic policies on weaker states over which they exercised military control. Now, international financial institutions and donor countries use the promise of economic assistance to secure the same end. In either case, the weaker party yields to the stronger.

The North–South Institute
www.nsi-ins.ca

Summary and Conclusion

Although there have been improvements in living standards throughout much of the Third World, particularly in the newly industrialized countries of East Asia, differences between the richest and the poorest countries continue to increase. About one-fifth of the world's population still lives in extreme poverty, with incomes of less than US$1 a day (UNDP, 2005). Feeding growing populations, creating employment, and providing housing and other services to those who have flocked to the slums of congested cities pose difficult challenges for many countries.

The problems of the world's poorest states are everyone's problems. A world of great wealth for some and grinding poverty for others is, potentially, a very unstable place. Political violence in Third World countries is not just local, but can affect people in all countries. Poverty, unemployment, or violence in underdeveloped countries leads to migration, legal or illegal, to the richer countries. Environmental problems, such as the destruction of rainforests to achieve rapid economic growth, affect the ecosystems of the world as a whole.

Political scientists do not fully understand how countries develop successfully. There does not seem to be a single, universally applicable route to solving the economic and political problems of underdevelopment. We know that some policies have worked for a while but also that none has fully delivered on its promises. Adopting the free-market policies of the United States and other rich Western countries has not generally been highly successful. In the past, the adoption of the state socialist approach of the Soviet Union failed. Although several Asian countries have achieved high rates of economic growth through export-led industrialization, it is unclear whether this approach can be replicated successfully elsewhere or, indeed, if successes of some Asian countries can be maintained. Despite improvements in the living standards of the Third World, only the city-state of Singapore has fully entered the ranks of the wealthy developed countries.

Development is a political and social issue as well as an economic one, thus abstract economic theories need to be qualified by an understanding of the political, social, and cultural realities of particular underdeveloped countries. Political problems such as corruption, wars, instability, ineffective government administration, and poorly regulated economic activity create serious obstacles to development. Political institutions, both governmental and non-governmental, need to be strengthened and reformed to involve the people in the process of development, to hold government accountable for its actions, and to ensure that sound policies are designed and implemented. The development of Third World countries can also be promoted by pressuring various international institutions to provide fairer opportunities for countries that are weak and poor. Social and cultural changes such as improving the status of women and encouraging the involvement of local communities in the development process can be very helpful.

Overall, the poorer countries face difficult problems in seeking the common good of their citizens. With limited wealth, it is difficult to meet even the most basic needs of the population. Governments often lack the resources needed for effective governing. The great inequalities found in many poor countries let the wealthy wield enormous political power, which hinders needed reforms. Further, underdeveloped countries face not only internal problems, but also problems resulting from global inequities in power. The poorer countries have faced domination and exploitation by the powerful wealthy countries, whether through imperialism or through the global economic system. Various forms of assistance to the poorer countries are often insufficient to overcome the challenges that they face.

In sum, if we want to achieve the common good of humanity, addressing global imbalances in economic and political power as well as providing meaningful assistance to developing countries is necessary. A key problem is that governments and citizens typically are concerned primarily with the good of their own country.

Key Terms

Discussion Questions

1. Why is global inequality so severe?

2. What should a poor country do to develop?

3. Why have some countries in the Third World prospered while others remain poor?

4. Should wealthy countries provide greater assistance to poor countries?

5. Should developed countries help less developed countries to become consolidated democracies?

6. Should poor countries have to meet certain standards of transparency and accountability before they can receive Official Development Assistance?

Further Reading

Bill, J.A., & Springborg, R. *Politics in the Middle East.* Upper Saddle River, NJ: Pearson, Allyn & Bacon, Longman, 2000.

Chazan, N., Lewis, P., Mortimer, R., Rothchild, D., & Stedman, S.J. (Eds.). *Politics and society in contemporary Africa.* Boulder, CO: Lynne Rienner Publishers, 1999.

De Rivero, O. *The myth of development: The non-viable economies of the 21st century.* London, UK: Zed Books, 2001.

Handelman, H., *The challenge of third world development,* 4th ed. Upper Saddle River, NJ: Pearson/PrenticeHall, 2006.

Huntington, S. *Political order in changing societies.* Boston: MIT Press, 1968.

North–South Institute. *Canadian development report.* Ottawa: North-South Institute, [annual].

Seligson, M., & Passe-Smith, J. (Eds.). *Development and underdevelopment: The political economy of global inequality.* Boulder, CO: Lynne Rienner Publishers, 1998.

Sen, A. *Development as freedom.* New York: Knopf, 1999.

Thomas, C. *In search of security: The Third World in international relations.* Boulder, CO: Lynne Rienner Publishers, 1987.

United Nations Development Programme. *Human development report.* New York: Oxford University Press, [annual].

Vanden, H., & Prevost, G. (Eds.). *Politics of Latin America: The power game,* 2nd ed. New York: Oxford University Press, 2005.

Wang, J.C.F. *Comparative Asian politics: Power, policy and change.* Upper Saddle River, NJ: Prentice Hall, 1998.

Wilber, C., & Jameson, K. (Eds.). *The political economy of development and underdevelopment.* New York: McGraw Hill, 1996.

World Bank. *World development report.* Washington: The World Bank, [annual].

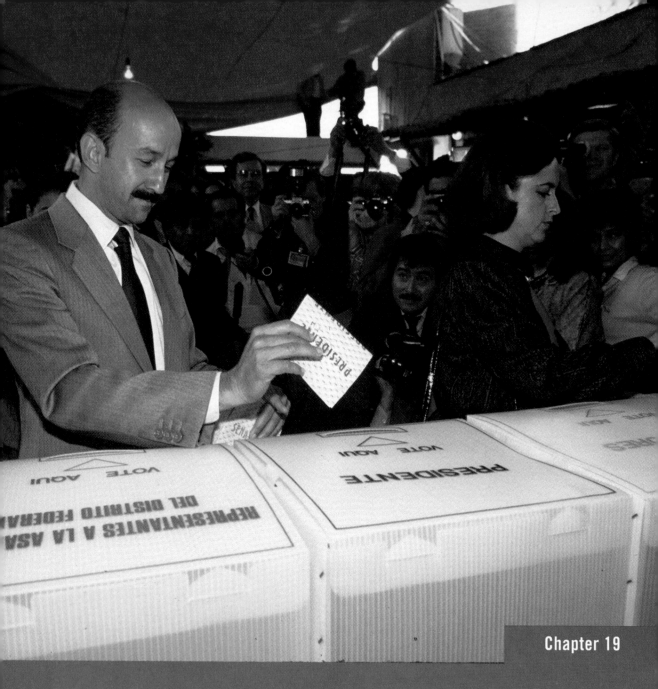

Chapter 19

NON-DEMOCRATIC SYSTEMS AND THE TRANSITION TO DEMOCRACY

PHOTO ABOVE: The power went out in Mexico, forcing a halt to the vote count just as an opposition candidate seemed to be winning the country's 1988 presidential election. But the lights went on in the Mexican electoral reform movement.

CHAPTER OBJECTIVES

After reading this chapter you should be able to:

1. distinguish among the various forms of authoritarian governments
2. understand what a democratic transition is
3. explain what democratic consolidation means and how it is different from a democratic transition
4. discuss democracy promotion and its strengths and weaknesses
5. outline what it takes to build and maintain a democratic political system

When the power went out, suspending the vote count just as an opposition candidate seemed to be winning the country's presidential election, the lights went on in the Mexican electoral reform movement. It was the scandal-ridden 1988 election, and the maxim of "the one who counts wins" was being applied just as it had been since 1929. But two innovations were about to help turn the Mexican system upside down: an independent national electoral authority and groups of citizen electoral observers.

The government party, the PRI (Institutional Revolutionary Party),* used to arrange the elections and count the votes in Mexico. The PRI went beyond "innovative" counting to ensure itself victory by excluding opponents from voters' lists, buying votes, and stuffing ballot boxes. But in 1990, Mexico's national electoral authority, the IFE (Federal Electoral Institute) was founded. It was further strengthened by reforms in 1993 and 1996 (Schedler, 2000). Where earlier electoral authorities had operated only during elections and had little independence from the governing party, the IFE is an autonomous institution operating on a permanent basis, just like Elections Canada.

The IFE's first big test came in 1997, when the PRI lost its majority in Mexico's lower house for the first time ever. Then, in 2000, Mexicans elected the first non-PRI president in more than seventy years. When the PRI regained much of its legislative strength in 2003, the IFE's reputation guaranteed that the results were accepted without question.

The other part of Mexico's success story involves the citizens who serve as independent electoral observers. As their name implies, electoral observers watch the campaign, witness the voting and vote

counting, and report any violations of a country's electoral laws that they see. The presence of these observers, who are organized by national or local civic organizations, seems to give voters confidence that the rules will be applied fairly. They work in many countries where free and competitive elections are new. In 2000, out of a total population of 100 million, about 80 000 Mexicans (excluding party poll watchers) acted as election observers (Polisource, 2003). This was proof of a strong commitment to making democracy work.

However, in Mexico's 2006 presidential election, serious conflict arose over the results and the IFE's neutrality was questioned. The winning candidate, Felipe Calderon of the National Action Party (PAN), defeated Andres Manuel Lopez Obrador of the Democratic Revolutionary Party (PRD) by 35.9 to 35.3 percent. Although domestic and foreign observers accepted the result, Lopez Obrador alleged fraud because a PRD lead of one point with 90 percent of the votes counted turned into a defeat when all of the ballots were counted. The candidate then led his supporters in a massive protest while his party asked Mexico's special electoral court to perform a full recount. When the court

(continued)

---

* The PRI was called the PNR (National Revolutionary Party) from 1928 to 1938 and then the PRM (Party of the Mexican Revolution) from 1938 to 1946, but through these name changes it has been the same organization.

(continued)

rejected that request, Lopez Obrador declared Calderon's win illegitimate and talked of creating a parallel administration.

If Mexico had runoff elections in cases where no presidential candidate had a majority or some specified plurality of the votes, as do Chile and France, there might have been no conflict. Having citizen observers who care enough about democracy to dedicate their time to ensuring that elections are properly run is plainly important. But a well-functioning democracy also needs a legal framework that guarantees that electoral results will be universally accepted. All of Mexico's political parties now agree that the country's electoral law must be changed before the next presidential election in 2012. Democracy doesn't just happen; it must be built.

DEMOCRATIC GOVERNMENT

Democracy is a relatively new form of government. As we saw in Chapter 4, the Athenians experimented with democratic rule about 2500 years ago, but from then until the late eighteenth century it was missing in action.

The idea of letting the people govern themselves grew during the nineteenth century, and by the end of the twentieth century most of the world's population lived in states that are widely accepted as democratic (see Table 19-1). All of these countries have:

- leaders chosen in competitive multiparty elections
- an opposition with a real chance to win
- a system in which no adult citizen is precluded from voting by reason of sex, race, religion, or wealth (Freedom House, 1999)

In fact, Table 19-1 underlines that it really was during the last century that democracy blossomed: if in 1900 there were no countries that we today would consider democratic (because none allowed women to vote), by 2000 there were one hundred and twenty democracies.

However, several questions immediately arise. Why has democracy taken so long to reach a majority of the world's people? Why are there still countries that are not democratic? Can a non-democratic government claim to seek the common good? Answering these questions requires that we examine some of

National Democratic Institute
www.ndi.org

TABLE 19-1
THE GROWTH OF DEMOCRACY IN THE TWENTIETH CENTURY

YEAR	NUMBER OF DEMOCRACIES	POPULATION (MILLIONS)
1900	0 (0%)	0 (0)
1950	22 (14.3%)	743.2 (31.0%)
2000	120 (62.5%)	3439.4 (58.2%)

SOURCE: *Democracy's century: A survey of political change in the 20th century*, by Freedom House, 1999, retrieved August 20, 2004, from *www.freedomhouse.org/reports/century.html*.

the non-democratic systems that have existed and then analyze the **Third Wave of Democracy** (Huntington 1991), the dramatic extension of democracy to many countries in the late twentieth century.

THIRD WAVE OF DEMOCRACY
The broad move to democratic government that began in 1974 and still continues.

The Waves of Democracy

Huntington (1991) notes that democracy has not spread throughout the world at a steady pace. Rather, it has expanded in large and long-lasting waves, the first two of which (1810 to 1926 and 1942 to 1962) spawned reverse waves in which the number of democracies shrank. The latest or Third Wave of democracy began in 1974, with the fall of dictatorships in Portugal and Greece. It gathered momentum throughout Latin America in the1980s and reached a crescendo between 1989 and 1991 as communism failed in the Soviet Union and its allies.

We refer to this process of change as *democratic transition*, which means simply abandoning authoritarian government (another name for non-democratic systems) for democratic rule. Since the early 1990s, the number of transitions has declined, as the world's remaining authoritarian states— forty-five in 2006, ruling 36.1 percent of the world's people (Freedom House, 2006)[1]—grow fewer but more resistant to change.

Consolidation Phase

Once a country has chosen democracy it embarks on the path of **democratic consolidation**. The concept of democratic consolidation is intuitively easy to grasp because it means that a country's commitment to democracy is strong and sure, and that citizens can use governmental processes to extend democracy to fit their needs. However, democratic consolidation is hard to measure. We have no problem deciding when a country has thrown off a dictatorship. However, it is far more difficult to be able to say with certainty that democracy is well entrenched in a country. Later in this chapter, we explain why it can be difficult to decide that a country has a consolidated democracy.

DEMOCRATIC CONSOLIDATION
The situation in which a country's commitment to democracy is strong and sure, such that democracy is likely to persist.

NON-DEMOCRATIC SYSTEMS

For most of human history people have lived within non-democratic systems. Such systems, whether ancient or modern, are often grouped under a single label: *authoritarian*. This term was originally employed by Juan Linz (1964) to refer only to those non-democratic governments that, unlike totalitarian

---

[1] Freedom House categorizes countries according to their levels of political rights and civil liberties. Canada, for example, is among the countries with the highest levels of freedom. It is scored Free and shares this rating with the United States, Chile, Botswana, and India. In contrast, countries such as Honduras, Tanzania, and Nepal are scored Partly Free. It is the countries scored Not Free that we take as being authoritarian governments. These forty-five countries in Freedom House's 2007 ratings include Pakistan, Russia, Belarus, the People's Republic of China, Saudi Arabia, and North Korea.

states, did not attempt to control all facets of life in a country. Using it now to describe any political system that is not democratic leaves us unable to distinguish a state that is murderously despotic from one that rules through electoral fraud, corruption, and legal manoeuvres to hobble the opposition.

Our first step, then, is to unpack the concept of authoritarian government to view its component parts. Specifically, we look at six types of authoritarian systems to grasp the variety of patterns of anti-democratic government:

- totalitarian states
- absolute monarchies
- personal dictatorships
- party dictatorships
- military dictatorships
- theocratic dictatorships

Totalitarian States

All dictatorships share one trait: a high level of concentration of political power. Ordinary citizens do not even have the right to select their governors, let alone participate more actively in making the laws that govern them. The distinguishing characteristic of a *totalitarian* dictatorship is that it seeks to control all aspects of life within a country (see Box 19-1, Totalitarianism versus Authoritarianism). Benito Mussolini, the founder of Italian fascism, neatly summed up the nature of totalitarianism with the slogan, "All within the state, nothing outside the state, nothing against the state!"

Such complete domination was probably always a tyrant's dream, but before the twentieth century it was impossible. During the last hundred years, advances in transportation and communications have made it possible to achieve an approximation of total control. Carl Friederich and Zbigniew Brzezinski (1956) identified six traits that characterized the totalitarian dictatorships of the first part of the twentieth century. All had:

1. an official ideology
2. a single mass party usually led by one man, the dictator, and made up of no more than 10 percent of the population
3. a police state that used terror to control the population
4. a nearly complete monopoly by the party over all means of mass communication
5. a similarly complete monopoly by the party over all means of armed combat
6. an economy planned and controlled by the party

MOST IMPORTANT PRACTITIONERS   The most important practitioners of totalitarian rule were the various fascist and communist movements that existed between 1920 and 1970. Although they differed in many ways, both communism and fascism sought to unite all of the people of a country in a common project commanded by an individual leader and a single political party.

Leading the totalitarian states were very powerful, unchecked rulers, dictators such as Benito Mussolini in Italy, Adolf Hitler in Germany, Joseph Stalin in the old Soviet Union, and Mao Zedong in the People's Republic of China. All were able to mobilize their populations and harness them to the needs of the state. As well, totalitarians ruled by force and violence. Leading great projects that were supposed to transform society, even remake human nature, totalitarians brooked no interference and wasted no time negotiating with their opponents. In this they acted as dictators always have. It was their ability to monitor and control the lives of their citizens that made the totalitarians distinctive.

Yet the totalitarians failed. The Second World War put an end to Mussolini and Hitler, and while communism in the Soviet Union and China lived on after Stalin and Mao, later rulers generally reduced repression and relaxed to a limited degree their control over their people. The Soviet Union joined the ranks of failed totalitarian regimes when it ceased to exist in December 1991.

PATHOLOGICAL TYRANTS It is not only big, powerful states that have flirted with totalitarianism. Perhaps the most shockingly bloodthirsty totalitarian of our age was Pol Pot, who terrorized Cambodia from 1975 to 1979 (Kiernan, 2002). He and his Khmer Rouge turned the Southeast Asian country into a killing field, murdering 1.5 million of its 8 million inhabitants.

Pathological tyrants are neither new nor especially uncommon, however. Nineteenth-century Paraguay produced José Gaspar Rodríguez de Francia, who styled himself *El Supremo* and shut his country off from the rest of the world for almost thirty years (White, 1978). More recently, the tiny African country of Equatorial Guinea fell under the control of Francisco Macias, who brutalized and impoverished his nation while persecuting educated individuals (Decalo, 1988).

CASTRO   Finally, our survey of totalitarian rulers comes to Cuba's Fidel Castro. Though he became ill and unable to rule in 2006, he governed for forty-seven years. Although Castro always looked out for Cubans' welfare, his regime conforms perfectly to Friedrich and Brzezinski's definition.[2]

EMERGENCE FROM A VACUUM   We should note here that totalitarian states, whether ruled by madmen or shrewd dictators, grow out of periods of turmoil and societal chaos. It is as if the vacuum caused by breakdown opens the way to those who would exercise total control over their people. This suggests that societies that are able to function are poor targets for totalitarians.

Absolute Monarchies

Historically, most people have been ruled by monarchs. Some contemporary monarchies, such as the British, Dutch, or Spanish, are constitutional, meaning that the monarch is subject to the law, like everyone else, and has very limited powers. The monarch is the symbolic leader of his or her country and not an active governor. However, some monarchies, such as Saudi Arabia's, are labelled absolute because the monarch has unlimited power. This was the sort of system that the French Revolution toppled in 1789. In fact, much of today's thinking about democratic government first arose to serve as an antidote to absolutism.

In absolute monarchies, political activity is severely constrained. Political parties are often prohibited, and there are no elections since government positions are filled by royal appointment. If there is a representative assembly, it is more likely to be a council of nobles than an elected body that speaks for the people. There is usually strict censorship and the liberties of those outside the ruling circle are radically circumscribed.

Given those characteristics, it will be no surprise to learn that in the twentieth century absolute monarchies were often victims of revolution. This fate befell the Russian empire in 1917, the Ethiopian empire in 1974, and the Iranian empire in 1979. However, in none of these cases was the ensuing regime democratic. Rather, absolutism gave way to other forms of dictatorship. It may be that

---

[2] Some might argue that the nearly permanent presence of thousands of Canadian and European tourists in Cuba suggests that Castro's is not a totalitarian regime. However, both Hitler and Mussolini welcomed travellers and, more to the point, although Castro allows visitors, he does not let Cubans out.

making political activity illegal forces those who want change into clandestine revolutionary movements. If successful, they may use their tight, disciplined organizational structure to control the state.

Four Kinds of Dictatorships

There has never been a true democratic dictatorship because all dictatorships vest power in the hands of rulers who are not accountable to the public. Dictatorships, like totalitarian regimes, often claim that they work on behalf of all of their citizens. However, these governments would not put their hold on power to the test of an open and honest election. Dictatorships can be built around one person or around an institution, such as a party, the military, or a religious elite. Thus, there are four kinds of dictatorships: personal, party, military, and theocratic.

PERSONAL DICTATORSHIPS **Personal dictatorships** are harder to find now, at the start of the twenty-first century, than they would have been even two or three decades ago. They are distinguished by being dominated by a single leader who rules according to personal preferences, rather than by following the law. Historically, personal dictators have always been men, but there is no reason to suppose that women could not fill the role. The great danger in this form of government is that, as in all dictatorships, there are no institutional constraints on the leader, who leaves power only when he dies or is overthrown by armed force.

PERSONAL DICTATORSHIP
An undemocratic government dominated by a single individual. Saddam Hussein's Iraq was a classic example of this kind of system.

PARTY DICTATORSHIPS **Party dictatorships** have their political life controlled by a single political party rather than by a lone individual. In the most unambiguous cases, only one party has the legal right to exist, or, if others do exist, only one party is legally able to exercise power. Communist states have provided the best-known party dictatorships, but they are not the only ones. Besides the obvious instances of Mussolini's Italy and Hitler's Germany, Portugal and Spain also had one-party dictatorships for extended periods in the twentieth century. One-party states were also very common in Africa from independence, usually in the 1960s, to the early 1990s. Rulers there generally justified one-party rule in terms of unifying the nation. They argued that the best way to build a strong nation out of the many tribes that often coexisted uncomfortably within the borders of their countries was to channel all political action through one party. Although this is a logical premise, in practice, eliminating other parties led to dictatorship. Throughout history, most dictatorships of this sort have met violent ends, but since the 1970s more of them are negotiating the conditions of their demise with other political forces.

PARTY DICTATORSHIP
An undemocratic political system that is controlled by one party. The most familiar examples are communist political systems.

MILITARY DICTATORSHIPS In **military dictatorships**, the military obviously provides the rulers (Fitch, 1998; Janowitz, 1977). As discussed in Chapter 18, these systems are established after a military seizure of power, or

MILITARY DICTATORSHIP
An undemocratic government run by the military.

coup d'état. Sometimes military dictatorships are run by committees of a country's armed forces, known as military juntas. Most military regimes start with a junta, but many are quickly dominated by a single leader. When this happens, the resulting government takes on some of the traits of a personal dictatorship, distinguishing itself mostly by giving the military special benefits. Unlike other dictatorships, however, military governments often leave power of their own volition. It is quite common for the military to oust a civilian government, rule for a few years, and then arrange elections for a new civilian government. Although the military frequently imposes restrictions on who may compete for power, the transition is at least peaceful.

THEOCRATIC DICTATORSHIP
An undemocratic state run by religious elites. The best contemporary example is Iran.

THEOCRATIC DICTATORSHIP   A **theocratic dictatorship** is run by religious elites (theocracy is government in the name of God or by priests). Iran is the best current example of a theocratic state (see Box 19-2, Theocratic Government in Iran: 1979–Present). Until overthrown in 2001 by U.S.-led forces that included Canada, the Taliban government in Afghanistan was the most extreme theocratic dictatorship of modern times. Basing its governing philosophy on a radical reading of the Quran, the Taliban was infamous for eliminating virtually all

"The people of this country are going to catch on to this thing called democracy . . . and if they don't we'll make them!"

BOX 19-2

Theocratic Government in Iran: 1979–Present

Iran's seventy million people have had little experience with democracy. Only under the Mossadegh government, which ruled for only a few short days in 1953, was there a respite from authoritarianism.

Although the 1979 Iranian Revolution promised greater freedom after overthrowing the increasingly repressive and autocratic monarchy headed by the Shah, it soon instituted a theocratic system, an Islamic Republic, headed by the religious leader Ayatollah Ruhollah Khomeini. Best known in the West for its uncompromising application of law based on religious doctrine, Iran's political system has also relied on the country's armed forces, the Revolutionary Guards, to use force to ensure compliance.

By 1997, however, there were signs that Iranians had had enough of strictly enforced religious principles. They elected Muhammad Khatami, a moderate cleric committed to reform, as president of Iran. The reformers were fought at every turn by conservatives who supported a theocratic dictatorship, but the forces of change and moderation made significant gains. The Majlis (legislative) elections of 2000 produced a pro-reform majority and Khatami himself was re-elected in 2001. A moderation of the radically religious regime seemed possible. However, Khatami and his allies in Majlis were not Iran's ultimate authority. That rested in the hands of a religious leader, Ayatollah Ali Khamenei, Iran's "Supreme Leader." The Supreme Leader is chosen by an elected, seventy-member Council of Experts, all of whom currently are clerics. Among his other roles, the Supreme Leader is commander-in-chief of the armed forces and the police, head of the state television and radio company, and the country's top jurist.

In 2003, university students led Iranians to the streets in a call for freedom and democracy. Their demonstrations were broken up not just by the police, but also by vigilantes who used clubs and chains. Then, before legislative elections in 2003, the Guardian Council (a twelve-member chamber, half of whom are appointed by the Supreme Leader and half by the Majlis, with absolute veto powers) struck four thousand reformist candidates from the lists. The remaining reformers boycotted the vote. The conservative candidates, approved by the Guardian Council, won in a landslide. In the 2005 presidential elections, hardliners won again, as Mahmoud Ahmadinejad took power. President Ahmadinejad has become best known for his efforts to make Iran a nuclear power.

In an authoritarian state, elites commonly and often legally disregard the public's wishes. Such systems also use force with impunity when challenged by their citizens. That in cases like Iran the authorities believe that they are acting morally, indeed in accordance with the will of God, may only strengthen their resolve and make achieving more rights for more people even more difficult.

rights for women. Both the Iranian and Taliban regimes emerged when a preceding secular authoritarian state was overthrown.

Although Islam is the faith underlying today's theocracies, other religions have been the basis for theocratic rule. North America produced one in the seventeenth-century Massachusetts Bay Colony, which was founded and run by the Puritans, a Protestant sect. As with any religious dictators, the Puritans declared that no one had the right to sin and were zealous in their pursuit of those who violated the colony's rigid moral codes (Parrington, 1987).

▶ Until overthrown in 2001 by U.S.-led forces that included Canada, the Taliban government in Afghanistan was the most extreme theocratic dictatorship of modern times.

Immigration and the establishment of religious tolerance in neighbouring colonies ended the Puritans' experiment. Thus, dictatorships based on religion can evolve into more democratic political systems.

Final Thoughts on Authoritarian Government

All of the non-democratic governments that we now label authoritarian share two characteristics:

1. All of them give the right to determine what constitutes the common good to a restricted number of people. Thus, in authoritarian systems the common good is less what is good for everyone than what the rulers believe is good. (Skeptics will say that the same thing happens in democracies, because elites set the agenda there as well.)

2. In general, authoritarian governments are more likely to use coercion as a normal governing instrument than are democracies. There are good reasons for this. A government that is unelected and unaccountable does not fear the judgment of its citizens. Therefore, it does not need to convince them that some policy is good for the country; it is enough to declare it so and punish those who object. In a democracy, persuasion and consultation are government's best and most useful tools. In an authoritarian state, although a government can try to persuade its people, coercion is easier and more effective, at least in the short term.

Rights & Democracy: International Centre for Human Rights and Democratic Development
www.ichrdd.ca

We can sum up the differences between democratic and authoritarian governments in this way: Democracy aims to be ruled by the people. Authoritarianism aims only to rule the people.

DEMOCRATIC TRANSITIONS

Any country that is now democratic has an undemocratic past. Even Canada and the United States, which along with Australia and New Zealand are the only countries never to have known authoritarian rule since they became independent, have all undeniably become far more democratic over the years, for example by eventually extending the right to vote to all citizens (see Box 19-3, Expanding Democracy in Canada).

Political science has always been interested in how political systems become democratic and how their democracies then develop. However, the democratic transitions of the 1970s and 1980s made political scientists take a fresh look at these questions.

BOX 19-3

Expanding Democracy in Canada

It is easy to take Canadian democracy for granted and assume that it has always been a part of our political life. Although it is true that Canada is one of the few countries in the world never to have suffered under a dictatorship, democracy as it exists today took time to develop. We can find evidence of this by looking at restrictions on the franchise, the right to vote (Elections Canada, 1997).

Until early in the twentieth century, Canada had a property franchise. This meant that those who did not own property worth a certain value or have an income of a specified level were unable to vote. Until the 1940s, some provinces restricted the rights of people of certain non-European ethnic backgrounds, especially Asians, even though those individuals were Canadian citizens. Women were denied the vote federally until 1918, and some Aboriginals were not enfranchised until 1960. (For more details, see Chapter 4, especially Figure 4-1.)

More than voting rights have been extended. Before the 1960s, official bilingualism had a limited reach. It was only in that same decade that laws were adopted promoting and protecting women's rights. Aboriginal rights only arrived on the national agenda in the 1970s, and gay and lesbian rights did not become an important issue until the 1980s and 1990s.

Canada is not alone in expanding democratic rights slowly. All of the world's historic democracies have done the same. This should make us question whether we are right to expect countries just completing their transitions to democracy to offer the same rights and freedoms that people enjoy in Canada, Britain, or the United States.

Democracy's Revival

Until the Portuguese revolution of April 25, 1974, the twentieth century had seen more democracies fail and fall into authoritarian rule than vice versa.[3] Not only did the Great Depression of the 1930s take its toll, but also the flood of new states that accompanied decolonization after the Second World War produced only a handful of long-lasting democracies.[4] Then, in 1973, two of Latin America's longest-lived democracies, Chile and Uruguay, crumbled before military coups. In fact, the failure of democracies was so common that a number of political scientists collaborated to write a book entitled *The Breakdown of Democratic Regimes* (Linz & Stepan, 1978).

As far as democracy's prospects went, then, a sombre panorama confronted the world in the early 1970s. States that had suffered under non-democratic regimes for a long time, such as the Soviet Union, showed no signs of being able to shake them. The new states of Africa and Asia proved, on the whole, unable to sustain democratic rule. Although the heartlands of democracy—northwestern Europe, North America, Australia, New Zealand, Japan, and India—were in no danger,[5] it would have taken a brave political scientist to have predicted in the early 1970s that most of the world's countries would enjoy some form of democratic rule by century's end. Yet that is precisely what happened.

SHRUGGING OFF CHAINS The first movement came from southern Europe as Portugal, then Greece, and finally Spain shrugged off the chains of dictatorship between 1974 and 1978. Next, the venue shifted to Latin America, where throughout the 1980s military dictatorships gave way to electoral democracies. In Asia, both South Korea and the Republic of China (Taiwan) joined the democratic procession. Even in Africa, a bastion of dictatorships of all sorts since the end of colonial rule in the 1960s, countries began to abandon authoritarian ways.

The big story, however, was the fall of communism in Europe,[6] first in the former satellites at the end of the 1980s and then in the Soviet Union itself, which ceased to exist at the end of 1991. Although some dictatorships have yielded to democratic rule since the early 1990s, most notably Indonesia in 1998, the Third Wave of democratic change seems to have subsided. Some

---

[3] However, many of these failed democracies collapsed only after having been invaded by Nazi Germany.

[4] Before 1974, only India, Botswana, and Sri Lanka had managed to maintain democratic government continuously since independence.

[5] Even in the historic, well-established democracies, some authors spoke of a "crisis of democracy" (Huntington, Crozier, & Watanuki, 1975).

[6] This also marked the fall of communism in Mongolia, which was closely allied to the Soviet Union.

very important countries are still not democracies—the People's Republic of China, Cuba, Iran, Syria, and Saudi Arabia—and, as we shall see later in this chapter, some countries have reverted to less democratic ways. Nevertheless, the world is far more democratic now than it was forty or fifty years earlier. Thus, it is fair to describe the last quarter of the twentieth century as the era of democratic transitions.

At the start of this chapter, we defined democratic transitions as the move from an authoritarian government of any kind to a democracy. While that is a handy definition, it raises two questions. First, why did the old regimes fail? They were, after all, authoritarians who repressed dissidents without a second thought. Second, how did the transitions occur—was there a recipe for democratic transition?

The Failure of Authoritarianism

It is sometimes hard for people who know only democratic politics to imagine an authoritarian system failing. After all, these governments worry about neither losing elections nor keeping their citizens happy. A substantial number of them had been working smoothly for many years. There are two explanations for why the clock ran out on so many non-democratic states at the same time: inability to manage an increasingly complex economy, and pressures—domestic and international—to open closed political systems. Looking at a few examples will explain how and why this occurred.

Managing the national economy well is important for any government, but for many years it was not seen as being related to democracy. In fact, commentators often asked whether democracy harmed a country's economic health by putting political concerns ahead of purely economic ones or suggested that democratic government could not produce rapid economic growth (Bhardwaj & Vijaykrishnan, 1998; Leftwich, 1996; Organski, 1967).[7]

By the 1980s, however, several forces pushed toward democracy. First, globalization demanded more open economies that could not be controlled by authoritarian governments. Thus, governments had to choose between being shut out of the global economy or adopting policies that were better managed by democracies.

Second, most authoritarian states were by then producing poor economic results. Even though some authoritarian governments had previously presided over rapid growth, by the last quarter of the twentieth century many, though not all, were facing economic hardship.

Finally, many international economic organizations were demanding democratic political systems either as a condition for entry, as with the European

---

[7] Those who argue that democracy impedes economic development assert that development demands sacrifices and that democracies are not very good at forcing people to make sacrifices. Research now suggests that this argument is ill founded. Remmer (1996) and Easterly (2006) discuss this.

Union, or as a qualification to keep receiving loans, the case with international financial institutions such as the International Monetary Fund.

EXTERNAL PRESSURE   External pressure for political change came not just from international lenders. During the Cold War between the West and the Soviet bloc, the world's democracies would accept any government that was anti-communist, but the West began to push countries to get on the democratic track as signs of reform emerged in the Soviet Union in the late 1980s. For example, in 1988, Chile's military dictatorship organized a plebiscite to determine whether the public wished to extend the government's mandate or preferred to return to the democracy it had lost in 1973. The United States government, which had once supported the dictatorship, changed sides and worked on behalf of those seeking a return to democracy, giving them financial aid to ensure "a level playing field" (Sater, 1990; Sigmund, 1993).

Despite this dramatic shift in outlook and behaviour, there are still times when democracies support authoritarian governments for strategic reasons such as fighting international terrorism. However, such cases are less common than before.

Bringing about Democratic Transition

Political science has charted two routes that people can take to bring about a democratic transition in their countries. One stresses the role of elites working from the top down (Di Palma, 1990). These are called **pacted transitions** because they are produced by pacts or agreements among elites that permit the establishment of democratic government. This form of transition was the norm in Latin America and Southern Europe.

The other route for democratic transition stresses the role of mobilized citizens forming a movement to overthrow authoritarian rule and build democracy. This was the route that was generally followed in the formerly communist-ruled countries of Eastern and Central Europe (Bunce, 2003).

Once the elites have agreed to proceed to democracy or the mass of citizens have proceeded there regardless of the wishes of the elites, democratic transitions are mostly about elections. The central event in a transition is the **transitional election**, which marks the official beginning of a democratic regime. Their role as cornerstones for a new system gives these elections great importance and makes it imperative to get them right.

Elections raise technical concerns, such as how to ensure a quick and honest count of the vote, guarantee all serious candidates some minimum of media time so that voters can learn about them, and ensure that those who run the polling stations are non-partisan and trained to do their jobs. Once this initial election is over, so is the transition.

Thus, democracy is equated with holding elections, a notion that can be traced back to Joseph Schumpeter (1943). Obviously, these elections must be

PACTED TRANSITION
A democratic transition that occurs when pacts or agreements among the elites of formerly undemocratic states permit the establishment of democratic government.

TRANSITIONAL ELECTION
An election that marks the official beginning of a democratic regime.

International Institute for Democracy and Electoral Assistance
www.idea.int

fair and open, and are often observed by foreign organizations to assess whether the vote was really free and the results represented the people's will (Montgomery, 2000). However, even with these provisions, treating elections as the principal condition a country must meet to be a democracy is problematic. First, elections exist outside democracies. This is true historically and it also applies even today to dictatorships that stage sham elections. Second, other parts of a political system are equally essential to building a democracy, including the institutions that administer justice and a political culture that encourages effective participation.

CONSTRAINED DEMOCRACY A system featuring free and competitive elections can coexist with a very thin and constrained sort of democracy. Even after broadening the concept of transition to include a democratic constitution and institutions such as a representative legislature, transition is still bones with no flesh. The institutions that form democracy's skeleton are there, but the outcomes and practices that are democracy's muscle still are not. As with any **procedural definition of democracy**, concentrating on institutions can lead to ignoring the results those institutions produce.

PROCEDURAL DEFINITION OF DEMOCRACY
A definition of democracy in terms of procedures and institutions (such as elections) rather than outcomes.

Instead of focusing on the transitional election, the transition to democracy may be thought of as multi-step process (Carothers, 2002):

1. An opening when an authoritarian regimes shows weakness.
2. A breakthrough when the authoritarian regime collapses.
3. The transitional election, which is the first experience with democratic politics.
4. Consolidation when democracy becomes widely accepted within the country.

Democratic Consolidation

There is no doubt that some democratic systems are so deeply embedded in their societies that it is scarcely possible to think of any other form of government existing. Further, consolidated democracies can extend democracy's reach by, for example, increasing opportunities for participation by the people in decision making. This has certainly happened in Canada. That knowledge, however, does not define consolidation more precisely or make it easier to measure accurately. However, if consolidation is the endpoint of any democratic transition, understanding the concept is critical (see Box 19-4, Democratic Consolidation).

Green and Luehrmann (2003) offer a different formulation. Specifically, these political scientists believe that a democratic transition is complete only when "all politically significant groups agree to abide by the procedural rules of the game (and) . . . no politically significant groups are trying to overthrow the democratic regime" (p. 309). Democracy is then broadly accepted as not just a good way to run public affairs, but as the only legitimate and acceptable way to govern. Once a country has reached this point, its citizens will defend

Democratic Consolidation

Democratic consolidation is a complex phenomenon. To be able to study it effectively and understand its workings, we look for indicators—something reflecting or revealing the presence of what we want to study. Perhaps the best indicator of democratic consolidation is persistence. A country that has maintained over a substantial time a series of the characteristics that most people agree are necessary for democracy would be deemed consolidated.

Two problems arise, however—first, deciding how long is long enough (ten years? twenty?), and then filling out the list of essential characteristics. Regarding the latter, we could choose the absence of a significant force opposed to democracy, or high popular support for democratic institutions as reflected in public opinion polls. However, there will always be debate about whether we use the right criteria to measure democracy, as well as concerns about whether we could collect the necessary data. Not even democratic countries produce the kind of information we would want.

These problems have led political scientists to propose a two-electoral-turnover guideline. Thus, a democracy would be deemed consolidated when a governing party lost an election and turned over power to an opponent twice. This is easy to understand and has readily available data on which to make a decision.

Unfortunately, reality is too complicated for this rule. For example, Botswana, generally considered the most robust democracy in Africa, has been governed by the Botswana Democratic Party since independence in 1966. And we know that in Canada, provincial political parties can have very long uninterrupted runs in office, such as the Ontario Conservatives' forty-two-year stretch from 1943 to 1985, but we do not believe that this means a province is undemocratic. So, while the electoral turnover rule is a good preliminary indicator of democratic consolidation, we must apply it carefully and watch for idiosyncrasies that could lead us to make erroneous conclusions.

the democratic system even when their government faces grave economic or political problems. There are no solutions outside democratic institutions and values in a consolidated democracy.

Even adding this helpful step still leaves two questions. The first is whether all transitions produce consolidated democracies. In other words, is consolidation the automatic, guaranteed outcome of a democratic transition? The second question is the logical counterpart of the first: Can a transition stop somewhere short of full democracy? For example, a country may have free and fair elections and all significant political actors may accept elections as the only legitimate way to gain power. Once in power, though, a government may pack the civil service and courts with its followers, amend laws to make corruption harder to punish, or rig the system to give itself permanent legal advantages. Such systems show enough signs of democracy that we cannot call them authoritarian—indeed, similar systems existed in Canada and the United States through the early twentieth century—but it still seems to fall short of what we instinctively believe a consolidated democracy should be.

If this were only a question of semantics or deciding which country goes into which pigeonhole, it would be unimportant. Unfortunately, there are numerous cases of democratic transitions stalling and leaving countries with political systems that have important non-democratic traits. Political science has to account for these partial, imperfect democracies.

Partial or Imperfect Democracy

Perhaps limited or imperfect democracies should not be counted as consolidated democracies. There are too many discrepancies between our notion of what a democracy should do and how some supposedly democratic governments behave. However, if the country is more democratic than it was before, giving people more freedom and equality, and if the institutional and procedural arrangements it has in place look set to last for some time, then it should either join the ranks of consolidated democracies or political scientists should change how they think about democratic consolidation. The latter view now predominates and we can identify two varieties of imperfect or partial democracies.

THIN DEMOCRACY Countries where the democratic transition stalled before taking full effect constitute one class of imperfect democracy. Ronaldo Munck (1997) uses the term "thin democracy" to characterize democracy in Argentina in the 1990s. Although the country seemed to have put a long history of military dictatorships behind it, Munck feared that democracy still did not penetrate all areas of the country's political life. Gill, Rocamora, and

◄ Thin democracy? In Guatemala, democracy depends on the backing of the military.

Wilson (1993) talk about "low-intensity democracies" whose existence depends on the real but extra-official backing of the military. Guatemala has exemplified this kind of system since abandoning direct military rule in 1986.

DELEGATIVE DEMOCRACY A second class of imperfect democracy contains countries where democratic achievements have been reversed, although not entirely obliterated. Guillermo O'Donnell (1994) coined the phrase "delegative democracy" to fit one set of these cases.

Delegative democracies have competitive elections, wide-ranging political opposition, free media, and functioning legislatures and courts. What they do not have is any serious control over their president or prime minister between elections. They are governed by a boss who has as free a hand as the boss dares to use.

In particular, when faced with a crisis, leaders in a delegative democracy will typically assume great powers to confront it. Although the same thing occurs in consolidated democracies, in a delegative democracy the leader tends to keep the added powers once the crisis has passed. Delegative democracies in effect adapt the pattern of one-person, unaccountable rule found in authoritarian states to the requirements of a democratic constitution.

The Failure to Consolidate Democracy

Governments do not always seek to extend or perfect democracy. They may be unwilling to go beyond a limited form of democracy either to retain power or to avoid raising levels of political conflict. This can lead governments to "undo democracy" (as discussed in Box 19-5, Undoing Democracy). What this suggests is that the sequence of events leading from the first tremors of a dictatorship to having a solid democracy is less certain than observers and analysts once thought.

Democracy Promotion and Democratic Strengthening

To maximize the chances that a country embarking on a democratic transition actually emerges as a consolidated democracy, a number of already consolidated, stable democracies have added a democracy promotion element to their foreign policies. In this endeavour they have been joined by some nongovernmental organizations (NGOs) and international organizations. The work has been under way since the early 1980s and still continues.

The National Endowment for Democracy
www.ned.org

Thomas Carothers, probably the world's leading expert on democracy promotion, argues that there is a "democracy template" (see Table 19-2) that embodies the "core strategy" of democratic strengthening (1999, pp. 86–88).[8] Translated into practice, this means focusing on the electoral process, state

---

[8] Perlin offers a slightly different and somewhat broader list of what he calls "the objectives of political aid" (2003, p. 9): good governance, human rights, democratization, and civil society.

BOX 19-5

Undoing Democracy

Governments can consciously work to make democracy more imperfect.* They do this by removing some of the impediments that democracy puts in the way of easy administration, thus letting them rule with less accountability and fewer restraints. It may seem odd that a democratically elected government should want to limit democracy, but there is a logic at work here. Governing is hard work and democracy makes it even harder. In a democracy, the government should be honest and transparent, and even encourage citizens to take part in running things. Worse, in democracies, governments have no job security. Ungrateful electors can turn them out in any election.

In poor countries with weak economies, government is often the best road to riches, so losing power is a daunting possibility. So too, however, are accountability and tolerating a free and active opposition and media that investigate what government does. It is no surprise, then, that a government would want to remove the constraints that democracy puts on it. With a little luck, and perhaps more than a little money, a government can simply ignore the rules. In some cases, however, it may believe that it has to change those rules.

There is one bit of good news, though. Whereas in the past governments that felt hemmed in by democracy simply abolished it and established dictatorships, today they seem more inclined simply to weaken democracy so that it does not work as intended. Now they may do so because many foreign aid agencies and international organizations will not deal with dictatorships. Yet even if the reason is unedifying, leaving the outward forms of democracy in place provides a foundation on which a future government more dedicated to democracy can build.

---

* This argument is developed more fully by David Close (2004).

---

institutions, and civil society. The United States is the most active proponent of democracy promotion, followed by Germany, the United Kingdom, the Scandinavian states, the Netherlands, and Canada.

United Nations Development Programme
www.undp.org

Among the countries that are important sources of economic aid, only Japan does not have a significant democracy promotion program (Perlin, 2003). Overall, these states, plus international organizations such as the United Nations Development Programme and the World Bank and NGOs such as George Soros's Open Society Foundation, dedicate about US$3 billion to democracy promotion every year. Is this money well spent?

According to Carothers (2002), at least in the case of the United States, funds for democracy promotion are not well spent. He believes that democracy promotion has fallen prey to a one-size-fits-all outlook that depends on all countries following the same steps and using the same institutions as they move toward democracy. Going beyond Carothers's critique, the very concept of democracy promotion raises difficult questions. Although it seems obvious that external aid to countries that are building new democracies is welcome and useful, it seems equally obvious that democracy must take different forms in different countries. Canada has different governmental institutions, political

TABLE 19-2
**THE DEMOCRACY
TEMPLATE**

SECTOR	SECTOR GOAL	TYPE OF AID
Electoral process	Free and fair elections	Electoral aid
	Strong national political parties	Political party building
State institutions	Democratic constitution	Constitutional assistance
	Independent effective judiciary and other law-oriented institutions	Rule-of-law aid
	Competent, representative legislature	Legislative strengthening
	Responsive local government	Local government development
	Prodemocratic military	Civil-military relations
Civil society	Active advocacy non-governmental organizations (NGOs)	NGO building
	Politically educated citizenry	Civic education
	Strong independent media	Media strengthening
	Strong independent unions	Union building

SOURCE: *T. Carothers, Aiding democracy abroad: The learning curve (Washington, DC: Carnegie Endowment for International Peace), p. 88.*

values, and processes than the United States. If two of the world's oldest and surest democracies can be democratic in quite different ways, why should new and struggling governments not seek their own paths? Similarly, we should ask whether democracy promoters give new democracies enough time to get their institutions right and to allow a democratic political culture to mature. America's recent efforts to transfer democracy to Iraq bear these points out (see Box 19-6, A Bungled Effort to Bring Democracy to Iraq?).

A Democratic Future?

Currently, all forms of dictatorship and other examples of non-democratic rule are in at least momentary decline. Does this mean that all of the world's countries will have at least openly elected governments, the minimum requirement for democracy, in the near future? At least one analyst thinks so.

Francis Fukuyama (1989, 1992), a political scientist who worked as an analyst for the United States' Department of State (foreign affairs), argued in 1989 that liberal democracy had proven its superiority and would soon be universally accepted. He based his conclusion on an analysis of key trends, notably globalization and the crisis of European communism, that were becoming evident.

A Bungled Effort to Bring Democracy to Iraq?

American political scientist Larry Diamond is a world-renowned expert on the practical aspects of building democracies. It was therefore natural that he was asked to serve with the Coalition Provisional Authority (CPA), the occupation government set up by Washington to run and democratize post-Saddam Iraq. In his book about his experiences in Iraq, Diamond (2005) argues that the CPA did too little to establish lines of communication with the Iraqi people and appeared to have less commitment to democracy that did the Iraqis. Arriving with a plan drafted in Washington before the war, the CPA proved inflexible and unable to adapt to the wishes and needs of the Iraqis, the people the invasion was intended to liberate.

Although Diamond's book is about America in Iraq, it raises the same questions about democracy and democracy promotion that Carothers does. We should therefore think carefully before prescribing our particular democratic forms and values to others.

Fukuyama's thesis sparked lively debate. Some argued that the norms of liberal democracy clash with Asian values, which place greater weight on duty and the family rather than on freedom and the individual. Others felt that Fukuyama was too quick to declare the liberal version of democracy the winner, believing that a different version of democracy emphasizing substantive outputs that contributed to the material well-being of the citizenry was still a viable option.

However, the terrorist attacks on the United States in 2001 most grievously undermined the hope that all of the world's peoples would soon live under democracies. Not only did some people prefer a theocracy, or at least reject liberal democratic values that they associated with the West, but they were ready to take extreme measures to make their preferences clear.

Summary and Conclusion

Canadians generally hope that democracy becomes the universal form of government. We view democracy as the best way to seek the common good because only democracy is committed to giving every man and woman a voice in saying how they should be governed and by whom. Thus, as more countries develop democratic political systems, more people will contribute to deliberations about the common good and the policies that governments enact will be more likely to work toward the common good of their countries.

Nevertheless, it is doubtless too soon to talk about democracy as a universal aspect of politics.

A wiser approach would be to lower our sights a little. Doing that will reveal that more people now live in democracies than ever before in human history. That should please all democrats, even if nothing less than universal democracy will satisfy them.

Key Terms

Democratic consolidation 453

Military dictatorship 457

Pacted transition 464

Party dictatorship 457

Personal dictatorship 457

Procedural definition of democracy 465

Theocratic dictatorship 458

Third Wave of Democracy 453

Transitional election 464

Discussion Questions

1. Do you think that most countries will become democratic in the next few decades?
2. What obstacles stand in the way of the democratic transition and consolidation?
3. Is totalitarianism likely to reappear as a significant type of political system?
4. Should Canada provide aid only to democratic countries and those moving toward democracy?

Further Reading

Brooker, P. *Non-democratic regimes: Theory, government and politics.* New York: St. Martin's Press, 2000.

Collier, D. (Ed.). *The new authoritarianism in Latin America.* Princeton, NJ: Princeton University Press, 1979.

Diamond, L. *Developing democracy: Toward consolidation.* Baltimore, MD: Johns Hopkins University Press, 1999.

Diamond, L., & Plattner, M. (Eds.). *The global divergence of democracies.* Baltimore, MD: Johns Hopkins University Press, 2001.

Gregor, A.J. *Contemporary radical ideologies: Totalitarian thought in the twentieth century.* New York: Random House, 1968.

Grugel, J., *Democratization: A critical introduction.* New York: Palgrave, 2002

Journal of Democracy, 1990–.

O'Donnell, G. *Counterpoints: Selected essays in authoritarianism and democratization.* Notre Dame, IN: Notre Dame University Press, 1999.

O'Donnell, G. "Democracy, law, and comparative politics." *Studies in Comparative International Development, 36*(1), 2001, pp. 7–36.

O'Donnell, G., Schmitter, P., & Whitehead, L. (Eds.). *Transitions from authoritarian rule*. Baltimore, MD: Johns Hopkins University Press, 1986.

Pinkney, R. *Democracy in the Third World*. Boulder, CO: Lynne Rienner, 2003.

Przeworski, A., with P. Bardhan, et al. *Sustainable democracy*. New York: Cambridge University Press, 1995.

Reuschmeyer, D., Stephens, E., & Stephens, J. *Capitalist development and democracy*. Chicago: University of Chicago Press, 1992.

Smith, P. *Democracy in Latin America*. New York: Oxford University Press, 2005.

Chapter 20

POLITICS AND GOVERNANCE
AT THE GLOBAL LEVEL

PHOTO ABOVE: The international conflict known as the turbot war broke out in March 1995. The Canadian Coast Guard seized the Spanish trawler *Estai* on the Grand Banks off Newfoundland, accusing it of contravening measures to conserve fish stocks.

1. discuss the differences between national politics and international politics
2. explain the differences between the realist and the liberal–internationalist approaches to the study of international politics
3. analyze contemporary international political issues by using the realist and liberal–internationalist approaches
4. assess the chances of international peace and the possibilities of order and governance at the global level

The international conflict known as the turbot war broke out on March 9, 1995, when the Canadian Coast Guard seized a Spanish trawler, the *Estai*, on the Grand Banks off Newfoundland, accusing it of contravening measures to conserve fish stocks. The Grand Banks used to be one of the richest and most popular fishing grounds in the world. By the 1970s, it became clear that unless rigorous conservation measures were adopted, its fish stocks would collapse. On January 1, 1977, Canada declared a 200-mile (320-kilometre) exclusive economic zone and imposed strict controls on fishing inside the zone. However, about 10 percent of the Grand Banks, known as the Nose and Tail, are beyond Canada's limit.

In 1979, the conservation of the fish stocks outside the 200-mile limit became the responsibility of an international organization, the Northwest Atlantic Fisheries Organization (NAFO). In February 1995, NAFO announced its allocation decision for the total allowable catch (TAC) for turbot for 1995, with a breakdown for Canada, the European Union (EU), and other countries that left the EU dissatisfied. Since NAFO procedures so allow, the EU unilaterally set itself a higher quota.

In part because of NAFO's inability to enforce its own quotas and conservation measures, Canada decided to act in defence of its interests. In May 1994, following the collapse of the cod stocks and the consequent adoption of a moratorium on cod fishing, the Canadian government decided to search, and if necessary seize, any foreign vessels using flags of convenience suspected of fishing in violation of conservation measures. Following the EU decision to set its own quota for turbot, the Canadian government reacted by suggesting a turbot fishing moratorium of sixty days and adding Spain and Portugal to the list of states whose ships could be searched and seized.

The EU refused to impose the moratorium. On March 9, 1995, the Canadian government seized the *Estai* in international waters and accused it of fishing with nets smaller than those permitted under conservation measures and of purposely misreporting its fish landings. The Spanish government brought a case against Canada before the International Court of Justice (ICJ) in The Hague, accusing it of piracy. Eventually, Canada dropped its charges and the ICJ decided not to act on Spain's case.

The turbot war exemplifies the predicament in which states find themselves in international politics, namely whether to entrust the defence of their interests to a weak international regime with limited enforcement abilities or to rely on themselves, which might at times require the use of force. This chapter examines politics at the global level, first pointing out the major differences between national and international politics and then illustrating the differences between the two main approaches to the study of international politics, namely the realist and the liberal–internationalist approaches.

INTERNATIONAL POLITICS AND GOVERNANCE

There is a major difference between national politics (politics within one state) and international politics (politics at the global level). States are entities composed of a population, a government, and a territory. They are sovereign, meaning that their governments have the final authority to make and enforce rules on the population living within their territorial boundaries. The world as a whole does not have such a central authority. There is, in other words, no world government; states live in an **anarchic** world.

ANARCHY
A situation in which there is no central authority.

This means that the organization of authority within the world is horizontal rather than vertical (that is, hierarchical), as within a state. The world has as many authorities as there are sovereign states—almost two hundred of them. The fact that the world is anarchic does not mean, however, that there are no rules in relations among states. Rules do exist. They are based on customary practices that have often been codified into law. They are also the result of agreements negotiated and signed by states directly (international treaties) or negotiated and agreed upon within the framework of international governmental organizations, which are associations of sovereign states, created to facilitate co-operation among them in specific issue areas. International rules also derive from interpretations of existing international law provided by the courts.

International Court of Justice
www.icj-cij.org

Because the world is anarchic, though, there is no certain mechanism to enforce international rules. An individual who breaks the law within a state will, more often than not, be apprehended by police, tried in a court of law, and punished. A state that chooses to ignore international rules either because it interprets them in a different way than other states or because it is in its interest to do so will, more often than not, escape punishment. Individuals cannot claim that certain rules do not apply to them or refuse to appear in court if summoned. A state can refuse to be bound by some rules by choosing not to be part of the treaty establishing them. A state may also refuse to submit to a court when accused of violating international law. The International Court of Justice (ICJ), which has the task of settling disputes among states (either in accordance with international law or, if so requested by the parties, *ex aequo et bono*—that is, simply on the basis of justice and equity), has no compulsory jurisdiction. This means that the ICJ cannot summon a state to appear before its fifteen judges who sit in The Hague, Netherlands, unless that state has voluntarily agreed to recognize the jurisdiction of the court and submit itself to its judgment.

GLOBAL GOVERNANCE
The process whereby a number of different actors (mainly states and international governmental and non-governmental organizations) compete and co-operate to provide a certain degree of order and predictability to relations among states.

Although the world as a whole does not have a government, it can be said to have **global governance**, which can be defined as the process whereby a number of different actors compete and co-operate to provide a certain degree of order and predictability to relations among states.

All scholars of international politics agree in defining the world as anarchic (that is, lacking a central authority). They also agree in recognizing that, anarchy notwithstanding, a certain degree of governance exists. When it comes to assessing the significance of anarchy, identifying its consequences, and making policy suggestions, however, scholars divide themselves into a number of different schools. Each one starts from different assumptions, adopts a different theoretical approach, and ends up making different policy recommendations. This chapter focuses on the two major schools: realism and liberal–internationalism.[1]

REALISM

The realist school assumes that, since the world is anarchic, states find themselves in the same predicament as that of individuals in the state of nature before the establishment of government imagined by English philosopher Thomas Hobbes (1588–1679). According to Hobbes, life in the state of nature is "solitary, poor, nasty, brutish, and short" (1651/1968, p. 186). Individuals must fend for themselves in this competitive and dangerous environment.

Realism also assumes that the main objective of states is their own security, understood primarily as the defence of their territorial borders and form of government and the protection of their population from external threats. This objective is the core of what is usually called the **national interest**, which realists view as the most important common good governments pursue when conducting foreign policy—that is, when acting in relation to other states or actors outside their national territories.

For realists, the pursuit of the national interest is a central and constant feature of the foreign policy of any state, regardless of changes of governments or political leaders. So, at least in regard to the quest for national security, realists regard each state as a unitary actor that makes decisions as if it were a single person, even if decisions are made by different individuals and institutions acting on behalf of the state.

If states must rely only on themselves for their security, it follows that they must seek to preserve and accumulate power. Power—that is, the ability of a state to get its way in the international arena when its interests or preferences clash with those of other states—derives from a variety of resources or capabilities. These may be tangible and measurable, such as economic and military resources, or intangible and unquantifiable, such as ideological and cultural resources. The European Union, for instance, believes that its security depends primarily on its ability to attract other states to copy its own political, economic, and social model. Thus, its security strategy calls for "spreading

REALISM
An approach to the study of international politics that assumes that because the international system is anarchic, security is the major preoccupation of states. Peace rests primarily on deterrence, and the possibility of international governance is limited because states are reluctant to put constraints on their sovereignty.

NATIONAL INTEREST
The goals a state pursues in the conduct of its foreign policy. The term is multi-faceted and, besides the quest for power and security, includes goals ranging from the pursuit of economic growth and wealth to the preservation and expansion of national culture.

---

[1] The most prominent representatives of the realist school are Carr (1939), Morgenthau (1948), Waltz (1979), and Gilpin (1981). The work of Keohane and Nye (1977) and Keohane (1984) have shaped the liberal-internationalist school. There are also constructivist, feminist, and radical schools. See, for example, Wendt (1999), Zehfuss (2002), Cox (1987), Wallerstein (1974–1980), Enloe (1989), and Sylvester (1994). For an overview of all theoretical approaches, see Sterling-Folker (2006).

good governance, supporting social and political reform, dealing with corruption and abuse of power, establishing the rule of law and protecting human rights" (European Council, 2003). Tangible resources or capabilities are usually defined as constituting hard power, whereas intangible resources are usually referred to as soft power. Both are important.

Since all states are sovereign, they are equal from a legal point of view. Equal in law, however, does not mean equal in fact. Some states have more power than others. This means, as first pointed out by the Greek historian Thucydides some 2400 years ago, that "the strong do what they have the power to do and the weak accept what they have to accept" (quoted in Goldstein, 1994, p. 48). According to the realist school,[2] a world divided into sovereign states constitutes an **international system**. How power is distributed among states affects the way the system works, that is, how states tend to relate to one another in it (see Box 20-1, Power Distribution in the Classroom and at the Pub).

The modern international system dates from the treaties of Münster and Osnabrück signed in 1648. They are collectively known as the Peace of Westphalia, and hence the system is sometimes referred to as the Westphalian system. The treaties put an end to the so-called wars of religion that had devastated Europe since the Protestant Reformation of 1517. Even more importantly, they recognized and incorporated the concept of state sovereignty, which had been developed by the French jurist Jean Bodin (1503–1596). Since then, sovereign states have been the major units of the international system. The distribution of power among the states in the system has undergone changes, however.

We distinguish among different types of international systems based on how power is distributed among states. Because each concentration of power is called a **pole**, we talk about multipolar, bipolar, and unipolar international systems (see Figure 20-1).

Multipolarity

From the Peace of Westphalia until the beginning of the twentieth century, the international system was **multipolar**, meaning that it contained at least four, and sometimes more than four, major poles.[3]

INTERNATIONAL SYSTEM
A concept referring to both the most important international actors (states and international governmental organizations) and the pattern of interactions among them. The latter depends primarily on how power is distributed among actors.

POLE A concentration of power in the international system. It could be a state or an alliance.

MULTIPOLAR SYSTEM
A multipolar system is a type of international system containing four or more major powers.

---

[2] To be more precise, one should make a distinction between two trends within the realist school. Traditional realism looked at the behaviour of states in the international system the way Hobbes speculated about the behaviour of individuals in a state of nature. The most representative work of this phase is Morgenthau (1948). More recently, a group of scholars, called neo-realists, have concentrated on examining the dynamics of different types of international systems and their impact on the behaviour of states. Their most representative work is Waltz (1979).

[3] Note that scholars do not regard a tripolar system, of which there is no historical example, as a type of multipolar system. The reason is that the policy of balancing, which is the central characteristic of a multipolar system, would be difficult to pursue since two states could ally and prevail on the third. A tripolar system is therefore considered a distinct type and inherently unstable.

Power Distribution in the Classroom and at the Pub

A university class—a group of students and their lecturer—can be regarded as a type of system. Its components or units in this case are not states but individuals. When these individuals move out of their normal environment, say to a local pub to celebrate the end of the academic year, the distribution of power among them will change.

When the group meets in a classroom, power is concentrated in one individual, the lecturer, while the students are in a subordinate position. When they meet at the pub at the end of the academic year, their behaviour will change. Most likely it will be much less formal and predictable than in the classroom.

In a classroom, the lecturer will speak most of the time and occasionally call upon students who signal their desire to speak. While some students will listen attentively, others will let their minds wander or even fall asleep. In the pub, the lecturer will no longer shape the interaction between himself or herself and the students and among the students themselves. Some students might continue debating the topic that occupied them in class, but they will be more willing to express their views and will not ask formal permission from the lecturer to intervene in the conversation. Others will strike up side conversations, maybe on a different topic.

Because the distribution of power among them has changed, the behaviour of the components of the system changes. Outside the classroom, power is no longer concentrated in one individual, the lecturer, but is equally distributed among all components of the system—students and lecturer. In the pub, the lecturer no longer has any official authority over students and consequently their behaviour is no longer constrained in the same way as in the classroom. The same thing happens in the international system. The range and type of foreign policy actions that states can pursue in an international system in which power is more or less equally distributed will be much larger, and less predictable, than those they can pursue in a system in which power is concentrated in one state, for instance.

States in a multipolar system tend to maintain what is called a **balance of power**—that is, they tend to behave in such a way as to prevent the emergence of a dominant power. On the one hand, a state must try to increase its power in order to guarantee its security. On the other hand, it must be careful not to be perceived by other states as representing a threat to them because in such a case it would eventually face a confrontation with them. States thus face what is called a **security dilemma**: they need power to feel secure, but the accumulation of power might undermine rather than increase their security if it leads other states to feel in danger and form an alliance to meet the perceived threat.

Power, in fact, can be augmented not only through an increase in capabilities, but also through the formation of alliances. Indeed, in a multipolar system, the formation of alliances plays a key role in the maintenance of a balance of power (see Box 20-2, Anatomy of Alliances).

BALANCE OF POWER
A situation in which no state is dominant in the global system.

SECURITY DILEMMA
The dilemma that arises when states need power to feel secure, but their accumulation of power might undermine rather than increase their security if it leads other states to feel that they are in danger and form an alliance to meet the perceived threat.

FIGURE 20-1
TYPES OF INTERNATIONAL SYSTEMS

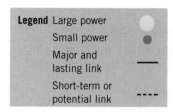

| Legend | Large power | Small power | Major and lasting link | Short-term or potential link |

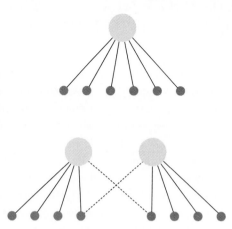

Unipolarity
One state (usually referred to as superpower or hyperpower) has a dominant or hegemonic position in the system.

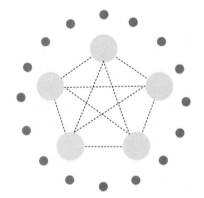

Bipolarity
Two superpowers have a number of lesser powers as allies or satellites. This was the type of international system during the Cold War.

Multipolarity
Four or more great powers compete and co-operate with one another to ensure that none of them emerges as a superpower. Smaller powers do not play a significant role.

SOURCE: *Adapted from* International politics on the world stage, *9th ed. (p. 65), by J.T. Rourke, 2003, Boston: McGraw-Hill.*

BOX 20-2
Anatomy of Alliances

Alliances in the realist perspective are not based on friendship or a commonality of ideology or views but on interest. Alliances are formed, in other words, whenever needed to meet a common threat. There are two main characteristics of alliances:

1. To be effective as a mechanism to balance power, they must not be permanent but be able to shift according to needs.

2. If war becomes necessary to prevent one state from becoming dominant, alliances ensure that the defeated state is not eliminated from the map, but simply cut down to size and reinstated in the system. This is, for instance, how European powers dealt with France after they had defeated Napoleon at the beginning of the nineteenth century.

Bipolarity

The distribution of power in the international system may of course change. This may occur when some states are unable to continue producing the power resources and capabilities needed to sustain their position in the system, or when changes in technology such as the development of the nuclear bomb lead to the rise of new power(s). At the end of the Second World War, the international system that had been multipolar since its inception became **bipolar**. The United States and the Soviet Union emerged as rival superpowers, so called because of their formidable nuclear arsenals, which no other country could match.

Their rivalry might have been compounded by the differences in their economic and political regimes—the U.S. was a liberal democracy with a free-market economy whereas the Soviets had a communist dictatorship with a command economy (an economy under the total control of the state). Realists, however, argue that in a bipolar system, the two superpowers are bound to compete with one another. The other states in the system will fall within the sphere of influence of one or the other of the two superpowers, and thus two opposing blocs will be formed. Some states might be able to remain non-aligned, but competition between the two superpowers and their respective blocs will be the major issue in a bipolar system and overshadow all others. Each superpower will try to keep the other in check, and at the same time try to increase its own power. It will also try to recruit new members to its respective bloc, while trying to prevent others from joining the rival one.

In the past, the rivalries between Sparta and Athens in the ancient Greek city-state system and between Rome and Carthage ended in direct military confrontation and the defeat (and, in the case of Carthage, destruction) of one of the two rivals. This was not the case with the confrontation between the Americans and the Soviets, which is why the period between 1946 and 1989 is known as the Cold War. Realists argue that the two superpowers did not clash militarily because of the presence of nuclear weapons. As Robert Oppenheimer (1953), one of the scientists who worked on the development of the atomic bomb in the U.S., put it, the two superpowers were like two scorpions in a bottle—if one attacked the other, it must do so at the price of its own destruction. While avoiding direct military confrontation, however, the two superpowers did fight each other by proxy. Military confrontation took place between some of their client states or even within one state that they were both trying to bring to their respective bloc, in the form of a civil war.

BIPOLARITY
A type of international system in which two superpowers compete with one another. The other states in the system fall within the sphere of influence of one or the other of the two superpowers.

Unipolarity

The economic collapse of the Soviet Union and its subsequent political disintegration at the beginning of the 1990s left the U.S. as sole superpower and

▶ At the end of the Second World War, the international system became bipolar. The U.S. and the Soviet Union emerged as rival superpowers: no other country could match their formidable atomic arsenals. With the economic collapse of the Soviet Union, the U.S. became the sole superpower and the system transformed from bipolar to unipolar.

UNIPOLARITY
An international system with a single superpower.

transformed the system from bipolar in **unipolar**. Given its overwhelming military superiority and economic size, no other state is capable of matching the U.S. in terms of power.

On the one hand, the sole superpower has the ability to act unilaterally (that is, without the formal approval of international organizations) to suppress any perceived threat to its status. On the other hand, it has an incentive to build as vast a consensus as possible around its choices. Thus, the sole superpower has an incentive to exercise power through authority (that is, through multilateral procedures that are perceived as legitimate by other states in the system) and persuasion rather than solely through coercion. The sole superpower must, in other words, act as much as possible as a hegemon. The repeated use of coercion, in fact, might solve problems in the short run, but in the longer run it will invite the formation of a countervailing bloc, and thus erode its position in the system as well as its security. It seems highly unlikely that France, Germany, Russia, and China, for instance, would be able to form a lasting coalition capable of rivalling the U.S., at least in the short term. Yet their collective attempt to hold the U.S. back from intervening in Iraq in the winter of 2002–03 provides an example of how a countervailing bloc might originate.

The Limits of International Co-operation

Realists recognize that during the twentieth century, **international governmental organizations** (IGOs) have come to play an increasingly more visible and important role in the international system. They also recognize that IGOs can, and often do, constrain the action of states.

Iraq, for instance, did not get away with its invasion and forced annexation of Kuwait in August 1990. Acting through its Security Council, the **United Nations (UN)** (see Box 20-3, The United Nations), the most visible and ambitious IGO, immediately called for Iraq's withdrawal (Security Council Resolution 660 of August 2, 1990). Since Iraq ignored this and subsequent resolutions, the Security Council, through Resolution 678 of November 29, 1990, called for member-states "to use all necessary means" (a euphemism for military force) to oust Iraq from Kuwait. Based on this resolution, a number of countries led by the U.S. assembled a military coalition, defeated Iraq in the 1991 Gulf War, and forced it to withdraw from Kuwait. What happened to Iraq, however, could not happen to any of the five permanent members of the Security Council, without whose vote no resolution could be approved. It would also be unlikely to happen to any state that is a close ally of any of the permanent five.

Realists also underline the fact that the UN is not a supranational body. Its members are sovereign states and respect of state sovereignty is one of the core principles on which the UN is based. The UN, in the realist view, is simply a multilateral political arena that states have established and in which they pursue their national interests, as they do in bilateral relations. Inevitably, therefore, the big powers enjoy as privileged a position within the UN as they do outside it.

IGOS AS TOOLS AND ARENAS Realists point out that IGOs usually have been established through the initiative of big powers. Their institutional structure and the way they work reflect the distribution of power in the international system—or at least the distribution that existed when they were founded. This means that the big powers occupy a key position and play a key role in the functioning of the organization. Thus, for example, the so-called Big Five, victors in the Second World War (the U.S., the Soviet Union, Great Britain, China, and France), gave themselves a permanent seat on the UN Security Council as well as the ability to block any of its resolutions through a veto. In the International Monetary Fund, each country has a number of votes proportional to the reserve funds it has contributed, which means that the U.S. has 371 743 votes, corresponding to 17.14 percent of the total number of votes, while the microstate of Palau has 281 votes, corresponding to 0.01 percent.

According to the realists, IGOs are best regarded as tools that big powers create in order to help them fulfill their responsibilities for the maintenance of international order. The role of IGOs is primarily to help foster international

INTERNATIONAL GOVERNMENTAL ORGANIZATION (IGO)
An organization created by states to facilitate co-operation among them.

UNITED NATIONS (UN)
An international governmental organization representing almost all of the world's states.

United Nations
www.un.org

International Monetary Fund
www.imf.org

BOX 20-3

The United Nations

The name United Nations was first used during the Second World War in the so-called Declaration by United Nations of January 1, 1942, when representatives of twenty-six countries pledged their willingness to continue fighting together against the Axis powers (Germany, Japan, Italy, and their allies).

In 1945, representatives of fifty countries met in San Francisco at the United Nations Conference on International Organization to draw up the United Nations Charter. The Charter, which is the international treaty that established the UN, was signed on June 26, 1945, and its ratification completed by October 24, 1945. The forerunner of and model on which the United Nations was based was the League of Nations, an organization conceived in similar circumstances during the First World War, and established in 1919 to promote international co-operation and to achieve peace and security.

The principal organs of the UN are:

- *The General Assembly*, which seats the permanent diplomatic representatives of all UN member countries (192 as of June 2007). The General Assembly can debate any topic that falls within the provisions of the Charter. Each member has one vote. Its decisions, called General Assembly Resolutions, have no legally binding force for member-states. They simply carry the weight of that body's opinion on major international issues and, since the General Assembly is the nearest thing the world has to a global Parliament, perhaps can also be said to carry the moral authority of the world community.

- *The Security Council,* which is the body responsible for peace and security issues. It is supposed to identify aggressors and situations that represent a threat to peace and decide on enforcement measures. It has fifteen members, five of which are permanent (the U.S., Russia, China, Britain, and France). The other ten rotating members are selected for a two-year period. A Security Council resolution needs nine votes, including those of the five permanent members or their abstention, to be approved. This means that any of the permanent five can block a resolution, and with it the activity of the Security Council. Security Council resolutions are binding on all UN members, but this does not mean that they can always be enforced. In case of non-compliance on the part of the state to which the resolution is addressed, in fact, enforcement depends on the willingness of other UN members to heed the provisions of the resolution, which might also mean readiness to put some of their military forces at the disposal of the UN.

- *The Secretariat,* which is the administrative organ of the organization. It has some eight thousand international civil servants headed by the secretary-general, who is elected for a five-year renewable term by the General Assembly and the Security Council.

consensus, and thus provide legitimacy for an order that inevitably reflects more closely the interests and preferences of the big powers than those of other states in the system.[4]

IGOs, once formed, might impose some constraints on the big powers, but such constraints are largely self-imposed. Even the U.S., in the current unipolar system, prefers to act either with the approval of the UN or at least with the political support of a coalition of allies. Realists, however, focus on the fact that, when states perceive that a certain action is necessary for their own security, they will act—if they have the power to do so—with or without UN approval, as the U.S. did in the spring of 2003 with regards to Iraq.

These cases might be infrequent but, according to realists, they prove that, in the final analysis, states are the main players in the system, not least because they have a monopoly on the use of force. The UN might authorize the use of coercion (whether in the form of economic sanctions or military intervention) against one of its members, but the UN has no ability to enforce its own resolutions and depends on the willingness of other member-states to do so. According to realists, therefore, states work with IGOs when it is in their interest to do so, but do not delegate responsibility for their own security to the UN or any other IGOs.

War and Peace in the International System

Realists view competition and rivalry, and hence conflict, as the normal mode of interaction among states. The fact that the international system is anarchic, moreover, means that there is no authority capable of taming conflict and that, consequently, rivalry can easily lead to war. To maintain peace, one cannot, and need not, replace competition and rivalry with co-operation and friendship or eliminate anarchy through the creation of a central authority in the system. For realists, the problem is how to ensure that competition and rivalry stop short of war. Their solution is to make war too costly an option for a would-be aggressor to choose. It follows that peace can only be attained through strength. Wolves cannot be turned into lambs, but they can be deterred from attacking if it is clear to them that they cannot possibly prevail.

MAINTAINING PEACE IN MULTIPOLAR AND BIPOLAR SYSTEMS
What keeps peace in a multipolar system is the relatively equal distribution of power among its "great powers" (the term *great power* is usually used instead of *big power* when talking about multipolar systems), which deters any of them from taking aggressive action. If one great power increases its power capabilities and begins to be perceived as a threat by the other great powers,

---

[4] The radical (or Marxist) school affirms the same thing. The difference between realists and radicals is that the former describe the existing order and regard it as an inescapable feature of how international politics works, while the latter denounce it as inequitable and oppressive and argue that it should be changed.

an alliance will be formed between two or more of the latter to counter the would-be aggressor. Formation of flexible alliances, in other words, keeps a balance of power among the great powers and hence maintains peace in the system.

The balance of terror, also known as the doctrine of mutual assured destruction (MAD), kept peace during the Cold War, or to be more precise, prevented a direct military confrontation between the U.S. and the Soviet Union. The two contenders had accumulated such vast arsenals of nuclear weapons that neither of them had an incentive to launch an attack since the initiator could not hope to survive a retaliatory strike from its adversary. War would mean mutual assured destruction, no matter who initiated it.

The knowledge that peace rested only on the balance of terror or MAD led the two states to sign the 1972 Anti-Ballistic Missile (ABM) Treaty, which purposely limited to two (later reduced to one) the number of strategic defence systems each country could deploy. Since ABM systems were supposed to neutralize incoming missiles while they were still in the air, it was thought that their deployment would destabilize the balance of terror and hence increase the probabilities of a nuclear exchange. The superpower that would succeed first in protecting all of its territory with such systems might in fact be tempted to launch an initial strike in the hope of being able to withstand the retaliatory one and escape from the exchange relatively unscathed.[5] The signing of the treaty was an implicit acknowledgment that the maintenance of peace did not depend on the simple desire for it—because in this case the two superpowers could have agreed to disarm completely. Peace rested instead on tying one's hands or, to put it differently, resisting any temptation one might have to resort to war by eliminating all advantages one might derive from an attack.

MAINTAINING PEACE IN A UNIPOLAR SYSTEM   It is more difficult to analyze how peace can be maintained in a unipolar system since such a system has been around only for slightly longer than a decade, and hence there are few data on which to base any conclusion. It would appear, however, that in a unipolar system the sole superpower confronts a rather difficult task. On one hand, it has primary responsibility for the maintenance of stability and order in the international system. On the other, any initiative the superpower takes for this purpose risks being perceived by other actors as nothing but the blatant pursuit of its national interests and hence as an aggressive action.

The UN, for instance, could hardly undertake any military operation with respect to breaches of the peace, threats to the peace, or acts of aggression (the so-called Chapter 7 operations) if it could not rely on the willingness of the

---

[5] The United States has continued to work on the technology needed for ABM systems and intends to deploy a type of ABM system designed to protect its territory and that of its allies from the threat represented by the missiles of the so-called "rogue" states, mainly North Korea and Iran.

U.S. to provide its military forces for such operations. This means, however, that the United States must be involved in all activities executing mandates under Chapter 7 of the UN Charter. As the United States also desires to retain command and control of its own troops in such operations, the impression is inevitably given that these interventions are not the duly authorized execution of a UN mandate but U.S. wars.

The 1950–53 Korean War and the 1991 Gulf War are often thought of as American wars rather than UN-mandated interventions. When the UN mandate *is* acknowledged, the suggestion is often made that the U.S. coerced and cajoled the members of the UN Security Council to obtain its authorization in order to legitimize an intervention it was ready to undertake unilaterally. Things are even worse, of course, when the sole superpower takes initiatives without explicit UN authorization—as was the case in 2003, when the United States and some of its allies invaded Iraq.

The provisional conclusion seems to be that in a unipolar system peace depends not only on the willingness of the superpower to intervene to maintain stability and order, but also on its ability to forge consensus around such order and the actions it undertakes to maintain it. A superpower in a unipolar system must act, in other words, as a hegemon. Without willing partners and eager followers, **hegemony** deteriorates into domination and a dominant power invites the formation of countervailing alliances, which leads to turbulence and war.

HEGEMONY OR HEGEMONIC SYSTEM
A type of unipolar system in which the superpower exercises power primarily through authority, leadership, and persuasion and thus creates a large consensus around its actions.

The Realist School and the Limits of Governance

Realists are skeptical about the possibility of global governance. They regard it at best as limited and based on the ability and willingness of big powers to take the lead in shaping and providing it. There are two reasons for such skepticism:

1. Realists focus primarily on the issue of security, which they assume to be the central concern of sovereign states and therefore unlikely to be completely delegated to any IGO, the UN included.
2. States are generally unwilling to put constraints on their sovereignty. Hence, the international system might change in terms of its distribution of power among states, but is unlikely to change in terms of its organization of authority. The system, in other words, is likely to remain anarchic.

For realists therefore, the possibility of global governance depends on the ability of bigger powers (whether many, two, or one) to develop rules and institutions, which, while conferring privileges on them, also enjoy a minimum of legitimacy among lesser powers in the international system. For realists, in other words, global governance means at best the benign rule of hegemons.

LIBERAL–INTERNATIONALISM

The liberal–internationalist school has a less sombre view of the consequences of international anarchy and is more optimistic about the possibilities of global governance. **Liberal–internationalism** differs from realism in a number of ways (see also Table 20-1):

- Liberal–internationalists believe that while states might still be the most important actors in the international arena, they are not the only ones. Other actors, such as IGOs, **international non-governmental organizations (INGOs)**—examples include Greenpeace and Amnesty International, to mention only two of the most well known[6]—specific state institutions such as parliaments and bureaucracies, societal groups, multinational corporations (MNCs), and even individuals, play an important role.

- For liberal-internationalists, states and societies interact in many different issue areas—political, economic, social, and cultural. Each of these issue areas affects the others, and none is dominant all the time. For this reason, liberal-internationalists tend to speak of international relations (conceived of as a vast array of interactions between states and societies) as opposed to simply international politics (which suggests primarily power relations). Hence, national security, although important, cannot be examined in isolation.

- Liberal–internationalists do not regard states as unitary actors but as a network of different actors—individuals, socio-economic groups, and governmental institutions and departments—each with different interests, priorities, and preferences. These actors interact with similar actors across national borders on many different issue areas, each of which is of primary importance to some actors and of lesser importance to others. Unlike realists, liberal-internationalists do not believe that there is a constant national interest. There are instead many different, shifting, and competing national interests. Thus, even if everyone might agree on the primacy of national security (that is, the need to defend one's state from external threats), disagreements will inevitably occur concerning the means that should be used to defend oneself from such threats. How a state behaves on the international scene, therefore, is always the result of a bargaining process among competing domestic groups and institutions.

- Liberal–internationalists believe that individuals, groups, and institutions learn from their experiences and mistakes, and hence are capable of modifying their behaviour accordingly.

LIBERAL–INTERNATIONALISM
An approach to the study of international politics that assumes that increased cultural and social connections as well as economic interdependence are leading to the emergence of a global civil society in which co-operation, the rule of law, and peace are valued and global governance is spreading both functionally and geographically.

INTERNATIONAL NON-GOVERNMENTAL ORGANIZATION (INGO)
An international organization whose members are not states but rather representatives of civil society.

---

[6] INGOs are distinguished from IGOs because they are established and controlled by individuals and/or groups in civil society rather than by national governments.

	REALISM	LIBERAL–INTERNATIONALISM
Key Actors	States	States, IGOs, INGOs, groups, individuals
View of the state	Unitary actor, power seeking, moved by national interest	Network of different actors, competing national interests
View of the international system	Anarchic	Interdependence of actors International society
Views on peace	Attainable through strength, deterrence, balance of power	Attainable through law
Views on possibility of international governance	Weak; provided by hegemonic powers	Strong; governance is spreading fast

TABLE 20-1

MAJOR DIFFERENCES BETWEEN REALISM AND LIBERAL–INTERNATIONALISM

An International Society in the Making

Liberal–internationalists agree with realists that the world is made up of sovereign states and that there is no authority above them. They disagree, however, on the question of how significant anarchy is for the functioning of the international system and the behaviour of its members. According to them, the principle of sovereignty, which has traditionally regulated interstate relations, is constantly evolving.

The idea has recently gained ground, for instance, that sovereign states have a responsibility to protect their own citizens from avoidable catastrophes as well as to guarantee their enjoyment of human rights. When states are unwilling or unable to do so, that responsibility must be borne by the international community as a whole. Thus, under certain circumstances it is appropriate for a state, a coalition of states, or an IGO to take action—including military action—against another state in order to protect that state's population or part of it.[7] This is, of course, an important limitation on state sovereignty. The intervention by a number of countries against the republic of Yugoslavia (at the time consisting of Serbia and Montenegro) in the spring of 1999, for instance, was justified precisely with the argument that intervention was necessary to protect the rights of the Albanian population in the Serbian region of Kosovo.

INTERDEPENDENCE Liberal–internationalists also point out that the range of international interactions is so vast and its reach is so deep that all actors in the international system are interdependent—that is, each is affected by the actions of others. The interdependence of actors, the fact that all of them face an increasing number of common challenges, such as environmental degradation, population explosion, and climate change, and the

---

[7] See International Commission on Intervention and State Sovereignty (2001).

shrinking of the time–space dimensions due to technological advances in communication and travel, have slowly led, according to liberal–internationalists, to the development of a common identity, a sense of "we-ness" on planet Earth.

For all of these reasons, liberal–internationalists think that the international system is not an almost immutable structure constraining the behaviour of its units, but an evolving one. The international system does constrain the behaviour of its units, but states, groups, and individuals are constantly modifying the system through their own ideas and actions. The increasing number and relevance of INGOs, moreover, is evidence of the rapid emergence of a vibrant global civil society, which will eventually give birth to a global and democratic political society. Thus, for liberal–internationalists the world is more than a system of independent sovereign states. It is also an **international or global society** in the making.

INTERNATIONAL OR GLOBAL SOCIETY
The idea that the increasing number and importance of international interactions and the rising degree of interdependence is creating a global common identity and leading to the development of a global society.

Why States Co-operate

Liberal–internationalists point out that although there are occasional exceptions, states usually comply with international law even in the absence of a central authority capable of enforcing it. They do so for two reasons:

1. States wish to do what is considered right and moral, and do not wish to lose prestige in the eyes of international public opinion.
2. Even more importantly, states have learned over time that it is in their interest to abide by international law because it is preferable to live in an ordered and predictable world rather than in a lawless, uncertain, and dangerous one.

Order and predictability allow states not to have to worry too much about the behaviour of other states, since it can be assumed that it will fall within the parameters allowed by the law.

JOINING INTERNATIONAL GOVERNMENTAL ORGANIZATIONS The desire to reduce uncertainty in interstate relations has pushed states to set up and join an increasing number of IGOs. Although IGOs can rarely enforce rules on states unwilling to abide by them, they are useful because they provide a context in which it is easier for states to co-operate with one another. That is, they can help to find a mutually satisfying adjustment in situations of conflicting interests or preferences.

Membership in IGOs does not weaken state sovereignty; it simply provides a different context in which to exercise it. More precisely, the context provided by IGOs reduces the costs of negotiating agreements by providing clear rules, better information, and opportunities for compromises and side payments through issue linkages. When different issues are on the table, in other words, states are more willing to make concessions on some if at the same time they get what they want on others. Membership in IGOs also improves the chances of voluntary compliance since the costs of defection (or non-compliance), in terms of reputation and credibility, are higher than they would be in a bilateral relationship. This explains why smaller powers like Canada seem to value membership in IGOs more than big powers do. Their sovereignty is enhanced because they gain more voice and hence influence, especially when acting in concert, than they would have in bilateral relationships with bigger powers.

The analysis of liberal–internationalists is undoubtedly very convincing when applied to the technical and even economic issue areas of international relations (Keohane, 1984). Thus, an effective **international regime** (defined as a set of principles, norms, and procedures regulating, usually but not necessarily through an IGO, international activity in a specific issue area) exists, for instance, in the area of telecommunications. International trade also has an increasingly effective regime centred on the World Trade Organization (see Box 20-4, The World Trade Organization). Indeed, as interdependence has increased, so have the need for IGOs and international regimes and the eagerness of states to form them. The proliferation of IGOs and international regimes reinforces the habit of co-operation, and this, according to liberal–internationalists, bodes well for an increasingly peaceful future (Brown, 1995).

INTERNATIONAL REGIME
A set of principles, norms, treaties, and IGOs that regulates international activities in a given issue area.

The Problem of Security and the Search for Peace

Unlike realists, who think that states can only rely on self-help for their security, liberal–internationalists believe that states can, and should, rely on IGOs and law. For them, state security is better achieved through a collective approach. The principle of **collective security** posits that states pledge to intervene on behalf of a member whose security is threatened by the aggressive actions of another state.

The UN is, among other things, a system of collective security, as was its predecessor, the League of Nations. The principle of collective security is also consistent with the realist reliance on deterrence to discourage aggression and maintain peace. If states can be certain that aggression will be punished by collective action, they will refrain from engaging in aggressive behaviour.

For a system of collective security to work, however, one must assume that participating members can always agree on establishing who the aggressor is when two states come to blows. Unfortunately, this is not always easy since states, much like individuals, are more likely to listen sympathetically to the arguments of friends than to those of foes. For collective security to work, one must also assume that participating members are always ready and willing to act against the aggressor. The historical record

COLLECTIVE SECURITY
The principle that all members of the collectivity of states (or simply a number of them) are jointly responsible for the security of each of them and therefore pledge to intervene on behalf of a member whose security is threatened by the aggressive actions of another state.

BOX 20-4

The World Trade Organization

Based in Geneva, Switzerland, the World Trade Organization (WTO) is charged with managing trade relations among its one hundred and fifty-one members (as of July 2007). At the same time, the WTO is an organization aimed at promoting free trade through the progressive dismantling of tariff and non-tariff barriers, a forum for governments to negotiate trade agreements, and a place and mechanism for them to settle trade disputes.

The WTO was established in 1995 but its origins date back to 1947, when twenty-three states negotiated a General Agreement on Tariffs and Trade (GATT) aimed at overcoming economic nationalism, which was perceived as one of the factors responsible for the outbreak of the Second World War, and promoting freer international trade. To this end, GATT sponsored a series of trade negotiations called "rounds" that reduced tariffs and non-tariff barriers and increased the total value of world exports from $53 billion in 1948 to $11 069 billion in 2004. At the end of the last successful round—the Uruguay round—the WTO was formed.

As discussed in Chapter 18, the current round of trade negotiations—the Doha round, launched in November 2001—has tackled trade in services and agricultural products, particularly the issue of subsidies that hurt the less developed counties. It is on this issue, however, that talks stalled in 2006. Trade liberalization is supposed to take place according to the principle of the "most favoured nation," which means that concessions granted to one WTO member must be extended to all other members. Exceptions exist, however, in the case of regional free-trade areas and in favour of less developed countries. Trade liberalization, moreover, can also be suspended when domestic industries face severe injury.

The WTO's top-level decision-making body is the Ministerial Conference, which is formed by member-states' ministers of international trade and meets at least once every two years. Day-to-day operations are conducted by the heads of national delegations, which meet as the General Council. Each member-state has the right to have one representative on the Council, whose work is supported by a Secretariat who is headed by a Director General and has about six hundred staff members.

An important innovation of the WTO as compared with GATT is its dispute-resolution mechanism. It provides fixed timetables for the various steps in the procedure, which means that any dispute is solved in a maximum of fifteen months. Disputes are submitted to the General Council, which then selects a panel to hear the dispute and submits a report for adoption. The procedure is repeated if there is an appeal of the first report. What is new with respect to the old GATT procedure is that disputes cannot be prolonged indefinitely, and no party to a dispute can block or veto the adoption of a report. Now, a report can only be blocked if every member agrees to do so. The procedure has changed, in other words, from negative to positive consensus and, as a result, the international trade regime has been strengthened.

on this point is not comforting. When Japan invaded Manchuria and Italy conquered Ethiopia in the 1930s, members of the League of Nations did not make good on their promise to intervene. Thus, the system of collective security effectively collapsed, leading to further aggression by Germany against Czechoslovakia and Poland and in the end to the Second World War.

Things did not fare any better with the UN Security Council during the Cold War, since the ideological and political rivalry between the U.S. and the Soviet Union effectively paralyzed the Council until the end of the Cold War. Only two acts of international aggression met with a collective response by the UN between 1945 and 1991:

- *The intervention against North Korea for its invasion of South Korea in 1950.* The UN was able to intervene only because, at the time, the Soviet Union was boycotting the meetings of the Security Council to protest the fact that Taiwan and not China had a seat at the UN. Had the Soviet Union been present, it almost surely would have vetoed an intervention against its North Korean ally.
- *The 1991 intervention against Iraq following its invasion of Kuwait.* The end of the Cold War rekindled liberal–internationalist hopes that the UN could finally fulfill its collective security responsibility, but these hopes did not last very long.

As the debate over what to do about Iraq's protracted defiance of the disarmament terms imposed by UN Security Council Resolution 687 at the end of the 1991 Gulf War showed, disagreements among Security Council members resurfaced and manifested themselves dramatically during the period immediately preceding the 2003 intervention against the Saddam Hussein's regime. Such disagreements were due partly to the ambiguity of the evidence available as to whether Iraq represented an immediate threat to regional and world peace, and partly to the desire of some permanent members of the Security Council—France and Russia, in particular—to try to constrain the range of action of the lone superpower.

Reducing the Likelihood of War: The Role of Economic Interdependence

Some liberal–internationalists believe that, as a method of solving interstate conflicts, war is losing legitimacy, just as the duel has lost legitimacy as a way of solving interpersonal disputes (Mueller, 1989). Indeed, states formally renounced recourse to war for the solution of international controversies and as an instrument of national policy in 1928 when they signed the General Treaty for the Renunciation of War (better known as the Briand-Kellogg Pact, from the names of the French and American foreign ministers instrumental in negotiating it). The treaty had little practical effect but was significant at the level of ideas since it indicated a rapidly changing attitude toward state-sanctioned violence. Liberal–internationalists, moreover, argue that interests, rather than just sensibilities, are changing. The high degree of economic interdependence that characterizes liberal–democratic states has made war a very costly mechanism for solving disputes because it can cause severe disruption to the functioning of the economies of the warring states.

For example, France and Germany went to war three times in less than a century, but war between the two countries—or any two European countries,

The European Union
http://europa.eu.int

▶ President George W. Bush and his consolation prize from the Iraq war.

for that matter—would be unthinkable today given their high degree of economic interdependence. Indeed, economic interdependence has also led to the building of a network of common political institutions (the countries belonging to the European Union being those who have gone farthest in this direction), which has made war an even more remote possibility.

Some liberals argue that the European Union represents an example of a **postmodern state**—that is, a state in which the meaning and practice of sovereignty has been redefined since tools of governance are shared, foreign and domestic policies have become inextricably intertwined, and security is no longer based on control of borders and deterrence (Cooper, 2000). The idea is that the example of the European Union could be replicated in other parts of the world, until the entire world would become a postmodern state.

Given also the traditional liberal idea—whose origins go back to the German philosopher Immanuel Kant (1724–1804)—that states with a liberal democratic government are less likely than states with other types of government to wage war, especially toward one another, liberal–internationalists believe that international peace can be promoted by fostering the development

POSTMODERN STATE
A state in which the meaning and practice of sovereignty have been redefined since tools of governance are shared, foreign and domestic policies have become inextricably intertwined, and security is no longer based on control of borders and deterrence.

of free-market economies and democratic institutions around the world.[8] Such a policy, however, if not pursued subtly and carefully, might lead, at least in some parts of the world, to resentment and resistance, and thus end up triggering, rather than preventing, disorders and even military hostilities.

The Liberal–Internationalist Promise of Governance

Liberal–internationalists are more optimistic than realists about the possibility of global governance. The world, they argue, does not resemble Hobbes' mythical state of nature. It also appears to be increasingly acquiring the features of a global civil society, as evidenced by a growing network of connections across national boundaries (Lipschutz, 2000).

These connections, which have traditionally linked organized groups, now involve single individuals thanks to the World Wide Web. One can see the slow but nevertheless sure emergence of a global consciousness that is increasingly bringing challenges to, and slowly eroding, the traditional primacy of the sovereign states. To be sure, the world does not yet have a central authority—and it might never have one. Yet it exhibits an increasing number of functional areas (for example, telecommunications or international trade) and geographic areas (for example, the European Union) in which the rule of law prevails. Such a trend, moreover, is self-reinforcing and hence unlikely to be reversed.

FOREIGN POLICY ANALYSIS

Both the realist and liberal–internationalist approaches capture some aspects of international relations. The liberal–internationalist analysis is certainly very effective in explaining the evolution of the international system in the twentieth century and is particularly convincing when applied to state relations in economic issue areas. The realist analysis is instead more effective in explaining security relations.

It should be remembered, however, that both approaches offer an explanation of how the international system as a whole works and of how states tend to behave in it over time. The approaches do not claim to explain how states make specific foreign policy decisions. In order to do that, one needs to open the so-called "black box," that is, the complex processes by which decisions are made. In other words, one needs to move beyond the assumptions that the state is rational and unitary (realism) or rational and made up of different actors (liberal–internationalism) and examine in more detail how actors—individuals, groups, and institutions—work to arrive at specific decisions (see, for instance, Box 20-5, The U.S. Decision to Intervene in Iraq). This is the task of a branch of the study of international relations called foreign policy analysis.

---

[8] It should be pointed out that, whereas liberal–internationalists see liberal democracy as a carrier of peace, radical Marxist scholars argue exactly the opposite. They believe that the free-market capitalist economy that usually characterizes liberal democracies is exactly what causes conflict and war, both among classes within states and among states within the international system.

BOX 20-5

The U.S. Decision to Intervene in Iraq

Iraq's protracted failure to comply with the disarmament terms imposed by UN Security Council Resolution 687 at the end of the 1991 Gulf War was met throughout the 1990s with a policy of containment centred on the imposition of economic sanctions. The terrorist attack of September 11, 2001, although not immediately related to Iraq, changed policy thinking, at least in the U.S. The Bush administration came to the conclusion that Iraq's defiance needed a more resolute response, a military one if necessary (Pollack, 2002).

The official rationale provided by the U.S. administration for its new course of action was that Iraq, rather than disarming, might be enhancing its chemical and biological capabilities and even developing nuclear weapons. Given Saddam Hussein's past willingness to use chemical weapons against his enemies both at home and abroad, Iraq was perceived as representing a threat to regional and international security. To those critics (among whom were realist scholars) who argued that the Iraq threat did not appear imminent enough to justify pre-emptive military action, the Bush administration answered that the concept of "imminent threat" needed to be adapted "to the capabilities and objectives of today's adversaries." Prudence, in other words, called for action before terrorists or rogue states obtained weapons of mass destruction (WMD).

The rationale for action, however, was not entirely based on (realist) security considerations. It also rested on a good dose of (liberal–internationalist) interventionism. The Bush administration, in fact, also argued that the replacement of Saddam Hussein's dictatorship with a liberal-democratic regime would bring similar changes in other countries in the region and thus promote peace both regionally and internationally. The administration also justified the intervention in "humanitarian" terms. This argument, however, was used sparingly since the Iraqi regime had committed its worst atrocities against Kurds and Shia Muslim groups between 1987 and 1991.

The option of moving from a policy of containment to one of regime change in Iraq had already been seriously considered by the Clinton administration at the end of the 1990s. Before September 11, 2001, however, it would have been difficult to convince the American public that a military intervention in Iraq was required for national security. After September 11, all that was needed was to emphasize the possibility that Saddam's WMD might be passed on to, or simply fall into the hands of, Islamic terrorists. Before the policy change could be implemented, the Bush administration had to overcome the skepticism of the State Department and some members of the uniformed military who thought that a military intervention in Iraq required a bigger allocation of military resources than senior staff thought necessary (Wallack, 2006). Finally, before the new policy was implemented, the U.S. tried to obtain an explicit UN approval. When this failed, it moved to the second-best option, that is, building a large political alliance—the so-called "coalition of the willing"—and arguing, not unconvincingly, that its intervention was in line with existing UN Security Council resolutions.

The study of foreign policy decisions includes findings from different levels of analysis. At the individual level, it examines the preferences of key decision-makers—for example, presidents or prime ministers and foreign ministers—as expressed, for instance, in parties' electoral platforms or speeches. These preferences, whether initiatives or responses to other states' actions, must pass various tests and go through a number of stages before they can become foreign policy decisions or choices.

At the systemic level, the foreign policy choices must be consistent with the structure of the international system—that is, they must be within the range of actions the state can comfortably take given the constraints represented by the distribution of power in the system. Thus, during the Cold War, a satellite of the Soviet Union or of the United States could not reasonably and safely pursue a foreign policy objective that was perceived as damaging to the interests of the superpower in whose sphere it orbited.

At the national level, implementation of the foreign policy choices cannot require more power capabilities than the country has at its disposal. There is little practical use—although the exercise can, of course, be worthwhile in symbolic terms—in giving oneself the objective, as Canada did when Lloyd Axworthy held the position of minister of foreign affairs, of promoting "human security," understood as the general improvement of the quality of life conditions experienced by individuals worldwide (Axworthy, 2003). Canada does not have the capabilities to improve "human security" worldwide; it could at best only bring attention to such an issue.

Preferences must also enjoy domestic consensus and hence be perceived as consistent with national identity and effective in promoting the country's national interest. Before they become foreign policy decisions, they must also go through a complex policy process whose institutional characteristics depend on the type of political system of the country in question. In general, it can be said that the more liberal democratic, and hence open, the political system is, the more likely it is that the original preferences will be adjusted and modified during the policy-making process. For all these reasons, a democratic country's foreign policy has a built-in bias in favour of continuity. A new foreign policy is likely to emerge only in the wake of a major change in the structure of the international system and/or in the country's capabilities, two events that happen only rarely.

Once decisions are made and implemented, they will have an impact on the external environment and on other states that are likely to react and hence begin the whole process anew.

Summary and Conclusion

This chapter has examined the difference between national politics and international politics: the fact that the respect for rules at the international level depends more on voluntary compliance on the part of states than on enforcement. It has also examined the differences between the two major approaches to the study of international politics: realism and liberal–internationalism.

Realists argue that the fact that states are sovereign makes the international system anarchic, and hence very similar to Hobbes' state of nature. In such a world, security, which is the major preoccupation of states, depends on self-help and hence on power. Peace depends on deterrence, namely making it clear to potential aggressors that the costs of aggression outweigh the potential benefits. Because states are jealous of their sovereignty, the possibilities of international governance are limited.

Liberal–internationalists argue that, although the world is still politically organized in states, each of whose governments claims to be the ultimate authority over its territory and population, increased cultural and social connections and economic interdependence are leading to the emergence of a global civil society—one that values co-operation, the rule of law, and peace. A world political federation might never emerge, but international governance is spreading both functionally and geographically.

Overall, international politics raises difficult issues for the pursuit of the common good. Given the problems that the world faces (such as war, global climate change, global inequality, international terrorism, and the protection of basic human rights), it would be desirable for the common good to be considered, at least in part, in terms of the common good of humanity or of the entire planet.

However, the realist perspective alerts us to the continuing importance of national interests. The common good of humanity can, at best, only be achieved to a limited degree in an anarchic world. In contrast, liberal–internationalists have a more optimistic outlook on achieving the common good. In their view, the development of international organizations and agreements, along with increased interaction among the peoples of the world in areas such as trade and communications and the spread of democracy, makes progress toward a more peaceful and prosperous world possible. However, international organizations and trade agreements do not necessarily lead to the global common good, as they may reflect the interests of the powerful. As well, international governmental organizations are often not particularly democratic. Achieving the global common good, therefore, presents us with difficult challenges.

Key Terms

Anarchy 476

Balance of power 479

Bipolarity 481

Collective security 491

Global governance 476

Hegemony or hegemonic system 487

International governmental organization (IGO) 483

International non-governmental organization (INGO) 488

International or global society 490

International regime 491

International system 478

Discussion Questions

1. What are the major differences between the realist and liberal–internationalist approaches to the study of world politics? What are the implications for policy suggestions?

2. What are the policy options and the dilemmas a state confronts in trying to guarantee its own security?

3. Can the United Nations be considered a world government? How significant is the lack of a central authority in world politics?

4. Is a peaceful world a realistic objective? How might a more peaceful world be achieved?

Further Reading

Baylis, J., & Smith, S. (Eds.). *The globalization of world politics*, 3rd ed. Oxford: Oxford University Press, 2005.

Baylis, J., Wirts, J., Cohen, E., & Gray, C.S. (Eds.). *Strategy in the contemporary world: An introduction to strategic studies.* Oxford: Oxford University Press, 2002.

Jackson, R., & Sørensen, G. *Introduction to international relations: Theories and approaches,* 2nd ed. Oxford: Oxford University Press, 2003.

Kennedy, P. *The rise and fall of the great powers: Economic change and military conflict from 1500 to 2000.* New York: Vintage Books, 1987

Ravenhill, J. (Ed.). *Global political economy.* Oxford: Oxford University Press, 2005.

GLOSSARY

Accountability Having to be responsible for one's actions and having to accept the consequences of failure to perform as expected.

Affirmative action The adoption of programs designed to make the workplace, universities, legislatures, or other institutions more representative of disadvantaged groups and groups that have suffered from discrimination.

Agenda setting The process by which potential problems come to the attention of policy-makers.

Agenda-setting effect The effect of the media on what the public thinks are the key issues or political priorities at a particular point in time.

Alternative service delivery New methods of delivering government programs, such as the establishment of service agencies that have considerable autonomy from the normal departmental structures and rules and establishing partnerships with business, other levels of government, and voluntary organizations to deliver services.

Anarchism An ideology that views the state as the key source of oppression and seeks to replace the state with a system based on voluntary co-operation.

Anarchy A situation in which there is no central authority.

Anthropocentrism The focus on human well-being that is at the centre of most political thought.

Asian model The economic model of export-led industrialization associated with a number of Asian countries.

Asymmetrical federalism A version of federalism in which some provincial or state governments have a greater degree of self-government than others..

Authoritarian government A non-democratic system of government.

Authority The right to exercise power. Those with political authority claim that they have been *authorized* to govern.

Balance of power A situation in which no state is dominant in the global system.

Binational and multinational states States whose population is composed of two or more nations.

Bipolarity A type of international system in which two superpowers compete with one another. The other states in the system fall within the sphere of influence of one or the other of the two superpowers.

Brokerage party A party that attempts to find compromises to accommodate a variety of interests (particularly regional and ethnic/cultural divisions) so as to try to build broad support across the country in a non-ideological manner.

Bureaucracy An organization in which people are hired and promoted based on their qualifications and merit, work is organized in terms of specialized positions, detailed rules and procedures are followed by all members of the organization, and there is a hierarchical chain of command so that those at the top can direct and supervise large numbers of people.

Cabinet The members of the political executive. The Cabinet is led by the prime minister, with many or most Cabinet ministers having the responsibility of heading a government department.

Cabinet secrecy The convention that the Cabinet meets behind closed doors, Cabinet documents normally remain secret for a lengthy period of time, and the advice given to the Cabinet is not usually released publicly.

Cabinet solidarity The convention in a parliamentary system that each member of the Cabinet is expected to fully support and defend the decisions and actions that the Cabinet takes.

Cadre party A loosely organized party established by members of a legislative body with the support of local notables concerned with electing members of the party to legislative bodies, rather than building a strong, centralized, membership-based organization outside of the legislature.

Catch-all party A party that tries to appeal to all segments of the population, particularly by downplaying or abandoning its ideology and emphasizing the qualities of its leaders.

Central agency An organization that tries to provide direction and coordination to government. In Canada, the key central agencies are the Privy Council Office, the Prime Minister's Office, the Treasury Board, and the Department of Finance.

Centrally planned state socialist economic system An economic system involving state ownership of almost all enterprises and centralized planning by state officials.

Charismatic authority Authority based on the perception that a leader has extraordinary or supernatural qualities.

Charlottetown Accord A package of constitutional changes, including recognition of the inherent right of Aboriginals to self-government and major changes to the Senate to provide for equal representation by each province regardless of population size. It was defeated in a referendum in 1992.

Charter of Rights and Freedoms As part of the Constitution Act, 1982, the Charter protects a variety of rights and freedoms. It is superior to ordinary legislation, explicitly allows the courts to invalidate legislation, and applies to the actions of all governments and organizations under the control of government.

Checks and balances A basic principle of the American presidential system in which each of the three branches of government is able to check the actions of the others so that no individual or institution becomes too powerful.

Citizens' jury A group of randomly selected persons that deliberate about and make recommendations concerning particular issues.

Citizenship The idea that the permanent residents of a country are full members of the political community, involving various duties and rights.

Civic nationalism Nationalism based on the shared political values and political history of those who are citizens of a country.

Civil disobedience Deliberate lawbreaking that accepts punishment by state authorities as part of the action.

Civil society The voluntary groups and organizations that are not controlled by the state.

Class consciousness The extent to which people see themselves as members of a particular social class.

Classical federalism A version of federalism in which the federal and provincial governments each concern themselves with their own areas of constitutional authority without infringing upon the areas of authority of the other level of government.

Classical liberalism A form of liberalism that emphasizes the desirability of limited government and the free marketplace.

Closure A procedure in a legislative body that cuts off debate if approved by a majority vote.

Coalition government A form of government in which two or more parties jointly govern, sharing the Cabinet positions.

Cohabitation The sharing of power between the French president and prime minister that occurs when the Assembly is controlled by a party opposed to the president.

Collective responsibility The convention that the Cabinet as a group will defend, explain, and take responsibility for the actions of the government in Parliament.

Collective security The principle that all members of the collectivity of states (or simply a number of them) are jointly responsible for the security of each of them and therefore pledge to intervene on behalf of a member whose security is threatened by the aggressive actions of another state.

Common good What is good for the entire political community.

Communism A system in which private property has been replaced by collective or communal ownership and in which everyone would be free to take from society what they need.

Confederal system A system of governing in which sovereign states have agreed to delegate some of their authority to a joint government with limited authority while retaining their sovereignty.

Congress The legislative branch of the American government.

Consensus model of democracy A model of governing featuring the sharing of governing power and a balance of power between the political executive and Parliament.

Conservatism A perspective or ideology that emphasizes the values of order, stability, respect for authority, and tradition, based on a view that humans are inherently imperfect, with a limited capacity to reason.

Consolidated democracies Countries with democratic governments that are stable, well accepted by both ordinary citizens and political elites, and unlikely to be overthrown.

Constitution The fundamental rules and principles by which a state is governed.

Constitution Act, 1867 An Act of the United Kingdom Parliament that established Canada by uniting the colonies of Canada (Ontario and Quebec), Nova Scotia, and New Brunswick. It also set out many of the features of Canada's system of governing.

Constitution Act, 1982 The Act that made the constitution fully Canadian, added the Charter of Rights and Freedoms to the constitution, and established procedures for amending the constitution.

Constitutional amendment A formal change to the constitution.

Constitutional convention A fundamental principle that is consistently followed even though it is not contained in a legal document and is not generally enforceable in the courts.

Constitutional government A government that consistently acts in accordance with the rules and principles established in its constitution.

Constitutional monarchy A governing system in which the powers of the monarch are greatly restricted by formal constitutional provisions or "unwritten" constitutional conventions. The monarch is primarily a symbolic figure rather than an active participant in the governing processes.

Contentious politics Protest involving ordinary citizens, often joined by more influential citizens, uniting to confront elites, authorities, and opponents.

Co-operative federalism A federal system in which the two levels of government are jointly involved in developing, financing, and administering many government services.

Corporate state A system associated with fascist Italy in which business and labour work harmoniously to achieve goals established by the state to advance the good of the nation.

Corporatism A political system in which the state actively collaborates with selected major interests (particularly the national organizations of business and labour) to seek a consensus concerning the country's major economic and social policies.

Corporatist system A political system in which the state actively collaborates with selected major interests to set the direction for the political community, particularly in terms of economic and social policies.

Cost–benefit analysis An economic technique that determines whether, and to what extent, the benefits of a policy exceed the costs.

Counter-insurgency A blend of military and political action taken by a government to defeat an insurgency. The tactics are usually described as a mixture of repression and reform.

Coup d'état A forcible seizure of power by the armed forces or occasionally the police.

Deep ecology An environmentalist perspective that views anthropocentrism as the fundamental cause of environmental degradation and advocates the cultivation of an environmental consciousness and a sense of oneness with the world that recognizes the unity of humans, plants, animals, and the Earth.

Deliberative democracy A political system in which decisions are made based on discussion by citizens rather than by elected representatives alone.

Democracy Rule by the people.

Democratic consolidation The situation in which a country's commitment to democracy is strong and sure, such that democracy is likely to persist.

Democratic socialism The perspective that socialism should be achieved by democratic rather than revolutionary means, and that a socialist society should be democratic in nature with political rights and freedoms respected.

Democratic transition A process of change involving abandoning authoritarian government for democratic rule.

Dependency theory A development model that views underdevelopment as a result of unequal power relations between the centre (dominant, capitalist countries) and the periphery (poor, dependent countries).

Deputy minister The executive head of a department of government appointed by the prime minister in consultation with the clerk of the Privy Council Office. The deputy minister runs the department with oversight by the Cabinet minister who is the political head of the department.

Developing countries Countries that have not reached the same level of development as the richer, advanced countries.

Development A condition that involves the satisfaction of the basic needs of all of the people as well as the means for them to live fulfilling and productive lives based on the creation of a more diversified, sophisticated, and sustainable economy.

Devolution A system of governing in which the central government grants some legislative (law-making) powers as well as administrative responsibilities to one or more regional bodies.

Direct democracy A system in which citizens make the governing decisions.

Disappearance The kidnapping by security forces of an individual who is never heard from again.

Dominant ideology perspective on the mass media The view that the major media convey the values of the powerful and serve the interests of those who benefit from the status quo.

Ecocentrism The view that nature has intrinsic value and should not be valued only in terms of its use for human beings.

Ecofeminism A combination of environmentalism and feminism that views male dominance as the basic cause of the degradation of the Earth.

Electoral college A body that elects the president of the United States. Members of the electoral college from each state are expected to vote for the presidential candidate who has won the most votes in their state.

Electoral system The system used to translate the votes that people cast into the composition of the legislature and the selection of the government.

Electoral–professional party A political party whose dominant concern is winning elections and that relies on professional experts to market the party to voters.

Elite media The newspapers and magazines that are read by decision-makers in government, business, and leading social institutions, as well as by those highly interested in public affairs.

Elitist perspective The view that power in all communities is concentrated in a small number of hands, particularly in the elites that hold the top positions in the major institutions of the economy, society, and politics.

Empirical analysis Analysis that involves explaining various aspects of politics, particularly by using careful observation and comparison to develop generalizations and testable theories.

Enlightenment An intellectual movement that developed in the mid eighteenth century, emphasizing the power of human reason to understand and improve the world.

Environmentalism A perspective based on the idea that humanity needs to change its relationship to nature so as to protect the natural environment and ensure that it can sustain all forms of life.

Equalization payments Payment made by the federal government to try to ensure that different provincial governments are able to provide an equivalent level of services to their populations without resorting to excessive levels of taxation.

Ethnic nationalism Nationalism based on common ancestry along with the cultural traditions and language associated with a particular ethnic group.

European Union (EU) The European Union (EU) is a unique system of governing in which many European countries have pooled some of their sovereignty while retaining their independence.

Executive dominance A descriptive term applied to the Canadian parliamentary system (and other countries that follow the Westminster model) because it places considerable power in the hands of the prime minister and Cabinet through their ability to control the House of Commons, particularly in a majority government situation.

Export-led industrialization (ELI) A model of economic development with a capitalist system in which government and the biggest businesses work very closely together to develop export industries. Government influences investments, provides incentives for exports, and can decide whether firms are allowed to export products.

Extraparliamentary party A political party organization outside of Parliament.

Failed state A state that no longer has the capacity to maintain order.

Fascism An ideology that combines an aggressive form of nationalism with a strong belief in the naturalness of inequality and opposition to both liberal democracy and communism.

Federal system A system of governing in which sovereign authority is divided or shared between the central government and regional governments, with each deriving its authority from the constitution.

Feminism A perspective that views society as patriarchal and seeks to achieve full independence and equality for women.

Filibuster The use of various delaying tactics by those opposed to the passage of a particular piece of legislation.

Framing Selecting and highlighting some facets of events or issues, and making connections among them so as to promote a particular interpretation, evaluation, and/or solution.

Free-market capitalist economic system An economic system involving private ownership and control of most businesses. Economic activity is coordinated primarily through market transactions, rather than by the commands of government or other authorities.

Free rider problem A problem with voluntary collective action that results because an individual can enjoy the benefits of group action without contributing.

Fundamentalism The revival of strict religious beliefs seeking to promote the fundamental principles of the faith, including the belief that sacred scriptures are the word of God and should be strictly followed in all areas of life.

Generational effect The effect on attitudes and behaviour of the views of different generations that persist throughout the life cycle.

Gerrymandering The manipulation of the division of the country into constituencies so as to benefit a particular party.

Global governance The process whereby a number of different actors (mainly states and international governmental and non-governmental organizations) compete and co-operate to provide a certain degree of order and predictability to relations among states.

Globalization The processes that are increasing the interconnectedness of the world.

Government The set of institutions that makes decisions and oversees their implementation of decisions on behalf of the state for a particular period of time.

Governor general The person who carries out the duties and responsibilities of the monarch at the national level in Canada.

Gross domestic product (GDP) The market value of goods and services produced in a country, excluding transactions with other countries.

Guerrilla warfare A form of highly political warfare built around lightly armed irregulars who oppose a government and use hit-and-run tactics and political work to take power.

Head of government The person who heads the executive side of government and is usually responsible for choosing the Cabinet. In Canada, the prime minister is the head of the Canadian government while the heads of provincial governments are known as premiers (in Quebec, *premier ministre*).

Head of state A largely ceremonial position as the official representative of the state. In a parliamentary system, the head of state is not usually involved in making governing decisions, but has the responsibility to ensure that a legitimate government is in place.

Hegemony or hegemonic system A type of unipolar system in which the superpower exercises power primarily through authority, leadership, and persuasion and thus creates a large consensus around its actions.

Historical materialism The view that historical development and the dynamics of society and politics can be understood in terms of the way society is organized to produce material goods.

Holocaust The systematic extermination of six million European Jews by the Nazis during the Second World War.

House of Commons The elected chamber of Parliament, with each member of the House representing a particular geographical constituency.

House of Commons committees Committees composed of government and opposition party members in proportion to their party's strength in the House of Commons; they provide detailed examination of proposed legislation, and often suggest modifications to the proposed legislation.

House of Representatives The lower chamber of the American Congress, elected for a two-year term from districts of approximately equal population size.

Human Development Index (HDI) An annual index for most countries, calculated by the United Nations Development Programme and based on literacy and education, life expectancy, and per capita GDP.

Hypodermic model The view that the messages conveyed by the mass media have a direct effect on the attitudes, opinions, and behaviour of the public.

Identity politics A perspective in which groups seek recognition and respect for their particular identity. Those involved in identity politics often seek to express their distinctiveness and gain a degree of autonomy from the rest of the community by developing their own institutions and services, obtaining recognition of their specific rights, and having their own means of political representation.

Impeachment A process by which a president and other public officials can be removed from office after being accused of criminal behaviour and convicted by a legislative body.

Import substitution industrialization (ISI) An economic development model that involves creating an industrial sector by placing tariffs on imported industrial products.

Incremental model of the policy process A policy-making model that suggests the policy process usually involves making minor changes to existing practices.

Individualist perspective A perspective that views human beings as acting primarily in accordance with their own interests.

Infotainment The merging of information and entertainment in news and public affairs programming of the mass media, particularly television.

Initiative A procedure that gives citizens the right, by obtaining a sizable number of signatures on a petition, to have a proposition that they have drafted put to a vote by the electorate for approval.

Inside strategies Strategies in which interest group leaders develop close contacts with key policy-makers in government and the public service in order to influence public policies.

Institutionalized interest group A group that has developed a formal organization, including such features as a well-established membership base, paid professional staff, permanent offices, and the capability to keep its members and the public aware of its views and activities.

Insurgency A rebellion or revolt, especially one employing the tools of guerrilla warfare.

Interest group A group of people who have joined together to pursue common interests and whose political activity is generally focused on trying to influence the making and implementation of the laws and policies of a political community.

International financial institution (IFI) An organization that has some ability to affect the global economic system; for example, the International Monetary Fund and the World Bank.

International governmental organization (IGO) An organization created by states to facilitate co-operation among them.

International non-governmental organization (INGO) An international organization whose members are not states but rather representatives of civil society.

International or global society The idea that the increasing number and importance of international interactions and the rising degree of interdependence is creating a global common identity and leading to the development of a global society.

International regime A set of principles, norms, treaties, and IGOs that regulates international activities in a given issue area.

International system A concept referring to both the most important international actors (states and international governmental organizations) and the pattern of interactions among them. The latter depends primarily on how power is distributed among actors.

Iron law of oligarchy A generalization that claims that all organizations, even those that appear democratic, inevitably become dominated by a small group of leaders.

Islamic fundamentalism The revival of Islam based on a strict, literal interpretation of the Quran and a belief that public and private life should be governed by the sharia (Islamic law).

Issue-oriented interest group An interest group that spontaneously develops to express the views of people on a particular issue, concern, or grievance.

Judicial activism The term used when the courts are active in invalidating legislation and government actions that are inconsistent with the constitution.

Judicial review The authority of the courts to strike down legislation or governmental actions that the courts deem to be in violation of the constitution.

Jurisdiction The state's governing and law-making authority over a particular geographic area and population.

Keynesian economic policies The idea that government can smooth out the ups and downs of the free-market economy by stimulating the economy when private business investment is low, and cooling down the economy when excessive investment is creating inflation.

Laissez-faire system A system in which privately owned businesses, workers, and consumers freely interact in the marketplace without government interference. The role of government is limited to such activities as maintaining order, enforcing contracts, and settling disputes.

Left The general ideological position associated with advocacy of greater social and economic equality, laws based on human rights rather than traditional morality, and opposition to state support for religious institutions.

Legal–rational authority The right to rule based on legal rules and procedures rather than on the personal qualities or characteristics of the rulers.

Legislature A body that is responsible for the formal approval of legislation and the raising and spending of funds by the government.

Legitimacy Acceptance by the members of a political community that those in positions of authority have the right to govern.

Leninism The version of Marxism that includes the belief that the capitalist system can only be overthrown through force by means of a tightly disciplined party controlled by a revolutionary vanguard.

Liberal democracy A political system that combines the liberal ideas of limited government, individual freedom, and the rule of law with a democratic system of governing based on the election of representatives.

Liberal feminism A version of feminism that advocates equal opportunities for women in such areas as education and employment as well as equal legal and political rights.

Liberal–internationalism An approach to the study of international politics that assumes that increased cultural and social connections as well as economic interdependence are leading to the emergence of a global civil society in which co-operation, the rule of law, and peace are valued and global governance is spreading both functionally and geographically.

Liberalism An ideological perspective advocating a high level of individual freedom, based on a belief in the inherent dignity and worth of each individual.

Liberation Freeing the human potential that has been stifled by the organization and values of society.

Libertarian perspective on the mass media The idea that if the mass media are free from government control and regulation, individuals will be able to obtain and assess the information and ideas they want.

Lieutenant-governor The person who carries out the duties and responsibilities of the monarch at the provincial level in Canada.

Life cycle effect The effect on attitudes and behaviour of one's age. As a person grows older, his or her attitudes and behaviours may change due to changing circumstances (such as education, marriage, employment, and retirement) related to age.

Lobbying An effort to persuade legislators, executives, or public officials, particularly through direct personal contact, to adopt and implement policies or decisions favoured by an individual, business, or group.

Majoritarian electoral system An electoral system designed to try to ensure that the winning candidate has the support of the majority of voters.

Majority government The government formed when the prime minister's party has a majority of the members of the House of Commons; thus, a single party forms the government.

Marginalization Exclusion from the mainstream.

Mass media Television, radio, and widely circulated newspapers that tend to reach a large audience that is not strongly differentiated by social characteristics.

Mass party A party that draws its support from a regular dues-paying membership and features a strong party organization outside of the legislature.

Meech Lake Accord A 1987 package of constitutional changes that was not passed. It contained controversial provisions, including the recognition of Quebec as a distinct society.

Mercantilist policies Pursuit of the interests of the nation-state through protectionist policies, the granting of monopolies to particular merchants, and the extraction of wealth from colonies.

Military dictatorship An undemocratic government run by the military.

Minimal effects model Through selective attention and selective perception, individuals filter out messages that might cause them to change their attitudes and behaviour. The effect of messages conveyed through the media is primarily to reinforce existing attitudes.

Minority government A single party governs, but that party does not have a majority of members in the House of Commons; thus, a minority government needs to gain the support of one or more other parties to pass legislation and to stay in office.

Mixed economy An economic system in which there is substantial state ownership or control of major elements of the economy along with a substantial degree of private ownership and some ability of private business to make their own decisions.

Mixed member proportional (MMP) system An electoral system in which voters cast one vote for the party they prefer and one vote for the candidate they prefer. Some legislators are elected to represent particular constituencies based on gaining the most votes in that constituency, while others are elected based on the popular vote received by their party.

Modernization theory A development model that views the traditional values, practices, and institutions of Third World countries as the basic cause of underdevelopment. To develop, poor countries should change their cultural outlook, social structure, economic organization, and political system based on the model of the advanced Western societies.

Monetarism An economic perspective based on the view that government's role in the economy should be largely restricted to controlling the supply of money.

Multiparty system A political party system featuring several parties that are significant actors in the competition for political power.

Multipolar system A multipolar system is a type of international system containing four or more major powers.

Nation A group of people who share a sense of common identity and who typically believe they should be self-governing within their homeland.

National interest The goals a state pursues in the conduct of its foreign policy. The term is multi-faceted and, besides the quest for power and security, includes goals ranging from the pursuit of economic growth and wealth to the preservation and expansion of national culture.

National self-determination The idea that nations should have the right to determine their political status, including choosing to have their own sovereign state.

Nationalism The idea that the nation-state is the best form of political community and that a nation should have its own self-governing state.

Nation-state A sovereign state based on people living in a country who share a sense of being a member of a particular nation.

Nazism A version of fascism associated with Adolf Hitler, the Nazi leader of Germany, emphasizing racial conflict and the superiority of the "Aryan race."

Neo-fascism A revival of fascism in contemporary times.

Neo-liberalism A perspective based on a strong belief in the free marketplace and opposition to government intervention in the economy.

Neo-Marxist theory A perspective that views politics as reflecting the conflicts that result from the way society is organized to produce goods. Public policies in a capitalist society will reflect the unequal power relations between the dominant capitalist forces and subordinate groups.

New public management The adoption of the practices of private business in the administrative activities of government.

New Right A perspective that combines, in various ways, the promotion of free-market capitalism and traditional cultural and moral values.

New style of citizen politics Changes in political culture related to postmaterialism, the development of a post-industrial, knowledge-based economy, greater access to higher education, and more effective means of mass communications. This new style includes greater activism, the questioning of authority, the development of new political parties and new social movements, the raising of new types of issues, and the development of more liberal social values.

News management The controlling and shaping of the presentation of news in order to affect the public's evaluation of news stories.

Non-confidence motion A motion put forward by the opposition members in a legislature expressing a lack of confidence in the government. If passed, the prime minister is expected to either resign or request that an election be held.

Non-governmental organization (NGO) Private organizations that often deliver public services but are independent of government. NGOs have been very active in international development activities.

Normative analysis Analysis that involves examining ideas about how the community should be governed and what values should be pursued through politics.

North The rich, developed countries.

Notwithstanding clause A provision in the Charter of Rights and Freedoms that allows a legislative body to explicitly declare that a particular law (related to some parts of the Charter) shall operate *notwithstanding* the provisions of the Charter. Such a declaration is only effective for five years, although it can be re-enacted as often asis desired.

Official Development Assistance (ODA) Aid to the poorer countries given by the governments of the richer countries.

Official opposition The party with the second-highest number of seats in the House of Commons is designated as the official opposition and leads off the questioning or criticism of government every day that the House is sitting.

One-party dominant system A party system in which a single party rules for long periods of time and the opposition parties are not likely to gain the support needed to successfully challenge the dominant party for control of the government.

Outside strategies Strategies in which interest group leaders appeal to the public for support in order to put pressure on decision-makers concerning public policies.

Pacted transition A democratic transition that occurs when pacts or agreements among the elites of formerly undemocratic states permit the establishment of democratic government.

Parliamentary party The organization of a political party's members who have seats in Parliament.

Parliamentary sovereignty A basic principle of the British system of governing, recognizing Parliament as the supreme law-making body.

Parliamentary system A system of governing in which there is a close interrelationship between the political executive (prime minister and Cabinet) and Parliament (the legislative or law-making body). The executive is generally composed of members of the House of Commons (the elected parliamentary body) and must maintain the support of the House of Commons.

Party caucus A meeting of the party's parliamentary members.

Party convention A meeting of delegates from party constituency associations as well as the party's legislators and party officials.

Party dictatorship An undemocratic political system that is controlled by one party. The most familiar examples are communist political systems.

Party discipline The expectation that legislators will vote in accordance with the position that the party has adopted in caucus.

Party identification A long-term psychological attachment to a particular political party.

Party system The pattern of competition among political parties.

Patriarchy A system in which power is in the hands of men and in which many aspects of women's lives are controlled by men.

Pay equity A policy that requires employers to provide equal pay for work of equal value; for example, by raising the pay of persons in occupations that are largely staffed by women to the same pay as persons in comparable occupations that are largely staffed by men.

Personal dictatorship An undemocratic government dominated by a single individual. Saddam Hussein's Iraq was a classic example of this kind of system.

Personalistic leader A political leader whose claim to rule is based on some presumed inherent personal qualities. It also implies a government in which all important decisions are made by the leader and according to the leader's wishes.

Personalistic party A party established to promote the election of a particular individual as prime minister or president.

Plebiscitary democracy A form of democracy in which citizens have greater control than in representative democracy through the use of such devices as referendums, initiatives, and recall elections.

Pluralist perspective The freedom of individuals to establish and join groups that are not controlled by the government results in a wide variety of groups having an ability to influence the decisions of government, with no group dominant.

Pole A concentration of power in the international system. It could be a state or an alliance.

Policy analysis Analysis that involves evaluating existing policies and assessing alternatives to deal with particular problems.

Policy cycle The analysis of the policy process as a continuous cycle of stages, with policies continually undergoing modification in response to evaluations of the policy.

Policy entrepreneur Someone who is ready to push a pet policy proposal whenever an opportunity arises.

Policy evaluation Determining the extent to which a policy is achieving its objectives and how it can be made more effective.

Policy formulation Developing and evaluating different courses of action to deal with a problem.

Policy implementation Taking measures to put a policy into effect, such as developing rules and regulations and establishing an administrative structure.

Policy legitimation Gaining acceptance of a policy proposal; for example, through formal approval by a legislative body.

Policy network The governmental and non-governmental actors that participate in the development of policies in a particular policy field.

Political agenda The issues that are considered important and given priority in political deliberations.

Political conflict A state of opposition, usually involving groups and the state, over something government is doing or proposes to do.

Political culture The general political values, attitudes, and beliefs that are widely held within a political community.

Political efficacy The attitude that individuals can have an impact on politics and that government is responsive to what people want.

Political ideology A package of interrelated ideas and beliefs about government, society, the economy, and human nature that affect political action. Each ideology provides a different perspective that is used to understand and evaluate how the world actually works. Most ideologies present a vision of what the world should be like and how political action can be used to achieve that vision.

Political institutions Behavioural patterns or established organizations associated with governing.

Political opportunity structures (POS) The openings that political institutions and processes offer to (or withhold from) movements.

Political parties Organizations that have a central role in the competition for political power in legislative bodies, and in governing.

Political protest Oppositional political action that takes place outside formal channels, generally seeking to have government make significant changes in its policies.

Political science The systematic study of politics.

Political socialization The processes by which the values, attitudes, and beliefs of the political culture are transmitted to members of the political community.

Political violence The use of physical force with a political objective.

Politics Activity related to influencing, making, or implementing collective decisions for a political community.

Populism A perspective that advocates putting power in the hands of the people rather than the elites who control politics and society.

Positive rights A right to services or benefits such as the right to education, health care, and employment.

Postmaterialist theory A theory that modern societies are undergoing a fundamental change in value priorities because generations that grew up in the relative security and affluence of the Western world since the Second World War are more likely to give priority to postmaterialist values than to materialist values.

Postmaterialist values Non-materialist values such as freedom of expression, participation, concern about the quality of life, and appreciation of a more beautiful environment.

Postmodern state A state in which the meaning and practice of sovereignty have been redefined since tools of governance are shared, foreign and domestic policies have become inextricably intertwined, and security is no longer based on control of borders and deterrence.

Power The ability to achieve an objective by influencing the behaviour of others, particularly to get them to do what they would not have otherwise done.

Preferential voting An electoral system in which voters rank candidates in order of preference. If no candidate has a majority of first preferences, the candidate with the least votes is dropped and the second preferences of those who voted for that candidate are added to the votes of other candidates. This process continues until one candidate has a majority.

Presidential system A system of governing in which the president and Congress each separately derive their authority from being elected by the people and have a fixed term of office. The president is both head of government and head of state.

Presidential veto The ability to prevent the passage of a bill. For example, the president of the U.S. has the authority to veto laws passed by Congress, although this veto can be overridden by a two-thirds majority in each House of Congress.

Primary election A state-run election in which American citizens select the candidates they want to represent their party in the general election.

Prime Minister's Office (PMO) The office that provides support and political advice to the prime minister.

Prime ministerial government The view that the prime minister has become the dominant member of the political executive, rather than the "first among equals" in the Cabinet.

Priming The potential capability of the media to affect the criteria by which people judge political events and personalities.

Private members Ordinary members of the House of Commons who are not in the Cabinet.

Privy Council Office (PCO) An administrative structure, directly responsible to the Canadian prime minister, that has a key role in coordinating and directing the activities of government and in providing policy advice to the prime minister.

Procedural definition of democracy A definition of democracy in terms of procedures and institutions (such as elections) rather than outcomes.

Programmatic party A party that has a distinct ideological perspective or a coherent set of policy goals that are consistently followed over time.

Proportional representation (PR) system An electoral system in which the proportion of seats a party receives in the legislature reflects the proportion of votes it has obtained.

Protest movement A group of people who mount a continuing challenge in opposition to some government policy or action by a private firm or individual.

Public choice theory A perspective based on the assumption that all political actors rationally pursue their own individual interests or preferences. Public policies will generally reflect the choices made by voters.

Public interest group A group that seeks to achieve goals that the group views as being for the good of the community as a whole rather than specific benefits for their members.

Public policy A course of action or inaction chosen by public authorities to address a given problem or interrelated set of problems.

Purchasing power parity (PPP) A measure of per capita income that shows the purchasing power of an income, instead of its worth at current exchange rates.

Radical feminism A version of feminism that views society as based fundamentally on the oppression of women, and seeks to liberate women through the fundamental transformation of social institutions, values, and personal relationships.

Radical Islamism The perspective often associated with those seeking to purge "degenerate" foreign elements from Muslim society and establish a "pure" Islamic state based strictly on the sharia (Islamic law).

Rational–comprehensive model of the policy process A policy-making model that involves establishing clear goals to deal with a problem, examining all possible alternatives, and choosing the best alternative. The policy is then monitored and evaluated to assess whether the goals have been achieved, and changed if necessary.

Reactionary A conservative who favours a return to the values and institutions of the past.

Realism An approach to the study of international politics that assumes that because the international system is anarchic, security is the major preoccupation of states. Peace rests primarily on deterrence, and the possibility of international governance is limited because states are reluctant to put constraints on their sovereignty.

Reasonable limits clause A provision of the Canadian Charter of Rights and Freedoms that allows for "reasonable limits" to be placed on rights and freedoms provided that the limits can be "demonstrably justified in a free and democratic society."

Recall A procedure that allows citizens to remove representatives from office. By gaining a sufficient number of signatures on a petition, citizens can require that their representative seek re-election before the representative's term is over.

Referendum A vote by citizens on a particular issue or law.

Reform environmentalism A perspective that views the solution to environmental problems primarily in terms of better science, technology, and environmental management.

Reform liberalism A version of liberalism that combines support for individual freedom with a belief that government action may be needed to help remove obstacles to individual development.

Regime violence Political violence used by a government against its citizens, generally as a way to repress dissent and maintain order.

Representative bureaucracy A bureaucracy that reflects the characteristics of society, particularly by trying to ensure that all levels of the public service have a proportion of women and various disadvantaged minority groups similar to that of the population as a whole.

Representative democracy A form of democracy in which citizens elect representatives to the legislature to make decisions on their behalf.

Responsible government A governing system in which the political executive (the prime minister and Cabinet) is accountable to Parliament for its actions based on the principle that the political executive must retain the support of the elected members of Parliament to remain in office.

Revolution The use of violence to overthrow a government, especially when the overthrow is followed by rapid and thorough social, economic, and political restructuring.

Right The general ideological position associated with opposition to imposing greater social and economic equality and with maintaining traditional (religious-based) moral values and institutions.

Rule of law The idea that we should be subject to known, predictable, and impartial rules of conduct, rather than to the arbitrary orders of particular individuals. Both the rulers and the ruled should be equally subject to the law.

Runoff election An election held if no candidate receives a majority of votes; generally, only the top two candidates appear on the ballot to ensure that the winning candidate has a majority of the votes cast.

Secessionist A person who favours separation of a territory from an existing state.

Secretaries of state Cabinet ministers who are not responsible for a particular government department.

Secular humanism The view that ethical principles and moral standards can be developed through human reason.

Security dilemma The dilemma that arises when states need power to feel secure, but their accumulation of power might undermine rather than increase their security if it leads other states to feel that they are in danger and form an alliance to meet the perceived threat.

Segregation The legal separation of blacks and whites, particularly in the southern United States.

Selective incentive A particular benefit that is made available to members of an interest group but is not available to the public as a whole.

Self-interest group An interest group whose primary objective is to promote the interests of the group and its members and to seek benefits that are primarily or exclusively for their members.

Semi-presidential system A governmental system in which an elected president shares power with a prime minister and Cabinet, which usually need to retain the support of the elected legislature.

Senate (Canada) The upper chamber of Parliament, appointed on the recommendation of the prime minister. Senators hold their positions until age seventy-five.

Senate (United States) The upper chamber of Congress. Two senators are elected by voters in each state for a six-year term.

Separation of powers A basic feature of presidential systems in which the executive, legislative, and judicial branches of government are separate from each other with each having different personnel and different bases of authority.

Single member plurality (SMP) system An electoral system in which voters in each geographical constituency elect a single representative to the legislature. The candidate with the most votes is elected, regardless of whether that candidate received the majority of votes.

Single transferable vote (STV) system An electoral system in which voters mark their preferences for candidates in a multi-member constituency. Candidates receiving a certain proportion of the vote are declared elected. The second preferences of voters that are surplus to what the winning candidates need are then transferred to candidates who have not reached the quota. The process is continued until all seats in the constituency are filled.

Social class A grouping of people who have a similar position in the economy and related social status.

Social Darwinism The use of Darwin's theory of evolution to argue that competition and conflict allow humanity to evolve through the "survival of the fittest."

Social democracy The belief that the capitalist economy should be reformed to ensure that it works for the common good of all and that greater social and economic equality is desirable to achieve a meaningful democracy.

Social ecology A perspective that views social, economic, and political relationships of hierarchy and domination as the cause of both human and environmental problems.

Social movement A network of groups and individuals that seeks major social and political changes, particularly by acting outside of established political institutions.

Social responsibility perspective on the mass media The view that the media have a responsibility to the public. Freeing the media from government regulation and control does not necessarily result in the public interest being served.

Social revolution A revolution that changes not just who governs but how a state, society, and economy are structured.

Socialism An ideological perspective based on the view that human beings are basically social in nature and that the capitalist system undermines the co-operative and community-oriented nature of humanity. Socialism advocates the establishment of an egalitarian society.

Socialist economic system An economic system based on social (usually state) ownership and control of the economy.

Socialist feminism A version of feminism that views women as oppressed by both the male-dominated character of society and the capitalist system. The liberation of women is connected to the transformation of capitalism into a more co-operative and egalitarian socialist system.

South Less developed, poorer countries.

Sovereign state A state that has the ability to govern its population and territory without outside interference.

Sovereignty The principle that states have the right to govern their population and territory without outside interference.

State An independent, self-governing political community whose governing institutions have the capability to make rules that are binding on the population residing within a particular territory.

State-centred theory This perspective views public policies as reflecting, to a considerable extent, the preferences and priorities of those in important positions of authority within various state institutions.

Streams and windows model of the policy process A policy-making model that views the policy process as fluid. Changes in the identification of problems, policy proposals, and political circumstances create windows of opportunity in which policy entrepreneurs may successfully push their pet proposals.

Structural adjustment program (SAP) A program administered by international financial institutions, which offer loans at very favourable interest rates to governments facing problems paying their debt if they adopt the programs espoused by the Washington Consensus.

Suicide terrorism A form of terrorist violence in which the attacker intends to die as well as killing the intended targets.

Sustainability Maintaining the integrity of ecosystems by ensuring that renewable resources are not being used at a rate that exceeds the ability of ecosystems to regenerate them, developing renewable substitutes to replace the consumption of non-renewable resources, and ensuring that the emission of pollutants does not exceed the ability of the ecosystem to handle them without damage.

Sustainable development Meeting the needs of the present without compromising the ability of future generations to meet their own needs; it involves development to ensure that the needs of the poor are fulfilled and protecting the environment for the well-being of future generations.

Tariff A tax on imports.

Terrorism The deliberate use of violence designed to induce fear in a population in order to achieve a political objective.

Theocratic dictatorship An undemocratic state run by religious elites. The best contemporary example is Iran.

Third Wave of Democracy The broad move to democratic government that began in 1974 and still continues.

Third World Less developed countries.

Three faces of power The argument that looking at who affects particular decisions is insufficient to analyze power. Power can also involve the ability to keep issues off the political agenda and the ability to affect the dominant values of society.

Totalitarian A type of state that attempts to control all aspects of life.

Traditional authority Authority based on customs that establish the right of certain persons to rule.

Transitional election An election that marks the official beginning of a democratic regime.

Transparency The visibility to the public of the governmental decision-making processes.

Treasury Board A permanent Cabinet committee with its own staff and minister that plays a central role in governing in Canada because of its responsibility for the expenditures and management practices of government.

Two-party system A party system in which two major parties contend to control the government. Two-party systems are competitive in the sense that a single party does not govern for a lengthy period of time.

Two-plus party system A party system in which there are two major contenders for control of the government but other parties also have a significant amount of support, which may at times prevent either of the larger parties from gaining a majority of legislative seats.

Underdeveloped countries A term often used to describe Third World countries.

Unipolarity An international system with a single superpower.

Unitary system A system of governing in which sovereign authority rests with the central government; regional and local governments are subordinate.

United Nations (UN) An international governmental organization representing almost all of the world's states.

Universal suffrage The right of all adult citizens to vote regardless of such characteristics as gender, ethnicity, wealth, or education.

Valence issues Issues on which there is a general consensus.

Washington Consensus A series of policies put together by the International Monetary Fund and the World Bank that encourages developing countries to generate more revenue for debt repayment by cutting government expenditures to balance their budgets, selling off government-owned enterprises (privatization), and fully opening their countries to foreign goods and investments.

Welfare state A term used to describe countries in which government ensures that all people have a minimum standard of living and are provided some protection from hardships resulting from unemployment, sickness, disability, and old age.

Westminster model A model of governing that developed in Britain, featuring majority rule, executive dominance, and an adversarial relationship between the government party and the opposition parties.

REFERENCES

Adams, I. (2001). *Political ideology today* (2nd ed.). Manchester, UK: Manchester University Press.

Adams, M. (2003). *Fire and ice: The United States, Canada and the myth of converging values.* Toronto: Penguin.

Adams, J., & Merrill, S. (2005). Candidate policy platforms and electoral outcomes: The three faces of policy representation. *European Journal of Political Research, 44*, 881–896.

Adolini, J.R., & Blake, C.H. (2001). *Comparing policies: Issues and choices in six industrialized countries.* Washington, DC: CQ Press.

Albritton, R.B. (2006). American federalism and intergovernmental relations. In G. Peele, C.J. Bailey, B. Cain & B.G. Peters (Eds.), *Developments in American politics 5.* Houndmills, Basingstoke, Hampshire, UK: Palgrave Macmillan.

Almond, G., & Verba, S. (1963). *The civic culture: Political attitudes and democracy in five nations.* Princeton, NJ: Princeton University Press.

Almond, G.A., Appleby, R.S., & Sivan, E. (2003). *Strong religions: The rise of fundamentalism around the world.* Chicago: University of Chicago Press.

Alterman, E. (2003). *What liberal media? The truth about bias and the news.* New York: Basic Books.

Andersen, V.N., & Hansen, K.M. (2007). How deliberation makes better citizens: The Danish Deliberative Poll on the euro. *European Journal of Political Research, 46*(4), 531–556.

Anderson, J.E. (1979). *Public policy-making* (2nd ed.). New York: Holt, Rinehart & Winston.

Ansolabehere, S., Iyengar, S., Simon, A., & Valentino, N. (1997). Does attack advertising demobilize the electorate? In S. Iyengar & R. Reeves (Eds.), *Do the media govern? Politicians, voters, and reporters in America* (pp. 195–207). Thousand Oaks, CA: Sage Publications.

Atkinson, A.B. (2000). Can welfare states compete in a global economy? In R.V. Ericson & N. Stehr (Eds.), *Governing modern societies* (pp. 259–275). Toronto: University of Toronto Press.

Aucoin, P. (2002). Beyond the "new" public management reform in Canada: Catching the next wave? In C. Dunn (Ed.), *The handbook of Canadian public administration* (pp. 37–52). Don Mills, ON: Oxford University Press.

Axworthy, L. (2003). *Navigating a new world: Canada's global future.* Toronto: Alfred A. Knopf.

Babbie, E. (1995). *The practice of social research* (7th ed.). Belmont, CA: Wadworth Publishing Company.

Bachrach, P., & Baratz, M. (1962). The two faces of power. *American Political Science Review, 56*, 947–952.

Baer, D., Curtis, J., & Grabb, E. (2001). Has voluntary association activity declined? Cross-national analysis for fifteen countries. *Canadian Review of Sociology and Anthropology, 38*, 249–272.

Ball, T., & Dagger, R. (2004). *Political ideologies and the democratic ideal* (5th ed.). New York: Pearson Longman.

Ball-Rokeach, S.J., Rokeach, M., & Grube, J.W. (1984). *The great American values test: Influencing behavior and belief through television.* London: Free Press.

Barber, B. (1995). *Jihad vs. McWorld: How globalization and tribalism are reshaping the world.* New York: Ballantine.

Barnard, F.M. (2001). *Democratic legitimacy: plural values and political power.* Montreal: McGill–Queen's University Press.

Barry, B. (1996). Political theory, old and new. In R.E. Goodin & H.-D. Klingemann (Eds.), *A new handbook of political science.* Oxford: Oxford University Press.

Beckett, I. (2001). *Modern insurgencies and counter-insurgencies: Guerrillas and their opponents since 1750.* London, UK: Routledge.

Bell, D. (1998). The end of ideology revisited. *Government and Opposition, 23*, 131–150; 321–328.

Bell, D.V.J. (2004). Political culture in Canada. In M. Whittington & G. Williams (Eds.), *Canadian politics in the 21st century* (6th ed.). Toronto: Nelson.

Bellini, E. (2004). The robustness of authoritarianism in the Middle East: Exceptionalism in comparative perspective. *Comparative Politics, 36*(2), 139–157.

Benedicto, J. (2004). Cultural structures and political life: The cultural matrix of democracy in Spain. *European Journal of Political Research, 43*(3), 287–307.

Bercuson, D., & Cooper, B. (1998, August 8). The logic behind an elected Senate. *Globe and Mail,* D2.

Berman, P. (2001). The passion of Joschka Fischer. *The New Republic* (August 27).

Bhardwaj, R., & Vijayakrishnan, K. (1998). *Democracy and development: Allies or adversaries?* Aldershot, UK: Ashgate.

Black, R. (2006). Carbon emissions show sharp rise. BBC News website, November 27, 2006. Retrieved November 27, 2006, from www.bbc.co.uk.

Blais, A. (2005). Accounting for the electoral success of the Liberal party in Canada. *Canadian Journal of Political Science, 38*(4), 821–840.

Blais, A., Gidengil, E., Nadeau, R, & Nevitte, N. (2002). *Anatomy of a Liberal victory: Making sense of the vote in the 2000 Canadian election.* Peterborough, ON: Broadview.

Blais, A, Gidengil, E., Nevitte, N., & Nadeau, R. (2004). Where does turnout decline come from? *European Journal of Political Research, 43,* 221–236.

Blais, A., & Massicotte, L. (2002). Electoral systems. In L. LeDuc, R.G. Niemi, & P. Norris (Eds.), *Comparing democracies 2: New challenges in the study of elections and voting* (pp. 40–69). London: Sage.

Blais, A., Massicotte, L., & Dobrzynska, A. (2003). *Why is election turnout higher in some countries than others?* Retrieved May 26, 2004, from www.elections.ca.

Borins, S. (2002). Transformation of the public sector: Canada in comparative perspective. In C. Dunn (Ed.), *The handbook of Canadian public administration* (pp. 3–17). Don Mills, ON: Oxford University Press.

Bosso, C.J. (1989). Setting the agenda: Mass media and the discovery of famine in Ethiopia. In M. Margolis & G.A. Mauser (Eds.), *Manipulating public opinion: Essays on public opinion as a dependent variable* (pp. 153–174). Belmont, CA: Wadsworth.

Bosso, C.J. (2005). *Environment, Inc.: From grassroots to beltway.* Lawrence, KS: University Press of Kansas.

Boyd, D.R. (2003). *Unnatural law: Rethinking Canadian environmental law and policy.* Vancouver: UBC Press.

Brady, D.W., & Volden, C. (2006). *Revolving gridlock: Politics and policy from Jimmy Carter to George W. Bush* (2nd ed.). Boulder, CO: Westview Press.

Brinton, C. (1965). *The anatomy of a revolution.* New York: Vintage.

Broadbent, E. (2001). Social democracy—The way ahead. Conference on the future of social democracy in Canada. Retrieved August 26, 2006, from www.misc-iecm. mcgill.ca/socdem/ebeng.htm.

Brodie, J., & Jenson, J. (1988). *Crisis, challenge and change: Party and class in Canada revisited.* Ottawa: Carleton University Press.

Brooks, S. (1998). *Public policy in Canada* (3rd. ed.). Toronto: Oxford University Press.

Brown, S. (1995). *New forces, old forces and the future of world politics.* New York: HarperCollins.

Brownmiller, S. (1975). *Against our will: Men, women and rape.* New York: Simon & Schuster.

Bryson, V. (2003). *Feminist political theory: An introduction* (2nd ed.). Houndmills, Basingstoke, Hampshire, UK: Palgrave Macmillan.

Bunce, V. (2003). Rethinking recent democratization: Lessons from the postcommunist experience. *World Politics, 55*(1), 167–192.

Burden, B.C., & Kimball, D.C. (2004). *Why Americans split their tickets: Campaigns, competition, and divided government.* Ann Arbor, MI: University of Michigan Press.

Burke, E. (1955). *Reflections on the revolution in France.* (T.H.D. Mahoney, Ed.). Indianapolis, IN: The Liberal Arts Press. (Original work published in 1790).

Bush, G.W. (2006). Address to the American Legion National Convention, August 31, 2006. Retrieved September 9, 2006, from www.whitehouse.gov/news/release/ 2006/08/31/20060831.html.

Cairns, A.C. (1968). The electoral system and the party system in Canada, 1921–1965. *Canadian Journal of Political Science, 1*(1), 55–80.

Cairns, A.C. (2000). *Citizens plus: Aboriginal peoples and the Canadian state.* Vancouver: UBC Press.

Calderisi, R. (2006). *The trouble with Africa.* New York: Palgrave Macmillan.

Canadian Broadcasting Corporation (2004). *CBC/Radio Canada pre-election poll.* Retrieved May 26, 2004, from www.cbc.ca/canadavotes/thepolls/democracypoll.htm.

Cappella, J.N., & Jamieson, K.H. (1997). *Spiral of cynicism: The press and the public good.* Oxford: Oxford University Press.

Cardoso, F.H., & Falletto, E. (1979). *Dependency and development in Latin America.* Berkeley: University of California Press.

Carens, J.H. (2000). *Culture, citizenship, and community: A contextual exploration of justice as evenhandedness.* Oxford, UK: Oxford University Press.

Carothers, T. (1999). *Aiding democracy abroad.* Washington, DC: Carnegie Endowment for International Peace.

Carothers, T. (2002). The end of the transition paradigm. *Journal of Democracy, 13*(1), 5–22.

Carr, E. H. (1939/2001).*The twenty years' crisis: 1919–39: An introduction to international relations.* New York: Harper and Row.

Carty, R.K. (1988). Three Canadian party systems. In G.C. Perlin (Ed.). *Party democracy in Canada.* Toronto: Prentice Hall.

Carty, R.K. (2002). Canadian political parties as franchise organizations. *Canadian Journal of Political Science, 35*(4), 723–745.

Castells, M. (2004). *The information age: Economy, society and culture. Volume II: The power of identity* (2nd ed.). Malden, MA: Blackwell.

Castle, B. (1987). *Sylvia and Cristabel Pankhurst.* New York: Penguin Books.

Caul, M.L., & Gray, M.M. (2000). From platform declarations to policy outcomes: Changing party profiles and partisan influence over policy. In R.J. Dalton & M.P. Wattenberg (Eds.), *Parties without partisans: Political change in advanced industrial democracies* (pp. 208–237). Oxford: Oxford University Press.

Centre for Research and Information on Canada (2002). *Portraits of Canada, 2002.* Retrieved August 18, 2003, from www.cric.ca/pdf/cahiers/cricpapers_dec2002.pdf.

Clark, S.D., Grayson, J.P., & Grayson, L. (1976). General introduction: The nature of social movements. In S.D. Clark, J.P. Grayson, & L.M. Grayson (Eds.), *Prophecy and protest: Social movements in twentieth-century Canada* (pp. 1–38). Toronto: Gage.

Clarke, H.D., Jenson, J., LeDuc, L., & Pammett, J.H. (1996). *Absent mandate: Canadian electoral politics in an era of restructuring* (3rd ed.). Toronto: Gage Educational Publishing.

Clarke, H.D., Kornberg, A., Scotto, T. & Twyman, J. (2006). Flawless campaign, fragile victory: Voting in Canada's 2006 federal election. *PS: Political Science and Politics, 39*(4), 815–819.

Clarke, T., & Barlow, M. (1997). *MAI: The multilateral agreement on investment and the threat to Canadian sovereignty.* Toronto: Stoddart.

Cleverdon, C.L. (1974). *The woman suffrage movement in Canada* (2nd ed.). Toronto: University of Toronto Press.

Close, D. (2004). Undoing democracy in Nicaragua. In D. Close & K. Deonandan (Eds.), *Undoing democracy: The politics of electoral caudillismo* (pp. 1–15). Lanham, MD: Lexington Books.

Close, D., & Deonandan, K. (Eds.). (2004). *Undoing democracy: The politics of electoral caudillismo.* Lanham, MD: Lexington Books.

Close, D., & Mintz, E. (2005). State sponsorship and community environmental groups: The Atlantic coastal action program in Newfoundland. *American Review of Canadian Studies, 35*(4), 621–639.

Code, L. (1988). Feminist theory. In S. Burt, L. Code, & L. Dorney (Eds.), *Changing patterns: Women in Canada.* Toronto: McClelland and Stewart.

Coleman, W.D. (2002). The politics of globalization. In R. Dyck (Ed.), *Studying politics: An introduction to political science* (pp. 389–405). Scarborough, ON: Thomson Nelson.

Compas. (2004). *The Global TV election day poll.* Retrieved August 16, 2004, from www.compas.ca/data/040628-GlobalTVEDayPollPart1-E.pdf.

Cook, D. (2005). *Understanding jihad.* Berkeley, CA: University of California Press.

Coombes, C. (2003). *Terrorism in the twenty-first century* (3rd ed.). Upper Saddle River, NJ: Prentice-Hall.

Cooper, R. (2000). *The post-modern state and world order.* London: Foreign Policy Centre.

Coupland, R. (1964). *The British anti-slavery movement.* London: Frank Cass

Courchene, T.J. (1992). *Rearrangements: The Courchene papers.* Oakville, ON: Mosaic Press.

Courchene, T.J. (2007). Global futures for Canada's global cities. *Policy Matters, 8*(2).

Cox, R.W. (1987). *Production, power, and world order: Social forces in the making of history.* New York: Columbia University Press.

Crick, B. (1963). *In defence of politics.* London: Weidenfield and Nicholson.

Crick, B. (1993). *In defence of politics* (4th American ed.). Chicago: University of Chicago Press.

Cross, W. (2004). *Political parties.* Vancouver: UBC Press.

Cross, W., & Young, L. (2002). Policy attitudes of party members in Canada: Evidence of ideological politics. *Canadian Journal of Political Science, 35*(4), 859–880.

Croteau, D. (1998). *Examining the "liberal media" claim: Journalists' views on politics, economic policy, and media coverage.* Retrieved November 15, 2003, from www.fair.org/reports/journalist-survey.html.

Crozier, M., Huntington, S.P., & Watanuki, J. (1975). *The crisis of democracy.* New York: New York University Press.

Dahl, R.A. (1961). *Who governs? Democracy and power in an American city.* New Haven: Yale University Press.

Dahl, R.A. (1984). *Modern political analysis* (4th ed.). Englewood Cliffs, NJ: Prentice-Hall.

Dalton, R.J. (2000). The decline of party identifications. In R.J. Dalton & M.P. Wattenberg (Eds.), *Parties without partisans: Political change in advanced industrial democracies* (pp. 19–36). Oxford: Oxford University Press.

Dalton, R.J. (2006). *Citizen politics: Public opinion and political parties in advanced industrial democracies* (4th ed.). Washington, DC: CQ Press.

Dalton, R.J., & Wattenburg, M.P. (2000). Partisan change and the democratic process. In R.J. Dalton & M.P. Wattenberg (Eds.), *Parties with partisans: Political change in advanced industrial democracies* (pp. 261–285). Oxford: Oxford University Press.

Daly, H.E., & Cobb, J.B. (1994). *For the common good: Redirecting the economy toward community, the environment, and a sustainable future* (2nd ed.). Boston: Beacon Press.

Decalo, S. (1988). *Psychoses of power: African personal dictatorships.* Boulder, CO: Westview Press.

Devall, B., & Sessions, G. (1998). Deep ecology. In D. VanDeVeer & C. Pierce (Eds.), *The environmental ethics and policy book: Philosophy, ecology, economics* (2nd ed.) (pp. 221–226). Belmont, CA: Wadsworth.

DeWeil, B. (2000). *Democracy: A history of ideas.* Vancouver: UBC Press.

Di Palma, G. (1990). *To craft democracies.* Berkeley, CA: University of California Press.

Diamond, L. (2005). *Squandered victory: The American occupation and the bungled effort to bring democracy to Iraq.* New York: Times Books, Henry Holt and Company.

Dietz, T., Ostrom, E., & Stern, P.C. (2003). The struggle to govern the commons. *Science, 302*(5652), 1907–1912.

Dobson, A. (2000). *Green political thought* (3rd ed.). New York: Routledge.

Domhoff, G.W. (2006). *Who rules America? Power, politics, and social change* (5th ed.). New York: McGraw-Hill.

Dowie, M. (1995). *Losing ground: American environmentalism at the close of the twentieth century.* Cambridge, MA: MIT Press.

Downs, A. (1957). *An economic theory of democracy.* New York: Harper.

Dowty, A. (2005). *Israel/Paelstine.* Cambridge, UK: Polity.

Doyle, T., & Kellow, A. (1995). *Environmental politics and policy making in Australia.* Melbourne: Macmillan.

Dryzek, J. (1997). *The politics of the earth: Environmental discourses.* Oxford: Oxford University Press.

Dunleavy, P., *et al.* (2006). New public management is dead—long live digital-era governance. *Journal of Public Administration Research and Theory, 16*(3), 467–494.

Duverger, M. (1964). *Political parties: Their organization and activity in the modern state* (3rd ed.). London: Methuen.

Dyck, R. (2004). *Canadian politics: Critical approaches* (4th ed.). Scarborough, ON: Nelson Canada.

Easterly, W. (2006). *The white man's burden.* New York: The Penguin Press.

Easton, A. (2005). *The twins who would lead Poland.* BBC online, June 16, 2005. Retrieved May 1, 2007, from www.bbc.co.uk/2/hi/europe14099646.stm.

Easton, D. (1953). *The political system: An enquiry into the state of political science.* New York: Knopf.

Eatwell, R. (1995). *Fascism: A history.* New York: Penguin Books.

Eckersley, R. (1992). *Environmentalism and political theory: Towards an ecocentric approach.* Albany, NY: State University of New York Press.

Ehrenreich, B., & English, D. (1979). *For her own good: 150 years of the experts' advice to women.* New York: Anchor Press.

Ekos. (2004). *Federal election poll #4: Final countdown.* Retrieved August 16, 2004, from www.ekos.com/admin/pressreleases/26june2004backgrounddoc.pdf.

Elections Canada. (1997). *A history of the vote in Canada.* Ottawa: Minister of Public Works and Government Services.

Elections Canada. (2005). *Estimates of voter turnout by age groups in the 38th federal general election (June 28, 2004): Final report.* Retrieved May 27, 2007, from www.elections.ca.

Elgie, R. (1999). Semi-presidentialism and comparative institutional engineering. In R. Elgie (Ed.), *Semi-presidentialism in Europe.* Oxford: Oxford University Press.

Elgie, R. (2005). The political executive. In A. Cole, P. Le Galès, & J. Levy (Eds.), *Developments in French politics 3.* Houndmills, Basingstoke, Hampshire, UK: Palgrave Macmillan.

Elkins, D.J. (1993). *Manipulation and consent: How voters and leaders manage complexity.* Vancouver: UBC Press.

Elkins, D.J. (1995). *Beyond sovereignty: Territory and political economy in the twenty-first century.* Toronto: University of Toronto Press.

Elster, J. (1998). *Deliberative democracy.* Cambridge: Cambridge University Press.

Enloe, C. (1989). *Bananas, beaches and bases: Making feminist sense of international relations.* London: Pandora.

Entman, R.M. (2004). *Projections of power: Framing news, public opinion, and U.S. foreign policy.* Chicago: University of Chicago Press.

Environics/CBC 2006 Federal Election Survey. Retrieved August 21, 2007, from www.environicsresearch.com/media_room/default.asp?aID=598.

European Council. (2003). *A secure Europe in a better world: European security strategy.* Retrieved August 15, 2007, from www.consilium.europa.eu/uedocs/cmsUpload/78367.pdf.

Evans, M. (2006). Elitism. In C. Hay, M. Lister, & D. Marsh (Eds.). *The state: Theories and issues.* Houndmills, Basingstoke, Hampshire, UK: Palgrave Macmillan.

Farcau, B.W. (1994). *The coup: Tactics in the seizure of power.* Westport, CT: Praeger.

Federation of Canadian Municipalities. (2006). *Building prosperity from the ground up: Restoring municipal fiscal balance.* Retrieved June 22, 2007, from www.fcm.ca.

Fitch, J.S. (1977). *The military coup d'etat as a political process.* Baltimore, MD: Johns Hopkins University Press.

Fitch, S. (1998). *The armed forces and democracy in Latin America.* Baltimore, MD: Johns Hopkins University Press.

Foreign Policy. (2006). Ranking the rich. *Foreign Policy, 156,* 68–75

Fortier, I. (2003). From skepticism to cynicism: Paradoxes of administrative reform. *Choices, 9*(6), 1–20.

Fournier, P. (2002). The uninformed Canadian voter. In J. Everitt & B. O'Neill (Eds.), *Citizen politics: Research and theory in Canadian political behaviour* (pp. 92–109). Don Mills, ON: Oxford University Press.

Frank, A.G. (1972). The development of underdevelopment. In D. Cockcroft, A.G. Frank, & D. Johnson (Eds.), *Dependence and underdevelopment.* New York: Anchor Books.

Frank, A.G. (1979). *Dependent accumulation and underdevelopment.* New York: Monthly Review Press.

Freedman, J. (2001). *Feminism.* Buckingham, UK: Open University Press.

Freedom House. (n.d.). Retrieved May 16, 2004, from www.freedomhouse.org.

Freedom House. (1999). *Democracy's century: A survey of political change in the 20th century.* Retrieved August 20, 2004, from www.freedomhouse.org/reports/century.html.

Freedom House. (2006). *Freedom in the world.* Retrieved July 9, 2007, from www.freedomhouse.org.

Friedan, B. (1963). *The feminine mystique.* New York: Dell.

Friedan, B. (1998). *It changed my life: Writings on the women's movement.* Cambridge, MA: Harvard University Press.

Friederich, C., & Brzezinski, Z. (1956). *Totalitarian dictatorship and democracy.* Cambridge, MA: Harvard University Press.

Friedman, T. (2000). *The Lexus and the olive tree.* New York: Anchor Books.

Frum, D. (1996). *What's right: The new conservatism and what it means for Canada.* Toronto: Random House.

Fukuyama, F. (1989). The end of history? *The National Interest, 16,* 3–18.

Fukuyama, F. (1992). *The end of history and the last man.* New York: Free Press.

Galligan, B. (2006). Comparative federalism. In R.A.W. Rhodes, S.A. Binder, & B.A. Rockman (Eds.). *The Oxford handbook of political institutions.* Oxford, UK: Oxford University Press.

Gamble, A. (1994). *The free economy and the strong state: The politics of Thatcherism* (2nd ed.). Houndsmills, Basingstoke, Hampshire, UK: Macmillan.

Gamble, A. (2006). The constitutional revolution in the UK. *Publius, 36*(1), 19–35.

Garrett, G. (1998). *Partisan politics in the global economy.* Cambridge: Cambridge University Press.

Gidengil, E., Blais, A., Everitt, J., Fournier, P., & Nevitte, N. (2006a). Back to the future? Making sense of the 2004 Canadian election outside Quebec. *Canadian Journal of Political Science, 39*(1), 1–25.

Gidengil, E., Blais, A., Everitt, J., Fournier, P., & Nevitte, N. (2006c). Is the concept of party identification applicable in Canada? A panel-based analysis. Presented at the ECPR 34th joint session workshop, Nicosia. Retrieved August 11, 2007, from www.ces-eec.umontreal.ca/ECPRGidengiletal.pdf

Gidengil, E., Blais, A., Nadeau, R., & Nevitte, N. (2002). Changes in the party system and anti-party sentiment. In W. Cross (Ed.), *Political parties, representation, and electoral democracy in Canada* (pp. 68–86). Don Mills, ON: Oxford University Press.

Gidengil, E., Blais, A., Nadeau, R., & Nevitte, N. (2003). Women to the left? Gender differences in political beliefs and policy preferences. In M.Tremblay & L.Trimble (Eds.), *Women and electoral politics in Canada* (pp. 140–159). Don Mills, ON: Oxford University Press.

Gidengil, E., & Everitt, J. (2002). Damned if you do, damned if you don't: Television news coverage of female party leaders in the 1993 federal election. In W. Cross (Ed.), *Political parties, representation, and electoral democracy in Canada* (pp. 223–237). Don Mills, ON: Oxford University Press.

Gidengil, E., Everitt, J., Blais, A., Fournier, P., & Nevitte, N. (2006b). Gender and vote choice in the 2006 Canadian election. Paper prepared for the annual meeting of the American Political Science Association. Retrieved August 10, 2007, from www.ces-eec.umontreal.ca/Gidengiletal/APSA2006.pdf.

Gill, B., Rocamora, J., & Wilson, R. (Eds.). (1993). *Low intensity democracy.* London, UK: Pluto Press.

Gilley, B. (2006). The meaning and measure of state legitimacy: Results for 72 countries. *European Journal of Political Research, 45*, 499–525.

Gilligan, C. (1982). *In a different voice.* Cambridge, MA: Harvard University Press.

Gilpin, R. (1981). *War and change in world politics.* Cambridge, UK: Cambridge University Press.

Glendon, M.A. (1995). Rights in twentieth century constitutions. In A. Etzioni (Ed.), *Rights and the common good: The communitarian perspective* (pp. 27–36). New York: St. Martin's Press.

Goldenberg, E. (2006). *The way it works.* Toronto: McClelland & Stewart.

Goldstone, J. (1995). Predicting revolution: Why we could and (and should) have foreseen the revolutions of 1989–1991 in the U.S.S.R. and Eastern Europe. In N. Keddie (Ed.),

Debating revolution (pp. 39–64). New York: New York University Press.

Grabb, E.C., & Curtis, J. (2005). *Regions apart: The four societies of Canada and the United States.* Toronto: Oxford University Press.

Graefe, P. (2007). Political economy and Canadian public policy. In M. Orsini & M. Smith (Eds.), *Critical policy studies.* Vancouver: UBC Press.

Grandin, G. (2006). *Empire's workshop: Latin America, the United States, and the rise of the new imperialism.* New York: Metropolitian Books.

Green, D., & Luehrmann, L. (2003). *Comparative politics of the Third World.* Boulder, CO: Lynne Rienner.

Grofman, B. (1996). Political economy: Downsian perspectives. In R.E. Goodin & H.-D. Klingemann (Eds.), *A new handbook of political science* (pp. 691–701). Oxford: Oxford University Press.

Gunther, R., & Diamond, L. (2001). Types and functions of parties. In L. Diamond & R. Gunther (Eds.), *Political parties and democracy.* Baltimore, MD: Johns Hopkins University Press.

Gunther, R., & Mughan, A. (2000). The political impact of the media: A reassessment. In R. Gunther & A. Mughan (Eds.), *Democracy and the media: A comparative perspective* (pp. 402–448). Cambridge, UK: Cambridge University Press.

Gurr, T.R. (1970). *Why men rebel.* Princeton: Princeton University Press.

Habermas, J. (1975). *Legitimation crisis* (T. McCarthy, Trans.). Boston: Beacon Press. (Original work published 1973)

Hackett, R.A., & Zhao, Y. (1998). *Sustaining democracy? Journalism and the politics of objectivity.* Toronto: Garamond Press.

Handelman, H. (2003). *The challenge of Third World development.* Upper Saddle River, NJ: Prentice-Hall.

Hardin, G. (1968, December 13). The tragedy of the commons. *Science, 162*, 1243–1248.

Harmes, A. (2004). *The return of the state: Protestors, powerbrokers and the new global compromise.* Vancouver: Douglas & McIntyre.

Harris, M. (1991). *Unholy orders: Tragedy at Mount Cashel.* Toronto: Penguin.

Harty, S., & Murphy, M. (2005). In defence of multinational citizenship. Vancouver: UBC Press.

Hartz, L. (1964). *The founding of new societies.* Toronto: Longmans.

Hauss, C., & Smith, M. (2000). *Comparative politics: Domestic responses to global challenges: A Canadian perspective.* Scarborough, ON: Nelson Thomson Learning.

Hay, C. (1997). Divided by a common language: Political theory and the concept of power. *Politics, 17*(1), 45–52.

Heberle, R. (1951). *Social movements.* New York: Appleton, Century, Crofts.

Heclo, H. (1978). Issue networks and the executive establishment. In A. King, (Ed.), *The new American political system* (pp. 87–124). Washington, DC: American Enterprise Institute.

Hedley, R.A. (2002). *Running out of control: Dilemmas of globalization.* Bloomfield, CT: Kumarian Press.

Held, D. (2000). The changing contours of political community: Rethinking democracy in the context of globalization. In R.V. Ericson & N. Stehr (Eds.), *Governing modern societies* (pp. 42–59). Toronto: University of Toronto Press.

Herman, E.S., & Chomsky, N. (2002). *Manufacturing consent* (updated ed.). New York: Pantheon Books.

Hess, G.R. (2005). Authorizing war: Congressional resolutions and presidential leadership, 1955–2002. In D.R. Kelley (Ed.), *Divided power: The presidency, Congress, and the formation of American foreign policy.* Fayetteville, AR: The University of Arkansas Press.

Hessing, M., Howlett M., & Summerville, T. (2005). *Canadian natural resource and environmental policy* (2nd. ed.). Vancouver: UBC Press.

Heywood, A. (2002). *Politics* (2nd ed.). Houndmills, Basingstoke, Hampshire, UK: Palgrave.

Heywood, A. (2003). *Political ideologies: An introduction* (3rd ed.). Houndmills, Basingstoke, Hampshire, UK: Palgrave.

Hinojosa, V.J., & Pérez-Liñán, A. (2005). Presidential impeachment and the politics of survival: The case of Columbia. In J.C. Baumgarner & N. Kada (Eds.), *Checking executive power: Presidential impeachment in comparative perspective.* Westport, CT: Praeger.

Hobbes, T. (1968/1651). *Leviathan.* C.B. Macpherson (Ed.). Harmondsworth, UK: Penguin.

Hoffman, B. (2004). *Insurgency and counterinsurgency in Iraq.* RAND Corporation Occasional Paper OP-127. Santa Monica, CA: Rand Corporation; www.rand.org/pubs/occasional_papers/2005/RAND_OP127.pdf.

Hooghe, L., & Marks, G. (2001). *Multi-level governance and European integration.* Boulder, CO: Rowman and Littlefield.

Horowitz, G. (1966). Conservatism, liberalism and socialism in Canada: An interpretation. *Canadian Journal of Economics and Political Science, 32*(2), 143–171.

Howlett, M., & Ramesh, M. (1995). *Studying public policy: Policy cycles and policy subsystems.* Toronto: Oxford University Press.

Hume, M. (2004, July 12). For whistle blower, it got personal. *Globe and Mail,* A4.

Huntington, S.P. (1991). *The third wave.* Norman, OK: University of Oklahoma Press.

Huntington, S.P. (1993). The clash of civilizations? *Foreign Affairs, 72*(3), 22–49.

Huntington, S.P. (1996). *The clash of civilizations and the remaking of world order.* New York: Simon & Schuster.

Huntington, S.P, Crozier, M., & Watanuki, J. (1975). *The crisis of democracy.* New York: New York University Press.

Inglehart, R.I. (1977). *The silent revolution: Changing values and political styles among Western publics.* Princeton, NJ: Princeton University Press.

Inglehart, R.I. (1990). *Culture shift in advanced industrial society.* Princeton, NJ: Princeton University Press.

Inglehart, R.I., & Norris, P. (2003). *The true clash of civilizations.* Retrieved on August 10, 2004, from www.globalpolicy.org/globaliz/cultural/2003/0304clash.htm.

Inglehart, R.I., & Welzel, C. (2005). *Modernization, cultural change and democracy: The human development sequence.* New York: Cambridge University Press.

International Commission on Intervention and State Sovereignty. (2001). *The responsibility to protect: Report of the International Commission on Intervention and State Sovereignty.* Retrieved August 20, 2004, from www.dfait-maeci.gc.ca/iciss-ciise/pdf/Commission-Report.pdf.

International Institute for Democracy and Electoral Assistance. (2007a). *Global database of quotas for women.* Retrieved July 10, 2007, from www.quotaproject.org/system.cfm.

International Institute for Democracy and Electoral Assistance. (2007b). *Voter turnout: Main findings.* Retrieved July 12, 2007, from www.idea.net/vt.

IPSOS Reid/Dominion Institute. (2007). *National citizenship exam: 10 year benchmark study.* Retrieved July 12, 2007, from www.dominion.ca/Dominion_Institute_Press_Release_Mock_Exam.pdf.

Iyengar, S., & Kinder, D. (1987). *News that matters.* Chicago: University of Chicago Press.

Janowitz, M. (1977). *Military institutions and coercion in the developing nations.* Chicago: University of Chicago Press.

Jennings, M.K. (1984). The intergenerational transfer of political ideologies in eight Western nations. *European Journal of Political Research 12,* 261–276.

Jennings, M.K., & Niemi, R.G. (1968). The transmission of political values from parent to child. *American Political Science Review, 62,* 169–184.

Jennings, M.K., & Niemi, R.G. (1981). *Generations and politics: A panel study of young adults and their parents.* Princeton, NJ: Princeton University Press.

Joes, A. (1992). *Modern guerrilla insurgency.* Westport, CT: Praeger Publishers.

Joes, A. (2004). *Resisting rebellion: The history and politics of counterinsurgency.* Lexington, KY: University of Kentucky Press.

Kampfner, J. (2003, May 15). The truth about Jessica. *The Guardian Unlimited.* Retrieved August 11, 2004, from www.guardian.co.uk/Iraq/Story/0,2763,956255,00.html.

Kara, N. (2005). Impeachment as punishment for corruption? The cases of Brazil and Venezuela. In J.C. Baumgarner & N. Kada (Eds.), *Checking executive power: Presidential impeachment in comparative perspective.* Westport, CT: Praeger.

Katz, R.S., & Mair, P. (1995). Changing models of party organization and party democracy: The emergence of the cartel party. *Party Politics, 1,* 5–28.

Keating, M. (1996). *Nations against the state: The new politics of nationalism in Quebec, Catalonia and Scotland.* Houndmills, Basingstoke, Hampshire, UK: Macmillan.

Keddie, N. (1995). Can revolutions be predicted; Can their causes be understood? In N. Keddie (Ed.), *Debating revolution* (pp. 1–26). New York: New York University Press.

Kent, A. (1996). *Risk and redemption: Surviving the network news wars.* Toronto: Penguin Books Canada.

Keohane, R.O. (1984). *After hegemony: Cooperation and discord in the world political economy.* Princeton, NJ: Princeton University Press.

Keohane, R.O., & Nye, J.S. (1977). *Power and interdependence: World politics in transition.* Boston: Little, Brown.

Kiernan, B. (2002). *The Pol Pot regime: Race, power, and genocide under the Khmer Rouge.* New Haven, CT: Yale University Press.

Kingdon, J.W. (1995). *Agendas, alternatives and public policies* (2nd ed.). New York: Longman.

Kirchheimer, O. (1966). The transformation of West European party systems. In J. LaPalombara & M. Weiner (Eds.), *Political parties and political development* (pp. 177–200). Princeton, NJ: Princeton University Press.

Kirkpatrick, J. (1979). Dictatorships and double standards. *Commentary, 68*(5), 34–45.

Kitschelt, H. (1986). Political opportunity structures and political protest: Anti-nuclear movements in four democracies. *British Journal of Political Science, 16*(1) 57–79.

Korten, D.C. (1996). *When corporations rule the world.* West Hartford, CT: Kumarian Press.

Kraft, M.E. (2004). *Environmental policy and politics* (3rd ed.). New York: Pearson Longman.

Kristof, N. (2006, October 5). Aid: Can it work? *The New York Review of Books, 53*, 15. www.nybooks.com/articles/ 19374.

Kushner, J., Siegel, D., & Stanwick, H. (1997). Ontario municipal elections: Voting trends and determinants of electoral success in a Canadian province. *Canadian Journal of Political Science, 30*, 539–559.

Ladd, E.C. (1999). *The Ladd report.* New York: Free Press.

Lane, J.-E., & Ersson, S. (2000). *The new institutional politics: Performance and outcomes.* London, UK: Routledge.

Lane, J.-E., & Ersson, S. (2005). *Culture and politics: A comparative approach* (2nd ed.). Aldershot, Hants, UK: Ashgate.

Laquer, W. (1977). *Guerrilla: A historical and critical study.* London, UK: Weidenfeld and Nicolson.

Lasswell, H. (1936). *Politics: Who gets what, when, how?* New York: McGraw-Hill.

Lau, R., Sigelman, L., Heldman, C., & Babbitt, P. (1999). The effects of negative political advertisements: A meta-analytic assessment. *American Political Science Review, 93*, 851–875.

Law Commission of Canada. *Voting counts: Electoral reform for Canada.* Retrieved May 17, 2004, from www.cc.gc.ca/en/ themes/gr/er/er_main.asp.

Laycock, D. (2002). *The new right and democracy in Canada: Understanding Reform and the Canadian Alliance.* Don Mills, ON: Oxford University Press.

Lazar, H., Telford, H., & Watts, R. (2003). Divergent trajectories: The impact of global and regional integration on federal systems. In H. lazar, H. Telford, & R. Watts (Eds.), *The impact of global and regional integration on federal systems.* Montreal & Kingston: McGill-Queen's University Press.

Leftwich, A. (1983). *Redefining politics: People, resources and power.* London: Methuen.

Leftwich, A. (Ed.). (1996). *Democracy and development: Theory and practice.* Cambridge, UK: Polity Press.

Leggett, W. (2007). British social democracy beyond new Labour: Entrenching a progressive consensus. *British Journal of Politics and International Relations, 9*, 346–364.

Leo, C., & Mulligan, S. (2006). City politics: Globalization and community democracy. In J. Grace & B. Sheldreck (Eds.), *Canadian politics: Democracy and dissent.* Toronto: Pearson Education.

Lewin, L. (1991). *Self-interest and public interest in Western politics* (D. Lavery, Trans.). Oxford: Oxford University Press.

Lewis, B. (2004). *The crisis of Islam: Holy war and unholy terror.* New York: Random House.

Lijphart, A. (1999). *Patterns of democracy: Government forms and performance in thirty-six countries.* New Haven, CT: Yale University Press.

Lindblom, C.E. (1959). The science of muddling through. *Public Administration Review, 19*(2), 79–88.

Lindblom, C.E. (1977). *Politics and markets: The world's political-economic systems.* New York: Basic Books.

Lindblom, C.E. (2001). *The market system: What it is, how it works and what to make of it.* New Haven, CT: Yale University Press.

Linz, J. (1964). An authoritarian regime: Spain. In E. Allardt & Y. Littunen (Eds.), *Cleavages, ideologies, and party systems: Contributions to comparative political sociology. Transactions of the Westermarck Society, 10*, 291–342.

Linz, J. (1994). Presidential or parliamentary democracy: Does it make a difference? In J.J. Linz & A. Valenzuela (Eds.), *The failure of presidential democracy: Vol. 1. Comparative perspectives* (pp. 3–87). Baltimore, MD: John Hopkins University Press.

Linz, J., & Stepan, A. (Eds.). (1978). *The breakdown of democratic regimes.* Baltimore. MD: Johns Hopkins University Press.

Lipschutz, R.D. (2000). *After authority: War, peace and global politics in the 21st century.* Albany, NY: State University of New York Press.

Lipschutz, R.D. (2004). *Global environmental politics: Power, perspectives, and practice.* Washington, DC: CQ Press

Lipset, S.M. (1950). *Agrarian socialism.* Berkeley, CA: University of California Press.

Lipset, S.M. (1990). *Continental divide: The values and institutions of the United States and Canada.* New York: Routledge.

Lipsky, R. (1968). Protest as a political resource. *American Political Science Review, 62*(4), 1144–1158.

Lobe, J. (2002. September 27). The arrogance of power. *Foreign Policy in Focus.*

Lukes, S. (1974). *Power: A radical view.* London: Macmillan.

Luttwak, E. (1969). *Coup d'etat.* New York: Alfred A. Knopf.

Lyons, W., Scheb, J.M., & Richardson, L.E. (1995). *American government: Politics and political culture.* St. Paul, MN: West Publishing.

Macaulay, N. (1986). *The Sandino Affair.* Durham, NC: Duke University Press.

MacIvor, H. (2006). *Canadian politics and government in the Charter era*. Toronto: Thomson Nelson.

Macpherson, C.B. (1954). *Democracy in Alberta*. Toronto: University of Toronto Press.

Mann, M. (1997). Has globalization ended the rise and rise of the nation-state? *Review of International Political Economy, 4*(3), 472–496.

Mann, M. (2004). *Fascists*. New York: Cambridge University Press.

Marletti, C., & Roncarolo, F. (2000). Media influence in the Italian transition from a consensual to a majoritarian democracy. In R. Gunther & A. Mughan (Eds.), *Democracy and the media: A comparative perspective* (pp. 195–240). Cambridge, UK: Cambridge University Press.

Martell, L. (1994). *Ecology and society: An introduction*. Amherst, MA: University of Massachusetts Press.

Martin, H.-P., & Schumann, H. (1997). *The global trap: Globalization and the assault on democracy and prosperity*. Montreal: Black Rose Books.

Marzolini, M. (2002, September). *Polling alone: Canadian values and liberalism*. Paper presented to the Conference on Securing the New Liberalism, Toronto. Retrieved August 10, 2004, from www.pollara.ca/new/POLLARA_NET.html.

McAllister, M.L. (2004). *Governing ourselves: The politics of local communities*. Vancouver, BC: UBC Press.

McQuail, D. (1994). *Mass communication theory: An introduction* (3rd ed.). London, UK: Sage.

Meadows, D.H., Meadows, D.L., Randers, J., & Behrens, W.H. (1972). *The limits to growth*. New York: Universe Books.

Medcalf, L.J., & Dolbeare, K.M. (1985). *Neopolitics: American political ideas in the 1980s*. Philadelphia, PA: Temple University Press.

Meisel, J., & Mendelsohn, M. (2001). Meteor? Phoenix? Chameleon? The decline and transformation of party in Canada. In H.G. Thorburn & A. Whitehorn (Eds.), *Party politics in Canada* (8th ed.) (pp. 163–178). Toronto: Prentice Hall.

Michels, R. (1962). *Political parties: a sociological study of the oligarchic tendencies of modern democracy* (E. Paul & C. Paul, Trans.). New York: Collier. (Original work published in 1911).

Miljan, L.A., & Cooper, B. (2003). *Hidden agendas: How journalists influence the news*. Vancouver: UBC Press.

Mill, J.S. (1912). *On liberty. Representative government. The subjection of women. Three essays*. London, UK: Oxford University Press. (*On Liberty* originally published in 1859).

Miller, W.L., & Niemi, R.G. (2002). Voting: Choice, conditioning, and constraint. In L. LeDuc, R.G. Niemi, & P. Norris (Eds.), *Comparing democracies 2: New challenges in the study of elections and voting* (pp. 169–188). London: Sage.

Millett, K. (1985). *Sexual politics*. London: Virago.

Mills, C.W. (1956). *The power elite*. New York: Oxford University Press.

Milner, H. (1997). Electoral systems, integrated institutions and turnout in local and national elections: Canada in comparative perspective. *Canadian Journal of Political Science, 30*(1, March), 89–106.

Milner, H. (2005). Fixing Canada's unfixed election dates: A political season to reduce the democratic deficit. *IRPP Policy Matters, 6*(6).

Milton-Edwards, B (2005). *Islamic fundamentalism since 1945*. London, UK: Routledge.

Mintz, E. (1993). Two generations: The political attitudes of high school students and their parents. *International Journal of Canadian Studies,* (special issue), 59–71.

Mishler, W., & Clarke, H.D. (1995). Political participation in Canada. In M.S. Whittington & G. Williams (Eds.), *Canadian politics in the 1990s* (4th ed.) (pp. 129–151). Toronto: Nelson Canada.

Mitchell, K. (2003). Educating the national citizen in neoliberal times: From the multicultural self to the strategic cosmopolitan. *Transactions of the Institute of British Geographers, 28*(4), 387–403.

Montgomery, T. (Ed.). (2000). *Peacekeeping and democratization in the Western hemisphere*. Coral Gables, FL: North–South Center Press, University of Miami.

Montpetit, É. (2004). Governance and interest group activities. In J. Bickerton and A-G. Gagnon (Eds.), *Canadian politics* (4th ed.). Peterborough, ON: Broadview Press.

More, T. (2004). *Utopia*. In T. Ball & R. Dagger (Eds.), *Ideals and ideologies: A reader* (5th ed.). New York: Pearson Longman. (Original work published in 1516).

Morgan, R. (1977). *Going too far: The personal chronicle of a feminist*. New York: Random House.

Morgan-Jones, E., & Schleiter, P. (2004). Governmental change in a president-parliamentary regime: The case of Russia 1994–2003. *Post-Soviet Affairs, 20*(2), 132–163.

Morgenthau, H.J. (1948). *Politics among nations: The struggle for power and peace*. New York: Knopf.

Morlan, R.L. (1984). Municipal vs. national election voter turnout: Europe and the United States. *Political Science Quarterly, 99*, 457–70.

Morris, J.C. (2007). Government and market pathologies of privatization: The case of prison privatization. *Politics & Policy, 35*(2), 318–341.

Morton, F.L. (2003). Can judicial supremacy be stopped? *Policy Options, 24*(9), 25–99.

Morton, W.L. (1950). *The Progressive Party in Canada*. Toronto: University of Toronto Press

Mueller, J. (1989). *Retreat from doomsday: The obsolescence of major war*. New York: Basic Books.

Munck, R. (1997). Introduction: A thin democracy. *Latin American Perspectives, 24*(6), 5–21.

Myers, R.A., & Worm, B. (2003). Rapid worldwide depletion of predatory fish communities. *Nature, 423*(6937), 280–283.

Nadeau, R. (2002). Satisfaction with democracy: The Canadian paradox. In N. Nevitte (Ed.), *Value change and governance in Canada* (pp. 37–70). Toronto: University of Toronto Press.

Nadeau, R., & Giasson, T. (2003). Canada's democratic malaise: Are the media to blame? *Choices, 9*(1, February), 3–32.

Naess, A., & Sessions, G. (1993). The deep ecology platform. In B. Devall (Ed.), *Clearcut: The tragedy of industrial forestry*. San Francisco: Sierra Book Club & Earth Island Press.

Needler, M.C. (1996). *Identity, interest, and ideology: An introduction to politics.* Westport, CT: Praeger.

Neocleous, M. (1997). *Fascism.* Minneapolis, MN: University of Minnesota Press.

Nevitte, N. (1996). *The decline of deference: Canadian value change in cross-national perspective.* Peterborough, ON: Broadview Press.

Nevitte, N., Blais, A., Gidengil, E., & Nadeau, R. (2000). *Unsteady state: The 1997 Canadian federal election.* Don Mills, ON: Oxford University Press.

Norris, P. (2000). *A virtuous circle: Political communications in postindustrial societies.* Cambridge, UK: Cambridge University Press, 2000.

Norris, P. (2001). *Digital divide: Civic engagement, information poverty, and the Internet worldwide.* Cambridge, UK: Cambridge University Press.

Norris, P. (2002). Campaign communications. In L. LeDuc, R.G. Niemi, & P. Norris (Eds.), *Comparing democracies 2: New challenges in the study of elections and voting* (pp. 127–147). London, UK: Sage.

Nye, J.S., Jr. (2004). *Soft power: The means to success in world politics.* New York: Public Affairs.

O'Donnell, G. (1994). Delegative democracy. *Journal of Democracy, 5*(1), 55–69.

O'Neill, B. (2002). Sugar and spice? Political culture and the political behaviour of Canadian women. In J. Everitt & B. O'Neill (Eds.), *Citizen politics: Research and theory in Canadian political behaviour* (pp. 40–55). Don Mills, ON: Oxford University Press.

Oeter, S. (2006). Federal republic of Germany. In K. Le Roy & C. Saunders (Eds.), *Legislative, executive, and judicial governance in federal countries.* Montreal & Kingston: McGill-Queen's University Press.

Ohmae, K. (1995). *The end of the nation state: The rise of regional economies.* London, UK: HarperCollins.

Olson, L.R., & Green, J.C. (2006). Gapology and the presidential vote. *PS: Political science and politics, 39*(3), 443–446.

Olson, M. (1965). *The logic of collective action: Public goods and the theory of groups.* Cambridge, MA: Harvard University Press.

Opp, K.-D. (1989). *The rationality of political protest.* Boulder, CO: Westview Press.

Oppenheimer, J.R. (1953). Atomic weapons and American policy. *Foreign Affairs, 31*(4), 525–535.

Organski, A.F.K. (1967). *The stages of political development.* New York: Knopf.

Osborne, D., & Gaebler, T. (1993). *Reinventing government: How the entrepreneurial spirit is transforming the public sector.* Reading, MA: Addison-Wesley.

Ostrom, E. (2000). *Governing the commons: The evolution of institutions for collective action.* New York: Cambridge University Press.

Oxfam. (2003). *Running into the sand: Why failure at the Cancun trade talks threatens the world's poorest people.* Retrieved May 9, 2004, from www.oxfam.org.uk/what_we_do/issue/trade/bp53_cancun.pdf.

Paehlke, R. (2003). *Democracy's dilemma: Environment, social equity and the global community.* Cambridge, MA: MIT Press.

Pal, L.A. (1992). *Public policy analysis: An introduction* (2nd ed.). Scarborough, ON: Nelson Canada.

Pal, L.A. (1993). *Interests of state: The politics of language, multiculturalism and feminism in Canada.* Montreal: McGill-Queen's University Press.

Palmer, D. (1994). *Shining Path of Peru.* New York: St. Martin's Press.

Pammett, J.H., & LeDuc, L. (2003). *Explaining the turnout decline in Canadian federal elections: A new survey of nonvoters.* Retrieved May 26, 2004, from www.elections.ca.

Panebianco, A. (1988). *Political parties: Organization and power.* Cambridge, UK: Cambridge University Press.

Panitch, L.V. (1995). Elites, classes, and power in Canada. In M.S. Whittington & G. Williams (Eds.), *Canadian politics in the 1990s* (4th ed.) (pp. 152–175). Toronto: Nelson Canada.

Parrington, V. (1987). *Main currents in American thought* (Vols. 1–2). Norman, OK: University of Oklahoma Press.

Pape, R.A. (2005). *Dying to win: The strategic logic of suicide terrorism.* New York: Random House.

Parenti, M. (1970). Power and pluralism: A view from the bottom. *Journal of Politics, 32*(3), 501–530.

Patterson, T.E. (2000). The United States: News in a free-market society. In R. Gunther & A. Mughan (Eds.), *Democracy and the media: A comparative perspective* (pp. 241–265). Cambridge, UK: Cambridge University Press.

Perlin, G. (2003). *International assistance to democratic development: A review.* IRPP Working Paper Series no. 2003-04. Montreal: Institute for Research on Public Policy.

Petter, A. (1990). When rights go wrong. *Policy Options, 11*(3), 33–34.

Pfau, M., Houston, J.B., & Semmler, S.M. (2007). *Mediating the vote: The changing media landscape in U.S. presidential campaigns.* Lanham, MD: Rowman & Littlefield.

Pharr, S., Putnam, R.D., & Dalton, R.J. (2000). A quarter century of declining confidence. *Journal of Democracy, 11*(2), 5–25.

Pierson, C. (1996). *The modern state.* London, UK: Routledge.

Plasser, F., with Plasser, G. (2002). *Global political campaigning: A worldwide analysis of campaign professionals and their practices.* Westport, CT: Praeger.

Polisource. (2003). *Background note: Mexico.* Retrieved August 20, 2004, from www.polisource.com/documents/BackgroundNotes/1838pf.shtml.

Pollack, K.M. (2002). *The threatening storm: The case for invading Iraq.* New York: Random House.

Porter, J. (1965). *The vertical mosaic.* Toronto: University of Toronto Press.

Postman, N. (1985). *Amusing ourselves to death: Public discourse in an age of show business.* New York: Penguin.

Potter, S.V. (2003). Judging the judiciary: The rule of law in the age of the Charter. *Policy Options, 24*(9), 34–38.

Pross, A.P. (1993). *Group politics and public policies* (2nd ed.). Toronto: Oxford University Press.

Putnam, R. (2000). *Bowling alone: The collapse and revival of American community.* New York: Simon & Schuster.

Qualter, T.J. (1986). *Conflicting political ideas in liberal democracies.* Toronto: Methuen.

Ranney, A. (2001). *Governing: An introduction to political science* (8th ed.). Upper Saddle River, NJ: Prentice-Hall.

Rasch. B.E., & Congleton, R.D. (2006). Amendment procedures and constitutional stability. In R.D. Congleton & B. Swedenborg (Eds.), *Democratic constitutional design and public policy: Analysis and evidence.* Cambridge, MA: MIT Press.

Rees, W., & Wackernagel, M. (1996). *Our ecological footprint: Reducing human impact on earth.* Gabriola Island, BC: New Society Publishers.

Remmer, K. (1996). The sustainability of political democracy: Lessons from South America. *Comparative Political Studies, 29*(6), 611–634.

Resnick, P. (1997). *Twenty-first century democracy.* Montreal: McGill-Queen's University Press.

Robinson, M.J. (1976). Public affairs television and the growth of political malaise: The case of "The Selling of the Pentagon." *American Political Science Review, 70*(2), 409–432.

Rochlin, J. (2003). *Vanguard revolutionaries in Latin America: Peru, Colombia, Mexico.* Boulder, CO: Lynne Reinner Publishers.

Roese, N.J. (2002). Canadians' shrinking trust in government: Causes and consequences. In N. Nevitte (Ed.), *Value change and governance in Canada* (pp. 149–163). Toronto: University of Toronto Press.

Rosenberg, T. (2006, November 16) How to fight poverty: 8 programs that work. *New York Times.* http://select.nytimes.com/2006/11/16/opinion/15talkingpoints.html.

Roth, D.F., Warwick, P.V., & Paul, D.W. (1989). *Comparative politics: Diverse states in an interdependent world.* New York: Harper and Row.

Rousseau, J.-J. (1968). *The social contract* (M. Cranston, Trans.). Harmondsworth, UK: Penguin. (Original work published in 1762).

Sabato, L. (1992). *Feeding frenzy: How attack journalism has transformed American politics.* New York: Free Press.

Sachs, J. (2005). *An end to poverty.* New York: Penguin.

Saint-Martin, D. (2007). From the welfare state to the social investment state. In M. Orsini & M. Smith (Eds.), *Critical policy studies.* Vancouver: UBC Press.

Sallot, J. (2004, March 27). Information commissioner wins access to documents. *Globe and Mail,* A11.

Sancton, A. (2002). Municipalities, cities, and globalization: Implications for Canadian federalism. In H. Bakvis & G. Skogstad (Eds.), *Canadian federalism: Performance, effectiveness, and legitimacy* (pp. 261–277). Don Mills, ON: Oxford University Press.

Sandbrook, R. (2003). Introduction: Envisioning a civilized globalization. In R. Sandbrook (Ed.), *Civilizing globalization: A survival guide.* Albany, NY: State University of New York Press.

Sater, W. (1990). *Chile and the United States: Empires in conflict.* Athens, GA: University of Georgia Press.

Savoie, D.J. (1999). *Governing from the centre: The concentration of power in Canadian politics.* Toronto: University of Toronto Press.

Savoie, D.J. (2003). *Breaking the bargain: Public servants, ministers and Parliament.* Toronto: University of Toronto Press.

Scarrow, S.E. (2000). Parties without members? Party organization in a changing electoral environment. In R.J. Dalton & M.P. Wattenberg (Eds.), *Parties without partisans: Political change in advanced industrial democracies* (pp. 79–101). Oxford, UK: Oxford University Press.

Scarrow, S.E., Webb, P., & Farrell, D.M. (2000). From social integration to electoral contestation: The changing distribution of power within political parties. In R.J. Dalton & M.P. Wattenberg (Eds.), *Parties without partisans: Political change in advanced industrial democracies* (pp. 129–153). Oxford, UK: Oxford University Press.

Schedler, A. (2000). The democratic revelation. *Journal of Democracy, 11*(4), 5–19.

Schleiter, P., & Morgan-Jones, E. (2005). *Semi-presidential regimes: Providing flexibility or generating representation and governance problems?* Centre for the Study of Democratic Government, *Working Paper Series Paper No. 01.*

Schlesinger, A.E. (1973). *The imperial presidency.* Boston: Houghton Mifflin.

Schumacher, E.F. (1973). *Small is beautiful: A study of economics as if people mattered.* London, UK: Sphere Books.

Schumpeter, J. (1943). *Capitalism, socialism and democracy.* New York: Harper & Row.

Scott, J. (2001). *Power.* Cambridge, UK: Polity Press.

Shaiko, R.G. (1999). *Voices and echoes for the environment: Public interest representation in the 1990s and beyond.* New York: Columbia University Press.

Shub, D. (1966). *Lenin: A biography.* Baltimore, MD: Penguin Books.

Shugart, M.S. (2006). Comparative executive-legislative relations. In R.A.W. Rhodes, S.A. Binder, & B.A. Rockman (Eds.), *The Oxford handbook of political institutions.* Oxford, UK: Oxford University Press.

Siaroff, A. (2003). Comparative presidencies: The inadequacy of the presidential, semi-presidential and parliamentary distinction. *European Journal of Political Research, 42*(3), 287–312.

Siebert, F., Peterson, T., & Schramm, W. (1956). *Four theories of the press.* Urbana, IL: University of Illinois Press.

Sigmund, P. (1993). *The United States and democracy in Chile.* Baltimore, MD: Johns Hopkins University Press.

Simeon, R. (1976). Studying public policy. *Canadian Journal of Political Science, 9*(3), 548–580.

Simeon, R., & Cameron, D. (2002). Intergovernmental relations and democracy: An oxymoron if there ever was one? In H. Bakvis & G. Skogstad (Eds.), *Canadian federalism: Performance, effectiveness, and legitimacy* (pp. 278–295). Don Mills, ON: Oxford University Press.

Simon, H.A. (1957). *Administrative behavior: A study of decision-making processes in administrative organization.* New York: Macmillan.

Simon, J.L., & Kahn, H. (1984). *The resourceful earth.* New York: Basil Blackwell.

Simpson, J. (2001). *The friendly dictatorship.* Toronto: McClelland & Stewart.

Skocpol, T. (1979). *States and social revolutions: A comparative analysis of France, Russia, and China.* New York: Cambridge University Press.

Smith, A. (2004). An inquiry into the nature and causes of the wealth of nations [excerpt]. In T. Ball & R. Dagger (Eds.), *Ideals and ideologies: A reader* (5th ed.) (pp. 104–106). New York: Pearson Education. (Original work published in 1776).

Smith, G., & Wales, C. (2002). Citizens' juries and deliberative democracy. In M.P. D'Entrèves (Ed.), *Democracy as public deliberation: New perspectives* (pp. 157–177). Manchester, UK: Manchester University Press.

Sniderman, P.M., Fletcher, J.F., Russell, P.H., & Tetlock, P. (1996). *The clash of rights: Liberty, equality, and legitimacy in pluralist democracy.* New Haven: Yale University Press.

Stephan, A., & Robertson, G.B. (2003). An "Arab" more than a "Muslim" electoral gap. *Journal of Democracy, 14*(3), 30–44.

Sterling-Folker, J. (Ed.). (2006). *Making sense of international relations theory.* Boulder, CO: Lynne Rienner.

Stewart, I. (2002). Vanishing points: Three paradoxes of political culture research. In J. Everitt & B. O'Neill (Eds.), *Citizen politics: Research and theory in Canadian political behaviour* (pp. 21–39). Don Mills, ON: Oxford University Press.

Stoker, G. (2006). Comparative local governance. In R.A.W. Rhodes, S.A. Binder, & B.A. Rockman (Eds.), *The Oxford handbook of political Institutions.* Oxford, UK: Oxford University Press.

Strauss, L. (1945). On classical political philosophy. *Social Research, 12,* 98–117.

Sunderlin, W.D. (2003). *Ideology, social theory, and the environment.* Lanham, MD: Rowman & Littlefield.

Suny, R.G. (2006). Nationalism, nation making and the post-colonial states of Asia, Africa, and Eurasia. In L. Barrington (Ed.), *Making and protecting the nation in postcolonial and postcommunist states.* Ann Arbor, MI: University of Michigan Press.

Swenden, W. (2006). *Federalism and regionalism in Western Europe: A comparative and thematic analysis.* Houndmills, Basingstoke, Hampshire, UK: Palgrave Macmillan.

Sylvester, C. (1994). *Feminist theory and international relations in a postmodern era.* New York: Cambridge University Press.

Taras, D. (1990). *The newsmakers: The media's influence on Canadian politics.* Scarborough, ON: Nelson Canada.

Tarrow, S. (1999). *Power in movement: Social movements and contentious politics.* Cambridge, UK: Cambridge University Press.

Taylor, D.M. (1992). Disagreeing on the basics: Environmental debates reflect competing world views. *Alternatives, 14*(3), 26–33.

Tessler, M. (2002). *Do Islamic orientations influence attitudes towards democracy in the Arab world? Evidence from Egypt, Jordan, Morocco, and Algeria.* Retrieved August 21, 2003, from www.worldvaluessurvey.org/Upload/5_TessIslamDem_2.pdf.

Thompson, D. (1984). *The Chartists.* New York: Pantheon.

Thucydides (1972). *History of the Peleponnesian war.* London: Penguin.

Tocqueville, A. (2000). *Democracy in America* (H.C. Mansfield & D. Winthrop, Trans. & Ed.). Chicago: University of Chicago Press. (Original work published in 1835.)

Tremblay, R.C., et al. (2004). *Mapping the political landscape: An introduction to political science.* Toronto: Thomson Nelson.

Trudeau, P.-E. (1993). *Memoirs.* Toronto: McClelland and Stewart.

Tully, J. (2003). Identity politics. In T. Ball & R. Bellamy (Eds.), *The Cambridge history of twentieth-century political thought.* Cambridge, UK: Cambridge University Press.

Turcotte, A. (2001). Fallen heroes: Leaders and voters in the 2000 Canadian federal election. In J.H. Pammett & C. Dornan (Eds.), *The Canadian general election of 2000* (pp. 277–292). Toronto: Dundurn.

UNDP [United Nations Development Programme] (1995, 2002, 2003, 2005). *Human development report, 1995, 2002, 2003, 2005.* New York: Oxford University Press.

UNMDG [United Nations Millennium Development Goals] (2005). *MDG Info 2005.* www.devinfo.org/facts.htm?IDX=13

UNMDG (2006). *Millennium Development Goals Report 2006.* http://mdgs.un.org/unsd/mdg/Resources/Static/Products/Progress2006/MDGReport2006.pdf

US Army. (2006). *Counterinsurgency.* Field Manual 3-24. Washington: Department of the Army. Available at http://usacac.army.mil/cac/repository/materials/coin-fm3-24.pdf.

Valaskakis, K. (2001, April 19). It's about world governance. *Globe and Mail,* A15.

Valiante, M. (2002). Legal foundations of Canadian environmental policy: Underlining our values in a shifting landscape. In D. L. VanNijnatten & R. Boardman (Eds.), *Canadian environmental policy: Context and cases* (2nd ed.) (pp. 3–24). Don Mills, ON: Oxford University Press.

Van Kersbergen, K., & Van Waarden, F. (2004). "Governance" as a bridge between disciplines: Cross-disciplinary inspiration regarding shifts in governance and problems of governability, accountability and legitimacy. *European Journal of Political Research, 43,* 143–171.

Verba, S., Nie, N., & Kim, J.O. (1978). *Participation and political equality.* New York: Cambridge University Press.

Wade, R. (1990). *Governing the market.* Princeton, NJ: Princeton University Press.

Walker, J.L. (1991). *Mobilizing interest groups in America: Patrons, professions, and social movements*. Ann Arbor, MI: The University of Michigan Press.

Wallack, M. (2006). From compellence to pre-emption: Kosovo and Iraq as U.S. responses to contested hegemony. In O. Croci & A. Verdun (Eds.), *The transatlantic divide: Foreign and security policies in the Atlantic Alliance from Kosovo to Iraq* (pp. 109–125). Manchester, UK: Manchester University Press.

Wallerstein, I. (1974–1980). *The modern world system* (Vol. 1–2). New York: Academic Press.

Waltz, K.N. (1979). *Theory of international politics*. Reading, MA: Addison-Wesley.

Ware, A. (1987). *Political parties: Electoral change and structural response*. Oxford: Basil Blackwell.

Warren, M. (2002). Deliberative democracy. In A. Carter & G. Stokes (Eds.), *Democratic theory today: Challenges for the 21st century* (pp. 173–202). Cambridge, UK: Polity Press.

Watts, R.L. (1999). *Comparing federal systems* (2nd ed.). Montreal: McGill–Queen's University Press.

Weale, A. (1992). *The new politics of pollution*. Manchester, UK: Manchester University Press.

Webb, P. (2002). Conclusion: Political parties and democratic control in advanced industrial societies. In P. Webb, D. Farrell, & I. Holliday (Eds.), *Political parties in advanced industrial democracies*. Oxford: Oxford University Press.

Weber, E. (1976). *Peasants into Frenchmen: The modernization of rural France, 1870–1914*. Stanford, CA: Stanford University.

Weber, M. (1958). In H.H. Gerth & C.W. Mills (Eds. & Trans.), *Max Weber: Essays in sociology*. New York: Oxford University Press.

Weir, S., & Beetham, D. (1999). *Political power and democratic control in Britain*. London, UK: Routledge.

Weller, P. (1985). *First among equals: Prime ministers in Westminster systems*. Sydney: George Allen & Unwin.

Wendt, A. (1999). *Social theory of international politics*. Cambridge, UK: Cambridge University Press, 1999.

Wheaton, B., & Z. Kavan (1992). *The Velvet Revolution: Czechoslovakia, 1988–1991*. Boulder, CO: Westview Press.

Whitaker, R. (1977). *The government party: Organizing and financing the Liberal party of Canada 1930–58*. Toronto: University of Toronto Press.

Whitaker, R. (1997). Canadian politics at the end of the millennium: Old dreams, new nightmares. In D. Taras & B. Rasporich (Eds.), *A passion for identity: An introduction to Canadian studies* (3rd ed.) (pp. 119–137). Toronto: ITP Nelson.

White, R. (1978). *Paraguay's autonomous revolution: 1810–1840*. Albuquerque, NM: University of New Mexico Press.

Wilensky, H. (1975*). The welfare state and equality: Structural and ideological roots of public expenditure*. Berkeley, CA: University of California Press.

Wilson, J. (2002). Continuity and change in the Canadian environmental movement: Assessing the effects of institutionalization. In D.L. VanNijnatten & R. Boardman (Eds.), *Canadian environmental policy: Context and cases*. Don Mills, ON: Oxford University Press.

Wiseman, N. (2001). The pattern of prairie politics. In H.G. Thorburn & A. Whitehorn (Eds.), *Party politics in Canada* (8th ed.). Toronto: Pearson Education Canada.

Wolin, S.S. (1960). *Politics and vision: Continuity and innovation in Western political thought*. Boston: Little, Brown.

Wood, G., & Sharit, I. (1997). *Who needs credit? Poverty and finance in Bangladesh*. London, UK: Zed Press.

World Bank. (2004). *World development report, 2004*. Washington, DC: The World Bank.

World Bank. (2005). *World development report, 2005*. Washington, DC: The World Bank

World Commission on Environment and Development. (1987). *Our common future*. Oxford: Oxford University Press.

Yunus, M. (1999). *Banker to the poor: Micro-lending and the battle against world poverty*. New York: Public Affairs Press.

Zehfuss, M. (2002). *Constructivism in international relations: The politics of reality*. Cambridge, UK: Cambridge University Press.

Zeidan, D. (2004). *Resurgence of religion: A comparative study of selected themes in Christian and Islamic fundamentalist discourses*. Leiden: Brill.

Zussman, D. (2002). Alternative service delivery. In C. Dunn (Ed.), *The handbook of Canadian public administration* (pp 53–76). Don Mills, ON: Oxford University Press.

PHOTO CREDITS

INDEX